Data Structures and Algorithms in Java

WORLDWIDE
SERIES IN
COMPUTER
SCIENCE

Series Editors **Professor David Barron, *Southampton University, UK***
Professor Peter Wegner, *Brown University, USA*

The Worldwide Series in Computer Science has been created to publish textbooks which both address and anticipate the needs of an ever evolving curriculum thereby shaping its future. It is designed for undergraduates majoring in Computer Science and practitioners who need to reskill. Its philosophy derives from the conviction that the discipline of computing needs to produce technically skilled engineers who will inevitably face, and possibly invent, radically new technologies throughout their future careers. New media will be used innovatively to support high quality texts written by leaders in the field.

Titles coming soon Winder, *Developing Java Software*
Kotonya & Sommerville, *Requirements Engineering*

Data Structures and Algorithms in Java

Michael T. Goodrich
Department of Computer Science
Johns Hopkins University

Roberto Tamassia
Department of Computer Science
Brown University

John Wiley & Sons, Inc.

New York • Chichester • Weinheim • Brisbane • Singapore • Toronto

Cover art: Anatjari Tjampitjinpa, *"Snake Dreaming,"* 1988. Reproduced courtesy of Patrick Corbally Stourton of Corbally Stourton Contemporary Art Ltd.

Java is a trademark of Sun Microsystems, Inc.
UNIX® is a registered trademark in the United States and other countries, licensed through X/Open Company, Ltd.
All other product names mentioned herein are the trademarks of their respective owners.

ACQUISITIONS EDITOR   Regina Brooks
MARKETING MANAGER   Jay Kirsch
SENIOR PRODUCTION MANAGER Lucille Buonocore
SENIOR PRODUCTION EDITOR   Monique Calello
SENIOR DESIGNER   Dawn Stanley
ILLUSTRATION COORDINATOR   Sigmund Malinowski
PREPRESS SERVICES   Color Associates
MANUFACTURING MANAGER   Monique Calello

This book was set in **Times Roman** by Michael Goodrich and Robert Tamassia and printed and bound by Quebecor Printing, Fairfield. The film was output by Color Associates. The cover was printed by Phoenix Color Corporation.

This book is printed on acid-free paper. ∞

The paper in this book was manufactured by a mill whose forest management programs include sustained yield harvesting of its timberlands. Sustained yield harvesting principles ensure that the numbers of trees cut each year does not exceed the amount of new growth.

ISBN 0-471-19308-9

Printed in the United States of America

10 9 8 7 6 5 4 3 2 1

To Karen and Paul
   – *Michael T. Goodrich*

To Isabel
   – *Roberto Tamassia*

About the Authors

Professors Goodrich and Tamassia are well-recognized researchers in data structures and algorithms, having published many papers in this field, with applications to geometric and combinatorial problems, including dynamic and external-memory environments. They have an extensive record of research collaboration and are co-principal investigators in the *Center for Geometric Computing*.

Michael Goodrich received his Ph.D. in Computer Science from Purdue University in 1987. He is currently a faculty member in the Department of Computer Science at Johns Hopkins University. He is an editor for *International Journal of Computational Geometry & Applications*, *Journal of Computer and System Sciences*, and *Journal of Graph Algorithms and Applications*.

Roberto Tamassia received his Ph.D. in Electrical and Computer Engineering from the University of Illinois at Urbana-Champaign in 1988. He is currently a faculty member in the Department of Computer Science at Brown University. He is an editor for *Computational Geometry: Theory and Applications*, *IEEE Transactions on Computers*, and *Journal of Graph Algorithms and Applications*.

In addition to their research accomplishments, the authors also have extensive experience in the classroom. For example, Dr. Goodrich has taught data structures and algorithms courses at Johns Hopkins University since 1987, including *Data Structures* as a feshman-sophomore level course and *Introduction to Algorithms* as a mid-to-upper level course. He has earned several teaching awards in this capacity. His teaching style is to involve the students in lively interactive classroom sessions that bring out the intuition and insights behind data structuring and algorithmic techniques, as well as in formulating solutions whose analysis is mathematically rigorous.

Dr. Tamassia has taught *Data Structures and Algorithms* as an introductory freshman-level course at Brown University since 1988. He has also attracted many students (including several undergraduates) to his advanced course on *Computational Geometry*, which is a popular graduate-level CS course at Brown. One thing that has set his teaching style apart is his effective use of interactive hypermedia presentations, continuing the tradition of Brown's "electronic classroom." The carefully designed Web pages of the courses taught by Dr. Tamassia have been used as reference material by students and professionals worldwide.

The authors, therefore, bring significant teaching experience to this book project so as to make this text appropriate for the study of data structure and algorithms, both at the introductory and at the intermediate levels.

Preface

The design and analysis of efficient data structures has long been recognized as a key subject in computer science, for the study of data structures is part of the core of every collegiate computer science major or minor program we are familiar with. Typically, in programs based upon semesters, elementary data structures are briefly introduced in the first programming or introduction to computer science course (CS1), and this is followed by a more in-depth introduction to data structures course (CS2). Furthermore, this introductory course is typically listed as a prerequisite for a host of other courses, and is often itself followed at a later point in the curriculum by a more in-depth study of data structures and algorithms (DS&A). Curricula based upon the quarter system follow a similar approach, but divide the subject matter into more courses. In either case, however, we feel that the central role of data structure design and analysis in the curriculum is fully justified, given the importance of efficient data structures in most software systems, including operating systems, databases, compilers, and scientific simulation systems.

Indeed, the importance of data structure design principles is actually increasing, with the emergence of the object-oriented paradigm as the framework of choice for the implementation of robust and reusable software. One of the main ideas of the object-oriented approach is that data should be presented as being encapsulated with the methods that access and modify them. That is, rather than simply viewing data as a collection of bytes and addresses, we think of data as instances of an *abstract data type* (*ADT*) that includes a repertory of methods for performing operations on the data. Given the powerful influence this paradigm is having on all areas of software engineering, we expect the central role of data structure design in the computer science curriculum to remain strong, and even increase, in the years ahead.

About The Book

This book is designed to provide a comprehensive introduction to data structures and algorithms, including their design, analysis, and implementation. In terms of the Computer Science curriculum, we have written this book so that it can be used in either a Freshman-Sophomore level Data Structures course (CS2) or in a Junior-Senior level Data Structures and Algorithms Course (CS7/DS&A). In particular, the early chapters, Chapters 1 through 6, are focused on developing fundamental data structuring concepts, including stacks, queues, linked lists, trees, priority queues, and heaps. We feel these chapters provide a solid core set of topics for a CS2 course.

Chapters 7 through 11 introduce the intermediate-level topics of dictionaries, balanced search trees, skip lists, hashing, sorting, selection, graphs, and strings. We believe that these chapters are appropriate concluding material for a CS2 course, with intermediate-paced courses ending in Chapter 7 or Chapter 8, and with fast-paced courses possibly getting as far as Chapter 10 or even 11. These intermediate chapters are also a starting point for a Junior-Senior level course on Data Structures and Algorithms (DS&A). Indeed, we feel these topics, which are at an intermediate level for CS2, should be considered core topics for a DS&A course.

The topics of Chapters 12 through 16 are intended primarily for a DS&A course, although we have written them in a way that allows selected topics from these chapters to be "folded" into a fast-paced CS2 course. These chapters cover fundamental techniques, such as amortization, divide-and-conquer, dynamic programming, the greedy method, balanced search trees, multi-dimensional search trees, computational geometry, and techniques for dealing with caches and disks.

Thus, we feel that this book can be used as a stand-alone text for either CS2 or DS&A, or as a single book that spans these two courses. In addition, because of its comprehensive nature, its use of established software engineering design patterns, and its numerous examples of data structure implementation details, we feel this book is also of use to software engineering practitioners.

Prerequisites

We have written this book assuming that the reader comes to it with certain knowledge. Namely, we assume that the reader is familiar with a high-level programming language, such as C, C++, or Java, and that he or she understands the main constructs from such a high-level language, including the following:

- variables and expressions,
- methods (also known as functions or procedures),
- decision structures (such as if-statements and switch-statements),
- iteration structures (for-loops and while-loops),
- arrays.

For readers who are familiar with these concepts, but not with how they are expressed in Java, we provide a primer on the Java language in Appendix A. We do not assume, however, that the reader is necessarily familiar with object-oriented design or with linked structures, such as linked lists, for these topics are covered in the core chapters of this book.

In terms of mathematical background, we assume the reader knows the fundamental topics of high-school mathematics, including exponents, logarithms, and elementary probability. Even so, we review most of these facts in Chapter 2, including exponents, logarithms, and summations, and we give a summary of other useful mathematical facts, including elementary probability, in Appendix B.

For the Instructor

As mentioned above, this book can be used as a textbook for either a Freshman-Sophomore Data Structures (CS2) course or for a Junior-Senior Data Structures and Algorithms (CS7/DS&A) course. Moreover, this book contains over 300 Java-code and pseudo-code fragments, and almost 450 exercises (with roughly 35% being reinforcement exercises, 45% being creativity exercises, and 20% being projects). This book is also structured to allow the instructor a great deal of freedom in how to organize and present the material. For example, we include in several chapters optional material that is somewhat mathematically more advanced. Such optional sections are indicated with a star ($\star$).

Chapter	Possible Options
A. Java Primer	skip if students all know Java
1. Design Principles	have students read a Therac-25 article
2. Analysis Techniques	skip justification methods
3. Stacks, Queues & Linked Lists	provide an alternate case study
4. Sequences	interact w/ the Sequence ADT at the web site
5. Trees	visit the tree drawing applet
6. Priority Queues	skip bottom-up heap construction
7. Dictionaries	visit AVL-tree applet or substitute red-black trees for AVL-trees; skip universal hashing
8. Sets, Sorting, and Selection	skip sorting lower bound
9. Graphs	skip discussion of directed graphs

Table 0.1: An example scenario for an intermediate-paced Freshman-Sophomore Data Structures (CS2) course.

There are also additional options that a creative instructor can exercise. An example of such an option includes substituting the AVL-tree discussion in Chapter 7 with one of the (2,4)-tree, red-black-tree, or splay tree sections of Chapter 13. Also, there are several topics from Chapters 11 through 16 that could easily be incorporated into an interesting CS2 course, such as Huffman coding, data compression, B-trees, or external sorting, to name just a few. We illustrate in Tables 0.1 and 0.2 some possible uses of this book for either a CS2 or DS&A course.

Chapter	Possible Options
Review topics in Chps. 1–6	include bottom-up heap construction
7. Dictionaries	include universal hashing
8. Sets, Sorting, and Selection	include sorting lower bound
9. Graphs	visit the graph drawing web site
10. Weighted graphs	skip one of the MST algorithms, include network flow
11. Strings	skip regular expression matching, visit pattern-matching animation web site
12. Fundamental Techniques	skip union-find analysis
13. Balanced search trees	visit other search tree web sites
14. Multi-dimensional search trees	skip partition trees
15. Computational Geometry	visit the computational geometry animation web site
16. Caches and Disks	skip competitive analysis

Table 0.2: An example scenario for an intermediate-paced Junior-Senior Data Structures and Algorithms (CS7/DS&A) course.

Since there are different ways of using this book in data structures and algorithms courses, we provide in Figure 0.1 the dependencies between different chapters. We include this figure primarily to give instructors an idea of the kinds of additional topics that can be included in an intermediate- or fast-paced CS2 course. This figure also provides a visual overview of the topics presented in this book.

Web Added-Value Education

This book comes accompanied by a CD-ROM and an extensive Web site. Included on the CD-ROM is a complete Java development environment—Microsoft's Visual J++, Publisher's Edition. Included on the Web site is an extensive collection of educational aids that augment the topics of this book. These educational aids include the following:

- all the Java source code presented in this book,
- overhead transparencies and additional figures for topics covered in this book,
- additional exercises and project ideas,
- Java animations and interactive applets for data structures and algorithms presented in this book,
- hyper-links to other data structures and algorithms resources on the Internet.

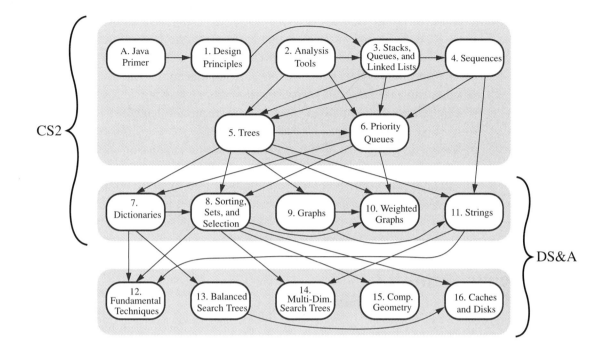

Figure 0.1: Dependencies between chapters. The shaded regions highlight the three major parts of the book.

We feel that the Java animations and interactive applets should be of particular interest, since they allow readers to interactively "play" with different data structures, which leads to better understanding of the different ADTs and the way they can be implemented.

Data Structures in Java

As mentioned earlier, the implementation language used in this book is Java. There are several important reasons for this. First, Java is object-oriented; hence, it incorporates the important software-engineering concepts that allow for code reuse. In addition, Java has a concise syntax like C, but it avoids a number of mechanisms that typically confuse beginning programmers, such as pointer arithmetic, unions and structs, and loosely-typed expressions. In addition, it builds in mechanisms for easily performing several tasks that are difficult to implement using C and C++, including window and mouse management, memory management and garbage collection, socket communication, and multiprogramming via threads. More importantly, unlike C and C++, Java is designed to be platform-independent, which is a feature that can greatly simplify class project implementation. Moreover, Java is supported by all modern Web-browsers. By using Java as our implementation language, then, we use a language that is simple, versatile, and fun.

Our use of Java is inspired by more than just the language itself, however. We present fundamental data structure interfaces in this book so as to conform to a simplified version of *JDSL, the Data Structures Library in Java*. JDSL is a library of ADT definitions and implementations that is inspired by the C++ libraries *STL, the Standard Template Library* [116] and *LEDA, the Library of Efficient Datatypes and Algorithms* [110]. JDSL also has some similarities to *JGL, a Generic Library in Java*, which was inspired by STL. Our use of terms such as "container," "sequence," and "iterator" are consistent with terminology used by these libraries. Thus, in addition to conveying the essentials of data structure design and implementation, this book also implicitly provides an introduction to data structure software libraries.

Acknowledgments

There are a number of individuals who have made contributions to this book. Many students at Brown University and Johns Hopkins University have used pre-publication versions of chapters of this text, and their experiences and responses have helped shape it. There are also a number of collaborators who made specific contributions to the book. Ryan Baker, Edward Bross, Natasha Gelfand, Mark Handy, Matthew Harris, Benoit Hudson, David Jackson, John Kloss, Russell Schwager, Amit Sobti, and Luca Vismara, developed Java code examples and animations. Also, Ryan, Natasha, Mark, Matthew, Benoit, and Luca provided valuable feedback and useful suggestions on drafts of book chapters. Lubomir Bourdev, Mike Demmer, Mark Handy, Michael Horn, and Scott Speigler developed a basic Java tutorial, which ultimately led to the Java Primer Appendix chapter.

We are grateful to all our former teaching assistants who helped us in developing exercises, programming assignments, and algorithm animation systems, and in particular to James Baker, Robert Cohen, Yi-Jen Chiang, Ashim Garg, Jeff Achter, Benjamin Boer, Lubomir Bourdev, Bryan Cantrill, Jody Fanto, Michael Horn, Jovanna Ignatowicz, Seth Padowitz, and Michael Shapiro.

There have been a number of friends and colleagues whose comments have lead to improvements in the text. We are particularly thankful to Karen Goodrich, Art Moorshead, and Scott Smith for their insightful comments. We are also truly indebted to the outside reviewers for their copious comments and constructive criticism, which were extremely useful in the early writing stages. We specifically thank the following reviewers for their comments and suggestions: Divy Agarwal, University of California, Santa Barbara; Bobby Blumofe, University of Texas, Austin; Michael Clancy, University of California, Berkeley; Larry Davis, University of Maryland; Scott Drysdale, Dartmouth College; Stan Kwasny, Washington University; Ken Slonneger, University of Iowa; C.V. Ravishankar, University of Michigan; Val Tannen, University of Pennsylvania; and Paul Van Arragon, Messiah College.

We are grateful to our editor, Regina Brooks, for her enthusiasm in this project, and for the resources she made available to us to complete it. The production team at Wiley has been great. Many thanks go to Monique Calello, Katherine Hepburn, Jay Kirsch, Madelyn Lesure, Charity Robey, and Jeri Uzzo.

The authors' research on data structures and algorithms was supported in part by the National Science Foundation and the U.S. Army Research Office. The advanced computing environments and excellent technical staff in the Computer Science Departments at Brown and Hopkins gave us a reliable working environment. This manuscript was prepared primarily with LaTeX, which is a macro package for TeX (for the text) and Adobe FrameMaker® (for the figures).

Finally, we would like to warmly thank Isabel Cruz, Karen Goodrich, Giuseppe Di Battista, Franco Preparata, Ioannis Tollis, and our parents for providing advice, encouragement, and support at various stages of the preparation of this book. We also thank them for reminding us that there are things in life beyond writing books.

Michael T. Goodrich
Roberto Tamassia

Contents

Chapter 1

Design Principles

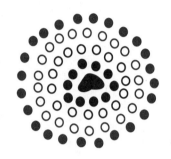

Contents

Figure 1.1: ENIAC, the first digital computer. Shown here are two women "programming" ENIAC. U.S. Army Photo.

The first digital computer, ENIAC (shown in Figure 1.1), did not use any data structures to speak of. Its primary function was to quickly perform long sequences of mathematical calculations, and it was able to perform such calculations at speeds that were truly remarkable for its time. As important an achievement as this was, the major impact of ENIAC is not in the actual calculations it performed, but in the computational era it ushered in.

Today, computers are utilized in a myriad of different ways. Computers are used in the home, providing real-time monitoring and control of washing machines, automobiles, and ovens. In science and engineering, computers are used to design new airplanes, to model complex molecules, and to simulate galaxies. And computers are essential for modern-day commerce, as they are employed to perform financial transactions, to book and schedule airline flights, and to facilitate a host of different modes of communication, not the least of which is the Internet. Indeed, we have come a long way since 1945 when ENIAC was first built.

Modern computers routinely have memory capacities that are tens of millions of times larger than ENIAC ever had,[1] and memory capacities continue to grow at astonishing rates. This growth in capacity has brought with it a new and exciting role for computers. Rather than simply being fast calculators, modern computers are *information processors*. They must be able to store, analyze, search, transfer, and update huge collections of complex data. Quickly performing these tasks requires that data be well organized and that the methods for accessing and maintaining data be fast and efficient. In short, modern computers need good data structures and algorithms.

1.1 Data Structures and Algorithms

Simply put, a *data structure* is a systematic way of organizing and accessing data, and an *algorithm* is a step-by-step procedure for performing some task in a finite amount of time. These concepts are central in computing, and this book is dedicated to the discussion of paradigms and principles for the design and implementation of good data structures and algorithms, which together form a framework for developing computer solutions to important problems.

1.1.1 High-Level Design Goals

Two fundamental goals are used in designing high-level descriptions of data structures and algorithms:

- Correctness
- Efficiency.

By correctness, we mean that a data structure or algorithm is designed, at a high level, to work correctly for all possible inputs that one might encounter within a certain domain of interest. For example, a data structure that is supposed to store a collection of numbers in order should never allow for elements to be stored out of order. Likewise, an algorithm for listing a collection of numbers in order should never output any numbers out of order. The precise meaning of correctness, then, will always depend on the specific problem the data structure or algorithm is intended to solve, but correctness should always be a primary goal.

---

[1]ENIAC's memory was upgraded around 1952 to be able to store a program of 1,800 two-digit instructions and a data set of 100 ten-digit numbers.

Useful data structure and algorithm solutions also need to be efficient. That is, they should be fast and not use any more of the computer's resources, such as memory space, than is necessary. In a competitive or real-time situation, the speed of a data structure or algorithm can make the difference between success and failure—a difference that can often be quite important. For example, the rocket-control algorithms used by the computers on a NASA space shuttle must be designed to run quickly in order to react to the rapidly changing conditions during a lift-off. We believe, therefore, that high-level solutions to data structure and algorithm problems should be based on correct and efficient designs.

Designing efficient data structures and algorithms is a rewarding and challenging endeavor. We have made one of the main goals of this book the development of skills for producing and evaluating quality data structure and algorithm solutions. We have organized subsequent chapters in this book to develop such skills, starting with some basic mathematical foundations, and building upon that with sound design and implementation principles for such structures as stacks, queues, sequences, priority queues, dictionaries, graphs, and strings. We follow that by discussing general algorithmic paradigms, binary search trees, multidimensional trees, computational geometry, and techniques for dealing with constraints imposed by caches and disks. Throughout this book we provide many exercises that reinforce concepts and nurture creativity for applying them in novel situations.

We believe that the skills for producing correct and efficient data structure and algorithm designs are almost useless if one does not also develop the skills to implement such designs. Thus, in addition to exercises that build design skills, we also include in this text several project-oriented exercises that are intended to develop implementation skills as well.

1.1.2 Implementation Goals

The fundamental goals of data structure and algorithm design are to produce solutions that are correct and efficient, and these goals certainly carry over to the production of quality software as well. Still, the production of quality data structure and algorithm implementations has additional goals, which are also fundamental. (See Figure 1.2.) In particular, software implementations should achieve

- Robustness
- Adaptability
- Reusability.

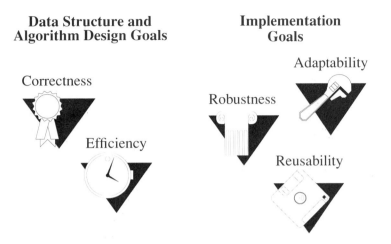

Figure 1.2: Data structure and algorithm design goals and implementation goals.

Robustness

Every good programmer wants to produce software that is ***robust***, which means that a program produces the correct output for all inputs and when run on all hardware platforms. In fact, robust software should be able to handle inputs that are not explicitly defined for its domain of interest. For example, if a program is expecting a number to be input as an integer and instead it is input as a floating point number, then the program should be able to recover gracefully from this error. A program that doesn't gracefully handle such unexpected-input errors can be embarrassing for the programmer. More importantly, in ***life-critical applications***, where a software error can lead to injury or loss-of-life, software that is not robust is deadly. This importance was driven home in the late 1980's in accidents involving Therac-25, a radiation-therapy machine, which severely overdosed six patients between 1985 and 1987, some of whom died from complications resulting from their radiation overdoses [97]. All six accidents were traced to software errors, with one of the most troubling being a user-interface error involving unexpected inputs.

The goal of robustness goes even beyond the need to handle unexpected inputs, however. Software should also be able to produce correct solutions given the well-known limitations of computers. For example, if a user (who could even be another programmer) wishes to store more elements in a data structure than originally expected, then the software should be able to expand the capacity of this structure to handle more elements. This philosophy of robustness is present, for example, in the Java Vector class, which defines an expandable array. Robustness does not come automatically, however. It must be designed in from the start.

Adaptability

Modern software projects, such as those for developing word processors, Web browsers, and Internet search engines, typically involve large software systems that are expected to last for many years. Software, therefore, needs to be able to evolve over time in response to changing conditions in its environment. These changes can be expected, such as the need to adapt to an increase in CPU or network speed, or they can be unexpected, such as the need to add a new functionality to software because of new market demands. Software should also be able to adapt to unexpected events that, in hindsight, really should have been expected, such as the coming of a new millennium and its effects on date calculations (the "year 2000" problem). Thus, another important goal of quality software is that it be ***adaptable***.

Reusability

Going hand-in-hand with adaptability is the desire that software be reusable, i.e., that the same code be a component of different systems in various application domains. Developing quality software can be an expensive enterprise, and its cost can be offset somewhat if the software is designed in a way that makes it easily reusable in future applications. Such reuse should be done with care, however, for one of the major sources of software errors in the Therac-25 came from inappropriate reuse of software from the Therac-20. So, for software to be truly reusable, we must be clear about what it does and does not do. Given this clarity, however, software reuse can be a significant cost-saving and time-saving technique.

1.2   Object-Oriented Design Principles

Much research in software engineering and programming languages has focused on the development of implementation methodologies that are ***simple*** enough to allow a programmer to easily produce software that meets the implementation goals listed above, and ***powerful*** enough to allow a programmer to fully express efficient high-level solutions. Achieving such a balance has not always been easy, but one methodology that is showing considerable promise in being able to strike a balance between simplicity and power is the ***object-oriented design*** approach. Chief among the principles of the object-oriented approach are the following:

- Abstraction
- Encapsulation
- Modularity.

1.2.1   Abstraction

The notion of ***abstraction*** is a powerful concept in computer science. The main idea of this concept is to distill a complicated system down to its most fundamental parts and describe these parts in a simple, precise language. Typically, describing the parts of a system involves naming the different parts and describing their functionality. For example, a typical text-editor graphical user interface (GUI) provides an abstraction of an "edit" menu that offers several specialized text-editing operations, including cutting and pasting portions of text or other graphical objects at different locations in the text. Without going into great details about the various complicated ways a GUI represents and displays text and graphical objects, the concepts of cutting and pasting are simple and precise; a cut operation deletes the selected text and graphics and places them into an external storage buffer, and a paste operation inserts the contents of the external storage buffer at a specific location in the text. Thus, the abstract functionality of an "edit" menu and its cutting and pasting operations is specified in a language precise enough to be clear, but simple enough to "abstract away" unnecessary details. This combination of clarity and simplicity benefits robustness, since it leads to understandable and correct implementations.

Applying this paradigm to the design of data structures gives rise to ***abstract data types*** (ADTs). An ADT is a mathematical model of a data structure that specifies the type of data stored, the operations supported on them, and the types of parameters of the operations. An ADT specifies ***what*** each operation does, but not ***how*** it does it. In Java, an ADT can be expressed by an ***interface***, which is simply a list of method declarations.

An ADT is realized by a concrete data structure, which is modeled in Java by a ***class***. A class defines the data stored and the operations supported by the objects that are instances of the class. Unlike interfaces, classes specify ***how*** the operations are performed. A Java class is said to implement an interface if its methods include those of the interface. It is possible for a class to implement multiple interfaces, provided its methods include all the methods declared in the interfaces.

1.2.2   Encapsulation

Another important principle of object-oriented design is the concept of ***encapsulation***, or ***information hiding***, which states that different components of a software system should implement an abstraction, as described above, without revealing the internal details of that implementation. Consider again our example of an edit menu with cutting and pasting functionality in a text-editor graphical user interface (GUI). One of the main reasons an edit menu is so useful is that one can completely understand how to use it without understanding exactly how it is implemented. One does not, for example, need to know how the menu is drawn, how selected text to be cut or pasted is represented, how selected portions of text are stored in the external buffer, or how various graphical objects, such as graphs, images, or drawings are identified, stored, and copied in and out of the external buffer. Indeed, the code associated with the edit menu should not depend on all of these details to work correctly. Instead, the edit menu should provide an interface that is sufficiently specified for other software components to use its methods effectively, while also requiring well-defined interfaces from other software components that it needs. In general terms, the principle of encapsulation states that all the different components of a large software system should operate on a strict need-to-know basis.

One of the main advantages of encapsulation is that it gives the programmer freedom in implementing the details of a system. The only constraint on the programmer is to maintain the abstract interface that outsiders see. For example, the programmer of the edit menu code in a text-editor GUI might at first implement the cut and paste operations by copying actual screen images in and out of an external buffer. Later, he or she may be dissatisfied with this implementation, since it does not allow one to store the selection compactly, and it does not allow one to distinguish between text and the various kinds of graphic objects. If the programmer has designed the cut and paste interface with encapsulation in mind, switching the underlying implementation to one that stores text as text and graphic objects in an appropriate compact format should not cause any problems to methods that need to interface with this GUI. Thus, encapsulation yields adaptability, for it allows the implementation details of parts of a program to change without adversely affecting other parts.

1.2.3 Modularity

In addition to abstraction and encapsulation, a principle fundamental to object-oriented design is *modularity*. Modern software systems typically consist of several different components that must interact correctly in order for the entire system to work properly. Keeping these interactions straight requires that these different components are well organized. In the object-oriented approach, this structure centers around two concepts, *modularity* and *hierarchy*. Modularity refers to an organizing structure, in which the different components of a software system are divided into separate functional units. For example, a house or apartment can be viewed as consisting of several interacting units, electrical, heating and cooling, plumbing, and structural. Rather than viewing these systems as one giant jumble of wires, vents, pipes, and boards, the organized architect designing a house or apartment will view them as separate modules that interact in well-defined ways. In so doing, he or she is using modularity to bring a clarity of thought that provides a natural way of organizing functions into distinct manageable units. In like manner, using modularity in a software system can also provide a powerful organizing framework that brings clarity to an implementation.

The structure imposed by modularity also enables software reusability, for if software modules are written in an abstract way to solve general problems, then it is likely that instances of these same general problems may arise in other contexts. For example, the structural definition of a wall is the same from house to house, typically being defined in terms of 2- by 4-inch studs, spaced a certain distance apart, etc. Thus, an organized architect can reuse his or her wall definitions from one house to another. In reusing such a definition, some parts may require redefinition, for example, a wall in a commercial building may be similar to that of a house, but the electrical system might be different. Thus, our architect may wish to organize the various structural components, such as electrical and structural, in a *hierarchical* fashion, that groups similar abstract definitions together in a level-by-level manner that goes from specific to more general as one traverses up the hierarchy. A common use of such hierarchies is in an organizational chart, where each link going up can be read as "is a," as in "a ranch is a house is a building." (See Figure 1.3.) Likewise, this kind of hierarchy is useful in software design, for it groups together common functionality at the most general level, and views specialized behavior as an extension of the general one. Thus, the organizing concepts of modularity and hierarchy enable software reusability.

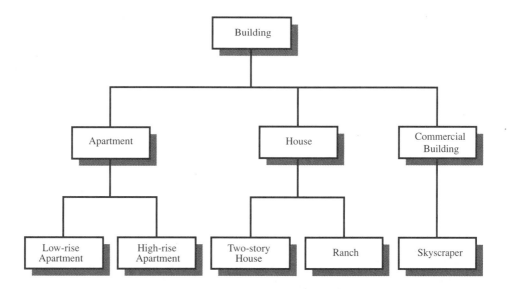

Figure 1.3: An example of an "is-a" hierarchy involving architectural buildings.

1.3   Object-Oriented Design Techniques

Achieving the principles of abstraction, encapsulation, and modularity requires some specific software techniques. The primary techniques of object-oriented design directed at enabling these principles include the following:

- Classes and objects
- Interfaces and strong typing
- Inheritance and polymorphism.

The techniques, principles, and goals of object-oriented design are illustrated in Figure 1.4. We offer this figure mainly as a visual device for remembering these different aspects of object-oriented design, and we discuss some of the techniques for achieving the goals of object-oriented design in the remainder of this section.

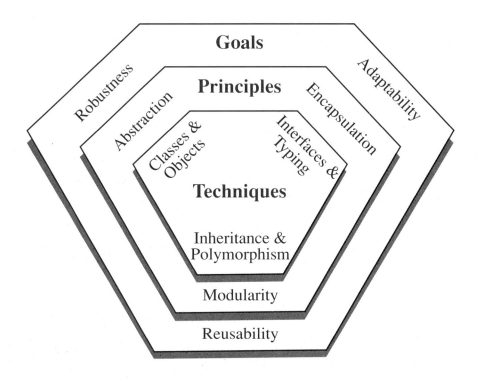

Figure 1.4: The goals, principles, and techniques of object-oriented design.

1.3.1 Classes and Objects

As the name implies, the main "actors" in the object-oriented paradigm are called ***objects***. An object comes from a ***class***, which is a specification of the data ***fields***, also called ***instance variables***, that the object contains, as well as of the operations that the object can execute. Each class should present to the outside world a concise and consistent view of the objects that are instances of this class, without going into too much unnecessary detail or giving others access to the inner workings of the objects.

When an object o is created, memory is allocated for its data fields, and these same fields are initialized to specific beginning values. Typically, one associates the new object o to a variable, which serves as a "link" to object o, and is said to ***reference*** o. When one wishes to access object o (for the purpose of accessing its fields or executing its methods), one can either request the execution of one of o's methods (defined by the class that o belongs to), or look up the fields of o. Indeed, the primary way that an object p interacts with another object o is for p to send a "message" to o that invokes one of o's methods, for example, for o to print a description of itself, for o to convert itself to a string, or for o to return the value of one of its data fields. The secondary way that p can interact with o is for p to access one of o's fields directly, but only if o has given other objects like p permission to do so. For example, an instance of the Java class Integer stores, as an instance variable, an integer, and it provides several operations for accessing this data, including methods for converting it into other number types, for converting it to a string of digits, and for converting strings of digits to a number. It does not allow for direct access of its instance variables, however, for these details are hidden. Thus, classes and the objects that are instances of them, implement the abstraction principle of object-oriented design.

1.3.2 Interfaces and Strong Typing

In order for two objects to interact, they must "know" about the various messages that each will accept, that is, the methods that each object supports. To enforce this "knowledge," the object-oriented design paradigm insists that classes specify the ***application programming interface*** (API), or simply ***interface***, that their objects present to other objects. In an ***ADT-based*** approach, this interface is specified as a class type definition and a collection of methods for this type, with the arguments for each method being of specified types. This specification is, in turn, enforced by the compiler or run-time system, which requires that the types of parameters that are actually passed to methods rigidly conform with the type specified in the interface. This requirement is known as ***strong typing***. Having to define interfaces and then having those definitions enforced by strong typing admittedly places a burden on the programmer, but this burden is offset by the rewards that it provides, for it enforces the encapsulation principle.

1.3.3   Inheritance and Polymorphism

To offset further the extra burden imposed by strong typing, the object-oriented design approach provides ways of reusing code in a software system. Reusing software saves programming time and reduces the probability of errors. Indeed, once a software component is completely debugged, it is better to reuse it than to copy it and slightly modify it at several different locations, for all this copying and modifying can introduce new errors into a program.

In order to avoid redundant code, the object-oriented paradigm provides a modular and hierarchical organizing structure for reusing code: namely, through a technique called *inheritance*. This technique involves the design of generic classes, like the Java Number class, that can then be specialized to more particular classes, such as the Java Float, Integer, and Long classes. The general class, which is also known as a *base* class or *superclass*, can define "generic" instance variables and methods that apply in a multitude of situations. The class that specializes, or *extends*, or *inherits from*, the superclass need not give new implementations for the general methods. It should only define those methods that are specialized for this particular *subclass* (which is also known as a *derived* class). Let us consider an example to illustrate these concepts.

Example 1.1: *Consider a class* S *that defines objects with a field,* x, *and three methods,* a(), b(), *and* c(). *(The particular type of* x *and the functionality of* a(), b(), *and* c() *are not important for this example.) Suppose we were to define a class* T *that extends* S *and includes an additional field,* y, *and two methods,* d() *and* e(). *This would imply that objects of the class* T *have two fields,* x *and* y, *and five methods,* a(), b(), c(), d(), *and* e(). *We illustrate the relationships between the class* S *and the class* T *in a* **class inheritance diagram** *in Figure 1.5. Each box in such a diagram denotes a class, with its name, fields (or instance variables), and methods included as subrectangles.*

An arrow from one box T *to another box* S *indicates that class* T *extends (or inherits from) class* S.

When a program wishes to invoke a certain method a() of some object o, it sends a "message" to o, which is usually denoted, using a procedure-call syntax, as "o.a()." In the compiled version of this program, the code corresponding to this invocation directs the run-time environment to examine o's class T to determine

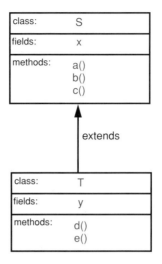

Figure 1.5: A class inheritance diagram. Each box denotes a class, with its name, fields, and methods. An arrow between two boxes denotes an inheritance relation.

if the class T supports an a() method, and, if so, to execute it. Specifically, the run-time environment examines the class T to see if it defines an a() method itself. If it does, then this method is executed. If T does not define an a() method, then the run-time environment examines the superclass T of S. If S defines a(), then this method is executed. If S does not define a(), on the other hand, then the run-time environment repeats the search at the superclass of S. This search continues up the hierarchy of classes until it either finds an a() method, which is then executed, or it reaches a topmost class (e.g., the Object class in Java) without an a() method, which generates a run-time error.

This simple algorithm for finding a method a() to process the message "*o*.a()" allows for another powerful technique of object-oriented programming, ***polymorphism***. Literally, "polymorphism" means "many forms," and in the context of object-oriented design, it refers to the ability of an object to take different forms. Object-oriented languages, such as Java, address objects using reference variables. The reference variable *o* must define which class of objects it is allowed to refer to in terms of some class S. But this implies that *o* can also refer to any object belonging to a class T that extends S. Now consider what happens if S defines an a() method and T also defines an a() method. Because the method invocation algorithm always starts its search from the most restrictive class that applies, when *o* refers to an object from class T, then it will use T's a() method when asked for *o*.a(). In this case, T is said to ***override*** method a() from S. However, when *o* refers to an object from class S, it will execute S's a() method when asked for o.a(). Thus, the object variable o can be polymorphic, or take many forms, depending on the specific class of the objects it is referring to. This kind of functionality is quite useful, actually, for it allows a specialized class T to extend a class S, inherit the "generic" methods from S, and redefine other methods from S to account for specific properties of objects of T. The algorithm that processes the message o.a() to find the specific method to invoke is called the ***dynamic dispatch*** algorithm.

Some object-oriented languages, such as Java, also provide a "watered down" kind of polymorphism, which is more accurately called method ***overloading***, where even a single class T can have multiple methods with the same name, provided each one has a different ***signature***. The signature of a method is a combination of its name and the type and number of arguments that are passed to it. Thus, even though multiple methods in a class can have the same name, they can be distinguished by a compiler, provided they have different signatures, that is, are different in actuality. In languages that allow for method overloading the run-time environment algorithm determines which actual method to invoke for a specific method call by searching up the class hierarchy to find the first method with a signature matching the method being invoked. For example, suppose a class T, which defines a method a(), extends a class U, which defines a method a(x, y). If an object o from class T receives the message "o.a(x, y)," then it is U's version of method a() that is invoked (and gets passed the two parameters x and y). Thus, true polymorphism applies only to methods that have the same signature, but are defined in different classes.

Inheritance, polymorphism, and method overloading support the development of reusable software. We can define classes that inherit the generic instance variables and methods and can then define new more-specific instance variables and methods that deal with special aspects of objects of the new class.

1.4   Java Examples of Object-Oriented Design

To make these notions more concrete, we consider some simple examples in Java.

1.4.1   Some Numeric Progression Classes

We consider as the first example a simple program that consists of several classes for stepping through and printing out a numeric progression. We begin by defining a class, Progression, shown in Code Fragment 1.1, which defines the "generic" fields and methods of a numeric progression. Specifically, it defines an integer cur field, which stores the current value, and the following four methods:

- first(): Reset the progression to the first value.

- nextValue(): Step the progression to the next value and return that value.

- valueAt(*i*): Set the progression to the *i*th value and return that value.

- printProgression(*n*): Print the first *n* values of the progression.

The Progression class also includes a method Progression(), which is a special *constructor* method that sets up all the instance variables at the time an object of this class is created. Note that the Progression class is declared as abstract, which indicates that we cannot directly create objects of this class. Indeed, the Progression class is meant to be a generic superclass from which specialized classes inherit.

```java
public abstract class Progression { // a simple class for numeric progressions.
  protected int cur;              // current value;

  Progression() {                 // constructor
    cur = 0;
  }
  protected int currentValue() { // return the current value
    return cur;
  }
  protected int first() {        // reset to the first value
    cur = 0;
    return cur;
  }
  protected int nextValue() { // should return the "next" value.
    return cur;                   // but this superclass just returns the current
  }
  protected int valueAt(int i) {// return the i-th value;
    first();                      // start with the first value
    for (int j=1; j<i; j++)       // and count i-1 more
      nextValue();
    return currentValue();
  }
  public void printProgression(int n) { // print first n values
    System.out.print(first() + " ");
    for (int i=1; i<n; i++)
      System.out.print(nextValue() + " ");
    System.out.println();
  }
}
```

Code Fragment 1.1: Generic numeric progression class.

Consider now the class ArithProgression, shown in Code Fragment 1.2, which defines a progression where each value is determined by adding a fixed increment, inc, to the previous value. Class ArithProgression inherits from the Progression class field cur and methods currentValue(), valueAt(*i*), and printProgression(*n*), adds a new field, inc, and overrides the first() and nextValue() methods.

```
class ArithProgression extends Progression { // arithmetic progression
  protected int inc; // increment value

  ArithProgression() { inc = 1; /* default increment */ }
  ArithProgression(int increment) { inc = increment; }
  protected int first() { // reset (overrides superclass method)
    cur = 0;
    return cur;
  }
  protected int nextValue() { // next (overrides superclass method)
    cur = cur + inc;
    return cur;
  }
  // Inherits: currentValue(), valueAt(int), and printProgression(int)
}
```

Code Fragment 1.2: The arithmetic progression.

In the definition of the ArithProgression class, we have added two constructor methods, a default method, which takes no parameters, and a parametric method, which can take an integer parameter as the increment for the progression. These two definitions illustrate method overloading, where a method name can have multiple versions inside the same class, since a method is actually specified by its name, the class of the object that calls it, and the types of arguments that are passed to it—its signature. In this case, the overloading is for constructor methods (a default constructor and a parametric constructor). Note that in these constructor methods the Java environment calls the default constructor for the superclass (Progression) before calling the constructor for the subclass. This call of the default constructor is not shown explicitly in the code, however. (See Appendix A for more details about constructors.)

Let us next define a class, GeomProgression, shown in Code Fragment 1.3, which steps through and prints out a geometric progression, that is, a progression where the next value is determined by multiplying the previous value by a fixed base b. A geometric progression is like a generic progression, except that the methods for determining the initial and the next value are different. Hence, GeomProgression is declared as a subclass of the Progression class. As with the

ArithProgression class, the GeomProgression class inherits from the Progression class the field cur and the methods currentValue, valueAt, and printProgression.

```
class GeomProgression extends Progression { // geometric progression
    int b; // the base of the progression.

    GeomProgression() { b = 2; /* default */ }
    GeomProgression(int base) { b = base; }
    protected int first() { // reset (overrides superclass method)
        cur = b;
        return cur;
    }
    protected int nextValue() { // next (overrides superclass method)
        cur = cur * b;
        return cur;
    }
    // Inherits: currentValue(), valueAt(int), and printProgression(int)
}
```

Code Fragment 1.3: The geometric progression.

As a further example, we define a FibonacciProgression class that represents another kind of progression, the Fibonacci progression, where the next value is defined as the sum of the previous two. In order to visualize how the three different progression classes are derived from the abstract Progression class, we give their inheritance diagram in Figure 1.6.

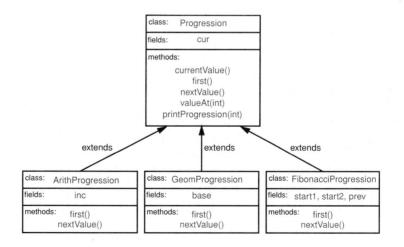

Figure 1.6: Inheritance diagram for class Progression and its subclasses.

We show the Fibonacci Progression class in Code Fragment 1.4. Note that the parameterized constructor in the FibonacciProgression class illustrates the handling of error conditions in Java by means of named *exceptions*, which are "thrown" when an error is detected. The exception BadFibonacciParameterException thrown by the parameterized constructor FibonacciProgression(int, int) indicates that either the first parameter is negative or the second parameter is nonpositive. Please see Appendix A for more information about exceptions.

```java
class FibonacciProgression extends Progression { // Fibonacci  progression
  int start1,start2; // starting values
  int prev; // previous value

  FibonacciProgression() { // default constructor.
    start1 = 0;
    start2 = 1;
  }
  FibonacciProgression(int i1, int i2) // parametric constructor.
    throws BadFibonacciParameterException {
      if ((i1< 0) || (i2 <= 0)) throw new BadFibonacciParameterException();
      start1 = i1;
      start2 = i2;
  }
  protected int first() { // reset (overrides superclass method)
    cur = start1; // starting value
    prev = start2 − cur; // "previous" value
    return cur;
  }
  protected int nextValue() { // next (overrides superclass method)
    int temp = prev;
    prev = cur;
    cur = cur + temp;
    return cur;
  }
  // Inherits: currentValue(), valueAt(int), and printProgression(int)
}
```

Code Fragment 1.4: The Fibonacci progression.

We define a class Tester, shown in Code Fragment 1.5, which performs a simple test of each of the three classes. In this class, variable prog is polymorphic during the execution of the main method, since it references in turn objects of class ArithProgression, GeomProgression, and FibonacciProgression. When the main method of the Tester class is invoked by the Java runtime system, the output shown in Code Fragment 1.6 is produced.

```java
class Tester {
  public static void main(String[] args) {
    Progression prog;

    System.out.println("Arithmetic progression with increment 5:");
    prog = new ArithProgression(5);
    prog.printProgression(10);
    System.out.println("Geometric progression with base 3:");
    prog = new GeomProgression(3);
    prog.printProgression(10);
    System.out.println("Fibonacci progression with default start values:");
    prog = new FibonacciProgression();
    prog.printProgression(10);
    try {
      System.out.println("Fibonacci progression starting with 4 and 6:");
      prog = new FibonacciProgression(4,6);
      prog.printProgression(10);
    } catch (BadFibonacciParameterException e) {
      System.out.println(e.getMessage());
    }
    try {
      System.out.println("Fibonacci progression starting with 2 and -1:");
      prog = new FibonacciProgression(2,-1);
      prog.printProgression(10);
    } catch (BadFibonacciParameterException e) {
      System.out.println(e.getMessage());
    }
    System.out.println("That is all.");
  }
}
```

Code Fragment 1.5: Testing the progression classes.

```
Arithmetic progression with increment 5:
0 5 10 15 20 25 30 35 40 45
Geometric progression with base 3:
3 9 27 81 243 729 2187 6561 19683 59049
Fibonacci progression with default start values:
0 1 1 2 3 5 8 13 21 34
Fibonacci progression starting with 4 and 6:
4 6 10 16 26 42 68 110 178 288
Fibonacci progression starting with 2 and −1:
Error: bad starting values for a Fibonacci progression.
That is all.
```

Code Fragment 1.6: Output of the testing program.

The example presented in this section is admittedly small, but it illustrates the main features of the object-oriented design paradigm as implemented in a stand-alone Java program.

We consider next another kind of Java program, which also illustrates object-oriented programming. This other style of programming uses Java applets, which are window-based programs that use inheritance to provide a software framework for designing programs that can safely be sent over the Internet.

1.4.2 A Simple Java Applet

One of the prime uses of the Java language is to write programs, called *applets*, that are embedded into HTML documents and are then viewed using a Web browser. Applets allow Web documents to come "alive" as interactive animations. It is beyond the scope of this book to discuss all the ways to perform interaction, input/output, and animation in Java applets.[2] Nevertheless, we give a simple example Java applet here, because the concepts of inheritance and polymorphism are central to the way that we define applets.

All applets in Java must be defined as classes that extend the built-in Java Applet class, because the built-in Applet class has a number of predefined methods for drawing and interacting with applets. To make a particular applet do interesting things, we need only override a few of these methods. Important methods defined for the Applet class include the following:

- init(): This method is called when the applet is first loaded. It should be considered equivalent to a constructor for the applet.
- start(): This method is called when the applet is started, which occurs when the applet is loaded, when the applet window is opened after being iconified or when the Web page containing the applet is revisited (for example, by hitting the "back" button in the Web browser).
- stop(): This method is called when the applet is stopped, for example, because the applet window is iconified or the Web browser leaves the Web page containing the applet.
- destroy(): This method is called just before an applet is terminated, for example, when the Web browser itself is closed.

There are a number of other Applet methods as well, but the methods listed above are the main ones governing the "milestones" in the life of a Java applet.

---

[2]A great way to learn about applets is to visit the Java tutorial site at Javasoft, Inc. (http://www.javasoft.com), which describes how to write applets and gives several "live" examples that include source code.

The Applet class derives from a chain of superclasses that, as depicted in Figure 1.7, ends with the Object class. We did not illustrate the Object class in the previous example, but it was there, because every object in Java is derived from this class. In Figure 1.7, we illustrate only a few of the many methods the Applet class inherits. A nice aspect of this framework for defining applets is that each class in the hierarchy from Applet to Object provides some level of functionality. The classes are separated in a modular fashion, with each superclass describing more-general objects than its subclass.

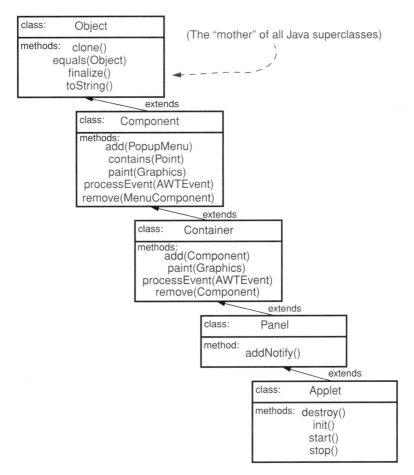

Figure 1.7: Class inheritance diagram for the Java Applet class.

Each class in the class hierarchy depicted in Figure 1.7 hides the details of how functionality for a graphical user interface is achieved. Thus, the hierarchy uses encapsulation to embed details that do not have to be known by an applet programmer.

We conclude this section by giving a simple Java applet that overrides a few of the built-in Applet methods to draw a number of nested rectangles equal to the number of milestones in the life of this applet. In addition, it outputs to the Java console of the browser the name of each milestone as it is occurring. This class does not have a main() method, because it is intended to be called inside an applet viewer or Web browser.

A snapshot of what this applet looks like after it has been iconified and opened a few times is shown in Figure 1.8. This is admittedly a simple Java applet, but it nevertheless illustrates a practical application of the power of inheritance and object-oriented design.

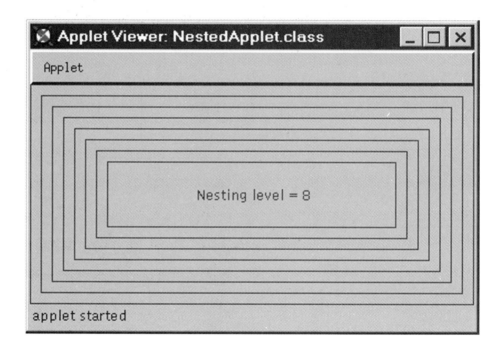

Figure 1.8: A screen snapshot of the NestedApplet Java applet.

In Code Fragment 1.7, we give the source code for the applet illustrated in Figure 1.8, and we show an example HTML document that has this applet embedded inside it in Code Fragment 1.8.

There are, of course, a number of other interesting things that applets can be used for besides illustrating object-orientivity. We encourage the reader to explore the many possibilities that Java applets provide, particularly for solving project exercises included in Chapters 3 through 16.

```java
import java.applet.*;
import java.awt.*;

public class NestedApplet extends Applet {
    int level = 0;            // the nesting level
    int inc = 10;             // the nesting increment
    int width = 400;          // the expected applet width
    int height = 200;         // the expected applet height

    public void init() {          // The applet initializer.
        System.out.println("Initializing.");
        incNesting();
    }
    public void start() {         // The start-up method
        System.out.println("Starting.");
        incNesting();
    }
    public void stop() {          // The stopping method
        System.out.println("Stopping.");
        incNesting();
    }
    public void destroy() {       // The applet shut-down method
        System.out.println("Shutting down...");
        incNesting();
    }
    public void incNesting() {  // Increment the nesting level & repaint
        level++;
        repaint();
    }
    public void paint(Graphics g) {     // Paint the nested rectangles
        int i, shift=0;                 // level indent amount
        g.setColor(Color.blue);
        for (i=0; i<level; i++) {
            g.drawRect(shift, shift, width-2*shift-1, height-2*shift-1);
            shift=shift+inc;
        }
        g.drawString("Nesting level = " + level, width/2-50, height/2+5);
    }
}
```

Code Fragment 1.7: A simple Java Applet.

```
<html>
<head>
   <title>A Nested Rectangle Applet</title>
</head>
<body>
<Applet CODE="NestedApplet.class" WIDTH=400 HEIGHT=200></Applet>
</body>
</html>
```

Code Fragment 1.8: Example of an HTML document that includes the applet of Code Fragment 1.7.

1.5   Object-Oriented Design Patterns

One of the main advantages of object-oriented design is to encourage organized code development skills for building software that is reusable, robust, and adaptable. Designing quality object-oriented code takes more than simply understanding the object-oriented design methodologies, however. It requires the effective use of these and other object-oriented techniques in powerful and elegant ways.

Software engineering researchers and practitioners have developed a variety of organizational concepts and methodologies for designing quality object-oriented software that is concise, correct, and reusable. Of special relevance to this book is the concept of a ***design pattern***, which describes a solution to a "typical" software design problem. A pattern provides a general template that can be applied in many different situations. It describes the main elements of a software architecture in an abstract way that can be specialized for the specific problem at hand. Design patterns are important but sometimes neglected in the discussion of data structures and algorithms.

We present several object-oriented design patterns in this book, and we show how they can be consistently applied to design quality implementations of data structures and algorithms. Some of the design patterns we discuss include:

- Adapter
- Position
- Iterator (also known as enumeration)
- Template method
- Locator
- Composition
- Comparator.

Rather than explain each of these concepts here, however, we will introduce them throughout the text as they are needed.

1.6 Exercises

Reinforcement

R-1.1 Give three examples of life-critical software applications.

R-1.2 Give an example of a software application where adaptability can mean the difference between a prolonged sales lifetime and bankruptcy.

R-1.3 Describe a component from a text-editor GUI (other than an "edit" menu) and the methods that it encapsulates.

R-1.4 Draw a class inheritance diagram for the following set of classes:

- Class Dog extends Object and adds an instance variable tail and methods bark() and jump().
- Class Cat extends Object and adds an instance variable nose and methods purr() and jump().
- Class Sheep extends Object and adds instance variables length and color, and methods clip() and clone() (which overrides the Object clone() method).
- Class Poodle extends Dog and adds a method groom().
- Class Puppy extends Dog and adds an instance variable weight and methods sleep() and isTrained().

R-1.5 Give a short fragment of Java code that uses the classes from Section 1.4.1 to find the 7th value of a Fibonacci progression that starts with 3 and 4 as its first two values.

Creativity

C-1.1 Explain why the dynamic dispatch algorithm that looks for the specific method to invoke for a message $o.a()$ will never get into an infinite loop.

C-1.2 Write a Java class that extends the Progression class to produce a progression where each value is the absolute value of the difference between the previous two values. You should include a default constructor that starts with 2 and 200 as the first two values and a parametric constructor that starts with a specified pair of numbers as the first two values.

C-1.3 Write a Java class that extends the Progression class to produce a progression where each value is the square root of the previous value. (Note that you can no longer represent each value with an integer.) You should include a default constructor that starts with $65,536$ as the first value, and a parametric constructor that starts with a specified (**double**) number as the first value.

C-1.4 Explain why the NestedApplet Java applet will almost always be displaying an even number of nested rectangles.

Projects

P-1.1 Write a Java applet to display a number of nested circles equal to the number of milestones in the life of this applet. (Make sure to define your viewing box large enough so as to show at least 16 nested circles.)

P-1.2 Write a Java applet to alternately draw a "happy" face and a "sad" face every other time it is iconified and restored or revisited in a Web browser.

P-1.3 Write a Java applet or stand-alone program that can take a positive number greater than 2 that is input from a text window and write out the number of times one must repeatedly divide this number by 2 before getting a value less than 2.

P-1.4 A common punishment given to school children is to write out the same sentence multiple times. Write a Java stand-alone program that will write out the sentence, "I will always use object-oriented design," one hundred times. Your program should number each sentence and it should "accidentally" make eight different random looking typos, at various points in the listing, so that it looks like a human typed it all by hand.

P-1.5 Write a Java applet or a stand-alone Java program that can "make change." Your program should take two numbers as input, one that is a monetary amount charged and the other that is a monetary amount given. It should then return the number of each kind of bill and coin to give back as change for the difference between the amount given and the amount charged. The values assigned to the bills and coins can be based on the monetary system of any current or former government. Try to design your program so that it returns the fewest number of bills and coins as possible.

Chapter Notes

The reader interested in learning more about the contribution to computing that was made by ENIAC and other historical computing devices is referred to the book by Williams [148] or the Web site (`http://ftp.arl.mil/~mike/comphist/`) for the Army Research Laboratory's "History of Computing Information." For a broad overview of recent developments in computer science and engineering we refer the reader to *The Computer Science and Engineering Handbook* [140].

The reader interested in further studying object-oriented programming is referred to the books by Booch [25], Budd [29], and Liskov and Guttag [100]. Liskov and Guttag [100] also provide a nice discussion of abstract data types, as does the survey paper by Cardelli and Wegner [32] and the book chapter by Demurjian [39] in the *The Computer Science and Engineering Handbook* [140]. Design patterns are described in the book by Gamma, *et al.* [55]. The class inheritance diagram notation we use is derived from the class diagram notation described in the book by Gamma, *et al.* book.

Readers who are unfamiliar with Java are encouraged to read one of the many fine introductory books about Java, including the books by Arnold and Gosling [10], Campione and Walrath [31], Cornell and Horstmann [37], Flanagan [49], and Horstmann [75]. It may also be instructive to visit the Javasoft Web site (`http://www.javasoft.com/`).

Chapter

2

Analysis Tools

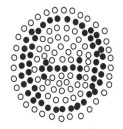

Contents

In a classic story, the famous mathematician Archimedes was asked to determine if a golden crown commissioned by the king was indeed pure gold, and not part silver, as an informant had claimed. Archimedes discovered a way to determine this while stepping into a (Greek) bath. He noted that water spilled out of the bath in proportion to the amount of him that went in. Realizing the implications of this fact, he immediately got out of the bath and ran naked through the city shouting, "Eureka, eureka!," for he had discovered an analysis tool (displacement), which, when combined with a simple scale, could determine if the king's new crown was good or not. This discovery was unfortunate for the goldsmith, however, for when Archimedes did his analysis, the crown displaced more water than an equal-weight lump of pure gold, indicating that the crown was not, in fact, pure gold.

In like manner, to classify some data structures and algorithms as "good," we must have precise ways of analyzing them. The primary analysis tool we will use in this book involves characterizing the running times of algorithms and data structure operations, with space usage also being of interest. Running time is a very natural measure of "goodness," since time is a precious resource—computer solutions should run as fast as possible. But focusing on running time as a primary measure of goodness raises an interesting question.

2.1 What Is Running Time Anyway?

The running time of an algorithm or data structure operation typically depends on a number of factors, so what should be the proper way of measuring it?

2.1.1 Experimental Studies

If an algorithm has been implemented, we can study its running time by executing it on various test inputs and recording the time spent in each execution. Such measurements can be taken in an accurate manner by using system calls that are built into the language or operating system for which the algorithm is written (for example, by using the Java System.currentTimeMillis() method or calling the Java run-time environment with profiling enabled). In general, we are interested in determining the dependency of the running time on the size of the input. In order to determine this, we can perform several experiments on many different test inputs of various sizes. We can then visualize the results of such experiments by plotting the performance of each run of the algorithm as a point with x-coordinate equal to the input size, n, and y-coordinate equal to the running time, t. (See Figure 2.1.) To be meaningful, this analysis requires that we choose good sample inputs and test enough of them to be able to make sound statistical claims about the algorithm.

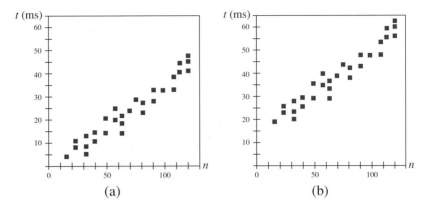

Figure 2.1: The results of an experimental study on the running time of an algorithm. A dot with coordinates (n, t) indicates that on an input of size n, the running time of the algorithm is t milliseconds (ms). (a) the algorithm executed on a fast computer; (b) the algorithm executed on a slow computer.

In general, the running time of an algorithm or data structure method increases with the input size, although it may also vary for distinct inputs of the same size. Also, the running time is affected by the hardware environment (processor, clock rate, memory, disk, etc.) and software environment (operating system, programming language, compiler, interpreter, etc.) in which the algorithm is implemented, compiled, and executed. All other factors being equal, the running time of the same algorithm on the same input data will be smaller if the computer has, say, a much faster processor or if the implementation is done in a program compiled into native machine code instead of an interpreted implementation run on a virtual machine.

2.1.2 Requirements for a General Methodology

While experimental studies on running times are useful, they have three major limitations:

- Experiments can be done only on a limited set of test inputs, and may not be indicative of the running time on other inputs that were not included in the experiment.
- It is difficult to compare the efficiency of two algorithms unless experiments on their running times have been performed in the same hardware and software environments.
- It is necessary to implement and execute an algorithm in order to study its running time.

In the rest of this chapter, we develop a general methodology for analyzing the running time of algorithms that:

- Takes into account all possible inputs
- Allows us to evaluate the relative efficiency of any two algorithms in a way that is independent from the hardware and software environment
- Can be performed by studying a high-level description of the algorithm without actually implementing it or running experiments on it.

This methodology aims at associating with each algorithm a function $f(n)$ that characterizes the running time of the algorithm as a function of the input size n. Typical functions that will be encountered include n and n^2. For example, we will write statements of the type "Algorithm A runs in time proportional to n," meaning that if we performed experiments, we would find that the actual running time of algorithm A on **any** input of size n never exceeds cn, where c is a constant that depends on the hardware and software environment used in the experiment. Given two algorithms A and B, where A runs in time proportional to n and B runs in time proportional to n^2, we will prefer A to B, since function n grows at a smaller rate than function n^2. These, of course, are intuitive notions of the growth of two familiar functions, but our methodology will make such notions precise.

Before we "roll up our sleeves" and start developing our methodology for algorithm analysis, we present a high-level notation for describing algorithms (Section 2.2) and review fundamental mathematical concepts (Section 2.3) as well as techniques for formal reasoning (Section 2.4).

2.2   Pseudo-Code

Computer scientists are often asked to describe algorithms in a way that is intended for human eyes only. Such descriptions are not computer programs, but are more structured than usual prose. In particular, these "high-level" descriptions combine natural language and familiar structures from a programming language, in a way that is both clear and informative. Such descriptions also facilitate the high-level analysis of a data structure or algorithm. We call these descriptions *pseudo-code*.

2.2.1   An Example of Pseudo-Code

The straightforward array-maximum problem is to find the maximum element in an array A storing n integers. To solve this problem we can use an algorithm called arrayMax, which scans through the elements of A using a **for** loop.

The pseudo-code description of algorithm arrayMax is shown in Code Fragment 2.1, while a complete Java implementation is shown in Code Fragment 2.2.

Algorithm arrayMax(A, n):
> *Input:* An array A storing n integers.
> *Output:* The maximum element in A.
>
> $currentMax \leftarrow A[0]$
> **for** $i \leftarrow 1$ **to** $n - 1$ **do**
>   **if** $currentMax < A[i]$ **then**
> $currentMax \leftarrow A[i]$
> **return** $currentMax$

Code Fragment 2.1: Algorithm arrayMax.

```java
public class ArrayMaxProgram {
    // test program for an algorithm that finds the maximum element in an array
    static int arrayMax(int[] A, int n) {
        // find the maximum element in array A of n integers by scanning
        // the cells of A while keeping track of the maximum element
        // encountered
        int currentMax = A[0];      // executed once
        for (int i=1; i < n; i++)   // executed once; n times; n-1 times, resp.
            if (currentMax < A[i])  // executed n-1 times
                currentMax = A[i];  // executed at most n-1 times
        return currentMax;          // executed once
    }
    public static void main(String args[]) {
        // testing method called when the program is executed
        int[] num = { 10, 15, 3, 5, 56, 107, 22, 16, 85 };
        int n = num.length;
        System.out.print("Array:");
        for (int i=0; i < n; i++)
            System.out.print(" " + num[i]); // prints one element of the array
        System.out.println(".");
        System.out.println("The maximum element is " + arrayMax(num,n) + ".");
    }
}
```

Code Fragment 2.2: Algorithm arrayMax within a complete Java program. The comments indicate how many times some statements are executed when the program is run.

Note that the pseudo-code is more compact than the Java code and is easier to read and understand. By inspecting the pseudo-code, we can argue about the correctness of algorithm arrayMax with a simple iteration argument. Variable *currentMax* starts out being equal to the first element of *A*. We claim that at the beginning of the *i*th iteration of the loop, *currentMax* is equal to the maximum of the first *i* elements in *A*. Since we compare *currentMax* to $A[i]$ in iteration *i*, if this claim is true before this iteration, it will be true after it for $i + 1$ (which is the next value of counter *i*). Thus, after $n - 1$ iterations *currentMax* will equal the maximum element in *A*.

2.2.2 What Is Pseudo-Code?

Pseudo-code is a mixture of natural language and high-level programming constructs that describe the main ideas behind a generic implementation of a data structure or algorithm. There really is no precise definition of the ***pseudo-code*** language, however, because of its reliance on natural language. At the same time, to help achieve clarity, pseudo-code mixes natural language with standard programming language constructs, such as:

- Expressions: We use standard mathematical symbols to express numeric and boolean expressions. We use the left arrow sign ($\leftarrow$) as the assignment operator in assignment statements (equivalent to the Java = operator) and we use the equal sign (=) as the equality relation in boolean expressions (which is equivalent to the "==" relation in Java).
- Method declarations: **Algorithm** name(*param1, param2, . . .*) declares a new method "name" and its parameters.
- Decision structures: **if** condition **then** true-actions [**else** false-actions]. We use indentation to indicate what actions should be included in the true-actions and false-actions.
- While-loops: **while** condition **do** actions. We use indentation to indicate what actions should be included in the loop actions.
- Repeat-loops: **repeat** actions **until** condition. We use indentation to indicate what actions should be included in the loop actions.
- For-loops: **for** variable-increment-definition **do** actions. We use indentation to indicate what actions should be included among the loop actions.
- Array indexing: $A[i]$ represents the *i*th cell in the array *A*. The cells of an *n*-celled array *A* are indexed from $A[0]$ to $A[n - 1]$ (consistent with Java).
- Method calls: object.method(args) (object is optional if it is understood).
- Method returns: **return** value. This operation returns the value specified to the method that called this one.

When we write pseudo-code, we must keep in mind that we are writing for a human reader, not a computer. Thus, we should strive to communicate high-level ideas, not low-level implementation details. At the same time, we should not gloss over important steps. Like many forms of human communication, finding the right balance is an important skill that is refined through practice. We provide several opportunities for such practice in the exercises included in this book.

In addition, to better communicate the essence of an algorithm or data structure operation, it is useful to begin an algorithm description with a brief abstract explaining the input/output behavior of the algorithm, as well as what it does and the main ideas that it uses.

2.3 A Quick Mathematical Review

In this section, we briefly review some of the fundamental concepts from discrete mathematics that will arise in several of our discussions. In addition to these fundamental concepts, we include in Appendix B a list of other useful mathematical facts that apply to a lesser degree in the context of data structure and algorithm analysis.

2.3.1 Logarithms and Exponents

One of the interesting, and sometimes even surprising aspects of the analysis of data structures and algorithms is the ubiquitous presence of logarithms and exponents, where we say

$$\log_b a = c \qquad \text{if} \qquad a = b^c.$$

As is the custom in computer science literature, we omit writing the base b of the logarithm when $b = 2$. For example, $\log 1024 = 10$.

There are a number of important rules for logarithms and exponents, including the following:

Proposition 2.1: *Let a, b, and c be positive real numbers. We have*

1. $\log_b ac = \log_b a + \log_b c$
2. $\log_b a/c = \log_b a - \log_b c$
3. $\log_b a^c = c \log_b a$
4. $\log_b a = (\log_c a)/\log_c b$
5. $b^{\log_c a} = a^{\log_c b}$
6. $(b^a)^c = b^{ac}$
7. $b^a b^c = b^{a+c}$
8. $b^a/b^c = b^{a-c}$

Also, as a notational shorthand, we use $\log^c n$ to denote the function $(\log n)^c$ and we use $\log\log n$ to denote $\log(\log n)$. Rather than show how we could derive each of the previous identities, which all follow from the definition of logarithms and exponents, let us instead illustrate these identities with a few examples of their usefulness.

Example 2.2: *We illustrate some interesting cases when the base of a logarithm or exponent is 2. The rules cited refer to Proposition 2.1.*

- $\log(2n\log n) = 1 + \log n + \log\log n$, *by rule 1 (twice)*
- $\log(n/2) = \log n - \log 2 = \log n - 1$, *by rule 2*
- $\log\sqrt{n} = \log(n)^{1/2} = (\log n)/2$, *by rule 3*
- $\log\log\sqrt{n} = \log(\log n)/2 = \log\log n - 1$, *by rules 1, 2, and 3*
- $\log_4 n = (\log n)/\log 4 = (\log n)/2$, *by rule 4*
- $\log 2^n = n$, *by rule 3*
- $2^{\log n} = n$, *by rule 5 (and 3)*
- $2^{2\log n} = (2^{\log n})^2 = n^2$, *by rule 6*
- $4^n = (2^2)^n = 2^{2n}$, *by rule 6*
- $n^2 2^{3\log n} = n^2 \cdot n^3 = n^5$, *by rule 7 and 6*
- $4^n/2^n = 2^{2n}/2^n = 2^{2n-n} = 2^n$, *by rules 8 and 6*

One additional comment concerning logarithms is in order. The value of a logarithm is typically not an integer, yet the running time of an algorithm is typically expressed by means of an integer quantity, such as the number of operations performed. Thus, an algorithm analysis may sometimes involve the use of the so-called "floor" and "ceiling" functions, which are defined respectively as

- $\lfloor x \rfloor$ = the largest integer less than or equal to x.
- $\lceil x \rceil$ = the smallest integer greater than or equal to x.

These functions give us a way to convert real-valued functions into integer-valued functions. Even so, functions used to analyze data structures and algorithms are often expressed simply as real-valued functions (for example, $n\log n$ or $n^{3/2}$). We should read such a running time as having a "big" ceiling function surrounding it.[1]

---

[1] Real-valued running-time functions are almost always used in conjunction with the asymptotic notation described in Section 2.6, for which the use of the ceiling function would usually be redundant anyway. (See Exercise R-2.17.)

2.3.2 Summations

Another notation that appears again and again in the analysis of data structures and algorithms is the summation, which is defined as

$$\sum_{i=a}^{b} f(i) = f(a) + f(a+1) + f(a+2) + \cdots + f(b).$$

Summations arise in data structure and algorithm analysis because the running times of loops naturally give rise to summations. For example, one type of summation that often arises in data structure and algorithm analysis is the summation of a geometric progression, which is characterized as follows:

Proposition 2.3: *For any integer $n \geq 0$ and any real number $0 < a \neq 1$, consider the summation*

$$\sum_{i=0}^{n} a^i = 1 + a + a^2 + \cdots + a^n$$

(remembering that $a^0 = 1$ if $a > 0$). This summation is equal to

$$\frac{1 - a^{n+1}}{1 - a}.$$

For example, every computer scientist should know that

$$1 + 2 + 4 + 8 + \cdots + 2^{n-1} = 2^n - 1,$$

for this is the largest integer that can be represented in binary notation using n bits. Summations such as this are called **geometric** summations, because each term in the summation is geometrically larger than the previous one if $a > 1$. That is, the terms in such a geometric summation exhibit exponential growth.

Another summation that arises in several different contexts is

$$\sum_{i=1}^{n} i = 1 + 2 + 3 + \cdots + (n-2) + (n-1) + n.$$

This summation often arises in the analysis of loops in cases where the number of operations performed inside the loop increases by a fixed, constant amount with each iteration. This summation also has an interesting history. In 1787, a German elementary school teacher decided to keep his 9- and 10-year-old pupils occupied with the task of adding up all the numbers from 1 to 100. But almost immediately after giving this assignment, one of the children claimed to have the answer! The teacher was suspicious, for the student had only the answer on his slate, with no calculations. But the answer was correct—5,050. That student was none other than Karl Gauss, who would grow up to be one of the greatest mathematicians of the 19th century. It is widely suspected that young Gauss derived the answer to his teacher's assignment using the following identity.

Proposition 2.4: *For any integer $n \geq 1$, we have*

$$\sum_{i=1}^{n} i = \frac{n(n+1)}{2}.$$

We give two "visual" justifications of Proposition 2.4 in Figure 2.2.

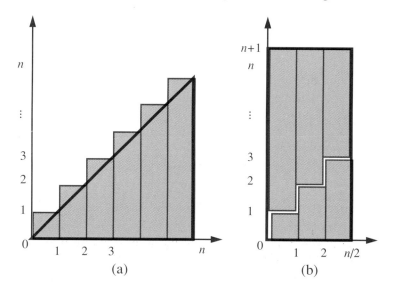

(a)   (b)

Figure 2.2: Visual justifications of Proposition 2.4. Both illustrations visualize the identity in terms of the total area covered by n unit-width rectangles with heights $1, 2, \ldots, n$. In (a) the rectangles are shown to cover a big triangle of area $n^2/2$ (base n and height n) plus n small triangles of area $1/2$ each (base 1 and height 1). In (b), which applies only when n is even, the rectangles are shown to cover a big rectangle of base $n/2$ and height $n+1$.

2.4 Simple Justification Techniques ⋆

Throughout this book, we will sometimes wish to make strong claims about a certain data structure or algorithm. We may, for example, wish to claim that our algorithm is 100% correct or make an argument about its running time. In order to rigorously make such claims, we must use mathematical language, and in order to back up such claims, we must justify or ***prove*** our statements. Fortunately, there are several simple ways to produce such justifications.

⋆We use a star (⋆) to indicate sections containing material more advanced than the material in the rest of the chapter; this material can be considered optional in a first reading.

2.4.1 By Example

Some claims are of the generic form, "There is an element x in a set S that has property P." To justify such a claim, we need only produce a particular $x \in S$ that has property P. Likewise, some hard-to-believe claims are of the generic form, "Every element x in a set S has property P." To justify that such a claim is false, we need to only produce a particular x from S, in this case one that does not have property P. Such an instance is called a ***counterexample***.

Example 2.5: *A certain Professor Amongus claims that every number of the form $2^i - 1$ is a prime, when i is an integer greater than 1. Professor Amongus is wrong.*

Justification: *To prove Professor Amongus is wrong, we need to find a counterexample. Fortunately, we need not look too far, for $2^4 - 1 = 15 = 3 \cdot 5$.* ∎

2.4.2 The "Contra" Attack

Another set of justification techniques involves the use of the negative. The two primary such methods are the use of the ***contrapositive*** and the ***contradiction***. The use of the contrapositive method is like looking through a negative mirror. To justify the statement "if p is true, then q is true" we instead establish that "if q is not true, then p is not true." Logically, these two statements are the same, but the latter, which is called the ***contrapositive*** of the first, may be easier to think about.

Example 2.6: *If ab is odd, then a is odd or b is even.*

Justification: *To justify this claim, consider the contrapositive, "If a is even and b is odd, then ab is even." So, suppose $a = 2i$, for some positive integer i. Then $ab = (2i)b = 2(ib)$; hence, ab is even.* ∎

Besides showing a use of the contrapositive justification technique, the previous example also contains an application of ***DeMorgan's Law***. This law helps us deal with negations, for it states that the negation of a statement of the form "p or q" is "not p and not q." Likewise, it states that the negation of a statement of the form "p and q" is "not p or not q."

Another negative justification technique is justification by ***contradiction***, which also often involves using DeMorgan's Law. In applying the justification by contradiction technique, we establish that a statement q is true by first supposing that q is false and then showing that this assumption leads to a contradiction (such as $2 \neq 2$ or $1 > 3$). By reaching such a contradiction, we show that no consistent world exists with q being false, so q must be true. Of course, in order to reach this conclusion, we must be sure the world is consistent before we assume q is false.

Example 2.7: *If ab is odd, then a is odd or b is even.*

Justification: *Suppose ab is odd. We wish to show that a is odd or b is even. So, with the hope of leading to a contradiction, let us assume the opposite, namely, suppose a is even and b is odd. Then $a = 2i$ for some positive integer i. Hence, $ab = (2i)b = 2(ib)$, that is, ab is even. But this is a contradiction: ab cannot simultaneously be odd and even. Therefore a is odd or b is even.* ∎

2.4.3 Induction and Loop Invariants

Most of the claims we make about a running time or a space bound involve an integer parameter n (usually denoting an intuitive notion of the "size" of the problem). Moreover, most of these claims are equivalent to saying some statement $q(n)$ is true "for all $n \geq 1$." Since this is making a claim about an infinite set of numbers, we cannot justify this exhaustively in a direct fashion.

Induction

We can often still justify claims such as those above as true, however, by using the technique of **induction**. This technique amounts to showing that, for any particular $n \geq 1$, there is a finite sequence of implications that starts with something known to be true and ultimately leads to showing that $q(n)$ is true.

A justification by induction, then, always has the same general form. We begin by justifying that $q(n)$ is true for $n = 1$ (and possibly some other values $n = 2, 3, \ldots, k$, for some constant k). Then we justify that the inductive "step" is true for $n > k$, namely, we show "if $q(i)$ is true for $i < n$, then $q(n)$ is true." The combination of these two pieces completes the justification by induction.

Example 2.8: *Consider the Fibonacci sequence: $F(1) = 1, F(2) = 2$, and $F(n) = F(n-1) + F(n-2)$ for $n > 2$. We claim that $F(n) < 2^n$.*

Justification: *We will show our claim is right by induction.*
Base cases: *($n \leq 2$). $F(1) = 1 < 2 = 2^1$ and $F(2) = 2 < 4 = 2^2$. Thus, our claim is true for $n \leq 2$.*
Induction step: *($n > 2$). Suppose our claim is true for $n' < n$. Consider $F(n)$. Since $n > 2$, $F(n) = F(n-1) + F(n-2)$. Moreover, since $n - 1 < n$ and $n - 2 < n$, we can apply the inductive assumption (sometimes called the "inductive hypothesis") to imply that $F(n) < 2^{n-1} + 2^{n-2}$. But, since $n > 2$,*
$$2^{n-1} + 2^{n-2} < 2^{n-1} + 2^{n-1} = 2 \cdot 2^{n-1} = 2^n.$$
This completes the justification. ∎

Let us do another inductive argument, this time for a fact we have seen before.

Proposition 2.9: *(which is the same as Proposition 2.4)*

$$\sum_{i=1}^{n} i = \frac{n(n+1)}{2}.$$

Justification: We will justify this equality by induction.
Base case: $n = 1$. Trivial, for $1 = n(n+1)/2$, if $n = 1$.
Induction step: $n \geq 2$. Assume the claim is true for $n' < n$. Consider n.

$$\sum_{i=1}^{n} i = n + \sum_{i=1}^{n-1} i.$$

By the induction hypothesis, then

$$\sum_{i=1}^{n} i = n + \frac{(n-1)n}{2},$$

which we can simplify as

$$n + \frac{(n-1)n}{2} = \frac{2n + n^2 - n}{2} = \frac{n^2 + n}{2} = \frac{n(n+1)}{2}.$$

This completes the justification. ∎

That's all there is to it. We may sometimes feel overwhelmed by the task of justifying something true for *all* $n \geq 1$. If we sense such feelings coming on, we should remember the concreteness of the inductive technique. It shows that, for any particular n we pick, there is a finite step-by-step sequence of implications that starts with something true and leads to the truth about n. In short, the inductive argument is a formula for building a sequence of little direct justifications.

Loop Invariants

The final justification technique we discuss in this section is the ***loop invariant***, which is used to analyze and prove the correctness of loops. Formally, the loop invariant technique is as follows:

> To prove some statement S about a loop is correct, define that statement in an inductive manner in terms of a series of smaller statements $S_0, S_1, \ldots, S_k$, where:
>
> 1. The ***initial*** claim, S_0, is true before the loop begins.
> 2. If S_{i-1} is true before iteration i begins, then one can show that S_i will be true after iteration i is over.
> 3. The final statement, S_k, implies the statement S that we wish to justify as being true.

We have already seen the loop-invariant justification technique at work in Section 2.2 (for arguing the correctness of Algorithm arrayMax), but let us nevertheless give one more example of its usage here. Algorithm arrayFind, shown in Code Fragment 2.3, solves the problem of finding an element x in an array A.

Algorithm arrayFind(x, A):
    Input: An element x and an n-element array, A.
    Output: The index i such that $x = A[i]$ or -1 if no element of A is equal to x.
    Abstract: This method uses a simple **while** loop to search through A from the beginning.
    $i \leftarrow 0$
    while $i < n$ **do**
        if $x \leftarrow A[i]$ **then**
            return i
        else
            $i \leftarrow i + 1$
    return -1

Code Fragment 2.3: Algorithm arrayFind.

To show that Algorithm arrayFind is correct, we use a loop invariant argument. We claim the following is true at the beginning of iteration i:

S_i: x is not equal to any of the first i elements of A.

This claim is true at the beginning of the first iteration of the loop, since there are no elements among the first 0 in A (this kind of a trivially-true claim is said to hold *vacuously*). In iteration i, we compare element x to element $A[i]$ and return the index i, if these two elements are equal, which is clearly correct and completes the algorithm in this case. If the two elements x and $A[i]$ are not equal, then we have found one more element not equal to x and we increment the index i. Thus, the claim S_i will be true for this new value of i; hence, it is true at the beginning of the next iteration. If the while-loop terminates without ever returning an index in A, then it must be true that $i = n$. That is, S_n is true—there are no elements of A equal to x. Therefore, the algorithm is correct to return the nonindex value -1, as required.

The above justification of correctness also shows the power of induction, this time as it is used in conjunction with the loop-invariant justification technique.

2.5   Analysis of Algorithms

Now that we have developed a high-level way of describing algorithms, let us address the different ways that we can analyze algorithms.

2.5.1   Primitive Operations

As we noted above, experimental analysis is valuable but it has its limitations. If we wish to analyze a particular algorithm without performing experiments on its running time, we can take the following more analytical approach:

1. Code up the algorithm in some high-level computer language (like Java).
2. Compile the program into some low-level executable language (like the bytecode language of the Java Virtual Machine).
3. Determine for each instruction i of the low-level language, the time t_i needed to execute the instruction.
4. Determine for each instruction i of the low-level language, the number of times n_i that instruction i gets executed when the algorithm is run.
5. Sum up the products $n_i \cdot t_i$ over all the instructions, which yields the running time of the algorithm.

This approach can often give us an accurate estimate of the running time but it is very complicated to pursue, since it requires a detailed understanding of the low-level language generated by a program's compilation and the environment in which it is to be run.

So, instead, we perform our analysis directly on the high-level code or pseudo-code. We define a set of high-level *primitive operations* that are largely independent from the programming language used and can be identified also in the pseudo-code. Primitive operations include the following:

- Assigning a value to a variable
- Calling a method
- Performing an arithmetic operation (e.g., adding two Numbers)
- Comparing two numbers
- Indexing into an array
- Following an object reference
- Returning from a method.

Specifically, a primitive operation corresponds to a low-level instruction with an execution time that depends on the hardware and software environment but is nevertheless constant. Instead of trying to determine the specific execution time of each primitive operation, we will simply ***count*** how many primitive operations are executed, and use this number t as a high-level estimate of the running-time of the algorithm. This operation count will correlate to an actual running time in a specific hardware and software environment, for each primitive operation corresponds to a constant-time instruction, and there are only a fixed number of primitive operations. The implicit assumption in this approach is that the running times of different primitive operations will be fairly similar. Thus, the number, t, of primitive operations an algorithm performs will be proportional to the actual running time of that algorithm.

Counting Primitive Operations

We now show how to count the number of primitive operations executed by an algorithm using as an example algorithm arrayMax, whose pseudo-code and Java implementation are given in Code Fragments 2.1 and 2.2, respectively, on page 33. The following analysis can be carried out looking either at the pseudo-code or at the Java implementation.

- Initializing variable *currentMax* to $A[0]$ corresponds to two primitive operations (indexing into an array and assigning a value to a variable) and is executed only once at the beginning of the algorithm. Thus, it contributes two units to the count.
- At the beginning of the for loop, counter i is initialized to 1. This action corresponds to executing one primitive operation (assigning a value to a variable).
- Before entering the body of the for loop, condition $i < n$ is verified. This action corresponds to executing one primitive instruction (comparing two numbers). Since counter i starts at 0 and is incremented by 1 at the end of each iteration of the loop, the comparison $i < n$ is performed n times. Thus, it contributes n units to the count.
- The body of the for loop is executed $n - 1$ times (for values $1, 2, \ldots, n - 1$ of the counter). At each iteration, $A[i]$ is compared with *currentMax* (two primitive operations, indexing and comparing), $A[currentMax]$ is possibly assigned to *currentMax* (two primitive operations, indexing and assigning), and the counter i is incremented (two primitive operations, summing and assigning). Hence, at each iteration of the loop, either four or six primitive operations are performed, depending on whether $A[i] \leq currentMax$ or $A[i] > currentMax$. Therefore, the body of the loop contributes between $4(n - 1)$ and $6(n - 1)$ units to the count.
- Returning the value of variable *currentMax* corresponds to one primitive operation, and is executed only once.

To summarize, the number of primitive operations $t(n)$ executed by algorithm arrayMax is at least

$$2+1+n+4(n-1)+1 = 5n-1$$

and at most

$$2+1+n+6(n-1)+1 = 7n-3.$$

The best case ($t(n) = 5n-1$) occurs when $A[0]$ is the maximum element, so that variable *currentMax* is never reassigned. The worst case ($t(n) = 7n-3$) occurs when the elements are sorted in increasing order, so that variable *currentMax* is reassigned at each iteration of the for loop.

2.5.2 Average-Case and Worst-Case Analysis

Like the arrayMax method, an algorithm may run faster on some inputs than it does on others. In such cases we may wish to express the running time of such an algorithm as an average taken over all possible inputs. Unfortunately, such an *average case* analysis is typically quite challenging. It requires us to define a probability distribution on the set of inputs, which is typically a difficult task. Figure 2.3 schematically shows how, depending on the input distribution, the running time of an algorithm can be anywhere between the worst-case time and the best-case time. For example, what if inputs are really only of types "A" or "D"?

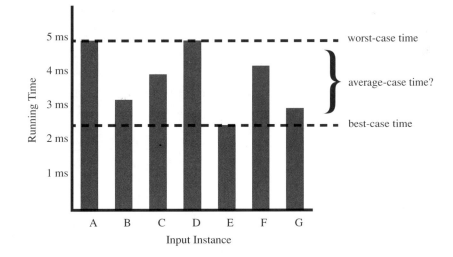

Figure 2.3: The difference between best-case and worst-case time. Each bar represents the running time of some algorithm on a different possible input.

An average-case analysis also typically requires that we calculate expected running times based on a given input distribution. Such an analysis often requires heavy mathematics and probability theory.

Therefore, for the remainder of this book, unless we specify otherwise, we will characterize running times in terms of the **worst case**. We shall say that algorithm arrayMax executes $t(n) = 7n - 3$ primitive operations **in the worst case**, meaning that the maximum number of primitive operations executed by the algorithm, taken over all inputs of size n, is $7n - 3$.

This type of analysis is much easier than an average case analysis, as it does not require probability theory; it just requires the ability to identify the worst-case input, which is often straightforward. In addition, taking a worst-case approach can actually lead to better algorithms. Making the standard of success that of having an algorithm perform well in the worst case necessarily requires that it perform well on **every** input. That is, designing for the worst case leads to stronger algorithmic "muscles," much like a track star who always practices by running up hill.

2.6 Asymptotic Notation

We have clearly gone into laborious detail for evaluating the running time of such a simple algorithm as the arrayMax algorithm. There are a number of questions that this analysis raises:

- Is this level of detail really needed?
- How important is it to figure out the exact number of primitive operations performed by an algorithm?
- How carefully must we define the set of primitive operations? For example, how many primitive operations are needed for the statement y = a∗x + b? (We may argue that two arithmetic operations and one assignment are executed, but we may be disregarding the additional "hidden" assignment of the result of a∗x to a temporary variable before performing the sum.)

In general, each step in a pseudo-code description and each statement in a high-level language implementation corresponds to a small number of primitive operations that does not depend on the input size. Thus, we can perform a simplified analysis that estimates the number of primitive operations executed up to a constant factor, by counting the steps of the pseudo-code or the statements of the high-level language executed. Going back to algorithm arrayMax, our simplified analysis indicates that between $5n - 1$ and $7n - 3$ steps are executed on an input of size n.

Simplifying the Analysis Further

It is useful in algorithm analysis to focus on the growth rate of the running time as a function of the input size n, taking a "big-picture" approach, rather than being bogged down with small details. It is often enough just to know that the running time of an algorithm such as arrayMax **grows proportionally to** n, with its true running time being n times a small constant factor that depends on the hardware and software environment and varies in a certain range depending on the specific input.

We will formalize our method for analyzing data structures and algorithms using a mathematical notation for functions that disregards constant factors. Namely, we characterize the running time and memory requirements of an algorithm by using functions that map integers to real numbers in a way that focuses attention on the primary "big-picture" aspects in a running time or space requirement function.

2.6.1 The "Big-Oh" Notation

Let $f(n)$ and $g(n)$ be functions mapping nonnegative integers to real numbers. We say that $f(n)$ is $O(g(n))$ if there is a real constant $c > 0$ and an integer constant $n_0 \geq 1$ such that $f(n) \leq cg(n)$ for every integer $n \geq n_0$. This definition is often referred to as the "big-Oh" notation, for it is sometimes pronounced as "$f(n)$ is **big-Oh** of $g(n)$." Alternatively, we can also say "$f(n)$ is **order** $g(n)$." (This definition is illustrated in Figure 2.4.)

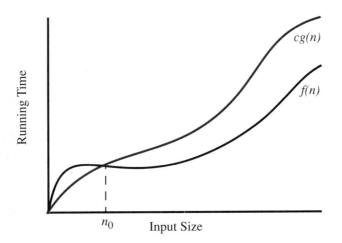

Figure 2.4: Illustrating the "big-Oh" notation. The function $f(n)$ is $O(g(n))$, because $f(n) \leq c \cdot g(n)$ for $n \geq n_0$.

Example 2.10: $7n - 3$ *is* $O(n)$.

Justification: *By the big-Oh definition, we need to find a real constant $c > 0$ and an integer constant $n_0 \geq 1$ such that $7n - 3 \leq cn$ for every integer $n \geq n_0$. It is easy to see that a possible choice is $c = 7$ and $n_0 = 1$. Indeed, this is one of infinitely many choices available because any real number greater than or equal to 7 will work for c, and any integer greater than or equal to 1 will work for n_0.* ∎

The big-Oh notation allows us to say that a function of n is "less-than-or-equal-to" another function (by the inequality "$\leq$" in the definition), up to a constant factor (by the constant c in the definition) and in the **asymptotic** sense as n grows towards infinity (by the statement "$n \geq n_0$" in the definition).

The big-Oh notation is used widely to characterize running times and space bounds in terms of some parameter n, which varies from problem to problem, but is usually an intuitive notion of the "size" of the problem. For example, if we are interested in finding the largest element in an array of integers (see arrayMax given in Code Fragments 2.1 and 2.2), it would be most natural to let n denote the number of elements of the array. The big-Oh notation allows us to ignore constant factors and lower order terms and focus on the main components of a function that affect its growth.

Using the big-Oh notation, we can write the following mathematically precise statement on the running time of algorithm arrayMax (see Code Fragment 2.1 and Code Fragment 2.2) in **any** hardware and software environment.

Proposition 2.11: *The running time of algorithm* arrayMax *for computing the maximum element in an array of n integers is $O(n)$.*

Justification: As shown in Section 2.5.1, the number of primitive operations executed by algorithm arrayMax is at most $7n - 3$. Hence, there is a positive constant a that depends on the time unit and on the hardware and software environment where the algorithm is implemented, compiled, and executed such that the running time of algorithm arrayMax on an input of size n is at most $a(7n - 3)$. We apply the big-Oh definition with $c = 7a$ and $n_0 = 1$ and conclude that the running time of algorithm arrayMax is $O(n)$. ∎

Let us consider a few additional examples that illustrate the big-Oh notation.

Example 2.12: $20n^3 + 10n \log n + 5$ *is* $O(n^3)$.

Justification: $20n^3 + 10n \log n + 5 \leq 35n^3$, *for* $n \geq 1$. ∎

In fact, any polynomial $a_k n^k + a_{k-1} n^{k-1} + \cdots + a_0$ will always be $O(n^k)$.

Example 2.13: $3\log n + \log\log n$ is $O(\log n)$.

Justification: $3\log n + \log\log n \le 4\log n$, for $n \ge 2$. *Note that* $\log\log n$ *is not even defined for* $n = 1$. *That is why we use* $n \ge 2$. ∎

Example 2.14: 2^{100} is $O(1)$.

Justification: $2^{100} \le 2^{100} \cdot 1$, for $n \ge 1$. *Note that variable* n *does not appear in the inequality, since we are dealing with constant-valued functions.* ∎

Example 2.15: $5/n$ is $O(1/n)$.

Justification: $5/n \le 5(1/n)$, for $n \ge 1$ *(even though this is actually a* **decreasing** *function).* ∎

In general, we should use the big-Oh notation to characterize a function as closely as possible. While it is true that the function $f(n) = 4n^3 + 3n^{4/3}$ is $O(n^5)$ or even $O(n^3\log n)$, it is more accurate to say that $f(n)$ is $O(n^3)$. Consider, by way of analogy, a scenario where a hungry traveler driving along a long country road happens upon a local farmer walking home from a market. If the traveler asks the farmer how much longer he must drive before he can find some food, it may be truthful for the farmer to say, "certainly no longer than 12 hours," but it is much more accurate (and helpful) for him to say, "you can find a market just a few minutes drive up this road." Thus, even with the big-Oh notation, we should strive as much as possible to tell the *whole* truth.

Instead of always applying big-Oh definition directly to simply a big-Oh characterization, we can use the following rules to simplify notation.

Proposition 2.16: *Let* $f(n)$, $g(n)$, *and* $h(n)$ *be functions mapping nonnegative integers to reals. Then*

1. $f(n)$ *is* $O(af(n))$ *for any constant* $a > 0$.
2. *If* $f(n) \le g(n)$ *and* $g(n)$ *is* $O(h(n))$, *then* $f(n)$ *is* $O(h(n))$.
3. *If* $f(n)$ *is* $O(g(n))$ *and* $g(n)$ *is* $O(h(n))$, *then* $f(n)$ *is* $O(h(n))$.
4. $f(n) + g(n)$ *is* $O(\max\{f(n), g(n)\})$.
5. *If* $g(n)$ *is* $O(h(n))$, *then* $f(n) + g(n)$ *is* $O(f(n) + h(n))$.
6. *If* $g(n)$ *is* $O(h(n))$, *then* $f(n)g(n)$ *is* $O(f(n)h(n))$.
7. *If* $f(n)$ *is a polynomial of degree* d *(i.e.,* $f(n) = a_0 + a_1 n + \cdots + a_d n^d$*), then* $f(n)$ *is* $O(n^d)$.
8. n^x *is* $O(a^n)$ *for any fixed* $x > 0$ *and* $a > 1$.
9. $\log n^x$ *is* $O(\log n)$ *for any fixed* $x > 0$.
10. $\log^x n$ *is* $O(n^y)$ *for any fixed constants* $x > 0$ *and* $y > 0$.

It is considered poor taste to include constant factors and lower order terms in the big-Oh notation. For example, it is not fashionable to say that the function $2n^2$ is $O(4n^2 + 6n\log n)$, although this is completely correct. We should strive instead to describe the function in the big-Oh in **simplest terms**.

Example 2.17: $2n^3 + 4n^2 \log n$ is $O(n^3)$.

Justification: *We apply the rules of Proposition 2.16 as follows:*

- $\log n$ is $O(n)$ *(Rule 10)*.
- $4n^2 \log n$ is $O(4n^3)$ *(Rule 6)*.
- $2n^3 + 4n^2 \log n$ is $O(2n^3 + 4n^3)$ *(Rule 5)*.
- $2n^3 + 4n^3$ is $O(n^3)$ *(Rule 7)*.
- $2n^3 + 4n^2 \log n$ is $O(n^3)$ *(Rule 3)*.

■

Some functions appear often in the analysis of algorithms and data structures, and we often use special terms to refer to them. The term **linear** is often used, for example, to refer to the class of functions that are $O(n)$. Table 2.1 shows this and other related terms commonly used in algorithm analysis.

logarithmic	linear	quadratic	polynomial	exponential
$O(\log n)$	$O(n)$	$O(n^2)$	$O(n^k)$ $(k \geq 1)$	$O(a^n)$ $(a > 1)$

Table 2.1: Terminology for classes of functions.

2.6.2 "Relatives" of the Big-Oh

Just as the big-Oh notation provides an asymptotic way of saying that a function is "less than or equal to" another function, the following notations provide asymptotic ways of making other types of comparisons.

Let $f(n)$ and $g(n)$ be functions mapping integers to real numbers. We say that $f(n)$ is $\Omega(g(n))$ (pronounced "$f(n)$ is big-Omega of $g(n)$") if $g(n)$ is $O(f(n))$, that is, there is a real constant $c > 0$ and an integer constant $n_0 \geq 1$ such that $f(n) \geq cg(n)$, for $n \geq n_0$. This definition allows us to say asymptotically that one function is greater than or equal to another, up to a constant factor.   Likewise, we say that $f(n)$ is $\Theta(g(n))$ (pronounced "$f(n)$ is big-Theta of $g(n)$") if $f(n)$ is $O(g(n))$ and $f(n)$ is $\Omega(g(n))$, that is, there are real constants $c' > 0$ and $c'' > 0$, and an integer constant $n_0 \geq 1$ such that $c'g(n) \leq f(n) \leq c''g(n)$, for $n \geq n_0$.

The big-Theta allows us to say that two functions are asymptotically equal, up to a constant factor. We consider some examples of these notations below.

Example 2.18: $3\log n + \log\log n$ is $\Omega(\log n)$.

Justification: $3\log n + \log\log n \geq 3\log n$, for $n \geq 2$. ∎

This example shows that lower order terms are not dominant in establishing lower bounds, with the big-Omega notation. Thus, as the next example sums up, lower order terms are not dominant in the big-Theta notation either.

Example 2.19: $3\log n + \log\log n$ is $\Theta(\log n)$.

Justification: *This follows from Examples 2.13 and 2.18.* ∎

"Distant Cousins" of the Big-Oh

There are also some ways of saying that one function is strictly less-than or strictly greater-than another asymptotically, but these are not used as often as the big-Oh, big-Omega, and big-Theta. Nevertheless, for the sake of completeness, we give their definitions as well.

Let $f(n)$ and $g(n)$ be functions mapping integers to real numbers. We say that $f(n)$ is $o(g(n))$ (pronounced "$f(n)$ is little-oh of $g(n)$") if, for any constant $c > 0$, there is a constant $n_0 > 0$ such that $f(n) \leq cg(n)$ for $n \geq n_0$. Likewise, we say that $f(n)$ is $\omega(g(n))$ (pronounced "$f(n)$ is little-omega of $g(n)$") if $g(n)$ is $o(f(n))$, that is, if, for any constant $c > 0$, there is a constant $n_0 > 0$ such that $g(n) \geq cf(n)$ for $n \geq n_0$. Intuitively, $o(\cdot)$ is analogous to "less than" in an asymptotic sense, and $\omega(\cdot)$ is analogous to "greater than" in an asymptotic sense.

Example 2.20: *The function* $f(n) = 12n^2 + 6n$ *is* $o(n^3)$ *and* $\omega(n)$.

Justification: *Let us first show that* $f(n)$ *is* $o(n^3)$. *Let* $c > 0$ *be any constant. If we take* $n_0 = 12/c + 6$, *then, for* $n \geq n_0$, *we have*
$$cn^3 \geq 12n^2 + 6n^2 \geq 12n^2 + 6n.$$
Thus, $f(n)$ *is* $o(n^3)$.

To show that $f(n)$ *is* $\omega(n)$, *let* $c > 0$ *again be any constant. If we take* $n_0 = c/12$, *then, for* $n \geq n_0$, *we have*
$$12n^2 + 6n \geq 12n^2 \geq cn.$$
Thus, $f(n)$ *is* $\omega(n)$. ∎

For the reader familiar with limits, we note that $f(n)$ is $o(g(n))$ if and only if

$$\lim_{n\to\infty} \frac{f(n)}{g(n)} = 0,$$

provided this limit exists.

The main difference between the little-oh and big-Oh notions is that $f(n)$ is $O(g(n))$ if **there exist** constants $c > 0$ and $n_0 \geq 1$ such that $f(n) \leq cg(n)$, for $n \geq n_0$; whereas $f(n)$ is $o(g(n))$ if **for all** constants $c > 0$ there is a constant n_0 such that $f(n) \leq cg(n)$, for $n \geq n_0$. Intuitively, $f(n)$ is $o(g(n))$ if $f(n)$ becomes insignificant compared to $g(n)$ as n grows towards infinity.

As previously mentioned, asymptotic notation is useful because it allows us to concentrate on the main factor determining a function's growth.

2.7 Asymptotic Analysis

Suppose that two algorithms solving the same problem are available: an algorithm A, which has a running time that is $\Theta(n)$, and an algorithm B, which has a running time that is $\Theta(n^2)$. Which one is better? The little-oh notation says that n is $o(n^2)$, which means that the ratio of the running times of algorithms A and B goes to zero as n grows to infinity. That is, algorithm A is **asymptotically better** than algorithm B, although for a given value of n, it is possible for algorithm B to have lower running time than algorithm A.

We can use the little-oh notation to order classes of functions by asymptotic growth rate. The following list of functions is ordered by increasing growth rate, that is, if a function $f(n)$ precedes a function $g(n)$ in the list, then $f(n)$ is $o(g(n))$.

$$\log n \quad \log^2 n \quad \sqrt{n} \quad n \quad n\log n \quad n^2 \quad n^3 \quad 2^n.$$

We illustrate the difference in the growth rate of the above functions in Table 2.2.

n	$\log n$	$\sqrt{n}$	n	$n\log n$	n^2	n^3	2^n
2	1	1.4	2	2	4	8	4
4	2	2	4	8	16	64	16
8	3	2.8	8	24	64	512	256
16	4	4	16	64	256	4,096	65,536
32	5	5.7	32	160	1,024	32,768	4,294,967,296
64	6	8	64	384	4,096	262,144	1.84×10^{19}
128	7	11	128	896	16,384	2,097,152	3.40×10^{38}
256	8	16	256	2,048	65,536	16,777,216	1.15×10^{77}
512	9	23	512	4,608	262,144	134,217,728	1.34×10^{154}
1,024	10	32	1,024	10,240	1,048,576	1,073,741,824	1.79×10^{308}

Table 2.2: Growth of several functions.

We further illustrate the importance of the asymptotic viewpoint in Table 2.3. This table explores the maximum size allowed for an input instance for various running times to be solved in 1 second, 1 minute, and 1 hour, assuming each operation can be processed in 1 microsecond (1 μs). It also shows the importance of good algorithm design, because an algorithm with an asymptotically-slow running time (for example, one that is $O(n^2)$) is easily beaten in the long run by an algorithm with an asymptotically-faster running time (for example, one that is $O(n\log n)$), even if the constant factor for the asymptotically-faster algorithm is worse.

Running	Maximum Problem Size (n)		
Time	1 second	1 minute	1 hour
$400n$	2,500	150,000	9,000,000
$20n\lceil\log n\rceil$	4,096	166,666	7,826,087
$2n^2$	707	5,477	42,426
n^4	31	88	244
2^n	19	25	31

Table 2.3: Maximum size of a problem that can be solved in 1 second, 1 minute, and 1 hour, for various running times of the algorithm, measured in microseconds.

The importance of good algorithm design goes beyond just what can be solved effectively on a given computer, however. As shown in Table 2.4, even if we achieve a dramatic speedup in hardware, we still cannot overcome the handicap of an asymptotically-slow algorithm. This table shows the new maximum problem size achievable for any fixed amount of time assuming algorithms with the given running times are now run on a computer 256 times faster than the previous one.

Running	New Maximum
Time	Problem Size
$400n$	$256m$
$20n\lceil\log n\rceil$	approx. $256((\log m)/(7+\log m))m$
$2n^2$	$16m$
n^4	$4m$
2^n	$m+8$

Table 2.4: Increase in the maximum size of a problem that can be solved in a certain fixed amount of time, by using a computer that is 256 times faster than the previous one, for various running times of the algorithm. Each entry is given as a function of m, the previous maximum problem size.

2.7.1   Using the Big-Oh Notation

It is considered poor taste, in general, to say "$f(n) \leq O(g(n))$," since the big-Oh already denotes the "less than or equal to" concept. Likewise, although common, it is not completely correct to say "$f(n) = O(g(n))$" (with the usual understanding of the "=" relation), and it is actually wrong to say "$f(n) \geq O(g(n))$" or "$f(n) > O(g(n))$." It is best to say "$f(n)$ **is** $O(g(n))$." For the more mathematically-inclined, it is also correct to say "$f(n) \in O(g(n))$," for the big-Oh notation is, technically speaking, denoting a whole collection of functions.

Even with this interpretation, there is considerable freedom in how we can use arithmetic operations with the big-Oh notation, provided the connection to the definition of the big-Oh is clear. For example, we can say that "$f(n)$ is $g(n) + O(h(n))$," which would mean that there are constants $c > 0$ and $n_0 \geq 1$ such that $f(n) \leq g(n) + ch(n)$ for $n \geq n_0$. Likewise, we can say that "$f(n)$ is $O(g(n)) + O(h(n))$," which means that there are constants $c_1, c_2 > 0$ and $n_0 \geq 1$ such that $f(n) \leq c_1 g(n) + c_2 h(n)$ for $n \geq n_0$. In fact, we can even say that "$f(n)$ is $O(g(n)) \cdot O(h(n))$, which means that there are constants $c_1, c_2 > 0$ and $n_0 \geq 1$ such that $f(n) \leq c_1 g(n) \cdot c_2 h(n)$ for $n \geq n_0$. Let us not belabor this point, however, other than to observe that if $f(n)$ is $O(g(n)) + O(h(n))$, then it is $O(g(n) + h(n))$, and if $f(n)$ is $O(g(n)) \cdot O(h(n))$, then it is $O(g(n) \cdot h(n))$.

In fact, we may sometimes wish to give the exact leading term in an asymptotic characterization, in which case we would say that "$f(n)$ is $g(n) + O(h(n))$," where $h(n)$ grows slower than $g(n)$. For example, we could say that $2n \log n + 4n + 10\sqrt{n}$ is $2n \log n + O(n)$.

Some Words of Caution

A few words of caution about asymptotic notation are in order at this point. First, note that the use of the big-Oh and related notations can be somewhat misleading should the constant factors they "hide" be very large. While it is true that the function $10^{100} n$ is $\Theta(n)$, if this is the running time of an asymptotically linear-time algorithm being compared to one whose running time is $10n \log n$, we should probably choose the $\Theta(n \log n)$-time algorithm[2], even though the linear-time algorithm is asymptotically faster. Thus, even when using these notations, we should at least be somewhat mindful of the constant factors and lower order terms.

The above observation raises the issue of what constitutes a "fast" algorithm. Generally speaking, any algorithm running in $O(n \log n)$ time (with a reasonable constant factor) should be considered efficient. Even an $O(n^2)$ time method may

---

[2]Some astronomers believe that 10^{100} is an upper bound on the number of atoms in the observable universe.

be fast enough in some contexts, that is, when n is small. But an algorithm running in $\Theta(2^n)$ time should never be considered efficient.

There is a famous story about the inventor of the game of chess. He asked only that his king pay him 1 grain of rice for the first square on the board, 2 grains for the second, 4 grains for the third, 8 for the fourth, and so on. It is an interesting test of programming skills to write a program to exactly compute the number of grains of rice the king would have to pay.[3] If we must draw a line between efficient and inefficient algorithms, therefore, it is natural to make this distinction be that between those algorithms running in polynomial time and those requiring exponential time. That is, make the distinction between algorithms with a running time that is $O(n^k)$, for some constant $k \geq 1$, and those with a running time that is $\Theta(c^n)$, for some constant $c > 1$. Like so many notions we have discussed in this section, this too should be taken with a "grain of salt," for an algorithm running in $\Theta(n^{100})$ time should probably not be considered "efficient." Even so, the distinction between polynomial-time and exponential-time algorithms is considered a robust measure of tractability.

To summarize, the asymptotic notations of big-Oh, big-Omega, and, big-Theta provide a convenient language for us to analyze data structures and algorithms. As mentioned earlier, these notations provide convenience because they let us concentrate on the "big picture" rather than low-level details.

2.7.2   Examples of Asymptotic Algorithm Analysis

We conclude this chapter by analyzing two algorithms that solve the same problem but have rather different running times. The problem we are interested in is the one of computing the so called ***prefix averages*** of a sequence of numbers. Namely, given an array X storing n numbers, we want to compute an array A such that $A[i]$ is the average of elements $X[0],\ldots,X[i]$, for $i = 0,\ldots,n-1$, that is,

$$A[i] = \frac{\sum_{j=0}^{i} X[j]}{i+1}.$$

Computing prefix averages has many applications in economics and statistics. For example, given the year-by-year returns of a mutual fund, an investor will typically want to see the fund's average annual returns for the last year, the last three years, the last five years, and the last ten years.

---

[3] Any Java program written to compute this number in a single integer value will cause an integer overflow to occur (although the run-time machine will probably not complain). To represent this number exactly as an integer requires using a BigInteger class.

A Quadratic-Time Algorithm

Our first algorithm for the prefix averages problem, called prefixAverages1, is shown in Code Fragment 2.4. It computes every element of A separately, following the definition.

Algorithm prefixAverages1(X):

  Input: An n-element array X of numbers.
  Output: An n-element array A of numbers such that $A[i]$ is
     the average of elements $X[0], \ldots, X[i]$.

  Let A be an array of n numbers.
  for $i \leftarrow 0$ **to** $n-1$ **do**
     $a \leftarrow 0$
     for $j \leftarrow 0$ **to** i **do**
        $a \leftarrow a + X[j]$
     $A[i] \leftarrow a/(i+1)$
  return array A

Code Fragment 2.4: Algorithm prefixAverages1.

Let us analyze the prefixAverages1 algorithm.

- Initializing and returning array A at the beginning and end can be done with a constant number of primitive operations per element and takes $O(n)$ time.
- There are two nested **for** loops, which are controlled by counters i and j, respectively. The body of the outer loop, controlled by counter i, is executed n times, for $i = 0, \ldots, n-1$. Thus, statements $a = 0$ and $A[i] = a/(i+1)$ are executed n times each. This implies that these two statements, plus the incrementing and testing of counter i, contribute a number of primitive operations proportional to n, that is, $O(n)$ time.
- The body of the inner loop, which is controlled by counter j, is executed $i+1$ times, depending on the current value of the outer loop counter i. Thus, statement $a = a + X[j]$ in the inner loop is executed $1 + 2 + 3 + \cdots + n$ times. By recalling Proposition 2.4, we know that $1 + 2 + 3 + \cdots + n = n(n+1)/2$, which implies that the statement in the inner loop contributes $O(n^2)$ time. A similar argument can be done for the primitive operations associated with incrementing and testing counter j, which also take $O(n^2)$ time.

The running time of algorithm prefixAverages1 is given by the sum of three terms. The first and the second term are $O(n)$, and the third term is $O(n^2)$. By a simple application of Proposition 2.16, the running time of prefixAverages1 is $O(n^2)$.

A Linear-Time Algorithm

In order to compute prefix averages more efficiently, we can observe that two consecutive averages $A[i-1]$ and $A[i]$ are similar:

$$A[i-1] = (X[0]+X[1]+\cdots+X[i-1])/i$$
$$A[i] = (X[0]+X[1]+\cdots+X[i-1]+X[i])/(i+1).$$

If we denote with S_i the **prefix sum** $X[0]+X[1]+\cdots+X[i]$, we can compute the prefix averages as $A[i] = S_i/(i+1)$. It is easy to keep track of the current prefix sum while scanning array X with a loop. We are now ready to present Algorithm prefixAverages2 in Code Fragment 2.5.

Algorithm prefixAverages2(X):
   Input: An n-element array X of numbers.
   Output: An n-element array A of numbers such that $A[i]$ is
      the average of elements $X[0],\ldots,X[i]$.

Let A be an array of n numbers.
$s \leftarrow 0$
for $i \leftarrow 0$ **to** $n-1$ **do**
   $s \leftarrow s+X[i]$
   $A[i] \leftarrow s/(i+1)$
return array A

Code Fragment 2.5: Algorithm prefixAverages2.

The analysis of the running time of algorithm prefixAverages2 follows:

- Initializing and returning array A at the beginning and end can be done with a constant number of primitive operations per element, and takes $O(n)$ time.
- Initializing variable s at the beginning takes $O(1)$ time.
- There is a single **for** loop, which is controlled by counter i. The body of the loop is executed n times, for $i = 0,\ldots,n-1$. Thus, statements $s = s+X[i]$ and $A[i] = s/(i+1)$ are executed n times each. This implies that that these two statements plus the incrementing and testing of counter i contribute a number of primitive operations proportional to n, that is, $O(n)$ time.

The running time of algorithm prefixAverages2 is given by the sum of three terms. The first and the third term are $O(n)$, and the second term is $O(1)$. By a simple application of Proposition 2.16, the running time of prefixAverages2 is $O(n)$, which is much better than the quadratic-time algorithm prefixAverages1.

2.8 Exercises

Most of the following exercises are designed to build the reader's comfort with using asymptotic notation and the other analysis tools developed in this chapter. For some additional mathematical tools, refer to Appendix B.

Reinforcement

R-2.1 Graph the functions $12n$, $6n \log n$, n^2, n^3, and 2^n using a logarithmic scale for the x- and y-axes, that is, if the function value $f(n)$ is y, plot this as a point with x-coordinate at $\log n$ and y-coordinate at $\log y$.

R-2.2 Algorithm A uses $10n \log n$ operations, while algorithm B uses n^2 operations. Determine the value N such that A is better than B for $n \geq n_0$.

R-2.3 Repeat the previous problem assuming B uses $n\sqrt{n}$ operations.

R-2.4 Show that the following two statements are equivalent:

1. The running time of algorithm A is $O(f(n))$.
2. In the worst case, the running time of algorithm A is $O(f(n))$.

R-2.5 Order the following list of functions by the big-Oh notation. Group together (for example, by underlining) those functions that are big-Theta of one another. (Hint: when in doubt about two functions $f(n)$ and $g(n)$, consider $\log f(n)$ and $\log g(n)$ or $2^{f(n)}$ and $2^{g(n)}$.)

$$6n \log n \quad 2^{100} \quad \log \log n \quad \log^2 n \quad 2^{\log n}$$
$$2^{2^n} \quad \lceil \sqrt{n} \rceil \quad n^{0.01} \quad 1/n \quad 4n^{3/2}$$
$$3n^{0.5} \quad 5n \quad \lfloor 2n \log^2 n \rfloor \quad 2^n \quad n \log_4 n$$
$$4^n \quad n^3 \quad n^2 \log n \quad 4^{\log n} \quad \sqrt{\log n}$$

R-2.6 For each function $f(n)$ and time t in the following table, determine the largest size n of a problem that can be solved in time t assuming that the algorithm to solve the problem takes $f(n)$ microseconds. Recall that $\log n$ denotes the logarithm in base 2 of n. Some entries have already been completed to get you started.

	1 Second	1 Hour	1 Month	1 Century
$\log n$	$\approx 10^{300000}$			
$\sqrt{n}$				
n				
$n \log n$				
n^2				
n^3				
2^n				
$n!$		12		

R-2.7 Show that $\log^3 n$ is $o(n^{1/3})$.

R-2.8 Show that if $f(n)$ is $O(g(n))$ and $d(n)$ is $O(h(n))$, then $f(n) + d(n)$ is $O(g(n) + h(n))$.

R-2.9 Show that $O(\max\{f(n), g(n)\}) = O(f(n) + g(n))$.

R-2.10 Show that $f(n)$ is $O(g(n))$ if and only if $g(n)$ is $\Omega(n)$.

R-2.11 Show that if $p(n)$ is a polynomial in n, then $\log p(n)$ is $O(\log n)$.

R-2.12 Show that $(n+1)^5$ is $O(n^5)$.

R-2.13 Show that 2^{n+1} is $O(2^n)$.

R-2.14 Show that n is $o(n \log n)$.

R-2.15 Show that n^2 is $\omega(n)$.

R-2.16 Show that $n^3 \log n$ is $\Omega(n^3)$.

R-2.17 Show that $\lceil f(n) \rceil$ is $O(f(n))$ if $f(n)$ is a positive nondecreasing function that is always greater than 1.

R-2.18 Characterize the following summation (exactly) in terms of n:
$$\frac{5}{2} + \frac{5}{4} + \frac{5}{8} + \frac{5}{16} + \cdots + \frac{5}{2^n}.$$

R-2.19 Characterize the following summation (exactly) in terms of n:
$$\sum_{i=1}^{n} (3i + 4).$$

R-2.20 Give a big-Oh characterization, in terms of *n*, of the running time of the Ex1 method shown in Code Fragment 2.6.

R-2.21 Perform a similar analysis for method Ex2 shown in Code Fragment 2.6.

R-2.22 Perform a similar analysis for method Ex3 shown in Code Fragment 2.6.

R-2.23 Perform a similar analysis for method Ex4 shown in Code Fragment 2.6.

R-2.24 Perform a similar analysis for method Ex5 shown in Code Fragment 2.6.

```java
class Reinforcable {

    public void Ex1(int n) {
        int a;
        for (int i=0; i < n; i++)
            a = i;
    }
    public void Ex2(int n) {
        int a;
        for (int i=0; i < n; i+=2)
            a = i;
    }
    public void Ex3(int n) {
        int a;
        for (int i=0; i < n*n; i++)
            a = i;
    }
    public void Ex4(int n) {
        int a;
        for (int i=0; i < n; i++)
            for (int j=0; j <= i; j++)
                a = i;
    }
    public void Ex5(int n) {
        int a;
        for (int i=0; i < n*n; i++)
            for (int j=0; j <= i; j++)
                a = i;
    }
}
```

Code Fragment 2.6: A collection of Java methods.

Creativity

C-2.1 Al and Bill are arguing about the performance of their sorting algorithms. Al claims that his $O(n \log n)$ time algorithm is *always* faster than Bill's $O(n^2)$ time algorithm. To settle the issue, they implement and run the two algorithms on many randomly generated data sets. To Al's dismay, they find that if $n < 100$ the $O(n^2)$ time algorithm actually runs faster, and only when $n \geq 100$ is the $O(n \log n)$ time one better. Explain why this scenario is possible. You may give numerical examples.

C-2.2 Communication security is extremely important in computer networks, and one way many network protocols achieve security is to encrypt messages. Typical *cryptographic* schemes for the secure transmission of messages over such networks are based on the fact that no efficient algorithms are known for factoring large integers. Hence, if we can represent a secret message by a large prime number p, we can transmit over the network the number $r = p \cdot q$, where $q > p$ is another large prime number that acts as the *encryption key*. An eavesdropper who obtains the transmitted number r on the network would have to factor r in order to figure out the secret message p.

Using factoring to figure out a message is very difficult without knowing the encryption key q. To understand why, consider the following naive factoring algorithm:

> For every integer p such that $1 < p < r$, check if p divides r. If so, print "The secret message is p!" and stop, if not, continue.

1. Suppose that the eavesdropper uses the above algorithm and has a computer that can carry out in 1 microsecond (1 millionth of a second) a division between two integers of up to 100 bits each. Give an estimate of the time that it will take in the worst case to decipher the secret message if r has 100 bits.
2. What is the worst-case time complexity of the above algorithm? Since the input to the algorithm is just one large number r, assume that the input size n is the number of bytes needed to store r, that is, $n = (\log_2 r)/8$, and that each division takes time $O(n)$.

C-2.3 Give an example of a positive function $f(n)$ such that $f(n)$ is neither $O(n)$ nor $\Omega(n)$.

C-2.4 Show that $\sum_{i=1}^{n} i^2$ is $O(n^3)$.

C-2.5 Show that $\sum_{i=1}^{n} i/2^i < 2$. (Hint: try to bound this sum term-by-term with a geometric progression.)

C-2.6 Show that $\log_b f(n)$ is $\Theta(\log f(n))$ if $b > 1$ is a constant.

C-2.7 Describe in pseudo-code, a method for finding both the minimum and maximum of n numbers using fewer than $3n/2$ comparisons. (Hint: first construct a group of candidate minimums and a group of candidate maximums.)

C-2.8 Given a set $A = \{a_1, a_2, \ldots, a_n\}$ of n integers, describe in pseudo-code an efficient method for computing each of partial sums

$$s_k = \sum_{i=1}^{k} a_i,$$

for $k = 1, 2, \ldots, n$. (Note: remember that we are assuming that arrays begin indexing from 0.) What is the running time of this method?

C-2.9 An n-degree *polynomial* $p(x)$ is an equation of the form

$$p(x) = \sum_{i=0}^{n} a_i x^i,$$

where x is a real number and each a_i is a constant.

1. Describe a simple $O(n^2)$ time method for computing $p(x)$ for a particular value of x.
2. Consider now a rewriting of $p(x)$ as

   $$p(x) = a_0 + x(a_1 + x(a_2 + x(a_3 + \cdots + x(a_{n-1} + xa_n)\cdots))),$$

   which is known as *Horner's method*. Characterize, using the big-Oh notation, the number of multiplications and additions this method of evaluation uses.

C-2.10 Consider the following induction "justification" that all sheep in a flock are the same color:

Base case: One sheep. It is clearly the same color as itself.

Induction step: A flock of n sheep. Take a sheep, a, out of the flock. The remaining $n - 1$ are all the same color by induction. Now put sheep a back in the flock, and take out a different sheep, b. By induction, the $n - 1$ sheep (now with a in their group) are all the same color. Therefore, a is the same color as all the other sheep; hence, all the sheep in the flock are the same color.

What is wrong with this "justification"?

C-2.11 Consider the following "justification" that the Fibonacci function $F(n)$, defined as $F(1) = 1, F(2) = 2, F(n) = F(n-1) + F(n-2)$, is $O(n)$:

Base case $(n \leq 2)$: $F(1) = 1$, which is $O(1)$, and $F(2) = 2$, which is $O(2)$.

Induction step $(n > 2)$: Assume claim is true for $n' < n$. Consider n. $F(n) = F(n-1) + F(n+2)$. By induction, $F(n-1)$ is $O(n-1)$ and $F(n-2)$ is $O(n-2)$. Then, $F(n)$ is $O((n-1) + (n-2))$, by the identity presented in Exercise R-2.8. Therefore, $F(n)$ is $O(n)$, since $O((n-1) + (n-2))$ is $O(n)$.

What is wrong with this "justification"?

C-2.12 Consider the Fibonacci function, $F(n)$, from the previous exercise. Show by induction that $F(n)$ is $\Omega((3/2)^n)$.

C-2.13 Draw a visual justification of Proposition 2.4 analogous to that of Figure 2.2(b) for the case when n is odd.

Chapter Notes

The methodology for analyzing algorithms is traditionally within a model of computation called the **RAM**, or *random access machine* (not to be confused with "random access memory"). Within this model, a computer consists of a *central processing unit* (or **CPU**) and a *memory*. The CPU performs elementary operations, such as loads, stores, additions, and comparisons, and the memory stores the program and data in *cells* that have integer addresses. The term "random access" refers to the ability of the CPU can access an arbitrary memory cell with one primitive operation. Each primitive operation executed by an algorithm corresponds to a constant number of elementary computations of the RAM. Our approach of counting primitive operations is equivalent to this approach theoretically, but does not require the conceptual burden of an abstract model like the RAM.

Our use of the Big-Oh notation is consistent with most authors' usage, but we have taken a slightly more conservative approach than some. The big-Oh notation has prompted several discussions in the algorithms and computation theory community over its proper use [28, 68, 91]. Knuth [89, 91], for example, defines it using the notation $f(n) = O(g(n))$, but he refers to this "equality" as being only "one way," even though he mentions that the big-Oh is actually defining a set of functions. We have chosen to take a more standard view of equality and view the big-Oh notation truly as a set, following the suggestions of Brassard [28]. The reader interested in studying average-case analysis is referred to the book chapter by Vitter and Flajolet [144].

We include a number of useful mathematical facts in Appendix B. The reader interested in further study into the analysis of algorithms is referred to the books by Graham, Knuth and Patashnik [66], and Sedgewick and Flajolet [132]. The reader interested in learning more about the history of mathematics is referred to the book by Boyer and Merzbach [26]. Our version of the famous story about Archimedes is taken from [113].

Chapter

3

Stacks, Queues, and Linked Lists

Contents

Stacks and queues are among the simplest of all data structures, but are also among the most important. Stacks and queues are used in a host of different applications that include many more sophisticated data structures. In addition, stacks and queues are among the few kinds of data structures that are often implemented in the hardware microinstructions inside a CPU. They are central to some important features of modern computing environments, like the Java runtime environment called the Java Virtual Machine.

In this chapter, we define stack and queue abstract data types in a general way and we give two alternative implementations for them: arrays and linked lists. To illustrate the usefulness of stacks and queues, we present examples of their application to realizations of the Java Virtual Machine. We also present a generalization of stacks and queues, called the double-ended queue, and show how it can be implemented using a doubly linked list. In addition, this chapter includes discussions of several programming concepts, including interfaces, casting, sentinels, and the adapter pattern. We conclude this chapter with a case study that uses the stack data structure to build a simple stock analysis applet.

3.1   Stacks

A *stack* is a container of objects that are inserted and removed according to the *last-in first-out* (*LIFO*) principle. Objects can be inserted into a stack at any time, but only the most-recently inserted (that is, "last") object can be removed at any time. The name "stack" is derived from the metaphor of a stack of plates in a spring-loaded, cafeteria plate dispenser. In this case, the fundamental operations involve the "pushing" and "popping" of plates on the stack. When we need a new plate from the dispenser, we "pop" the top plate off the stack, and when we add a plate, we "push" it down on the stack to become the new top plate. Perhaps an even better metaphor would be a PEZ® candy dispenser which stores mint candies in a spring-loaded container that "pops" out the top-most candy in the stack when the top of the dispenser is lifted. (See Figure 3.1.) Stacks are fundamental and used in many applications, including the following.

Example 3.1: *Internet Web browsers store the addresses of recently visited sites on a stack. Each time a user visits a new site, that site's address is "pushed" onto the stack of addresses. The browser then allows the user to "pop" back to previously visited sites using the "back" button.*

Example 3.2: *Text editors usually provide an "undo" mechanism that cancels recent editing operations and reverts to former states of a document. This undo operation is accomplished in more powerful editors by keeping text changes in a stack.*

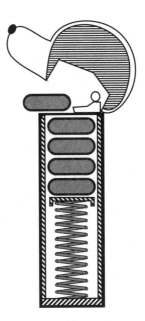

Figure 3.1: A schematic drawing of a PEZ® dispenser; a physical implementation of the stack ADT. (PEZ® is a registered trademark of PEZ Candy, Inc.)

3.1.1 The Stack Abstract Data Type

A stack S is an abstract data type (ADT) that supports the following two fundamental methods:

> push(o): Insert object o at the top of the stack.
> *Input:* Object; *Output:* None.

> pop(): Remove from the stack and return the top object on the stack; an error occurs if the stack is empty.
> *Input:* None; *Output:* Object.

Additionally, let us also define the following supporting methods:

> size(): Return the number of objects in the stack.
> *Input:* None; *Output:* Integer.

> isEmpty(): Return a boolean indicating if the stack is empty.
> *Input:* None; *Output:* Boolean.

> top(): Return the top object on the stack, without removing it; an error occurs if the stack is empty.
> *Input:* None; *Output:* Object.

Example 3.3: *The following table shows a series of stack operations and their effects on an initially empty stack S of integer objects. For simplicity, we show integers as arguments of the operations.*

Operation	Output	S
push(5)	–	(5)
push(3)	–	(5,3)
pop()	3	(5)
push(7)	–	(5,7)
pop()	7	(5)
top()	5	(5)
pop()	5	()
pop()	"error"	()
isEmpty()	true	()
push(9)	–	(9)
push(7)	–	(9,7)
push(3)	–	(9,7,3)
push(5)	–	(9,7,3,5)
size()	4	(9,7,3,5)
pop()	5	(9,7,3)

A Stack Interface in Java

Because of its importance, the stack data structure is included as a "built-in" class in the java.util package of Java. Class java.util.Stack is a data structure that stores generic Java objects and includes, among others, the methods push(obj), pop(), peek() (equivalent to top()), size(), and empty() (equivalent to isEmpty()). Methods pop() and peek() throw exception StackEmptyException if they are called on an empty stack. In Section 3.5.3, we show an example of a Stack object. While it is convenient to just use the built-in class java.util.Stack, it is instructive to learn how to design and implement a stack "from scratch."

Implementing an abstract data type in Java involves two steps. The first step is the definition of a Java *Application Programming Interface* (API), or simply *interface*, which describes the names of the methods that the ADT supports and how they are to be declared and used. A Java interface for the stack ADT is given in Code Fragment 3.1. Note that this interface is very general since it specifies that objects of arbitrary and possibly heterogeneous classes can be inserted into the stack.

The error condition that occurs when calling method pop() or top() on an empty stack is signaled by throwing an exception of type StackEmptyException, which is defined in Code Fragment 3.2.

```
public interface Stack {
    // accessor methods
    public int size(); // return the number of elements stored in the stack
    public boolean isEmpty(); // test whether the stack is empty
    public Object top() // return the top elemet
        throws StackEmptyException; // thrown if called on an empty stack
    // update methods
    public void push (Object element); // insert an element onto the stack
    public Object pop() // return and remove the top element of the stack
        throws StackEmptyException; // thrown if called on an empty stack
}
```

Code Fragment 3.1: Interface Stack.

```
public class StackEmptyException extends RuntimeException {
    public StackEmptyException(String err) {
        super(err);
    }
}
```

Code Fragment 3.2: Exception thrown by methods pop() and top() of the Stack interface when called on an empty stack.

For a given ADT to be of any use, we need to provide a concrete class that implements the methods of the interface associated with that ADT. We give a simple implementation of the Stack interface in the following subsection.

3.1.2 A Simple Array-Based Implementation

In this subsection, we show how to realize a stack by storing its elements in an array. Since an array's size needs to be determined when it is created, one of the important details of our implementation is that we specify some maximum size N for our stack, say, $N = 1,000$ elements. Our stack then consists of an N-element array S plus an integer variable t that gives the index of the top element in array S. (See Figure 3.2.)

Figure 3.2: Realization of a stack by means of an array S. The top element in the stack is stored in the cell $S[t]$.

Recalling that arrays start at index 0 in Java, we initialize t to -1. We also introduce a new type of exception, called StackFullException, to signal the error condition that arises if we try to insert a new element and the array S is full. We can then implement the stack ADT methods as described in Code Fragment 3.3.

Algorithm size():
>   **return** $t + 1$

Algorithm isEmpty():
>   **return** $(t < 0)$

Algorithm top():
>   **if** isEmpty() **then**
>>   throw a StackEmptyException
>
>   **return** $S[t]$

Algorithm push(o):
>   **if** size() $= N$ **then**
>>   throw a StackFullException
>
> $t \leftarrow t + 1$
> $S[t] \leftarrow o$

Algorithm pop():
>   **if** isEmpty() **then**
>>   throw a StackEmptyException
>
> $e \leftarrow S[t]$.
> $S[t] \leftarrow$ **null**
> $t \leftarrow t - 1$
>   **return** e

Code Fragment 3.3: Implementation of a stack by means of an array.

The correctness of these methods follows immediately from the definition of the methods themselves. There is, nevertheless, a mildly interesting point in this implementation involving the implementation of the pop method. Note that we could have avoided resetting the old $S[t]$ to **null** and we would still have a correct method. There is a trade-off in being able to avoid this assignment in Java, however. The trade-off involves the Java *garbage collection* mechanism that searches memory for objects that are no longer referenced by active objects, and reclaims their space for future use. (For more details, see Section 9.4.5.) Let $e = S[t]$ be the top element before the pop method is called. By making $S[t]$ a null reference, we indicate that the stack no longer needs to hold a reference to object e. Indeed, if there are no other active references to e, then the memory space taken by e will be reclaimed by the garbage collector. A concrete Java implementation of the above pseudo-code specification, by means of Java class ArrayStack implementing the Stack interface, is given in Code Fragment 3.4.

Table 3.1 shows the running times for methods in a realization of a stack by an array. Each of the stack methods in the array realization executes a constant number of statements involving arithmetic operations, comparisons, and assignments. Thus, in this implementation of the Stack ADT, each method runs in constant time, that is, they each run in $O(1)$ time.

Method	Time
size	$O(1)$
isEmpty	$O(1)$
top	$O(1)$
push	$O(1)$
pop	$O(1)$

Table 3.1: Performance of a stack realized by an array. The space usage is $O(N)$, where N is the size of the array, is determined at the time the stack is instantiated. Note that the space usage is independent from the number $n \leq N$ of elements that are actually in the stack.

The array implementation of a stack is both simple and efficient, and is widely used in a variety of computing applications. Nevertheless, this implementation has one negative aspect; it must assume a fixed upper bound N on the ultimate size of the stack. In Code Fragment 3.4 we chose the capacity value $N = 1,000$ more-or-less arbitrarily. An application may actually need much less space than this, in which case we would be wasting memory. Alternatively, an application may need more space than this, in which case our stack implementation may "crash" the application with an error as soon as it tries to push its $(N+1)$st object on the stack. Thus, even with its simplicity and efficiency, the array-based stack implementation is not necessarily ideal. Fortunately, there are other implementations, discussed later in this chapter, that do not have a size limitation and use space proportional to the actual number of elements stored in the stack. In cases where we have a good estimate on the number of items needing to go in the stack, however, the array-based implementation is hard to beat. Stacks serve a vital role in a number of computing applications, so it is helpful to have a fast stack ADT implementation, such as the simple array-based implementation.

```java
public class ArrayStack implements Stack {
  // Implementation of the Stack interface using an array.

    public static final int CAPACITY = 1000; // default capacity of the stack
    private int capacity;                     // maximum capacity of the stack.
    private Object S[ ];                       // S holds the elements of the stack
    private int top = −1;                      // the top element of the stack.

    public ArrayStack() {        // Initialize the stack with default capacity
       this(CAPACITY);
    }
    public ArrayStack(int cap) {  // Initialize the stack with given capacity
       capacity = cap;
       S = new Object[capacity];
    }
    public int size() {           // Return the current stack size
       return (top + 1);
    }
    public boolean isEmpty() {    // Return true iff the stack is empty
       return (top < 0);
    }
    public void push(Object obj) {  // Push a new object on the stack
       if (size() == capacity)
          throw new StackFullException("Stack overflow.");
       S[++top] = obj;
    }
    public Object top()            // Return the top stack element
      throws StackEmptyException {
    if (isEmpty())
       throw new StackEmptyException("Stack is empty.");
    return S[top];
    }
    public Object pop()            // Pop off the stack element
      throws StackEmptyException {
    Object elem;
    if (isEmpty())
       throw new StackEmptyException("Stack is Empty.");
    elem = S[top];
    S[top−−] = null;               // Dereference S[top] and decrement top
    return elem;
    }
}
```

Code Fragment 3.4: Array-based Java implementation of the Stack interface.

Casting with a Generic Stack

One of the strong points of our realization of the stack ADT by means of a Java class that implements the Stack interface is that we can store generic objects in the stack, each belonging to an arbitrary class. (See again Code Fragments 3.1 and 3.4.) Namely, an ArrayStack can store Integer objects, Student objects, or even Planet objects.

We must take care, however, that we are consistent in how we use our generic stack, because any elements that are stored in it are viewed as instances of the Java Object class. This causes no trouble when we are adding elements to the stack, because every class in Java inherits from the Object class. However, when we retrieve an object from the stack (with either the top or pop method), we always get back an instance of the Object class, no matter what the specific class of the object is. Thus, in order to use the retrieved element as an instance of the specific class it really belongs to, we must perform a ***cast***, which forces the object to be viewed as a member of a specific class rather than a more general superclass Object. (Casting in Java is discussed in more detail in Appendix A.)

In the example of Code Fragment 3.5, we illustrate the need for casting in applications that use a stack realizing the Stack interface.

```java
public static Integer[] reverse(Integer[] a) {
    ArrayStack S = new ArrayStack(a.length);
    Integer[] b = new Integer[a.length];
    for (int i=0; i < a.length; i++)
        S.push(a[i]);
    for (int i=0; i < a.length; i++)
        b[i] = (Integer) (S.pop());
    return b;
}
```

Code Fragment 3.5: A method that reverses the ordering of the elements in an array using an auxiliary ArrayStack. Casting is performed to force the object returned by pop to be viewed as an Integer object. Note that a Java array has a field length that stores the size of the array.

The reverse method, shown in Code Fragment 3.5, illustrates a small application of the stack data structure, but this data structure has many more-important applications than this. In fact, the stack data structure plays an important role in the implementation of the Java language itself.

3.1.3   Stacks in the Java Virtual Machine

A Java program is typically compiled into a sequence of byte codes that are defined as "machine" instructions for a well-defined machine model—the **Java Virtual Machine**. The definition of the Java Virtual Machine is at the heart of the definition of the Java language itself. By compiling Java code into the Java Virtual Machine byte codes, rather than the machine language of a specific CPU, a Java program can be run on any computer, such as a PC or UNIX workstation, that can emulate the Java Virtual Machine. Interestingly, the stack data structure plays a central role in the definition of the Java Virtual Machine.

The Java Method Stack

Stacks are an important application to the runtime environment of Java programs. A running Java program (more precisely, a running Java thread) has a private stack, called the **Java method stack** or just **Java stack** for short, which is used to keep track of local variables and other important information on methods, as they are invoked during execution. (See Figure 3.3.)

More specifically, during the execution of a Java program, the Java Virtual Machine maintains a stack whose elements are descriptors of the currently active (that is, nonterminated) invocations of methods. These descriptors are called *frames*. A frame for some invocation of method "fool" stores the current values of the local variables and parameters of method fool, as well as information on the method that called fool and on what needs to be returned to this method.

The Java Virtual Machine keeps in a special register called the **program counter** the address of the statement currently being executed in the program. When a method "cool" invokes another method "fool", the current value of the program counter is recorded in the frame of the current invocation of cool (so the Java Virtual Machine will know where to return to when method fool is done). At the top of the Java stack is the frame of the **running method**, that is, the method that currently has control of the execution. The remaining elements of the stack are frames of the **suspended methods**, that is, methods that have invoked another method and are currently waiting for it to return control to them upon its termination. The order of the elements in the stack corresponds to the chain of invocations of the currently active methods. When a new method is invoked, a frame for this method is pushed onto the stack. When it terminates, its frame is popped from the stack and the Java Virtual Machine resumes the processing of the previously suspended method.

The Java stack performs parameter passing to methods. Specifically, Java uses the **call-by-value** parameter passing protocol. This means that the current **value** of a variable (or expression) is what is passed as an argument to a called method.

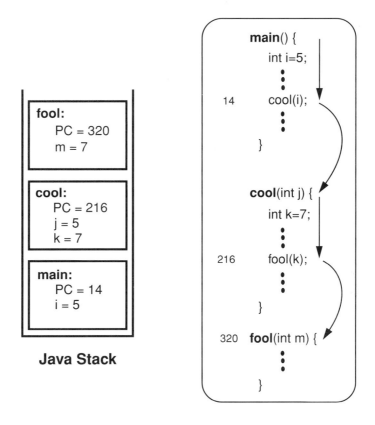

Java Stack

Java Program

Figure 3.3: An example of a Java stack: Method fool has just been called by method cool, which itself was previously called by method main. Note the values of the program counter, parameters, and local variables stored in the stack frames. When the invocation of method fool terminates, the invocation of method cool will resume its execution at instruction 217, which is obtained by incrementing the value of the program counter stored in the stack frame.

In the case of a variable *x* of a primitive type, such as an int or float, the current value of *x* is simply the number that is associated with *x*. When such a value is passed to the called method, it is assigned to a local variable in the called method's frame. (This simple assignment is also illustrated in Figure 3.3.) Note that if the called method changes the value of this local variable, it will **not** change the value of the variable in the calling method.

In the case of a variable *x* that refers to an object, however, the current value of *x* is the memory address of object *x*. (We will say more about where in memory this address actually is in Section 3.2.3.) Thus, when object *x* is passed as a parameter to some method, the address of x is actually passed. When this address is assigned to some local variable y in the called method, y will refer to the same object that x refers to. Therefore, if the called method changes the internal state of the object that y refers to, it will simultaneously be changing the internal state of the object that x refers to (which is the same object). Nevertheless, if the called program changes y to refer to some other object, x will remain unchanged—it will still refer to the same object it was referencing before.

Thus, the Java Method Stack is used by the Java Virtual Machine to implement method calls and parameter passing. Incidentally, method stacks are not a specific feature of Java. They are used in the runtime environment of most modern programming languages, including C and C++.

Recursion

One of the benefits of using a stack to implement method invocation is that it allows programs to use **recursion**. That is, it allows a method to call itself as a subroutine. Recursion can be very powerful, as it often allows us to design simple and efficient programs for fairly difficult problems.

For example, we can use recursion to compute the classic factorial function, $n! = n(n-1)(n-2)\cdots 1$, as shown in Code Fragment 3.6.

```java
public static long factorial(long n) {
    if (n <= 1)
        return 1;
    else
        return n*factorial(n−1);
}
```

Code Fragment 3.6: Recursive method factorial.

The method factorial calls itself recursively to compute the factorial of $n-1$. When the recursive call terminates, it returns $(n-1)!$, which is then multiplied by n to compute $n!$. In turn, the recursive invocation calls itself to compute the factorial of $n-2$, etc. The chain of recursive invocations, and thus the Java stack, grows only up to size n, because calling factorial(1) returns 1 immediately without invoking itself recursively. The Java stack in the Java Virtual Machine allows for the method factorial to exist simultaneously in several active frames (as many as n at some point). Each frame stores the value of the parameter n as well as the value to be returned.

This example also illustrates an important property that a recursive method should always possess—the method terminates. We ensured this property in method factorial by writing nonrecursive statements for the case $n \leq 1$, and always performing the recursive call on a smaller value of the parameter $(n-1)$ than that which we were given (n), so that, at some point (at the "bottom" of the recursion) we will perform the nonrecursive part of the computation (returning 1). We must always design a recursive method so that it is guaranteed to terminate at some point (for example, by always making recursive calls for "smaller" instances of the problem and handling the "smallest" instances nonrecursively as special cases). We note that if we design an "infinitely recursive" method, it will not actually run forever. It will instead, at some point, use up all the memory available for the Java stack and generate an out-of-memory error. If we use recursion with care, however, the method stack will implement recursive methods without any trouble.

The Operand Stack

Interestingly, there is actually another place where the Java Virtual Machine uses a stack. An *operand stack* is used to evaluate arithmetic expressions, such as the expression $((a+b)*(c+d))/e$. A simple binary operation, such as $a+b$, is computed by pushing a on the operand stack, pushing b on the operand stack, and then calling an instruction that pops the top two items from the operand stack, performs the binary operation on them, and pushes the result back onto the operand stack. Likewise, instructions for writing and reading elements to and from memory involve the use of pop and push methods for the operand stack.

In Chapter 5 we discuss the evaluation of arithmetic expression in a more general framework. For now, however, let us simply note that the operand stack plays a crucial role in this computation. Thus, the operand stack and the Java (method) stack are fundamental components of the Java Virtual Machine.

3.2 Queues

Another fundamental data structure is the *queue*. It is a close "cousin" of the stack, as a queue is a container of objects that are inserted and removed according to the *first-in first-out* (*FIFO*) principle. That is, elements can be inserted at any time, but only the element that has been in the queue the longest can be removed at any time. We usually say that elements enter the queue at the *rear* and are removed from the *front*. The metaphor for this terminology is a line of people waiting to get on an amusement park ride. People enter at the rear of the line and get on the ride from the front of the line.

3.2.1   The Queue Abstract Data Type

Formally, the queue abstract data type defines a sequence-oriented object container where element access and deletion is restricted to the first element in the sequence, which is called the ***front*** of the queue, and element insertion is restricted to the end of the sequence, which is called the ***rear*** of the queue. This restriction enforces the rule that items are inserted and deleted in a stack according to the first-in first-out (FIFO) principle.

The ***queue*** abstract data type (ADT) supports the following two fundamental methods:

enqueue(o): Insert object o at the rear of the queue.
Input: Object; *Output:* None.

dequeue(): Remove and return from the queue the object at the front; an error occurs if the queue is empty.
Input: None; *Output:* Object.

Additionally, the queue ADT includes the following supporting methods:

size(): Return the number of objects in the queue.
Input: None; *Output:* Integer.

isEmpty(): Return a boolean value that indicates whether the queue is empty.
Input: None; *Output:* Boolean.

front(): Return, but do not remove, the front object in the queue; an error occurs if the queue is empty.
Input: None; *Output:* Object.

There are several possible applications for queues. Stores, theaters, public offices, reservation centers, and other similar service organizations typically serve customers according to the FIFO principle.[1] A queue would therefore be a convenient data structure to handle transaction processing for such applications. For example, it would be a natural choice for handling incoming calls to an automated airline reservation center, where callers are requesting seats on flights for a particular airline.

---

[1]This policy is true in most Western countries, such as France, Germany, the UK, and the U.S.A., with the notable exception of Italy, where customers at a post office are usually loath to form a line and instead typically choose more creative arrangements.

Example 3.4: *The following table shows a series of queue operations and their effects on an initially empty queue Q of integer objects. For simplicity, we use integers instead of integer objects as arguments of the operations.*

Operation	Output	Q
enqueue(5)	–	(5)
enqueue(3)	–	(5,3)
dequeue()	5	(3)
enqueue(7)	–	(3,7)
dequeue()	3	(7)
front()	7	(7)
dequeue()	7	()
dequeue()	"error"	()
isEmpty()	true	()
enqueue(9)	–	(9)
enqueue(7)	–	(9,7)
size()	2	(9,7)
enqueue(3)	–	(9,7,3)
enqueue(5)	–	(9,7,3,5)
dequeue()	9	(7,3,5)

A Queue Interface in Java

A Java interface for the queue ADT is given in Code Fragment 3.7. This interface specifies that objects of arbitrary and possibly heterogeneous classes can be inserted into the queue.

```java
public interface Queue {
  // accessor methods
  public int size(); // return the number of elements stored in the queue
  public boolean isEmpty(); // test whether the queue is empty
  public Object front() // return the front element of the queue
    throws QueueEmptyException; // thrown if called on an empty queue
  // update methods
  public void enqueue (Object element); // insert an element at the rear
  public Object dequeue() // return and remove the front element
    throws QueueEmptyException; // thrown if called on an empty queue
}
```

Code Fragment 3.7: Interface Queue.

3.2.2   A Simple Array-Based Implementation

As we did with stacks, let us present a simple realization of a queue by means of an array. We again use a fixed-size array, this time called Q, of N entries, say, $N = 1,000$, to store the elements. Since the main rule with the queue ADT is that we insert and delete objects according to the FIFO principle, we must decide how we are going to keep track of the front and rear of the queue.

One possibility would be to adapt the approach we used for the stack implementation, letting $Q[0]$ be the front of the queue and then letting the queue grow from there. This would not be an efficient solution, however, for it would require that we move all the elements forward one array cell each time we perform a dequeue operation. Such an implementation would therefore require $\Theta(n)$ time to perform the dequeue method, where n is the current number of objects in the queue. Thus, if we want to achieve constant time for each queue method, we need a different solution.

To avoid moving objects once they are placed in Q, we define two variables f and r, which have the following meanings:

- f is an index to the cell of Q storing the first element of the queue (which is the next candidate to be removed by a dequeue operation), unless the queue is empty (in which case $f = r$).

- r is an index to the next available array cell in Q.

Initially, we assign $f = r = 0$, which indicates that the queue is empty. Now, when we remove an element from the front of the queue, we can simply increment f to index the next cell. Likewise, when we add an element, we can simply increment r to index the next available cell in Q. This scheme allows us to implement the enqueue and dequeue methods in constant time, that is, $O(1)$ time. However, there is still a problem with this approach.

Consider, for example, what happens if we repeatedly enqueue and dequeue a single element $N - 1$ different times. We would have $f = r = N - 1$. If we were then to try to insert the element just one more time, we would get an array-out-of-bounds error (since the N valid locations in Q are from $Q[0]$ to $Q[N-1]$), even though there is plenty of room in the queue in this case. To avoid this problem and be able to utilize all of the array Q, we let the f and r indices "wrap around" the end of Q. That is, we now view Q as a "circular array" that goes from $Q[0]$ to $Q[N-1]$ and then immediately back to $Q[0]$ again. (See Figure 3.4.)

Implementing this circular view of Q is actually pretty easy. Each time we increment f or r, we simply need to compute this increment as "$(f+1) \bmod N$" or "$(r+1) \bmod N$," respectively, where the operator "mod" is the *modulo* operator,

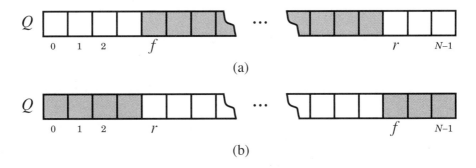

Figure 3.4: Using array Q in a circular fashion: (a) the "normal" configuration with $f \leq r$; (b) the "wrapped around" configuration with $r \leq f$. The cells storing queue elements are highlighted.

computed by taking the remainder after an integral division, so that, if y is nonzero, then

$$x \bmod y = x - \lfloor x/y \rfloor y.$$

Java uses "%" to denote the modulo operator. By using the modulo operator, we can view Q as a circular array and implement each queue method in a constant amount of time (that is, $O(1)$ time). Thus, we can solve the array-overflow problem by using the modulo operator, but one small problem yet remains with this approach.

Consider now the situation that occurs if we enqueue N objects into Q without dequeuing any of them. We would have $f = r$, which is the same condition that occurs when the queue is empty. Hence, we would not be able to tell the difference between a full queue and an empty one in this case. Fortunately, this is not a big problem, and a number of ways for dealing with it exist. The solution we describe here is to insist that Q can never hold more than $N - 1$ objects. (We explore another solution in an exercise.) This simple rule takes care of the final problem with our implementation, and leads to pseudo-coded descriptions of the queue methods given in Code Fragment 3.8. Note the introduction of a new type of exception, called QueueFullException, to signal that no more elements can be inserted, and the computation of the size of the queue by means of the expression $(N - f + r) \bmod N$, which gives the correct result both in the "normal" configuration ($f \leq r$) and in the "wrapped around" configuration ($r \leq f$). The Java implementation of a queue by means of an array is similar to that of a stack, and is left as an exercise.

Table 3.2 shows the running times of methods in a realization of a queue by an array. As with our array-based stack implementation, each of the queue methods in the array realization executes a constant number of statements involving arithmetic operations, comparisons, and assignments. Thus each method in this implementation runs in $O(1)$ time.

Algorithm size():
    return $(N - f + r) \bmod N$

Algorithm isEmpty():
    return $(f = r)$

Algorithm front():
    if isEmpty() **then**
        throw a QueueEmptyException
    return $Q[f]$

Algorithm dequeue():
    if isEmpty() **then**
        throw a QueueEmptyException
    $temp \leftarrow Q[f]$
    $Q[f] \leftarrow$ **null**
    $f \leftarrow (f + 1) \bmod N$
    return $temp$

Algorithm enqueue(o):
    if size() $= N - 1$ **then**
        throw a QueueFullException
    $Q[r] \leftarrow o$
    $r \leftarrow (r + 1) \bmod N$

Code Fragment 3.8: Implementation of a queue by means of an array.

Method	Time
size	$O(1)$
isEmpty	$O(1)$
front	$O(1)$
enqueue	$O(1)$
dequeue	$O(1)$

Table 3.2: Performance of a queue realized by an array. The space usage is $O(N)$, where N is the size of the array, which is determined at the time the queue is created. Note that the space usage is independent from the number $n \leq N$ of elements that are actually in the stack.

As with the array-based stack implementation, the only real disadvantage of the array-based queue implementation is that we artificially set the capacity of the queue to be some number N. In a real application, we may actually need more or less queue capacity than this, but if we have a good estimate of the number of elements that will be in the queue at the same time, then the array-based implementation is quite efficient. One such possible application of a queue is dynamic memory allocation in Java.

3.2.3 Memory Allocation in Java

We have already discussed (in Section 3.1.3) how the Java Virtual Machine allocates a method's local variables in that method's frame on the Java stack. The Java stack is not the only kind of memory available for program data in Java, however. Memory for an object can also be allocated dynamically during a method's execution, by having that method utilize the special **new** operator built into Java. For example, we can create a new 12-element Vector object in Java using the statement

Vector items = **new** Vector(12);

A Vector object can be treated much like an array, except that its capacity grows and shrinks as necessary. Moreover, this object continues to exist even after the method that created it terminates. Thus, the memory for this object cannot be allocated on the Java stack.

Instead of using the Java stack for this object's memory, Java uses memory from another area of storage—the ***memory heap*** (which should not be confused with the "heap" data structure we will discuss in Chapter 6). We illustrate this memory area, together with the other memory areas, in a Java Virtual Machine in Figure 3.5. The storage available in the memory heap is divided into ***blocks***, which are contiguous array-like "chunks" of memory that may be of variable or fixed sizes. To simplify the discussion, let us assume that blocks in the memory heap are of a fixed size, say, $1,024$ bytes, and that one block is big enough for any object we might want to create. (Efficiently handling the more general case is actually an interesting research problem.)

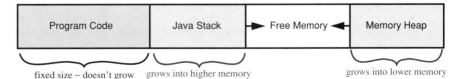

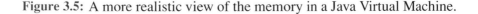

Figure 3.5: A more realistic view of the memory in a Java Virtual Machine.

The Java Virtual Machine definition requires that the memory heap be able to quickly allocate memory blocks for new objects, but it does not specify the algorithm that we should use to do this. So each implementor of a Java Virtual Machine is free to choose the implementation thought to be best. We therefore exercise this freedom and choose to use a queue to manage the unused blocks in the memory heap. When a method uses the **new** operator to request a block of memory for some new object, we will perform a dequeue operation on the queue of unused blocks to provide a free block of memory in the memory heap. Likewise, when the Java Virtual Machine determines that a block of memory previously allocated is no longer being used (by use of its "garbage collector," discussed in more detail in Section 9.4.5), then the Java Virtual Machine performs an enqueue operation to return this block to the queue of available blocks. As long as there are enough blocks available in the memory heap, this scheme is guaranteed to efficiently allocate memory for newly created objects. Thus, the queue data structure can be applied in the implementation of Java itself. There are other applications for queues in Java, as well.

3.2.4   Java Threads ★

Multiprogramming is a way of achieving a limited form of parallelism, even on a computer that has only one CPU. This mechanism allows us to have multiple tasks or computational *threads* running at the same time, with each thread being responsible for some specific computation. Multiprogramming is useful in graphical applications. For example, one thread can be responsible for catching mouse clicks while several others are responsible for moving parts of an animation around in a screen canvas. Even if the computer has only one CPU, these different computational threads can all seem to be running at the same time because:

1. The CPU is so fast relative to our perception of time.
2. The operating system is providing each thread with a different "slice" of the CPU's time.

The time slices given to each different thread occur with such rapid succession that the different threads appear to be running simultaneously, in parallel.

Java has a built-in mechanism for achieving multiprogramming—Java threads. Java threads are computational objects that can cooperate and communicate with one another to share other objects in memory, the computer's screen, or other kinds of resources and devices. Switching between different threads in a Java program occurs rapidly because each thread has its own Java stack stored in the memory of

---

★We use a star (★) to indicate sections containing material more advanced than the material in the rest of the chapter; this material can be considered optional in a first reading.

the Java Virtual Machine. The Java stack for each thread contains the local variables and the frames for the methods that that thread is currently running. Thus, to switch from a thread T to another thread U, all the CPU needs to do is to "remember" where it left off in the thread T before it switches to the thread U. We have already discussed a way for this to be done, namely, by storing the current value of T's program counter, which is a reference to the next instruction T is to perform, at the top of T's Java stack. By saving the program counter for each active thread in the top of its Java stack, the CPU can pick up where it left off in some other thread U, by restoring the value of the program counter to the value that was stored at the top of U's Java stack (and using U's stack as the "current" Java stack).

A Java thread will always be in one of four different states:

- New
- Runnable
- Blocked
- Dead

When a thread is first created, it is in a *new* state, and it remains in this state until the thread that created it sends it a start message. Once it starts, a Java thread becomes *runnable*, which means that it is a candidate to perform computations when given a slice of the CPU's time. When a thread is in the runnable state and it becomes the active thread, then it executes its instructions. These instructions can be regular primitive operations, or they can be special operations that put the thread into a *blocked* state so that it is no longer runnable (until some event or thread puts it back in the runnable state). These blocking operations include calls to sleep, suspend, and wait methods or any instruction that causes the thread to have to wait for some input-output (I/O) action. A thread can be brought back into the runnable state by having its sleep event terminate (that is, it "wakes up"), having some other thread send it a resume or notify message, or having an I/O it was waiting for complete. Finally, when a thread is done performing its computations, it enters a *dead* state.

When designing a program that uses multiple threads, we must be careful not to allow an individual thread to monopolize the CPU. Such CPU monopolization can lead to an application or applet *hanging*, where it is technically running, but not actually doing anything.

However, in some operating systems, CPU monopolizing by threads is not an issue. These operating systems utilize a queue to allocate CPU time to the runnable threads in a *round robin* protocol. The main idea of this protocol is to store all runnable threads in a queue Q. When the CPU is ready to provide a time slice to a thread, it performs a *dequeue* operation on the queue Q to get the next available runnable thread; let's call it T. Before the CPU actually starts executing instructions for T, however, it starts a timer running in hardware that is set to expire a short time later. If the thread T blocks itself (by one of the blocking methods mentioned above) before the timer expires, then the CPU saves the current value of T's program counter at the top of its Java stack and repeats the above process by performing another dequeue operation on Q. If, on the other hand, the timer expires before T voluntarily releases the CPU, then the CPU saves the current value of T's program counter and performs an enqueue operation to place T at the end of the line of currently runnable threads. Then the CPU repeats the process with the next available runnable thread in Q. In this way, the CPU ensures that each runnable thread is given its fair share of time. Thus, by using a simple queue data structure and a hardware stopwatch, the operating system can avoid CPU monopolization.[2]

3.3 Linked Lists

In the previous sections, we presented the stack and queue ADTs and discussed some important applications of them. We also showed how to implement these abstract data types with concrete data structures based on arrays. While these implementations are quite simple, they have the drawback of not being very adaptable since the size N of the array must be fixed in advance. There are other ways to implement these data structures, however, that do not have this drawback. In this section, we explore an important alternate implementation—the linked list.

3.3.1 Singly Linked Lists

A ***linked list*** in its simplest form is a collection of ***nodes*** that together form a linear ordering. The ordering is determined as in the children's game "Follow the Leader," in that each node is a compound object that stores a reference to an element and a reference, called ***next***, to another node. (See Figure 3.6.)

It might seem like circular reasoning to have a node reference another node, but such a scheme easily works. The ***next*** reference inside a node can be viewed as a ***link*** or ***pointer*** to another node. Likewise, moving from one node to another by following a ***next*** reference is known as ***link hopping*** or ***pointer hopping***. The first and last node of a linked list usually are called the ***head*** and ***tail*** of the list, respectively. We identify the tail as the node having a null ***next*** reference, which indicates the termination of the list. A linked list defined in this way is known as a ***singly linked list***.

---

[2]This queue-based policy is actually an oversimplification of the protocol used by most operating systems that do round-robin time slicing, as most systems give threads priorities; hence, they use a ***priority queue*** to implement time slicing; we discuss priority queues in Chapter 6.

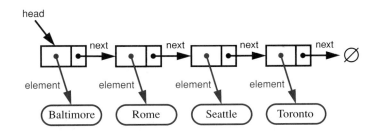

Figure 3.6: A singly linked list. References to elements are shown with blue arrows; next references are shown with black arrows. The **null** object is denoted as $\emptyset$.

Like an array, a singly linked list keeps the elements in a certain linear order, which is determined by the chain of next references between the nodes. Unlike an array, a singly linked list does not have a predetermined fixed size, and uses space proportional to the number of its elements. More precisely, the space usage of a singly linked list with n elements is $O(n)$ since it has n nodes and each node uses $O(1)$ space to store references to an element and to the next node. To implement a singly linked list in Java, we define a Node class, as shown in Code Fragment 3.9, which specifies the format of the objects associated with the nodes of the list, and a LinkedList class, which keeps a reference to the head node of the list and other information for the list, such as the number of elements.

```
class Node {
  private Object element;  // element stored in this node
  private Node next; // reference to the next node in the list

  // constructors
  Node() {  // create a node with a null element and next reference
    this(null, null);
  }
  public Node(Object e, Node n) { // create a node given element and next
    element = e;
    next = n;
  }
  // update methods
  void setElement(Object newElem) { element = newElem; }
  void setNext(Node newNext) { next = newNext; }
  // accessor methods
  Object getElement() { return element; }
  Node getNext() { return next; }
}
```

Code Fragment 3.9: Implementation of a node of a singly linked list.

With a singly linked list, we can easily insert or delete an element at the head of the list in $O(1)$ time, as shown in Figure 3.7.

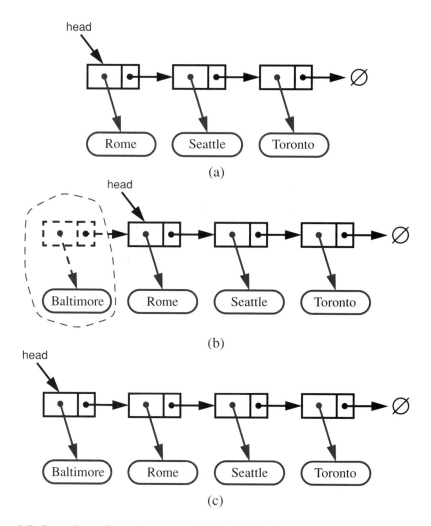

Figure 3.7: Insertion of an element at the head of a singly linked list: (a) before the insertion; (b) creation of a new node; (c) after the insertion. Deleting an element from the head of the list is a symmetric operation, which can be visualized by looking first at (c), then (b), and finally (a).

We can also insert an element at the tail of the list in $O(1)$ time, provided we keep a reference to the tail node, as shown in Figure 3.8.

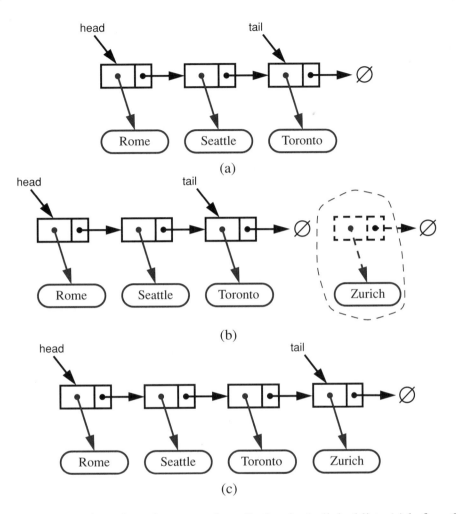

Figure 3.8: Insertion of an element at the tail of a singly linked list: (a) before the insertion; (b) creation of a new node; (c) after the insertion.

We cannot delete the tail node of a singly linked list in $O(1)$ time, however. Even if we have a tail reference directly to the last node of the list, we must be able to access the node *before* the last node, in order to remove the last node. This is one time when it is appropriate to say, "you can't get there from here," for we cannot reach the node before a node v by following next links from v. The only way to access the node before v is to start from the head of the list and search all the way through the list until coming to a node whose *next* reference points to v. But if v is the last node, such link hopping takes an amount of time proportional to the number of elements in the list, that is, $\Theta(n)$ time.

3.3.2   Implementing a Stack with a Singly Linked List

Let us explore using a singly linked list to implement the stack ADT. In principle, the top of the stack could be either at the head or at the tail of the list. However, since we can insert and delete elements in $O(1)$ time only at the head, it is more efficient to have the top of the stack at the head. Also, in order to perform operation size in $O(1)$ time, we keep track of the current number of elements in an instance variable. A Java implementation of a stack, by means of a singly linked list, is given in Code Fragment 3.10. All the methods of the Stack interface are executed in $O(1)$ time, and the space requirement is $O(n)$, where n is the current number of elements in the stack.

We use a reference variable to refer to the head of the list (which points to the null object if the list is empty). When we push a new element e on the stack, we simply create a new node n for e, reference e from n, and insert n at the head of the list. Likewise, when we pop an element from the stack, we simply remove the node at the head of the list and return its element. This implementation of a stack, by means of a singly linked list, has an important advantage over the array-based one: it does not require that we place an explicit upper bound on the size of the stack.

3.3.3   Implementing a Queue with a Singly Linked List

We can efficiently implement the queue ADT using a singly linked list, as well. For efficiency reasons, we choose the front of the queue, where we delete only, to be at the head of the list, and the rear of the queue, where we insert only, to be at the tail of the list. (Why would it be bad to insert at the head and remove at the tail?) Note that we need to maintain references to both the head and tail nodes of the list.

Rather than go into every detail of this implementation, we simply give a Java implementation for the fundamental methods of the queue ADT in Code Fragment 3.11.

As with the singly linked list implementation of the stack ADT, each of the methods of the singly linked list implementation of the queue ADT runs in $O(1)$ time. In addition, we avoid the need to specify a maximum size for the queue, as was done in the array-based queue implementation, but again this benefit comes at the expense of increasing the amount of space used per element in the queue. The methods in the singly linked list queue implementation are more complicated than those in the linked-list stack implementation. We must take extra care in how we deal with those special cases where the queue is empty before an enqueue or where the queue becomes empty after a dequeue.

```java
public class LinkedStack implements Stack {
    private Node top;           // reference to the top node
    private int size;           // number of elements in the stack

    public LinkedStack() {      // Initialize the stack
        top = null;
        size = 0;
    }
    public int size() {                 // Returns the current stack size
        return size;
    }
    public boolean isEmpty() {          // Returns true iff the stack is empty
        if (top == null)
            return true;
        return false;
    }
    public void push(Object obj) {    // Push a new object on the stack
        Node n = new Node();
        n.setElement(obj);
        n.setNext(top);
        top = n;
        size++;
    }
    public Object top()        // Return the top stack element
throws StackEmptyException {
        if (isEmpty())
            throw new StackEmptyException("Stack is empty.");
        return top.getElement();
    }
    public Object pop()        // Pop off the top stack element
throws StackEmptyException {
        Object temp;
        if (isEmpty())
            throw new StackEmptyException("Stack is empty.");
        temp = top.getElement();
        top = top.getNext();               // link-out the top node
        size--;
        return temp;
    }
}
```

Code Fragment 3.10: Class LinkedStack, which implements the Stack interface using a singly linked list.

```
public void enqueue(Object obj) {
  // Place a new object at the rear of the queue
  Node node = new Node();
  node.setElement(obj);
  node.setNext(null);       // node will be new tail node
  if (size == 0)
    head = node;          // special case of a previously empty queue
  else
    tail.setNext(node);   // add node at the tail of the list
  tail = node;     // update the reference to the tail node
  size++;
}
```

. . .

```
public Object dequeue() throws QueueEmptyException {
  // Remove the first object from the queue
  Object obj;
  if (size == 0)
    throw new QueueEmptyException("Queue is empty.");
  obj = head.getElement();
  head = head.getNext();
  size−−;
  if (size == 0)
  tail = null;        // the queue is now empty
  return obj;
}
```

Code Fragment 3.11: Methods enqueue and dequeue in the implementation of the queue ADT by means of a singly linked list. Variable size keeps track of the current number of elements in the queue.

3.4 Double-Ended Queues

Consider now a queue-like data structure that supports insertion and deletion at both the front and the rear of the queue. Such an extension of a queue is called a ***double-ended queue***, or ***deque***, which is usually pronounced "deck" to avoid confusion with the dequeue method of the regular queue ADT.

3.4.1 The Deque Abstract Data Type

The deque abstract data type is richer than both the stack and the queue ADTs. The fundamental methods of the deque ADT are as follows (where we use D to denote the deque):

insertFirst(e): Insert a new element e at the beginning of D.
Input: Object; *Output:* None.

insertLast(e): Insert a new element e at the end of D.
Input: Object; *Output:* None.

removeFirst(): Remove and return the first element of D.
Input: None; *Output:* Object.

removeLast(): Remove and return the last element of D.
Input: None; *Output:* Object.

Additionally, the deque ADT may also support the following methods:

first(): Return the first element of D.
Input: None; *Output:* Object.

last(): Return the last element of D.
Input: None; *Output:* Object.

size(): Return the number of elements of D.
Input: None; *Output:* Integer.

isEmpty(): Determine if D is empty.
Input: None; *Output:* Boolean.

We illustrate a series of deque operations performed on an initially empty deque in the following example.

Example 3.5: *The following table shows a series of operations and their effects on an initially empty deque D of integer objects.*

Operation	Output	D
insertFirst(3)	–	(3)
insertFirst(5)	–	(5, 3)
removeFirst()	5	(3)
insertLast(7)	–	(3, 7)
removeFirst()	3	(7)
removeLast()	7	()
removeFirst()	"error"	()
isEmpty()	true	()
insertFirst(9)	–	(9)
insertLast(7)	–	(9, 7)
size()	2	(9, 7)
insertFirst(3)	–	(3, 9, 7)
insertLast(5)	–	(3, 9, 7, 5)
removeLast()	5	(3, 9, 7)

3.4.2 Implementing Stacks and Queues with Deques

There is a simple mapping that takes the methods of the stack and queue ADTs and implements them using deque operations. Specifically, there are the following simple correspondences for the stack ADT:

Stack Method	Deque Implementation
size()	size()
isEmpty()	isEmpty()
top()	last()
push(e)	insertLast(e)
pop()	removeLast()

Likewise, we have the following simple correspondences for the queue ADT:

Queue Method	Deque Implementation
size()	size()
isEmpty()	isEmpty()
front()	first()
enqueue(e)	insertLast(e)
dequeue()	removeFirst()

With any implementation MyDeque of the deque ADT, we can easily implement the Stack interface with the class DequeStack shown in Code Fragment 3.12. All the methods of DequeStack are essentially one-line calls to methods of the Deque interface. This implementation assumes that Some methods of Deque throw a DequeEmptyException when we try to access or delete elements in an empty deque.

```java
public class DequeStack implements Stack {
    private Deque D; // holds the elements of the stack
    public DequeStack() {    // Initialize the stack
        D = new MyDeque();
    }
    public int size() {  // Return the number of elements if the stack
        return D.size();
    }
    public boolean isEmpty() {  // Return true iff the stack has no elements
        return D.isEmpty();
    }
    public void push(Object obj) {  // Insert an element into the stack
        D.insertLast(obj);
    }
    public Object top()    // Access the top element of the stack
      throws StackEmptyException {   // thrown if the stack is empty
        try {
            return D.last();
        }
        // since the deque throws its own exception, we catch it
        // and throw the StackEmptyException
        catch (DequeEmptyException ece) {
            throw new StackEmptyException("Stack is empty!");
        }
    }
    public Object pop()  // Remove and return the top element of the stack
      throws StackEmptyException {  // thrown if the stack is empty
        try {
            return D.removeLast();
        }
        catch (DequeEmptyException ece) {
            throw new StackEmptyException("Stack is empty!");
        }
    }
}
```

Code Fragment 3.12: Implementation of the Stack interface by means of a deque.

3.4.3   The Adapter Pattern

The DequeStack methods shown in Code Fragment 3.12 also illustrate an important design pattern—the *adapter* pattern. The adapter pattern adjusts methods from one class so they can be used to implement methods of another class. The adaptation is expected to be a simple one, involving what are essentially one-line method calls to implement each method.

There are several situations for which the adapter pattern comes in handy. One is the situation illustrated in the DequeStack class, where we want to specialize a general class and simplify its usage by changing the names of some of its methods. This typically also involves *not* using several of the methods from the more general class. In the case of the DequeStack class, we adapt class MyDeque, which implements the more complex Deque interface, so that it can be used to implement the simpler Stack interface.

Another useful application of the adapter pattern is to specialize the types of objects that are used by a general class. We can use this kind of adapter, for example, to define an IntegerArrayStack class that adapts the ArrayStack class (see Code Fragment 3.4) so that the stack only stores Integer objects. Such a class can then be used in a method, such as the reverse method of Code Fragment 3.5, to avoid the extra typing and possible confusion associated with casting, since the casting would be done internally by the class. In general, adapter classes should be defined to use general classes in specialized applications so as to simplify programming tasks.

3.4.4   Implementing Deques with Doubly Linked Lists

When we use a singly linked list as described in the previous section, deletions at the tail of the list cannot be done in constant time, even if we keep a reference to the tail node. (See Section 3.3.1.) There is a variant of the singly linked list, however, that allows for a great variety of operations, including inserting and deleting at the head and tail of the list, to run in $O(1)$ time—the *doubly linked* list. A node in a doubly linked list is like a node in a singly linked list except that, in addition to the *next* link, it also has a *prev* link to the previous node in the list. A Java implementation of a node of a doubly linked list is shown in Code Fragment 3.13.

To simplify programming, it is convenient to add special nodes at both ends of the list; a *header* node just before the head of the list, and a *trailer* node just after the tail of the list. These "dummy" or *sentinel* nodes do not store any element. The header has a valid *next* reference but a null *prev* reference, while the trailer has a valid *prev* reference but a null *next* reference. A doubly linked list with sentinels is shown in Figure 3.9.

```
class DLNode {
  // node of a doubly-linked list
  private Object element;
  private DLNode next, prev;
  DLNode() { this(null, null, null); }
  DLNode(Object e, DLNode p, DLNode n) {
    element = e;
    next = n;
    prev = p;
  }
  void setElement(Object newElem) { element = newElem; }
  void setNext(DLNode newNext) { next = newNext; }
  void setPrev(DLNode newPrev) { prev = newPrev; }
  Object getElement() { return element; }
  DLNode getNext() { return next; }
  DLNode getPrev() { return prev; }
}
```

Code Fragment 3.13: Implementation of a node of a doubly linked list.

It is easy to see that we can insert elements at both ends of a doubly linked list in $O(1)$ time. (See Figure 3.9.) Indeed, the *prev* links eliminate the need to traverse the list to get to the node just before the tail. Thus, a doubly linked list can be used to implement all the methods of the deque ADT in $O(1)$ time. We show in Code Fragment 3.14 portions of the implementation of a deque by means of a doubly linked list. Table 3.3 shows the running times of methods in a realization of a deque by a doubly linked list.

Method	Time
size	$O(1)$
isEmpty	$O(1)$
first	$O(1)$
last	$O(1)$
insertFirst	$O(1)$
insertLast	$O(1)$
removeFirst	$O(1)$
removeLast	$O(1)$

Table 3.3: Performance of a deque realized by a doubly linked list. The space usage is $O(n)$, where n is number of elements in the deque.

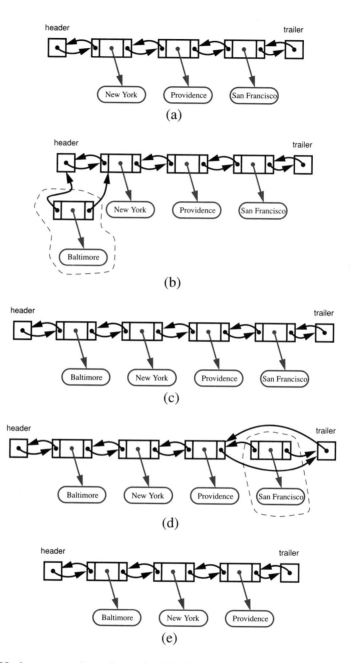

Figure 3.9: Update operations for a doubly linked list with header and trailer sentinels: (a) before inserting at the head; (b) creating a new node; (c) after the insertion and before deleting at the tail; (d) deletion of the tail node; (e) after the deletion.

```
public class MyDeque implements Deque {

   // implementation of the Deque interface by means of a doubly-linked list

    DLNode header, trailer;  // sentinels
    int size;     // number of elements

    public MyDeque() {      // constructor
        header = new DLNode();
        trailer = new DLNode();
        header.setElement(null);
        header.setPrev(null);
        header.setNext(trailer);  // make header point to trailer
        trailer.setElement(null);
        trailer.setNext(null);
        trailer.setPrev(header);  // make trailer point to header
        size = 0;
    }
...
    public void insertFirst(Object o) {
        DLNode second = header.getNext();
        DLNode first = new DLNode(o, header, second);
        second.setPrev(first);
        header.setNext(first);
        size++;
    }

...
    public Object removeLast() throws DequeEmptyException {
        if (isEmpty())
            throw new DequeEmptyException("Illegal removal request.");
        DLNode last = trailer.getPrev();
        Object o = last.getElement();
        DLNode secondtolast = last.getPrev();
        trailer.setPrev(secondtolast);
        secondtolast.setNext(trailer);
        size--;
        return o;
    }
...
```

Code Fragment 3.14: Portions of the implementation of the deque ADT by means of a doubly linked list. Note that thanks to the use of sentinels we do not need to check for "special cases" of an empty, or about to become empty, list. Methods insertFirst and removeLast are illustrated in Figure 3.9.

3.5   Case Study: A Stock Analysis Applet

In this section, we demonstrate a stack application used to solve a simple financial analysis problem, and we present an applet that visualizes the results of the analysis with a bar chart.

The Problem

Given a series of n daily price quotes for a stock, we call the ***span*** of the stock's price on a certain day the maximum number of consecutive days up to the current day that the price of the stock has been less than or equal to its price on that day. (See Figure 3.10.) More formally, assume that price quotes begin with day 0 and that p_i denotes the price on day i. The span s_i on day i is equal to the maximum integer k such that $k \leq i+1$ and $p_j \leq p_i$ for $j = i-k+1, \ldots, i$. Given the prices $p_0, p_1, \ldots, p_{n-1}$, consider the problem of computing the spans $s_0, s_1, \ldots, s_{n-1}$.

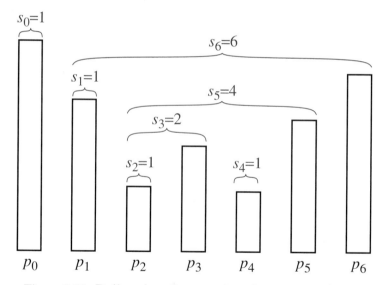

Figure 3.10: Daily prices for a stock and span on each day.

3.5.1   A Quadratic-Time Algorithm

We show a straightforward solution to our problem in computeSpans1, which is shown in Code Fragment 3.15. This method computes each span separately, directly applying the definition given above.

Algorithm computeSpans1(P):

Input: An n-element array P of numbers

Output: An n-element array S of numbers such that $S[i]$ is the largest integer k such that $k \leq i+1$ and $P[j] \leq P[i]$ for $j = i-k+1,\ldots,i$

Let S be an array of n numbers.

for $i = 0$ **to** $n-1$ **do**

    $k \leftarrow 0$

    done $\leftarrow$ **false**

    repeat

        if $P[i-k] \leq P[i]$ **then**

            $k \leftarrow k+1$

        else

            done$\leftarrow$**true**

    until $(k = i)$ **or** *done*

    $S[i] \leftarrow k$

return array S

Code Fragment 3.15: Algorithm computeSpans1.

We analyze the running time of algorithm computeSpans1 as follows.

- Initializing the array S at the beginning and returning it at the end requires a constant number of primitive operations per element; hence, takes $O(n)$ time.
- There is a **repeat** loop nested within a **for** loop. The **for** loop, controlled by counter i, is executed n times, for $i = 0,\ldots,n-1$. The statements inside the **for** loop but outside the **repeat** loop are executed n times. That is, these statements, plus the incrementing and testing of counter i, contribute $O(n)$ primitive operations to the total running time.
- In iteration i of the outer **for** loop, the body of the inner **repeat** loop is executed at most $i+1$ times. Indeed, in the worst case, element $S[i]$ is larger than or equal to all the preceding elements. Thus, testing for the **if** condition $(S[i-k] \leq S[i])$, executing one of the ensuing statements, and testing for the **until** condition is performed $i+1$ times during iteration i of the outer loop ($i = 0,\ldots,n-1$). Therefore, the number of operations performed is proportional to $1+2+3+\cdots+n$. By recalling Proposition 2.4, the total time contributed by the statements in the inner loop is $O(n(n+1)/2)$, which is $O(n^2)$.

The running time of computeSpans1 is therefore given by the sum of three terms. The first and the second term are $O(n)$, and the third term is $O(n^2)$. Thus, the running time of algorithm computeSpans1 is $O(n^2)$.

3.5.2   A Linear-Time Algorithm

To compute spans more efficiently, we observe that the span s_i on a certain day i can be easily computed if we know the closest day preceding i, such that the price on that day is higher than the price on day i. (See Figure 3.11.) If such a preceding day exits for a day i, let us denote it with $h(i)$, and otherwise let us define $h(i) = -1$. The span on day i is given by $s_i = i - h(i)$.

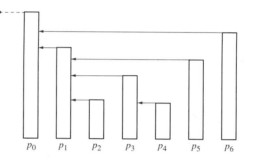

p_0 p_1 p_2 p_3 p_4 p_5 p_6

Figure 3.11: Daily prices for a stock with arrows pointing to the closest previous higher price.

Our second algorithm, computeSpans2, shown in Code Fragment 3.16, uses a stack to store days $i, h(i), h(h(i))$, etc. When going from day i to day $i + 1$, we pop days with prices less than or equal to p_{i+1}, and then push day $i + 1$. An example run of computeSpans2 is shown in Figure 3.12.   We assume that stack D is implemented so that each method of the stack ADT takes $O(1)$ time. With this assumption, our analysis of the running time of algorithm computeSpans2 is as follows:

- Initializing the array S at the beginning and returning it at the end can be done with $O(1)$ primitive operations per element, and takes $O(n)$ time.

- There is a **while** loop nested within a **for** loop. The **for** loop, controlled by counter i, is executed n times, for $i = 0, \ldots, n - 1$. Thus, the statements in the **for** loop outside the **while** loop are executed at most n times, that is, such statements (plus the incrementing and testing of counter i) take $O(n)$ time.

- Consider now the execution of the inner **while** loop during iteration i of the **for** loop. Statement $done \leftarrow$ **true** is executed at most once, since this causes a subsequent exit from the loop. Let t_i be the number of times statement D.pop() is executed. Conditions (**not** (D.isEmpty() **or** $done$)) and ($P[i] \geq P[D$.top()]) are each tested at most $t_i + 1$ times.

Algorithm computeSpans2(P):

> *Input:* An n-element array P of numbers
>
> *Output:* An n-element array S of numbers such that $S[i]$ is the largest integer k such that $k \leq i+1$ and $P[j] \leq P[i]$ for $j = i-k+1,\ldots,i$
>
> Let S be an array of n numbers, and let D be an empty stack.
>
> **for** $i = 0$ **to** $n-1$ **do**
> > $done \leftarrow$ **false**
> > **while** **not** (D.isEmpty() **or** $done$) **do**
> > > **if** $P[i] \geq P[D.\text{top}()]$ **then**
> > > > D.pop()
> > >
> > > **else**
> > > > $done \leftarrow$ **true**
> >
> > **if** D.isEmpty() **then**
> > > $h \leftarrow -1$
> >
> > **else**
> > > $h \leftarrow D$.top()
> >
> > $S[i] \leftarrow i - h$
> > D.push(i)
>
> **return** array S

Code Fragment 3.16: Algorithm computeSpans2.

Thus, the total running time contribution of the statements in the **while** loop is

$$O\left(\sum_{i=0}^{n-1} (t_i + 1) \right).$$

Once an element is popped out from stack D, it is never pushed in again by the algorithm. Hence,

$$\sum_{i=0}^{n-1} t_i \leq n.$$

In other words, the total time spent performing statements in the **while** loop is $O(n)$. The running time of algorithm computeSpans2 is given by the sum of three terms, each of which is $O(n)$. Therefore, the running time of computeSpans2 is $O(n)$.

3.5.3 Java Implementation

In this section, we present a Java applet based on algorithm computeSpans2. The complete code for the applet is given in Code Fragments 3.17–3.19. Examples of outputs generated by the applet are shown in Figure 3.13. The applet uses the java.util.Stack class instead of the stack class presented in this chapter.

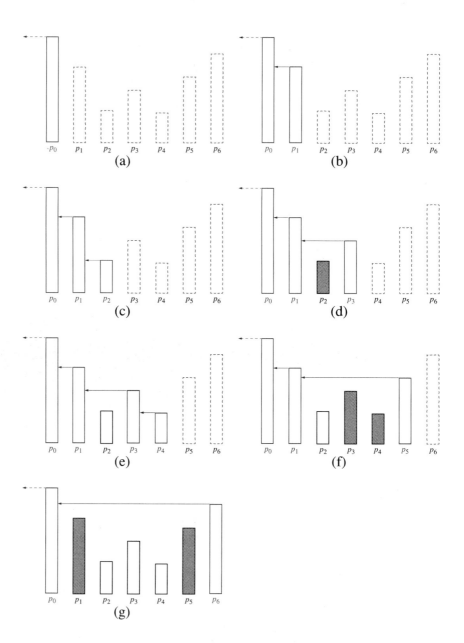

Figure 3.12: A sample run of algorithm computeSpans2. The contents of the stack D at the end of each iteration of the **for** loop are visualized by highlighting and connecting with arrows the bars associated with the days stored in D. The dashed bars denote days not yet examined by the algorithm. The shaded bars denote days popped from D in the current iteration.

```java
public class StockAnalysis extends Applet implements ActionListener {
  /* This applet performs the following computations: (1) randomly
   * generates daily price quotes for a stock over a period of N
   * days; (2) computes, for each day i, the span of the price on day i,
   * which is the maximum number of consecutive days up to day i
   * such that the price of the stock has been less than or equal to
   * that on day i; this computation is performed by means of a
   * stack; (3) visualizes the daily stock prices and spans by means of
   * a chart where the prices are drawn as vertical bars and the
   * spans are drawn as horizontal lines (bars associated with
   * prices higher than those in all the previous days are highlighted). */
  // configuration variables for the applet
  private static int numDays = 60; // number of days
  private static int startPrice = 160; // price for first day
  private static int maxVariation = startPrice/8 ; // max daily price change
  private static Color barColor = Color.blue; // color of bars
  private static Color highBarColor = Color.red; // color of bars for price highs
  private static Color lineColor = Color.green; // color of span lines
  private static int barWidth = 5; // width of bars
  private static int xOff = 20; // horizontal offset for first bar
  private static int xSep = 10; // horizontal separation between bars
  private static int yOff = startPrice*2+100; // baseline for bars
  private Quote[] currQuote; // quote that is currently displayed

  public StockAnalysis() { // constructor
      setLayout(new BorderLayout());
      currQuote = randomDailyPrices(numDays, startPrice, maxVariation);
      // create a button that will make a new quote when it is clicked
      Panel p = new Panel();
      p.setLayout(new FlowLayout());
      Button newQuote = new Button("New Quote");
      newQuote.addActionListener(this);
      p.add(newQuote);
      add("South", p);
  }
  public void paint(Graphics g) { // randomly generate daily price quotes
      // compute the daily span of the stock price
      computeDailyHighSpan(currQuote);
      // draw a bart chart visualizing daily stock prices and spans
      for (int i=0 ; i<currQuote.length ; i++) {
          drawQuote(g, currQuote[i]);
      }
  }
}
```

Code Fragment 3.17: Applet based on algorithm computeSpans2 (part 1).

```
public void actionPerformed(ActionEvent e) {
    currQuote = randomDailyPrices(numDays, startPrice, maxVariation);
    repaint();
}
public Quote[] randomDailyPrices(int N, int startPrice, int maxVariation) {
    // generate an array of randomly generated Quote objects storing
    // price quotes for N days as follows:
    //
    // - the price on day 0 is startPrice;
    //
    //    the price on day i (i > 0) is obtained by adding to the price
    //    on day i-1 a randomly generated number in the range
    //    [-maxVariation,+maxVariation]; however, if this yields a
    // - negative number, then the price is set equal to 0
    //
    Random gen = new Random();  // random number generator
    Quote[] Q = new Quote[N];   // initialize the array of price quotes
    Q[0] = new Quote(0, startPrice);
    for (int i=1 ; i<Q.length ; i++) {
        int price = Math.max(0, Q[i−1].getPrice()+gen.nextInt() % maxVariation);
        Q[i] = new Quote(i, price);
    }
    return Q;
}
public void computeDailyHighSpan (Quote Q[]) {
    // compute the span of the stock price on each day by means of a
    // stack, and stores the information in the Quote objects
    int prevHigh; // closest preceding day when the stock price was higher
    Stack D = new ArrayStack(); // creates an empty jdsl.simple.api.Stack
    for (int i=0 ; i<Q.length ; i++) {  // process the current day i
        while (!D.isEmpty() && Q[i].getPrice() >= ((Quote) D.top()).getPrice())
            // note that if the first condition !D.empty() evaluates to
            // false, then the second condition is not evaluated
            D.pop(); // remove quote from the stack because the price is
        // lower than the current one
        if (D.isEmpty())
            prevHigh = −1; // day i is a new high for the stock price
        else
            prevHigh = ((Quote) D.top()).getDay();
        Q[i].setSpan(i−prevHigh); // computed and store the span
        D.push(Q[i]); // add to the stack the current quote
    }
}
```

Code Fragment 3.18: Applet based on algorithm computeSpans2 (part 2).

```
    public void drawQuote(Graphics g, Quote q) {
        // visualize price (vertical bar) and span (horizontal line)
        int x = xOff+q.getDay()*xSep;
        int y = yOff − q.getPrice();
        int w = barWidth;
        int h = q.getPrice();
        int l = q.getSpan()*xSep − barWidth;
        if (q.getSpan() == q.getDay() + 1)
            g.setColor(highBarColor); // the bar for a price high has a special color
        else
            g.setColor(barColor);
        g.fillRect(x,y,w,h); // draw a vertical bar representing the price
        g.setColor(lineColor);
        g.drawLine(x−1,y,x−l,y); // draw a horizontal line representing the span
    }
} // end class StockAnalysis

// Stock quote
public class Quote {
    private int day, price, span;
    public Quote(int d, int p) {
        setDay(d);
        setPrice(p);
    }
    public void setDay(int d) {
        day = d;
    }
    public int getDay() {
        return day;
    }
    public void setPrice(int p) {
        price = p;
    }
    public int getPrice() {
        return price;
    }
    public void setSpan(int s) {
        span = s;
    }
    public int getSpan() {
        return span;
    }
} // end class Quote
```

Code Fragment 3.19: Applet based on algorithm computeSpans2 (part 3).

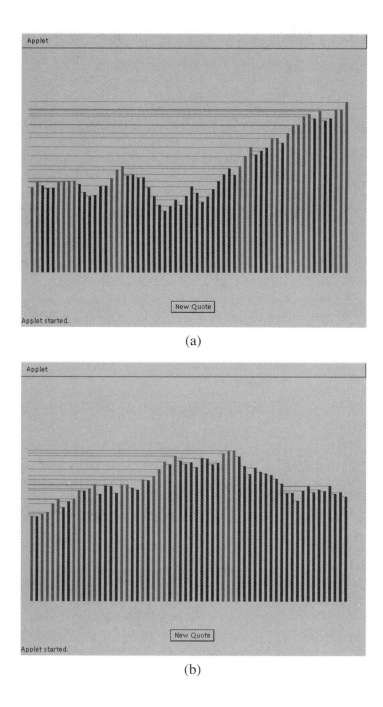

Figure 3.13: Examples of outputs generated by applet StockAnalysis.

3.6 Exercises

Reinforcement

R-3.1 Describe the output of the following series of stack operations: push(5), push(3), pop(), push(2), push(8), pop(), pop(), push(9), push(1), pop(), push(7), push(6), pop(), pop(), push(4), pop(), pop().

R-3.2 Describe the output for the following sequence of queue operations: enqueue(5), enqueue(3), dequeue(), enqueue(2), enqueue(8), dequeue(), dequeue(), enqueue(9), enqueue(1), dequeue(), enqueue(7), enqueue(6), dequeue(), dequeue(), enqueue(4), dequeue(), dequeue().

R-3.3 Describe in pseudo-code, how to insert an element at the beginning of a singly linked list, assuming that the list does **not** have a sentinel header node, and instead uses a reference variable head to reference the first node in the list.

R-3.4 Give a Java method for finding the penultimate node in a singly linked list where the last element is indicated by a null *next* reference.

R-3.5 Give a Java method for determining, just by link hopping, whether a doubly linked list with header and trailer sentinels is empty (that is, do not make use of a *size* instance variable).

Creativity

C-3.1 Describe in pseudo-code, a method for finding the middle node of a doubly linked list with header and trailer sentinels and an odd number of real nodes between them. (Note: this method must only use link hopping; it cannot use a counter.) What is the running time of this method?

C-3.2 Give a Java code fragment for concatenating two singly linked lists L and M, with header sentinel nodes, into a single list L' that contains all the nodes of L (in their original order) followed by all the nodes of M (also in their original order). What is the running time of this method, if we let n denote the number of nodes in L and we let m denote the number of nodes in M?

C-3.3 Describe how to implement the queue ADT using two stacks. What is the running time of the enqueue() and dequeue() methods in this case?

C-3.4 Describe in pseudo-code how to swap two nodes x and y in a singly linked list L given references only to x and y. Repeat this exercise for the case when L is a doubly linked list. What are the running times of each of these methods in terms of n, the number of nodes in L?

C-3.5 In most programming languages, parenthetic symbols (), [] and {} must be balanced and properly nested. We define a ***parenthetically correct*** string of characters as a string that matches one of the following patterns, where S denotes a (possibly empty) string without any parenthetic symbols, and P, P', and P'' recursively denote parenthetically correct strings:

- S
- $P'(P)P''$
- $P'[P]P''$
- $P'\{P\}P''$

Design an algorithm that checks whether a string is parenthetically correct in time proportional to the size of the string using a stack as an auxiliary data structure.

C-3.6 Give a Java code fragment for concatenating two doubly linked lists L and M, with header and trailer sentinel nodes, into a single list L', as in the previous exercise. What is the running time of this method?

C-3.7 Describe in pseudo-code a linear-time algorithm for reversing a singly linked list L, so that the ordering of the nodes becomes exactly opposite of what it was before.

C-3.8★ Describe in pseudo-code an algorithm for reversing a singly linked list L using only a constant amount of additional space and not using any recursion. What is the running time of this method?

C-3.9 Give a pseudo-code description for an array-based implementation of the double-ended queue ADT described in the previous exercise. What is the running time for each operation?

C-3.10 Describe how to implement the stack ADT using two queues. What is the running time of the push() and pop() methods in this case?

Projects

P-3.1 Implement the stack ADT with a simply linked list (without using the built-in Java Stack class).

P-3.2 When a share of common stock of some company is sold, the *capital gain* is the difference between the share's selling price and the price originally paid to buy it. This rule is easy-to-understand for a single share, but if we sell multiple shares of stock bought over a long period of time, then we must identify the shares actually being sold. A standard accounting principle for identifying which shares of a stock were sold in such a case is to use a FIFO protocol—the shares sold are the ones that have been held the longest (indeed, this is the default method built into several personal finance software packages). For example, suppose we buy 100 shares at $20 each on day 1, 20 shares at $24 on day 2, 200 shares at $36 on day 3, and then sell 150 shares on day 4 at $30 each. Then applying the FIFO protocol means that of the 150 shares sold, 100 were bought on day 1, 20 were bought on day 2, and 30 were bought on day 3. The capital gain in this case would therefore be $100 \cdot 10 + 20 \cdot 6 + 30 \cdot (-6)$, or $940. Write a program that takes as input a sequence of transactions of the form

$$\text{buy } x \text{ share(s) at } \$y \text{ each}$$

or

$$\text{sell } x \text{ share(s) at } \$y \text{ each}$$

assuming that the transactions occur on consecutive days and the values x and y are integers. Given this input sequence, the output should be the total capital gain (or loss) for the entire sequence, using the FIFO protocol to identify shares.

P-3.3 Design an ADT for a two-color, double-stack ADT that consists of two stacks—one "red" and one "blue"—and has as its operations color-coded versions of the regular stack ADT operations. For example, this ADT should allow for both a red push operation and a blue push operation. Give an efficient implementation of this ADT using a single array whose capacity is set at some value N that is assumed to always be larger than the sizes of the red and blue stacks combined.

P-3.4 Implement the stack ADT using the Java Vector class.

P-3.5 Implement the queue ADT using an array.

P-3.6 Implement the queue ADT using a simply linked list.

P-3.7 Implement the deque ADT with a doubly linked list.

P-3.8 Implement the deque ADT with an array used in a circular fashion.

Chapter Notes

The fundamental data structures of stacks, queues, and linked lists discussed in this chapter belong to the folklore of computer science. They were first chronicled by Knuth in his seminal book on *Fundamental Algorithms* [88]. In this chapter, we have taken the approach of defining the fundamental data structures of stacks, queues, and deques, first in terms of their ADTs and then in terms of concrete implementations. This approach to data structure specification and implementation is an outgrowth of software engineering advances brought on by the object-oriented design approach, and is now considered a standard approach for teaching data structures. We were introduced to this approach to data structure design by the classic books by Aho, Hopcroft, and Ullman on data structures and algorithms [6, 7]. For further study of abstract data types, please see the book by Liskov and Guttag [100], the survey paper by Cardelli and Wegner [32], or the book chapter by Demurjian [39]. The naming conventions we use for the methods of the stack, queue, and deque ADTs are taken from JDSL. JDSL is a data structures library in Java that builds on approaches taken for C++ in the libraries STL [116] and LEDA [111]. We shall use this convention throughout this text. In this chapter, we motivated the study of stacks and queues from implementation issues in Java. The reader interested in learning more about the Java run-time environment known as the Java Virtual Machine (JVM) is referred to the book by Lindholm and Yellin [99] that defines the JVM.

Chapter

4

Sequences

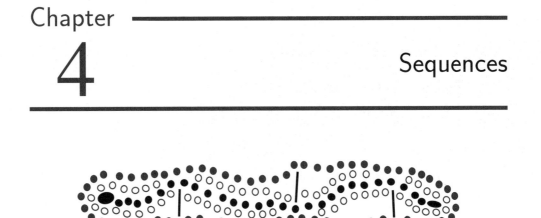

Contents

The concept of a sequence, where each object comes before or after another, is fundamental in human society and in computing. We see it in a city parade, as each float and marching band passes along a central street in a prescribed order. We also see it in a chronology of important events in the history of a nation, where each event is succeeded by another. We see it in computing in a line-by-line listing of the code of a computer program, where the order of instructions determines the computation that this program represents. We also see it in the sequence of network packets that together comprise an e-mail message from a friend, which, if it is to make sense, requires that the packets be assembled in the same order in which they are sent. Sequences are interesting, then, for they represent the important relationships of "next" and "previous" between related objects. In addition, sequences are widely used to realize and implement other data structures; hence, they are foundational building-blocks for data structure design.

In this chapter, we present the *sequence* ADT, which represents a collection of linearly arranged elements and provides methods for accessing, inserting, and removing arbitrary elements. Formally, a *sequence* (which is also called a *list*) is a data structure that represents a collection of elements arranged in a linear order. Thus, each element of a sequence has a previous element (unless it is the first element) and a next element (unless it is the last element). Stacks, queues, and deques, studied in Chapter 3, can be viewed as restricted types of sequences that access only the first and/or last element of a sequence. An important property of a sequence is that, just as with stacks, queues, and deques, the order of the elements in a sequence is determined by the operations in the abstract data type specification, and not by the values of the elements.

We give two basic ways of implementing a sequence, with an array and with a doubly linked list, and we point out performance trade-offs between the two implementations. In order to specify certain methods of the sequence ADT in a way that abstracts away implementation details, we introduce the concepts of *rank* and *position*. The rank indicates the relative ordering of an object in a sequence, and the position concept abstracts the location of objects in a sequence. In particular, a rank is always an integer, whereas a position is an object that provides a unified way of referring to the "place" where the element is stored, independent of the specific implementation of the sequence. For example, the place of an element could be a cell of an array or a node of a doubly linked list.

We illustrate the use of the sequence ADT through the implementation of a well-known sorting algorithm known as *bubble-sort*. We also discuss the concept of an *iterator* and mention its realization by means of a sequence.

4.1 Ranked Sequences

If a sequence S has n elements, each element e of S is uniquely associated with an integer **rank** in the range $[0, n-1]$, which is equal to the number of elements of S that precede e in S. It is important to note that this association does **not** imply that we are necessarily using an array to implement a sequence, although that is one possibility. We adopt the convention that the first element in a sequence has rank 0 and the last element has rank $n-1$. If an element is the rth element in the sequence, then it has rank $r-1$. This convention is in keeping with the indexing convention for arrays in Java. Clearly, if an element of the sequence has rank r, its previous element (if it exists) has rank $r-1$, and its next element (if it exists) has rank $r+1$. The rank of an element may change whenever the sequence is updated, however. For example, if we insert a new element at the beginning of the sequence, the rank of each of the other elements increases by one.

Caution

A sequence that supports access to its elements by their ranks is a called a **ranked sequence**. Rank is a simple yet powerful notion, since it can be used to specify where to insert a new element into a sequence or where to remove an old element. For example, we can give the rank that a new element will have after it is inserted (for example, insert at rank 2). We could also use rank to specify an element to be removed (for example, remove the element at rank 2).

Example 4.1: *In the following, we show a series of rank-based insert and delete operations on an initially empty sequence S.*

Operation	Output	S
insert 7 at rank 0	–	(7)
insert 4 at rank 0	–	(4,7)
return the element at rank 1	7	(4,7)
insert 2 at rank 2	–	(4,7,2)
return the element at rank 3	"error"	(4,7,2)
remove the element at rank 1	7	(4,2)
insert 5 at rank 1	–	(4,5,2)
insert 3 at rank 1	–	(4,3,5,2)
insert 9 at rank 4	–	(4,3,5,2,9)
return the element at rank 2	5	(4,3,5,2,9)

Note that the rank of an element in a sequence is a function of the time and place that it and other elements were placed in the sequence, and not on the element's value. We provide the specific methods of the ranked sequence ADT in the next subsection.

4.1.1   The Ranked Sequence Abstract Data Type

A ranked sequence S is an ADT that supports the following fundamental methods.

elemAtRank(r): Return the element of S with rank r; an error condition occurs if $r < 0$ or $r > n - 1$, where n is the current number of elements.
Input: Integer; *Output:* Object.

replaceElemAtRank(r, e): Replace with e the element at rank r and return it; an error condition occurs if $r < 0$ or $r > n - 1$, where n is the current number of elements.
Input: Integer r and object e; *Output:* Object.

insertElemAtRank(r, e): Insert a new element e into S to have rank r; an error condition occurs if if $r < 0$ or $r > n$, where n is the number of elements before the insertion.
Input: Integer r and object e; *Output:* None.

removeElemAtRank(r): Remove from S the element at rank r; an error condition occurs if $r < 0$ or $r > n - 1$, where n is the current number of elements.
Input: Integer; *Output:* Object.

In addition, a ranked sequence supports the usual methods size() and isEmpty().

The repertory of methods we have given for the ranked sequence is small, but it is sufficient for us to define an adapter class (see Section 3.4.3) that realizes the deque ADT. One possible adaptation is given in Table 4.1. (See also Exercise C-4.3.)

Deque Method	*Realization with Ranked Sequence Methods*
size()	size()
isEmpty()	isEmpty()
first()	elemAtRank(0)
last()	elemAtRank(size() − 1)
insertFirst(e)	insertElemAtRank(0, e)
insertLast(e)	insertElemAtRank(size(), e)
removeFirst()	removeElemAtRank(0)
removeLast()	removeElemAtRank(size() − 1)

Table 4.1: Realization of a deque by means of a ranked sequence.

4.1.2 A Simple Array-Based Implementation

An obvious choice for implementing the ranked sequence ADT is for us to use an array S, where $S[i]$ stores (a reference to) the element with rank i. We choose the size N of array S sufficiently large, and we keep the number n of actual elements of the sequence in an instance variable. The details for performing each of the methods of the ranked sequence ADT in this case are fairly simple. To implement the elemAtRank(r) operation, for example, all we need to do is return $S[r]$. Implementations of methods insertElemAtRank(r, e) and removeElemAtRank(r), given in Code Fragment 4.1, involve shifting elements up or down to keep the occupied cells in the array contiguous. (See Figure 4.1 and also Exercise R-4.5.)

Algorithm insertElemAtRank(r, e):

    for $i = n-1, n-2, \ldots, r$ **do**

        $S[i+1] \leftarrow S[i]$ {make room for the new element}

    $S[r] \leftarrow e$

    $n \leftarrow n+1$

Algorithm removeElemAtRank(r):

    $e \leftarrow S[r]$ {e is a temporary variable}

    for $i = r, r+1, \ldots, n-2$ **do**

        $S[i] \leftarrow S[i+1]$ {fill-in for the removed element}

    $n \leftarrow n-1$

    return e

Code Fragment 4.1: Methods insertElemAtRank(r, e) and removeElemAtRank(r) in the array-based implementation of the ranked sequence ADT.

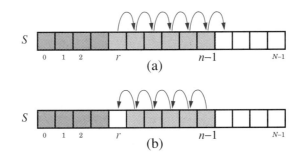

Figure 4.1: Array-based implementation of a ranked sequence storing n elements: (a) shifting up for an insert at rank r; (b) shifting down for a removal at rank r.

Table 4.2 shows the worst-case running times of methods in a realization of a ranked sequence by means of an array. The methods isEmpty, size, and elemAtRank clearly run in $O(1)$ time. However, insertElemAtRank(r, e) runs in time $O(n)$. Indeed, the worst case for this operation occurs when $r = 0$, since we have to shift forward all the existing n elements. A similar argument applies to the method removeElemAtRank(r), which runs in $O(n)$ time, because we have to shift backward $n - 1$ elements in the worst case ($r = 0$). In fact, the average running time of these operations is $\Theta(n)$, for we will have to shift $n/2$ elements on average.

Method	Time
size, isEmpty	$O(1)$
elemAtRank, replaceElemAtRank	$O(1)$
insertElemAtRank, removeElemAtRank	$O(n)$

Table 4.2: Performance of a ranked sequence realized by an array. The space usage is $O(N)$, where N is the size of the array.

Looking closer at insertElemAtRank(r, e) and removeElemAtRank(r), we note that they each run in time $O(n - r + 1)$; hence, methods insertElemAtRank(n, e) and removeElemAtRank$(n - 1)$ each take $O(1)$ time. Moreover, this observation has an interesting consequence for the adaptation of the ranked sequence ADT to the deque ADT given in Section 4.1.1. If the ranked sequence ADT is implemented by means of an array, then methods insertLast and removeLast of the deque each run in $O(1)$ time. But using the implementation given above, the methods insertFirst and removeFirst of the deque each run in $O(n)$ time. Nevertheless, with a little effort, we can produce an array-based implementation of the ranked sequence ADT that achieves $O(1)$ time for insertions and removals at rank 0, as well as insertions and removals at the end of the sequence. We leave the details for an exercise.

4.1.3 The Java Vector Class

Java has a built-in class java.util.Vector that provides methods similar to those of the ranked sequence ADT. A Vector is an array-based data structure that allows for rank-based access, insertion, and deletion of general objects. It does not specify a rigid capacity constraint, however, as is required by a strict array-based implementation. Instead, a Vector can grow dynamically, much like a hermit crab that moves into a larger shell when it outgrows its previous one. Specifically, if an insertion into a Vector V overflows V's current capacity, then V copies all of its contents to a new larger array, which is typically twice as big as the previous one.

4.1.4   Implementation with a Doubly Linked List

A ranked sequence can also be implemented with a doubly linked list. (See Section 3.4.4.) Of course, using this implementation means that we no longer explicitly store the ranks of the elements in the sequence. Hence, to perform the operation elemAtRank(r), we must do link hopping from one of the ends of the list until we locate the node storing the element with rank r. For efficiency reasons, we start hopping from the closest end of the sequence, achieving a running time that is

$$O(\min(r+1, n-r)),$$

which is $O(n)$. The worst case occurs when $r = \lfloor n/2 \rfloor$.

Operations insertElemAtRank(r, e) and removeElemAtRank(r) also perform link hopping to locate the node storing the element with rank r, and then insert or delete a node, as shown in Figure 4.2. The running time of this implementation of insertElemAtRank(r, e) and removeElemAtRank(r) is also

$$O(\min(r+1, n-r+1)),$$

which is $O(n)$. One advantage of this approach is that, if $r = 0$ or $r = n-1$, as is the case in the adaptation of the ranked sequence ADT to the deque ADT given in Section 4.1.1, then insertElemAtRank and removeElemAtRank run in $O(1)$ time.

We show in Code Fragment 4.2 selected portions of a Java implementation of the RankedSequence interface by means of a doubly linked list. Note that this implementation is a class, NodeRankedSequence, that extends (through class inheritance) the implementation of a deque given in Code Fragments 3.13 and 3.14. Like its parent class MyDeque, class NodeRankedSequence uses class DLNode for the implementation of the nodes of a doubly linked list.

Method checkRank(r) is a private method of NodeRankedSequence that throws a BoundaryViolationException when its argument r is an invalid rank, that is,

$$r < 0 \ \textbf{ or } \ r > n-1.$$

The worst-case running times of the methods of a ranked sequence implemented by means of a doubly linked list are the same as those of the implementation with an array (see Table 4.2), except for the method elemAtRank. The doubly linked list implementation has the advantage that it requires space $O(n)$, proportional to the number of elements effectively present in the sequence, whereas an array needs space proportional to the size of the array. The trade-off is that operation elemAtRank is more efficient in the array implementation, since this operation requires $O(n)$ time in the worst case when we use a doubly linked list. Still, implementing a sequence with a doubly linked list allows other kinds of insertion and deletion operations to be performed very quickly.

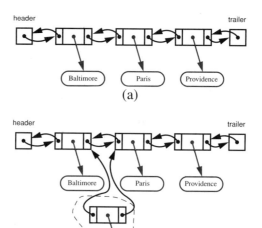

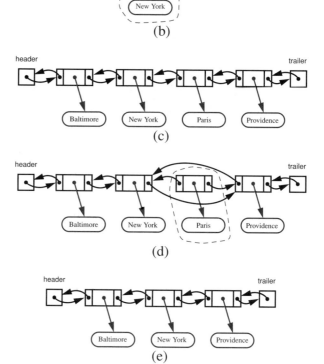

Figure 4.2: Update operations in a doubly linked list with header and trailer sentinels: (a) before the insertion of a node; (b) creating a new node; (c) after the insertion and before the deletion a node; (d) deleting a node; (e) after the deletion.

```
public class NodeRankedSequence
  extends MyDeque implements Deque, RankedSequence {
. . .
    public void insertElemAtRank (int rank, Object element)
    throws BoundaryViolationException {
      if (rank != size()) // rank size() is OK for insertion
        checkRank(rank);
      DLNode next = nodeAtRank(rank); // the new node will be right before this
      DLNode prev = next.getPrev(); // the new node will be right after this
      DLNode node = new DLNode(element, prev, next);
      next.setPrev(node);
      prev.setNext(node);
      size++;
    }
    public Object removeElemAtRank (int rank)
      throws BoundaryViolationException {
      checkRank(rank);
      DLNode node = nodeAtRank(rank); // node to be removed
      DLNode next = node.getNext(); // node before it
      DLNode prev = node.getPrev(); // node after it
      prev.setNext(next);
      next.setPrev(prev);
      size--;
      return node.getElement();
    }
    private DLNode nodeAtRank (int rank) {
      // auxiliary method to find the node of the element with the given rank
      DLNode node;
      if (rank <= size()/2) { // scan forward from the head
        node = header.getNext();
        for (int i=0; i < rank; i++)
          node = node.getNext();
      }
      else { // scan backward from the tail
        node = trailer.getPrev();
        for (int i=0; i < size()-rank-1 ; i++)
          node = node.getPrev();
      }
      return node;
    }
. . .
```

Code Fragment 4.2: Methods insertElemAtRank, removeElemAtRank, and check-Rank of class NodeRankedSequence, which implements a ranked sequence by means of a doubly linked list. Their execution is illustrated in Figure 4.2.

4.2 Positional Sequences

Ranks are not the only way of referring to the place where an element appears in a sequence. If we have a sequence S implemented with a (singly or doubly) linked list, for example, then it would be natural and efficient to use **nodes** instead of ranks. In this section, we explore a way of abstracting the concept of "place" of an element in a sequence without revealing whether it is implemented with an index in an array or a reference to a node of a linked list.

4.2.1 Node-Based Operations

Let S be a sequence implemented using a doubly linked list. It would be convenient to define methods for S that take nodes of the list as parameters. For instance, we could define a hypothetical method removeAtNode(v) that removes the element of S stored at node v of the list. Using a node as a parameter allows us to remove an element in $O(1)$ time by simply "linking out" the old node through an update of the *next* and *prev* links of its neighbors (recall Figure 4.2). Similarly, we could insert in $O(1)$ time a new element e into S with an operation such as insertAfterNode(v, e), which specifies the node v after which the node of the new element should be inserted. In this case, we simply "link in" the new node (as shown in Figure 4.2).

Augmenting the repertory of operations of the sequence ADT by adding the above node-based operations raises a very serious issue. If a method takes a reference to a node as an argument, then it can be executed on a sequence implemented with a doubly linked list, but this would be meaningless in an array-based implementation, for there are no "nodes" in an array. Thus, such a method should not be included in a generic sequence ADT, since it would violate the object-oriented principle of abstracting the behavior of a data structure away from its implementation.

Caution

So now we are faced with a dilemma. If we do not extend the repertory of operations of a sequence beyond the rank-based operations, then we cannot take advantage of the efficiency of doubly linked lists, yet if we do extend the repertory of operations to refer to individual nodes, then we violate an important principle of object-oriented design. Fortunately, there is a simple way out of this dilemma.

In order to abstract and unify the different mechanisms for storing elements in the various implementations of a sequence, we introduce the concept of **position** in a sequence, which formalizes the intuitive notion of "place" of an element relative to others in a sequence.

4.2.2   Positions

So as to safely expand the set of operations for sequences, we encapsulate a notion of "position" that allows us to enjoy the efficiency of a doubly linked list sequence implementation without violating object-oriented design principles. In this framework, we view a sequence as a ***container*** of elements that stores each element at a position and that keeps these positions arranged in a linear order. A position is itself an abstract data type that supports the following two methods:

> element(): Return the element stored at this position.
> ***Input:*** None; ***Output:*** Object.

> container(): Return the sequence that contains this position.
> ***Input:*** None; ***Output:*** Sequence.

A position is always defined ***relatively***, that is, in terms of its neighbors. In a sequence, a position p will always be "after" some position q and "before" some position s (unless p is the first or last position). A position p, which is associated with some element e, in a sequence S does not change, even if the rank of e changes in S, unless we explicitly remove e (and, hence, have no more need for p). Moreover, the position p does not change even if we replace or swap the element e stored at p with another element. These facts about positions allows us to define a rich set of positional sequence methods that take position objects as parameters.

4.2.3   The Positional Sequence Abstract Data Type

Using the concept of position, we can define another type of sequence ADT, called a ***positional sequence***. This ADT supports the following methods:

> first(): Return the position of the first element of S; an error occurs if S is empty.
> ***Input:*** None; ***Output:*** Position.

> last(): Return the position of the last element of S; an error occurs if S is empty.
> ***Input:*** None; ***Output:*** Position.

> before(p): Return the position of the element of S preceding the one at position p; an error occurs if $p =$ first.
> ***Input:*** Position; ***Output:*** Position.

> after(p): Return the position of the element of S following the one at position p; an error occurs if $p =$ last.
> ***Input:*** Position; ***Output:*** Position.

The above methods allow us to refer to relative positions in a sequence and to be able to move between them. Note that there are no references to pointers in these methods. In addition to the above methods, and generic container methods size and isEmpty, we also include the following update methods for the positional sequence ADT, which take position objects as parameters and/or return position objects as values:

replace(p, e): Replace the element at position p with e, returning the element formerly at position p.
Input: Position p and object e; *Output:* Object.

swap(p, q): Swap the elements stored at positions p and q, so that the element that is at position p moves to position q and the element that is at position q moves to position p.
Input: Two positions; *Output:* None.

insertFirst(e): Insert a new element e into S as the first element.
Input: Object e; *Output:* Position of the newly inserted element e.

insertLast(e): Insert a new element e into S as the last element.
Input: Object e; *Output:* Position of the newly inserted element e.

insertBefore(p, e): Insert a new element e into S before position p in S.
Input: Position p and Object e; *Output:* Position of the newly inserted element e.

insertAfter(p, e): Insert a new element e into S after position p in S.
Input: Position p and Object e; *Output:* Position of the newly inserted element e.

remove(p): Remove from S the element at position p.
Input: Position; *Output:* The removed element.

In a complete ADT we should probably also include two boolean functions: isFirst(p) and isLast(p), which determine if a position is respectively the first or last in a sequence. These methods are not strictly needed, however, for such determinations can be decided by comparing for equality the position p to the positions returned by the first and last methods, respectively. Nevertheless, their inclusion in the ADT could improve code readability.

We illustrate the operations of a positional sequence in the following example.

Example 4.2: *We show below a series of operations for an initially empty positional sequence S. We use variables p_1, p_2, and so on, to denote different positions, and we show, in parentheses, the object that is currently stored at such a position.*

Operation	Output	S
insertFirst(8)	$p_1(8)$	(8)
insertAfter(p_1,5)	$p_2(5)$	(8,5)
insertBefore(p_2,3)	$p_3(3)$	(8,3,5)
insertFirst(9)	$p_4(9)$	(9,8,3,5)
before(p_3)	$p_1(8)$	(9,8,3,5)
last()	$p_2(5)$	(9,8,3,5)
remove(p_4)	9	(8,3,5)
swap(p_1,p_2)	–	(5,3,8)
replace(p_3,7)	3	(5,7,8)
insertAfter(first(),2)	$p_5(2)$	(5,2,3,8)

There are a number of different ways to implement positional sequences. Two of the most natural ways are to use an array or a doubly linked list.

4.2.4   Array Implementation

Suppose we want to implement a positional sequence S by storing each element e of S in a cell $A[i]$ of an array A. A position object p holds an index i as an instance variables, together with an instance variable referencing S. We can then implement method element(p) by simply returning $S.A[i]$. A major drawback with this approach, however, is that the cells in A have no way to reference their corresponding positions. Thus, after performing an insertFirst operation we have no way of informing the existing positions in S that their ranks each went up by 1 (remember that positions in a sequence are always defined relative to their neighboring positions, not their ranks). Hence, if we are going to implement a positional sequence with an array, we need a different approach.

Consider an alternate solution in which, instead of storing the elements of S in array A, we store position objects in A and we store elements in positions. Now, in addition to references to S and an index i, a position object $p = A[i]$ holds the element e associated with p. With this data structure, illustrated in Figure 4.3, we can easily scan through the array to update the i variable for each position whose rank changes because of an insertion or deletion.

In this array implementation of a positional sequence, the methods insertFirst, insertBefore, insertAfter, and remove take $O(n)$ time because we have to shift position objects to make room for the new position or to fill-in the hole created by the removal of the old position. All the other methods take $O(1)$ time.

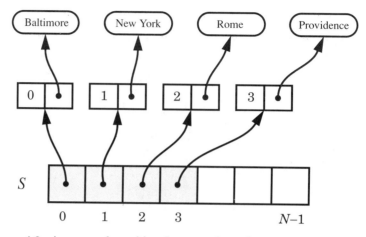

Figure 4.3: An array-based implementation of a positional sequence.

Note that we can use an array in a circular fashion, like we did for implementing a deque (see Section 3.2.2). With a little work, we can then perform method insertFirst in $O(1)$ time. Note that methods insertBefore, insertAfter, and remove still take $O(n)$ time. The worst case occurs now when the element to be inserted or removed has rank $\lfloor n/2 \rfloor$. The running times of methods of a positional sequence implemented by means of an array used in a circular fashion are shown in Table 4.3.

4.2.5 Doubly Linked List Implementation

Suppose now that we wish to implement a positional sequence using a doubly linked list. In this case we can use inheritance to design an elegant implementation of a positional sequence, by simply making the nodes of the linked list implement the position ADT. That is, we have each node store a reference to the object S representing the sequence and defining methods element(), which returns the element stored at the node, and container(), which returns the reference to the sequence. Thus, the nodes themselves act as positions. They are viewed internally by the linked list as nodes, but from the outside they are viewed only as generic positions. For example, given a position p in S, we can implement the method before(p) by returning p.prev (unless p is the first position, in which case we signal an error). Therefore, positions in a doubly linked list implementation can be supported without any additional time or space overhead. Moreover, this approach has the advantage of hiding the implementation details of the sequence from a user, which aids in code reuse.

We show in Code Fragment 4.3 a Java class for the nodes of a doubly linked list that implements the position ADT.

```
class NSNode implements Position {
    private NSNode prev, next; // References to the nodes before and after
    private Object element;    // Element stored in this positin
    private Container cont;     // Container of this position
    NSNode(NSNode newPrev, NSNode newNext,
            Container container, Object elem) { // Initialize the node
        prev = newPrev;
        next = newNext;
        cont = container;
        element = elem;
    }
    // Methods from interface Position
    public Container container() throws InvalidPositionException {
        if (cont == null)
            throw new InvalidPositionException
                ("Position has no container!");
        return cont;
    }
    public Object element() throws InvalidPositionException {
        if (cont == null)
            throw new InvalidPositionException
                ("Position has no container!");
        return element;
    }
    // Accesor methods
    NSNode getNext() { return next; }
    NSNode getPrev() { return prev; }
    void setNext(NSNode newNext) { next = newNext; }
    // Update methods
    void setPrev(NSNode newPrev) { prev = newPrev; }
    void setElement(Object newElement) { element = newElement; }
    void setContainer(Container newCont) { cont = newCont; }
}
```

Code Fragment 4.3: Class NSNode realizing a node of a doubly linked list and implementing the Position interface (ADT).

Note that all the methods of the positional sequence ADT can be implemented in $O(1)$ time by means of a doubly linked list. Hence, a doubly linked list is preferable to an array for implementing a positional sequence. (See Table 4.3.)

Operations	Array	List
size, isEmpty	$O(1)$	$O(1)$
first, last	$O(1)$	$O(1)$
before, after	$O(1)$	$O(1)$
replace, swap	$O(1)$	$O(1)$
insertFirst, insertLast	$O(1)$	$O(1)$
insertAfter, insertBefore	$O(n)$	$O(1)$
remove	$O(n)$	$O(1)$

Table 4.3: Comparison of the running times of the methods of a positional sequence implemented with either an array (used in a circular fashion) or a doubly linked list. We denote with n the number of elements in the sequence. The space usage is $O(n)$ for the doubly linked list and $O(N)$ for the array, where N is the size of the array.

Portions of a Java implementation of a positional sequence by means of a doubly linked list are shown in Code Fragments 4.4–4.7. Error conditions are signaled by the following exceptions:

EmptyContainerException: thrown if the sequence is empty and an attempt is made at accessing an element of it (for example, via the first method).

BoundaryViolationException: thrown if an attempt is made at accessing an element whose position is outside the range of positions of the sequence.

InvalidPositionException: thrown if a position provided as argument is not valid (for example, it is a null reference or it has no associated container).

The following instance variables are also used:

```
private int numElts;      // Number of items in the sequence
private NSNode head, tail; // Special sentinels
```

Code Fragment 4.4 shows method replace and two "convenience" methods, checkPosition and checkRank, which perform some safety checks. Code Fragment 4.5 shows methods first, last, before, and after. Code Fragment 4.6 shows methods insertAfter, insertFirst, and remove. Finally, Code Fragment 4.7 shows how methods insertLast and insertBefore can be realized by simple combinations of methods insertAfter and insertFirst.

```
// Replace the element of the given position with the new element and
// return the old value of element
public Object replace (Position p, Object element)
  throws InvalidPositionException {
    NSNode n = checkPosition (p);
    Object oldElt = n.element();
    n.setElement(element);
    return oldElt;
}
// Check if position is valid for this sequence
protected NSNode checkPosition(Position p)
  throws InvalidPositionException {
    // position must belong to this container
    // and cannot be head or tail of the sequence
    if (p == head)
        throw new InvalidPositionException
            ("Head of the sequence is not a valid position");
    if (p == tail)
        throw new InvalidPositionException
            ("Tail of the sequence is not a valid position");
    if (p.container() != this)
        throw new InvalidPositionException
            ("Position does not belong to this container");
    try {
        NSNode temp = (NSNode)p;
        return temp;
    } catch (ClassCastException e) {
        throw new InvalidPositionException
            ("Position is of wrong type for this container.");
    }
}


// Check that rack is in the range 0 <= rank < numElts
protected void checkRank(int rank)
  throws BoundaryViolationException {
    if (rank < 0 || rank >= numElts)
        throw new BoundaryViolationException
        ("Rank " + rank + " is invalid for this sequence of " +
        numElts + " elements.");
}
```

Code Fragment 4.4: Method replace and auxiliary methods checkPosition and checkRank in the implementation of a positional sequence by means of a doubly linked list. The implementation of the nodes of the list is shown in Code Fragment 4.3.

```
public Position first()  // Return the first position in the sequence
  throws EmptyContainerException {  // Thrown if the sequence is empty
    if(isEmpty())
        throw new EmptyContainerException("Sequence is empty");
    return head.getNext();
}

public Position last() // Return the last position in the sequence
  throws EmptyContainerException {  // Thrown if the sequence is empty
    if (isEmpty())
        throw new EmptyContainerException("Sequence is empty");
    return tail.getPrev();
}
public Position before (Position p)  // Return position before this one
  throws InvalidPositionException, BoundaryViolationException {
    NSNode n = checkPosition(p);
    NSNode prev = n.getPrev();
    if (prev == head)
        throw new BoundaryViolationException
            ("Cannot go past the beginning of the sequence");
    return prev;
}

public Position after (Position p)  // Return position after this one
  throws InvalidPositionException, BoundaryViolationException {
    NSNode n = checkPosition(p);
    NSNode next = n.getNext();
    if (next == tail)
        throw new BoundaryViolationException
            ("Cannot go past the end of the sequence");
    return next;
}
```

Code Fragment 4.5: Methods first, last, before, and after in the implementation of a positional sequence by means of a doubly linked list. The implementation of the nodes of the list is shown in Code Fragment 4.3.

```
// Create a new position with the given element and insert it after the
// given position, returning a reference the new position
public Position insertAfter (Position p, Object element)
  throws InvalidPositionException {
    NSNode n = checkPosition(p);
    numElts++;
    NSNode newNode = new NSNode(n, n.getNext(), this, element);
    n.getNext().setPrev(newNode);
    n.setNext(newNode);
    return newNode;
}

// Create a new position with the given element and insert it as the
// first position in the sequence.
public Position insertFirst(Object element) {
    numElts++;
    NSNode newNode = new NSNode(head, head.getNext(), this, element);
    head.getNext().setPrev(newNode);
    head.setNext(newNode);
    return newNode;
}

public Object remove(Position p)  // Remove this position from the sequence
  throws InvalidPositionException {
    NSNode n = checkPosition(p);
    numElts--;
    NSNode nPrev = n.getPrev();
    NSNode nNext = n.getNext();
    nPrev.setNext(nNext);
    nNext.setPrev(nPrev);
    Object nElem = n.element();
    // unlink the position from the list and make it invalid
    n.setNext(null);
    n.setPrev(null);
    n.setContainer(null);
    return nElem;
}
```

Code Fragment 4.6: Methods insertAfter, insertFirst, and remove in the implementation of a positional sequence by means of a doubly linked list. The implementation of the nodes of the list is shown in Code Fragment 4.3.

```
public Position insertLast(Object element) {
  if (isEmpty())
    return insertFirst(element);
  else
    return insertAfter(last(), element);
}
public Position insertBefore (Position p, Object element)
  throws InvalidPositionException {
    if (isEmpty())
      throw new InvalidPositionException("Invalid position.");
    else  if (p == first())
      return insertFirst(element);
    else
      return insertAfter(before(p), element);
}
```

Code Fragment 4.7: Methods insertLast and insertBefore realized by simple combinations of methods insertAfter and insertFirst.

4.3   General Sequences

In this section, we define a generalized sequence that includes all the methods of the ranked sequence and positional sequence. This generalized sequence therefore provides access to its elements using both ranks and positions and is a versatile data structure for a wide variety of applications.

4.3.1   The Sequence Abstract Data Type

A *sequence* is an ADT that supports all the methods of the ranked sequence (discussed in Section 4.1) and positional sequence (discussed in Section 4.2), plus the following methods that provide "bridging" connections between ranks and positions:

atRank(r): Return the position of the element with rank r.
Input: Integer; *Output:* Position.

rankOf(p): Return the rank of the element at position p.
Input: Position; *Output:* Integer.

The definition of the sequence ADT is an example of ***multiple inheritance***, since the sequence inherits methods from two other "super" ADTs. Therefore, its methods include the union of the methods of its super ADTs.

4.3.2 Comparing Sequence Implementations

Table 4.4 compares the running times of the implementations of the general sequence ADT, by means of an array (used in a circular fashion) and by means of a doubly linked list.

Operations	Array	List
size, isEmpty	$O(1)$	$O(1)$
atRank, rankOf,elemAtRank	$O(1)$	$O(n)$
first, last	$O(1)$	$O(1)$
before, after	$O(1)$	$O(1)$
replace, replaceElemAtRank, swap	$O(1)$	$O(1)$
insertElemAtRank, removeElemAtRank	$O(n)$	$O(n)$
insertFirst, insertLast	$O(1)$	$O(1)$
insertAfter, insertBefore	$O(n)$	$O(1)$
remove	$O(n)$	$O(1)$

Table 4.4: Comparison of the running times of the methods of a sequence implemented with either an array (used in a circular fashion) or a doubly linked list. We denote with n the number of elements in the sequence at the time the operation is performed. The space usage is $O(n)$ for the doubly linked list implementation, and $O(N)$ for the array implementation, where N is the size of the array.

Summarizing this table, we see that the array-based implementation is superior to the linked-list implementation on the rank-based access operations (atRank, rankOf, and elemAtRank), and it is equal in performance to the linked-list implementation on all the other access operations. Regarding update operations, the linked-list implementation beats the array-based implementation in the position-based operations (insertAfter, insertBefore, and remove). Even so, the array-based and link-list implementations have the same worst-case performance on the rank-based update methods (insertElemAtRank and removeElemAtRank), albeit for different reasons. In update operations insertFirst and insertLast, the two implementations have comparable performance.

Considering space usage, note that an array requires $O(N)$ space, where N is the size of the array, while a doubly linked list uses $O(n)$ space, where n is the number of elements in the sequence. Since n is less than or equal to N, this implies that the asymptotic space usage of a linked list implementation is superior to that of an array, although there is a small constant factor overhead that is larger for linked lists, since arrays do not need pointers to maintain the ordering of their cells.

The array and linked list implementations each have their advantages and disadvantages. The correct one for a particular application depends on the kinds of operations that are to be performed and the memory space available. Designing the sequence ADT in a way that does not depend on the way it is implemented allows us to easily switch between implementations, so as to always use the implementation that best suits our applications with few changes to our program.

4.4   Case Study: Bubble-Sort on a Sequence

In this section, we illustrate the use of the sequence ADT and its implementation trade-offs with sample Java methods, using the well-known *bubble-sort* algorithm.

4.4.1   The Bubble-Sort Algorithm

Consider a sequence such that any two elements in the sequence can be compared according to an order relation (for example, companies compared by revenue, states compared by population, students compared by age, or words compared lexicographically). The *sorting* problem is to reorder the sequence so that the elements are in nondecreasing order. The *bubble-sort* algorithm (see Figure 4.4) solves this problem by performing a series of *passes* over the sequence. In each pass, the elements are scanned by increasing rank, from rank 0 to the end of the sequence of unordered items. At each position in a pass, an element is compared with its neighbor, and if these two consecutive elements are found to be in the wrong relative order (that is, the preceding element is larger than the succeeding one), then the two elements are swapped. The sequence is sorted by completing n such passes.

pass	swaps	sequence
		$(5,7,2,6,9,3)$
1st	$7 \leftrightarrow 2 \;\; 7 \leftrightarrow 6 \;\; 9 \leftrightarrow 3$	$(5,2,6,7,3,9)$
2nd	$5 \leftrightarrow 2 \;\; 7 \leftrightarrow 3$	$(2,5,6,3,7,9)$
3rd	$6 \leftrightarrow 3$	$(2,5,3,6,7,9)$
4th	$5 \leftrightarrow 3$	$(2,3,5,6,7,9)$

Figure 4.4: The bubble-sort algorithm on a sequence of integers. For each pass, the swaps performed and the sequence after the pass are shown.

Let n denote the number of elements in the sequence. The bubble-sort algorithm has the following property:

- In the first pass, once the largest element is reached, it will keep on being swapped until it gets to the last position of the sequence.
- In the second pass, once the second largest element is reached, it will keep on being swapped until it gets to the second last position of the sequence.
- And so on.

Thus, at the end of the ith pass, the rightmost i elements of the sequence (that is, those with ranks from $n-1$ down to $n-i$) are in final position. This observation implies that it is correct to limit the number of passes made by a bubble-sort on an n-element sequence to n. Moreover, it allows the ith pass to be limited to the first $n-i+1$ elements of the sequence.

4.4.2 A Sequence-Based Analysis of Bubble-Sort

Assume that the implementation of the sequence is such that the accesses to elements and swaps of elements performed by bubble-sort take $O(1)$ time each. That is, the running time of the i-th pass is $O(n-i+1)$. Hence, the overall running time of bubble-sort is

$$O\left(\sum_{i=1}^{n}(n-i+1)\right).$$

We can rewrite the above sum as

$$O\left(n+(n-1)+\cdots+2+1\right),\text{ that is, it is } O\left(\sum_{i=1}^{n}i\right).$$

By Proposition 2.4 we have

$$\sum_{i=1}^{n}i = \frac{n(n+1)}{2}.$$

Thus, bubble-sort runs in $O(n^2)$ time provided that accesses and swaps can each be implemented in $O(1)$ time.

Code Fragment 4.8 contains two Java implementations of bubble-sort on a sequence of Integer objects. The two implementations differ in the preferred choice of methods to access and modify the sequence.

- Method BubbleSort1 accesses the elements only through the interface method atRank. It is a rank-based implementation of the bubble-sort algorithm, and it is suitable only for the array implementation of the sequence, where atRank takes $O(1)$ time. Given such an array-based implementation, this method will run in $O(n^2)$ time. If we implement the sequence used by this algorithm using a doubly linked list, on the other hand, then each atRank call takes $O(n)$ time in the worst case; hence, the entire algorithm would actually run in $O(n^3)$ worst-case time with a linked-list implementation.

```
public void static bubbleSort1(IntegerSequence s) {
  int n = s.size();
  for (int i=0; i<n; i++)        // i-th pass
    for (int j=0; j<n-i; j++)
      if (s.atRank(j).element().intValue() > s.atRank(j+1).element().intValue())
        swap(s.positionAtRank(j), s.positionAtRank(j+1));
}

public void static bubbleSort2(IntegerSequence s) {
  int n = s.size();
  IntegerSequencePosition prec, succ;

  for (int i=0; i<n; i++) {      // i-th pass
    prec = s.firstPosition();
    for (int j=0; j<n-i; j++) {
      succ = s.after(prec);
      if (prec.element().intValue() > succ.element().intValue())
        swap(prec,succ);
      else
        prec = succ;
    }
  }
}
```

Code Fragment 4.8: Java implementations of bubble-sort on a sequence of integers.

- Method BubbleSort2 accesses the elements through the Sequence interface methods first and after. It is a position-based implementation of the bubble-sort algorithm, and it is suitable for both the array and the linked-list implementation of the sequence. This is because both implementations support constant-time performance for the first and after methods. Thus, this implementation runs in $\Theta(n^2)$ time, no matter which implementation is used for the sequence.

The two bubble-sort implementations given above show the importance of providing efficient implementations of ADTs, as well as the importance of designing algorithms to take advantage of those implementations.

Bubble-sort is very simple to implement. Nevertheless, computer scientists generally feel that it is not a good sorting method, because, even if implemented in the best possible way, it still takes quadratic time. Indeed, there are sorting algorithms that run in $O(n \log n)$ time, and are thus much more efficient than bubble-sort. We explore some of them in Chapters 6 and 8.

4.5   Iterators and Enumerations

A typical computation on a sequence is to march through its elements in order, one at a time, for example, to look for a specific element, or to sum the values associated with its elements. An *iterator* is a software design pattern that abstracts the process of scanning through a collection of elements one element at the time. An iterator consists of a sequence S, a current position in S, and a way of stepping to a next position in S and making it the current position. Thus, an iterator is similar to the position ADT we introduce in Section 4.2. In fact, a position object can be thought of as an iterator that doesn't go anywhere. An iterator encapsulates the concepts of "place" and "next" in a container of objects.

Java provides a simplified version of an iterator through an *enumeration* ADT (java.util.Enumeration), which defines the following two methods:

hasMoreElements(): Return true if and only if there are elements left in the enumeration.
Input: None; *Output:* Boolean.

nextElement(): Return and remove the next element in the enumeration.
Input: None; *Output:* Object.

This ADT is an example of an iterator, since it has a notion of the "current" element in its traversal through the sequence, even though it does not provide a specific method to access the current element (just the next one). The first element in the enumeration is returned by the first call to the nextElement method, assuming of course that the enumeration contains at least one element. Elements in a sequence are enumerated according to the linear ordering of that sequence, while elements in an unordered collection of objects are enumerated in an order specific to the collection. Thus, an enumeration provides a unified scheme to access all the elements of a collection in a way that is independent from the specific organization of the collection. We provide an example use of an enumeration in Code Fragment 4.9, for printing out each element in a vector.

```
public PrintCollection(Vector vec) {
    Enumeration enum = vec.elements();
    while (enum.hasMoreElements()) {
        System.out.println(enum.nextElement());
    }
}
```

Code Fragment 4.9: An example of an enumeration.

Since an enumeration can be defined for any container, we can add to each container ADT a method elements() that returns an enumeration of the elements in the container. Likewise, we can add to other ADTs extra methods that return enumerations of various kinds. These extra methods can therefore provide unified ways of scanning through sets of elements of a container.

We can use many of the data structures presented in this and the previous chapter to implement an enumeration. For example, we can implement an enumeration by inserting all the elements of the collection into a stack. Method hasMoreElements() corresponds to isEmpty, while method nextElement() corresponds to pop. In case there is a given order in which the elements should be returned by the enumeration, we should insert the elements into the stack in reverse order. Alternatively, we can realize an enumeration with a queue, which allows us to insert the elements in order.

An enumeration is a restricted type of iterator that allows only one pass through the elements. More powerful iterators can also be defined, which allow one to move forward and backward over a certain ordering of the elements, and that provide access to the "current" element. An important application of a sequence is to realize such iterators: namely, an iterator can be implemented with a sequence S and a position *cur* that keeps track of the current element.

When it is created, an iterator may or may not be a "snapshot" of its corresponding container at that time. It is therefore generally considered dangerous programming practice to use an iterator while modifying the contents of its container. If insertions, deletions, or replacements are required at a certain "place" in a container, it is safer to use a position object to specify this location, since we do not expect a position object to be able to step through a set of elements of its container (without using methods from the container itself, of course).

4.6   Exercises

Reinforcement

R-4.1 Give a detailed justification of the running times shown in Table 4.2 for the methods of a ranked sequence implemented with an array.

R-4.2 Give an adapter class to support the Stack interface using the methods of the ranked sequence ADT.

R-4.3 Provide the details of the array implementation of a positional sequence. In particular, describe how the index fields of the position objects are updated after an insertion or deletion of an element.

R-4.4 Let MySequence be a sequence of 99 Dalmatian puppies, and let Boiler be a Dalmatian puppy. Give the value returned or the exception thrown by each of the following statements that make calls to methods of MySequence:

1. size()
2. isEmpty()
3. rankOf(first())
4. rankOf(last())
5. rankOf(atRank(0))
6. rankOf(atRank(99))
7. rankOf(atRank(100))
8. rankOf(atRank(size()))
9. rankOf(before(last()))
10. rankOf(after(before(first())))
11. rankOf(insertFirst(Boiler))
12. rankOf(insertBefore(first(), Boiler))
13. remove(first())
14. remove(insertElemAtRank(1, Boiler))

R-4.5 Give pseudo-code describing how to implement all the operations in the general sequence ADT using an array. What is the running time for each of these methods?

R-4.6 Using the Sequence ADT, describe a recursive way for determining if a sequence S of n integer objects contains a given integer k. Your method should not contain any loops. How much space does your method use in addition to the space used for S?

R-4.7 Give a short fragment of Java code describing a new sequence method makeFirst(p) that moves the element of a sequence S at position p to be the first element in S while keeping the relative ordering of the remaining elements in S unchanged. Your method should run in $O(1)$ time if S is implemented with a doubly linked list.

Creativity

C-4.1 Compare the methods of the java.util.Vector class with the methods of the Sequence interface presented in this chapter by answering the following questions:

1. Show with an example why indices in Vector are not equivalent to positions in Sequence.
2. Which methods of Vector and Sequence are completely equivalent?
3. Which methods of Vector do not have an equivalent in Sequence?
4. Which methods of Sequence do not have an equivalent in Vector?
5. Suppose we want to extend Sequence with methods indexOf(e), contains(e), and removeElement(e) (where e is an element) with the same functionality as the methods of Vector. Show how to implement these methods by expressing them in terms of other methods of the Sequence interface.

C-4.2 Consider the following fragment of Java code, where the constructor My-Sequence() creates an empty sequence of integer objects. Recall that "/" denotes integer division (for example, $7/2 = 3$):

```
Sequence seq = new MySequence();
for (int i=0; i<n; i++)
    seq.insertAtRank(i/2)+1,Integer(i));
```

1. Assume that the **for** loop is executed 10 times, that is, n=10, and show the sequence after each iteration of the loop.
2. Draw a schematic illustration of the sequence at the end of the **for** loop, for a generic number n of iterations. (Hint: consider separately the cases of n being even and n being odd.)

C-4.3 Give an adaptation of the sequence ADT to the deque ADT that is different from that given in Section 4.1.1.

C-4.4 You are asked to design an algorithm for reversing a sequence that accesses the sequence only through a restricted set of methods. The algorithm should rearrange the elements of the sequence. Returning a new sequence is not allowed. However, using other sequences for auxiliary storage is allowed.

1. Reverse a sequence using only methods size, first, last, remove, and insertFirst.
2. Reverse a sequence using only methods size, first, remove, and insertFirst.

C-4.5 Describe the structure and pseudo-code for an array-based implementation of the ranked sequence ADT that achieves $O(1)$ time for insertions and removals at rank 0, as well as insertions and removals at the end of the sequence. Your implementation should also provide for a constant time elemAtRank method. (Hint: think about how to extend the circular array implementation of the queue given in Section 3.2.)

C-4.6 In the children's game "hot potato," a group of n children sit in a circle passing an object, called the "potato," around the circle (say in a clockwise direction). The children continue passing the potato until a leader rings a bell, at which point the child holding the potato must leave the game, and the other children close-up the circle. This process is then continued until there is only one child remaining, who is declared the winner. Using the sequence ADT, describe an efficient method for implementing this game. Suppose the leader always rings the bell immediately after the potato has been passed k times. (Determining the last child remaining in this variation of hot potato is known as the ***Josephus problem***.) What is the running time of your method, in terms of n and k, assuming the sequence is implemented with a doubly linked list? What if the sequence is implemented with an array?

C-4.7 Using the Sequence ADT, describe an efficient algorithm for putting a sequence representing a deck of n cards into random order. You may assume the existence of a function, random(), which returns a random number between 0 and $n - 1$, inclusive. Your method should guarantee that every possible ordering of the cards is equally likely. What is the worst-case running time of your method assuming the sequence is implemented with an array? What if the sequence is implemented with a linked list?

C-4.8 Show that only $n - 1$ passes are needed in the execution of bubble-sort on a sequence with n elements.

C-4.9 Using the Enumeration ADT, describe an algorithm for finding the minimum and maximum of a sequence of integer elements using at most $3n/2$ comparisons between elements. (Hint: consider the elements in pairs.)

Projects

P-4.1 Implement the sequence ADT by means of an array used in a circular fashion, so that insertions and deletions at the beginning and end of the sequence run in constant time.

P-4.2 Implement the sequence ADT by means of a singly linked list.

P-4.3 Write a complete adapter class that implements the sequence ADT using a Java Vector.

Chapter Notes

Sequences and iterators are pervasive concepts in the C++ Standard Template Library (STL) [116], and they play fundamental roles in JDSL, the data structures library in Java. The sequence ADT is a generalization and extension of the Java Vector API (for example, see the book by Arnold and Gosling [10]) and the list ADT used by several other data structures and algorithms authors, including Aho, Hopcroft, and Ullman [7], who introduce the "position" abstraction, and Wood [149], who defines a list ADT similar to our positional sequence ADT. Implementations of sequences via arrays and linked lists are discussed in Knuth's seminal book, *Fundamental Algorithms* [89]. Knuth's companion volume, *Sorting and Searching* [90], describes the bubble-sort method and the history of this and other sorting algorithms.

Chapter

5

Trees

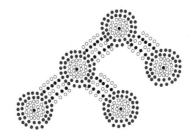

Contents

Productivity experts say that breakthroughs come by thinking "nonlinearly." In this chapter, we discuss the most important nonlinear concept in computer science—*trees*. Tree structures are indeed a breakthrough in data organization, for they allow us to implement a host of algorithms much faster than when using linear data structures, such as sequences. Trees also provide a natural organization for data, and consequently have become ubiquitous structures in file systems, graphical user interfaces, databases, Web sites, and other computer programs.

It is not always clear what productivity experts mean by "nonlinear" thinking, but when we say that trees are "nonlinear," we are referring to an organizational relationship that is richer than the simple "before" and "after" relationships that exist between objects in sequences. The relationships in a tree are *hierarchical*, with some objects being "above" and some "below" others. Actually, the main terminology for tree data structures comes from family trees, with the terms "parent," "child," "ancestor," and "descendent" being the most common words used to describe relationships. We show an example of a family tree in Figure 5.1.

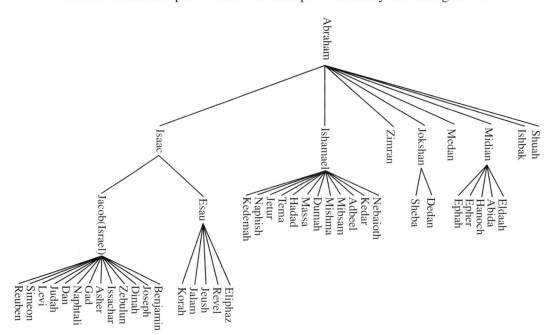

Figure 5.1: A family tree showing some descendents of Abraham, as recorded in Genesis, chapters 25–36.

5.1 The Tree Abstract Data Type

A tree is an abstract data type that stores elements hierarchically. With the exception of the top element, each element in a tree has a **parent** element and zero or more **children** elements. A tree is usually visualized by placing elements inside ovals or rectangles, and by drawing the connections between parents and children with straight lines. (See Figure 5.2.) Computer scientists typically call the top element the **root** of the tree, but it is drawn as the highest element, with the other elements being connected below (just the opposite of a botanical tree).

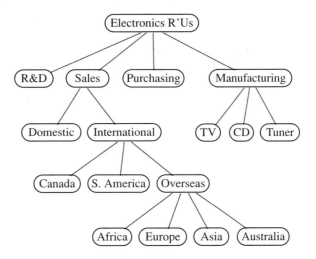

Figure 5.2: A tree with 17 nodes representing the organizational structure of a fictitious corporation. *Electronics R'Us* is stored at the root. The children of the root store *R&D*, *Sales*, *Purchasing*, and *Manufacturing*. The internal nodes store *Sales*, *International*, *Overseas*, *Electronic R'Us*, and *Manufacturing*. The other nodes are external nodes.

5.1.1 Terminology and Basic Properties

A tree T is a set of **nodes** storing elements in a **parent-child** relationship with the following properties:

- T has a distinguished node r, called the **root** of T, that has no parent.
- Each node v of T distinct from r has a **parent** node u.
- For every node v of T, the root r is an **ancestor** of v.

A precise definition of an ancestor can be formulated using recursion. Namely, an ancestor of a node is either the node itself or an ancestor of the parent of the node. Conversely, we say that a node v is a ***descendent*** of a node u if u is an ancestor of v. For example, in Figure 5.2, *Sales* is an ancestor of *Europe*, and *Europe* is a descendent of *Sales*.

Example 5.1: *The inheritance relation between classes in a Java program forms a tree. The class* java.lang.Object *is an ancestor of all other classes.*

If node u is the parent of node v, then we say that v is a ***child*** of u. Two nodes that are children of the same parent are ***siblings***. A node is ***external*** if it has no children, and it is ***internal*** if it has one or more children. External nodes are also known as ***leaves***. The ***subtree*** of T ***rooted*** at a node v is the tree consisting of all the descendents of v in T (including v itself).

Example 5.2: *In most operating system, files are organized hierarchically into nested directories, which are presented to the user in the form of a tree. (See Figure 5.3.) Directories form the internal nodes of the tree, and the files are the external nodes. In the UNIX operating system, the root of the tree is appropriately called the "root directory," and is represented by the symbol "/." It is the ancestor of all directories and files in a UNIX file system.*

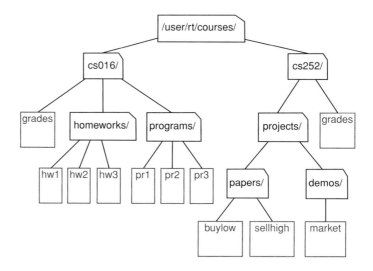

Figure 5.3: Tree representing a portion of a UNIX file system. Note that the subtree rooted at cs016/ contains 10 nodes.

A tree is ***ordered*** if there is a linear ordering defined for the children of each node in such a way that we can identify children of a node as being the first, second, third, and so on. Such an ordering is determined by the use we wish to make for the tree, and it is usually indicated in a drawing of a tree by arranging siblings left-to-right, corresponding to their linear relationship. Ordered trees typically indicate the linear order relationship existing between siblings by listing them in a sequence or enumeration in the correct order.

Example 5.3: *A structured document, such as a book, is hierarchically organized as a tree whose internal nodes are chapters, sections, and subsections, and whose external nodes are paragraphs, tables, figures, the bibliography, and so on. (See Figure 5.4.) The root of the tree corresponds to the book itself. We could in fact consider expanding the tree further to show paragraphs consisting of sentences, sentences consisting of words, and words consisting of characters. In any case, such a tree is an example of an ordered tree, because there is a well-defined ordering among the children of each node.*

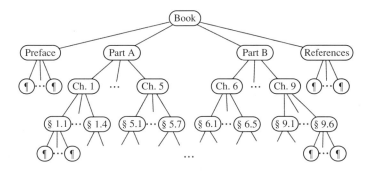

Figure 5.4: A tree associated with a book.

A ***binary tree*** is an ordered tree in which each internal node has either zero or two children. In a binary tree, the first child of an internal node is called the ***left child***, and the second child is called the ***right child***. The subtrees rooted at the left and right child of a node are called the ***left subtree*** and ***right subtree***, respectively. We note that a slightly different definition of a binary tree can be made by allowing for internal nodes to have one child. We will consider such a tree as not being a true "binary" tree, however; we consider it simply as a general tree where each internal node has at most two children.

Binary trees have a number of useful applications. Two are discussed in the examples below.

Caution

Example 5.4: *An important instance of binary trees arises in contexts where we wish to represent a number of different outcomes that can result from answering a collection of yes-or-no questions. Each internal node is associated with a question. Starting at the root, we go to the left or right child of the current node, depending on whether the answer to the question is "Yes" or "No." Such trees are known as* **decision** *trees, because each external node v in such a tree represents a decision of what to do if the questions associated with v's ancestors are answered in a way that leads to v. Figure 5.5 illustrates a binary decision tree that provides a prospective investor with investment recommendations. Each external node contains a recommended investment based on the answers provided.*

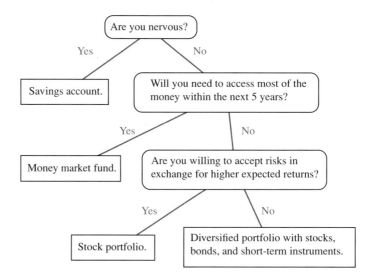

Figure 5.5: A binary decision tree providing investment advice.

Example 5.5: *An arithmetic expression can be represented by a tree whose external nodes are associated with variables or constants, and whose internal nodes are associated with one of the operators $+$, $-$, $\times$, and $/$. (See Figure 5.6.) Each node in such a tree has a value associated with it.*

- *If a node is external, then its value is that of its variable or constant.*
- *If a node is internal, then its value is defined by applying its operation to the values of its children.*

Such an arithmetic expression tree is a binary tree, since each of the operators $+$, $-$, $\times$, and $/$ take exactly two operands. Also, note that the two children of a node associated with the $-$ or $/$ operator must be ordered.

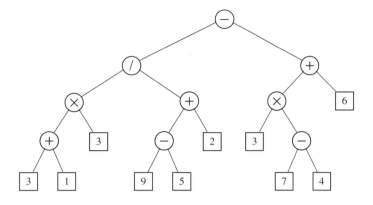

Figure 5.6: A binary tree representing an arithmetic expression. This tree represents the expression $((((3+1) \times 3)/((9-5)+2)) - ((3 \times (7-4))+6))$. The value associated with the internal node labeled "/" is 2.

5.1.2 Tree Methods

The tree ADT stores elements at positions, which, as with positions in a sequence, are defined relative to neighboring positions. The *positions* in a tree are its *nodes*, and neighboring positions satisfy the parent-child relationships that define a valid tree. Therefore we use the terms "position" and "node" interchangeably for trees. As with a sequence position, a position object for a tree supports the methods:

> element(): Return the object at this position.
> *Input:* None; *Output:* Object.

> container(): return a reference to the tree that contains this position.
> *Input:* none; *Output:* Tree.

The real power of node positions in a tree, however, comes from the methods of the tree ADT that return and accept positional objects, such as the following:

> root(): Return the root of T; if T is empty, an error occurs.
> *Input:* None; *Output:* Position.

> parent(v): Return the parent of node v; an error occurs if $v = $ root().
> *Input:* Position; *Output:* Position.

> children(v): Return an enumeration of the children of node v.
> *Input:* Position; *Output:* Enumeration of positions.

If a tree T is ordered, then the enumeration children(v) provides access to the children of v in order. If v is an external node, then children(v) is an empty enumeration.

In addition to the above fundamental query methods, we also include the following query methods:

isInternal(v): Test whether position v is internal.
        Input: Position; ***Output:*** Boolean.

isExternal(v): Test whether position v is external.
        Input: Position; ***Output:*** Boolean.

isRoot(v): Test whether position v is the root.
        Input: Position; ***Output:*** Boolean.

These methods make programming with trees easier and more readable, since we can use them in the conditionals of if-statements and while-loops, rather than using a nonintuitive conditional or trying to catch an error condition. For instance, isInternal(v) and isExternal(v) can be performed by checking whether the enumeration returned by method children(v) has elements or not.

There are also a number of methods a tree should probably support that are not necessarily related to its tree structure. Such methods for a tree T include the following:

size(): Return the number of nodes in T.
        Input: None; ***Output:*** Integer.

isEmpty(): Test whether T has any nodes or not.
        Input: None; ***Output:*** Boolean.

elements(): Return an enumeration of all the elements stored at nodes of T.
        Input: None; ***Output:*** Enumeration of objects.

positions(): Return an enumeration of all the positions (nodes) of T.
        Input: None; ***Output:*** Enumeration of positions.

swap(v, w): Swap the elements stored at the nodes v and w in T.
        Input: Two positions; ***Output:*** None.

replace(v, e): Replace the elements stored at the node v with e, returning the element previously stored at v.
        Input: A position and an object; ***Output:*** Object.

We do not define any specialized update methods for a tree here. Instead, we prefer to describe different tree update methods in conjunction with specific applications of trees in subsequent chapters. In fact, we can imagine several kinds of tree update operations beyond those given in this book. Even though we are not including any update operations here, we nevertheless consider in the next section how we might organize this set of tree ADT methods into a set of Java interfaces.

5.1.3 A Tree Interface in Java

The tree ADT methods given above can be used to define a simple Java interface SimpleTree, which defines the methods every tree should implement. Rather than include all of the above tree methods directly in the SimpleTree interface, however, we divide the tree-specific methods from the generic methods. The generic methods of the tree ADT are also shared by the Sequence ADT, for example. Therefore, let us put the generic methods in a separate PositionalContainer interface, which SimpleTree extends. We show the PositionalContainer interface in Code Fragment 5.1, and we show the SimpleTree interface in Code Fragment 5.2. Thus, a SimpleTree stores elements that are arbitrary Java objects, and supports the position abstraction.

```java
public interface PositionalContainer {
    // query methods
    public int size(); // return the size of the container
    public boolean isEmpty(); // return whether the container is empty or not
    public Enumeration elements(); // return the elements in the container
    public Enumeration positions(); // return the positions in the container
    // update methods
    public void swap(Position v, Position w); // swap elements at v and w
    public Object replace(Position v, Object e);
    // replace with e and return the element at v
}
```

Code Fragment 5.1: Interface PositionalContainer.

```java
public interface SimpleTree extends PositionalContainer {
    // accessor methods
    public Position root(); // return the root of the tree
    public Position parent(Position v); // return the parent of v
    public Enumeration children(Position v); // return the children of v
    // query methods
    public boolean isInternal(Position v); // test whether v is internal
    public boolean isExternal(Position v); // test whether v is external
    public boolean isRoot(Position v); // test whether v is the root of the tree
}
```

Code Fragment 5.2: Interface SimpleTree.

5.2   Basic Algorithms on Trees

In this section, we present algorithms that perform computations on a tree by accessing it through the SimpleTree interface. The algorithms will be expressed in Java and/or pseudo-code.

We make the following assumptions on the running time of the methods of any class that implements the SimpleTree interface.

- The generic methods size(), isEmpty(), swap(v, w), and replace(v, e) run in $O(1)$ time.
- The reference methods root() and parent(v) take $O(1)$ time.
- The Boolean methods isInternal(v), isExternal(v), and isRoot(v) take $O(1)$ time, as well.
- The enumeration methods elements() and positions() take $O(n)$ time, where n is the number of nodes in the tree.
- The enumeration method children(v) takes $O(c_v)$ time, where c_v is the number of children of v.
- For the enumerations returned by the methods elements() and children(v), the methods hasMoreElements() and nextElement() take $O(1)$ time each. (We do not make this assumption for the positions() enumeration, however.)

In Section 5.4, we will present data structures for trees that satisfy the above assumptions. Before we describe how to implement the tree ADT using a concrete data structure, however, let us describe how we can use the methods of the tree ADT to answer some interesting problems for trees.

5.2.1   Depth and Height

Let v be a node of a tree T. The ***depth*** of v is the number of ancestors of v, excluding v itself. For example, in the tree of Figure 5.2, the node storing *International* has depth 2. Note that this definition implies that the depth of the root of T is 0. The depth of a node v can also be recursively defined as follows:

- If v is the root, then the depth of v is 0.
- Otherwise, the depth of v is one plus the depth of the parent of v.

Based on the above definition, the recursive algorithm depth, shown in Code Fragment 5.3, computes the depth of a node v of T by invoking itself recursively on the parent of v, and adding 1 to the value returned. Thus, each ancestor of v is visited by a recursive call, and contributes a value of 1 to the depth, as it should. The running time of the algorithm depth(v) (Code Fragment 5.3) is $O(d_v)$, where d_v denotes the depth of a node v of tree T, because the algorithm performs a constant-time recursive step for each ancestor of v.

```
public int depth (SimpleTree T, position v) {
// recursive computation of the depth of node v
  if (T.isRoot(v))
    return(0);
  else
    return(1+depth(T.parent(v)));
}
```

Code Fragment 5.3: Method depth.

The *height* of a node v in a tree T is also defined recursively:

- If v is an external node, then the height of v is 0.
- Otherwise, the height of v is one plus the maximum height of a child of v.

The *height* of an entire tree T is defined to be the height of the root of T. For example, the tree of Figure 5.2 has height 4. Another way to view the height of a tree T is as the maximum depth of a node of T, which is achieved at one or more external nodes.

```
public int height1 (SimpleTree T) {
  // computation of the height of a tree by taking the maximum of the
  // depths of its external nodes
    int h = 0;
    Enumeration nodes_of_T = T.positions();
    while (nodes_of_T.hasMoreElements()) {
      Position v = (Position) nodes_of_T.nextElement();
      if (T.isExternal(v))
          h = Math.max(h,depth(T,v));
    }
    return h;
}
```

Code Fragment 5.4: Method height1. Note the casting from a generic Object returned by hasMoreElements() into a Position object and the use of the max method of class java.lang.Math.

We present two algorithms for computing the height of a tree T. Algorithm height1, shown in Code Fragment 5.4, is very simple. It is based on the fact that the height of T is equal to the maximum depth of a node of T. Algorithm height1 uses an enumeration of all the nodes in the tree and computes the depth of each external node by using algorithm depth (Code Fragment 5.3) as a subroutine, keeping track of the maximum depth seen so far. When it terminates, it will have computed the depth of a maximum-depth node in T, which is equal to the height of T. Thus, this algorithm correctly computes the height of T.

Unfortunately, the height1 algorithm is not very efficient. Let d_v again denote the depth of a node v. Since $d_v \leq h + 1 \leq n$, where h is the height of T and n is the number of nodes of T, we can also say that algorithm depth(v) has worst-case running time $O(h)$, which is $O(n)$. As a consequence, algorithm height1 (Code Fragment 5.4) runs in time $O(\sum_{v \in T} d_v)$, which is $O(nh)$, that is, it is $O(n^2)$ in the worst case.

Algorithm height2, shown in Code Fragment 5.5, computes the height of tree T in a more efficient manner by using the recursive definition of height. The algorithm is expressed by a recursive method height2(T,v) that computes the height of the subtree of T rooted at a node v. If the node v is external, then the algorithm returns the height of the subtree rooted at v as 0. Otherwise, it gets an enumeration of the children of v, recursively computes the height of each child, and returns 1 plus the maximum height returned from a recursive call. The height of T is obtained by calling height2(T,T.root()).

```
public int height2 (SimpleTree T; Position v) {
  // recursive computation of the height of the subtree rooted at node v
  if (T.isExternal(v))
    return(0);
  else {
    int h = 0;
    Enumeration children_of_v = T.children(v);
    while (children_of_v.hasMoreElements()) {
      Position w = (Position) children_of_v.nextElement();
      h = Math.max(h,T.height(w));
    }
    return 1 + h;
  }
}
```

Code Fragment 5.5: Method height2.

Algorithm height2 (from Code Fragment 5.5) is much more efficient than Algorithm height1 (from Code Fragment 5.4). The algorithm is recursive, and if it is initially called on the root of T, it will eventually be called on each node of T. Thus, we can determine the running time of this method by first determining the amount of time spent at each node (on the nonrecursive part), and then summing this time bound over all the nodes. The computation of the enumeration children_of_v takes $O(c_v)$ time, where c_v denotes the number of children of node v. Also, the **while** loop has c_v iterations, and each iteration takes time $O(1)$ time plus the time for the recursive call on a child of v. Thus, algorithm height2 spends $O(c_v)$ time at each node v, and its running time is

$$O\left(\sum_{v \in T} c_v\right).$$

In order to complete the analysis, we make use of the following property.

Proposition 5.6: *Let T be a tree with n nodes, and let c_v denote the number of children of a node v of T. Then*

$$\sum_{v \in T} c_v = n - 1.$$

Justification: Each node of T, with the exception of the root, is a child of another node, and thus contributes one unit to the above sum. ∎

By Proposition 5.6, the running time of algorithm height2, when called on the root of T, is $O(n)$, where n is the number of nodes of T.

5.2.2 Preorder Traversal

A *traversal* of a tree T is a systematic way of accessing, or "visiting," all the nodes of T. In this section, we present a basic traversal scheme for trees, called preorder traversal. In the next section, we will study another basic traversal scheme, called postorder traversal.

In a *preorder* traversal of a tree T, the root of T is visited first and then the subtrees rooted at its children are traversed recursively. If the tree is ordered, then the subtrees are traversed according to the order of the children. The specific action associated with the "visit" of a node v depends on the application of this traversal, and could involve anything from incrementing a counter to performing some complex computation for v. The pseudo-code for the preorder traversal of the subtree rooted at a node v is shown in Code Fragment 5.6. We initially call this routine as preorder$(T, T.\text{root}())$.

Algorithm preorder(T, v):
    perform the "visit" action for node v
    for each child w of v **do**
        recursively traverse the subtree rooted at w by calling preorder(T, w)

Code Fragment 5.6: Algorithm preorder.

The preorder traversal algorithm is useful for producing a linear ordering of the nodes of a tree where parents must always come before their children in the ordering. Such orderings have several different applications; we explore a simple instance of such an application in the next example. (See Figure 5.7.)

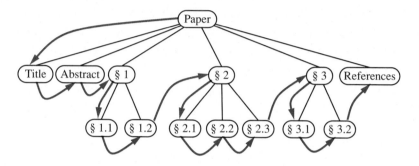

Figure 5.7: Preorder traversal of an ordered tree, where the children of each node are ordered from left to right.

Example 5.7: *The preorder traversal of the tree associated with a document, as in Example 5.3, examines an entire document sequentially, from beginning to end. If the external nodes are removed before the traversal, then the traversal examines the table of contents of the document. (See Figure 5.7.)*

The preorder traversal is also an efficient way to visit the nodes of a tree. To justify this, let us consider the running time of the preorder traversal of a tree T with n nodes under the assumption that visiting a node takes $O(1)$ time. The analysis of the preorder traversal algorithm is actually similar to that of algorithm height2 (Code Fragment 5.5), given in Section 5.2.1. At each node v, the nonrecursive part of the preorder traversal algorithm requires time $O(c_v)$, where c_v is the number of children of v. Thus, by Proposition 5.6, the overall running time of the preorder traversal of T is $O(n)$.

Algorithm preorderPrint, shown in Code Fragment 5.7, performs the preorder traversal of the subtree rooted at node v, and prints the element stored at a node when the node is visited. The algorithm is recursive and calls the standard Java method toString to return a string associated with an element, that is, its "name" or "label" (method toString has a default implementation in java.lang.Object and is typically overridden by subclasses to print some useful information about the object). The algorithm also assumes that for an ordered tree T, method T.children(v) correctly returns an enumeration that accesses the children of v in order. Given these assumptions, method preorderPrint will perform a preorder printing of the elements stored at the nodes of a tree.

```
public void preorderPrint (SimpleTree T, Position v) {
    // Preorder traversal of the subtree rooted at node v that prints to
    // the standard output the elements stored at the nodes in the order
    // they are visited.  It assumes that the elements support toString()
    System.out.println(T.element(v));
    Enumeration children_of_v = T.children(v);
    while (children_of_v.hasMoreElements()) {
        Position w = (Position) children_of_v.nextElement();
        preorderPrint(T, w); // recursive call
    }
}
```

Code Fragment 5.7: Algorithm preorderPrint.

There is an interesting application of a variation of the preorderPrint method that uses the preorder traversal to produce a string representation of an entire tree. Let us assume again that for each element e stored in tree T, calling e.toString() returns a string associated with e. The **parenthetic string representation** $P(T)$ of tree T is recursively defined as follows. If T consists of a single node v, then

$$P(T) = v.\text{element}().\text{toString}().$$

Otherwise,

$$P(T) = v.\text{element}().\text{toString}() + "(" + P(T_1) + P(T_2) + \cdots + P(T_k) + ")",$$

where v is the root of T and $T_1, T_2, \ldots, T_k$ are the subtrees rooted at the children of v, which are given in order if T is an ordered tree. Since the parenthetic representation of T is defined in terms of parenthetic representations of some of T's subtrees, this is a recursive definition. Also, we are using "+" here to denote string concatenation. (See Chapter 11 for details.) The parenthetic representation of the tree of Figure 5.2 is shown in Figure 5.8.

Electronics R'Us (R&D
Sales (Domestic
International (Canada S._America
Overseas (Africa Europe Asia Australia)))
Purchasing
Manufacturing (TV CD Tuner))

Figure 5.8: Parenthetic representation of the tree of Figure 5.2. Line breaks and spaces have been added for clarity.

The Java method parentheticRepresentation shown in Code Fragment 5.8 is a variation of algorithm preorderPrint (Code Fragment 5.7). It implements the definition given above to output a parenthetic string representation of a tree T.

```java
public void parentheticRepresentation (SimpleTree T, Position v) {
    // Print the parenthetic representation of the subtree rooted at v using
    // a preorder traversal, which assumes that elements implement toString().
    if (T.isExternal(v))
        System.out.print(v.element().toString());
    else {
        System.out.print(v.element() + "( ");  // implicitly calls toString()
        Enumeration children_of_v = T.children(v);
        while (children_of_v.hasMoreElements()) {
            Position w = (Position) children_of_v.nextElement();
            System.out.print(" ");  // prints a space before processing the subtree
            parentheticRepresentation(T, w); // recursive call
        }
        System.out.print(" )");
    }
}
```

Code Fragment 5.8: Algorithm parentheticRepresentation. Note the use of the $+$ operator to concatenate two strings.

Preorder traversal is useful for solving a tree problem where we must perform a computation for each node before performing any computations for its descendents.

5.2.3   Postorder Traversal

Another important tree traversal algorithm is the ***postorder*** traversal. This algorithm can be viewed as the opposite of the preorder traversal, because it recursively traverses the subtrees rooted at the children of the root first, and then visits the root. Still, as with the preorder traversal, if the tree is ordered, we make recursive calls for the children of a node v according to their specified order. Pseudo-code for the postorder traversal is given in Code Fragment 5.9.

Algorithm postorder(T, v):
    for each child w of v **do**
        recursively traverse the subtree rooted at w by calling postorder(T, w)
    perform the "visit" action for node v

Code Fragment 5.9: Algorithm postorder.

The name of the postorder traversal comes from the fact that this traversal method will visit a node *v* after it has visited all the other nodes in the subtree rooted at *v*. (See Figure 5.9.) The analysis of the running time of a postorder traversal is analogous to that of a preorder traversal. (See Section 5.2.2.) The total time spent in the nonrecursive portions of the algorithm is proportional to the time spent visiting the children of each node in the tree. Thus, a postorder traversal of a tree *T* with *n* nodes takes $O(n)$ time, assuming that visiting each node takes $O(1)$ time.

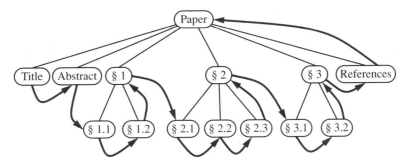

Figure 5.9: Postorder traversal of the ordered tree of Figure 5.7.

As an example instance of a postorder traversal, the Java method postorder-Print, shown in Code Fragment 5.10, performs a postorder traversal of a tree *T*, and prints the element stored at a node when it is visited. The algorithm is recursive and calls method toString to get the string associated with an element. Recall that for an ordered tree *T*, method *T*.children(*v*) returns an enumeration that accesses the children of *v* in order.

```
public void postorderPrint (SimpleTree T, Position v) {
    // Postorder traversal of the subtree rooted at node v that prints to
    // the standard output the elements stored at the nodes in the order
    // they are visited.
    Enumeration children_of_v = T.children(v);
    while (children_of_v.hasMoreElements()) {
        Position w = (Position) children_of_v.nextElement();
        postorderPrint(T, w); // recursive call
    }
    System.out.println(v.element());        // Assumes elements implement toString()
}
```

Code Fragment 5.10: Algorithm postorderPrint.

The postorder traversal method is useful for solving problems where we wish to compute some property for each node v in a tree, but computing that property for v requires that we have already computed that same property for v's children. Such an application is illustrated in the following example.

Example 5.8: *Consider a UNIX file system tree (see Example 5.2) whose external nodes represent files, and whose internal nodes represent directories. The UNIX command* du *("disk usage") computes the amount of disk space allocated to a directory, which is the sum of the sizes of the files in the subtree rooted at the directory plus the size of the directory itself. (See Figure 5.10.) Command* du *performs a postorder traversal of the tree associated with the file system. After the subtrees of a node v have been traversed, it computes the disk space allocated to v by summing the size of v to the disk space allocated to each child of v, which was computed by the recursive postorder traversals of the children of v.*

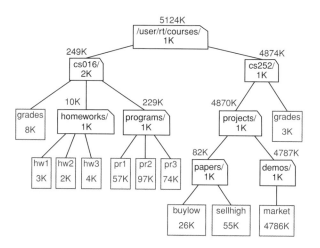

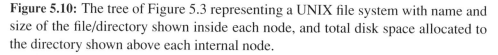

Figure 5.10: The tree of Figure 5.3 representing a UNIX file system with name and size of the file/directory shown inside each node, and total disk space allocated to the directory shown above each internal node.

Motivated by the above example, algorithm totalSize, shown in Code Fragment 5.11, performs a postorder traversal of a tree T and prints for each internal node v of T the name of v and the sum of the sizes of all the nodes in the subtree rooted at v (including v itself). The totalSize algorithm assumes that T stores objects of class Descriptor that support methods size() (which returns an integer) and name() (which returns a string). Since these methods spend a constant amount of time per node visit, the total time for performing the traversal is $O(n)$, where n is the number of nodes of the tree.

```
public int totalSize (SimpleTree T, Position v) {
    // Compute and return the total size of node v, defined as the sum
    // of the sizes of the nodes in the subtree rooted at v .  The computation
    // is based on a postorder traversal.  The elements stored at the nodes are
    // assumed to be Descriptor objects that support methods name() and size().
    int v_total_size = ((Descriptor) v.element()).size(); // start with node size
    Enumeration children_of_v = T.children(v);
    while (children_of_v.hasMoreElements()) {
        Position w = (Position) children_of_v.nextElement();
        // add recursively computed total size of the subtree rooted at w
        v_total_size += totalSize(T, w);
    }
    if (T.isInternal(v))  // print name and total size
        System.out.println(((Descriptor) v.element()).name() + ": " + v_total_size);
    return v_total_size;
}
```

Code Fragment 5.11: Method totalSize. Note the casting of a generic object returned by T.element(v) into an object of class Descriptor and the use of the $+=$ operator.

The preorder and postorder traversals are the two most common ways of visiting the nodes of a general tree. We can also imagine other generic traversal methods, however. For example, we could imagine visiting the nodes in a tree so that we visit all nodes at depth d before we visit any on depth $d+1$. Such a traversal could be implemented, for example, using a queue, whereas the preorder and postorder traversals use a stack. This stack is implicit in our use of recursion to describe these methods, although the use of a stack can be made explicit to avoid recursion. In addition, binary trees, which we discuss next, naturally support an additional traversal method, known as the inorder traversal.

5.3 Binary Trees

One kind of tree that is of particular interest to computer scientists is the binary tree. A **binary tree** is an ordered tree in which each internal node has two children. As we mention above, in Section 5.1.1, we consider a tree where internal nodes have only one child to not be a proper binary tree, even if each internal node has at most two children. Thus, we take the convention that internal nodes in a binary tree must each have exactly two children. This convention is made without any loss of generality, however, for we can easily convert any "improper" binary tree into a proper one, as we explore in a simple exercise.

Binary trees arise naturally in many different applications. For example, the expression tree of Example 5.5 is a binary tree, since each of the operators used to define this tree are binary operators. Also, a decision tree is a binary tree, since the outcome of a decision is always "yes" or "no." Thus, computer scientists have developed specialized terminology, data structures, and algorithms for binary trees. We discuss some of the specialized topics for binary trees below.

5.3.1   Properties of Binary Trees

Binary trees have several interesting properties, including the following:

Proposition 5.9: *In a binary tree T, the number of external nodes is 1 more than the number of internal nodes.*

Justification: We justify this proposition by dividing up the nodes of a binary tree into two "piles:" an internal-node pile and an external-node pile, as if we were dividing pieces of candy between two pre-schoolers. If T itself has only one node v, then v is external, and the proposition clearly holds. Otherwise, we remove from T an (arbitrary) external node w and its parent v, which is an internal node. We imagine placing w on the external-node pile and v on the internal-node pile. If v has a parent u, then we reconnect u with the former sibling z of w, as shown in Figure 5.11. This operation, which we call removeAboveExternal(w), removes one internal node and one external node, and it leaves the tree being a proper binary tree. Repeating this operation, we eventually are left with a single external node. Since the same number of external and internal nodes are removed and placed on their respective piles by the sequence of operations leading to this final tree, the number of external nodes of T is 1 more than the number of internal nodes.   ■

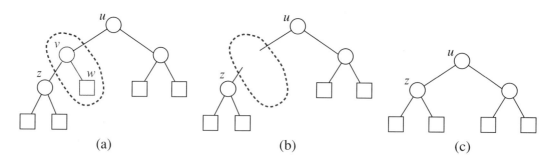

(a)   (b)   (c)

Figure 5.11: The operation removeAboveExternal(w), that removes an external node and an internal node in the justification of Proposition 5.9.

We denote the set of all nodes of a tree T at the same depth d as the *level d* of T. In a binary tree, level 0 has one node (the root), level 1 has at most two nodes (the children of the root), level 2 has at most four nodes, and so on. (See Figure 5.12.) In general, level d has at most 2^d nodes.

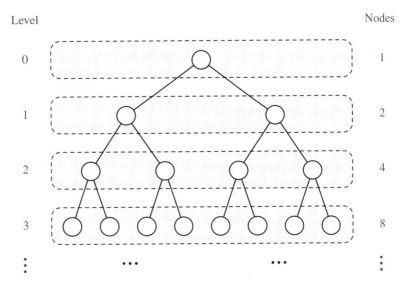

Figure 5.12: Maximum number of nodes in the levels of a binary tree.

From the observation above, the following properties relating the height of T with the number of nodes can be derived. A detailed justification of these properties is left as an exercise.

Proposition 5.10: *Let T be a binary tree with n nodes, and let h denote the height of T. Then T has the following properties:*

1. *The number of external nodes in T is at least $h + 1$ and at most 2^h.*
2. *The number of internal nodes in T is at least h and at most $2^h - 1$.*
3. *The total number of nodes in T is at least $2h + 1$ and at most $2^{h+1} - 1$.*
4. *The height of T is at least $\log(n + 1) - 1$ and at most $(n - 1)/2$, that is,* $\log(n + 1) - 1 \leq h \leq (n - 1)/2$.

An important consequence of Proposition 5.10 is that the minimum height for a binary tree with n nodes is $\Theta(\log n)$. In Section 6.3, we will see an important application of binary trees with minimum height. Before we discuss this application, however, let us discuss more about how binary trees are represented and traversed.

5.3.2 A Binary Tree Interface in Java

As an abstract data type, a binary tree is a specialization of a tree that supports two additional accessor methods:

leftChild(v): Return the left child of v; an error condition occurs if v is an external node.
Input: Position; *Output:* Position.

rightChild(v): Return the right child of v; an error condition occurs if v is an external node.
Input: Position; *Output:* Position.

We also include the following insertion update method:

expandExternal(v): Transforms v from an external node into an internal node by creating two new external nodes and making them the left and right children of v, respectively; an error condition occurs if v is an internal node.
Input: Position; *Output:* None.

Likewise, we include the following removal update method:

removeAboveExternal(v): Remove the external node v together with its parent u, replacing u with the sibling of v (see Figure 5.11); this operation returns the element previously stored at u, and it generates an error condition if v is an internal node.
Input: Position; *Output:* Object.

We assume that there is a binary tree constructor that returns a binary tree consisting of a single external node that stores no element. From this single node, we can construct any binary tree using the expandExternal method. Likewise, we can dismantle any binary tree T using the removeAboveExternal operation, ultimately reducing such a tree T to a single external node. There are other types of binary tree update methods that are useful for restructuring binary search trees, but let us defer the discussion of these methods until Chapter 7.

We model a binary tree as an abstract data type with the Java interface BinaryTree, shown in Code Fragment 5.12, which extends the SimpleTree interface, shown previously in Code Fragment 5.2. Since the BinaryTree interface extends the SimpleTree interface, it inherits all the methods from this superclass. Moreover, since binary trees are ordered trees, the enumeration returned by method children(v) and inherited from interface SimpleTree accesses the left child of v before the right child of v.

```
public interface BinaryTree extends SimpleTree {
    // Simplified interface for a binary tree whose nodes (positions)
    // store arbitrary elements.
    // Accessor methods:
    public Position leftChild(Position v);
    public Position rightChild(Position v);
    // Update methods:
    public void expandExternal(Position v);
    public void removeAboveExternal(Position v);
}
```

Code Fragment 5.12: Interface BinaryTree, which extends interface SimpleTree (from Code Fragment 5.2).

We make the following assumptions on the running time of the methods of any class that implements the BinaryTree interface.

- All the assumptions on the running time of the methods of the SimpleTree interface made in Section 5.2 hold. For a binary tree, method children(v) takes $O(1)$ time, because each node has either zero or two children.
- Methods leftChild(v) and rightChild(v) each take $O(1)$ time.
- Methods expandExternal(v) and removeAboveExternal(v) each take $O(1)$ time.

We next explore traversals for binary trees.

5.3.3 Traversals of a Binary Tree

As with general trees, computations performed on binary trees often involve tree traversals. In this section, we present algorithms that perform traversal computations on binary trees. The algorithms will be expressed in Java and/or pseudo-code, and will use the BinaryTree interface.

Preorder Traversal of a Binary Tree

Since any binary tree can also be viewed as a general tree, the preorder traversal for general trees can be applied to any binary tree. We can simplify the algorithm in the case of a binary tree traversal, however, as we show in Code Fragment 5.13. As is the case for general trees, there are many applications of the preorder traversal for binary trees. For example, we can use a preorder traversal to "clone" a binary tree T, to construct an exact copy T' of T. We do this recursively, starting with T' being a single external node v'. We call the recursive algorithm shown in Code Fragment 5.14 on the root v of T, which clones T using a preorder traversal.

Algorithm binaryPreorder(T, v):

   perform the "visit" action for node v

   if v is an internal node **then**

     binaryPreorder$(T, T.\text{leftChild}(v))$ {recursively traverse left subtree}

     binaryPreorder$(T, T.\text{rightChild}(v))$ {recursively traverse right subtree}

Code Fragment 5.13: Algorithm binaryPreorder.

In Java, every object implementing an important Clonable interface must be able to duplicate itself using the clone() method. The default implementation of clone() is simply to copy the instance variables for an object. Thus, an implementation of an algorithm like that given in Code Fragment 5.14 should be used for cloning a binary tree. Such an implementation would be quite efficient, for it spends $O(1)$ time per node visited; hence, it runs in $O(n)$ time to clone a binary tree with n nodes.

Algorithm clone(T, T', v, v'):

   Input: A binary tree T containing a node v and a binary tree T' containing an external node v'

   Output: An augmentation of T' so that the subtree rooted at v' is an exact copy of the subtree of T rooted at v

  if v is an internal node **then**

   expandExternal(v')

   $v'.\text{element} \leftarrow v.\text{element}()$

   clone$(T, T', T.\text{leftChild}(v), T'.\text{leftChild}(v'))$

   clone$(T, T', T.\text{rightChild}(v), T'.\text{rightChild}(v'))$

Code Fragment 5.14: Algorithm clone.

Postorder Traversal of a Binary Tree

Analogously, the postorder traversal for general trees can be specialized for binary trees. We give the pseudo-code for this specialized postorder traversal of the subtree rooted at a node v in a binary tree T in Code Fragment 5.15.

The postorder traversal of a binary tree can be used to solve the expression evaluation problem. In this problem, we are given a binary tree T that represents an arithmetic expression. Each external node of T has an arithmetic value associated with it and each internal node of T has an arithmetic operation associated with it. The problem arises when we must compute the value represented by the root of T.

Algorithm binaryPostorder(T, v):

    if v is an internal node **then**
        binaryPostorder(T, T.leftChild(v))   {recursively traverse left subtree}
        binaryPostorder(T, T.rightChild(v))   {recursively traverse right subtree}
    perform the "visit" action for the node v

Code Fragment 5.15: Algorithm binaryPostorder.

The algorithm evaluateExpression, expressed in Code Fragment 5.16, evaluates the arithmetic expression stored in the subtree rooted at a node v in a binary tree T (see Example 5.5) by performing a postorder traversal of T starting at v.

Algorithm evaluateExpression(T, v):

    if v is an internal node storing operator $\circ$ **then**
        $x \leftarrow$ evaluateExpression(T, T.leftChild(v))
        $y \leftarrow$ evaluateExpression(T, T.rightChild(v))
        return $x \circ y$
    else
        return the value of the variable stored at v

Code Fragment 5.16: Algorithm evaluateExpression.

The expression-tree evaluation application of the postorder traversal provides an $O(n)$ time algorithm for evaluating an arithmetic expression represented by a binary tree with n nodes. Indeed, like the general postorder traversal, the postorder traversal for binary trees can be applied to other "bottom-up" evaluation problems (such as the size computation given in Example 5.8) as well. The specialization of the postorder traversal for binary trees simplifies that for general trees, however, because we use the leftChild and rightChild methods to avoid a **for** loop that iterates through an enumeration of the children of an internal node.

Interestingly, this specialization of the general preorder and postorder traversal methods to binary trees suggests a third traversal in a binary tree that is different from both the preorder and postorder traversals.

Inorder Traversal of a Binary Tree

An additional traversal method for a binary tree is the ***inorder*** traversal. In this traversal, we visit a node between the recursive traversals of its left and right subtrees. Pseudo-code for the inorder traversal of the subtree rooted at a node v in a binary tree T is given in Code Fragment 5.17.

Algorithm inorder(T, v):

    if v is an internal node **then**

        inorder(T, T.leftChild(v))   {recursively traverse left subtree}

    perform the "visit" action for node v

    if v is an internal node **then**

        inorder(T, T.rightChild(v))   {recursively traverse right subtree}

Code Fragment 5.17: Algorithm inorder.

The inorder traversal of a binary tree T can be informally viewed as visiting the nodes of T "from left to right". Indeed, for every node v, the inorder traversal visits v after all the nodes in the left subtree of v and before all the nodes in the right subtree of v. (See Figure 5.13.)

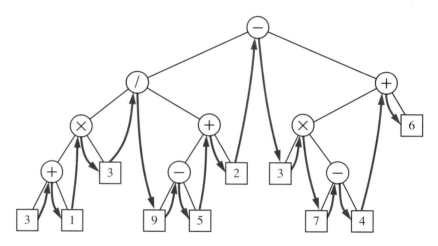

Figure 5.13: Inorder traversal of a binary tree.

The inorder traversal algorithm also has several applications. One of the most important applies when we store an ordered sequence of elements in a binary tree, defining a structure we call a ***binary search tree***. (See Figure 5.14.) In a binary search tree, each internal node v stores an element e such that the elements stored in the left subtree of v are less than or equal to e, and the elements stored in the right subtree of v are greater than or equal to e. An inorder traversal of a binary search tree visits the elements in such a tree in nondecreasing order. A binary search tree can be viewed as a binary decision tree (recall Figure 5.5) that supports searching, where the question asked at each internal node is whether the element at that node is less than, equal to, or larger than the element being searched for.

We can use a binary search tree T to locate an element with a certain value by traversing down the tree T. At each internal node we compare the value of the current node to our search element. If the answer to the question is "smaller," then the search continues in the left subtree. If the answer is "equal," then the search terminates successfully. If the answer is "greater," then the search continues in the right subtree. Finally, if we reach an external node, then the search terminates unsuccessfully. Note that the running time of searching in a binary search tree T is proportional to the height of T. We illustrate an example search operation in a binary search tree in Figure 5.14, and we study binary search trees in more detail in Section 7.3.

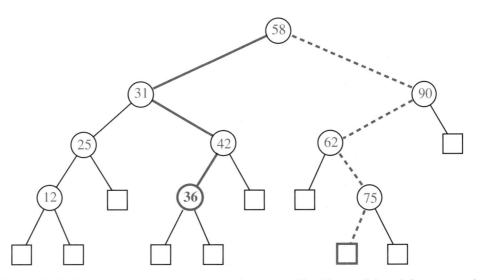

Figure 5.14: A binary search tree storing integers. The blue solid path is traversed when searching (successfully) for 36. The blue dashed path is traversed when searching (unsuccessfully) for 70.

Part of the way traversal algorithms achieve their efficiency (and their simplicity) is by using recursion. This use of recursion is not strictly necessary, however, as we can alternately use an explicit stack (as opposed to the implicit stack used to implement recursion) to keep track of the ancestor nodes we have yet to finish visiting in a tree traversal. Using an explicit stack in this way will still result in linear-time algorithms, but it can possibly save some space over recursive implementations of the three traversal algorithms (depending on the implementations). We leave the details of this conversion as an exercise.

The Euler Tour Traversal of a Binary Tree

Viewed in an object-oriented framework, the tree-traversal algorithms we have discussed so far are all forms of iterators (or enumerations in Java). Each traversal visits the nodes of a tree in a certain order, and is guaranteed to visit each node exactly once. We can unify the tree-traversal algorithms given above into a single framework, however, by relaxing the requirement that each node be visited exactly once. The resulting traversal method is called the *Euler tour traversal*. The advantage of the Euler tour traversal is that it allows for more general kinds of tree traversals to be expressed easily.

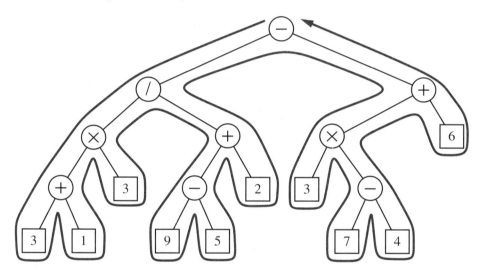

Figure 5.15: Euler tour of a binary tree.

Intuitively, the Euler tour traversal of a binary tree T can be informally defined as a walk around T, where we start by going from the root towards its left child, viewing the edges of T as being "walls" that we always keep to our left. (See Figure 5.15.) Each node v of T is encountered three times by the Euler tour:

- "On the left" (before the Euler tour of v's left subtree)
- "From below" (between the Euler tours of v's two subtrees)
- "On the right" (after the Euler tour of v's right subtree).

If v is external, then these three "visits" actually all happen at the same time. We give pseudo-code for the Euler tour of the subtree rooted at a node v in Code Fragment 5.18.

Algorithm eulerTour(T, v):

    perform the action for visiting node v on the left

    if v is an internal node **then**

        recursively tour the left subtree of v by calling eulerTour(T, T.leftChild(v))

    perform the action for visiting node v from below

    if v is an internal node **then**

        recursively tour the right subtree of v by calling eulerTour(T, T.leftChild(v))

    perform the action for visiting node v on the right

Code Fragment 5.18: Algorithm eulerTour.

The preorder traversal of a binary tree T is equivalent to an Euler tour, such that each node has an associated "visit" action occur only when it is encountered on the left. Likewise, the inorder and postorder traversals of a binary tree T are equivalent to an Euler tour, such that each node has an associated "visit" action occur only when it is encountered on from below or on the right, respectively.

The running times of the preorder, postorder, inorder, and Euler tour traversals of a binary tree with n nodes are easy to analyze. Suppose that visiting a node takes $O(1)$ time, which was the case for all the applications of binary tree traversals we presented above. In each traversal, we spend a constant amount of time at each node of the tree during the traversal, so the overall running time for each is $O(n)$.

The Euler tour traversal extends the preorder, inorder, and postorder traversals, because it can easily be used to implement those traversals, but it can also be used for other kinds of traversals. For example, in a binary tree T, we can use this traversal to compute the number of descendents belonging to each node v in T. Specifically, we can initialize a counter variable count to 0, and then increment this variable each time we visit a node on the left. To determine the number of descendents of a node v, we compute the difference between the value of the count variable when v is visited on the left and when it is visited on the right. This simple rule gives us the number of descendents of v, because each node in the subtree rooted at v is counted in a visit on the left, between v's visit on the left and v's visit on the right. Therefore, we have another $O(n)$ time method for computing the number of descendents for each node in a binary tree.

Another application of the Euler tour traversal is to convert a binary tree representing an arithmetic expression into its equivalent fully parenthesized expression. Algorithm printExpression, shown in Code Fragment 5.19, prints the arithmetic expression stored in a binary expression tree. (See Example 5.5.)

```
public void printExpression (BinaryTree T, Position v) {
  // Prints the arithmetic expression stored in binary T treee by
  // performing an inorder traversal.  It assumes that the elements
  // stored in the nodes of T support a toString method that
  // prints the variable at an external node or the operator at the
  // internal node.
  if (T.isExternal(v))
    System.out.print(v.element());
  else {
    System.out.print("(");
    printExpression (T,T.leftChild(v)); // recursive call
    System.out.print(v.element());
    printExpression (T,T.rightChild(v)); // recursive call
    System.out.print(")");
  }
}
```

Code Fragment 5.19: Algorithm printExpression.

5.3.4   The Template Method Pattern

The tree traversal methods described above are actually examples of an interesting object-oriented software design pattern, the ***template method pattern***. The template method pattern describes a generic computation mechanism that can be specialized for a particular application by redefining certain steps.

Following the template method pattern, class BinaryTreeTraversal, shown in Code Fragment 5.20, implements a generic Euler tour traversal of a binary tree. Processing a node of the tree is accomplished by the recursive traverseNode method, which invokes several other auxiliary methods at different phases of the traversal. For an external node, traverseNode invokes method external, followed by method result, which returns the output of traverseNode. For an internal node, method traverseNode executes the following steps:

- method left is executed, which performs the computations associated with encountering the node on the left;
- method traverseNode is recursively invoked on the left subtree;
- method below is executed, which performs the computations associated with encountering the node from below;
- method traverseNode is recursively invoked on the right subtree;
- method right is executed, which performs the computations associated with encountering the node on the right;
- method result is executed, which returns the output of traverseNode.

```
public abstract class BinaryTreeTraversal {
  // Template for algorthims traversing a binary tree using an Euler
  // tour. The subclasses of this class will redefine some of the
  // methods of this class to create a specific traversal.
  protected BinaryTree tree;
  public Object execute(BinaryTree T) {
    tree = T;
    return null;  // nothing interesting to return
  }
  protected Object traverseNode(Position p) {
    TraversalResult r = initResult();
    if (tree.isExternal(p)) {
      external(p, r);
    } else {
      left(p, r);
      r.leftResult = traverseNode(tree.leftChild(p)); // recursive traversal
      below(p, r);
      r.rightResult = traverseNode(tree.rightChild(p)); // recursive traversal
      right(p, r);
    }
    return result(r);
  }
  // methods that can be redefined by the subclasses
  protected void external(Position p, TraversalResult r) {}
  protected void left(Position p, TraversalResult r) {}
  protected void below(Position p, TraversalResult r) {}
  protected void right(Position p, TraversalResult r) {}
  protected TraversalResult initResult() { return new TraversalResult(); }
  protected Object result(TraversalResult r) { return r.finalResult; }
}
```

Code Fragment 5.20: Class BinaryTreeTraversal defining a generic Euler tour of a binary tree. This class realizes the template method pattern and must be specialized in order to get an interesting computation.

As shown in Code Fragment 5.20, an object of class TraversalResult is shared by the auxiliary methods left, below, and right. Code Fragment 5.21 shows the definition of the TraversalResult class. Note that an object from this class stores as instance variables references to three other objects, leftResult, rightResult, and finalResult, which hold temporary data for the computation. By default, a new TraversalResult object is created at the beginning of each invocation of the method traverseNode.

```
public class TraversalResult {
  public Object leftResult;
  public Object rightResult;
  public Object finalResult;
}
```

Code Fragment 5.21: Class TraversalResult used to hold temporary data for the computation performed by an invocation of method traverseNode.

The auxiliary methods left, below, and right have default implementations that do nothing. Hence, method traverseNode of class BinaryTreeTraversal can be viewed as a *template* or "skeleton" of an Euler tour. Indeed, we can implement a variety of algorithms based on an Euler tour of a binary tree by creating a subclass of BinaryTreeTraversal that redefines some of the auxiliary methods.

We give two examples of specializations of the generic BinaryTreeTraversal, as described below:

- Evaluating the arithmetic expression associated with an expression tree (see Example 5.5), can be done by defining a subclass EvaluateExpressionTraversal of BinaryTreeTraversal where methods external and right are suitably redefined. See Code Fragments 5.22–5.24 and compare them with Code Fragment 5.16. Note that EvaluateExpressionTraversal does not redefine methods left and below.

- Printing the arithmetic expression stored in a binary expression tree can be done by defining a subclass PrintExpressionTraversal of BinaryTreeTraversal where methods external, left, below, and right are suitably redefined. See Code Fragment 5.25 and compare it with Code Fragment 5.19.

After presenting these code fragments, we describe in the next section a number of efficient ways of realizing the tree abstract data type by concrete data structures, such as sequences and linked structures.

```java
public interface OperatorInfo {
// Generic operator stored at an internal node of an expression tree
  public Integer operation(Integer x, Integer y);
}
public class AdditionOperator implements OperatorInfo {
    public Integer operation(Integer x, Integer y) {
      return new Integer(x.intValue() + y.intValue());
    }
    public String toString() {
      return new String("+");
    }
}
public class MultiplicationOperator implements OperatorInfo {
    public Integer operation(Integer x, Integer y) {
      return new Integer(x.intValue() * y.intValue());
    }
    public String toString() {
      return new String("*");
    }
}
```

Code Fragment 5.22: Interface OperatorInfo and classes AdditionOperator and MultiplicationOperator representing the operators of an arithmetic expression tree.

```java
public class VariableInfo {
  // Variable stored at an external node of an expression tree
  private Integer var;
  public VariableInfo(int newVar) {
    var = new Integer(newVar);
  }
  public Integer variable() {
    return var;
  }
  public String toString() {
    return var.toString();
  }
}
```

Code Fragment 5.23: Class VariableInfo representing the variables of an arithmetic expression tree.

```
public class EvaluateExpressionTraversal extends BinaryTreeTraversal {
  // This traversal specializes BinaryTreeTraversal to compute the
  // value of an arithmetic expression stored in the tree. It assumes
  // that the elements stored at the external nodes are of type
  // VariableInfo (supporting method variable() that returns the value
  // of the int variable stored at that node), and that the elements
  // stored at the internal nodes are of type OperatorInfo (supporting
  // method operation(x, y) that applies the arithmetic operation
  // stored at that node to operands x and y, both of type int)
  public Object execute(BinaryTree T) {
    super.execute(T);
    System.out.print("The value is: ");
    Integer theResult = (Integer)traverseNode(tree.root());
    System.out.println(theResult);
    return null;  // nothing interesting to return
  }
  protected void external(Position p, TraversalResult r) {
    r.finalResult = ((VariableInfo)p.element()).variable();
  }
  protected void right(Position p, TraversalResult r) {
    r.finalResult = ((OperatorInfo)p.element()).operation
        ((Integer)r.leftResult, (Integer)r.rightResult);
  }
}
```

Code Fragment 5.24: Class EvaluateExpressionTraversal, which specializes BinaryTreeTraversal.

```
public class PrintExpressionTraversal extends BinaryTreeTraversal {
  // This traversal specialized BinaryTreeTraversal to print out the
  // arithmetic expression stored in the tree. It assumes that the
  // elements stored in the nodes of the tree support a toString
  // method that prints the variable at an external node or the
  // operator at the internal node.
  public Object execute(BinaryTree T) {
    super.execute(T);
    System.out.print("Expression: " );
    traverseNode(T.root());
    System.out.println();
    return null;    // nothing interesting to return
  }
  protected void external(Position p, TraversalResult r) {
    System.out.print(p.element());
  }
  protected void left(Position p, TraversalResult r) {
    System.out.print("(");
  }
  protected void below(Position p, TraversalResult r) {
    System.out.print(p.element());
  }
  protected void right(Position p, TraversalResult r) {
    System.out.print(")");
  }
}
```

Code Fragment 5.25: Class PrintExpressionTraversal, which specializes Binary-
TreeTraversal.

5.4   Data Structures for Representing Trees

In this section, we describe concrete data structures for representing trees and implementing the tree ADT and the binary tree ADT. We begin by describing a simple data structure for representing binary trees.

5.4.1   A Sequence-Based Structure for Binary Trees

A simple concrete data structure for realizing a binary tree T is based on a certain way of numbering the nodes of T. For every node v of T, let $p(v)$ be the integer defined as follows (see Figure 5.16):

- If v is the root of T, then $p(v) = 1$.
- If v is the left child of node u, then $p(v) = 2p(u)$.
- If v is the right child of node u, then $p(v) = 2p(u) + 1$.

The numbering function p is known as a ***level numbering*** of the nodes in a binary tree T, for it numbers the nodes on each level of T in increasing order from left to right (although it may skip some numbers).

The level numbering function p suggests a representation of a binary tree T by means of a sequence S such that node v of T is associated with the element of S at rank $p(v)$. (See Figure 5.17.) Typically, we implement the sequence S by means of an array. Such an implementation is simple and fast, for we can use it to easily perform the methods root, parent, leftChild, rightChild, isInternal, isExternal, and isRoot by using simple arithmetic operations on the numbers p associated with the nodes involved in the operation. We leave the details of such implementations as a simple exercise, but we note here that each such method takes $O(1)$ time.

Let n be the number of nodes of T, and let N be the maximum value of $p(v)$ over all the nodes of T. If we implement the sequence S as described above, then its underlying array has size N, which is at least $n + 1$ (the element of S at rank 0 is not associated with any node of T) and could be much larger. The sequence S will in general contain a number of empty positions, which do not refer to existing nodes of T. In fact, in the worst case, $N = 2^{(n-1)/2}$ (the justification of this fact is left as an exercise). In Section 6.3, we will see a class of binary trees, called "heaps" for which $N = n + 1$; hence, in spite of this worst-case space usage, there are applications for which the sequence representation of a binary tree is space efficient. Still, for general binary trees, the exponential worst-case space requirement of this representation is prohibitive.

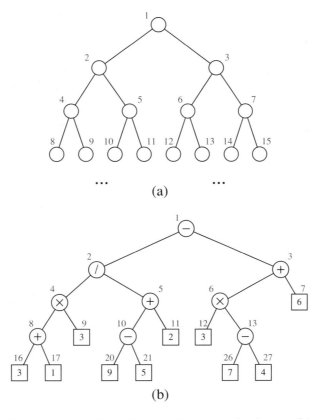

(a)

(b)

Figure 5.16: Binary tree level numbering: (a) general scheme; (b) an example.

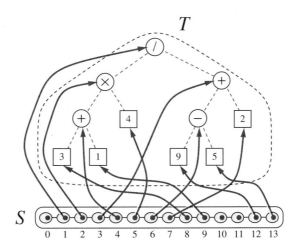

Figure 5.17: Representation of a binary tree T by means of a sequence S.

Operation	Time
size, isEmpty	$O(1)$
positions, elements	$O(n)$
swap, replace(v,e)	$O(1)$
root, parent, children	$O(1)$
leftChild, rightChild	$O(1)$
isInternal, isExternal, isRoot	$O(1)$
expandExternal, removeAboveExternal	$O(1)$

Table 5.1: Running times of the methods of a binary tree T implemented with a sequence S, where S is realized by means of an array. We denote with n the number of nodes of T, and N denotes the size of sequence S. Methods hasMoreElements() and nextElement() of the enumerations elements(), positions(), and children(v) take $O(1)$ time. The space usage is $O(N)$, which is $O(2^{(n-1)/2})$ in the worst case.

Table 5.1 summarizes the running times of the methods of a binary tree implemented with a sequence. The sequence implementation of a binary tree is thus a fast and easy way of realizing the binary tree ADT, but it can be very space inefficient if the height of the tree is large. The next data structure we discuss does not have this drawback.

5.4.2   A Linked Structure for Binary Trees

A natural way to realize a binary tree T is to use a ***linked structure***. In this approach we represent each node v of T by an object with references to the element stored at v and to the objects associated with the children and parent of v. (See Figure 5.18.) If v is the root of T, then the reference to the parent node is null, and if v is an external node, then the references to the children of v are null.

Class Node (Code Fragment 5.26) represents a node v by an object implementing the position ADT and having instance variables element, left, right, and parent, which reference the element stored at v, the parent of v, the left child of v, and the right child of v, respectively. Class Node also has methods that get and set these variables. Class LinkedBinaryTree, shown in Code Fragment 5.27, stores in internal variables the size of the tree and a reference to the Node object associated with the root of the tree. Also, it implements methods replace, root, parent, leftChild, rightChild, isInternal, isExternal, isRoot, and expandExternal of the BinaryTree interface (Code Fragment 5.12), by making straightforward calls to the methods of class Node (Code Fragment 5.26). We can easily verify that the above methods each use a constant number of instructions and thus take $O(1)$ time each.

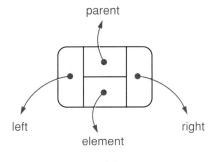

(a)

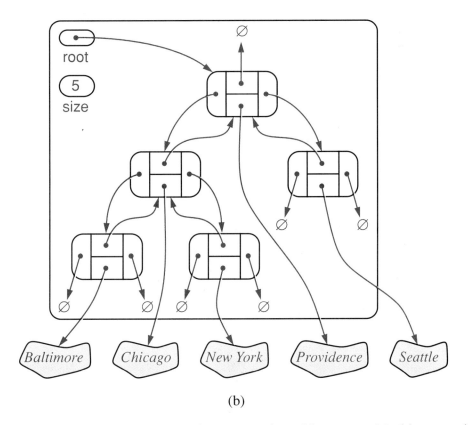

(b)

Figure 5.18: Linked data structure for representing a binary tree: (a) object associated with a node; (b) complete data structure for a binary tree with five nodes.

```java
public class Node implements Position {
    // node of a binary tree realized by means of a linked structure
    private Container container; // container storing this node
    private Object element; // element stored at the node
    private Node left; // left child
    private Node right; // right child
    private Node parent; // parent node
    public Node() { } // default constructor
    public Node(Object o, Node u, Node v, Node w, Container c) {
        // constructor with parameters
        setElement(o);
        setContainer(c);
        setParent(u);
        setLeft(v);
        setRight(w);
    }
    public Object element() { return element; }
    protected void setElement(Object o) { element=o; }
    public Container container() { return container; }
    protected void setContainer(Container c) { container=c; }
    protected Node getLeft() { return left; }
    protected void setLeft(Node v) { left=v; }
    protected Node getRight() { return right; }
    protected void setRight(Node v) { right=v; }
    protected Node getParent() { return parent; }
    protected void setParent(Node v) { parent=v; }
}
```

Code Fragment 5.26: Class Node.

```
public class LinkedBinaryTree implements BinaryTree {
  private Position root; // reference to the root
  private int size; // number of nodes
  public LinkedBinaryTree() {
    root = new Node(null,null,null,null,this);
    size = 1;
  }
  public int size() { return size; }
  public boolean isEmpty() { return (size==0); }
  public Object  replace(Position v, Object o) {
    Object temp = ((Node) v).element();
    ((Node) v).setElement(o);
    return temp;
  }
  public Position leftChild(Position v) { return ((Node) v).getLeft(); }
  public Position rightChild(Position v) { return ((Node) v).getRight(); }
  public Position parent(Position v) { return ((Node) v).getParent(); }
  public boolean isInternal(Position v) {
    return (((Node) v).getLeft()!=null || ((Node) v).getRight()!=null);
  }
  public boolean isExternal(Position v) {
    return (((Node) v).getLeft()==null && ((Node) v).getRight()==null);
  }
  public boolean isRoot(Position v) { return (v==root()); }
  public Position root() { return root; }
  public void expandExternal(Position v) {
    if (isExternal(v)) {
      ((Node) v).setLeft(new Node(null,(Node) v,null,null,this));
      ((Node) v).setRight(new Node(null,(Node) v,null,null,this));
      size++;
    }
  }
  ...
}
```

Code Fragment 5.27: A portion of class LinkedBinaryTree, including the implementation of selected methods of the BinaryTree interface.

We left a number of simple methods out of Code Fragment 5.27. We discuss these methods below, but leave their implementations as an exercise.

- Methods size() and isEmpty() use an instance variable storing the number of nodes of T, and each take $O(1)$ time.
- Method swap(v, w) is straightforward to implement (we just swap the element references of v and w), and also takes $O(1)$ time. Likewise, the method replace(v, e) can be implemented in $O(1)$ time.
- We can realize enumerations elements(), positions(), and children(v) by using a sequence and a position in that sequence as instance variables. Thus, the two methods hasMoreElements() and nextElement() of such enumerations each take $O(1)$ time.
- Method positions() can be implemented by performing a traversal of the binary tree. When a node v is visited, we insert a reference to v at the end of a sequence. Any one of the three traversals discussed in Section 5.3.3 (preorder, inorder, and postorder) will serve the purpose. Method elements() is similar. Thus methods positions() and elements() take $O(n)$ time each.
- Class LinkedBinaryTree (Code Fragment 5.27) has a constructor with no arguments that returns a binary tree consisting of a single node.

Consider now the space required by this data structure. There is an object of class Node (Code Fragment 5.26) for every node of tree T, plus an object of class LinkedBinaryTree (Code Fragment 5.27) for the the tree T itself. Such objects each use a constant amount of space. Thus, the overall space requirement is equal to $c_1 n + c_2$ for some constants c_1 and c_2, and is thus $O(n)$. Table 5.2 summarizes the performance of this implementation of a binary tree.

Operation	Time
size, isEmpty	$O(1)$
positions, elements	$O(n)$
swap, replace(v, e)	$O(1)$
root, parent, children	$O(1)$
leftChild, rightChild	$O(1)$
isInternal, isExternal, isRoot	$O(1)$
expandExternal, removeAboveExternal	$O(1)$

Table 5.2: Running times for the methods of an n-node binary tree implemented with a linked structure. The space usage is $O(n)$.

5.4.3 A Linked Structure for General Trees

We can extend the linked structure for binary trees to represent general trees. Since there is no limit on the number of children that a node v in a general tree can have, we use a container (for example, a sequence) to store the children of v, instead of using instance variables. This structure is schematically illustrated in Figure 5.19. By using a container to store the children of each node v, we can implement the children(v) method simply by calling the elements() method of the children container that v stores.

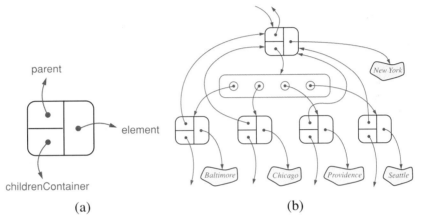

parent

element

childrenContainer

(a)   (b)

Figure 5.19: The linked structure for a tree: (a) the object associated with a node; (b) the portion of the data structure associated with a node and its children.

Table 5.3 summarizes the performance of the implementation of a tree by means of a linked structure. The analysis is left as an exercise.

Operation	Time
size, isEmpty	$O(1)$
positions, elements	$O(n)$
swap, replace(v, e)	$O(1)$
root, parent	$O(1)$
children(v)	$O(c_v)$
isInternal, isExternal, isRoot	$O(1)$

Table 5.3: Running times of the methods of an n-node tree implemented with a linked structure. We let c_v denote the number of children of a node v. The space usage is $O(n)$.

5.4.4 Representing General Trees with Binary Trees

An alternative representation of a general tree T is obtained by transforming T into a binary tree T'. (See Figure 5.20.) We assume that either T is ordered or that it has been arbitrarily ordered. The transformation is as follows:

- For each node u of T, there is an internal node u' of T' associated with u.
- If u is an external node of T, then the children of u' in T' are external nodes.
- If u is an internal node of T and v is the first child of u in T, then v' is the left child of u' in T.
- If node v has a sibling w immediately following it, then w' is the right child of v' in T'.

Note that the external nodes of T' are not associated with nodes of T, and serve only as placeholders.

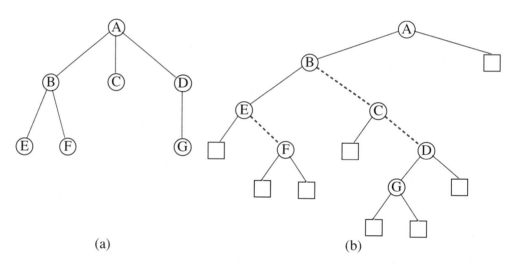

(a)   (b)

Figure 5.20: Representation of a tree by means of a binary tree: (a) tree T; (b) binary tree T' associated with T. The dashed edges connect nodes of T' associated with sibling nodes of T.

It is easy to maintain the correspondence between T and T', and to express operations in T in terms of corresponding operations in T'. Intuitively, we can think of the correspondence in terms of a conversion of T into T' that takes each set of siblings $\{v_1, v_2, \ldots, v_k\}$ in T with parent v and replaces it with a chain of right children rooted at v_1, which then becomes the left child of v.

Table 5.4 summarizes the performance of the implementation of a tree by means of a binary tree. The analysis is left as an exercise.

Operation	Time
size, isEmpty	$O(1)$
positions, elements	$O(n)$
swap, replace(v, e)	$O(1)$
root	$O(1)$
parent(v)	$O(s_v)$
children(v)	$O(c_v)$
isInternal, isExternal, isRoot	$O(1)$

Table 5.4: Running times of the methods of a tree represented by means of a binary tree, which is in turn implemented with a linked structure. We denote with n the number of nodes of the tree, with c_v the number of children of a node v, and with s_v the number of siblings of v. The methods hasMoreElements() and nextElement() of the enumerations returned by elements(), positions(), and children(v) take $O(1)$ time. The space usage is $O(n)$.

5.5 An Applet that Draws a Binary Tree ★

In this section, we present an applet that generates a random binary tree and draws it in the applet's canvas window. The algorithm used for generating a random binary tree T with a given number of external nodes, m, is summarized as follows:

Create the root node v of T.
if $m \geq 2$ **then**
　Generate a random number l between 1 and $m - 1$.
　$r \leftarrow m - l$
　Recursively create a random binary tree T_l with l external nodes.
　Recursively create a random binary tree T_r with r external nodes.
　Make T_l and T_r the left and right subtree of v, respectively.

In our Java implementation of this algorithm, shown in Code Fragments 5.28 and 5.29, we also generate a random color for every internal node, while the external nodes are colored black.

★We use a star (★) to indicate sections containing material more advanced than the material in the rest of the chapter; this material can be considered optional in a first reading.

The drawing algorithm assigns x- and y-coordinates to a node v of T using the following two rules (see Figure 5.21):

- $x(v)$ is equal to the number of nodes visited before v in the inorder traversal of T.
- $y(v)$ is equal to the depth of v in T.

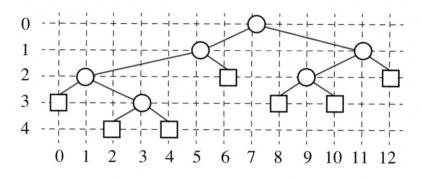

Figure 5.21: Illustrating the inorder drawing algorithm.

We implement the drawing algorithm as a specialization of the generic Euler tour traversal. Namely, we define a subclass InorderDrawTraversal of BinaryTreeTraversal (Code Fragment 5.20), as shown in Code Fragment 5.30.

The drawing produced by Code Fragment 5.30 has x- and y-coordinates that refer to an ideal grid with unit spacing. In order to draw the tree in the applet's window, we need to transform these coordinates by means of an appropriate scaling and translation, and to call methods for drawing the nodes of the tree and the edges joining them. This transformation is accomplished by another specialization of the generic Euler tour traversal obtained by defining a subclass CanvasDrawTraversal of BinaryTreeTraversal, as shown in Code Fragments 5.31 and 5.32.

Finally, we show the drawing information class in Code Fragment 5.29 and the main module of the applet in Code Fragment 5.33, and we give a sample image produced by it in Figure 5.22.

```
public class RandomTreeBuilder {
  protected Random gen = new Random();
  protected BinaryTree tree;
  public BinaryTree randomBinaryTree(int n) {
    // Create a random binary tree with n external nodes
    System.out.println
      ("Building random binary tree with " + n + " external nodes . . .");
    tree = new BTNodeBinaryTree();
    build(tree.root(), n);  // auxiliary recursive method
    return tree;
  }
  protected void build(Position p, int n) {
    // Auxiliary method used by randomBinaryTree that recursively builds
    // a tree rooted at position p with n external nodes
    if (tree.isExternal(p) && n > 1) {
      // make a new internal node and assign to it a random color
      tree.expandExternal(p);
      tree.replace(p, new DrawingInfo(randomColor()));
      // color black the newly created external nodes
      tree.replace(tree.leftChild(p), new DrawingInfo(Color.black));
      tree.replace(tree.rightChild(p), new DrawingInfo(Color.black));
      // generate random sizes for left and right subtrees
      int leftsize = randomInteger(1, n − 1);
      int rightsize = n−leftsize;
      // recursively build the left and right subtrees
      build(tree.leftChild(p), leftsize);
      build(tree.rightChild(p), rightsize);
    }
  }
  protected Color randomColor() {
    // Make a new color with random red, green and blue values
    int r = randomInteger(50, 255);
    int g = randomInteger(50, 255);
    int b = randomInteger(50, 255);
    return new Color(r, g, b);
  }
  protected int randomInteger(int min, int max) {
    // Return a random integer i such that min <= i <= max
    float r1 = gen.nextFloat();
    float r2 = min + r1*(max+1−min);
    return (int) r2;
  }
}
```

Code Fragment 5.28: Class RandomTreeBuilder.

```java
import java.awt.Color;
public class DrawingInfo {
  // Element stored at a node of a drawable binary tree.
  private int x;
  private int y;
  private Color c;
  public DrawingInfo(Color col) { this.setColor(col); }
  public int getX() { return x; }
  public int getY() { return y; }
  public Color getColor() { return c; }
  public void setX(int newX) { x = newX; }
  public void setY(int newY) { y = newY; }
  public void setColor(Color newCol) { c = newCol; }
}
```

Code Fragment 5.29: Class DrawingInfo.

```java
public class InorderDrawTraversal extends BinaryTreeTraversal {
  // Computation of a straight-line drawing of a binary tree where the
  // the x-coordinate of a node is its inorder rank and the
  // y-coordinate is its depth. .
  protected int rank  = 0;
  protected int depth = 0;
  public Object execute(BinaryTree T) {
    super.execute(T);
    rank = 0;
    depth = 0;
    this.traverseNode(T.root());
    return null;    // nothing interesting to return
  }
  protected void external(Position p, TraversalResult r) {
    ((DrawingInfo)p.element()).setX(rank++);
    ((DrawingInfo)p.element()).setY(depth);
  }
  protected void left(Position p, TraversalResult r) { depth++; }
  protected void below(Position p, TraversalResult r) {
    depth−−;
    ((DrawingInfo)p.element()).setX(rank++);
    ((DrawingInfo)p.element()).setY(depth);
    depth++;
  }
  protected void right(Position p, TraversalResult r) { depth−−; }
}
```

Code Fragment 5.30: Class InorderDrawTraversal.

```
public class CanvasDrawTraversal extends BinaryTreeTraversal {
  // Traversal of a binary tree that is specialized to draw a binary
  // tree within an applet. It is assumed that the elements stored at
  // the nodes of the binary tree are of type DrawingInfo
  protected int offset = 20; // size of the grid squares
  protected int radius = 16; // radius of circles and side of squares
  protected Graphics g;
  public CanvasDrawTraversal(Graphics gg) { g = gg; }
  public Object execute(BinaryTree T) {
    super.execute(T);
    traverseNode(tree.root());
    return null;  // nothing interesting to return
  }
  protected void external(Position p, TraversalResult r) {
    // Draw an external node as a black square
    g.setColor(((DrawingInfo)p.element()).getColor());
    g.fillRect(xCorner(p),yCorner(p),radius,radius);
  }
  protected void left(Position p, TraversalResult r) {
    // Draw the edge to the left child
    g.setColor(Color.black);
    g.drawLine(xPos(p), yPos(p), xPos(tree.leftChild(p)),
               yPos(tree.leftChild(p)));
  }
  protected void below(Position p, TraversalResult r) {
    // Draw the edge to the right child
    g.setColor(Color.black);
    g.drawLine(xPos(p), yPos(p), xPos(tree.rightChild(p)),
               yPos(tree.rightChild(p)));
  }
  protected void right(Position p, TraversalResult r) {
    // Draw the internal node as a colored circle
    g.setColor(((DrawingInfo)p.element()).getColor());
    g.fillOval(xCorner(p), yCorner(p), radius, radius);
    g.setColor(Color.black);
    g.drawOval(xCorner(p), yCorner(p), radius, radius);
  }
  . . .
```

Code Fragment 5.31: Class CanvasDrawTraversal, which is continued in Code Fragment 5.32.

```
    . . .
    // Auxiliary methods for drawing the nodes
    protected int xCorner(Position p) {
      return (1+((DrawingInfo) p.element()).getX())*offset−radius/2;
    }
    protected int yCorner(Position p) {
      return (1+((DrawingInfo)p.element()).getY())*offset−radius/2;
    }
    protected int xPos(Position p) {
      return (1+((DrawingInfo)p.element()).getX())*offset;
    }
    protected int yPos(Position p) {
      return (1+((DrawingInfo)p.element()).getY())*offset;
    }
}
```

Code Fragment 5.32: Class CanvasDrawTraversal, continued.

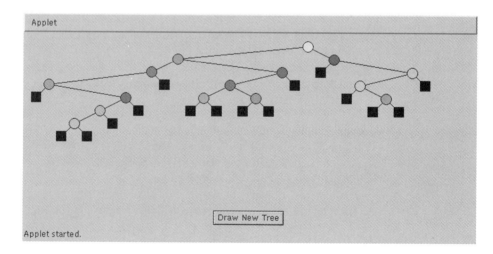

Figure 5.22: A sample screen image from the tree-drawing applet.

```java
public class InorderDrawApplet extends Applet implements ActionListener {
  private int numExt = 16;
  private RandomTreeBuilder builder;
  private InorderDrawTraversal inorder;
  private CanvasDrawTraversal canvas;
  private BinaryTree tree;
  public void init() {
    setLayout(new BorderLayout());
    // create a random tree and draw it
    builder = new RandomTreeBuilder();
    inorder = new InorderDrawTraversal();
    canvas = new CanvasDrawTraversal(getGraphics());
    tree = builder.randomBinaryTree(numExt);
    inorder.execute(tree);
    canvas.execute(tree);
    // create a button that will draw a new tree when it is clicked
    Panel p = new Panel();
    p.setLayout(new FlowLayout());
    Button newTree = new Button("Draw New Tree");
    newTree.addActionListener(this);
    p.add(newTree);
    add("South", p);
  }
  public void paint(Graphics g) {
    canvas.execute(tree);
  }
  public void actionPerformed(ActionEvent e) {
    repaint();
    tree = builder.randomBinaryTree(numExt);
    inorder.execute(tree);
    canvas.execute(tree);
  }
}
```

Code Fragment 5.33: Class InorderDrawApplet.

5.6   Exercises

Reinforcement

R-5.1 The following questions refer to the tree of Figure 5.3.

1. Which node is the root?
2. What are the internal nodes?
3. How many descendants does node cs016/ have?
4. How many ancestors does node cs016/ have?
5. What are the siblings of node homeworks/?
6. Which nodes are in the subtree rooted at node projects/?
7. What is the depth of node papers/?
8. What is the height of the tree?

R-5.2 What is the value of the arithmetic expression associated with the binary tree of Figure 5.6?

R-5.3 Let T be a tree such that each internal node has one or two children. Describe how to convert T into a proper binary tree, where each internal node has exactly two children, without adding any additional internal nodes to T.

R-5.4 Let T be the tree of Figure 5.3.

1. Give the output of algorithm preorderPrint(T, T.root()) (Code Fragment 5.7).
2. Give the output of algorithm parentheticRepresentation(T, T.root()) (which is shown in Code Fragment 5.8).

R-5.5 Modify the Java method preorderPrint given in Code Fragment 5.7 so that it will print the strings associated with nodes of a tree indented as shown in Figure 5.8.

R-5.6 Let T be the tree of Figure 5.3.

1. Give the output of algorithm postorderPrint(T, T.root()) (see Code Fragment 5.7).
2. Give the output of algorithm totalSize(T, T.root()) (see Code Fragment 5.11).

R-5.7 Let T be a general ordered tree with more than one node. Is it possible that the preorder traversal of T visits the nodes in the same same order as the postorder traversal of T? If so, give an example; otherwise, argue why this cannot occur. Likewise, is it possible that the preorder traversal of T visits the nodes in the reverse order of the postorder traversal of T? If so, give an example; otherwise, argue why this cannot occur.

R-5.8 Answer the previous question for the case when T is a binary tree.

R-5.9 Let T be a tree with n nodes.

1. What is the running time of parentheticRepresentation(T, T.root())? (See Code Fragment 5.8.)
2. What is the running time of totalSize(T, T.root())? (See Code Fragment 5.11.)

R-5.10 Draw a (single) binary tree T such that

- each internal node of T stores a single character;
- a *preorder* traversal of T yields EXAMFUN; and
- an *inorder* traversal of T yields MAFXUEN

R-5.11 Answer the following questions so as to justify Proposition 5.10.

1. Draw a binary tree with height 7 and minimum number of external nodes.
2. Draw a binary tree with height 7 and maximum number of external nodes.
3. What is the minimum number of external nodes for a binary tree with height h? Justify your answer.
4. What is the maximum number of external nodes for a binary tree with height h? Justify your answer.
5. Let T be a binary tree with height h and n nodes. Show that
$$\log(n+1) - 1 \le h \le (n-1)/2.$$
6. For which values of n and k can the above lower and upper bounds on h be attained with equality?

R-5.12 Let T be the binary tree of Figure 5.6.

1. Give the output of algorithm preorderPrint(T, T.root()) (which is given in Code Fragment 5.7).
2. Give the output of algorithm parentheticRepresentation(T, T.root()) (which is given in Code Fragment 5.8).

R-5.13 Let T be a complete binary tree, that is, a binary tree such that all the external nodes have the same depth. Let D_e be the sum of the depths of all the external nodes of T, and let D_i be the sum of the depths of all the internal nodes of T. Find constants a and b such that

$$D_e = aD_i + bn,$$

where n is the number of nodes of T. (Hint: try to gain some intuition by drawing a few different complete binary trees.)

R-5.14 Let T be the binary tree of Figure 5.6.

1. Give the output of algorithm postorderPrint(T, T.root()) (which is given in Code Fragment 5.7).
2. Give the output of algorithm printExpression(T, T.root()) (which is given in Code Fragment 5.19).

R-5.15 Answer the following questions with reference to the following line of method isExternal from class LinkedBinaryTree (Code Fragment 5.27):

return ((Node) v).getLeft()==**null** && ((Node) v).getRight()==**null**;

1. Can we replace the above line with

   return ((Node) v).getLeft()==**null**;

   and still get a correct behavior?
2. Can we replace the above line with

   return ((Node) v).getRight()==**null**;

   and still get a correct behavior?
3. Can we replace the above line with

   return ((Node) v).getParent()==**null**;

   and still get a correct behavior?

R-5.16 Show that the level numbering p of the nodes of a binary tree given in Section 5.4.1 assigns a unique integer to every node, that is, $p(u) \neq p(v)$ whenever $u \neq v$.

R-5.17 Let T be a binary tree with n nodes, and let p be the level numbering of the nodes of T, as given in Section 5.4.1.

1. Show that, for every node v of T, $p(v) \leq 2^{(n-1)/2}$.
2. Show an example of a binary tree with at least five nodes that attains the above upper bound on the maximum value of $p(v)$ for some node v.

R-5.18 Let T be a binary tree with n nodes that is realized with a sequence, S, and let p be the level numbering of the nodes in T, as given in Section 5.4.1. Give pseudo-code descriptions of each of the methods root, parent, leftChild, rightChild, isInternal, isExternal, and isRoot.

R-5.19 Draw a binary tree representation of the general tree shown in Figure 5.2 using the binary-tree representation scheme described in Section 5.4.4.

Creativity

C-5.1 Let T be a tree whose nodes store strings. Give an algorithm that computes and prints, for every internal node v of T, the string stored at v and the height of the subtree rooted at v.

C-5.2 The *indented parenthetic representation* of a tree T is a variation of the parenthetic representation of T (see Figure 5.8) illustrated in Figure 5.23.

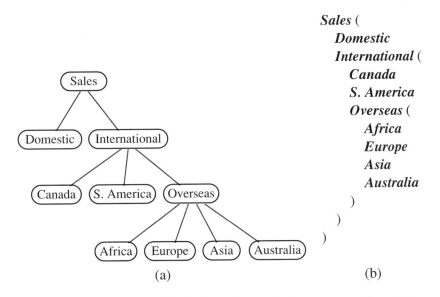

Figure 5.23: (a) Tree T; (b) indented parenthetic representation of T.

Give an algorithm that prints the indented parenthetic representation of a tree.

C-5.3 Give an $O(n)$-time algorithm for computing the depth of all the nodes of a tree T, where n is the number of nodes of T.

C-5.4 The *balance factor* of an internal node v of a binary tree is the difference between the heights of the right and left subtrees of v. Show how to specialize the generic binary tree traversal of Section 5.3.4 to print the balance factors of all the nodes of a binary tree.

C-5.5 Two ordered trees T' and T'' are said to be *isomorphic* if one of the following holds:

- Both T' and T'' consist of a single node
- Both T' and T'' have the same number k of subtrees, and the ith subtree of T' is isomorphic to the ith subtree of T'', for $i = 1, \ldots, k$.

Design an algorithm that tests whether two given ordered trees are isomorphic. What is the running time of your algorithm?

C-5.6 Algorithm PreorderDraw draws a binary tree T by assigning x- and y-coordinates to each node v as follows:

- Set $y(v)$ equal to the depth of v in T.
- Set $x(v)$ equal to the rank of v in the preorder traversal of T, that is, $x(v) = k$ if v is the hth node visited in the preorder traversal of T.

1. Show that the drawing of T produced by algorithm PreorderDraw has no pairs of crossing edges.
2. Redraw the binary tree of Figure 5.21 using algorithm Preorder-Draw.
3. Redraw the binary tree of Figure 5.21 using algorithm Postorder-Draw, which is similar to PreorderDraw but assigns y-coordinates using a postorder traversal.

C-5.7 Design algorithms for performing the following operations on a binary tree T:

- tourNext(v): return the node visited after node v in an Euler tour of T
- preorderNext(v): return the node visited after node v in a preorder traversal of T
- inorderNext(v): return the node visited after node v in an inorder traversal of T
- postorderNext(v): return the node visited after node v in a postorder traversal of T.

What is the time complexity of your algorithms?

C-5.8 Consider a variation of the linked data structure for binary trees where each Node object has references to the Node objects of the children but not to the Node object of the parent. Describe an implementation of the methods of a binary tree with this data structure and analyze the time complexity for these methods.

C-5.9 Extend the concept of an Euler tour to an ordered tree that is not necessarily a binary tree, and design a generic traversal of an ordered tree.

C-5.10 Design an alternative implementation of the linked data structure for binary trees using a class for nodes that specializes into subclasses for an internal node, an external node, and the root node.

C-5.11 Within the linked data structure for binary trees, explore an alternative design for the enumerations returned by methods elements(), positions(), and positions(o) such that each of the above methods takes $O(1)$ time. Can you still achieve $O(1)$ time complexity for the two enumeration methods hasMoreElements() and nextElement() of the enumerations returned?

C-5.12 Justify the bounds in Table 5.2 by providing a detailed analysis of the running times of the methods of a binary tree T implemented with a sequence S, where S is realized by means of an array.

C-5.13 Justify Table 5.3, summarizing the running time of the methods of a tree represented with a linked structure, by providing, for each method, a description of its implementation, and an analysis of its running time.

C-5.14 Justify the bounds in Table 5.4 for the running times of the methods of a tree represented by means of a binary tree, which is in turn implemented with a linked structure, by providing, for each method, a description of its implementation and an analysis of its running time.

C-5.15 Let T' be the binary tree representing a tree T (see Section 5.4.4).

1. Is a preorder traversal of T' equivalent to a preorder traversal of T?
2. Is a postorder traversal of T' equivalent to a postorder traversal of T?
3. Is an inorder traversal of T' equivalent to some kind of traversal of T?

C-5.16 Describe in pseudo-code a non-recursive method for performing an Euler tour traversal of a binary tree that runs in linear time and does not use a stack. (Hint: you can tell which visit action to perform at a node by taking note of where you are coming from.)

C-5.17 Describe in pseudo-code a non-recursive method for performing an in-order traversal of a binary tree in linear time. (Hint: use a stack.)

C-5.18 Let T be a binary tree with n nodes that may or may not be realized with a sequence. Give a linear-time method that uses the methods of the Binary-Tree interface to traverse the nodes of T by increasing values of the level numbering function p given in Section 5.4.1. This traversal is known as the *level order traversal*.

Projects

P-5.1 Implement the general tree ADT using a linked structure.

P-5.2 Implement the binary tree ADT using a linked structure.

P-5.3 Implement the binary tree ADT using a sequence.

P-5.4 Implement the binary tree ADT using a linked structure and then use this binary tree representation to implement the general tree ADT.

P-5.5 A *slicing floorplan* is a recursive decomposition of a floorplan (rectangle with horizontal and vertical sides) by means of horizontal and vertical *cuts* (segments). (See Figure 5.24a.) A slicing floorplan can be represented by a binary tree, called a *slicing tree*, whose internal nodes represent the cuts, and whose external nodes represent the *basic rectangles* into which the floorplan is decomposed by the cuts. (See Figure 5.24b.) Slicing floor-plans and their compaction have applications to the layout of integrated circuits.

The *compaction problem* for a *slicing floorplan* is defined as follows. Assume that each basic rectangle of a slicing floorplan is assigned a minimum width w and a minimum height h. Find the smallest possible height and width for each rectangle of the slicing floorplan that is compatible with the minimum dimensions of the basic rectangles. Namely, assign values $h(v)$ and $w(v)$ to each node v of the slicing tree such that:

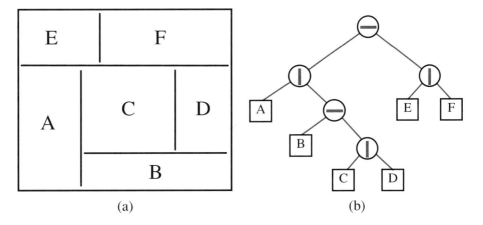

Figure 5.24: (a) Slicing floorplan; (b) slicing tree associated with the floorplan.

$$w(v) = \begin{cases} w & \text{if } v \text{ is an external node whose basic rectangle has minimum width } w \\[2ex] \max(\mathsf{w}(w), \mathsf{w}(z)) & \text{if } v \text{ is an internal node associated with a horizontal cut with left child } w \text{ and right child } z \\[2ex] \mathsf{w}(w) + \mathsf{w}(z) & \text{if } v \text{ is an internal node associated with a vertical cut with left child } w \text{ and right child } z \end{cases}$$

$$h(v) = \begin{cases} h & \text{if } v \text{ is an external node whose basic rectangle has minimum height } h \\[2ex] \mathsf{h}(w) + \mathsf{h}(z) & \text{if } v \text{ is an internal node associated with a horizontal cut with left child } w \text{ and right child } z \\[2ex] \max(\mathsf{h}(w), \mathsf{h}(z)) & \text{if } v \text{ is an internal node associated with a vertical cut with left child } w \text{ and right child } z \end{cases}$$

Design a data structure for slicing floorplans that supports the following operations:

- Create a floorplan consisting of a single basic rectangle.
- Decompose a basic rectangle by means of a horizontal cut.
- Decompose a basic rectangle by means of a vertical cut.
- Assign minimum height and width to a basic rectangle.
- Draw the slicing tree associated with the floorplan.
- Compact the floorplan.
- Draw the compacted floorplan.

Chapter Notes

The concept of viewing data structures as containers (and other principles of object-oriented design) can be found in object-oriented design books by Booch [25] and Budd [29]. The concept also exists under the name "collection class" in books by Golberg and Robson [58] and Liskov and Guttag [100]. Our use of the "position" abstraction derives from the "position" and "node" abstractions introduced by Aho, Hopcroft, and Ullman [7].

Discussions of tree representations and the classic preorder, inorder, and postorder tree traversal methods can be found in Knuth's *Fundamental Algorithms* book [89]. The Euler tour traversal technique actually comes from the parallel algorithms community, and is discussed in the book by JáJá [81] and a book chapter by Karp and Ramachandran [86]. The algorithm we described for drawing a tree is generally considered to be a part of the "folklore" of graph drawing algorithms. The reader interested in better methods for drawing trees is referred to the chapter by Tamassia [135], the annotated bibliography of Di Battista *et al.* [40], or the book by Di Battista *et al.* [41].

Chapter

6

Priority Queues

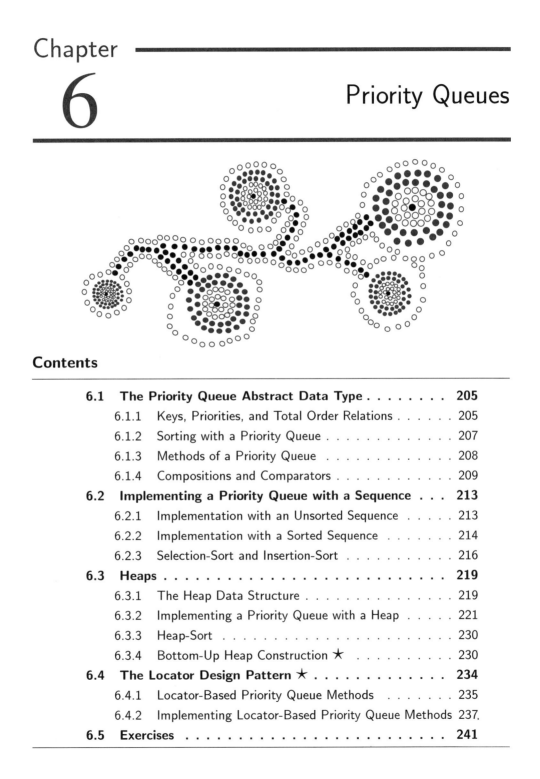

Contents

Having the right priorities is important to succeeding in life. On a quiet Saturday afternoon, presented with the opportunity of taking a nap, watching TV, playing soccer, or studying this chapter, the zealous student will certainly give first priority to the latter task. Outside of comfortable campus boundaries, priorities are an even more serious matter. Consider, for example, an air-traffic control center that has to decide which flight should be cleared for landing from among the many approaching the airport. The priority of a flight may depend not only on its distance from the runway, but also on the amount of fuel it has left. Choosing the next flight to land may be a life-critical application. There is also the example inside an airport of a standby passenger who has arrived first for a fully booked flight. When she checks in, the gate agent tells her that she is "first" in line. Thus, she thinks she will be given top priority if seats become available. Little does she know that the airline will give first priority to a standby passenger who has arrived later, if such a passenger is given better priority by the gate agent (priority in this context is measured in terms of the fare paid and frequent-flyer status, in addition to check-in time).

In this chapter, we study data structures that store "prioritized elements," that is, elements that have priorities assigned to them. Such a priority is typically a numerical value, and we take the view that the smallest numerical value should have first priority. However, as we show in this chapter, we can support the opposite viewpoint just as easily. More generally, priorities can be viewed as general objects, so long as there is a consistent way of comparing pairs of such objects to see if one is less than or equal to the other. This general viewpoint allows us to define a fairly generic ADT for storing prioritized elements.

A *priority queue* is an abstract data type for storing a collection of prioritized elements that supports arbitrary element insertion but supports removal of elements only in order of priority; that is, only the element with first priority can be removed at any time. This ADT is fundamentally different from the position-based data structures we discuss in previous chapters, such as stacks, queues, deques, sequences, and even trees. These other data structures store elements at specific positions, which are often positions in a linear arrangement of the elements that is determined by the insertion and deletion operations performed. The priority queue ADT stores elements according to their priorities, and has no notion of "position."

We present the priority queue abstract data type in Section 6.1. In Section 6.2, we present two implementations of a priority queue using sequences. These implementations are simple, but unfortunately not very efficient. Even so, these implementations allow us to easily describe two well-known sorting algorithms, insertion-sort and selection-sort, both of which have the same worst-case quadratic time performance as bubble-sort. In Section 6.3, we give a more efficient implementation of a priority queue, based on a concrete data structure known as a *heap*. A heap uses the hierarchical power of binary trees to support all the priority queue operations in logarithmic time, which leads to a fast sorting algorithm known as heap-sort. We conclude this chapter with a discussion of an interesting design pattern, known as the locator, and show how to augment the priority queue ADT to support this pattern.

6.1 The Priority Queue Abstract Data Type

In this section, we provide the framework for studying priority queues, based on the concepts of key and comparator, and we define the methods of a priority queue as an abstract data type (ADT).

6.1.1 Keys, Priorities, and Total Order Relations

Applications commonly require that we perform computations on collections of objects that can be compared and ranked according to a parameter or property that is defined for each object in the collection. We call such a parameter for an object the *key* for that element. The key an application assigns to an element is not necessarily unique, however, and an application may even change an element's key if it needs to. For example, we can compare companies by earnings or by number of employees; hence, either of these parameters can be used as a key for a company, depending on the information we wish to extract. Likewise, we can compare restaurants by a critic's food quality rating or by average entrée price. To achieve the most generality, then, we allow a key to be of any type that is appropriate for a particular application.

In the above examples, the key used for comparisons is often a single numerical value, such as price, length, weight, or speed, but a key is sometimes a more complex property that cannot be quantified with a single number. For example, the priority of standby passengers is usually determined by taking into account a host of different factors, including frequent-flyer status, the fare paid, and check-in time. In some applications, the key for an object is part of the the object itself (for example, it might be an instance variable storing the list price of a book, or the weight of a car). In other applications, the key is not part of the object but the object gets assigned its key by the application (for example, the quality rating given to a stock by a financial analyst, or the priority assigned to a standby passenger by a gate agent). The concept of a key as an arbitrary type is therefore quite general. But, in order to deal consistently with such a general definition for keys and still be able to discuss when one key has priority over another, we need a way of robustly defining a rule for comparing keys.

In particular, a priority queue needs a comparison rule that will never contradict itself. In order for a comparison rule, which we denote by $\leq$, to be robust in this way, it must define a **total order** relation, which is to say that it must satisfy the following properties:

- **Reflexive property**: $k \leq k$.
- **Antisymmetric property**: if $k_1 \leq k_2$ and $k_2 \leq k_1$, then $k_1 = k_2$.
- **Transitive property**: if $k_1 \leq k_2$ and $k_2 \leq k_3$, then $k_1 \leq k_3$.

Any comparison rule, $\leq$, that satisfies these three properties will never lead to a comparison contradiction. In fact, such a rule defines a linear ordering relationship among a set of keys; hence, if a collection of elements has a total order defined for it, then the notion of a **smallest** key, k_{min}, is well-defined as a key in which $k_{min} \leq k$, for any other key k in our collection.

A **priority queue** is a container of elements, each having an associated key that is provided at the time the element is inserted. The name "priority queue" comes from the fact that keys determine the "priority" used to pick elements to be removed. The two fundamental methods of a priority queue P are as follows:

- insertItem(k, e): insert an element e with key k into P.
- removeMinElement(): return and remove from P an element with the smallest key, that is, an element whose key is less than or equal to that of every other element in P.

By the way, some computer scientists refer to the removeMinElement method as the extractMin method, so as to stress that this method simultaneously removes and returns a smallest element in P. There are many applications where the operations insertItem and removeMinElement play an important role. We consider one such application in the example that follows.

Example 6.1: *Suppose a certain flight is fully booked an hour prior to departure. Because of the possibility of cancellations the airline maintains a priority queue of standby passengers hoping to get a seat. The priority of each passenger is determined by the airline taking into account the fare paid, the standby passenger's frequent-flyer status, and the time when the passenger requested to fly standby. A reference to a standby passenger is inserted into the priority queue with an insertItem operation as soon as he or she requests to fly standby. Shortly before the flight departure, if seats become available (for example, due to no-shows or last-minute cancellations), the airline removes from the priority queue a standby passenger with first priority using a removeMinElement operation and lets this person board. This process is then repeated until all available seats have been filled or the priority queue becomes empty.*

6.1.2 Sorting with a Priority Queue

Another important application of a priority queue is sorting, where we are given a sequence S of n elements that can be compared according to a total order relation, and we want to rearrange them in increasing order (or at least in nondecreasing order if there are ties). The algorithm for sorting S with a priority queue Q is quite simple and consists of the following two phases:

1. In the first phase, we put the elements of sequence S into an initially-empty priority queue P by means of a series of n insertItem operations, one for each element.

2. In the second phase, we extract the elements from P in nondecreasing order by means of a series of n removeMinElement operations, putting them back into S in order.

We show the pseudo-code for this algorithm in Code Fragment 6.1. The algorithm works correctly for any priority queue P, no matter how P is implemented. However, the running time of the algorithm is determined by the running times of operations insertItem and removeMinElement, which do depend on how P is implemented. Indeed, PriorityQueueSort should be considered more a sorting "scheme" than a sorting "algorithm" because it does not specify how the priority queue P is implemented. The PriorityQueueSort scheme is the paradigm of several popular sorting algorithms, including selection-sort, insertion-sort, and heap-sort, which we discuss later in this chapter.

Algorithm PriorityQueueSort(S, P):

    Input: A sequence S storing n elements, on which a total order relation is defined, and a priority queue, P, that compares keys using the same total order relation

    Output: The sequence S sorted by the total order relation

    while S is not empty **do**
        $e \leftarrow S.\text{removeFirst}()$ {remove an element e from S}
        $P.\text{insertItem}(e, e)$ {the key is the element itself}
    while Q is not empty **do**
        $e \leftarrow P.\text{removeMinElement}()$ {remove a smallest element from Q}
        $p.\text{insertLast}(e)$ {add the element at the end of S}

Code Fragment 6.1: Algorithm PriorityQueueSort.

6.1.3   Methods of a Priority Queue

Having described the priority queue abstract data type at an intuitive level, we now describe it in more detail. As an ADT, a priority queue P supports the following methods:

size(): Return the number of elements in P.
Input: None; *Output:* Integer.

isEmpty(): Test whether P is empty.
Input: None; *Output:* Boolean.

insertItem(k, e): Insert a new element e with key k into P.
Input: Objects k (key) and e (element); *Output:* None.

minElement(): Return (but do not remove) an element of P with smallest key; an error condition occurs if the priority queue is empty.
Input: None; *Output:* Object (element).

minKey(): Return a smallest key in P; an error condition occurs if the priority queue is empty.
Input: None; *Output:* Object (key).

removeMinElement(): Remove from P and return an element with smallest key; an error condition occurs if the priority queue is empty.
Input: None; *Output:* Object (element).

As mentioned above, the primary methods of the priority queue ADT are the insertItem and removeMinElement operations. The other operations are either secondary query methods (operations minElement and minKey) or are generic container methods (operations size and isEmpty).

One of the interesting aspects of the priority queue ADT, which should now be obvious, is that the priority queue ADT is much simpler than the sequence ADT. This simplicity is due to the fact that elements in a priority queue are inserted and deleted based entirely on their keys, whereas elements are inserted and removed in a sequence based on their positions and ranks. Thus, only one insertion method and one deletion method is needed in the priority queue ADT, whereas the sequence ADT has many different methods for inserting and removing elements. We leave as an exercise the writing of a Java interface for the priority queue ADT. The operations of the priority queue abstract data type are illustrated in the following example.

Example 6.2: *The following table shows a series of operations and their effects on an initially empty priority queue P, where an element e and its key k are indicated by the pair (k,e). The "Contents of P" column is somewhat deceiving since it shows the items sorted by key. This is more than is required of a priority queue. A priority queue need only have the minimum pair available, while storing the remaining pairs in an implementation-dependent manner.*

Operation	*Output*	*Contents of P*
insertItem$(5,A)$	–	$\{(5,A)\}$
insertItem$(9,C)$	–	$\{(5,A),(9,C)\}$
insertItem$(3,B)$	–	$\{(3,B),(5,A),(9,C)\}$
insertItem$(7,D)$	–	$\{(3,B),(5,A),(7,D),(9,C)\}$
minElement$()$	B	$\{(3,B),(5,A),(7,D),(9,C)\}$
minKey$()$	3	$\{(3,B),(5,A),(7,D),(9,C)\}$
removeMinElement$()$	B	$\{(5,A),(7,D),(9,C)\}$
size$()$	3	$\{(5,A),(7,D),(9,C)\}$
removeMinElement$()$	A	$\{(7,D),(9,C)\}$
removeMinElement$()$	D	$\{(9,C)\}$
removeMinElement$()$	C	$\{\}$
removeMinElement$()$	*"error"*	$\{\}$
isEmpty$()$	*true*	$\{\}$

There are still two important issues that we have left undetermined to this point:

- How do we keep track of the associations between keys and elements?
- How do we compare keys so as to determine a smallest key?

Answering these questions involves the use of two interesting design patterns.

6.1.4 Compositions and Comparators

The priority queue ADT implicitly makes use of two design patterns, compositions and comparators, which we discuss in this subsection.

The Composition Pattern

One such pattern is the **composition pattern**. In this pattern, we define a single object *e* that is a composition of other objects. We use this pattern in the priority queue ADT when we define the objects being stored in the priority queue to actually be **pairs**. A pair (k,e) is the simplest composition, for it composes two objects into a single **pair** object. To implement this concept we define a class that stores two objects in its first and second instance variables, respectively, and which provides methods to access and update these variables. We show in Code Fragment 6.2 an example Java implementation of the pair pattern as applied to key-element pairs used in a priority queue. Other kinds of compositions include triples, which store three objects, quadruples, which store four objects, and general compositions, which can store an arbitrary number of objects (using, say, a sequence).

```java
public class Item {
  private Object key, elem;
  protected Item (Object k, Object e) {
    key = k;
    elem = e;
  }
  public Object key() { return key; }
  public Object element() { return elem; }
  public void setKey(Object k) { key = k; }
  public void setElement(Object e) { elem = e; }
}
```

Code Fragment 6.2: Class for the key-element pairs stored in a priority queue.

We can also allow composition objects to store other composition objects as elements, which would give rise to a hierarchical tree relationship defined on compositions, but we will not explore this usage in this book.

The Comparator Pattern

Another important issue in the priority queue ADT that we have so far left undefined is how to specify the relation for comparing keys. We have a number of design choices concerning how to compare keys that we can make at this point.

One possibility, and the one that is the most concrete, is to implement a different priority queue for each key type we want to use and each possible way of comparing keys of such types. The problem with this approach is that it is not very general and it requires that we create a lot of similar code.

An alternative strategy is to require that keys be able to compare themselves to one another. This solution allows us to write a general priority queue class that can store instances of a key class that implements some kind of Comparable interface and encapsulates all the usual comparison methods. This solution is an improvement over the specialized approach, for it allows us to write a single priority queue class that can handle lots of different types of keys. But there are contexts in which this solution is asking too much of the keys, as keys often do not "know" how they ought to be compared. Two examples follow.

Example 6.3: *Given keys* 4 *and* 11 *we have that* $4 \leq 11$ *if the keys are integer objects (to be compared in the usual manner), but* $11 \leq 4$ *if the keys are string objects (to be compared lexicographically).*

Example 6.4: *A geometric algorithm may compare points* p *and* q *in the plane, by their x-coordinate (i.e.,* $p \leq q$ *if* $x(p) \leq x(q)$*), to sort them from left to right, while another algorithm may compare them by their y-coordinate (i.e.,* $p \leq q$ *if* $y(p) \leq y(q)$*), to sort them from bottom to top. In principle, there is nothing pertaining to the concept of a point that says whether points should be compared by x- or y-coordinate. Also, many other ways of comparing points can be defined (for example, we can compare the distances of* p *and* q *from the origin).*

Thus, for the most general and reusable form of a priority queue, we should not rely on the keys to provide their comparison rules. Instead, we use special *comparator* objects that are external to the keys to supply the comparison rules. A comparator is an object that compares two keys. We assume that a priority queue P is given a comparator when P is constructed, and we might also imagine the ability of a priority queue to be given a new comparator if its old one ever becomes "out-of-date." When P needs to compare two keys, it uses the comparator it was given to perform the comparison. Thus, a programmer can write a general priority queue implementation that can work correctly in a wide variety of contexts. Formally, a comparator object provides the following methods, each of which takes two keys and compares them (or reports an error if the keys are incomparable). The methods of the comparator ADT include:

isLessThan(a,b): True if and only if a is less than b.
>*Input:* Pair of objects; *Output:* Boolean.

isLessThanOrEqualTo(a,b): True if and only if a is less than or equal to b.
>*Input:* Pair of objects; *Output:* Boolean.

isEqualTo(a,b): True if and only if a and b are equal.
>*Input:* Pair of objects; *Output:* Boolean.

isGreaterThan(a,b): True if and only if a is greater than b.
>*Input:* Pair of objects; *Output:* Boolean.

isGreaterThanOrEqualTo(a,b): True if and only if a is greater than or equal to b.
>*Input:* Pair of objects; *Output:* Boolean.

isComparable(a): True if and only if a can be compared.
>*Input:* Object; *Output:* Boolean.

We provide an example of a comparator in Java in Code Fragment 6.3.

```java
public class Lexicographic implements Comparator {
  int xa, ya, xb, yb;
  // Comparator for points in the plane with the standard lexicographic order.
  // Assumes a Point2D has getX() and getY() methods returning its coordinates.
  private void getXY(Object a, Object b) {
    if (a == null || b == null)
      throw new InvalidElementException("Null Argument");
    try{
      xa = ((Point2D) a).getX();
      ya = ((Point2D) a).getY();
      xb = ((Point2D) b).getX();
      yb = ((Point2D) b).getY();
    }
    catch (ClassCastException e)
      { throw new InvalidElementException("Argument not a Point2D"); }
  }
  public boolean isLessThan(Object a, Object b) {
    getXY(a, b);
    if (xa == xb)
      return (ya < yb);
    else
      return (xa < xb);
  }
  public boolean isLessThanOrEqualTo(Object a, Object b) {
    getXY(a, b);
    if (xa == xb)
      return (ya <= yb);
    else
      return (xa <= xb);
  }
  public boolean isEqualTo(Object a, Object b) {
    getXY(a, b);
    return (xa == xb) && (ya == yb);
  }
  ...
  public boolean isComparable(Object a){
    if (a==null)
      return false;
    else {
      try{ Point2D p = (Point2D) a; }
      catch (ClassCastException e) { return false; }
      return true;
    }
  }
}
```

Code Fragment 6.3: Portions of a comparator for points in the plane.

The comparator pattern offers a general, dynamic, reusable way to compare objects. This pattern therefore provides us with a powerful tool for constructing a generic priority queue that uses a comparator object to order the elements in the priority queue so as to always be able to find and/or remove the minimum element. In fact, the comparator pattern provides additional functionality to the priority queue, allowing it to be used in applications where we are interested in an element with ***maximum*** key instead of minimum key. By defining our priority queue ADT to use comparator objects to compare elements, we can reuse our minimum-finding priority queue in such applications to find and/or remove maximum elements just by using a "reverse" comparator (which reverses the meaning of the operations $\leq$ and $\geq$ in the normal comparator).

6.2 Implementing a Priority Queue with a Sequence

In this section, we show how to implement a priority queue by storing the elements and keys in a sequence S. (See Chapter 4.3.) We provide two alternative realizations, depending on whether the sequence is kept sorted by keys or not.

6.2.1 Implementation with an Unsorted Sequence

As our first attempt at implementing a priority queue P, let us consider storing the elements of P and their keys in a sequence S. Thus, the elements of S are pairs (k, e), where e is an element of P and k is its key. A simple way of implementing method insertItem(k, e) of P is to add the new pair object $p = (k, e)$ at the end of sequence S, by executing method insertLast(p) on S. This implementation of method insertItem takes $O(1)$ time, independent of whether the sequence is implemented using an array or a linked list (Section 4.3). However, by always inserting at the end of S, the linear arrangement of the elements in S does not take into account the ordering of the keys. As a consequence, to perform operation minElement, minKey, or removeMinElement on P, we must inspect all the elements of sequence S to find an element $p = (k, e)$ of S with minimum k. Thus, no matter how the sequence S is implemented, performing these methods on P takes $O(n)$ time, where n is the number of elements in P at the time the method is executed. Moreover, these methods run in $\Omega(n)$ in the worst case, since they each require that we search the entire sequence to find a minimum element. Thus, in the worst case, these methods run in $\Theta(n)$ time. Finally, we implement methods size and isEmpty by simply returning the output of the corresponding methods executed on sequence S. In summary, by using an unsorted sequence to implement a priority queue, we achieve constant-time insertion, but the removeMinElement operation takes linear time.

6.2.2 Implementation with a Sorted Sequence

An alternative implementation of a priority queue P also uses a sequence S, but keeps S sorted by keys, which means that the first element of S has a smallest key. Thus, we can implement methods minElement and minKey simply by accessing the first element of the sequence with the first method of S. Likewise, we can implement the removeMinElement method of P with the remove method of S on the position returned by first. Assuming that S is implemented with a linked list or an array that supports constant-time front-element removal (Section 4.3), finding and removing the minimum in P takes $O(1)$ time. Thus, using a sorted sequence allows for simple and fast implementations of priority queue access and removal methods.

This benefit comes at a cost, however, for now the method insertItem of P requires that we scan through the sequence S to find the appropriate position to insert the new element and key. Thus, implementing the insertItem method of P now requires $O(n)$ time, where n is the number of elements in P at the time the method is executed. In summary, when using a sorted sequence to implement a priority queue, insertion runs in linear time whereas finding and removing the minimum can be done in constant time.

We show in Code Fragments 6.4 portions of a priority queue implementation that uses a sorted sequence (and the key-element items of Code Fragment 6.2).

Table 6.1 compares the running times of the methods of a priority queue realized by means of a sorted and unsorted sequence, respectively. We see an interesting trade-off when we use a sequence to implement the priority queue ADT. An unsorted sequence allows for fast insertions but slow queries and deletions, while a sorted sequence allows for fast queries and deletions, but slow insertions.

Method	Unsorted Sequence	Sorted Sequence
size, isEmpty	$O(1)$	$O(1)$
insertItem	$O(1)$	$O(n)$
minElement, minKey, removeMinElement	$\Theta(n)$	$O(1)$

Table 6.1: Comparison of the running times of the methods of a priority queue, realized by means of a sorted and unsorted sequence, respectively. We assume that the sequence is in turn implemented by means of an array or a doubly linked list. We use n to denote the number of elements in the priority queue at the time a method is executed. The space requirement is $O(n)$ if the sequence is implemented with a doubly linked list, and $O(N)$ if the sequence is implemented with an array of size $N \geq n$.

```
public class SequenceSimplePriorityQueue implements SimplePriorityQueue {
// Implementation of a priority queue using a sorted sequence
  protected Sequence seq = new NodeSequence();
  protected Comparator comp;
// auxiliary methods
  protected Object extractKey (Position pos) {
    return ((Item)pos.element()).key();
  }
  protected Object extractElem (Position pos) {
    return ((Item)pos.element()).element();
  }
  protected Object extractElem (Object kep) {
    return ((Item)kep).element();
  }
// methods of the SimplePriorityQueue ADT
  public SequenceSimplePriorityQueue (Comparator c) { this.comp = c; }
  public int size () {return seq.size(); }
  public boolean isEmpty () { return seq.isEmpty(); }
  public void insertItem (Object k, Object e) throws InvalidKeyException {
    if (!comp.isComparable(k))
      throw new InvalidKeyException("The key is not valid");
    else
      if (seq.isEmpty())
        seq.insertFirst(new Item(k,e));
      else
        if (comp.isGreaterThan(k,extractKey(seq.last())))
          seq.insertAfter(seq.last(),new Item(k,e));
        else {
          Position curr = seq.first();
          while (comp.isGreaterThan(k,extractKey(curr)))
            curr = seq.after(curr);
          seq.insertBefore(curr,new Item(k,e));
        }
  }
  public Object removeMinElement () throws EmptyContainerException {
    if (seq.isEmpty())
      throw new EmptyContainerException("The priority queue is empty");
    else
      return extractElem(seq.remove(seq.first()));
  }
...
```

Code Fragment 6.4: Portions of the Java implementation of a priority queue by means of a sorted sequence. Class SequenceSimplePriorityQueue implements the interface SimplePriorityQueue, which defines the basic priority queue methods.

6.2.3 Selection-Sort and Insertion-Sort

Recall the PriorityQueueSort scheme introduced in Section 6.1.2. We are given an unsorted sequence S containing n elements, which we sort using a priority queue P in two phases. In phase 1 we insert all the elements, one by one, and in phase 2 we repeatedly remove elements using the removeMinElement operation. In this section we consider two variations of this sorting algorithm.

Selection-Sort

If we implement the priority queue P with an unsorted sequence, then the first phase takes $O(n)$ time, for we can insert each element in constant time. In the second phase, assuming we can compare two keys in constant time, the running time of each removeMinElement operation is proportional to the number of elements currently in P. Thus, the bottleneck computation in this implementation is the repeated "selection" of the minimum element from an unsorted sequence in phase 2. For this reason, this algorithm is better known as ***selection-sort***. (See Figure 6.1.)

		Sequence S	**Priority Queue P**
Input		$(7,4,8,2,5,3,9)$	$()$
Phase 1	(a)	$(4,8,2,5,3,9)$	(7)
	(b)	$(8,2,5,3,9)$	$(7,4)$
	...	...	...
	(g)	$()$	$(7,4,8,2,5,3,9)$
Phase 2	(a)	(2)	$(7,4,8,5,3,9)$
	(b)	$(2,3)$	$(7,4,8,5,9)$
	(c)	$(2,3,4)$	$(7,8,5,9)$
	(d)	$(2,3,4,5)$	$(7,8,9)$
	(e)	$(2,3,4,5,7)$	$(8,9)$
	(f)	$(2,3,4,5,7,8)$	(9)
	(g)	$(2,3,4,5,7,8,9)$	$()$

Figure 6.1: An illustration of selection-sort run on sequence $S = (7,4,8,2,5,3,9)$. This algorithm follows the two-phase PriorityQueueSort scheme and uses a priority queue P implemented by means of an unsorted sequence. In the first phase we repeatedly remove the first element from S and insert it into P (as the last element of the sequence implementing P). Note that at the end of the first phase P is a copy of what was initially S. In the second phase we repeatedly perform removeMinElement operations on P (each of which requires that we scan the entire sequence implementing P) and we add the elements returned at the end of S.

Let us analyze the selection-sort algorithm more carefully. As noted above, the bottleneck is the second phase, where we repeatedly remove an element with smallest key from the priority queue P. The size of P starts at n and incrementally decreases with each removeMinElement until it becomes 0. Thus, the first removeMinElement operation takes time $O(n)$, the second one takes time $O(n-1)$, and so on, until the last (nth) operation takes time $O(1)$. Therefore, the total time need for this second phase takes is

$$O(n + (n-1) + \cdots + 2 + 1) = O\left(\sum_{i=1}^{n} i\right).$$

By Proposition 2.4 we have

$$\sum_{i=1}^{n} i = \frac{n(n+1)}{2}.$$

Thus, the second phase takes time $O(n^2)$ and so does the entire algorithm. That is, the version of the PriorityQueueSort scheme known as selection-sort, where we implement the priority queue P with an unsorted sequence, runs in $O(n^2)$ time.

Insertion-Sort

If we implement the priority queue P using a sorted sequence, then we improve the running time of the second phase to $O(n)$, for each operation removeMinElement on P now takes $O(1)$ time. Unfortunately, the first phase now becomes the bottleneck for the running time. Indeed, in the worst case, the running time of each insertItem operation is proportional to the number of elements that are currently in the priority queue, which starts out having size zero and increases in size until it has size n. The first insertItem operation takes time $O(1)$, the second one takes time $O(2)$, and so on, until the last (nth) operation takes time $O(n)$, in the worst case. Thus, if we use a sorted sequence to implement P, then the first phase becomes the bottleneck phase. This sorting algorithm is therefore better known as *insertion-sort* (see Figure 6.2), for the bottleneck in this sorting algorithm involves the repeated "insertion" of a new element at the appropriate position in a sorted sequence.

Analyzing the running time of phase 1 of insertion-sort, we note that it is

$$O\left(\sum_{i=1}^{n} i\right),$$

in the worst case. Again, by recalling Proposition 2.4, the first phase runs in $O(n^2)$ time, and hence so does the entire algorithm.

In other words, the running time of the PriorityQueueSort scheme implemented with a sorted sequence is $O(n^2)$. Therefore, both selection-sort and insertion-sort have running time $O(n^2)$. That is, their worst-case performance is similar to that of bubble-sort (Section 4.4), which also runs in $O(n^2)$ time.

		sequence S	priority queue P
Input		$(7,4,8,2,5,3,9)$	$()$
Phase 1	(a)	$(4,8,2,5,3,9)$	(7)
	(b)	$(8,2,5,3,9)$	$(4,7)$
	(c)	$(2,5,3,9)$	$(4,7,8)$
	(d)	$(5,3,9)$	$(2,4,7,8)$
	(e)	$(3,9)$	$(2,4,5,7,8)$
	(f)	(9)	$(2,3,4,5,7,8)$
	(g)	$()$	$(2,3,4,5,7,8,9)$
Phase 2	(a)	(2)	$(3,4,5,7,8,9)$
	(b)	$(2,3)$	$(4,5,7,8,9)$
	...	...	...
	(g)	$(2,3,4,5,7,8,9)$	$()$

Figure 6.2: Schematic visualization of the execution of insertion-sort on sequence $S = (7,4,8,2,5,3,9)$. This algorithm follows the two-phase PriorityQueueSort scheme and uses a priority queue P, implemented by means of a sorted sequence. In the first phase, we repeatedly remove the first element of S and insert it into P, by scanning the sequence implementing P, until we find the correct position for the element. In the second phase, we repeatedly perform removeMinElement operations on P, each of which returns the first element of the sequence implementing P, and we add the element at the end of S.

In comparing selection-sort and insertion-sort, we note that selection-sort always takes $\Omega(n^2)$ time, no matter what the input sequence is, for selecting the minimum requires scanning the entire priority-queue sequence in each step of the second phase. The running time of insertion-sort, on the other hand, varies depending on the input sequence. For example, if the input sequence S is in reverse order, then insertion-sort runs in $O(n)$ time, for we are always inserting the next element at the beginning of the priority-queue sequence in the first phase.

Alternately, we could change our definition of insertion-sort so that we insert elements starting from the end of the priority-queue sequence in the first phase, in which case performing insertion sort on a sequence that is already sorted would run in $O(n)$ time. Indeed, the running time of insertion sort in this case is $O(n+I)$, where I is the number of ***inversions*** in the sequence, that is, the number of pairs of elements that start out in the input sequence in the wrong relative order. The number of inversions in a small sequence is relatively small; hence, insertion-sort is fairly efficient for small sequences. Its $O(n^2)$ worst-case performance makes insertion-sort inefficient for sorting large sequences, however.

The two implementations of the PriorityQueueSort scheme presented in this section suggest a possible way of improving the running time for priority-queue sorting. For one algorithm (selection-sort) achieves a fast running time for the first phase, but has a slow second phase, whereas the other algorithm (insertion-sort) has a slow first phase, but achieves a fast running time for the second phase. If we can somehow balance the running times of the two phases, we might be able to significantly speed up the overall running time for sorting. This is, in fact, exactly what we can achieve using the priority-queue implementation discussed in the next section.

6.3 Heaps

An efficient realization of a priority queue uses a data structure called a *heap*. This data structure allows us to perform both insertions and removals in logarithmic time, which is a significant improvement over the sequence-based implementations discussed in Section 6.2. The fundamental way the heap achieves this improvement is to abandon the idea of storing elements and keys in a sequence and take the approach of storing elements and keys in a binary tree instead.

6.3.1 The Heap Data Structure

A heap (see Figure 6.3) is a binary tree T that stores a collection of keys at its internal nodes and that satisfies two additional properties: a relational property defined in terms of the way keys are stored in T and a structural property defined in terms of the nodes of T itself. We assume that a total order relation on the keys is given, for example, by a comparator. Also, note that in our definition of a heap the external nodes of T do not store keys or elements and serve only as "place-holders."

The relational property of T, defined in terms of the way keys are stored, is the following:

Heap-Order Property: In a heap T, for every node v other than the root, the key stored at v is greater than or equal to the key stored at v's parent.

As a consequence of the heap-order property, the keys encountered on a path from the root to an external node of T are in nondecreasing order. Also, a minimum key is always stored at the root of T. This is the most important key and is informally said to be "at the top of the heap;" hence, the name "heap" for the data structure. By the way, the heap data structure defined here has nothing to do with the memory heap (Section 3.2.3) used in the run-time environment supporting a programming language like Java.

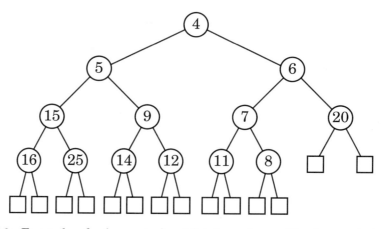

Figure 6.3: Example of a heap storing 13 integer keys. The last node is the one storing key 8.

If we define our comparator to indicate the opposite of the standard total order relation between keys (so that isLessThan$(3,2)$ would, for example, return true), then the root of the heap stores the largest key. This versatility comes essentially "for free" from our use of the comparator pattern. By defining the minimum key in terms of the comparator, we get that the minimum key with a reversing comparator is the largest. Thus, without loss of generality, we assume that we are always interested in the minimum key, which will always be at the root of the heap.

Caution

For the sake of efficiency, as will become clear later, we want the heap T to have as small a height as possible. We can enforce this desire by insisting that the heap T satisfy an additional structural property: it must be **complete**. Recalling that level i of a binary tree T is the set of nodes that have depth i, we can define this structural property as follows:

Complete Binary Tree: A binary tree T with height h is **complete** if the levels $0, 1, 2, \ldots, h-1$ have the maximum number of nodes possible (that is, level i has 2^i nodes, for $0 \leq i \leq h-1$) and in level $h-1$ all the internal nodes are to the left of the external nodes.

By saying that all the internal nodes on level $h-1$ are "to the left" of the external nodes, we mean that all the internal nodes on this level will be visited before any external nodes on this level in any standard tree traversal (for example, an inorder traversal). That is, in a standard drawing of a binary tree, all the internal nodes on level $h-1$ are drawn to the left of any of the external nodes on level $h-1$. (See Figure 6.3.) By insisting that a heap T be complete, we identify another important node in a heap T other than the root, namely, the **last node** of T, which we define to be the right-most, deepest internal node of T. Insisting that T be complete also has an important consequence, as shown in Proposition 6.5.

Proposition 6.5: *A heap T storing n keys has height*
$$h = \lceil \log(n+1) \rceil.$$

Justification: From the fact that T is complete, we know the number of internal nodes of T is at least

$$1 + 2 + 4 + \cdots + 2^{h-2} + 1 = 2^{h-1} - 1 + 1 = 2^{h-1}.$$

This lower bound is achieved when there is only one internal node on level $h - 1$. Alternately, but also following from T being complete, we can say that the number of internal nodes of T is at most

$$1 + 2 + 4 + \cdots + 2^{h-1} = 2^h - 1.$$

This upper bound is achieved when all the 2^{h-1} nodes on level $h - 1$ are internal. Since the number of internal nodes is equal to the number n of keys, we therefore have

$$2^{h-1} \leq n \quad \text{and} \quad n \leq 2^h - 1.$$

Thus, by taking logarithms of both sides of these two inequalities, we obtain

$$\log(n+1) \leq h \leq \log n + 1,$$

which implies that $h = \lceil \log(n+1) \rceil$. ∎

Proposition 6.5 has an important consequence, for it implies that if we can perform update operations on a heap in time proportional to its height, then those operations will run in logarithmic time. Let us therefore turn to the problem of how to efficiently perform various priority queue methods using a heap.

6.3.2 Implementing a Priority Queue with a Heap

In this section, we show how to implement the priority queue ADT using a heap. Our heap-based data structure for a priority queue P consists of the following (see Figure 6.4 and Code Fragment 6.5):

- a heap T, where we store with each internal node v of T an element of the priority queue and the key of that element, denoted $k(v)$ (see Code Fragment 6.2)
- a reference to the position of the last node of T
- a comparator that defines the total order relation among the keys.

We assume that heap T is in turn implemented by means of one of the data structures for binary trees presented in Section 5.4 (either the linked structure or the sequence-based structure). In addition, we assume the elements stored in this binary tree are key-element items, as shown in Code Fragment 6.2.

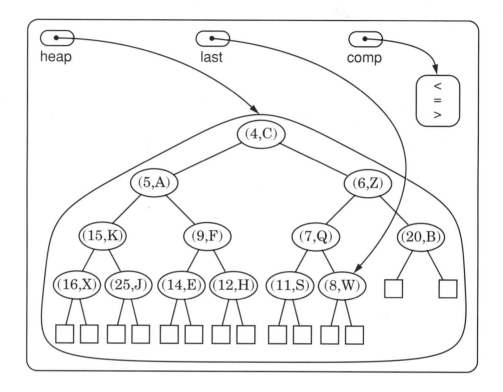

Figure 6.4: Heap-based implementation of a priority queue with integer keys and character elements. Each node of the heap stores a key-element pair. The heap-order property takes only the keys into account and ignores the elements.

public class HeapSimplePriorityQueue **implements** SimplePriorityQueue {

    BinaryTree T;
    Position last;
    Comparator comparator;

      ⋮

    Code Fragment 6.5: Instance variables of a heap implementation.

Because T is a complete binary tree, the sequence associated with heap T in a sequence-based implementation of a binary tree has $2n + 1$ elements, and it has no empty cells.

Insertion

Let us consider how to perform method insertItem of the priority queue ADT using the heap T. The algorithm is illustrated in Figure 6.5. In order to store a new key-element pair (k, e) into T, we need to add a new internal node to T. In order to keep T as a complete binary tree, we must add this new node so that it becomes the new last node of T. That is, we must identify the correct external node z where we can perform an expandExternal(z) operation and insert the new element at z while keeping T complete. (See Figure 6.5a–b.) Node z is called the **insertion position**.

Usually, node z is the external node immediately to the right of the last node w (see Fig. 6.6(b)). However, there are two special cases where this rule does not hold, as follows:

- If the current last node w is defined and is the right-most node on its level, then z is the left-most node of the bottom-most level (see Fig. 6.6(a)).
- If T has no internal nodes (that is, the priority queue is empty and the last node in T is not defined), then z is the root of T.

The details of how to find the insertion position z starting from the last node w will be given shortly. In any event, after performing expandExternal(z), node z becomes the last node, and we store in it the new key-element pair (k, e), so that $k(z) = k$.

After this action, the tree T is complete, but it may violate the heap-order property. Hence, unless node z is the root of T (that is, the priority queue was empty before the insertion), we compare key $k(z)$ with the key $k(u)$ stored at the parent u of z. If $k(u) > k(z)$, then we need to restore the heap-order property, which can be locally achieved by swapping the key-element pairs stored at z and u. (See Figure 6.5c–d.) This swap causes the new key-element pair (k, e) to move up one level. Again, the heap order property may be violated, and we continue swapping going up in T until no violation of heap-order property occurs. (See Figures 6.5e–h.)

The upward movement by means of swaps is conventionally called ***up-heap bubbling***. A swap either resolves the violation of the heap-order property or propagates it one level up in the the heap. In the worst case, up-heap bubbling causes the new key-element pair to move all the way up to the root of heap T. (See Figure 6.5.) Thus, in the worst case, the running time of method insertItem is proportional to the height of T, that is, it is $O(\log n)$ because T is complete.

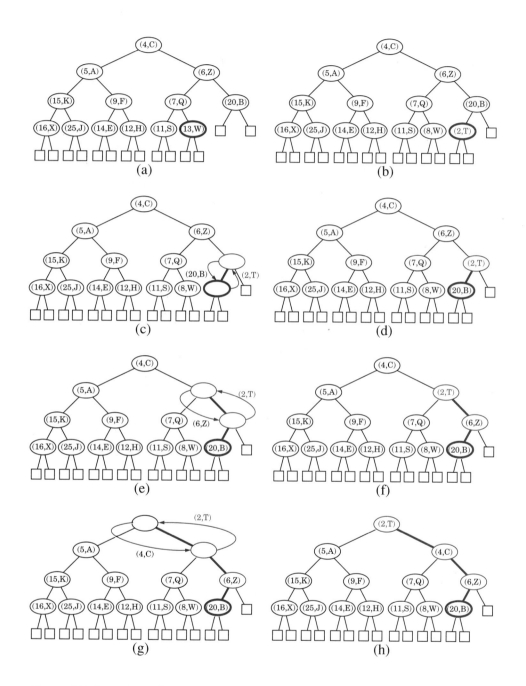

Figure 6.5: Insertion of a new element with key 2 into the heap of Figure 6.4: (a) initial heap; (b) adding a new last node to the right of the old last node; (c–d) swap to locally restore the partial order property; (e–f) another swap; (g–h) final swap.

Finding the Insertion Position

The first step in the insertion algorithm is to find the insertion position z, at which to perform operation expandExternal(z) and store the new key-element pair. If we know that the heap T is implemented using a sequence (Section 5.4.1), then finding the insertion position z is straightforward, since z is the node given number $n + 1$. (Recall Figure 5.16.) This nice property is true both in the general case and in the two special cases previously discussed.

If instead we implement T by means of a linked structure (Section 5.4.2), or if we do not know the implementation of T and we can access T only through the binary tree ADT methods, then finding the insertion position z is not as easy. In the special case where the root of T is an external node, then z is the root of T. Otherwise, starting at the current last node w of T, we identify the insertion position z as follows (see Figure 6.6):

1. Starting at the last node w, go up the tree repeatedly calling method parent until the root or a left child is reached.

    (a) If the root has been reached, let u be the root. This is the special case where the last node is the right-most internal node of its level.

    (b) Otherwise (a left child has been reached), let u be the sibling of the node reached.

2. Starting at u, go down the tree repeatedly calling method leftChild until an external node z is reached.

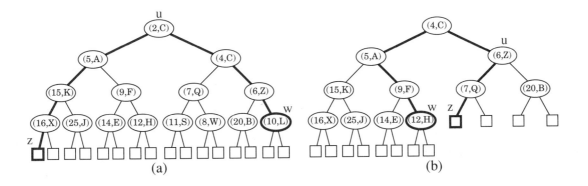

Figure 6.6: Finding the insertion position z in a heap: (a) going up until the root is reached, and then going down leftward; (b) going up until a left child is reached, then moving to the sibling, and finally going down leftward.

In summary, if T is implemented with an array-based sequence, then we can find the new last node z immediately in $O(1)$ time. Otherwise, if the heap T is implemented with a linked structure, we can find z with one march up T followed by another march down T, which takes a total of $O(\log n)$ time. In Code Fragment 6.6, we show how we can use this algorithm to implement method insertItem.

```
public void insertItem(Object k, Object e) throws InvalidKeyException {
  if (!comparator.isComparable(k))
    throw new InvalidKeyException("Invalid Key");
  Position z; // insertion position
  if (isEmpty())
    z = T.root();
  else {
    z = last;
    while (!T.isRoot(z) && !isLeftChild(z))
      z = T.parent(z);
    if (!T.isRoot(z))
      z = T.rightChild(T.parent(z));
    while (!T.isExternal(z))
      z = T.leftChild(z);
  }
  T.expandExternal(z);
  T.replace(z, new KeyElementPair(k, e));
  last = z;
  Position u;
  while (!T.isRoot(z)) { // up-heap bubbling
    u = T.parent(z);
    if (comparator.isLessThanOrEqualTo(keyOfPosition(u),
                                       keyOfPosition(z))) break;
    T.swap(u, z);
    z = u;
  }
}
private Object keyOfPosition(Position p) throws InvalidPositionException {
  return ((KeyElementPair) p.element()).key(); // cast shouldn't fail
}

private boolean isLeftChild(Position p) throws InvalidPositionException {
  try {
    return T.leftChild(T.parent(p)).equals(p);
  } catch (BoundaryViolationException e) {
    return false; // happens when p is the root
  }
}
```

Code Fragment 6.6: Method insertItem and its auxiliary methods.

By "reversing" the procedure for locating the new last node in an insertion, we can update the last node after a removal, which we discuss next.

Removal

Let us now turn to method removeMinElement of the priority queue ADT. The algorithm for performing method removeMinElement using heap T is illustrated in Figure 6.7.

We know that an element with the smallest key is stored at the root r of T. However, unless r is the only internal node of T, we cannot simply delete node r, because this action would disrupt the binary tree structure. Instead, we access the last node w of T, copy its key-element pair to the root r, and then delete the last node by performing operation removeAboveExternal(T.rightChild(w)) of the binary tree ADT. This operation removes w and its right child, and replaces w with its left child. (See Figure 6.7a–b.) After this action, we need to update our reference to the last node, which can be done with the "reverse" of the procedure described in Section 6.3.2.

We are not done, however, for, even though T is still complete, T may now violate the heap order property. To determine whether we need to restore the heap-order property, we examine the root r of T. If both children of r are external nodes, then the heap-order property is trivially satisfied and we are done. Otherwise, we distinguish two cases:

- If the left child of r is internal and the right child is external, let s be the left child of r.
- Otherwise (both children of r are internal), let s be a child of r with the smallest key.

If $k(r) > k(s)$, then we need to restore the heap-order property, which can be locally achieved by swapping the key-element pairs stored at r and s. (See Figure 6.7c–d.) (Note that we shouldn't swap r with s's sibling.) The swap we perform restores the heap order property for node r and its children, but it may violate this property at s; hence, we may have to continue swapping down T until no violation of the heap-order property occurs. (See Figure 6.7e–h.) This downward swapping process is called ***down-heap bubbling***. A swap either resolves the violation of the heap-order property or propagates it one level down in the heap. In the worst case, a key-element pair moves all the way down to the level immediately above the bottom level. (See Figure 6.7.) Thus, the running time of method removeMinElement is, in the worst case, proportional to the height of heap T, that is, it is $O(\log n)$.

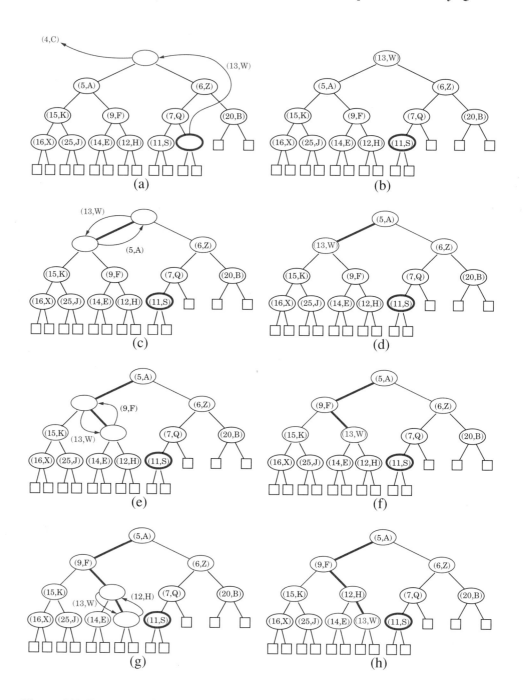

Figure 6.7: Removal of the element with the smallest key from a heap: (a–b) deletion of the last node, whose key-element pair gets stored into the root; (c–d) swap to locally restore the heap-order property; (e–f) another swap; (g–h) final swap.

Analysis

Table 6.2 shows the running time of the priority queue ADT methods for the heap implementation of a priority queue, assuming that the heap T is realized by a data structure for binary trees that supports the binary tree ADT methods (except for elements()) in $O(1)$ time. The linked structure and sequence-based structure from Section 5.4 easily satisfy this requirement.

Operation	Time
size, isEmpty	$O(1)$
minElement, minKey	$O(1)$
insertItem	$O(\log n)$
removeMinElement	$O(\log n)$

Table 6.2: Performance of a priority queue realized by means of a heap, which is in turn implemented with a linked or sequence-based structure for binary trees. We denote with n the number of elements in the priority queue at the time a method is executed. The space requirement is $O(n)$ if the heap is realized with a linked structure, and is $O(N)$ if the heap is realized with a sequence-based structure, where $N \geq n$ is the size of the array used to implement the sequence.

In short, each of the priority queue ADT methods can be performed in $O(1)$ or in $O(\log n)$ time, where n is the number of elements at the time the method is executed. The analysis of the running time of the methods is based on the following:

- The height of heap T is $O(\log n)$, since T is complete.
- In the worst case, up-heap and down-heap bubbling take time proportional to the height of T.
- Finding the insertion position in the execution of insertItem and updating the last node position in the execution of removeMinElement takes, in the worst case, time proportional to twice the height of T.
- The heap T has n internal nodes, each storing a reference to a key and a reference to an element, and $n+1$ external nodes.

We conclude that the heap data structure is a very efficient realization of the priority queue ADT, independent of whether the heap is implemented with a linked structure or a sequence. The heap implementation achieves fast running times for both insertion and removal, unlike the sequence-based priority queue implementations. Indeed, an important consequence of the efficiency of the heap-based implementation is that it can speed up priority-queue sorting to be much faster than the sequence-based insertion-sort and selection-sort algorithms.

6.3.3   Heap-Sort

As we have just observed, realizing a priority queue with a heap has the advantage that all the methods in the priority queue ADT run in logarithmic time or better. Hence, this realization is suitable for applications where fast running times are sought for all the priority queue methods. Therefore, let us again consider the PriorityQueueSort sorting scheme from Section 6.1.2, which uses a priority queue P to sort a sequence S.

If we implement the priority queue P with a heap, then both the first phase (n insertItem operations) and the second phase (n removeMinElement operations) take time $O(\log k)$, where k is the number of elements in the heap at the time. Since we always have $k \le n$, each such operation runs in $O(\log n)$ time in the worst case. Thus, each phase takes $O(n \log n)$ time, so the entire priority-queue sorting algorithm runs in $O(n \log n)$ time when we use a heap to implement the priority queue. This sorting algorithm is better known as ***heap-sort***, and its performance is summarized in the following proposition.

Proposition 6.6:   *The heap-sort algorithm sorts a sequence S of n comparable elements in $O(n \log n)$ time.*

Recalling Table 2.3, we stress that the $O(n \log n)$ running time of heap-sort is considerably better than the $O(n^2)$ running time of bubble-sort (Section 4.4), selection-sort, and insertion-sort (Section 6.2.3).

6.3.4   Bottom-Up Heap Construction ⋆

The analysis of the heap-sort algorithm shows that we can construct a heap storing n key-element pairs in $O(n \log n)$ time, by means of n successive insertItem operations, and then use that heap to extract the elements in order. However, if all the keys to be stored in the heap are given in advance, there is an alternative ***bottom-up*** construction method that runs in $O(n)$ time. We describe this method here, observing that it could be included as one of the constructors in a Heap class. For simplicity of exposition, we describe bottom-up heap construction for the case when the number n of keys is an integer of the type

$$n = 2^h - 1,$$

that is, the heap is a complete binary tree with every level being full. This implies that the heap has height $h = \log(n+1)$.

⋆We use a star (⋆) to indicate sections containing material more advanced than the material in the rest of the chapter; this material can be considered optional in a first reading.

We describe bottom-up heap construction as the recursive algorithm shown in Code Fragment 6.7, which we call by passing a sequence storing the keys for which we wish to build a heap. We describe the construction algorithm as acting on keys, with the understanding that their elements accompany them.

Algorithm BottomUpHeap(S):

> ***Input:*** A sequence S storing $n = 2^h - 1$ keys
> ***Output:*** A heap T storing the keys in S.
>
> **if** S is empty **then**
> > **return** an empty heap (consisting of a single external node).
> Remove the first key, k, from S.
> Split S into two sequences, S_1 and S_2, each of size $(n-1)/2$.
> $T_1 \leftarrow$ BottomUpHeap(S_1)
> $T_2 \leftarrow$ BottomUpHeap(S_2)
> Create binary tree T with root r storing k, left subtree T_1, and right subtree T_2.
> Perform a down-heap bubbling from the root r of T, if necessary.
> **return** T

Code Fragment 6.7: Recursive bottom-up heap construction.

Viewed nonrecursively, bottom-up heap construction consists of the following $h = \log(n+1)$ steps, which are illustrated in the example of Figure 6.8 for $h = 4$:

1. In the first step (see Figure 6.8a), we construct $(n+1)/2$ elementary heaps storing one key each.
2. In the second step (see Figure 6.8b–c), we form $(n+1)/4$ heaps, each storing three keys, by joining pairs of elementary heaps and adding a new key. The new key is placed at the root and may have to be swapped with the key stored at a child to preserve the heap-order property.
3. In the third step (see Figure 6.8d–e), we form $(n+1)/8$ heaps, each storing 7 keys, by joining pairs of 3-key heaps (constructed in the previous step) and adding a new key. The new key is placed initially at the root, but may have to move down with a down-heap bubbling to preserve the heap-order property.

> $\vdots$

i. In the generic ith step, $2 \leq i \leq h$ (see Figure 6.8f–g, where $i = 4$), we form $(n+1)/2^i$ heaps, each storing $2^i - 1$ keys, by joining pairs of heaps storing $(2^{i-1} - 1)$ keys (constructed in the previous step) and adding a new key. The new key is placed initially at the root, but may have to move down with a down-heap bubbling to preserve the heap-order property.

We illustrate bottom-up heap construction in Figure 6.8.

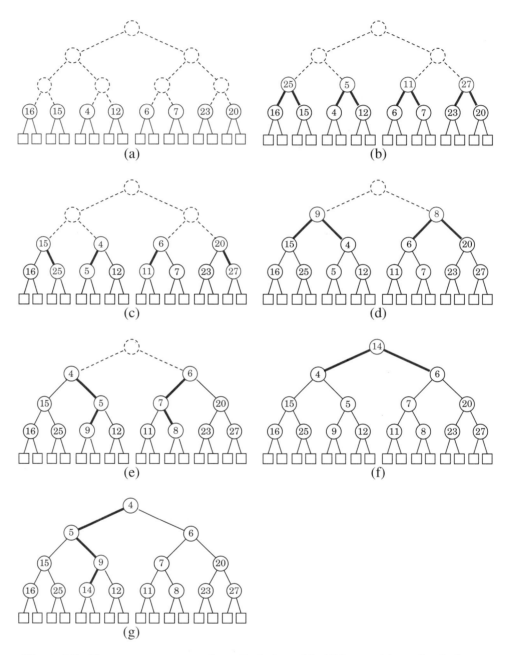

Figure 6.8: Bottom-up construction of a heap with 15 keys: (a) we begin by constructing 1-key heaps on the bottom level, (b–c) we combine these heaps into 3-key heaps and then (d–e) 7-key heaps, until (f–g) we create the final heap. We highlight the paths of the down-heap bubblings.

Bottom-up heap construction is asymptotically faster than incrementally inserting n keys into an initially empty heap, as the following proposition shows.

Proposition 6.7: *Bottom-up heap construction with n keys takes $O(n)$ time.*

Justification: We analyze bottom-up heap construction using a "visual" approach, which is illustrated in Figure 6.9.

Let T be the final heap, let v be an internal node of T, and let $T(v)$ denote the subtree of T rooted at v. In the worst case, the time for forming $T(v)$ from the two recursively formed subtrees rooted at v's children is proportional to the height of $T(v)$. The worst case occurs when down-heap bubbling from v traverses a path from v all the way to a bottom-most external node of $T(v)$. Consider now the path $p(v)$ of T from node v to its inorder successor external node, that is, the path that starts at v, goes to the right child of v, and then goes down leftward until it reaches an external node. We say that path $p(v)$ is ***associated with*** node v. Note that $p(v)$ is not necessarily the path followed by down-heap bubbling when forming $T(v)$. Clearly, the length (number of edges) of $p(v)$ is equal to the height of $T(v)$. Hence, forming $T(v)$ takes time proportional to the length of $p(v)$, in the worst case. Thus, the total running time of bottom-up heap construction is proportional to the sum of the lengths of the paths associated with the internal nodes of T.

Note that for any two internal nodes u and v of T, paths $p(u)$ and $p(v)$ do not share edges, although they may share nodes. (See Figure 6.9.) Therefore, the sum of the lengths of the paths associated with the internal nodes of T is no more than the number of edges of heap T, that is, no more than $2n$. We conclude that the bottom-up construction of heap T takes $O(n)$ time. ∎

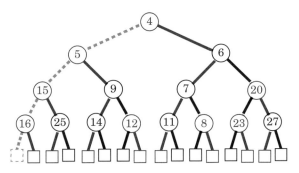

Figure 6.9: Visual justification of the linear running time of bottom-up heap construction, where the paths associated with the internal nodes have been highlighted with alternating colors. For example, the path associated with the root consists of the internal nodes storing keys 4, 6, 7, and 11, plus an external node.

To summarize, Proposition 6.7 states that the running time for the first phase of heap-sort can be reduced to be $O(n)$. Unfortunately, the running time of the second phase of heap-sort cannot be made asymptotically better than $O(n \log n)$ (that is, it will always be $\Omega(n \log n)$ in the worst case). We will not justify this lower bound until Chapter 8, however. Instead, we conclude this chapter by discussing a design pattern that allows us to extend the priority queue ADT to have additional functionality.

6.4   The Locator Design Pattern ★

As we saw with sequences and binary trees, abstracting positional information in a container is a very powerful tool. The position ADT, described in Section 4.2.2, allows us to identify a specific "place" in a container that can store an element. A position can have its element changed, for example, as a consequence of a swap operation, but the position stays the same. In Section 4.4 we gave applications of the position abstraction to implementations of the bubble-sort algorithm.

There are also applications where we need to keep track of elements as they are being moved around inside a positional container, however. For example, suppose we want to remove an element e from a sequence S. The deletion methods of the sequence ADT require that we specify either the position or the rank of e in S. If sequence S is modified by a series of swap operations after the insertion of e, then element e is, in general, at a position and/or rank different from the one it had at the time it was inserted. Thus, in order to perform the deletion of element e, we would have to search for e inside S (spending time proportional to the size of S in the worst case), which is rather inefficient. Instead, we would like to have a mechanism for keeping track of the position of an element in a container.

A design pattern that fulfills this need is the ***locator***. A locator is a mechanism for maintaining the association between an element and its current position in a container. A locator "sticks" with a specific element, even if the element changes its position in the container. A locator is like a coat check; we can give our coat to a coat room attendant, and we receive back a coat check, which is a "locator" for our coat. The position of our coat relative to the other coats can change, as other coats are added and removed, but our coat check can always be used to retrieve our coat. The important thing to remember about a locator is that it follows its item, even if it changes position.

Like a coat check, we can now imagine getting something back when we insert an element in a container—we can get back a locator for that element. This locator in turn can be used later to refer to the element within the container, for example, to specify that this element should be removed from the container. Thus, we can conveniently extend the repertory of operations of a positional container, such as a sequence or a binary tree, with methods that support the locator design pattern. For example, we can define insertion operations that return a locator to the element inserted, and deletion operations that take a locator as an argument.

Another important use of locators is to keep track of the items stored in a container whose operations do not refer to positions, but only to keys and elements, such as a priority queue. Indeed, the locator design pattern provides a generic mechanism for accessing an element, or key-element item, stored in a container in a way that abstracts from the concrete implementation of the container.

As an abstract data type, a locator ℓ supports the following fundamental methods:

> element(): Return the element of the item associated with ℓ.
> **Input:** None; **Output:** Object.
>
> key(): Return the key of the item associated with ℓ.
> **Input:** None; **Output:** Object.
>
> isContained(): Return true if and only if ℓ is associated with a container.
> **Input:** none; **Output:** Boolean.
>
> container(): Return the container associated with ℓ.
> **Input:** None; **Output:** Container.

For the sake of concreteness, we next discuss how we can use locators to extend the repertory of operations of the priority queue ADT to include methods that return locators and take locators as arguments.

6.4.1 Locator-Based Priority Queue Methods

We can use locators in a very natural way in the context of a priority queue. A locator in such a scenario stays attached to an item inserted in the priority queue, and allows us to access the item in a generic manner, independent of the specific implementation of the priority queue. This ability is important for a priority queue implementation, for there are no positions, *per se*, in a priority queue, since we do not refer to items by any notions of "rank," "index," or "node."

Although the implementations of the priority queue ADT that we have seen are based on underlying positional containers (sequences and trees), the position abstraction does not apply to the priority queue itself. Thus, we use locators to provide direct access to the items in a priority queue. A container class can give locators out when items are inserted and accept them as parameters to fast update methods.

By using locators, we can extend the priority queue ADT with the following methods that access and modify a priority queue P:

min(): Return the locator to an item of P with smallest key.
Input: None; *Output:* Locator.

insert(k,e): Insert a new item with element e and key k into P and return a locator to the item.
Input: Objects k (key) and e (element); *Output:* Locator.

remove(ℓ): Remove from P the item with locator ℓ.
Input: Locator; *Output:* None.

replaceElement(ℓ,e): Replace with e and return the element of the item of P with locator ℓ.
Input: Locator, object; *Output:* Object.

replaceKey(ℓ,k): Replace with k and return the key of the item of P with locator ℓ.
Input: Locator, object; *Output:* Object.

Example 6.8: *Consider the following series of locator-based operations and their effects on an initially empty priority queue P, where an item with element e and key k are indicated by the pair (k,e).*

Operation	Output	P
insert($5,A$)	ℓ_1	$\{(5,A)\}$
insert($3,B$)	ℓ_2	$\{(3,B),(5,A)\}$
insert($7,C$)	ℓ_3	$\{(3,B),(5,A),(7,C)\}$
min()	ℓ_2	$\{(3,B),(5,A),(7,C)\}$
key(ℓ_2)	3	$\{(3,B),(5,A),(7,C)\}$
remove(ℓ_1)	A	$\{(3,B),(7,C)\}$
replaceKey($\ell_2,9$)	3	$\{(7,C),(9,B)\}$
key(ℓ_2)	9	$\{(7,C),(9,B)\}$
replaceElement(ℓ_3,D)	C	$\{(7,D),(9,B)\}$
remove(ℓ_2)	B	$\{(7,D)\}$
remove(ℓ_3)	D	$\{\}$

There are several applications in which the above locator-based methods are useful. For example, in a priority queue of standby airline passengers, a passenger with a pessimistic attitude may decide to leave ahead of the boarding time (requiring us to perform operation remove). At the same time, the priority of another passenger may have to be increased (requiring our performing operation replaceKey) after she pulls out her frequent-flyer gold card. If we are maintaining a database of standby passengers, we can implement these removal and replacement methods much faster if we access the items via their locators. The reason that such locator-based lookup methods are more efficient is that, as the implementers of the locators, we can encode in our locators information about our priority-queue implementation that provides for fast lookup. These locator-based lookups are often much faster than lookups using a key value, because key values are provided by the user, whereas we provide the locators. For example, if we implement the priority queue with an unsorted sequence, then the locator for our priority queue can store the position of the item in the sequence. In this case, a locator-based access runs in $O(1)$ time, while a key-based access, which must look for the element via a search in the sequence, runs in $O(n)$ time in the worst case.

Finally, we point out that locator-based methods can be used to implement nonlocator-based container methods. Some of the methods of the priority queue ADT given in Section 6.1.3, for instance, can be expressed by simple combinations of the locator-based methods given above. For example, operation minElement() is equivalent to min().element(), and operation removeMinElement() is equivalent to a combination of remove and min. In addition, some applications call for us to restrict the operation replaceKey so that it only increases or decreases the key. This restriction can be done by defining new methods increaseKey or decreaseKey, for example, which would take a locator as an argument. Further applications of priority queues extended with locator-based methods are given in Chapter 10.

6.4.2 Implementing Locator-Based Priority Queue Methods

We can easily extend the sequence-based and heap-based implementations of a priority queue to support locators. Specifically, we can take advantage of inheritance to implement locators. Recall that sequences and binary trees are positional containers and we can use them to realize the priority queue ADT by storing key-element pairs (that is, items) as their elements. We can realize a locator, therefore, by extending the key-element item of Code Fragment 6.2 to implement the locator ADT and adding as instance variables a position reference and a container reference, as shown in Code Fragment 6.8. With this implementation, the methods of the locator ADT are straightforward to implement, and each take $O(1)$ time. The most significant overhead is that, while the locators automatically stay attached to the items (indeed, they store the items) in this implementation, we must keep track of the positions where items are placed in the sequence or heap. For example, we show such updates in Code Fragments 6.9–6.10 a Java implementation of a priority queue that supports locator-based methods. This implementation is obtained by extending class SequenceSimplePriorityQueue shown in Code Fragment 6.4.

```
public class LocItem extends Item implements Locator {
  private Container cont;
  private Position pos;
  LocItem (Object k, Object e, Position p, Container c) {
    super(k, e);
    pos = p;
    cont = c;
  }
  public boolean isContained() throws InvalidLocatorException {
    return cont != null;
  }
  public Container container() throws InvalidLocatorException { return cont; }
  protected Position position() {return pos; }
  protected void setPosition(Position p) { pos = p; }
  protected void setContainer(Container c) { cont = c; }
}
```

Code Fragment 6.8: Class LocItem realizing locators in the sequence- and heap-based implementations of a priority queue.

In Table 6.3, we compare the running times of the priority queue ADT methods defined in this section and in Section 6.1.3, for the unsorted-sequence, sorted-sequence, and heap implementations. The justification is left as an exercise.

Method	Unsorted Sequence	Sorted Sequence	Heap
size, isEmpty, key, replaceElement	$O(1)$	$O(1)$	$O(1)$
minElement, min, minKey	$O(n)$	$O(1)$	$O(1)$
insertItem, insert	$O(1)$	$O(n)$	$O(\log n)$
removeMinElement	$O(n)$	$O(1)$	$O(\log n)$
remove	$O(1)$	$O(1)$	$O(\log n)$
replaceKey	$O(1)$	$O(n)$	$O(\log n)$

Table 6.3: Comparison of the running times of the priority queue ADT methods for the unsorted sequence, sorted sequence, and heap implementations. We denote with n the number of elements in the priority queue at the time a method is executed.

```java
public class SequenceLocPriorityQueue
  extends SequenceSimplePriorityQueue implements PriorityQueue {
    // priority queue with locators implemented with a sorted sequence
    public SequenceLocPriorityQueue (Comparator comp) { super(comp); }
    // auxiliary methods
    protected Locator locInsert(LocItem locit) throws InvalidKeyException {
      Position p, curr;
      Object k = locit.key();
      if (!comp.isComparable(k))
        throw new InvalidKeyException("The key is not valid");
      else
        if (seq.isEmpty())
          p = seq.insertFirst(locit);
        else if (comp.isGreaterThan(k,extractKey(seq.last())))
          p = seq.insertAfter(seq.last(),locit);
        else {
          curr = seq.first();
          while (comp.isGreaterThan(k,extractKey(curr)))
            curr = seq.after(curr);
          p = seq.insertBefore(curr,locit);
        }
      locit.setPosition(p);
      locit.setContainer(this);
      return (Locator) locit;
    }
    protected LocItem locRemove(Locator loc) {
      checkLocator(loc);
      seq.remove(((LocItem) loc).position());
      ((LocItem) loc).setContainer(null);
      return (LocItem) loc;
    }
```

... continues in Code Fragment 6.10

Code Fragment 6.9: Java implementation of a priority queue supporting locator-based methods by means of a sorted sequence (part 1). Class SequenceLocPriorityQueue extends class SequenceSimplePriorityQueue (Code Fragment 6.4) and implements the Java interface PriorityQueue, which includes the locator-based methods of the priority queue ADT given in Section 6.4.1.

... continued from Code Fragment 6.9

```java
// methods of the PriorityQueue interface
public Locator min () throws EmptyContainerException {
if (seq.isEmpty())
  throw new EmptyContainerException("The priority queue is empty");
else
  return (Locator) seq.first().element();
}
public void insert(Locator loc) throws InvalidKeyException {
  locInsert((LocItem) loc);
}
public Locator insert(Object k, Object e) throws InvalidKeyException {
  LocItem locit = new LocItem(k, e, null, null);
  return locInsert(locit);
}
public void insertItem (Object k, Object e) throws InvalidKeyException {
  insert(k, e);
}
public void remove(Locator loc) throws InvalidLocatorException {
  locRemove(loc);
}
public Object removeMinElement () throws EmptyContainerException {
  Object toReturn = minElement();
  remove(min());
  return toReturn;
}
public Object replaceElement (Locator loc, Object newElement)
  throws InvalidLocatorException {
    checkLocator(loc);
    Object oldElement = ((LocItem) loc).element();
    ((LocItem) loc).setElement(newElement);
    return oldElement;
}
public Object replaceKey(Locator loc, Object newKey)
  throws InvalidLocatorException, InvalidKeyException {
    LocItem locit = locRemove(loc);
    Object oldKey = ((LocItem) loc).key();
    locit.setKey(newKey);
    locInsert(locit);
    return oldKey;
  }
}
```

Code Fragment 6.10: Java implementation of a priority queue supporting locator-based methods by means of a sorted sequence (part 2).

6.5 Exercises

Reinforcement

R-6.1 Although it is correct to use a "reverse" comparator with our priority queue ADT so that we retrieve and remove an element with the maximum key each time, it is confusing to have an element with maximum key returned by a method named "removeMinElement." Write a short adapter class that can take any priority queue P and an associated comparator C and implement a priority queue that concentrates on the element with maximum key, using methods with names like removeMaxElement. (Hint: define a new comparator C' in terms of C.)

R-6.2 Give an example of a worst-case sequence with n elements for insertion-sort, and show that insertion-sort runs in $\Omega(n^2)$ time on such a sequence.

R-6.3 Is there a heap T storing seven distinct elements such that a preorder traversal of T yields the elements of T in sorted order? How about an inorder traversal? How about a postorder traversal?

R-6.4 Consider the numbering of the nodes of a binary tree defined in Section 5.4.1, and show that the insertion position in a heap with n keys is the node with number $n+1$.

R-6.5 Show that the sum

$$\sum_{i=1}^{n} \log i,$$

which appears in the analysis of heap-sort, is $\Omega(n \log n)$.

R-6.6 An airport is developing a computer simulation of air-traffic control that handles events such as landings and takeoffs. Each event has a *time-stamp* that denotes the time when the event occurs. The simulation program needs to efficiently perform the following two fundamental operations:

- Insert a new event with a given time-stamp (that is, add a future event).
- Extract the event with smallest time-stamp (that is, determine the next event to process).

Which data structure would you use to support the above operations? Justify your answer.

R-6.7 Show all the steps of the algorithm for removing key 16 from the heap of Figure 6.3.

R-6.8 Show all the steps of the algorithm for replacing 5 with 18 in the heap of Figure 6.3.

Creativity

C-6.1 An alternative method for finding the insertion position in a heap T is to store in each external node of T a reference to the external node immediately to its right. If such references are in place, then the insertion position is the external node referenced by the right child of the last node. Show how to maintain such references in $O(1)$ time per operation of the priority queue ADT.

C-6.2 Describe in detail the procedure to update the last node of a heap during the execution of method removeMinElement.

C-6.3 We can represent a path from the root to a given node of a binary tree by means of a binary string, where 0 means "go the the left child" and 1 means "go the the right child". For example, the path from the root to the node storing 8 in the heap of Figure 6.3 is represented by the binary string 101. Design a logarithmic-time algorithm for finding the last node of a heap based on the above representation.

C-6.4 Develop an algorithm that computes the kth smallest elements of a sequence of n distinct integers in $O(n + k \log n)$ time.

C-6.5 Tamarindo Airlines has the policy of giving generous rewards to their most loyal customers. In particular, at the end of each year, Tamarindo Airlines gives a booklet of first-class upgrade coupons to their top $\log n$ frequent flyers, and a gift basket full of bananas and coconuts to the next $\sqrt{n}$ frequent flyers, based on the number of miles accumulated that year, where n is the total number of Tamarindo Airlines' frequent flyers. Since Tamarindo Airlines cannot afford an expensive computer, they need the fastest possible algorithm to determine which customers will receive the rewards. The algorithm they currently use first sorts the flyers by the number of miles flown, and then scans the sorted list to pick the top $\log n$ and the next $\sqrt{n}$ flyers. This algorithm has time-complexity $O(n \log n)$. Can you suggest a more efficient algorithm that runs in $O(n)$ time? Describe your algorithm informally and justify its running time.

C-6.6 Let T be a heap storing n keys. Give an efficient algorithm for reporting all the keys in T that are smaller than or equal to a given query key x (which is not necessarily in T). For example, given the heap of Figure 6.3 and query key $x = 7$, the algorithm should report 4, 5, 6, 7. Note that the keys do not need to be reported in sorted order. Ideally, your algorithm should run in $O(k)$ time, where k is the number of keys reported

C-6.7 Show that the following summation, which arises in the analysis of bottom-up heap construction, is $O(1)$ for any positive integer h:

$$\sum_{i=1}^{h} \left(\frac{i}{2^i} \right).$$

C-6.8 Provide a justification of the time bounds in Table 6.3.

Projects

P-6.1 Give a Java implementation of a priority queue based on an unsorted sequence.

P-6.2 Complete the Java implementation of a heap-based priority queue, given in part in Code Fragments 6.5 and 6.6.

P-6.3 Develop a Java implementation of a priority queue that is based on a heap and supports the locator-based methods.

Chapter Notes

Knuth's book on sorting and searching [90] describes the motivation and history for the selection-sort, insertion-sort, and heap-sort algorithms. The heap-sort algorithm is due to Williams [147], and the linear-time heap construction algorithm is due to Floyd [51]. Additional algorithms and analyses for heaps and heap-sort variations can be found in papers by Bentley [22], Carlsson [33], Gonnet and Munro [60], McDiarmid and Reed [106], and Schaffer and Sedgewick [128]. The locator pattern appears to be new.

Chapter

7

Dictionaries

Contents

"Go look it up."

This phrase might be heard when a lazy student requests the definition of a particular word from an equally lazy teacher. This phrase is also the underlying principle behind the ***dictionary*** abstract data type, which we discuss in this chapter.

As the name implies, the primary use of a dictionary is to store elements so that they can be located quickly using keys. The motivation for such searches is that each element in a dictionary typically stores additional useful information besides its search key, but the only way to get at that information is to use the search key. For example, a dictionary may hold bank accounts. Each account is an object that is identified by an account number and stores a wealth of additional information, including the current balance, the name and address of the account holder, and the history of deposits and withdrawals performed. An application wishing to operate on an account would have to provide the account number as a search key to get the account object from the dictionary.

As another example, a dictionary might hold a set of windows open in a graphical interface. The window objects are stored in the dictionary according to some identifier (like a process number), to determine a unique key value, but additional information is stored with each window object, including its dimensions, descriptions of its pull-down menus, its fonts, and its colors. A process wishing to send a message to a particular window object would need to be given a reference to this object, which it could request from the dictionary using the window's ID as a key.

Like a priority queue, a dictionary is a container of key-element pairs. However, although a total order relation on the keys is always required for a priority queue, it is optional for a dictionary. Indeed, the simplest form of a dictionary only assumes that we can determine whether two keys are equal. When a total order relation on the keys is actually defined, then we can talk about an ***ordered dictionary***, and we can specify additional ADT methods that refer to the ordering of the keys in such cases.

A computer dictionary is similar to a paper dictionary of words in the sense that both are used to look things up. The paper dictionary metaphor is not fully appropriate, however, for we typically desire a computer dictionary to be dynamic, so as to support element insertion and removal. Thus, the dictionary abstract data type has methods for the insertion, removal, and searching of elements with keys.

In this chapter, we describe several different techniques for realizing dictionaries. We show, for example, how to realize dictionaries using sequences and binary search trees. These implementations are simple, but they are not very efficient. So we introduce AVL trees and skip lists, in Sections 7.4 and 7.5, showing how these data structures can be used to realize ordered dictionaries with logarithmic-time query and update times. Incidentally, we discuss other data structures for achieving logarithmic-time dictionary-operation performance in Chapter 13, including

$(2,4)$ trees, red-black trees, and splay trees; some readers may wish to complement their reading of Sections 7.4 and 7.5 with sections from Chapter 13. In Section 7.6, we introduce hash tables and show how they can be used to realize unordered dictionaries with constant expected-time performance for queries and updates. We conclude the chapter with Section 7.7, which discusses how the locator pattern presented in the previous chapter can be used to expand the collection of methods that are included in the dictionary ADT. As with the priority queue, this expansion provides additional functionality for a dictionary.

7.1   The Dictionary Abstract Data Type

A dictionary stores key-element pairs (k, e), which we call ***items***, where k is the key and e is the element. In order to achieve the highest level of generality, we allow both the keys and the elements stored in a dictionary to be of any object type. For example, in a dictionary storing student records (such as the student's name, address, and course grades), the key might be the student's ID number. In some applications, the key may be the element itself. For example, if we had a dictionary storing prime numbers, we could use the numbers themselves as keys (and also as the elements).

We distinguish two types of dictionaries, the ***unordered dictionary*** and the ***ordered dictionary***. In the ordered dictionary we assume that a total order relation is defined on the keys, and we provide additional methods that refer to this ordering. An ordered dictionary determines the relative order of two keys by means of a comparator (see Section 6.1.4), which is provided to the dictionary as a parameter of the ordered dictionary constructor's method. In an unordered (generic) dictionary, however, no order relation is assumed on the keys, and only equality testing between keys is used. Likewise, the methods included in the abstract data type of the unordered dictionary form a proper subset of those included in the ordered dictionary ADT.

For the sake of generality, our definition allows a dictionary to store multiple items with the same key. Nevertheless, there may be applications in which we want to disallow items with the same key (for example, in a dictionary storing student records, we would probably want to disallow two students having the same ID). In such cases when keys are unique, then the key associated with an object is viewed as an "address" for that object in memory. Indeed, such dictionaries are sometimes referred to as "associative stores," for the key associated with an object determines where it belongs in the dictionary.

7.1.1   Methods of a Dictionary

As an abstract data type, a generic unordered dictionary D supports the following operations:

size(): Return the number of items in D.
Input: None; *Output:* Integer.

isEmpty(): Test whether D is empty.
Input: None; *Output:* Boolean.

findElement(k): If D contains an item with key equal to k, then return the element of such an item, else (there is no item with key equal to k in D) return a special element NO_SUCH_KEY to denote that the search was unsuccessful.
Input: Object (key); *Output:* Object (element).

findAllElements(k): Return an enumeration of all the elements in D with key equal to k.
Input: Object (key); *Output:* Enumeration (of elements).

insertItem(k, e): Insert an item with element e and key k into D.
Input: Objects k (key) and e (element); *Output:* None.

remove(k): Remove from D an item with key equal to k, and return its element. If D has no such item, then return the special element NO_SUCH_KEY.
Input: Object (key); *Output:* Object (element).

removeAll(k): Remove from D the items with key equal to k, and return an enumeration of their elements.
Input: Object (key); *Output:* Enumeration (of elements).

When operations findElement(k) and remove(k) are unsuccessful (i.e., the dictionary D has no item with key equal to k), we use the convention of returning a special element NO_SUCH_KEY. Such a special element is known as a ***sentinel***. We could have used the alternative convention of returning a null element, but this would prevent us from storing in D an item whose element is null. Another choice, of course, would be to throw an exception when someone requests a key that is not in our dictionary. This would probably not be an appropriate use of an exception, however, since it is normal to ask for something that might not be in our dictionary. Moreover, throwing and catching an exception is typically slower than a test against a sentinel; hence, using a sentinel is more efficient (and in this case more conceptually correct).

Note that, as we have defined it, a dictionary D can contain different items with equal keys. In this case, operations findElement(k) and remove(k) return an *arbitrary* element whose associated key is equal to k. Also, if we wish to store an item e in a dictionary, so that the item is itself its own key, then we would insert e using a call D.insertItem(e, e).

Example 7.1: *In the following, we show the effect of a series of operations on an initially empty dictionary storing integer keys and single-character elements.*

Operation	Output	Dictionary
insertItem$(5, A)$		$\{(5,A)\}$
insertItem$(7, B)$		$\{(5,A),(7,B)\}$
insertItem$(2, C)$		$\{(5,A),(7,B),(2,C)\}$
insertItem$(8, D)$		$\{(5,A),(7,B),(2,C),(8,D)\}$
insertItem$(2, E)$		$\{(5,A),(7,B),(2,C),(8,D),(2,E)\}$
findElement(7)	B	$\{(5,A),(7,B),(2,C),(8,D),(2,E)\}$
findElement(4)	NO_SUCH_KEY	$\{(5,A),(7,B),(2,C),(8,D),(2,E)\}$
findElement(2)	C	$\{(5,A),(7,B),(2,C),(8,D),(2,E)\}$
findAllElements(2)	C, E	$\{(5,A),(7,B),(2,C),(8,D),(2,E)\}$
size$()$	5	$\{(5,A),(7,B),(2,C),(8,D),(2,E)\}$
remove(5)	A	$\{(7,B),(2,C),(8,D),(2,E)\}$
removeAll(2)	C, E	$\{(7,B),(8,D)\}$
findElement(2)	NO_SUCH_KEY	$\{(7,B),(8,D)\}$

7.1.2 Equality Testers

Each of the standard dictionary operations given above requires that we have a mechanism for deciding whether two keys are equal. If the dictionary is ordered, then the areEqual method of the comparator (Section 6.1.4) associated with the dictionary serves the purpose. Otherwise, for a generic dictionary, we shall use an *equality tester* object that supports the operation areEqual on keys.

A comparator can be viewed as an extension of an equality tester, and can be used in lieu of an equality tester for an ordered dictionary. When a dictionary is instantiated, we associate with it an equality tester or a comparator, so that checking whether two keys are equal is a well-defined concept.

Beyond the Standard Java Dictionary

Our definition of a dictionary is more general than the standard Java abstract class java.util.Dictionary. Namely, a java.util.Dictionary does not allow multiple items with the same key, and uses method equals, supported by any Java object, to decide whether two keys are equal. Thus, if we use a java.util.Dictionary, we must "hard-code" an equality testing method within each key. This approach is not flexible, however, since there are contexts in which keys do not "know" when they are equal. For example, a geometric algorithm may consider points as "equal" if they have the same *x*-coordinate, while another algorithm may consider them equal if they have the same *y*-coordinate. (See the related discussion in Section 6.1.4.) A dictionary *D* could be provided an equality tester (or even a comparator) when *D* is created. Moreover, if *D* is not provided with an equality tester, we should include as our default tester an object that simply uses the built-in equals method to test if objects are equal. Thus, an equality tester provides a general, reusable, and adaptive way of testing for object equality.

Methods of an Ordered Dictionary

As mentioned above, an ordered dictionary can use a comparator to order its elements, and, as we will see, use such an ordering to efficiently implement the dictionary ADT. In addition, an ordered dictionary also supports the following methods beyond those included in the generic dictionary ADT:

closestKeyBefore(k): Return the key of the item with largest key less than or equal to k.
Input: Object (key); *Output:* Object (key).

closestElemBefore(k): Return the element for the item with largest key less than or equal to k.
Input: Object (key); *Output:* Object (element).

closestKeyAfter(k): Return the key of the item with smallest key greater than or equal to k.
Input: Object (key); *Output:* Object (key).

closestElemAfter(k): Return the element for the item with smallest key greater than or equal to k.
Input: Object (key); *Output:* Object (element).

Each of these methods returns the special NO_SUCH_KEY object if no item in the dictionary satisfies the query.

Having defined the dictionary abstract data type, let us now discuss different ways of implementing this ADT, pointing out the strengths and weaknesses of each approach.

7.2   Implementing a Dictionary with a Sequence

One simple way of realizing a dictionary uses a sequence. (See Chapter 4.) Such an implementation is simple but, as we will see, is not necessarily the most efficient.

7.2.1   Unordered and Ordered Sequences

There are actually several ways to realize a dictionary using a sequence.

Unordered Sequence Implementation

The simplest way to implement a dictionary D with n items using a sequence S is to store the items of D into S in arbitrary order. (See Figure 7.1a.) We assume, in turn, that S is implemented with either an array or a doubly-linked list (see Section 4.3). We refer to this implementation of D as the ***unordered sequence implementation***, since the keys have no influence on the linear arrangement of the items in S.

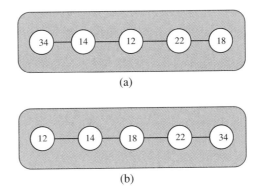

(a)

(b)

Figure 7.1: Realization of a dictionary D by means of a sequence: (a) unordered sequence implementation; (b) ordered sequence implementation. For simplicity, we show the integer keys stored in D but not their associated elements.

The space requirement of the unordered sequence implementation is $\Theta(n)$ if the sequence is implemented with a doubly linked list, and $\Theta(N)$ if the sequence is implemented with an array of size $N \geq n$.

With the unordered sequence implementation, we can realize operation insertItem(k,e) easily and efficiently, by a single call to the insertFirst or insertLast method on S, thus obtaining $O(1)$ running time for the insertItem(k,e) operation on D. Unfortunately, this implementation does not allow for an efficient execution of the findElement method. A findElement(k) operation must be performed by scanning through the sequence S, examining each of its items (for example, iteratively using the after sequence operation) until we either find an item with key equal to k or reach the end of the sequence. The worst case for the running time of this method clearly occurs when the search is unsuccessful, and we reach the end of the sequence having examined all of its n items. Thus, the findElement method runs in $O(n)$ time. A linear amount of time is needed in the worst case to perform a remove(k) operation on D as well, for in order to remove an item with a given key, we must first find it by scanning through sequence S. Operations findAllElements and removeAll always require scanning the entire sequence S, and hence their running time is $\Theta(n)$.

In conclusion, implementing a dictionary with an unordered sequence provides for fast insertions, but at the expense of slow searches and removals. Thus, it is appropriate for us to use this implementation only in situations where we either expect the dictionary to always be very small or we expect the number of insertions to be very large relative to the number of searches and removals.

Ordered Sequence Implementation

If the dictionary D is ordered, we can store its items in a sequence S by nondecreasing order of the keys. (See Figure 7.1b.) Again, we assume that S is implemented with either an array or a doubly linked list (Section 4.3). We refer to this implementation of D as the ***ordered sequence implementation***, since the keys determine the linear arrangement of the items in S.

As with the unordered sequence implementation, the space requirement of the unordered sequence implementation is $\Theta(n)$ if the sequence is implemented with a doubly linked list, and is $\Theta(N)$ if the sequence is implemented with an array of size $N \geq n$.

Unlike the unordered sequence implementation, operation insertItem(k,e) now requires $O(n)$ time in the worst case. Indeed, if S is implemented with a doubly linked list, it takes this long in the worst case just to find the place to insert the new item (k,e), and if S is implemented using an array, it takes this long in the worst case to shift all the items in the array with key greater than k to make room for the new item (k,e).

Similar observations apply to operations remove(k) and removeAll(k). If S is implemented with a doubly linked list, then it takes $O(n)$ time in the worst case just to find the item (or items) to remove, and if S is implemented using an array, it takes this long in the worst case to shift all the items in the array with key greater than k to close the "hole" left by the removed item (or items).

The ordered sequence implementation is inferior to the unordered sequence implementation in terms of the worst-case running times of the fundamental dictionary operations. If the sequence S is implemented with a doubly linked list, then searching for an item with key k requires a scan through the sequence and takes $O(n)$ time in the worst case (unsuccessful search). Thus, operations findElement and findAllElements run in $O(n)$ time, as does any operation must first perform a search for an item with key k. Therefore, realizing an ordered dictionary with an ordered sequence implemented with a doubly linked list is inefficient. As we show next, we can perform the operations findElement and findAllElements much faster if the sequence S is implemented by means of an array.

7.2.2 Binary Search

A significant advantage of using an array-based sequence S to implement an ordered dictionary D with n items is that accessing an element of S by its **rank** takes $O(1)$ time. We recall from Section 4.1 that the rank of an element in a sequence is the number of elements preceding it. Thus, the first element has rank 0 and the last element has rank $n-1$.

The elements of the sequence S are the items of dictionary D, and since S is ordered according to the keys, the item of S at rank i has a key that is no smaller than the keys of the items at ranks $0, \ldots, i-1$ and no larger than the keys of the items at ranks $i+1, \ldots, n-1$. This observation will allow us to significantly speed up the execution of the findElement(k) method. Specifically, instead of scanning through sequence S in search of an item with key k, we can quickly "home in" on such an item using a variant of the children's game "high-low." Let us call an item of D a **candidate** if, at the current stage of the search, we have not ruled out that it has key equal to k. The main idea of the algorithm is to maintain two parameters, low and high, such that all the candidate items in the dictionary have rank at least low and at most high in sequence S.

Initially, low $= 0$ and high $= n-1$. We then compare k to the key of the "middle item" of S, that is, the item with rank

$$\text{mid} = \lfloor (\text{low} + \text{high})/2 \rfloor.$$

Let us denote with key(mid) the key of the middle item and with elem(mid) the element of the middle item. We consider three cases:

- If $k =$ key(mid), then we have found the item we were looking for, and the search terminates successfully returning elem(mid).
- If $k <$ key(mid), then we recurse on the first half of the sequence, that is, on the range of ranks from low to mid $- 1$.
- If $k >$ key(mid), we recurse on the range of ranks from mid $+ 1$ to high.

The above search technique is called **binary search**. We give a pseudo-code description of binary search in Code Fragment 7.1, and illustrate it in Figure 7.2.

Algorithm BinarySearch($S, k,$ low, high):

    Input: A sequence S storing n items in nondecreasing order of the keys, a search key k, and integers low and high

    Output: An element of S with key k and rank between low and high, if such an element exists, and otherwise the special element NO_SUCH_KEY

    if low $>$ high **then**

        return NO_SUCH_KEY

    else

        mid $\leftarrow \lfloor (\text{low} + \text{high})/2 \rfloor$

        if $k = \text{key}(\text{mid})$ **then**

            return elem(mid)

        else if $k < \text{key}(\text{mid})$ **then**

            return BinarySearch($S, k,$ low, mid $- 1$)

        else

            return BinarySearch($S, k,$ mid $+ 1,$ high)

Code Fragment 7.1: Binary search in an ordered sequence.

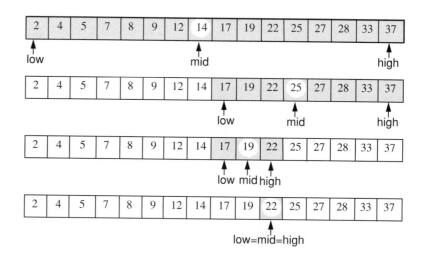

Figure 7.2: Example of a binary search to perform operation findElement(22), in a dictionary with integer keys, implemented with an array-based ordered sequence. For simplicity, we show the keys stored in the dictionary but not the elements.

Operation findElement(k) on an n-item dictionary implemented with an array-based sequence S consists of calling BinarySearch($S,k,0,n-1$).

To characterize the running time of binary search, we observe that a constant number of primitive operations are executed at each recursive call of method BinarySearch. Hence, the running time is proportional to the number of recursive calls performed. A crucial fact is that with each recursive call the number of candidate items still to be searched in the sequence S is given by the value

$$\text{high} - \text{low} + 1.$$

Moreover, the number of remaining candidates is reduced by at least one half with each recursive call. Specifically, from the definition of mid the number of remaining candidates is either

$$(\text{mid} - 1) - \text{low} + 1 = \left\lfloor \frac{\text{low} + \text{high}}{2} \right\rfloor - \text{low} \leq \frac{\text{high} - \text{low} + 1}{2}$$

or

$$\text{high} - (\text{mid} + 1) + 1 = \text{high} - \left\lfloor \frac{\text{low} + \text{high}}{2} \right\rfloor \leq \frac{\text{high} - \text{low} + 1}{2}.$$

Initially, the number of candidate items is n; after the first call to BinarySearch, it is at most $n/2$, after the second call, it is at most $n/4$, and so on. In general, after the ith call to BinarySearch, the number of candidate items remaining is at most $n/2^i$. In the worst case (unsuccessful search), the recursive calls stop when there are no more candidate items. Hence, the maximum number of recursive calls performed, is the smallest integer m such that

$$n/2^m < 1.$$

In other words (recalling that we omit a logarithm's base when it is 2),

$$m > \log n.$$

Thus, we have

$$m = \lfloor \log n \rfloor + 1,$$

which implies that BinarySearch($S,k,0,n-1$), and hence method findElement runs in $O(\log n)$ time.

There is a simple variation of binary search that performs findAllElements(k) in time $O(\log n + s)$, where s is the number of elements in the enumeration returned. The details are left as an exercise.

Table 7.1 compares the running times of the methods of a dictionary realized by an unsorted sequence (implemented with either a doubly linked list or an array), a sorted sequence implemented with an array, and a sorted sequence implemented with a doubly linked list. An unsorted sequence allows for fast insertions but slow searches and removals, while a sorted array-based sequence allows for fast searches but slow insertions and removals. A sorted sequence based on a doubly linked list is slow in performing all the operations.

Method	Unsorted Sequence		Sorted Sequence	
	Array	**Doubly Linked List**	**Array**	**Doubly Linked List**
size, isEmpty	$\Theta(1)$	$\Theta(1)$	$\Theta(1)$	$\Theta(1)$
findElement	$O(n)$	$O(n)$	$O(\log n)$	$O(n)$
findAllElements	$\Theta(n)$	$\Theta(n)$	$O(\log n + s)$	$O(n)$
insertItem	$\Theta(1)$	$\Theta(1)$	$O(n)$	$O(n)$
remove	$O(n)$	$O(n)$	$O(n)$	$O(n)$
removeAll	$\Theta(n)$	$\Theta(n)$	$O(n)$	$O(n)$

Table 7.1: Comparison of the running times of the methods of a dictionary realized by means of a sorted and unsorted sequence. We assume that the sequence is in turn implemented by means of an array or a doubly linked list. We denote with n the number of items in the dictionary at the time a method is executed, and with s the size of the enumeration returned by operations findAllElements and removeAll. The space requirement is $O(n)$ if the sequence is implemented with a doubly linked list, and is $O(N)$ if the sequence is implemented with an array of size $N \geq n$.

7.3 Binary Search Trees

Binary trees are an alternative data structure for storing the items of an ordered dictionary. As we have seen in Section 5.3.3, a ***binary search tree*** is a binary tree T such that each internal node v of T stores an item (k,e) of D, and

- Keys stored at nodes in the left subtree of v are less than or equal to k.
- Keys stored at nodes in the right subtree of v are greater than or equal to k.

Note that the external nodes of T do not store any key or element of D, and serve only as "placeholders." It is easy to verify that an inorder traversal (Section 5.3.3) of T visits the keys in nondecreasing order. (See Figure 7.3a.)

7.3.1 Search

To perform operation findElement(k) in a dictionary D represented with a binary search tree T we view the tree T as a decision tree (recall Figure 5.5), where the question asked at each internal node v of T is whether the search key k is less than, equal to, or greater than the key, key(v), stored at node v. If the answer is "smaller," then the search continues in the left subtree. If the answer is "equal," then the search terminates successfully. If the answer is "greater," then the search continues in the right subtree. Finally, if we reach an external node, then the search terminates unsuccessfully. (See Figure 7.3b.)

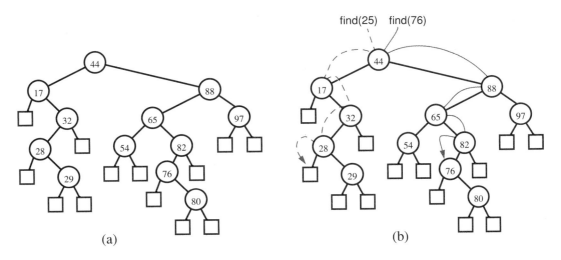

Figure 7.3: (a) A binary search tree T representing an ordered dictionary D with integer keys; (b) nodes of T visited when executing operations findElement(76) (successful) and findElement(25) (unsuccessful) on D. For simplicity, we show the keys but not the elements of D and refer to findElement as "find."

In Code Fragment 7.2, we give a recursive method TreeSearch, based on the above strategy for searching in a binary search tree T. Given a search key k and a node v of T, method TreeSearch returns a node (position) w of the subtree $T(v)$ of T rooted at v such that one of the following two cases occurs:

- w is an internal node of $T(v)$ that stores key k.
- w is an external node of $T(v)$, all the internal nodes of $T(v)$ that precede w in the inorder traversal have keys smaller than k, and all the internal nodes of $T(v)$ that follow w in the inorder traversal have keys greater than k.

Thus, method findElement(k) can be performed on dictionary D by calling the method TreeSearch($k, T.\text{root}()$) on T. Let w be the node of T returned by this call of the TreeSearch method. If node w is internal, we return the element stored at w from this call of the findElement method. Otherwise, if w is external, then we let findElement return the special element NO_SUCH_KEY.

The analysis of the worst-case running time of searching in a binary search tree T is simple. Algorithm TreeSearch is recursive and executes a constant number of primitive operations for each recursive call. Each recursive call of TreeSearch is on a child of the previous node. Hence, TreeSearch is called on the nodes of a path of T, and the number of such nodes is bounded by $h+1$, where h is the height of T. Thus, method findElement on dictionary D runs in $O(h)$ time, where h is the height of the binary search tree T used to implement D.

Algorithm TreeSearch(k, v):

   Input: A search key k, and a node v of a binary search tree T

   Output: A node w of the subtree $T(v)$ of T rooted at v, such that either w is an internal node storing key k or w is the external node encountered in the inorder traversal of $T(v)$ after all the internal nodes with keys smaller than k and before all the internal nodes with keys greater than k

   if v is an external node **then**
       return v
   if $k = \text{key}(v)$ **then**
       return v
   else if $k < \text{key}(v)$ **then**
       return TreeSearch($k, T.\text{leftChild}(v)$)
   else
       $\{$we know $k > \text{key}(v)\}$
       return TreeSearch($k, T.\text{rightChild}(v)$)

Code Fragment 7.2: Recursive search in a binary search tree.

We can also show that a variation of the above algorithm performs operation findAllElements(k) in time $O(h + s)$, where s is the number of elements in the enumeration returned. However, this method is slightly more complicated, and the details are left as an exercise.

Admittedly, the height h of T can be as large as n, but we expect that it is usually much smaller. Indeed, we will show in Section 7.4 how to maintain an upper bound of $O(\log n)$ on the height of a search tree T. Before we describe such a scheme, however, let us describe implementations for the update operations in the dictionary ADT.

7.3.2 Update Operations

Binary search trees support implementations of the insertItem and remove operations using algorithms that are slightly more complicated than those for a sequence implementation.

Insertion

To perform the operation insertItem(k, e) on a dictionary D implemented with a binary search tree T, we start by calling the method TreeSearch($k, T.\text{root}()$) on T. Let w be the node returned by TreeSearch.

- If w is an external node (no item with key k is stored in T), we replace w with a new internal node storing the item (k,e) and two external children, by means of operation expandExternal(w) on T. Note that this is the appropriate place to insert key k because of the property satisfied by the external node returned by TreeSearch.

- If w is an internal node (another item with key k is stored at w), we call TreeSearch(k, rightChild(w)) and recursively apply the algorithm to the node returned by TreeSearch.

The above insertion algorithm eventually traces a path from the root of T down to an external node, which gets replaced with an internal node accommodating the new item. Hence, an insertion adds the new item at the "bottom" of the search tree T. An example of insertion into a binary search tree is shown in Figure 7.4.

The analysis of the insertion algorithm is analogous to that of the search algorithm. We spend $O(1)$ time at each node visited, and, in the worst case, the number of nodes visited is proportional to the height h of T. Thus, in a dictionary D implemented with a binary search tree T, the method findElement runs in $O(h)$ time, where h is the height of T.

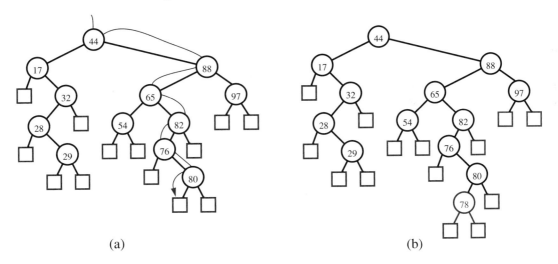

(a)   (b)

Figure 7.4: Insertion of an element with key 78 into the binary search tree of Figure 7.3. Finding the position to insert is shown in (a), and the resulting tree is shown in (b).

Removal

The implementation of the remove(k) operation on a dictionary D implemented with a binary search tree T is a bit more complex, since we do not wish to create any "holes" in the tree T. The operation starts out simple enough, since we begin by executing algorithm TreeSearch(k, T.root()) on T to find a node storing key k. If TreeSearch returns an external node, then there is no element with key k in dictionary D, and we return the special element NO_SUCH_KEY. If instead TreeSearch returns an internal node w, then w stores an item we wish to remove.

We distinguish two cases (of increasing difficulty):

- If one of the children of node w is an external node, say node z, we simply remove w and z from T by means of operation removeAboveExternal(z) on T. This operation restructures T by replacing w with the sibling of z, removing both w and z from T. This case is illustrated in Figure 7.5.
- If both children of node w are internal nodes, we cannot simply remove the node w from T, since this would create a "hole" in T. Instead, we proceed as follows (see Figure 7.6):
  - We find the first internal node y that follows w in the inorder traversal of T. Node y is the left-most internal node in the right subtree of w, and can be found by going first to the right child of w and then down T from there, following left children. Also, the left child x of y is the external node that immediately follows node w in the inorder traversal of T.
  - We save the element stored at w in a temporary variable t, and move the item of y into w. This action has the effect of removing the former item stored at w.
  - We remove nodes x and y from T by means of operation removeAboveExternal(x) on T. This action replaces y with x's sibling, and removes both x and y from T.
  - We return the element previously stored at w, which we had saved in the temporary variable t.

The analysis of the removal algorithm is analogous to that of the insertion and search algorithms. We spend $O(1)$ time at each node visited, and, in the worst case, the number of nodes visited is proportional to the height h of T. Thus, in a dictionary D implemented with a binary search tree T the remove method runs in $O(h)$ time, where h is the height of T.

We can also show that a variation of the above algorithm performs operation removeAll(k) in time $O(h + s)$, where s is the number of elements in the enumeration returned. The details are left for a (somewhat difficult) exercise.

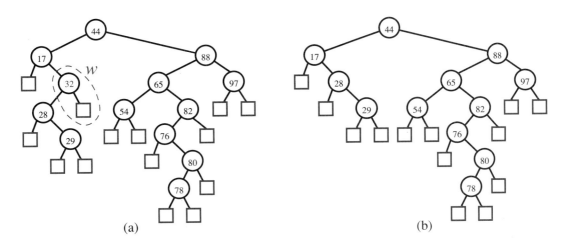

Figure 7.5: Removal from the binary search tree of Figure 7.4b, where the key to remove (32) is stored at a node (w) with an external child: (a) before the removal; (b) after the removal.

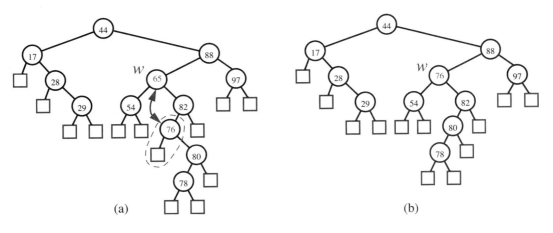

Figure 7.6: Removal from the binary search tree of Figure 7.4b, where the key to remove (65) is stored at a node whose children are both internal: (a) before the removal; (b) after the removal.

In conclusion, a binary search tree T is an efficient implementation of an ordered dictionary with n items but only if the height of T is small. In the best case, T has height $h = \lceil \log(n+1) \rceil$, which yields logarithmic time performance for all the dictionary operations. In the worst case, however, T has height n; hence, it looks and feels like an ordered sequence. Such a worst-case configuration arises, for example, if we insert a set of keys in increasing or decreasing order.

Java Implementation

Class SimpleBinarySearchTree, portions of which are shown in Code Fragments 7.4 and 7.5, is a Java implementation of a binary search tree. This implementation uses a binary tree T that stores as the elements stored at its positions (nodes) key-element pairs of class Item (shown again in Code Fragment 7.3). Note that T is used only through the binary tree interface. Thus, class SimpleBinarySearchTree is independent from the specific implementation of the binary tree T, and it takes extensive advantage of code reuse.

The dictionary methods in this implementation use the algorithms presented above. The auxiliary method findPosition, which performs the TreeSearch algorithm, is invoked by the findElement, insertItem and remove methods. The instance variable actionPos stores the position where the most recent search insertion, or deletion ended. This instance variable is not necessary to the implementation of a binary search tree, but is useful to classes that extend SimpleBinarySearchTree, as we shall see in Section 7.4.3.

```java
public class Item {
  private Object key, elem;
  protected Item (Object k, Object e) {
    key = k;
    elem = e;
  }
  public Object key() { return key; }
  public Object element() { return elem; }
  public void setKey(Object k) { key = k; }
  public void setElement(Object e) { elem = e; }
}
```

Code Fragment 7.3: Class for the key-element pairs stored in a dictionary.

We note that the performance of a dictionary implemented with a binary search tree varies dramatically depending on the tree's height. We can nevertheless take comfort that on average, a binary search tree with n keys generated from a random series of insertions and deletions of keys has expected height $O(\log n)$. Such a statement requires careful mathematical language to precisely define what we mean by a random series of insertions and deletions, and sophisticated probability theory to justify; hence, its justification is beyond the scope of this book. Thus, we can be content knowing that random update sequences give rise to binary search trees that are on average balanced, but, keeping in mind their poor worst-case performance, we should also take care in using standard binary search trees in applications where updates are not random.

Caution

```
public class SimpleBinarySearchTree implements Dictionary {
  Comparator C;  // comparator
  BinaryTree T; // binary tree
  protected Position actionPos; // insertion position or parent of removed position
  public SimpleBinarySearchTree(Comparator c) {
    C = c;
    T = (BinaryTree) new BTNodeBinaryTree();
  }
// auxiliary methods:
  protected Object key(Position position) {
    return ((Item) position.element()).key();
  }
  protected Object element(Position position) {
    return ((Item) position.element()).element();
  }
  protected void checkKey(Object key) throws InvalidKeyException {
    if(!C.isComparable(key))
      throw new InvalidKeyException("Key "+key+" is not comparable");
  }
  protected Position findPosition(Object key, Position pos) {
    if (T.isExternal(pos))
      return pos; // key not found and external node reached returned
    else {
      Object curKey = key(pos);
      if(C.isLessThan(key, curKey))
        return findPosition(key, T.leftChild(pos));
      else if(C.isGreaterThan(key, curKey)) // search in left subtree
        return findPosition(key, T.rightChild(pos)); // search in right subtree
      else
        return pos; // return internal node where key is found
    }
  }
// methods of the dictionary ADT
  public int size() { return (T.size()-1)/2; }
  public boolean isEmpty() { return T.size() == 1; }
  public Object findElement(Object key) throws InvalidKeyException {
    checkKey(key); // may throw an InvalidKeyException
    Position curPos = findPosition(key, T.root());
    actionPos = curPos;
    if (T.isInternal(curPos))
      return key(curPos);
    else
      return NO_SUCH_KEY;
  }
}
```

Code Fragment 7.4: Initial portions of a binary search tree implementation.

```
public void insertItem(Object key, Object element)
  throws InvalidKeyException  {
  checkKey(key); // may throw an InvalidKeyException
  Position insPos = T.root();
  // if the insertion key already exists, insert the new item to the
  // right of all the existing items with the same key
  do {
    insPos = findPosition(key, insPos);
    if (T.isExternal(insPos))
      break;
    else
      insPos = T.rightChild(insPos);
  } while (true);
  T.expandExternal(insPos);
  Item newItem = new Item(key, element);
  T.replace(insPos, newItem);
  actionPos = insPos;
}
public Object remove(Object key) throws InvalidKeyException  {
  Object toReturn;
  checkKey(key); // may throw an InvalidKeyException
  Position remPos = findPosition(key, T.root());
  if(T.isExternal(remPos)) {
    actionPos =remPos;
    return NO_SUCH_KEY;
  }
  else{
    toReturn = element(remPos); // element to be returned
    if (T.isExternal(T.leftChild(remPos)))
      remPos = T.leftChild(remPos);
    else if (T.isExternal(T.rightChild(remPos)))
      remPos = T.rightChild(remPos);
    else { // key is at a node with internal children
      // find node for swapping items
      Position swapPos = remPos;
      remPos = T.rightChild(swapPos);
      do
        remPos = T.leftChild(remPos);
      while (T.isInternal(remPos));
    }
    actionPos = T.sibling(remPos);
    T.removeAboveExternal(remPos);
    return toReturn;
  }
}
```

Code Fragment 7.5: Primary methods for a binary search tree.

The relative simplicity of their dictionary implementation, combined with good average-case performance, make binary search trees a rather attractive dictionary data structure in applications where the keys inserted and deleted follow a random pattern and occasionally slow response time is acceptable. There are, however, applications where it is essential to have a dictionary with fast worst-case search and update time. The data structure presented in the next section addresses this need (as do all the structures discussed in Chapter 13).

7.4 AVL Trees

In the previous section, we discussed what should be an efficient dictionary data structure, but the worst-case performance it achieves for the various operations is linear time, which is no better than the worst-case performance of the sequence implementations. In this section, we describe a simple way of correcting this problem so as to achieve logarithmic time for all the fundamental dictionary operations.

The simple correction is to add a rule to the binary search tree definition that will maintain a logarithmic height for the tree. The rule is the following height-balance property, which characterizes the structure of a binary search tree T in terms of the heights of its internal nodes (recall that the height of a node v in a tree is the length of a longest path from v to an external node):

Height-Balance Property: For every internal node v of T, the heights of the children of v can differ by at most 1.

Any binary search tree T that satisfies this property is said to be an ***AVL tree***, which is a concept named after the initials of its inventors: Adel'son-Vel'skii and Landis. An example of an AVL tree is shown in Figure 7.7.

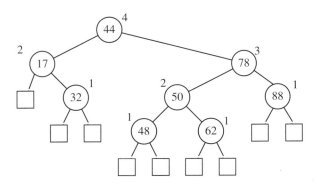

Figure 7.7: An example of an AVL tree. The keys are shown inside the nodes, and the heights are shown next to the nodes.

An immediate consequence of the height-balance property is that a subtree of an AVL tree is itself an AVL tree. The height-balance property has also the important consequence of keeping the height small, as shown in the following proposition.

Proposition 7.2: *The height of an AVL tree T storing n keys is $O(\log n)$.*

Justification: Instead of trying to find an upper bound on the height of an AVL tree directly, it turns out to be easier to work on the "inverse problem" of finding a lower bound on the minimum number of internal nodes $n(h)$ of an AVL tree with height h. We will show that $n(h)$ grows at least exponentially, that is, $n(h)$ is $\Omega(c^h)$ for some constant $c > 1$. From this, it will be an easy step to derive that the height of an AVL tree storing n keys is $O(\log n)$.

To start with, notice that $n(1) = 1$ and $n(2) = 2$, for an AVL tree of height 1 must have at least one internal node and an AVL tree of height 2 must have at least two internal nodes. Now, for $h \geq 3$, an AVL tree with height h and the minimum number of nodes is such that both its subtrees are AVL trees with the minimum number of nodes: one with height $h - 1$ and the other with height $h - 2$. Taking the root into account, we obtain the following formula that relates $n(h)$ to $n(h - 1)$ and $n(h - 2)$, for $h \geq 3$:

$$n(h) = 1 + n(h - 1) + n(h - 2). \tag{7.1}$$

The reader familiar with the properties of Fibonacci progressions (Section 1.4.1 and Exercise C-2.12) will already see at this point that $n(h)$ is a function exponential in h, but for the rest of the readers, let us proceed with our reasoning.

Formula 7.1 implies that $n(h)$ is a strictly increasing function of h. Thus, we have that $n(h - 1) > n(h - 2)$. Replacing $n(h - 1)$ with $n(h - 2)$ in Formula 7.1 and dropping the 1, we get, for $h \geq 3$,

$$n(h) > 2 \cdot n(h - 2). \tag{7.2}$$

Formula 7.2 indicates that $n(h)$ at least doubles each time h increases by 2, which intuitively means that $n(h)$ grows exponentially. To show this fact in a formal way, we apply Formula 7.2 repeatedly, yielding the following series of inequalities:

$$
\begin{aligned}
n(h) \quad &> \quad 2 \cdot n(h - 2) \\
&> \quad 4 \cdot n(h - 4) \\
&> \quad 8 \cdot n(h - 6) \\
&\;\;\vdots \\
&> \quad 2^i \cdot n(h - 2i). \tag{7.3}
\end{aligned}
$$

That is, $n(h) > 2^i \cdot n(h - 2i)$, for any integer i such that $h - 2i \geq 1$. Since we already know the values of $n(1)$ and $n(2)$, we pick i so that $h - 2i$ is equal to either 1 or 2.

That is, we pick

$$i = \left\lceil \frac{h}{2} \right\rceil - 1.$$

By substituting the above value of i in formula 7.3, we obtain, for $h \geq 3$,

$$
\begin{aligned}
n(h) &> 2^{\left\lceil \frac{h}{2} \right\rceil - 1} \cdot n\left(h - 2\left\lceil \frac{h}{2} \right\rceil\right) \\
&\geq 2^{\left\lceil \frac{h}{2} \right\rceil - 1} n(1) \\
&\geq 2^{\frac{h}{2} - 1}. \tag{7.4}
\end{aligned}
$$

By taking logarithms of both sides of formula 7.4, we obtain

$$\log n(h) > \frac{h}{2} - 1,$$

from which we get

$$h < 2\log n(h) + 2, \tag{7.5}$$

which implies that an AVL tree storing n keys has height at most $2\log n + 2$. ∎

By Proposition 7.2 and the analysis of binary search trees given in Section 7.3, the operations findElement and findAllElements, in a dictionary implemented with an AVL tree, run in time $O(\log n)$ and $O(\log n + s)$, respectively, where n is the number of items in the dictionary and s is the size of the enumeration returned by findAllElements. The important issue remaining is to show how to maintain the height-balance property of an AVL tree after an insertion or removal.

7.4.1 Insertion

The method for performing an insertion in an AVL tree T begins by performing an insertItem operation, as described in Section 7.3.2, for (general) binary search trees. Recall that this operation always inserts the new item at a node w in T that was previously an external node, and it makes w become an internal node with operation expandExternal. That is, it adds two external node children to w. This action may violate the height-balance property, however, as the heights of some nodes are increased by one. (See Figure 7.8a.) In particular, node w and possibly some of its ancestors increase their heights by one. Therefore, let us describe how to restructure T to restore the height-balance property.

Given the binary search tree T, we say that a node v of T is **balanced** if the absolute value of the difference between the heights of the children of v is at most 1, and we say that it is **unbalanced** otherwise. Thus, the height-balance property is equivalent to saying that every internal node is balanced. More importantly, if every node in a binary search tree T is balanced, then clearly the tree T is balanced, and, by Proposition 7.2, the tree T has $O(\log n)$ height.

Suppose that T satisfies the height-balance property, and hence is an AVL tree, prior to our inserting the new item. As we have mentioned, after performing the operation expandExternal(w) on T, the heights of some nodes of T, including w, increase. All such nodes are on the path of T from w to the root of T, and these are the only nodes of T that may have just become unbalanced. (See Figure 7.8a.) Of course, if this happens, then T is no longer an AVL tree; hence, we need a mechanism to fix the "unbalance" that we have just caused.

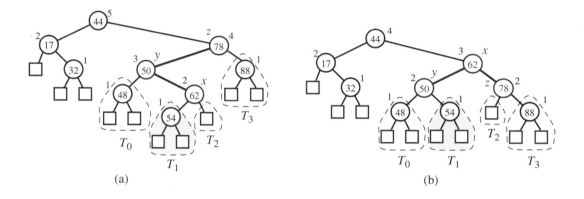

Figure 7.8: An example insertion of an element with key 54 in the AVL tree of Figure 7.7: (a) after adding a new node for key 54, the nodes storing keys 78 and 44 become unbalanced; (b) a (double) rotation restores the height-balance property. We show the heights of nodes next to them, and we identify the nodes x, y, and z.

We restore the balance of the nodes in the binary search tree T by a simple "search-and-repair" strategy. Let x be the first node we encounter in going up from w toward the root of T such that the grandparent z of x is unbalanced. (See Figure 7.8a.) Note that node x could be equal to w. Also, let y denote the parent of x, so that y is a child of z. Since node z became unbalanced because of an insertion in the subtree rooted at its child y, the height of y is equal to 2 plus the height of the sibling of y. We now "rebalance" the subtree currently rooted at z by performing a *rotation* operation, using the restructure method described in Code Fragment 7.6 and illustrated in Figures 7.8 and 7.9. A rotation temporarily renames the nodes x, y, and z as a, b, and c, so that a precedes b and b precedes c in an inorder traversal of T. There are four possible ways of mapping x, y and z to a, b, and c, as shown in Figure 7.9, which are unified into one case by our relabeling. The rotation then replaces z with the node called b, makes the children of this node be a and c, and makes the children of a and c be the four previous children of x, y, and z (other than x and y) while maintaining the inorder relationships of all the nodes in T.

Algorithm restructure(x):

> *Input:* A node x of a binary search tree T that has both a parent y and a grandparent z
>
> *Output:* Tree T restructured by a rotation (either single or double) involving nodes x, y, and z.

1: Let (a, b, c) be a left-to-right (inorder) listing of the nodes x, y, and z, and let (T_0, T_1, T_2, T_3) be a left-to-right (inorder) listing of the four subtrees of x, y, and z not rooted at x, y, or z.

2: Replace the subtree rooted at z with a new subtree rooted at b.

3: Let a be the left child of b and let T_0 and T_1 be the left and right subtrees of a, respectively.

4: Let c be the right child of b and let T_2 and T_3 be the left and right subtrees of c, respectively.

Code Fragment 7.6: Rotation in a binary search tree.

This rebalancing operation is called a ***rotation*** because of the geometric way it restructures T. If $b = y$ (see Code Fragment 7.6), the execution of the restructure method is called a ***single rotation***, for it can be visualized as "rotating" y over z. (See Figure 7.9a–b.) Otherwise, if $b = x$, this operation is called a ***double rotation***, for it can be visualized as first "rotating" x over y and then over z. (See Figure 7.9c–d, and Figure 7.8.) Some computer scientists separate these two kinds of rotations as separate methods; we have chosen, however, a restructure method that unifies these two types of rotations. In either case, a rotation modifies the parent-child relationships of $O(1)$ nodes in T, while preserving the inorder traversal ordering of all the nodes in T. While this order preservation is necessary, it is not actually the main reason we use a rotation.

The prime reason for a rotation is to change the heights of nodes in T so as to restore balance. Recall that we execute a rotation operation with restructure(x) because z, the grandparent of x, is unbalanced. Moreover, this unbalance is due to one of the children of x now having too large a height relative to the height of z's other child. As a result of a rotation, we move up the "tall" child of x while pushing down the "short" child of z. Thus, after performing restructure(x), all the nodes in the subtree now rooted at the node we called b are balanced. (See Figure 7.9.) Thus, the rotation restores the height-balance property ***locally*** at the nodes x, y, and z. In addition, since after performing the new item insertion the subtree rooted at b replaces the one formerly rooted at z, which was taller by one unit, all the ancestors of z that were formerly unbalanced become balanced. (See Figure 7.8.) (A detailed justification of this latter fact is left as an exercise.) Therefore, this one rotation also restores the height-balance property ***globally***.

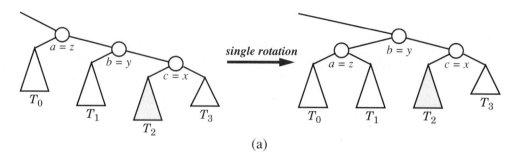

(a)

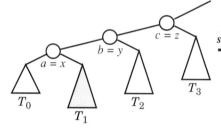

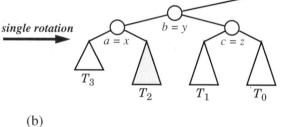

(b)

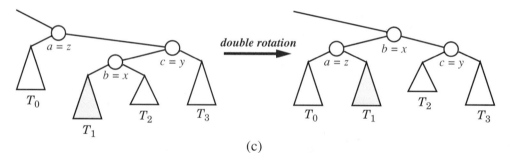

(c)

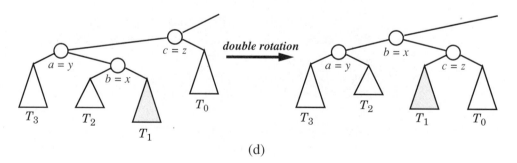

(d)

Figure 7.9: Schematic illustration of a rotation operation (method restructure of Code Fragment 7.6). Parts (a) and (b) show a single rotation, and parts (c) and (d) show a double rotation.

7.4.2 Removal

As was the case for the insertItem dictionary operation, we begin the implementation of the remove dictionary operation on an AVL tree T by using the algorithm for performing this operation on a regular binary search tree. The added difficulty in using this approach with an AVL tree is that it may violate the height-balance property. In particular, after deleting an internal node with operation removeAbove-External and elevating one of its children into its place, there may be an unbalanced node in T on the path from the parent w of the previously deleted node to the root of T. (See Figure 7.10a.) In fact, there can be at most one such unbalanced node (the justification of this fact is left as an exercise).

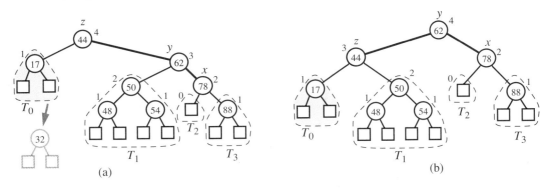

Figure 7.10: Deletion of the element with key 32 from the AVL tree of Figure 7.7: (a) after deleting the node storing key 32, the root becomes unbalanced; (b) a (single) rotation restores the height-balance property.

As with insertion in an AVL tree, we will use rotation to restore balance in the tree T. Let z be the first unbalanced node encountered going up from w toward the root of T. Also, let y be the child of z with larger height (note that node y is the child of z that is not an ancestor of w), and let x be a child of y with largest height. Note that the choice of x may not be unique, since the subtrees of y may have the same height. In any case, we then perform a restructure(x) operation, which restores the height-balance property *locally*, at the subtree that was formerly rooted at z and is now rooted at the node we temporarily called b. (See Figure 7.10b.)

Unfortunately, the rotation may actually reduce the height of the subtree rooted at b by 1, and hence may cause an ancestor of b to become unbalanced. Thus, in the case of removals, a rotation does not necessarily restore the height-balance property globally, and we may have to perform repeated rotations going up T until no more nodes are unbalanced. Since the height of T is $O(\log n)$ by Proposition 7.2, $O(\log n)$ rotations are sufficient to restore the height-balance property.

7.4.3 Implementation and Analysis

Having presented the algorithms for performing update operations in an AVL tree, let us now turn to the implementation details and analysis of using an AVL tree T to implement a dictionary. We denote with n the number of items in the dictionary, which is also the number of internal nodes of T. Some details are left as exercises.

The insertion and removal algorithms for T require that we are able to perform rotations and determine the difference between the heights of two sibling nodes. Regarding rotations, we should extend the collection of operations of the binary tree ADT by adding the method restructure. It is easy to see that a restructure operation can be performed in $O(1)$ time if T is implemented with the linked structure we describe in Section 5.4.2, while it would take $\Omega(n)$ time in the worst case if T is implemented with the sequence-based structure of Section 5.4.1. Thus, for efficiency reasons, we prefer the linked structure for representing an AVL tree.

Regarding height information, we can explicitly store with each internal node v its height. Alternatively, we can store at v the **balance factor** of v, which is defined as the height of the left child of v minus the height of the right child of v. Thus, the balance factor of v is always equal to -1, 0, or 1, except during an insertion or removal, when it may become **temporarily** equal to -2 or $+2$. During the execution of an insertion or removal, the heights and balance factors of $O(\log n)$ nodes are affected, and can be maintained in $O(\log n)$ time.

In Code Fragments 7.7–7.8, we show a Java implementation of a dictionary realized by means of an AVL tree. Class AVLItem, shown in Code Fragment 7.7, extends the Item class used to represent a key-element item of a binary search tree. It defines an additional instance variable height, representing the height of the node, and methods to set and return it.

Class SimpleAVLTree, shown in full in Code Fragments 7.8–7.9, extends SimpleBinarySearchTree (Code Fragments 7.4–7.5). The constructor of SimpleAVLTree executes first the superclass' constructor, and then assigns to T a RestructurableNodeBinaryTree, which is a class that implements the binary tree ADT, and in addition supports method restructure for performing rotations (its implementation is left as an exercise). Class SimpleAVLTree inherits methods size, isEmpty, findElement, findAllElements, and removeAll from its superclass SimpleBinarySearchTree but overrides methods insertItem and remove.

Method insertItem (Code Fragment 7.5) begins by calling the superclass' insertItem method, which inserts the new item and assigns the insertion position (node storing key 54 in Figure 7.8) to instance variable actionPos. The auxiliary method rebalance is then used to traverse the path from the insertion position to the root. This traversal updates the heights of all the nodes visited, and performs a rotation if necessary. Similarly, method remove (Code Fragment 7.5) begins by calling the

```
public class AVLItem extends Item  {
  int height;
  AVLItem(Object k, Object e, int h)  {
    super(k, e);
    height = h;
  }
  public int height()  {
    return height;
  }
  public int setHeight(int h)  {
    int oldHeight = height;
    height = h;
    return oldHeight;
  }
}
```

Code Fragment 7.7: Java implementation of a node of an AVL tree. Note that we store as an instance variable the height of this node in the tree.

superclass' remove method, which performs the deletion of the item and assigns the position replacing the deleted one (right child of node storing key 17 in Figure 7.10) to instance variable actionPos. The auxiliary method rebalance is then used to traverse the path from the insertion position to the root.

So, to sum up, with the implementation outlined above, dictionary operations insertItem and remove involve visiting the nodes along a root-to-leaf path of T, and spending $O(1)$ time per node. Thus, since the height of T is $O(\log n)$ by Proposition 7.2, insertItem and remove take $O(\log n)$ time each in an AVL tree dictionary implementation. We leave the implementation and analysis of operations findAllElements and removeAll, as interesting exercises. In Table 7.2, we summarize the performance of a dictionary implemented with an AVL tree.

Operation	Time
size, isEmpty	$\Theta(1)$
findElement, insertItem, remove	$O(\log n)$
findAllElements, removeAll	$O(\log n + s)$

Table 7.2: Performance of an n-element dictionary realized by an AVL tree, where s denotes the size of the enumerations returned. The space usage is $O(n)$.

```java
public class SimpleAVLTree
  extends SimpleBinarySearchTree implements Dictionary  {
    public SimpleAVLTree(Comparator c)  {
      super(c);
      T = new RestructurableNodeBinaryTree();
    }
    private int height(Position p)  {
      if(T.isExternal(p))
        return 0;
      else
        return ((AVLItem) p.element()).height();
    }
    private void setHeight(Position p)  { // called only if p is internal
      ((AVLItem) p.element()).setHeight(1+Math.max(height(T.leftChild(p)),
                                                   height(T.rightChild(p))));
    }
    private boolean isBalanced(Position p)  {
      // test whether node p has balance factor between -1 and 1
      int bf = height(T.leftChild(p)) − height(T.rightChild(p));
      return ((−1 <= bf) &&  (bf <= 1));
      }
    private Position tallerChild(Position p)  {
      // return a child of p with height no smaller than that of the other child
      if(height(T.leftChild(p)) >= height(T.rightChild(p)))
        return T.leftChild(p);
      else
        return T.rightChild(p);
    }
    private void rebalance(Position zPos) {
      // traverse the path of T from zPos to the root; for each node encountered,
      // recompute its height and perform a rotation if it is unbalanced
        while (!T.isRoot(zPos)) {
          zPos = T.parent(zPos);
          setHeight(zPos);
          if (!isBalanced(zPos)) { // perform a rotation
            Position xPos =  tallerChild(tallerChild(zPos));
            zPos = ((RestructurableNodeBinaryTree) T).restructure(xPos);
            setHeight(T.leftChild(zPos));
            setHeight(T.rightChild(zPos));
            setHeight(zPos);
          }
        }
    }
```

Code Fragment 7.8: Instance variables and auxiliary methods of class SimpleAVL-Tree.

```
public void insertItem(Object key, Object element)
  throws InvalidKeyException  {
    super.insertItem(key, element); // may throw an InvalidKeyException
    Position zPos = actionPos; // start at the insertion position
    T.replace(zPos, new AVLItem(key, element, 1));
    rebalance(zPos);
}
public Object remove(Object key) throws InvalidKeyException {
  Object toReturn = super.remove(key); // may throw an InvalidKeyException
  if(toReturn != NO_SUCH_KEY) {
    Position zPos = actionPos; // start at the removal position
    rebalance(zPos);
  }
  return toReturn;
}
```

Code Fragment 7.9: Methods insertItem and remove of class SimpleAVLTree.

7.5 Skip Lists

An interesting alternative to balanced binary search trees for efficiently realizing the ordered dictionary ADT is the ***skip list***. This data structure makes random choices in arranging the items in such a way that search and update times are $O(\log n)$ ***on average***, where n is the number of items in the dictionary. Interestingly, the notion of average time complexity used here does not depend on the probability distribution of the keys in the input. Instead, it depends on the use of a random-number generator in the implementation of the insertions to help decide where to place the new item. The running time is averaged over all possible outcomes of the random numbers used when inserting items.

The technique of using random numbers in an algorithm is called ***randomization***. Because they are used extensively in computer games and computer simulations, methods that generate numbers that can be viewed as random numbers are built-in operations in most modern computers. Such methods are called ***pseudo-random number generators***, and, for the sake of our discussions, we will assume that the numbers they return really are random. The main advantage of using randomization in data structure and algorithm design is that the structures and methods that result are usually simple and efficient. As we discuss in this section, the randomized data structure called skip lists have the same logarithmic time bounds for dictionary operations as balanced binary search trees (such as AVL trees). Nevertheless, the bounds are ***expected*** for skip lists, while they are ***worst-case*** bounds for AVL trees. On the other hand, skip lists are much simpler to implement than AVL trees.

A *skip list* S for dictionary D consists of a series of sequences $\{S_0, S_1, \ldots, S_h\}$. Each sequence S_i stores a subset of the items of D sorted by nondecreasing key plus items with two special keys, denoted $-\infty$ and $+\infty$, where $-\infty$ is smaller than every possible key that can be inserted in D and $+\infty$ is larger than every possible key that can be inserted in D. In addition, the sequences in S satisfy the following:

- Sequence S_0 contains every item of dictionary D (plus the special items with keys $-\infty$ and $+\infty$).
- For $i = 1, \ldots, h-1$, sequence S_i contains (in addition to $-\infty$ and $+\infty$) a randomly generated subset of the items in sequence S_{i-1}.
- Sequence S_h contains only $-\infty$ and $+\infty$.

An example of a skip list is shown in Figure 7.11. It is customary to visualize a skip list S with sequence S_0 at the bottom and sequences $S_1, \ldots, S_{h-1}$ above it. Also, we refer to h as the **height** of skip list S.

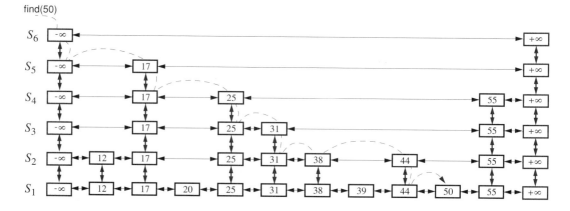

Figure 7.11: Example of a skip list. The dashed lines show the traversal of the structure performed when searching for key 50.

Intuitively, the sequences are set up so that S_{i+1} contains more or less every other item in S_i. As we shall see in the details of the insertion method, the items in S_{i+1} are chosen at random from the items in S_i by picking each item from S_i to also be in S_{i+1} with probability $1/2$. That is, in essence, we "flip a coin" for each item in S_i and place that item in S_{i+1} if the coin comes up "heads." Thus, we expect S_1 to have about $n/2$ items, S_2 to have about $n/4$ items, and, in general, S_i to have about $n/2^i$ items. In other words, we expect the height h of S to be about $\log n$. The halving of the number of items from one sequence to the next is not enforced as an explicit property of skip lists, however. Instead, randomization is used.

Using the position abstraction already used for sequences and trees, we view a skip list as a two-dimensional collection of positions arranged horizontally into *levels* and vertically into *towers*. Each level corresponds to a sequence S_i and each tower contains positions storing the same item across consecutive sequences. The positions in a skip list can be traversed using the following operations that would be included in a skip list ADT:

> after(p): Return the position following p on the same level.
>
> before(p): Return the position preceding p on the same level.
>
> below(p): Return the position below p in the same tower.
>
> above(p): Return the position above p in the same tower.

We conventionally assume that the above operations return a **null** position if the position requested does not exist. Without going into the details, we note that we can easily implement a skip list by means of a linked structure such that the above traversal methods each take $O(1)$ time, given a skip-list position p. Such a linked structure is essentially a collection of h doubly linked lists aligned at towers, which are also doubly linked lists.

7.5.1 Searching

The skip list structure allows for simple dictionary search algorithms. In fact, all of the skip list search algorithms are based on an elegant SkipSearch method that takes a key k and finds the item in a skip list S with the largest key (which is possibly $-\infty$) that is less than or equal to k. Suppose we are given such a key k. We begin the SkipSearch method by setting a position variable p to the top-most, left position in the skip list S. That is, p is set to the position of the special item with key $-\infty$ in S_h. We then perform the following steps (see Figure 7.11):

1. If S.below(p) is null, then the search terminates—we are *at the bottom* and have located the largest item in S with key less than or equal to the search key k. Otherwise, we *drop down* to the next lower level in the present tower by setting $p \leftarrow S$.below(p).
2. Starting at position p, we move p forward until it is at the right-most position on the present level such that key(p) $\leq k$. We call this the *scan forward* step. Note that such a position always exists, since each level contains the special keys $+\infty$ and $-\infty$. In fact, after we perform the scan forward for this level, p may remain where it started. In any case, we then repeat the previous step.

Algorithm SkipSearch(k):

> *Input:* A search key k
>
> *Output:* Position p in S such that the item at p has the largest key less than or equal to k
>
> Let p be the topmost-left position of S (which should have at least 2 levels).
> **while** below(p) $\neq$ **null do**
> > $p \leftarrow$ below(p)   {drop down}
> > **while** key(after(p)) $\leq k$ **do**
> > > Let $p \leftarrow$ after(p)   {scan forward}
>
> **return** p.

Code Fragment 7.10: A Generic Search method for a skip list S.

We give a pseudo-code description of the skip-list search algorithm in Code Fragment 7.10.

Given the SkipSearch method, it is easy to now implement the operation findElement(k). We simply perform $p \leftarrow$ SkipSearch(k) and test whether key(p) = k or not. If these two keys are equal, we return p.element; otherwise, we return the sentinel NO_SUCH_KEY. As it turns out, the expected running time of algorithm SkipSearch is $O(\log n)$. We postpone the justification of this fact, however, until after we discuss the implementation of the update methods for skip lists.

7.5.2   Update Operations

Another feature of the skip list data structure is that, besides having an elegant search algorithm, it also provides simple algorithms for dictionary updates.

Insertion

The insertion algorithm for skip lists uses randomization to decide how many references to the new item (k, e) should be added to the skip list. We begin the insertion of a new item (k, e) into a skip list by performing a SkipSearch(k) operation. This gives us the position p of the bottom-level item with the largest key less than or equal to k (note that p may be the position of the special item with key $-\infty$). We then insert (k, e) in this bottom-level list immediately after position p. After inserting the new item at this level we "flip" a coin. That is, we call a method random() that returns a number between 0 and 1, and if that number is less than $1/2$, then we consider the flip to have come up "heads;" otherwise, we consider the flip to have come up "tails." If the flip comes up tails, then we stop here. If the flip comes up heads, on the other hand, then we backtrack to the previous (next higher) level and insert (k,e) in this level at the appropriate position. We again flip a coin; if it comes up heads, we go to the next higher level and repeat. Thus, we continue to insert the new item (k,e) in lists until we finally get a flip that comes up tails. We link together all the references to the new item (k,e) created in this process to create the **tower** for (k,e). We give the pseudo-code for this insertion algorithm for a skip list S in Code Fragment 7.11 and we illustrate this algorithm in Figure 7.12. Our insertion algorithm uses an operation insertAfterAbove$(p,q,(k,e))$ that inserts a position storing the item (k,e) after position p (on the same level as p) and above position q, returning the position r of the new item (and setting internal references so that after, before, above, and below methods will work correctly for p, q, and r).

Algorithm SkipInsert(k,e):

    Input: Item (k,e)

    Output: None

      $p \leftarrow$ SkipSearch(k)

      $q \leftarrow$ insertAfterAbove$(p, null, (k,e))$ {we are at the bottom level}

      while random$() < 1/2$ **do**

        while above$(p) = null$ **do**

          $p \leftarrow$ before(p) {scan backward}

          $p \leftarrow$ above(p) {jump up to higher level}

          $q \leftarrow$ insertAfterAbove$(p,q,(k,e))$ {insert new item}

Code Fragment 7.11: Insertion in a skip list, assuming random$()$ returns a random number between 0 and 1, and we never insert past the top level.

A skip-list S must maintain as an instance variable a reference to the top-most, left position in S, and must have a policy for any insertion that wishes to continue inserting a new item past the top level of S. There are two possible courses of action we can take, both of which have their merits. One possibility is to restrict the top level, h, to be some fixed value that is a function of n, the number of elements currently in the dictionary (from the analysis we will see that $h = \max\{10, 2\lceil \log n \rceil\}$ is a reasonable choice, and picking $h = 3\lceil \log n \rceil$ is even safer). Implementing this choice means that we must modify the insertion algorithm to stop inserting a new item once we reach the topmost level (unless $\lceil \log n \rceil < \lceil \log(n+1) \rceil$, in which case we can now go one more level). The other possibility is to let an insertion continue inserting a new element as long it keeps getting heads returned from the random number generator. As we show in the analysis of skip lists, the probability that an insertion will go to a level that is more than $O(\log n)$ is very low, so this design choice should also work. Either choice will still result in our being able to perform element search, insertion, and removal in expected $O(\log n)$ time, however.

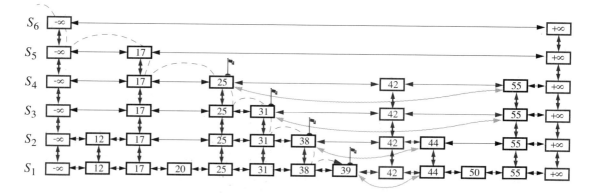

Figure 7.12: Insertion of an element with key 42 into the skip list of Figure 7.11. We assume that the random "coin flip" for the new item came up heads three times in a row. The dashed lines show the positions visited, and we flag the positions after which positions holding the new item are inserted, and we highlight these newly created positions.

Removal

Like the search and insertion algorithms, the removal algorithm for a skip list S is quite simple. In fact, it is even easier than the insertion algorithm. Namely, to perform a remove(k) operation, we begin by performing a search for the given key k. If a position p with key k is not found, then we return the NO_SUCH_KEY element. Otherwise, if a position p with key k is found (on the bottom level), then we remove all the positions above p, which are easily accessed by using above operations to climb up the tower of this item in S starting at position p. The removal algorithm is illustrated in Figure 7.13 and a detailed description of it is left as an exercise. As we show in the next subsection, the running time for removal in a skip list is expected to be $O(\log n)$.

Before we give this analysis, however, there are some minor improvements to the skip list data structure we would like to discuss. First, we don't actually need to store references to items at the levels of the skip list above 0, because all that is needed at these levels are references to keys. Second, we don't actually need the above method. In fact, we don't need the before method either. We can perform item insertion and removal in strictly a top-down, scan-forward fashion, thus saving space for "up" and "prev" references. We explore the details of this optimization in an exercise. Neither of these optimizations improve the asymptotic performance of skip lists by more than a constant factor, but these improvements can, nevertheless, be meaningful in practice. In fact, experimental evidence suggests that optimized skip lists are faster in practice than AVL trees and other balanced search trees.

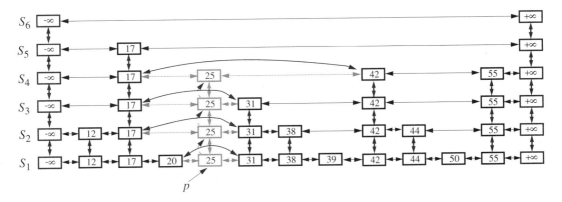

Figure 7.13: Removal of the item with key 25 from the skip list of Figure 7.12. The positions visited are those of the tower associated with key 25.

7.5.3 A Probabilistic Analysis of Skip Lists ⋆

As we have just shown, skip lists provide a simple alternative dictionary implementation to balanced search trees. In terms of worst-case performance, however, skip lists are not a superior data structure. In fact, if we don't officially prevent an insertion from continuing significantly past the current highest level, then the insertion algorithm can go into what is almost an infinite loop (it is not actually an infinite loop, however, since the probability of having a fair coin repeatedly come up heads forever is 0). If we terminate item insertion at the highest level h, then the **worst-case** running time for performing the findElement, insertItem, and remove operations in a skip list S with n items and height h is $O(n + h)$. This worst-case performance is due to the very low probability event when every item belongs to every level in S. Judging from this worst-case, then, we might conclude that the skip list structure is strictly inferior to the AVL tree. But this would not be a fair analysis, for this worst-case behavior is a gross over-estimate.

Because the insertion step involves randomization, a more honest analysis of skip lists involves a bit of probability. At first, this might seem like a major undertaking, for a complete and thorough probabilistic analysis could require deep mathematics (and, indeed, there are several such deep analyses that have appeared in data structures and algorithms literature). Fortunately, such an analysis is not necessary to understand the expected asymptotic behavior of skip lists. The informal and intuitive probabilistic analysis we give below uses only basic concepts of probability theory.

⋆We use a star (⋆) to indicate sections containing material more advanced than the material in the rest of the chapter; this material can be considered optional in a first reading.

Let us begin by determining the expected value of the height h of S (assuming that we do not terminate insertions early). The probability that a given item is stored in a position at level i is equal to the probability of getting i consecutive heads when flipping a coin, that is, this probability is $1/2^i$. Hence, the probability P_i that level i has at least one item is at most

$$P_i \leq \frac{n}{2^i},$$

for the probability that any one of n different events occurs is at most the sum of the probabilities that each occurs.

The probability that the height h of S is larger than i is equal to the probability that level i has at least one item, that is, it is no more than P_i. This means that h is larger than, say, $3 \log n$ with probability at most

$$P_{3\log n} \leq \frac{n}{2^{3\log n}} = \frac{n}{n^3} = \frac{1}{n^2}.$$

More generally, given a constant $c > 1$, h is larger than $c \log n$ with probability at most $1/n^{c-1}$. That is, the probability that h is smaller than or equal to $c \log n$ is at least $1 - 1/n^{c-1}$. Thus, with high probability, the height h of S is $O(\log n)$.

Consider the running time of a search in skip list S, and recall that such a search involves two nested **while** loops. The inner loop performs a scan forward on a level of S as long as the next key is no greater than the search key k, and the outer loop drops down to the next level and repeats the scan forward iteration. Since the height h of S is $O(\log n)$ with high probability, the number of drop-down steps is $O(\log n)$ with high probability.

So we have yet to bound the number of scan-forward steps we make. Let n_i be the number of keys examined while scanning forward at level i. Observe that, after the key at the starting position, each additional key examined in a scan-forward at level i cannot also belong to level $i+1$. If any of these items were on the previous level, we would have encountered them in the previous scan-forward step. Thus, the probability that any key is counted in n_i is $1/2$. Therefore, the expected value of n_i is exactly equal to the expected number of times we must flip a fair coin before it comes up heads. This expected value is 2. Hence, the expected amount of time spent scanning forward at any level i is $O(1)$. Since S has $O(\log n)$ levels with high probability, a search in S takes the expected time $O(\log n)$. By a similar analysis, we can show that the expected running time of an insertion or a removal is $O(\log n)$.

Finally, let us turn to the space requirement of a skip list S. As we observed above, the expected number of items at level i is $n/2^i$, which means that the expected total number of items in S is

$$\sum_{i=0}^{h} \frac{n}{2^i} = n \sum_{i=0}^{h} \frac{1}{2^i} < 2n.$$

Hence, the expected space requirement of S is $O(n)$.

Table 7.3 summarizes the performance of a dictionary realized by a skip list.

Operation	Time
size, isEmpty	$O(1)$
findElement, insertItem, remove	$O(\log n)$ (expected)
findAllElements, removeAll	$O(\log n + s)$ (expected)

Table 7.3: Performance of a dictionary implemented with a skip list. We denote with n the number of items in the dictionary at the time the operation is performed, and with s the size of the enumeration returned by operations findAllElements and removeAll. The expected space requirement is $O(n)$.

7.6 Hash Tables

Whereas almost all of the dictionary implementations we have considered so far in this chapter have assumed ordered dictionaries, unordered dictionaries are nevertheless useful in many scenarios. Such scenarios often require that elements be addressed by keys, but they do not assume a strict ordering on the keys. Examples of such scenarios include a compiler's symbol table and a list of keyword-value pairs (such as a properties list or a collection of environment variables).

One of the most efficient ways to implement a dictionary in such circumstances is to use a ***hash table***. Although the worst-case running time of the dictionary ADT operations is $O(n)$ when using a hash-table, where n is the number of items in the dictionary, a correctly implemented hash table should be able to perform these operations in $O(1)$ expected time. A hash table consists of two major components: a bucket array and a hash function, which we now discuss.

The Bucket Array

The ***bucket array*** of a hash table is an array A of size N, where each cell of A is thought of as a "bucket." The integer N defines the ***capacity*** of the bucket array. If the keys handled by the dictionary are integers in the range $[0, N-1]$, this bucket array is all that is needed. An element e with key k is simply inserted into bucket $A[k]$. Any bucket cells associated with keys not present in the dictionary are assumed to hold the special NO_SUCH_KEY object.

Of course, if the keys are not unique, then two different elements may get mapped to the same bucket of A. In this case we say that a ***collision*** between two elements has occurred.

Clearly, if each bucket of A stores only a single element, then we cannot associate more than one element with a single bucket, which is a problem in the case of collisions. A simple and efficient way for dealing with collisions is to store a *sequence* of elements in bucket $A[k]$ instead, each member of which has key k. Using this *collision resolution* rule, which is known as *chaining*, we can perform the fundamental dictionary operations as follows:

- Operation findElement(k) consists of returning an *arbitrary* element of $A[k]$ if $A[k]$ is nonempty, and the special NO_SUCH_KEY object if $A[k]$ is empty.
- Operation insertItem(k, e) consists of inserting e in sequence $A[k]$.
- Operation remove(k) consists of removing and returning an *arbitrary* element of $A[k]$ if $A[k]$ is nonempty, and of returning the NO_SUCH_KEY object if $A[k]$ is empty.

Thus, if keys are unique, then searches, insertions, and removals take worst-case time $O(1)$. This sounds like a great achievement, but it has two major drawbacks. The first is that it uses space $\Theta(N)$, which is not necessarily related to the number of items n actually present in the dictionary. Indeed, if N is large relative to n, then this implementation is wasteful of space. The second drawback is that the bucket array requires keys be integers in the range $[0, N-1]$, which is often not the case.

7.6.1   Hash Functions

If we want to store arbitrary keys in a bucket array A of size N, we have to find a way to map a key k of a given type into an integer in the range $[0, N-1]$. Before we can get to this point, however, we must have a consistent way of assigning integers to keys. The integer assigned to a key k is called the *hash code* for k. To be consistent, the specific hash code function $f(k)$ we use for a key k should have the property that $f(k_1) = f(k_2)$, if the two keys k_1 and k_2 are *equal* (in a generic sense). Of course, $f(k_1)$ can equal $f(k_2)$ even if $k_1 \neq k_2$. Since the notion of equality between two keys k_1 and k_2 depends on the equality tester used, the assignment of hash codes to keys must take the equality tester into account.

Every object defined in a Java program comes equipped with a default hash-Code method for mapping the object to an integer. We should take care, however, in using the default Object version of a hash-code function, as this could just be an integer interpretation of the object's location in memory (as is the case in many Java implementations). This type of hash code works poorly with character strings, for example, because two different string objects in memory might actually be equal, in which case we would like them to have the same hash code. Indeed, the Java String class overrides the hashCode method of the Object class to be something more appropriate for character strings.

Example 7.3: *Consistent hash codes for the following key types are:*

- **Floating-Point Number**: *Sum the mantissa and exponent, treating them as integers.*
- **Character String**: *Sum the ASCII (or Unicode) values of the characters of the string.*
- **Keyword-Value Pair**: *Use the hash code of the keyword (assuming the keyword is a string).*

Equipped with a way of assigning hash codes, we can apply the bucket array method to arbitrary keys using the hash code $f(k)$, instead of the key k. Thus, we store an item (k, e) in the sequence referenced by the cell $A[f(k)]$ indexed by the hash code $f(k)$.

When hash codes are used instead of the keys themselves, the occurrence of collisions makes the dictionary operations findElement and remove more complicated. Indeed, two distinct keys, k_1 and k_2, may be mapped to the same hash code $i = f(k_1) = f(k_2)$, and thus stored in the same bucket $A[i]$. When performing operation findElement(k_1), we cannot simply return the element of an *arbitrary* item from bucket $A[i]$, since such an item could have key k_2. Instead, we should treat bucket $A[i]$ as a dictionary and perform a findElement(k_1) operation on it. Similar considerations apply to operation remove. Hence, we can view a hash table of size N as a collection of N sequence-based dictionaries, each storing items whose keys have the same hash function value.

We still have a problem, however, in that the range of possible hash code values may exceed the capacity N of the bucket array A; hence, naively using a hash code $f(k)$ may result in an array out-of-bounds exception being thrown. Thus, once we have determined an integer hash-code value for a key object k, there is still the issue of mapping that integer into the range $[0, N-1]$. This compression step, which is called **hashing**, should map the hash codes down to the range $[0, N-1]$ in a uniform manner. The function that does this compression is called a **hash function**.

Since the dictionary operations in a sequence-based dictionary take time proportional to the size of the sequence (Section 7.2), we should aim at storing as few keys as possible in each bucket of a hash table. Unfortunately, the number of keys in a bucket $A[i]$ is equal to n in the worst case. The worst case occurs when all the keys inserted into the dictionary collide, that is, they have the same hash code.

Let us take a probabilistic "look" at the situation then. If the hash codes were uniformly distributed in the range $[0, N-1]$, then the expected number of keys in a bucket would be n/N, which is $O(1)$ if n is $O(N)$. The quantity n/N, which is the ratio of the number of items to the number of buckets, is called the **load factor** of the hash table. To reduce the probability of collisions, the load factor is typically kept below 1. A common choice is to maintain a load factor below 0.75.

If the load factor of a hash table goes significantly above the specified threshold, then it is common to require that the table be resized (to regain the specified load factor) and all the objects **rehashed** using this new size. A good requirement for the new array's size is that it be at least double the previous size.

To achieve a uniform distribution of the hash codes in the range $[0, N-1]$, the hash function must be suitably chosen. Since we have seen mechanisms for assigning integers to keys, let us assume, without loss of generality, that we now are dealing exclusively with keys that are themselves integers. One simple hash function to use in this case is

$$h(k) = k \bmod N.$$

Additionally, if we take N to be a prime number, then this hash function helps "spread out" the distribution of hashed values. Indeed, if N is not prime, there is a higher likelihood that patterns in the distribution of keys will be repeated in the distribution of hash codes, thereby causing collisions. For example, if we hash the keys $\{200, 205, 210, 215, 220, \ldots, 600\}$ to a bucket array of size 100, then each hash code will collide with three others. But if this same set of keys is hashed to a bucket array of size 101, then there will be no collisions. If a hash function is chosen well, it should guarantee that the probability that two different keys get hashed to the same bucket is at most $1/N$. We give an illustration of a simple hash table that uses this hash function in Figure 7.14.

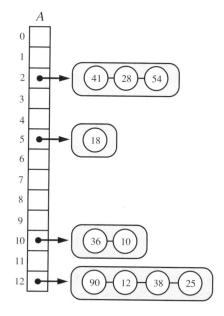

Figure 7.14: Example of a hash table of size 13 storing 10 integer keys, with collisions resolved by the chaining method. The hash function is $h(k) = k \bmod 13$.

Choosing N to be a prime number is not always enough, however, for if there is a repeated pattern of key values of the form $iN + j$ for several different i's, then there will still be collisions. For this reason, another common hash function is

$$h(k) = (ak + b) \bmod N,$$

where N is a prime number, and $a \neq 0$ and b are nonnegative integers, which are chosen at random at the time the hash function is determined. This hash function is chosen so as to hopefully eliminate repeated patterns in the set of hash codes and get us closer to having a "good" hash function, that is, one with the property that the probability that any two different keys collide is at most $1/N$ (which we would have if these keys were "thrown" into A uniformly at random).

Given a hash function, such as this, that spreads n elements fairly evenly in the range $[0, N-1]$, the expected running time of operations findElement, insertItem, and remove in a dictionary implemented with a hash table that uses this function is $O(\lceil n/N \rceil)$. Thus, given a good hash function and a bucket array we can implement the standard dictionary operations to run in $O(1)$ expected time, provided we know that n is $O(N)$.

7.6.2 Universal Hashing ★

We have admittedly "waved our hands" a bit in discussing how to choose a good hash function. In this section, we show how to pick a hash function that is guaranteed to be good. In order to do this carefully, we need to make our discussion a bit more mathematical.

As we mentioned earlier, we can assume without loss of generality that our set of keys are integers in some range. Let $[0, M-1]$ be this range. Thus, we can view a hash function h as a mapping from integers in the range $[0, M-1]$ to integers in the range $[0, N-1]$, and we can view the set of candidate hash functions we are considering as a *family* H of hash functions. Such a family is *universal* if for any two integers j and k in the range $[0, M-1]$ and for a hash function chosen uniformly at random from H,

$$\Pr(h(j) = h(k)) \leq \frac{1}{N}.$$

(Such a family is also known as a *2-universal* family of hash functions.) The goal of choosing a good hash function can therefore be viewed as the problem of selecting a small universal family H of hash functions that are easy to compute. The reason universal families of hash functions are useful is that they result in a low expected number of collisions. This notion of a low expected number of collisions is made precise in proposition that follows.

Proposition 7.4: *Let j be an integer in the range $[0, M-1]$, let S be a set of n integers in this same range, and let h be a hash function chosen uniformly, at random, from a universal family of hash functions from integers in the range $[0, M-1]$ to integers in the range $[0, N-1]$. Then the expected number of collisions between j and the integers in S is at most n/N.*

Justification: Let $c_h(j, S)$ denote the number of collisions between j and integers in S (i.e., $c_h(j, S) = |\{k \in S : h(j) = h(k)\}|$). The quantity we are interested in is the expected value $\mathbf{E}(c_h(j, S))$. We can write $c_h(j, S)$ as

$$c_h(j, S) = \sum_{k \in S} X_{j,k},$$

where $X_{j,k}$ is a random variable that is 1 if $h(j) = h(k)$ and is 0 otherwise (i.e., $X_{j,k}$ is an **indicator** random variable for a collision between j and k). By the linearity of expectation,

$$\mathbf{E}(c_h(j, S)) = \sum_{s \in S} \mathbf{E}(X_{j,k}).$$

Also, by the definition of a universal family of hash functions,

$$\mathbf{E}(X_{j,k}) \leq \frac{1}{N}.$$

Thus,

$$\begin{aligned} \mathbf{E}(c_h(j, S)) &\leq \sum_{s \in S} \frac{1}{N} \\ &= \frac{n}{N}. \end{aligned}$$

∎

Put another way, this proposition states that the expected number of collisions between a hash code j and the keys already in a hash table (using a hash function chosen at random from a universal family H) is at most the current load factor of the hash table. Since the time to perform a search, insertion, or deletion for a key j in a hash table that uses the chaining collision-resolution rule is proportional to the number of collisions between j and the other keys in the table, this implies that the expected running time of any such operation is proportional to the hash table's load factor. This is exactly what we want.

Let us turn our attention, then, to the problem of constructing a small universal family of hash functions that are easy to compute. The set of hash functions we construct is actually similar to the final family we considered at the end of the previous section. Let p be a prime number greater than or equal to the number of hash codes M but less than $2M$ (and there must always be such a prime number, according to a mathematical fact known as **Bertrand's Postulate**).

Define H as the set of hash functions of the form
$$h_{a,b}(k) = (ak + b \bmod p) \bmod N.$$
The following proposition establishes that this family of hash functions is universal.

Proposition 7.5: *The family $H = \{h_{a,b}: 0 < a < p \text{ and } 0 \le b < p\}$ is universal.*

Justification: Let Z denote the set of integers in the range $[0, p-1]$. Let us separate each hash function $h_{a,b}$ into the functions
$$f_{a,b}(k) = ak + b \bmod p$$
and
$$g(k) = k \bmod N$$
so that $h_{a,b}(k) = g(f_{a,b}(k))$. The set of functions $f_{a,b}$ defines a family of hash functions F that map integers in Z to integers in Z. We claim that each function in F causes no collisions at all. To justify this claim, consider $f_{a,b}(j)$ and $f_{a,b}(k)$ for some pair of different integers j and k in Z. If $f_{a,b}(j) = f_{a,b}(k)$, then we would have a collision. But, recalling the definition of the modulus operation, this would imply that
$$aj + b + \left\lfloor \frac{aj+b}{p} \right\rfloor p = ak + b + \left\lfloor \frac{ak+b}{p} \right\rfloor p.$$
Without loss of generality, we can assume that $j < k$, which implies that
$$\left(\left\lfloor \frac{aj+b}{p} \right\rfloor - \left\lfloor \frac{ak+b}{p} \right\rfloor \right) p = a(k - j).$$
Since $a \ne 0$ and $j < k$, this in turn implies that $a(k - j)$ is a multiple of p. But $a < p$ and $k - j < p$, so there is no way that $a(k - j)$ can be a multiple of p, because p is prime (remember that every positive integer can be factored into a product of primes). So it is impossible for $f_{a,b}(j) = f_{a,b}(k)$ if $j \ne k$. To put this another way, each $f_{a,b}$ maps the integers in Z to the integers in Z in a way that defines a one-to-one correspondence. Since the functions in F cause no collisions, the only way that a function $h_{a,b}$ can cause a collision is for the function g to cause a collision.

Let j and k be two different integers in Z. Also, let $c(j, k)$ denote the number of functions in H that map j and k to the same integer (that is, that cause j and k to collide). We can derive an upper bound for $c(j, k)$ by using a simple counting argument. If we consider any integer x in Z, there are p different functions $f_{a,b}$ such that $f_{a,b}(j) = x$ (since we can choose a b for each choice of a to make this so). Let us now fix x and note that each such function $f_{a,b}$ maps k to a unique integer $y = f_{a,b}(k)$ in Z with $x \ne y$. Moreover, of the p different integers of the form $y = f_{a,b}(k)$, there are at most $\lceil p/N \rceil - 1$ such that $g(y) = g(x)$ and $x \ne y$ (by the definition of g). Thus, for any x in Z, there are at most $\lceil p/N \rceil - 1$ functions $h_{a,b}$ in H such that $x = f_{a,b}(j)$ and $h_{a,b}(j) = h_{a,b}(k)$.

Since there are p choices for the integer x in Z, the above counting arguments imply that

$$c(j,k) \le p\left(\left\lceil \frac{p}{N} \right\rceil - 1\right) \le \frac{p(p-1)}{N}.$$

There are $p(p-1)$ functions in H, since each function $h_{a,b}$ is determined by a pair (a,b) such that $0 < a < p$ and $0 \le b < p$. Thus, picking a function uniformly at random from H involves picking one of $p(p-1)$ functions. Therefore, for any two different integers j and k in Z,

$$\Pr(h_{a,b}(j) = h_{a,b}(k)) \le \frac{p(p-1)/N}{p(p-1)} = \frac{1}{N}.$$

That is, the family H is universal. ∎

In addition to being universal, the functions in H have a number of other nice properties. Each function in H is easy to select, since doing so simply requires that we select a pair of random integers a and b such that $0 < a < p$ and $0 \le b < p$. In addition, each function in H is easy to compute in $O(1)$ time, requiring just one multiplication, one addition, and two applications of the modulus function. Thus, any hash function chosen uniformly at random in H will result in an implementation of the dictionary ADT so that the fundamental operations all have expected running times that are $O(\lceil n/N \rceil)$, since we are using the chaining rule for collision resolution.

7.6.3 Alternate Collision-Handling Schemes ⋆

We have given our hash table implementation assuming that collisions are handled using the chaining rule. We can handle collisions in other ways besides using the chaining rule, however. The chaining rule has many nice properties, as discussed above, but it nevertheless has one slight disadvantage: it requires the use of an auxiliary data structure, a sequence, to hold items with colliding keys.

An alternative scheme is to store directly, in each bucket, only one item. This scheme saves space because no auxiliary structures are employed, but it requires a bit more complication to handle collisions.

Linear Probing

In one collision-handling strategy, which is called **linear probing**, if we try to insert an item (k, e) and bucket $A[i]$ is already occupied, where $i = f(k)$, then we try $A[(i + 1) \bmod N]$. If $A[(i + 1) \bmod N]$ is occupied, then we try $A[(i + 2) \bmod N]$, and so on, until we find an empty bucket in A that can accept the new item. This strategy requires that the load factor always be no more than 1, that is, $n \le N$.

The linear probing approach saves space, but it has the disadvantage of complicating removals, since removing an item creates an empty bucket in A that prematurely terminates a findElement operation. We can get around this problem by replacing the deleted item with a special "deactivated item" object, with the understanding that searches must continue probing, even when encountering a deactivated item, and insertions must stop instead at a deactivated item and replace it with the new item to be inserted. Even when applying this lazy deletion trick, the linear-probing collision-handling strategy suffers from an additional disadvantage. It tends to cluster the items of the dictionary into long contiguous runs, which causes searches to slow down considerably.

Quadratic Probing

Another strategy, known as *quadratic probing*, involves iteratively trying the buckets $A[(i+f(j)) \bmod N]$, for $j = 1, 2, 3, \ldots$, where $f(j) = j^2$, until finding an empty bucket. As with linear probing, the quadratic probing strategy complicates the removal operation, but it does avoid the kinds of clustering patterns that occur with linear probing. Nevertheless, it creates its own kind of clustering, called *secondary clustering*, where the set of filled array cells "bounces" around the array in a fixed pattern. Also, if N is not chosen as a prime, then the quadratic probing strategy may not find an empty bucket in A even if one exists.

Double Hashing

Another strategy that does not cause clustering of the kind produced by linear probing or the kind produced by quadratic probing is the *double hashing* strategy. In this approach, we choose a secondary hash function h', and if h maps some key k to a bucket $A[i]$ (i.e., $i = h(k)$) that is already occupied, then we iteratively try the buckets $A[i + f(j)]$ next, for $j = 1, 2, 3, \ldots$, where $f(j) = j \cdot h'(k)$. In this scheme, the secondary hash function is not allowed to evaluate to zero; a common choice is $h'(k) = q - (k \bmod q)$, for some prime number $q < N$. Also, N must again be a prime.

These alternate collision-handling methods, which are collectively called *open addressing* strategies, save some space over the chaining method, but they are not necessarily faster. In experimental and theoretical analyses, the chaining method is either competitive or significantly faster than the other methods, depending on the load factor of the bucket array. So, if memory space is not a major issue, the chaining method of choice seems to be the collision-handling method. Still, if memory space is in short supply (such as in an application that must run on a very small device), then one of these open addressing methods might be worth implementing.

7.7 Supporting Locators in a Dictionary ⋆

As we did for priority queues, we can also use the locator pattern (Section 6.4) in the context of dictionaries. In the dictionary ADT, locators offer additional functionality for both unordered and ordered dictionaries. In an unordered dictionary locators allow for a remove method that need not begin with an implicit search, but can instead be immediately given a locator to the item being removed. Likewise, locators in an ordered dictionary allow us to refer to items before and after some specified item.

Locator-Based Dictionary Methods

We can extend the set of operations for a dictionary D with methods that refer to locators and are akin to similar methods for priority queues, such as insert(k,e), remove(ℓ), replaceElement(ℓ,e), replaceKey(ℓ,k), find(k), and findAll(k), with the obvious meanings of the operations (Section 6.4.1).

For an ordered dictionary D, we can also define the following specialized methods that refer to the total order relation on the keys:

before(ℓ): Return a locator to an item whose key is the largest key in D smaller than ℓ.key$()$.
Input: Locator; *Output:* Locator.

after(ℓ): Return a locator to an item whose key is the smallest key in D larger than ℓ.key$()$.
Input: Locator; *Output:* Locator.

closestBefore(k): Return a locator to an item whose key is the largest key in D smaller than or equal to k.
Input: Object; *Output:* Locator.

closestAfter(k): Return a locator to an item whose key is the smallest key in D greater than or equal to k.
Input: Object; *Output:* Locator.

min$()$: Return a locator to an item with smallest key in D.
Input: None; *Output:* Locator.

max$()$: Return a locator to an item with largest key in D.
Input: None; *Output:* Locator.

Implementing Locator-Based Dictionary Methods

We can extend the dictionary implementations based on sequences, binary search trees, and AVL trees discussed in this chapter with an approach similar to that used to extend the implementations of priority queues in Section 6.4.2. Namely, we can realize a locator by extending the key-element item object with a position reference and a container reference. While the locators always stay attached to the items (indeed, they store the items), we have to keep track of the positions where the items are placed in the sequence or binary tree, and update the position references in the locators. We leave these extensions as exercises.

7.8 Exercises

Reinforcement

R-7.1 Assuming that an ordered dictionary D is implemented with an ordered sequence, describe how to implement the following operations in $O(1)$ time:

minElement(): Return the element of an item of D with smallest key.

Input: None; *Output:* Object.

maxElement(): Return the element of an item of D with the largest key.

Input: None; *Output:* Object.

Argue why your implementation of these operations runs in $O(1)$ time, independent of whether the sequence is itself implemented with an array or a linked list.

R-7.2 Insert into an initially empty binary search tree items with the following keys (in this order): 30, 40, 24, 58, 48, 26, 11, 13. Draw the tree after each insertion.

R-7.3 A certain Professor Amongus claims that the order in which a fixed set of elements is inserted into a binary search tree does not matter—the same tree results every time. Give a small example that proves Professor Amongus wrong.

R-7.4 Professor Amongus claims he has a "patch" to his claim from the previous exercise, namely, that the order in which a fixed set of elements is inserted into an AVL tree does not matter—the same AVL tree results every time. Give a small example that proves that Professor Amongus is still wrong.

R-7.5 Is the rotation done in Figure 7.8 a single or a double rotation? What about the rotation in Figure 7.10?

R-7.6 Draw the AVL tree resulting from the insertion of an item with key 52 into the AVL tree of Figure 7.10b.

R-7.7 Draw the AVL tree resulting from the removal of the item with key 62 from the AVL tree of Figure 7.10b.

R-7.8 Explain why performing a rotation in an n-node binary tree represented using a sequence takes $\Omega(n)$ time.

R-7.9 Draw an example of a skip list that results from performing the following sequence of operations on the skip list shown in Figure 7.13: remove(38), insertItem(48,x), insertItem(24,y), remove(55). Remember to flip a coin in the insertion operations.

R-7.10 Give a detailed pseudo-code description of the remove dictionary operation, assuming the dictionary is implemented by a skip-list structure.

R-7.11 Draw the 11-item hash table that results from using the hash function
$$h(i) = (2i+5) \bmod 11,$$
to hash the keys 12, 44, 13, 88, 23, 94, 11, 39, 20, 16, and 5, assuming collisions are handled by chaining.

R-7.12 What is the result of the previous exercise, assuming collisions are handled by linear probing? What if we use quadratic probing?

R-7.13 What is the result of Exercise R-7.11 assuming collisions are handled by double hashing?

R-7.14 What is the worst-case running time for inserting n items into an initially empty hash table, where collisions are resolved by chaining? What if each sequence is stored in sorted order?

Creativity

C-7.1 Give a Java implementation of the binary search algorithm using only methods from the Position and Sequence classes (that is, your implementation cannot explicitly use array indexing).

   1. What is the running time of this method assuming the sequence is implemented as an array?
   2. What is the running time of this method assuming the sequence is implemented as a linked list?

C-7.2 Suppose we are given two ordered dictionaries S and T, each with n items, and that S and T are implemented by means of array-based ordered sequences. Describe an $O(\log^2 n)$-time algorithm for finding the kth smallest key in the union of the keys from S and T (assuming no duplicates).

C-7.3★ Give an $O(\log n)$ time solution for the previous problem.

C-7.4 Design a variation of binary search for performing findAllElements(k) in an ordered dictionary implemented with an ordered sequence, and show that it runs in time $O(\log n + s)$, where n is the number of elements in the dictionary, and s is the size of the enumeration returned.

C-7.5 Design a variation of algorithm TreeSearch for performing the operation findAllElements(k) in an ordered dictionary implemented with a binary search tree T, and show that it runs in time $O(h + s)$, where h is the height of T, and s is the size of the enumeration returned.

C-7.6 Draw an example of an AVL tree such that a single remove operation could require $\Theta(\log n)$ rotations from a leaf to the root in order to restore the height-balance property. (Use triangles to represent subtrees that are not affected by this operation.)

C-7.7 Show how to perform operation removeAll(k) in a dictionary implemented by means of an AVL tree in time $O(\log n + s)$, where n is the number of elements in the dictionary at the time the operation is performed and s is the size of the enumeration returned by the operation.

C-7.8★ Show that any n-node binary tree can be converted to any other n-node binary tree using $O(n)$ rotations. (Hint: show that $O(n)$ rotations suffice to convert any binary tree into a *left chain*, where each internal node has an external right child.)

C-7.9 Let D be an ordered dictionary with n items implemented by means of an AVL tree. Show how to implement the following operation on D in time $O(\log n + s)$, where s is the size of the enumeration returned:

findAllInRange(k_1, k_2): Return an enumeration of all the elements in D with key k such that $k_1 \leq k \leq k_2$.
Input: Objects; *Output:* Enumeration.

C-7.10★ Let D be an ordered dictionary with n items implemented by means of an AVL tree. Show how to implement the following operation on D in time $O(\log n)$:

countAllInRange(k_1, k_2): Compute and return the number of items in D with key k such that $k_1 \leq k \leq k_2$.
Input: Objects; *Output:* Integer.

Note that this method returns a single integer. You will need to extend the AVL tree data structure.

C-7.11 Show that at most one node in an AVL tree becomes unbalanced after operation removeAboveExternal is performed within the execution of a remove dictionary operation.

C-7.12 Show that at most one (single or double) rotation is needed after any insertion in an AVL tree.

C-7.13 Show that the methods above(p) and before(p) are not actually needed to efficiently implement a dictionary using a skip list. That is, we can implement item insertion and removal in a skip list using a strict top-down, scan-forward approach, without ever using the above or before methods. (Hint: in the insertion algorithm, first repeatedly flip the coin to determine the level where you should start inserting the new item.)

C-7.14 The hash table dictionary implementation requires that we find a prime number between a number M and a number $2M$. Implement a method for finding such a prime by using the *sieve algorithm*. In this algorithm, we allocate a $2M$ cell boolean array A such that cell i is associated with the integer i. We then initialize the array cells to all be "true" and we "mark off" all the cells that are multiples of 2, 3, 5, 7, and so on. This process can stop after it reaches a number larger than $\sqrt{2M}$. (Hint: consider a bootstrapping method for finding the primes up to $\sqrt{2M}$.)

C-7.15 Assuming a dictionary D is implemented as an unordered sequence, describe how to implement the following operation:

> locAtRank(r): Return a locator to an item (k, e) of D, such that D has exactly r items with key less than k.
> *Input:* Integer; *Output:* Locator.

What is the worst-case running time of this method?

C-7.16 Describe how to implement the locator-based method before(ℓ) as well as the locator-based method closestBefore(k) in a dictionary realized using an ordered sequence. Do the same using an unordered sequence implementation. What are the running times of these methods?

C-7.17 Repeat the previous exercise using a skip list. What are the expected running times of the two locator-based methods in your implementation?

C-7.18 If we keep the position to the leftmost internal node of an AVL tree, then operation min can be performed in $O(1)$ time. Describe how the implementation of the other dictionary methods needs to be modified to maintain the leftmost position.

Projects

P-7.1 Implement a class that realizes the Comparator ADT so as to be able to compare objects that are numeric strings (see Section 11.1). In this case, the character strings should be interpreted as numbers in some base, such as base 2 (binary strings) or base 10 (decimal numbers). In addition to the comparator operations, the StringNumberComparator should support a method setBase(b) that takes a positive integer less than or equal to 10 as the base for the numeric strings to be compared.

P-7.2 Implement the methods of the ordered dictionary ADT using an ordered sequence.

P-7.3 Implement a class RestructurableNodeBinaryTree that supports the methods of the binary tree ADT, plus a method restructure for performing a rotation operation. This class is a component of the implementation of an AVL tree given in Section 7.4.3.

P-7.4 Implement the methods of the ordered dictionary ADT using an AVL tree.

P-7.5 Implement the methods of the ordered dictionary ADT using a skip list.

P-7.6 Implement the methods of the dictionary ADT using a hash table (but not the built-in java.util.Hashtable class of Java).

P-7.7 Implement a dictionary that supports locator-based methods by means of an ordered sequence.

P-7.8 Implement a dictionary that supports locator-based methods by means of a binary search tree.

P-7.9 Implement a dictionary that supports locator-based methods by means of an AVL tree.

Chapter Notes

Interestingly, the binary search algorithm was first published in 1946, but was not published in a fully correct form until 1962. For further discussions on the lessons to be learned from this history, please see the discussions in Knuth's book [90] and the papers by Bentley [21] and Levisse [98].

AVL trees are due to Adel'son-Vel'skii and Landis [1], who invented this class of balanced search trees in 1962. Binary search trees, AVL trees, and hashing are described in Knuth's *Sorting and Searching* [90] book. Average-height analyses for binary search trees can be found in the books by Aho, Hopcroft, and Ullman [7] and Cormen, Leiserson, and Rivest [36]. The handbook by Gonnet and Baeza-Yates [59] contains a number of theoretical and experimental comparisons among dictionary implementations.

Skip lists were introduced by Pugh [125]. Our analysis of skip lists is a simplification of a presentation given in the book by Motwani and Raghavan [115]. In addition, our discussion of universal hashing is also a simplification of a presentation given in that book. The reader interested in other probabilistic constructions for supporting the dictionary ADT (including more information about universal hashing) is referred to the text by Motwani and Raghavan [115]. For a more in-depth analysis of skip lists, the reader is referred to papers on skip lists that have appeared in the data structures literature [87, 120, 122].

Chapter

8

Sorting, Sets, and Selection

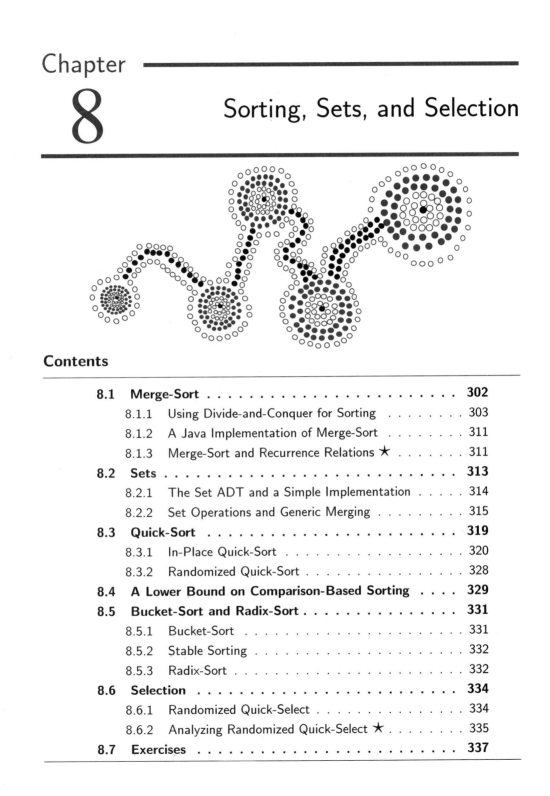

Contents

The Second Law of Thermodynamics suggests that Nature tends towards disorder. Humans, on the other hand, prefer order. Indeed, there are several advantages to keeping data in order. For example, the binary search algorithm, discussed in Section 7.2, works correctly only for an ordered sequence. Since computers are intended to be tools for humans, we devote this chapter to the study of sorting algorithms and their applications. We recall that the sorting problem is defined as follows. Let S be a sequence of n elements that can be compared to each other according to a total order relation, that is, it is always possible to compare two elements of S to see which is larger or smaller, or if the two of them are equal. We want to rearrange S in such a way that the elements appear in increasing order (or in nondecreasing order if there are equal elements in S).

We have already presented several sorting algorithms in the previous chapters. In particular, in Section 6.1.2, we presented a simple sorting scheme, called PriorityQueueSort, which consists of inserting elements into a priority queue and then extracting them in nondecreasing order, by means of a series of removeMinElement operations. If the priority queue is implemented by means of a sequence, then PriorityQueueSort runs in $O(n^2)$ time and corresponds to the sorting method known as either insertion-sort or selection-sort, depending on whether the sequence realizing the priority queue is kept ordered or not (Section 6.2.3). If instead the priority queue is implemented by means of a heap (Section 6.3), then PriorityQueueSort runs in $O(n \log n)$ time and corresponds to the sorting method known as heap-sort (Section 6.3.3).

In this chapter, we present four other sorting algorithms, called ***merge-sort***, ***quick-sort***, ***bucket-sort***, and ***radix-sort***. We also introduce the ***set*** abstract data type and show how the merge technique used in the merge-sort algorithm can be used in the implementation of its methods. Throughout this chapter, we assume that a total order relation is defined over the elements to be sorted. If this relation is induced by a comparator (Section 6.1.4), we assume that a comparison test takes $O(1)$ time.

8.1   Merge-Sort

We have already seen the power of recursion to describe algorithms in an elegant manner. (See, for example, the tree traversal techniques presented in Chapter 5.) In this section, we present a sorting technique, called ***merge-sort***, which can be described in a simple and compact way using recursion. This algorithm is also based upon our using an algorithm design technique called divide-and-conquer, which is both powerful and general.

8.1.1 Using Divide-and-Conquer for Sorting

Merge-sort is based on a general technique for algorithm design called ***divide-and-conquer***. The divide-and-conquer paradigm can be described in general terms as consisting of the following three steps:

1. ***Divide:*** If the input size is smaller than a certain threshold (say, one or two elements), solve the problem directly using a straightforward method and return the solution so obtained. Otherwise, divide the input data into two or more disjoint subsets.
2. ***Recurse:*** Recursively solve the subproblems associated with the subsets.
3. ***Conquer:*** Take the solutions to the subproblems and "merge" them into a solution to the original problem.

This technique has several applications, and we explore it in more detail in Chapter 12. The merge-sort algorithm applies the divide-and-conquer technique to the sorting problem. For the problem of sorting a sequence S with n elements, the above three steps are specialized as follows:

1. ***Divide:*** If S has at least two elements (nothing needs to be done if S has zero or one element), remove all the elements from S and put them into two sequences, S_1 and S_2, each containing about half of the elements of S, that is, S_1 contains the first $\lceil n/2 \rceil$ elements of S, and S_2 contains the remaining $\lfloor n/2 \rfloor$ elements.
2. ***Recurse:*** Recursively sort sequences S_1 and S_2.
3. ***Conquer:*** Put back the elements into S by merging the sorted sequences S_1 and S_2 into a unique sorted sequence.

As shown in Figures 8.1 through 8.4, we can visualize an execution of merge-sort by means of a binary tree T, called the ***merge-sort tree***. Each node of T represents a recursive invocation (or call) of the merge-sort algorithm. We associate with each node v of T the input sequence S that is passed to the invocation associated with v. The children of node v are associated with the recursive calls that are input the subsequences S_1 and S_2 of S. The external nodes of T are associated with individual elements of S, corresponding to instances of the algorithm that make no recursive calls.

This algorithm visualization in terms of the tree T also helps us analyze the running time of the merge-sort algorithm. In particular, since the size of the input sequence roughly halves at each recursive invocation of merge-sort, the height of the merge-sort tree is about $\log n$ (recall that the base of log is 2 if omitted).

Proposition 8.1: *The merge-sort tree associated with an execution of merge-sort on a sequence of size n has height $\lceil \log n \rceil$.*

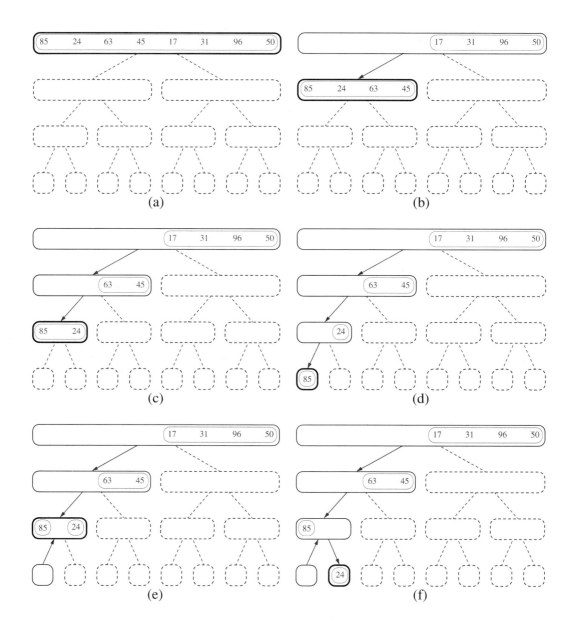

Figure 8.1: Visualization of an execution of merge-sort. Each node of the tree represents a recursive call of merge-sort. The nodes drawn with dashed lines represent calls that have not been made yet. The node drawn with thick lines represents the current call. The empty nodes drawn with thin lines represent completed calls. The remaining nodes (drawn with thin lines and not empty) represent calls that are waiting for a child invocation to return).

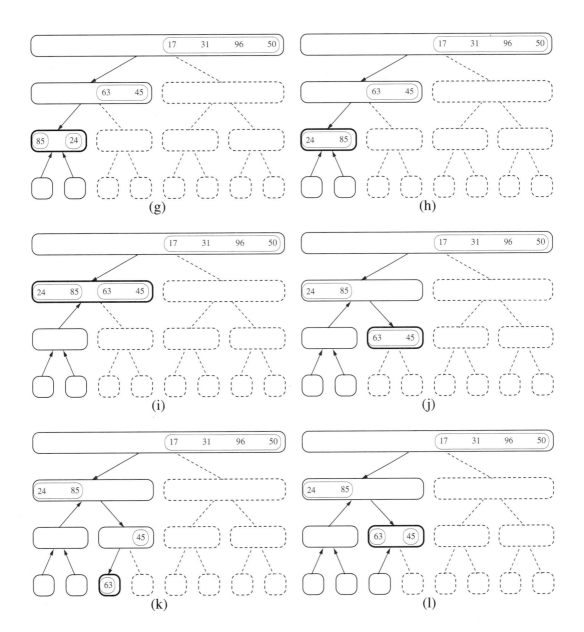

Figure 8.2: (Continued from Figure 8.1.) Visualization of an execution of merge-sort. Note the conquer step performed in (h).

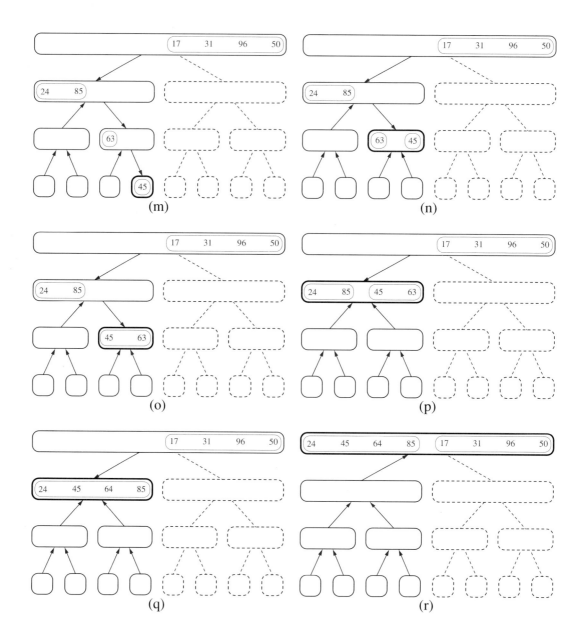

Figure 8.3: (Continued from Figure 8.2.) Visualization of an execution of merge-sort. Note the conquer steps performed in (o) and (q).

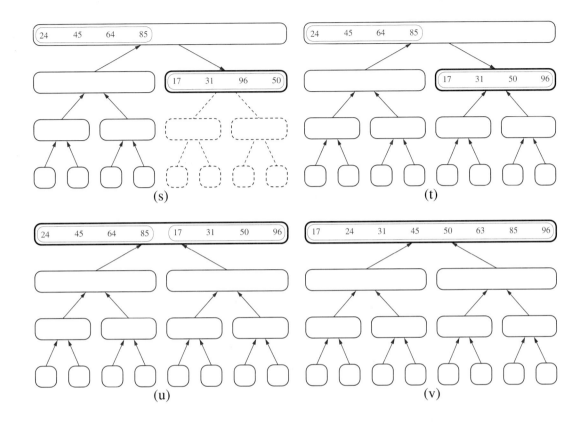

Figure 8.4: (Continued from Figure 8.3.) Visualization of an execution of merge-sort. Several invocations are omitted between (s) and (t). Note the conquer steps performed in (t) and (v).

We leave the justification of Proposition 8.1 as an interesting exercise. The importance of this proposition is that, once we have analyzed the details for performing the conquer step, we can apply this proposition to help derive the overall running time for the merge-sort algorithm.

Merging Two Sorted Sequences

Having given the high-level overview of merge-sort and an illustration of how it works, let us now consider each of the steps in this divide-and-conquer algorithm in more detail. The divide and recurse steps of the merge-sort algorithm are simple; dividing a sequence of size n involves separating it just after the element at rank $\lceil n/2 \rceil - 1$, and the recursive calls simply involve correctly passing these smaller sequences as parameters. The difficult step is the conquer step, which merges two sorted sequences into a single sorted sequence. Algorithm merge, shown in Code Fragment 8.1, accomplishes this task. It merges two sorted sequences by iteratively removing a smallest element from one of these two and adding it to the end of the output sequence until one of these two sequences is empty, at which point we copy the remainder of the other sequence to the end of the output sequence. A Java implementation of algorithm merge is given in Code Fragment 8.3. In addition, we show in Figure 8.5 an example execution of algorithm merge.

Algorithm merge(S_1, S_2, S):

    Input: Sequences S_1 and S_2 (on whose elements a total order relation is defined) sorted in nondecreasing order, and an empty sequence S

    Output: Sequence S containing the union of the elements from S_1 and S_2 sorted in nondecreasing order; sequences S_1 and S_2 become empty at the end of the execution

    while S_1 is not empty **and** S_2 is not empty **do**

      if S_1.first().element() $\leq$ S_2.first().element() **then**

        { move the first element of S_1 at the end of S }

        S.insertLast(S_1.remove(S_1.first()))

      else

        { move the first element of S_2 at the end of S }

        S.insertLast(S_2.remove(S_2.first()))

    { move the remaining elements of S_1 to S }

    while S_1 is not empty **do**

      S.insertLast(S_1.remove(S_1.first()))

    { move the remaining elements of S_2 to S }

    while S_2 is not empty **do**

      S.insertLast(S_2.remove(S_2.first()))

Code Fragment 8.1: Algorithm merge for merging two sorted sequences into a unique sorted sequence.

We can analyze the running time of the merge algorithm by making a simple observation. Let n_1 and n_2 be the number of elements of S_1 and S_2, respectively. Also, let us assume that the input sequences S_1 and S_2 and the output sequence S are implemented in such a way that access to, insertion into, and deletion from the first and last positions of the sequence each take $O(1)$ time. This is the case for sequences based on circular arrays or a doubly linked list (Section 4.3). Algorithm merge has three **while** loops. Because of our assumptions, the operations performed inside each loop take $O(1)$ time each. The key observation for our analysis is that during each iteration of one of the loops, one element is removed from either S_1

or S_2. Since no insertions are performed into S_1 or S_2, this observation implies that the overall number of iterations of the three loops is $n_1 + n_2$. Thus, the running time of algorithm merge is $O(n_1 + n_2)$.

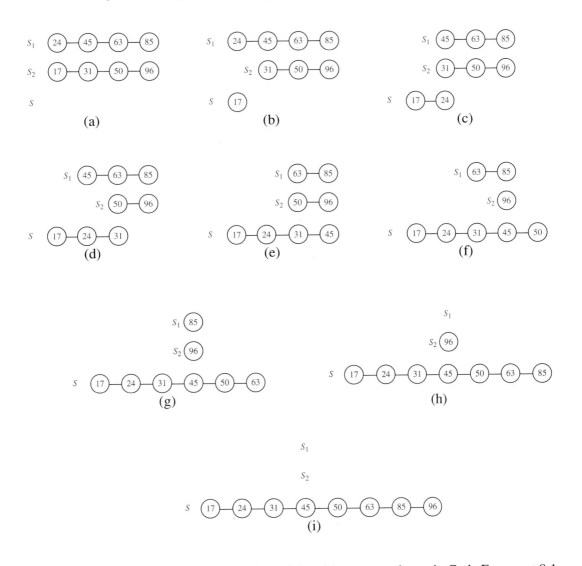

Figure 8.5: Example of execution of algorithm merge shown in Code Fragment 8.1.

The Running Time of Merge-Sort

Now that we have given the details of the merge-sort algorithm and have even analyzed the running time of the crucial merge algorithm used in the conquer step, let us analyze the running time of the entire merge-sort algorithm, assuming it is given an input sequence of n elements. For simplicity, we restrict our attention to the case where n is a power of 2. We leave it to an exercise to show that the result of our analysis also holds when n is not a power of 2.

As we did in the analysis of the merge algorithm, we assume that the input sequence S and the auxiliary sequences S_1 and S_2, created by each recursive call of merge-sort, are implemented in such a way that access to, insertion into, and deletion from the first and last positions of the sequence each take $O(1)$ time. This is the case for the implementations based on a circular array and a doubly linked list (Section 4.3).

As we mentioned earlier, we analyze the merge-sort procedure by referring to the merge-sort tree T. (Recall Figures 8.1 through 8.4.) We call the ***time spent at a node*** v of T the running time of the recursive call associated with v, excluding the time taken waiting for the recursive calls associated with the children of v to terminate. In other words, the time spent at node v includes the running times of the divide and conquer steps, but excludes the running time of the recurse step. We have already observed that the details of the divide step are straightforward; this step runs in time proportional to the size of the sequence for v. Also, as shown above, the conquer step, which consists of merging two sorted subsequences, also takes linear time. That is, letting i denote the depth of node v, the time spent at node v is $O(n/2^i)$, since the size of the sequence handled by the recursive call associated with v is equal to $n/2^i$.

Looking at the tree T more globally, we see that, given our definition of "time spent at a node," the running time of merge-sort is equal to the sum of the times spent at the nodes of T. Observe that T has exactly 2^i nodes at depth i. This simple observation has an important consequence, for it implies that the overall time spent at all the nodes of T at depth i is $O(2^i \cdot n/2^i)$, which is $O(n)$. By Proposition 8.1, the height of T is $\lceil \log n \rceil$. Thus, since the time spent at each of the $\lceil \log n \rceil + 1$ levels of T is $O(n)$, we have the following:

Proposition 8.2: *Algorithm merge-sort sorts a sequence of size n in $O(n \log n)$ time.*

In other words, the merge-sort procedure asymptotically matches the fast running time of the heap-sort algorithm.

8.1.2   A Java Implementation of Merge-Sort

In Code Fragment 8.3, we show a complete Java implementation of merge-sort. Class ListMergeSort implements the SortObject interface shown in Code Fragment 8.2, which defines a method sort(S,c) for sorting a sequence S using comparator c. Class ListMergeSort defines two methods: method sort, which is the merge-sort algorithm itself, and method merge, which is the associated merge procedure. Method sort assumes that the input sequence S supports a method newContainer that returns a new empty sequence of the same class as S. The sort method directly applies the divide-and-conquer paradigm to S using the built-in methods in the sequence ADT.

```
public interface SortObject {
   // sort sequence S in nondecreasing order using comparator c
    public void sort(Sequence S, Comparator c);
}
```

Code Fragment 8.2: Interface SortObject.

8.1.3   Merge-Sort and Recurrence Relations ⋆

There is another way to justify that the running time of the merge-sort algorithm is $O(n \log n)$ (Proposition 8.2). Namely, there is a justification that deals more directly with the recursive nature of the merge-sort algorithm. In this section, we present such an analysis of the running time of merge-sort, and in so doing introduce the mathematical concept of a ***recurrence relation***.

Let the function $t(n)$ denote the worst-case running time of merge-sort on an input sequence of size n. Since merge-sort is recursive, we can characterize function $t(n)$ by means of the following equalities, where function $t(n)$ is recursively expressed in terms of itself, as follows:

$$t(n) = \begin{cases} b & \text{if } n \leq 1 \\ t(\lceil n/2 \rceil) + t(\lfloor n/2 \rfloor) + cn & \text{otherwise} \end{cases}$$

where $b \geq 1$ and $c \geq 1$ are constants. A characterization of a function such as the one above is called a ***recurrence relation***, since the function appears on both the left- and right-hand sides of the equal sign. While such a characterization is correct and accurate, what we really desire is a big-Oh type of characterization of $t(n)$ that does not involve the function $t(n)$ itself (that is, we want a ***closed-form*** characterization of $t(n)$).

```java
public class ListMergeSort implements SortObject {

  public void sort(Sequence S, Comparator c) {
    int n = S.size();
    // a sequence with 0 or 1 element is already sorted
    if (n < 2) return;
    // divide
    Sequence S1 = (Sequence)S.newContainer();
    for (int i=1; i <= (n+1)/2; i++) {
      S1.insertLast(S.remove(S.first()));
    }
    Sequence S2 = (Sequence)S.newContainer();
    for (int i=1; i <= n/2; i++) {
      S2.insertLast(S.remove(S.first()));
    }
    // recur
    sort(S1,c);
    sort(S2,c);
    //conquer
    merge(S1,S2,c,S);
  }

  public void merge(Sequence S1, Sequence S2, Comparator c, Sequence S) {
    while(!S1.isEmpty() && !S2.isEmpty()) {
      if(c.isLessThanOrEqualTo(S1.first().element(),S2.first().element())) {
        S.insertLast(S1.remove(S1.first()));
      }
      else {
        S.insertLast(S2.remove(S2.first()));
      }
    }
    if(S1.isEmpty()) {
      while(!S2.isEmpty()) {
        S.insertLast(S2.remove(S2.first()));
      }
    }
    if(S2.isEmpty()) {
      while(!S1.isEmpty()) {
        S.insertLast(S1.remove(S1.first()));
      }
    }
  }
}
```

Code Fragment 8.3: Class ListMergeSort that implements the merge-sort algorithm.

In order to provide a closed-form characterization of $t(n)$, let us restrict our attention to the case when n is a power of 2 (we leave as an exercise the problem of showing that our asymptotic characterization still holds in the general case). In this case, we can simplify the definition of $t(n)$ to be

$$t(n) = \begin{cases} b & \text{if } n \leq 1 \\ 2t(n/2) + cn & \text{else,} \end{cases}$$

but, even so, we must still try to characterize this recurrence equation in a closed-form way. One way to do this is to iteratively apply this equation, assuming n is relatively large. For example, after one more application of this equation we can write a new recurrence for $t(n)$ as follows:

$$\begin{aligned} t(n) &= 2(2t(n/2^2) + (cn/2)) + cn \\ &= 2^2 t(n/2^2) + 2(cn/2) + cn \\ &= 2^2 t(n/2^2) + 2cn. \end{aligned}$$

If we apply the equation again we get

$$t(n) = 2^3 t(n/2^3) + 3cn.$$

At this point, we see a pattern emerging, so that after applying this equation i times we get

$$t(n) = 2^i t(n/2^i) + icn.$$

The issue that remains, then, is to determine when to stop this process. To see when to stop, recall that we switch to the closed form $t(n) = b$ when $n \leq 1$, which will occur when $2^i = n$. In other words, this will occur when $i = \log n$. Making this substitution, then, yields

$$t(n) = nb + cn \log n.$$

That is, we get an alternative justification of the fact that $t(n)$ is $O(n \log n)$. We study recurrence relations in more detail in Chapter 12.

In the next section we show how sorting and the merge algorithm can be used to implement an abstract data type for sets.

8.2 Sets

A *set* is a container that models the mathematical notion of a set. Thus, a set object stores a collection of elements so as to support fundamental set operations such as union and intersection. In this section, we introduce the set ADT, and show how its methods can be efficiently implemented using variations of the merge algorithm. The operations of a set do not refer to a total order relation among the elements, but that does not necessarily mean we cannot use ordering information to implement a set.

8.2.1 The Set ADT and a Simple Implementation

The specific operations supported by the set ADT include some operations similar to those of the dictionary ADT (Section 7.1) plus other operations that only make sense for sets. The fundamental set operations are set ***union***, set ***intersection***, and set ***subtraction***, which are respectively defined as follows for two sets A and B:

$$
\begin{aligned}
A \cup B &= \{x : x \in A \text{ or } x \in B\}, \\
A \cap B &= \{x : x \in A \text{ and } x \in B\}, \\
A - B &= \{x : x \in A \text{ and } x \notin B\}.
\end{aligned}
$$

The specific methods for a set A include the following:

size(): Return the number of elements in the set A.
Input: None; ***Output:*** Integer.

isEmpty(): Return if the set A is empty or not.
Input: None; ***Output:*** Boolean.

insertElement(e): Insert the element e into the set A, unless e is already in A.
Input: Object; ***Output:*** None.

elements(): Return an enumeration of the elements in the set A.
Input: None; ***Output:*** Enumeration.

isMember(e): Determine if e is in A.
Input: Object; ***Output:*** Boolean.

union(B): Return $A \cup B$.
Input: Set; ***Output:*** Set.

intersect(B): Return $A \cap B$.
Input: Set; ***Output:*** Set.

subtract(B): Return $A - B$.
Input: Set; ***Output:*** Set.

isEqual(B): Return true if and only if $A = B$.
Input: Two set objects; ***Output:*** Boolean.

We define the set methods union, intersect, and subtract above so that they are ***nondestructive***—they do not change the contents of the sets involved. If we wish to have a destructive version of one of these operations, say to union one set into another, destroying both, we can assign the result of the operation to one of the sets involved, and set equal to null the (reference to) the other set so that inactive elements will be garbage-collected.

If we wish to support the locator pattern (Section 6.4), then we can add the following methods to the repertory:

insert(e): Insert the element e into the set A, unless e is already in A, and return a locator to e in A.
Input: Object; *Output:* Locator.

remove(ℓ): Remove the element with locator ℓ, returning that element.
Input: Locator; *Output:* Object.

locators(): Return an enumeration of all the locators of the elements in A.
Input: None; *Output:* Enumeration (of locators).

One of the simplest and most versatile ways of implementing a set of elements is to store them in an ordered sequence. Even if the elements themselves do not naturally come from a total order, there is almost always a canonical way of ordering them (even if it is by their addresses in memory). Therefore, let us consider implementing the set ADT using an ordered sequence. The implementations for the methods size(), isEmpty(), elements(), remove(ℓ), and locators() can therefore be the same as in the ordered sequence implementation of a dictionary (Section 7.2). The methods insert(e) and insertElement(e) can also be done by essentially the same implementation as for the dictionary ADT, except that we require each element in a set to be unique. The interesting part of implementing a set with an ordered sequence is how it allows us to perform the union, intersection, and subtraction operations.

8.2.2 Set Operations and Generic Merging

We implement each of the set operations by using a generic version of the merge algorithm that takes as input two sorted sequences representing the input sets and constructs a sequence representing the output set, be it the union, intersection, or subtraction of the input sets. The ordering for the two sequences can be based upon any consistent ordering rule (that is, a total order), provided the same ordering rule is used for the two sets on which we wish to perform a union, intersection, or subtraction. We describe in detail the generic merge method in Code Fragment 8.4.

The generic merge method iteratively examines and compares the current elements a and b of enumerations A and B, respectively, and finds out whether $a < b$, $a = b$, or $a > b$. Then, based upon the outcome of this comparison, it determines

Algorithm genericMerge(A, B):

    Input: Sorted sequences A and B

    Output: Sorted sequence C

    {We won't destroy A and B}

    let A' be a copy of A

    let B' be a copy of B

    while A' and B' are not empty **do**

      $a \leftarrow A'$.first()

      $b \leftarrow B'$.first()

      if $a < b$ **then**

        firstIsLess(a,C)

        A'.removeFirst()

      else if $a = b$ **then**

        bothAreEqual(a,b,C)

        A'.removeFirst()

        B'.removeFirst()

      else

        firstIsGreater(b,C)

        B'.removeFirst()

    while A' is not empty **do**

      $a \leftarrow A'$.first()

      firstIsLess(a,C)

      A'.removeFirst()

    while B' is not empty **do**

      $b \leftarrow B'$.first()

      firstIsGreater(b,C)

      B'.removeFirst()

Code Fragment 8.4: Generic merge algorithm, parametrized by methods firstIsLess, bothAreEqual, and firstIsGreater.

whether it should copy one or none of the elements a and b to the end of the output sequence C. This determination is made based upon the particular operation we are performing, be it a union, intersection, or subtraction. For example, in a union operation, we copy the smaller of a and b to the output sequence, and, if they are equal, we copy just one (say a). This ensures that we will copy each element that is in one of the two sets, but we will not create duplicate entries. We specify the copy actions to perform using methods firstIsLess, bothAreEqual, and firstIsGreater, which we define depending upon the operation we wish to perform.

The generic merge algorithm is based on the template method pattern (see Section 5.3.4). The template pattern describes a generic computation mechanism that can be specialized by redefining certain steps. In this case we describe a method that merges two sequences into one modulated by the behavior of three abstract methods.

We give a Java implementation of the generic merge algorithm in Code Fragments 8.5, describing it as an abstract Merger class.

To convert the generic abstract Merger class into useful classes, we must extend it with concrete classes that implement the three abstract methods, firstIsLess, bothAreEqual, and firstIsGreater. We show how each of the operations of union, intersection, and subtraction can be easily described in terms of these methods in Code Fragment 8.6. These methods are defined so that the merge method for a UnionMerger object will copy every element from A and B, but will not duplicate any elements. An IntersectMerger object is defined so that the merge method will copy every element that is in both A and B, but will "throw away" any elements that are in one set but not in the other. Finally, a SubtractMerger object is defined so that the merge method will copy every element in A but not in B.

Each of the implementations of the generic merge method removes an element from A or B (or both) with each iteration. Assuming that comparisons between elements take $O(1)$ time, this implies that the total running time of a generic merge operation is $O(n_A + n_B)$, where n_A is the size of A and n_B is the size of B, that is, merging takes time proportional to the number of elements involved. Therefore, the generic merge method provides a linear-time implementation of the fundamental set operations. It can also be used to implement the isEqual method in linear time, but we leave the details of this fact to an exercise.

We summarize the performance of using an ordered sequence and the generic merge method to implement the set ADT in Table 8.1.

Methods	Time
size, isEmpty	$O(1)$
insertElement	$O(n)$
elements, isMember	$O(n)$
union, intersect, subtract	$O(n)$
isEqual	$O(n)$

Table 8.1: Performance of sets realized by ordered sequences. We let n denote the size of the set(s) involved in the respective operations.

```java
public abstract class Merger {
  protected abstract void firstIsLess(Object a, Sequence C);
  protected abstract void bothAreEqual(Object a, Object b, Sequence C);
  protected abstract void firstIsGreater(Object b, Sequence C);
  private Object a, b;
  private boolean advanceA(Enumeration enumA) {
    if (enumA.hasMoreElements()) { a = enumA.nextElement(); return true; }
    else { a = null; return false; } // for garbage collection
  }
  private boolean advanceB(Enumeration enumB) {
    if (enumB.hasMoreElements()) { b = enumB.nextElement(); return true; }
    else { b = null; return false; } // for garbage collection
  }
  public void merge(Sequence A, Sequence B, Sequence C, Comparator comp) {
    Enumeration enumA = A.elements(), enumB = B.elements();
    boolean aExists = advanceA(enumA), bExists = advanceB(enumB);
    while (aExists && bExists) {
      if (comp.isLessThan(a, b)) {
        firstIsLess(a, C);
        aExists = advanceA(enumA);
      } else if (comp.isEqualTo(a, b)) {
        bothAreEqual(a, b, C);
        aExists = advanceA(enumA);
        bExists = advanceB(enumB);
      } else {
        firstIsGreater(b, C);
        bExists = advanceB(enumB);
      }
    }
    while (aExists) {
      firstIsLess(a, C);
      aExists = advanceA(enumA);
    }
    while (bExists) {
      firstIsGreater(b, C);
      bExists = advanceB(enumB);
    }
  }
}
```

Code Fragment 8.5: The abstract Merger class.

```
public class UnionMerger extends Merger {
  protected void firstIsLess(Object a, Sequence C) {
    C.insertLast(a);
  }
  protected void bothAreEqual(Object a, Object b, Sequence C) {
    C.insertLast(a);
  }
  protected void firstIsGreater(Object b, Sequence C) {
    C.insertLast(b);
  }
}
public class IntersectMerger extends Merger {
  protected void firstIsLess(Object a, Sequence C) { } // null method
  protected void bothAreEqual(Object a, Object b, Sequence C) {
    C.insertLast(a);
  }
  protected void firstIsGreater(Object b, Sequence C) { } // null method
}
public class SubtractMerger extends Merger {
  protected void firstIsLess(Object a, Sequence C) {
    C.insertLast(a);
  }
  protected void bothAreEqual(Object a, Object b, Sequence C) {
  } // null method
  protected void firstIsGreater(Object b, Sequence C) { } // null method
}
```

Code Fragment 8.6: Concrete classes extending the abstract Merger class.

8.3 Quick-Sort

The next sorting algorithm we discuss is called *quick-sort*. Like merge-sort, this algorithm is also based on the divide-and-conquer paradigm, but it uses this technique in a somewhat backwards manner, as all the hard work is done *before* the recursive calls.

High-Level Description of Quick-Sort

The quick-sort algorithm sorts a sequence S using a simple recursive approach. The main idea is to apply the divide-and-conquer technique, whereby we divide S into subsequences whose range of elements are disjoint, recurse to sort each subsequence, and then combine the sorted subsequences by a simple concatenation.

In particular, the quick-sort algorithm consists of the following three steps:

1. ***Divide:*** If S has at least two elements (nothing needs to be done if S has zero or one element), select a specific element x from S, which is called the ***pivot***. For instance, let the pivot x be the last element. Remove all the elements from S and put them into three sequences:

   - L, storing the elements in S less than x
   - E, storing the elements in S equal to x
   - G, storing the elements in S greater than x.

   Of course, if the elements of S are all distinct, then E holds just one element—the pivot itself.

2. ***Recurse:*** Recursively sort sequences L and G.

3. ***Conquer:*** Put back the elements into S in order by first inserting the elements of L, then those of E, and finally those of G.

Like merge-sort, the execution of quick-sort can be visualized by means of a binary recursion tree, called the ***quick-sort tree***, as shown in Figures 8.6, 8.7, and 8.8. Unlike merge-sort, however, the height of the quick-sort tree associated with an execution of quick-sort is linear in the worst-case. This happens, for example, if the sequence consists of n distinct elements and is already sorted. Indeed, in this case, the pivot is the largest element, so that the size of subsequence L is $n - 1$, while subsequence E has size 1 and subsequence G has size 0. At each invocation of quick-sort on subsequence L, the size decreases by 1. Hence, the height of the quick-sort tree is $n - 1$.

8.3.1   In-Place Quick-Sort

There is an important implementation detail that we have avoided discussing so far: namely, the amount of additional space needed to implement a particular sorting algorithm. We say that a sorting algorithm is ***in-place*** if it uses only a constant amount of memory in addition to the memory needed for the objects being sorted themselves. A sorting algorithm is considered very space-efficient if it can be implemented to be in-place.

The merge-sort algorithm, as we have described it, is not in-place, and turning it into an in-place algorithm requires a more-complicated merging method than the one we discuss in Section 8.1.1. In-place sorting is not inherently difficult, however, for the sorting algorithm heap-sort, which is described in Section 6.3.3, can easily be made to be in-place if we use the sequence-based structure for the heap, where the sequence is in turn realized by means of an array. Likewise, the quick-sort algorithm can also be implemented so as to be in-place.

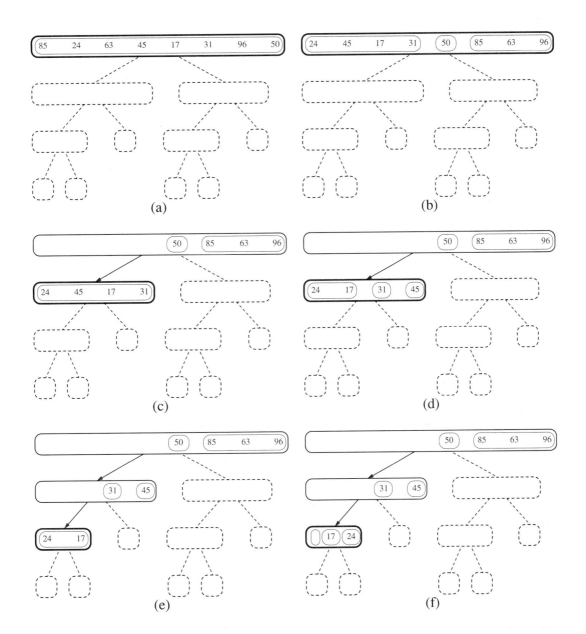

Figure 8.6: Visualization of quick-sort. Each node of the tree represents a recursive call of quick-sort. The nodes drawn with dashed lines represent calls that have not been made yet. The node drawn with thick lines represents the running invocation. The empty nodes drawn with thin lines represent terminated calls. The remaining nodes represent suspended calls (i.e., active invocations that are waiting for a child invocation to return). Note the divide steps performed in (b), (d), and (f).

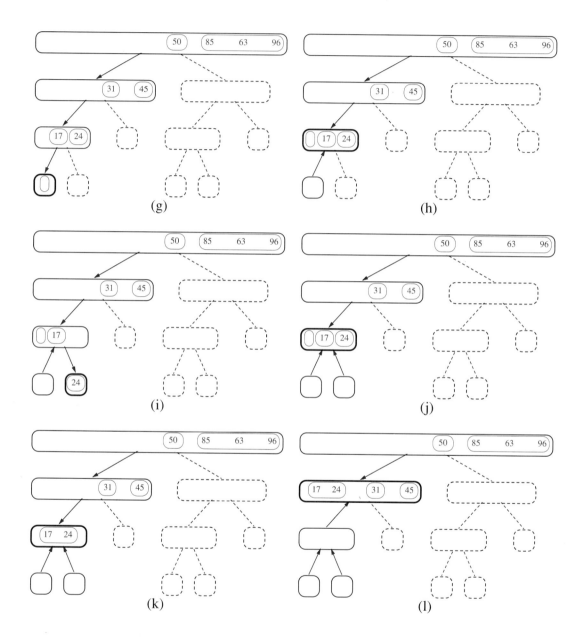

Figure 8.7: (Continued from Figure 8.6.) Visualization of an execution of quick-sort. Note the conquer step performed in (k).

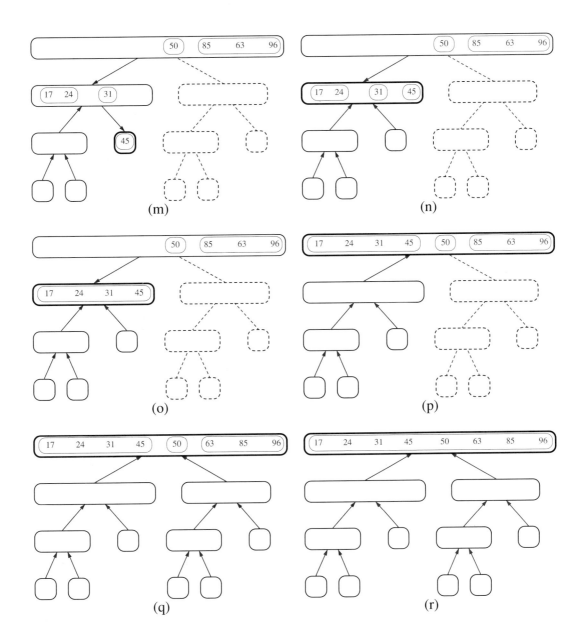

Figure 8.8: (Continued from Figure 8.7.) Visualization of an execution of quick-sort. Several invocations between (p) and (q) have been omitted. Note the conquer steps performed in (o) and (r).

Performing the quick-sort algorithm in-place requires a bit of ingenuity, for we must use the input sequence itself to store the subsequences for all the recursive calls of the quick-sort algorithm. We show such a quick-sort implementation in Code Fragment 8.7.

In-place quick-sort modifies the input sequence strictly by means of swap operations and does not explicitly create subsequences. Indeed, a subsequence of the input sequence can be implicitly represented by a range of positions specified by a left-most rank l and a right-most rank r. The divide step can be performed by scanning the sequence simultaneously from l forward and from r backward, swapping pairs of elements that are in reverse order, as shown in Figure 8.9. When these two indices "meet," the subsequences L and G are on opposite sides of this meeting point. The algorithm completes, then, by recursing on these two subsequences. In-place quick-sort reduces by a constant factor the overhead on the running time and the space requirement caused by the creation of new sequences and the movement of elements between them.

Technically speaking, the above implementation of quick-sort is still not quite in-place, as it still requires more than a constant amount of space. This additional space usage may not be immediately obvious, for we are using no additional space for the subsequences and we are using only a constant amount of additional space for local variables (such as l and r). Where does this additional space come from? It comes from the recursion, for, recalling the discussion from Section 3.1.3, we note that we need space proportional to the depth of the recursion tree for quick-sort, which is at least $\log n$ and at most $n - 1$.

In order to make quick-sort truly in-place, we must implement it in a non-recursive way (and not use a stack). The key detail for constructing such a non-recursive quick-sort implementation is to be able to determine the bounds for the left and right boundaries of the "current" subsequence. We leave the details of this implementation to an exercise.

Running Time of Quick-Sort

We can analyze the running time of quick-sort with the same technique used for merge-sort in Section 8.1.1. Namely, we identify the time spent at each node of the quick-sort tree T (Figures 8.6, 8.7, and 8.8), and we sum up the running times for all the nodes.

The divide step and the conquer step of quick-sort are easy to implement in linear time. Thus, the time spent at a node v of T is proportional to the ***input size*** $s(v)$ of v, defined as the size of the sequence handled by the invocation of quick-sort associated with node v. Since subsequence E has at least one element (the pivot), the sum of the input sizes of the children of v is at most $s(v) - 1$.

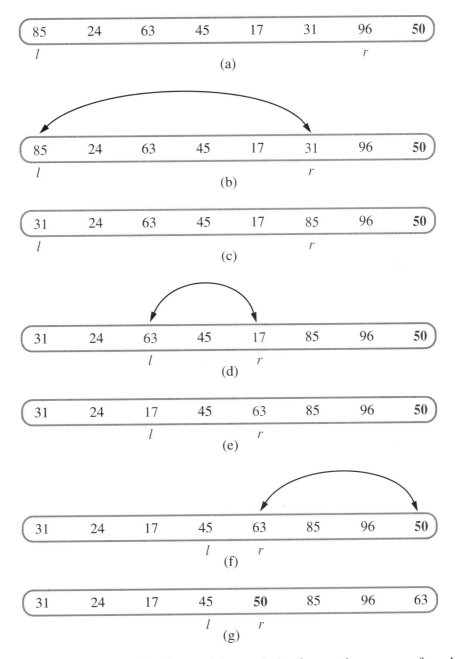

Figure 8.9: Divide step of in-place quick-sort. Index *l* scans the sequence from left to right, and index *r* scans the sequence from right to left. A swap is performed when *l* is at an element larger than the pivot and *r* is at an element smaller than the pivot. A final swap with the pivot completes the divide step.

```
public class ArrayQuickSort implements SortObject {
  public void sort (Sequence S, Comparator c) {
    quicksort(S, c, 0, S.size()−1);
  }
  private void quicksort (Sequence S,
                          Comparator c,
                          int leftBound, //  leftmost rank of sorting range
                          int rightBound // rightmost rank of sorting range
                          ) {
    // a sequence with 0 or 1 element is already sorted
    if (S.size() < 2) return;
    if (leftBound >= rightBound) return; // terminate recursion
    // pick the pivot as the current last element in the sorting range
    Object pivot = S.atRank(rightBound).element();
    // indices used to scan the sorting range
    int leftIndex = leftBound;        // will scan rightward
    int rightIndex = rightBound−1; // will scan leftward
    // outer loop
    while (leftIndex <= rightIndex) {
      // scan rightward until an element larger than the pivot is found
      // or the indices cross
      while ( (leftIndex <= rightIndex) &&
              c.isLessThanOrEqualTo(S.atRank(leftIndex).element(), pivot) )
        leftIndex++;
      // scan leftward until an element smaller than the pivot is found
      // or the indices cross
      while ( (rightIndex >= leftIndex) &&
              c.isGreaterThanOrEqualTo(S.atRank(rightIndex).element(), pivot) )
        rightIndex−−;
      // if an element larger than the pivot and an element smaller
      // than the pivot have been found, swap them
      if (leftIndex < rightIndex)
        S.swap ( S.atRank(leftIndex), S.atRank(rightIndex) );
    } // the outer loop continues until the indices cross
    // put the pivot in its place by swapping it with the element at
    // leftIndex
    S.swap ( S.atRank(leftIndex), S.atRank(rightBound) );
    // the pivot is now at leftIndex, so recur on both sides of it
    quicksort (S, c, leftBound, leftIndex−1);
    quicksort (S, c, leftIndex+1, rightBound);
  } // end quicksort
}
```

Code Fragment 8.7: Class ArrayQuickSort implementing in-place quick-sort.

Given a quick-sort tree T, let $s_i(n)$ denote the sum of the input sizes of the nodes at depth i in T. Clearly, $s_0(n) = n$, since the root r of T is associated with the entire sequence. Also, $s_1(n) \le n - 1$, since the pivot is not propagated to the children of r. Consider next $s_2(n)$. If both children of r have nonzero input size, then $s_2(n) = n - 3$. Otherwise (one child of the root has zero size, the other has size $n - 1$), $s_2(n) = n - 2$. Thus, $s_2(n) \le n - 2$. Continuing this line of reasoning, we obtain that $s_i(n) \le n - i$. As observed in Section 8.3, the height of T is $n - 1$ in the worst case. Thus, the worst-case running time of quick-sort is

$$O\left(\sum_{i=0}^{n-1} s_i(n)\right),$$

which is

$$O\left(\sum_{i=0}^{n-1}(n - i)\right) = O\left(\sum_{i=1}^{n} i\right).$$

By Proposition 2.4,

$$\sum_{i=1}^{n} i = \frac{n(n+1)}{2}.$$

Thus, quick-sort runs in $O(n^2)$ time in the worst case.

Given its name, we would expect quick-sort to run quickly. However, the above quadratic bound indicates that quick-sort is slow in the worst case. Paradoxically, this worst-case behavior occurs for problem instances when sorting should be easy—if the sequence is already sorted. Moreover, one can show that quick-sort performs poorly even if the sequence is just "almost" sorted.

Going back to our analysis, note that the best case for quick-sort occurs when subsequences L and G happen to have the same size for each invocation of the method. Indeed, in this case we save one pivot at each internal node and make two equal-sized calls for its children. Thus, we save 1 pivot at the root, 2 at level 1, 2^2 at level 2, and so on. That is, in the best case, we have:

$$
\begin{aligned}
s_0(n) &= n \\
s_1(n) &= n - 1 \\
s_2(n) &= n - (1+2) = n - 3 \\
s_3(n) &= n - (1+2+2^2) = n - 7 \\
&\ \vdots \\
s_i(n) &= n - (1 + 2 + 2^2 + \cdots + 2^{i-1}) = n - 2^i - 1 \\
&\ \vdots
\end{aligned}
$$

The above formulas imply that, in the best case, T has height $O(\log n)$ and quick-sort runs in $O(n \log n)$ time (we leave the justification for this as an exercise).

The informal intuition behind the expected behavior of quick-sort is that at each invocation the pivot will probably divide the input sequence about equally. Thus, we expect the average running time quick-sort to be similar to the best-case running time, that is, $O(n \log n)$. We will see in the next section that introducing randomization makes quick-sort behave exactly as described above.

8.3.2   Randomized Quick-Sort

One common method for analyzing quick-sort is to assume that the pivot will always divide the sequence almost equally. We feel such an assumption would presuppose knowledge about the input distribution that is typically not available, however. For example, we would have to assume that we will rarely be given "almost" sorted sequences to sort, which will be unlikely in practice as such sequences are common in many applications. Fortunately, this assumption is not needed in order for us to match our intuition to merge-sort's behavior.

Since the intuitive goal of the partition step of the quick-sort method is to divide the sequence S almost equally, let us introduce randomization into the algorithm and pick as the pivot a ***random element*** of the input sequence. This variation of quick-sort is called ***randomized quick-sort***.

The following proposition shows that the expected running time of randomized quick-sort on a sequence with n elements, is $O(n \log n)$, where this expectation is taken over all the possible random choices the algorithm makes, and is independent of any assumptions about the distribution of input sequences that the algorithm is likely to encounter.

Proposition 8.3: *The expected running time of randomized quick-sort on a sequence of size n is $O(n \log n)$.*

Justification: To justify this statement we will make use of a simple fact from probability theory:

> The expected number of times that a fair coin must be flipped until it shows "heads" k times is $2k$.

Consider now a single recursive invocation of randomized quick-sort, and let m denote the size of the input sequence for this invocation. Say that this invocation is "good" if the pivot chosen is such that subsequences L and G have size at least $m/4$ and at most $3m/4$ each. Thus, since the pivot is chosen uniformly at random and there are $m/2$ pivots for which this invocation is good, the probability that an invocation is good is $1/2$ (the same as the probability a coin comes up heads).

If a node v of the quick-sort tree T is associated with a "good" recursive call, then the input sizes of the children of v are each at most $3s(v)/4$ (which is the same as $(s(v)/(4/3))$). If we take any path in T from the root to an external node, then the length of this path is at most the number of invocations that have to be made (at each node on this path) until achieving $\log_{4/3} n$ good invocations. Applying the probabilistic fact reviewed above, the expected number of invocations we must make until this occurs is at most $2\log_{4/3} n$. Thus, the expected length of any path from the root to an external node in T is $O(\log n)$. Recalling that the time spent at each level of T is $O(n)$, the expected running time of randomized quick-sort is $O(n\log n)$. ∎

Actually, by using more-powerful facts from probability, one can show that the running time of randomized quick-sort is $O(n\log n)$ with very high probability. We leave this analysis as an exercise for the more mathematically inclined reader.

8.4 A Lower Bound on Comparison-Based Sorting

Recapping our discussions on sorting to this point, we have described several methods with either a worst-case or expected running time of $O(n\log n)$ on an input sequence of size n. These methods include merge-sort and quick-sort, described in this chapter, as well as heap-sort, described in Section 6.3.3. A natural question to ask, then, is whether it is possible to sort any faster than in $O(n\log n)$ time.

In this section, we show that if the basic computational primitive of a sorting algorithm is the comparison of two elements, then this is the best we can do—comparison-based sorting has an $\Omega(n\log n)$ worst-case lower bound on its running time. To focus in on the main cost of comparison-based sorting, let us only count the comparisons that a sorting algorithm performs. Since we want to derive a lower bound, this will certainly be sufficient.

Suppose we are given a sequence $S = (x_0, x_1, \ldots, x_{n-1})$. Each time a sorting algorithm compares two elements x_i and x_j (that is, it asks, "is $x_i \leq x_j$?"), there are two outcomes: "yes" or "no." Based on the result of this comparison, the sorting algorithm may perform some internal calculations (which we are not counting here) and will eventually perform another comparison between two other elements of S, which again will have two outcomes. Therefore, we can represent a comparison-based sorting algorithm with a decision tree T. (Recall Figure 5.5.) It is important to note that the hypothetical sorting algorithm in question probably has no explicit knowledge of the tree T. We simply use T to represent all the possible sequences of comparisons that a sorting algorithm might make, starting from the first comparison (associated with the root) and ending with the last comparison (associated with the parent of an external node) just before the algorithm outputs an answer.

Let us fix a set of objects that may belong to the sequence S, and, to simplify the arguments somewhat, let us assume the elements in S are distinct (which will be sufficient to establish the lower bound). Each possible initial ordering, or *permutation*, of the elements in S will result in the comparisons of our hypothetical sorting algorithm, proceeding in T from the root to some external node. Let us associate with each external node v in T, then, the set of permutations of S that cause our sorting algorithm to end up in v. The most important observation in our lower-bound argument is that each external node v in T can represent the sequence of comparisons for at most one permutation of S. The justification for this claim is simple; if two different permutations P_1 and P_2 of S are associated with the same external node, then there are at least two objects x_i and x_j, such that x_i is before x_j in P_1 but x_i is after x_j in P_2. At the same time, the output associated with v must be a specific reordering of S, with either x_i or x_j appearing before the other. But if P_1 and P_2 both cause the sorting algorithm to output the elements of S in this order, then that implies there is a way to trick the algorithm into outputting x_i and x_j in the wrong order. Since this cannot be allowed by a correct sorting algorithm, each external node of T can be associated with at most one permutation of S. We use this property of the decision tree associated with a sorting algorithm to prove the following result:

Proposition 8.4: *The running time of any comparison-based algorithm for sorting an n-element sequence is $\Omega(n \log n)$ in the worst case.*

Justification: The running time of a comparison-based sorting algorithm must be greater than or equal to the height of the decision tree T associated with this algorithm, as described above. By the above argument, each external node in T must be associated with at most one permutation of S. Moreover, each permutation of S must result in a different external node in T. Thus, T must have at least $n! = n(n-1)(n-2) \cdots 2 \cdot 1$ external nodes, which implies that the height of T is at least $\log(n!)$. This immediately justifies the proposition, for in the product $n!$, there are at least $n/2$ terms that are greater than or equal to $n/2$; hence

$$\log(n!) \geq \log(n/2)^{n/2} = (n/2) \log(n/2),$$

which is $\Omega(n \log n)$.   ■

So we cannot sort asymptotically faster than $O(n \log n)$ time with a comparison-based sorting algorithm. A natural question to ask, then, is whether there are other kinds of sorting algorithms that can be designed to asymptotically run faster than in $O(n \log n)$ time.

8.5 Bucket-Sort and Radix-Sort

Interestingly, it is indeed possible to asymptotically sort faster than $O(n \log n)$ time, but this requires some fairly restrictive assumptions about the format of the input sequence to be sorted. Even so, this restricted scenario often arises in practice, so discussing it is worthwhile.

8.5.1 Bucket-Sort

We consider the problem of sorting a sequence of items, each a key-element pair, where sorting takes into account only the keys. Note that all the sorting algorithms previously presented can be easily adapted to this scenario.

Consider a sequence S of n items whose keys are integers in the range $[0, N-1]$, for some integer $N \geq 2$, and suppose that S should be sorted according to the keys of the items. In this case, it is possible to sort S in $O(n+N)$ time. It might seem surprising, but this implies, for example, that if N is $O(n)$, then we can sort S in $O(n)$ time. Of course, the crucial point is that, because of the restrictive assumption about the format of the elements, we can avoid using comparisons.

The main idea is to use an algorithm called **bucket-sort**, which is based not upon comparisons, but on using keys as indices into a bucket array B that has entries from 0 to $N-1$. An item with key k is placed in the "bucket" $B[k]$, which itself is a sequence (of elements with key k).

After inserting each item of the input sequence S into its bucket, we can put back the items into S in sorted order by enumerating in order the contents of the buckets $B[0], B[1], \ldots, B[N-1]$. We describe the bucket-sort algorithm in Code Fragment 8.8.

Algorithm bucketSort(S):
    Input: Sequence S of items with integers keys in the range $[0, N-1]$
    Output: Sequence S sorted in nondecreasing order of the keys

    let B be an array of N sequences, each of which is initially empty
    for each item x in S **do**
        let k be the key of x
        remove x from S and insert it at the end of sequence $B[k]$
    for $i \leftarrow 0$ to $N-1$ **do**
        for each item x in sequence $B[i]$ **do**
            remove x from $B[i]$ and insert it at the end of S

Code Fragment 8.8: Bucket-sort.

It is easy to see that bucket-sort runs in $O(n+N)$ time and uses $O(n+N)$ space. Hence, bucket-sort is very efficient when the range N of values for the keys is small compared to the sequence size n, say $N = O(n)$ or $N = O(n\log n)$. However, its performance deteriorates as N grows compared to n.

An important property of the bucket-sort algorithm is that it works correctly even if there are many different elements with the same key. Indeed, we described it in a way that anticipates such occurrences.

Our informal description of bucket-sort in Code Fragment 8.8 does not guarantee stability. This is not inherent in the bucket-sort method itself, however, for we can easily modify our description to make bucket-sort be stable, while still preserving its $O(n+N)$ running time. Indeed, we obtain a stable bucket-sort algorithm by always removing the *first* element from sequence S and from the sequences $B[i]$ during the execution of the algorithm.

8.5.2   Stable Sorting

When sorting key-element items, an important issue is how equal keys are handled. Let $S = ((k_0, e_0), \ldots, (k_{n-1}, e_{n-1}))$ be a sequence of items. We say that a sorting algorithm is *stable* if, for any two items (k_i, e_i) and (k_j, e_j) of S such that $k_i = k_j$ and (k_i, e_i) precedes (k_j, e_j) in S before sorting, item (k_i, e_i) also precedes item (k_j, e_j) after sorting. Stability is important for a sorting algorithm because different elements with the same key will most likely have other data or methods that distinguish them from each other—so we wish to keep them straight.

8.5.3   Radix-Sort

One of the reasons that stable sorting is so important is that it allows the bucket-sort approach to be applied to more general contexts than to sort integers. Suppose, for example, that we want to sort items that are pairs (k, l), where k and l are integers in the range $[0, N-1]$, for some parameter $N \geq 2$. In a context such as this, it is natural to define an ordering on these items using the *lexicographical* (dictionary) convention, where we say that $(k_1, l_1) < (k_2, l_2)$ if $k_1 < k_2$ or if $k_1 = k_2$ and $l_1 < l_2$ (Section 6.1.4). This is a pair-wise version of the comparison function, usually applied to equal-length character strings (and it easily generalizes to tuples of d numbers for $d > 2$).

The *radix-sort* algorithm sorts a sequence such as S by applying a stable bucket-sort on the sequence twice; first using one component of the pair as the ordering key and then using the second component. But which order is correct? Should we first sort on the k's (the first component) and then on the l's (the second component), or should it be the other way around? Before we answer this question, we consider the following example.

Example 8.5: *Consider the following sequence S:*
$$S = ((3,3),(1,5),(2,5),(1,2),(2,3),(1,7),(3,2),(2,2)).$$
If we sort S stably on the first component, then we get the sequence
$$S_1 = ((1,5),(1,2),(1,7),(2,5),(2,3),(2,2),(3,3),(3,2)).$$
If we then stably sort this sequence S_1 using the second component, then we get the sequence
$$S_{1,2} = ((1,2),(2,2),(3,2),(2,3),(3,3),(1,5),(2,5),(1,7)),$$
which is not exactly a sorted sequence. On the other hand, if we first stably sort S using the second component, then we get the sequence
$$S_2 = ((1,2),(3,2),(2,2),(3,3),(2,3),(1,5),(2,5),(1,7)).$$
If we then stably sort sequence S_2 using the first component, then we get the sequence
$$S_{2,1} = ((1,2),(1,5),(1,7),(2,2),(2,3),(2,5),(3,2),(3,3)),$$
which is indeed sequence S lexicographically ordered.

So, from this example, we are led to believe that we should first sort using the second component and then again using the first component. This intuition is exactly right. By first stably sorting by second component and then again by first component, we guarantee that if two elements are equal in the second sort (by first component), then their relative order in the starting sequence (which is sorted by second component) is preserved. Thus, the resulting sequence is guaranteed to be sorted lexicographically every time. We leave to a simple exercise the determination of how this approach can be extended to triples and other d-tuples of numbers. We can summarize this section as follows:

Proposition 8.6: *Let S be a sequence of n key-element items, each of which has a key $(k_1, k_2, \ldots, k_d)$, where k_i is an integer in the range $[0, N-1]$ for some integer parameter $N \geq 2$. We can sort S lexicographically in time $O(d(n+N))$ using radix-sort.*

As important as it is, sorting is not the only interesting problem dealing with a total order relation on a set of elements. There are some applications, for example, that do not require an ordered listing of an entire set, but nevertheless call for some amount of ordering information about the set.

8.6   Selection

There are a number of applications in which we are interested in identifying a single element in terms of its rank relative to the entire set. Examples of this type of query that we have already seen include identifying the minimum and maximum elements. But we may also be interested in, say, identifying the *median* element, that is, the element such that half of the other elements are smaller and the remaining half are larger. In general, queries that ask for an element with a given rank in a set are called *order statistics*.

In this section, we discuss the general order-statistic problem of selecting the kth smallest element from a collection of n comparable elements. This is known as the *selection* problem. Of course, we can solve this problem by sorting the collection and then indexing into the sorted sequence at rank k. Using the best comparison-based sorting algorithms, this approach would take $O(n \log n)$ time, which is obviously an overkill for the cases where $k = 1$ or $k = n$ (or even $k = 2$, $k = 3$, $k = n - 1$, or $k = n - 5$), because we can easily solve the selection problem for these values of k in $O(n)$ time. Thus, a natural question to ask is whether we can achieve an $O(n)$ running time for all values of k (including the interesting case of finding the median, where $k = \lfloor n/2 \rfloor$).

8.6.1   Randomized Quick-Select

This may come as a small surprise, but we can indeed solve the selection problem in $O(n)$ time for any value of k. We describe here a simple and practical method, called *randomized quick-select*, for finding the kth smallest element in an unordered sequence of n elements on which a total order relation is defined. Randomized quick-select runs in $O(n)$ *expected* time, taken over all possible random choices taken by the algorithm, and this expectation does not depend whatsoever on any randomness assumptions about the input distribution. It should be noted though that randomized quick-select runs in $O(n^2)$ *worst-case* time (the justification is left as an exercise). We provide an exercise for modifying randomized quick-select to get a *deterministic* selection algorithm that runs in $O(n)$ *worst-case* time. The existence of this deterministic algorithm is mostly of theoretical interest, however, since the constant factor hidden by the big-Oh notation is relatively large in this case.

Suppose we are given an unsorted sequence S of n comparable elements together with an integer $k \in [1, n]$. At a high level, the quick-select algorithm for finding the kth smallest element in S is similar in structure to the randomized quicksort algorithm described in Section 8.3.2. We pick an element x from S at random, and use this as a "pivot" to subdivide S into three subsequences L, E, and G, storing the elements of S less than x, equal to x, and greater than x, respectively. Then, based upon the value of k, we then determine which of these sets to recurse on. Randomized quick-sort is described in Code Fragment 8.9.

Algorithm quickSelect(S, k):

> ***Input:*** Sequence S of n comparable elements, and an integer $k \in [1, n]$
> ***Output:*** The kth smallest element of S
>
> **if** $n = 1$ **then**
> > **return** the (first) element of S.
>
> pick a random integer r in the range $[0, n-1]$
> let x be the element of S at rank r.
> remove all the elements from S and put them into three sequences:
>
> > - L, storing the elements in S less than x
> > - E, storing the elements in S equal to x
> > - G, storing the elements in S greater than x.
>
> **if** $k \leq |L|$ **then**
> > quickSelect(L, k)
> **else if** $k \leq |L| + |E|$ **then**
> > **return** x {each element in E is equal to x}
> **else**
> > quickSelect($G, k - |L| - |E|$)   {note the new selection parameter}

Code Fragment 8.9: Randomized quick-select algorithm.

8.6.2 Analyzing Randomized Quick-Select ⋆

We mentioned above that the randomized quick-select algorithm runs in expected $O(n)$ time. Fortunately, justifying this claim requires only the simplest of probabilistic arguments. The main probabilistic fact that we use is the ***linearity of expectation***. This fact states that if X and Y are random variables and c is a number, then

$$E(X + Y) = E(X) + E(Y)$$

and

$$E(cX) = cE(X),$$

where we use $E(\mathcal{Z})$ to denote the expected value of the expression $\mathcal{Z}$.

Let $t(n)$ denote the running time of randomized quick-select on a sequence of size n. Since the randomized quick-select algorithm depends on the outcome of random events, its running time, $t(n)$, is a random variable. We are interested in bounding $E(t(n))$, the expected value of $t(n)$. Say that a recursive invocation of randomized quick-select is "good" if it partitions S, so that the size of L and G is at most $3n/4$. Clearly, a recursive call is good with probability $1/2$. Let $g(n)$ denote the number of consecutive recursive invocations (including the present one) before getting a good invocation. Then

$$t(n) \le bn \cdot g(n) + t(3n/4),$$

where $b \ge 1$ is a constant (to account for the overhead of each call). We are, of course, focusing in on the case where n is larger than 1, for we can easily characterize in a closed form that $t(1) = b$. Applying the linearity of expectation property to the general case, then, we get

$$E(t(n)) \le E(bn \cdot g(n) + t(3n/4)) = bn \cdot E(g(n)) + E(t(3n/4)).$$

Since a recursive call is good with probability $1/2$, and whether a recursive call is good or not is independent of its parent call being good, the expected value of $g(n)$ is the same as the expected number of times we must flip a fair coin before it comes up "heads." This implies that $E(g(n)) = 2$. Thus, if we let $T(n)$ be a shorthand notation for $E(t(n))$ (the expected running time of the randomized quick-select algorithm), then we can write the case for $n > 1$ as

$$T(n) \le T(3n/4) + 2bn.$$

As with the merge-sort recurrence relation, we would like to convert this relation into a closed form. To do this, let us again iteratively apply this equation assuming n is large. So, for example, after two iterative applications, we get

$$T(n) \le T((3/4)^2 n) + 2b(3/4)n + 2bn.$$

At this point, we see that the general case is

$$T(n) \le 2bn \cdot \sum_{i=0}^{\lceil \log_{4/3} n \rceil} (3/4)^i.$$

In other words, the expected running time of randomized quick-select is $2bn$ times the sum of a geometric progression whose base is a positive number less than 1. Thus, an identity from Chapter 2 gives the result that $T(n)$ is $O(n)$. To summarize, we have:

Proposition 8.7: *The expected running time of randomized quick-select on a sequence of size n is $O(n)$.*

As we mentioned earlier, there is a variation of quick-select that does not use randomization and runs in $O(n)$ worst-case time. Exercise C-8.18 walks the interested reader through the design and analysis of this algorithm.

8.7 Exercises

Reinforcement

R-8.1 Give a complete justification of Proposition 8.1.

R-8.2 In the merge-sort tree shown in Figures 8.1 through 8.4, some edges are drawn as arrows. What is the meaning of a downward arrow? How about an upward arrow?

R-8.3 Show by induction that the running time of the merge-sort algorithm is $O(n \log n)$.

R-8.4 Suppose we are given two n-element sorted sequences A and B that should be viewed as sets (that is, A and B contain no duplicate entries). Describe an $O(n)$ time method for computing a sequence representing the set $A \cup B$ (with no duplicates).

R-8.5 Suppose we modify the deterministic version of the quick-sort algorithm so that, instead of selecting the last element in an n-element sequence as the pivot, we choose the element at rank $\lfloor n/2 \rfloor$. What is the running time of this version of quick-sort on a sequence that is already sorted?

R-8.6 Consider again the modification of the deterministic version of the quick-sort algorithm so that, instead of selecting the last element in an n-element sequence as the pivot, we choose the element at rank $\lfloor n/2 \rfloor$. Describe the kind of sequence that would cause this version of quick-sort to run in $\Theta(n^2)$ time.

R-8.7 Show that the best-case running time of quick-sort on a sequence of size n is $O(n \log n)$.

R-8.8 Which, if any, of the algorithms bubble-sort, heap-sort, merge-sort, and quick-sort are stable?

R-8.9 Describe a radix-sorting scheme for lexicographically sorting a sequence S of triplets (k, l, m), where k, l, and m are integers in the range $[0, N - 1]$, for some parameter $N \geq 2$. How could this scheme be extended to sequences of d-tuples $(k_1, k_2, \ldots, k_d)$ and where each k_i is an integer in the range $[0, N - 1]$?

R-8.10 Is the bucket-sort algorithm in-place? Why or why not?

R-8.11 Give a pseudo-code description of the quick-select algorithm that is in-place.

R-8.12 Show that the worst-case running time of quick-select is $\Omega(n^2)$.

Creativity

C-8.1 Show how to implement the isEqual(B) method on a set A in $O(|A| + |B|)$ time by means of a concrete class extending the abstract Merger class.

C-8.2 Give a concrete class extending the abstract Merger class for computing $A \oplus B$, which is the set of elements that are in A or B, but not in both.

C-8.3★ Describe a non-recursive in-place version of the quick-sort algorithm. The algorithm should still be based upon the same divide-and-conquer approach. (Hint: think about how you can "mark" the left and right boundaries of the current subsequence before making a recursive call from this one.)

C-8.4★ Show that randomized quick-sort runs in $O(n \log n)$ time with probability $1 - 1/n^2$. (Hint: use the ***Chernoff bound*** that states that if we flip a coin k times, then the probability that we get fewer than $k/16$ heads is less than $2^{-k/8}$.)

C-8.5 Suppose we are given a sequence S of n elements, each of which is colored red or blue. Assuming S is represented as an array, give an in-place method for ordering S so that all the blue elements are listed before all the red elements. Can you extend your approach to three colors?

C-8.6 Suppose we are given an n-element sequence S such that each element in S represents a different vote for class president, where each vote is given as an integer representing the student ID of the chosen candidate. Without making any assumptions about who is running or even how many candidates there are, design an $O(n \log n)$ time algorithm to see who wins the election S represents, assuming the candidate with the most votes wins.

C-8.7 Consider the voting problem from the previous exercise, but now suppose that we know the number $k < n$ of candidates running. Describe an $O(n \log k)$ time algorithm for determining who wins the election.

C-8.8 Show that any comparison-based sorting algorithm can be made to be stable, without affecting the asymptotic running time of this algorithm. (Hint: change the way elements are compared with each other.)

C-8.9 Suppose we are given two sequences A and B of n elements, on which a total order relation is defined. Describe an efficient algorithm for determining if A and B contain the same set of elements (possibly in different orders). What is the running time of this method?

C-8.10 Suppose we are given a sequence S of n elements, each of which is an integer in the range $[0, n^2 - 1]$. Describe a simple method for sorting S in $O(n)$ time. (Hint: think of alternate ways of viewing the elements.)

C-8.11 Let $S_1, S_2, \ldots, S_k$ be k different sequences, whose elements have integer keys in the range $[0, N - 1]$, for some parameter $N \geq 2$. Describe an algorithm running in $O(k + n + N)$ time for sorting all the sequences, where n denotes the total size of all the sequences.

C-8.12 Suppose we are given a sequence S of n elements, on which a total order relation is defined. Describe an efficient method for determining whether there are two equal elements in S. What is the running time of your method?

C-8.13 Let S be a sequence of n elements on which a total order relation is defined. An *inversion* in S is a pair of elements x and y such that x appears before y in S but $x > y$. Describe an algorithm running in $O(n \log n)$ time for determining the *number* of inversions in S. (Hint: try to modify the merge-sort algorithm to solve this problem.)

C-8.14 Let S be a sequence of n elements on which a total order relation is defined. Describe a comparison-based method for sorting S in $O(n + k)$ time, where k is the number of inversions in S (recall the definition of inversion from the previous problem). (Hint: think of a modification of the bubble-sort algorithm that, after an $O(n)$ preprocessing step, only swaps elements that are inverted.)

C-8.15 Give a sequence of n integers with $\Omega(n^2)$ inversions. (Recall the definition of inversion from Exercise C-8.13.)

C-8.16 Let A and B be two sequences of n integers each. Given an integer m, describe an $O(n \log n)$ time algorithm for determining if there is an integer a in A and an integer b in B such that $m = a + b$.

C-8.17 Given a sequence S of n comparable elements, describe an efficient method for finding the $\lceil \sqrt{n} \rceil$ items whose rank in S is closest to that of the median. What is the running time of your method?

C-8.18 This problem deals with the modification of the quick-select algorithm so as to make it deterministic yet still run in $O(n)$ time. The idea is to modify the way we choose the pivot so that it is chosen deterministically, not randomly, as follows:

> Partition the set S into $\lceil n/5 \rceil$ groups of size 5 each (except possibly for one group). Sort each little set and identify the median element in this set. From this set of $\lceil n/5 \rceil$ "baby" medians, apply the selection algorithm recursively to find the median of the baby medians. Use this element as the pivot and proceed as in the quick-select algorithm.

Show that this deterministic method runs in $O(n)$ time by answering the following questions (please ignore floor and ceiling functions if that makes the mathematics easier, for the asymptotics will remain the same either way):

1. How many baby medians are less than or equal to the chosen pivot? How many are greater than or equal to the pivot?

2. For each baby median less than or equal to the pivot, how many other elements are less than or equal to the pivot? Is the same true for those greater than or equal to the pivot?

3. Argue why the method for finding the deterministic pivot and using it to partition S takes $O(n)$ time.

4. Based upon these estimates, write a recurrence relation that bounds the worst-case running time $t(n)$ for this selection algorithm (note that in the worst-case there are two recursive calls—one to find the median of the baby medians and one to then recurse on the larger of either L or G).

5. Using this recurrence relation, show by induction that $t(n)$ is $O(n)$.

C-8.19 Show how a deterministic $O(n)$ time selection algorithm can be used to design a quick-sort-like sorting algorithm that runs in $O(n \log n)$ **worst-case** time.

C-8.20 Given a sequence S of n comparable elements, give an $O(n \log k)$ expected-time algorithm for finding the $O(k)$ elements that have rank $\lceil n/k \rceil$, $2\lceil n/k \rceil$, $3\lceil n/k \rceil$, and so on.

Projects

P-8.1 Design and implement the merge-sort algorithm. Perform a series of benchmarking time trials to test whether this method does indeed run in $O(n \log n)$ time, and write a short report describing the code and the results of these trials.

P-8.2 Design and implement a stable version of the bucket-sort algorithm for sorting a sequence of n elements with integer keys taken from the range $[0, N-1]$, for $N \geq 2$. The algorithm should run in $O(n+N)$ time. Perform a series of benchmarking time trials to test whether this method does indeed run in this time, for various values of n and N, and write a short report describing the code and the results of these trials.

P-8.3 Implement merge-sort and deterministic quick-sort and perform a series of benchmarking tests to see which one is faster. Your tests should include sequences that are very "random" looking, as well as ones that are "almost" sorted. Write a short report describing the code and the results of these trials.

P-8.4 Implement deterministic and randomized versions of the quick-sort algorithm and perform a series of benchmarking tests to see which one is faster. Your tests should include sequences that are very "random" looking as well as ones that are "almost" sorted. Write a short report describing the code and the results of these trials.

P-8.5 Implement an in-place version of insertion-sort and an in-place version of quick-sort. Perform benchmarking tests to determine the range of values of n where quick-sort is on average better than insertion-sort.

P-8.6 Design and implement an animation for one of the sorting algorithms described in this chapter. Your animation should illustrate the key properties of this algorithm in an intuitive manner, and should be annotated with text or sound so as to explain this algorithm to someone unfamiliar with it. Write a short report describing this animation.

P-8.7 Implement the randomized quick-sort and quick-select algorithms. Design a series of benchmarking tests to test the relative speed of solving the selection problem either directly, by the quick-select method, or indirectly, by first sorting via the quick-sort method and then returning the element at the requested rank. Write a short report describing the code and the results of these trials.

P-8.8 Implement the set ADT. In addition to the methods given in Section 8.2.1, your implementation should also support the following mutable-set methods that change the set A that they act upon:

unionWith(B): Assign $A \leftarrow A \cup B$.
Input: Set; *Output:* Set.

intersectWith(B): Assign $A \leftarrow A \cap B$.
Input: Set; *Output:* Set.

differenceFrom(B): Assign $A \leftarrow A - B$.
Input: Set; *Output:* Set.

Chapter Notes

Knuth's classic text on *Sorting and Searching* [90] contains an extensive history of the sorting problem and algorithms for solving it, starting with the census card sorting machines of the late 19th century. Huang and Langston [79] describe how to merge two sorted lists in-place in linear time. Our set ADT is derived from the set ADT of Aho, Hopcroft, and Ullman [7]. The standard quick-sort algorithm is due to Hoare [72]. A tighter analysis of randomized quick-sort can be found in the book by Motwani and Raghavan [115]. Gonnet and Baeza-Yates [59] provide experimental comparisons and theoretical analyses of a number of different sorting algorithms.

Chapter

9

Graphs

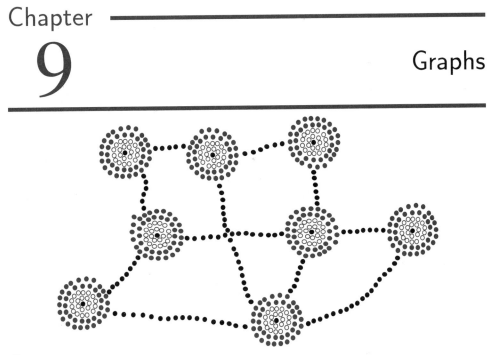

Contents

Greek mythology tells of an elaborate labyrinth that was built to house the monstrous part bull, part man Minotaur. This labyrinth was so complex that neither beast nor human could escape it. No human, that is, until the Greek hero, Theseus, with the help of the king's daughter, Ariadne, decided to implement one of the algorithms discussed in this chapter. Theseus fastened a ball of thread to the door of the labyrinth and unwound it as he traversed the twisting passages in search of the monster. Theseus obviously knew about good algorithm design, for, after finding and defeating the beast, Theseus easily followed the string back out of the labyrinth to the loving arms of Ariadne.

Being able to determine which objects, such as labyrinth passages, are connected to which other objects, may not always be as vitally important as it was in this story, but it is nevertheless fundamental. Connectivity information is present, for example, in city maps, where the objects are roads, and also in the routing tables for the Internet, where the objects are computers. Connectivity information is also present in the parent-child relationships defined by a binary tree, where the objects are tree nodes. Indeed, connectivity information can be defined by all kinds of relationships that exist between pairs of objects. The topic we study in this chapter—graphs—is therefore focused on representations and algorithms for dealing efficiently with such relationships.

9.1   The Graph Abstract Data Type

Viewed abstractly, a *graph* G is simply a set V of *vertices* and a collection E of pairs of vertices from V, called *edges*. Thus, a graph is simply a way of representing connections or relationships between pairs of objects from some class V. Incidentally, some books use a different terminology for graphs and refer to what we call vertices as *nodes* and what we call edges as *arcs*. We use the terms "vertices" and "edges."

The notion of a "graph," introduced here, should not be confused with bar charts and function plots, by the way, as these kinds of "graphs" are unrelated to the topic of this chapter.

9.1.1   Terminology and Basic Properties

Graphs have applications in a host of different domains, including mapping (in geographic information systems), transportation (in road and flight networks), electrical engineering (in circuits), and computer networking (in the connections of the Internet). Because applications for graphs are so widespread and diverse, people have developed a great deal of terminology to describe different components and properties of graphs. Fortunately, since most graph applications are relatively recent developments, this terminology is fairly intuitive. In this section, we introduce some of the more important terms used with graphs, and we provide several examples to illustrate these terms. We also state, as propositions, some elementary properties of graphs.

Edges in a graph are either ***directed*** or ***undirected***. An edge (u, v) is said to be ***directed*** from u to v if the pair (u, v) is ordered, with u preceding v. An edge (u, v) is said to be ***undirected*** if the pair (u, v) is not ordered. Undirected edges are sometimes denoted with set notation, as $\{u, v\}$, but for simplicity we use the pair notation (u, v), noting that, in the undirected case, (u, v) is the same as (v, u). Graphs are typically visualized by drawing the vertices as ovals or rectangles and the edges as segments or curves connecting pairs of ovals and rectangles. The following are some examples of directed and undirected graphs.

Example 9.1: *We can visualize collaborations among the researchers of a certain discipline by constructing a graph whose vertices are associated with the researchers themselves, and whose edges connect pairs of vertices associated with researchers who have coauthored a paper or book. (See Figure 9.1.) Such edges are undirected because coauthorship is a* **symmetric** *relation, that is, if A has coauthored something with B, then B necessarily has coauthored something with A.*

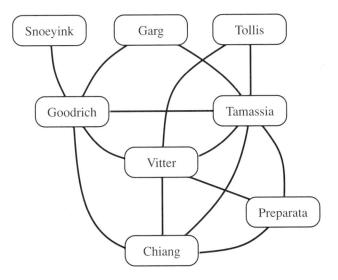

Figure 9.1: Graph of coauthorships among the authors of this book and some of their colleagues.

Example 9.2: *We can associate with an object-oriented program a graph whose vertices are associated with the classes defined in the program, and whose edges indicate inheritance between classes. There is an edge from a vertex v to a vertex u if the class for v extends the class for u. Such edges are directed because the inheritance relation only goes in one direction (that is, it is* **asymmetric***).*

If all the edges in a graph are undirected, then we say the graph is an ***undirected graph***. Likewise, a ***directed graph***, also called a ***digraph***, is a graph whose edges are all directed. A graph that has both directed and undirected edges is often called a ***mixed graph***. Note that an undirected or mixed graph can be converted into a directed graph by replacing every undirected edge (u, v) by the pair of directed edges (u, v) and (v, u). It is, nevertheless, often useful to keep undirected and mixed graphs represented as they are, however, for such graphs have several applications.

Example 9.3: *A city map can be modeled by a graph whose vertices are intersections or dead-ends, and whose edges are stretches of streets without intersections. This graph has both undirected edges, which correspond to stretches of two-way streets, and directed edges, which correspond to stretches of one-way streets. Thus, in this way, a graph modeling a city map is a mixed graph.*

Example 9.4: *Physical examples of graphs are present in the electrical wiring and plumbing networks of a building. Such networks can be modeled as graphs, where each connector, fixture, or outlet is viewed as a vertex, and each uninterrupted stretch of wire or pipe is viewed as an edge. Such graphs are actually components of much larger graphs, namely the local power and water distribution networks. Depending on the specific aspects of these graphs that we are interested in, we may consider their edges as undirected or directed, for, in principle, water can flow in a pipe and current can flow in a wire in either direction.*

The two vertices joined by an edge are called the ***end vertices*** of the edge. The end vertices of an edge are also known as the ***endpoints*** of that edge. If an edge is directed, its first endpoint is its ***origin*** and the other is the ***destination*** of the edge.

Two vertices are said to be ***adjacent*** if they are endpoints of the same edge. An edge is said to be ***incident*** on a vertex if the vertex is one of the edge's endpoints. The ***outgoing edges*** of a vertex are the directed edges whose origin is that vertex. The ***incoming edges*** of a vertex are the directed edges whose destination is that vertex. The ***degree*** of a vertex v, denoted $\deg(v)$, is the number of incident edges of v, which is the same as the number of the adjacent vertices of v. The ***in-degree*** and ***out-degree*** of a vertex v are the number of the incoming and outgoing edges of v, and are denoted $\mathrm{indeg}(v)$ and $\mathrm{outdeg}(v)$, respectively.

Example 9.5: *We can study air transportation by constructing a graph G, called a* **flight network**, *whose vertices are associated with airports, and whose edges are associated with flights. (See Figure 9.2.) In graph G, the edges are directed because a given flight has a specific travel direction (from the origin airport to the destination airport). The endpoints of an edge e in G correspond respectively to the origin and destination for the flight corresponding to e. Two airports are adjacent in G if there is a flight that flies between them, and an edge e is incident upon a vertex v in G if the flight for e flies to or from the airport for v. The outgoing edges of a vertex v correspond to the outbound flights from v's airport, and the incoming edges correspond to the inbound flights to v's airport. Finally, the in-degree of a vertex v of G corresponds to the number of inbound flights to v's airport, and the out-degree of a vertex v in G corresponds to the number of outbound flights.*

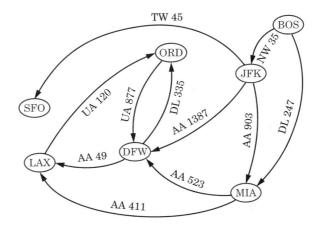

Figure 9.2: Example of a directed graph representing a flight network. The endpoints of edge UA 120 are LAX and ORD; hence, LAX and ORD are adjacent. The in-degree of DFW is 3, and the out-degree of DFW is 2.

The definition of a graph refers to the group of edges as a **collection**, not a **set**, thus allowing for two undirected edges to have the same end vertices, and for two directed edges to have the same origin and the same destination. Such edges are called **parallel edges** or **multiple edges**. Parallel edges can be in a flight network (Example 9.5), in which case multiple edges between the same pair of vertices could indicate different flights operating on the same route at different times of the day. Another special type of edge is one that connects a vertex to itself. Namely, we say that an edge (undirected or directed) is a **self-loop** if its two endpoints coincide. A self-loop may occur in a graph associated with a city map (Example 9.3), where it would correspond to a "circle" (a curving street that returns to its starting point).

With few exceptions, like those mentioned above, graphs do not have parallel edges or self-loops. Such graphs are said to be *simple*. Thus, we can usually say that the edges of a simple graph are a *set* of vertex pairs (and not just a collection). Throughout this chapter, we shall assume that a graph is simple unless otherwise specified. This assumption greatly simplifies the presentation of data structures and algorithms for graphs. Extending the results of this chapter to general graphs that admit self-loops and/or parallel edges is straightforward, though the details can be tedious.

Caution

We explore, in the propositions that follow, a few important properties of degrees and the number of edges in a graph. These properties relate the number of vertices and edges to each other and to the degrees of the vertices in a graph.

Proposition 9.6: *If G is a graph with m edges, then*

$$\sum_{v \in G} deg(v) = 2m.$$

Justification: An edge (u, v) is counted twice in the above summation; once by its endpoint u and once by its endpoint v. Thus, the total contribution of the edges to the degrees of the vertices is twice the number of edges.   ■

Proposition 9.7: *If G is a directed graph with m edges, then*

$$\sum_{v \in G} indeg(v) \;=\; \sum_{v \in G} outdeg(v) = m.$$

Justification: In a directed graph, an edge (u, v) contributes one unit to the out-degree of its origin u and one unit to the in-degree of its destination v. Thus, the total contribution of the edges to the out-degrees of the vertices is equal to the number of edges, and similarly for the out-degrees.   ■

Proposition 9.8: *Let G be a simple graph with n vertices and m edges. If G is undirected, then $m \leq n(n-1)/2$, and if G is directed, then $m \leq n(n-1)$.*

Justification: Suppose that G is undirected. Since no two edges can have the same endpoints and there are no self-loops, the maximum degree of a vertex in G is $n-1$ in this case. Thus, by Proposition 9.6, $2m \leq n(n-1)$. Now suppose that G is directed. Since no two edges can have the same origin and destination, and there are no self-loops, the maximum in-degree of a vertex in G is $n-1$ in this case. Thus, by Proposition 9.7, $m \leq n(n-1)$.   ■

Put another way, this last proposition states that a simple graph with n vertices has $O(n^2)$ edges.

A *path* of a graph is a sequence of alternating vertices and edges that starts at a vertex and ends at a vertex such that each edge is incident to its predecessor and successor vertex. A *cycle* is a path such that its start and end vertices are the same. We say that a path is *simple* if each vertex in the path is distinct, and we say that a cycle is *simple* if each vertex in the cycle is distinct, except for the first and last one. A *directed path* is a path such that all the edges are directed and are traversed along their direction. A *directed cycle* is defined similarly. For example, in the flight network of Figure 9.2, (BOS, NW 35, JFK, AA 1387, DFW) is a directed simple path, and (LAX, UA 120, ORD, UA 877, DFW, AA 49, LAX) is a directed simple cycle.

Example 9.9: *Given a graph G representing a city map (see Example 9.3), we can model a couple driving from their home to dinner at a recommended restaurant as traversing a path though G. If they know the way, and don't accidentally go though the same intersection twice, then they traverse a simple path in G. Likewise, we can model the entire trip the couple takes, from their home to the restaurant and back, as a cycle. If they go home from the restaurant in a completely different way than how they went, not even going through the same intersection twice, then their entire round trip is a simple cycle. Finally, if they travel along one-way streets for their entire trip, then we can model their night out as a directed cycle.*

A *subgraph* of a graph G is a graph H whose vertices and edges are subsets of the vertices and edges of G, respectively. For example, in the flight network of Figure 9.2, vertices BOS, JFK, and MIA, and edges AA 903 and DL 247 form a subgraph. A *spanning subgraph* of G is a subgraph of G that contains all the vertices of the graph G. A graph is *connected* if, for any two vertices, there is a path between them. If a graph G is not connected, its maximal connected subgraphs are called the *connected components* of G. A *forest* is a graph without cycles. A *tree* is a connected forest, that is, a connected graph without cycles. Note that this definition of a tree is somewhat different from the one given in Chapter 5. Namely, in the context of graphs, a tree has no root. Whenever there is ambiguity, the trees of Chapter 5 should be referred to as *rooted trees*, while the trees of this chapter should be referred to as *free trees*. The connected components of a forest are (free) trees. A *spanning tree* of a graph is a spanning subgraph that is a (free) tree.

| Caution |

Example 9.10: *Perhaps the most talked about graph today is the Internet, which can be viewed as a graph whose vertices are computers and whose (undirected) edges are communication connections between pairs of computers on the Internet. The computers and the connections between them in a single domain, like wiley.com, form a subgraph of the Internet. If this subgraph is connected, then two users on computers in this domain can send e-mail to one another without having*

their information packets ever leave their domain. Suppose the edges of this sub-graph form a spanning tree. This implies that, if even a single connection goes down (for example, because someone pulls a communication cable out of the back of a computer in this domain), then this subgraph will no longer be connected.

There are a number of simple properties of trees, forests, and connected graphs. We explore a few of them in the following proposition.

Proposition 9.11: *Let G be an undirected graph with n vertices and m edges. Then we have the following:*

- *If G is connected, then $m \geq n - 1$.*
- *If G is a tree, then $m = n - 1$.*
- *If G is a forest, then $m \leq n - 1$.*

We leave the justification of this proposition as an exercise.

9.1.2 Graph Methods

As an abstract data type, a graph is a positional container of elements that are stored at the graph's vertices and edges. Namely, the *positions* in a graph are its vertices and edges. Hence, we can store elements in a graph at either its edges or its vertices (or both). In terms of a Java implementation, this implies that we can define Vertex and Edge interfaces that each extend the Position interface. Recall that a position has an element() method, which returns the element that is stored at this position.

Since a graph is a positional container (Section 5.1.3), the graph ADT supports the following methods: size(), isEmpty(), elements(), positions(), replace(p, o), and swap(p, q), where p and q denote positions, and o denotes an object (element).

Graphs are a much richer abstract data type than we have discussed in previous chapters. Their richness derives mostly from the different kinds of objects that help define a graph, such as vertices and edges. So as to present the methods for the graph ADT in as organized a way as possible, we divide the graph methods into three main categories: general methods, methods dealing with directed edges, and methods for updating and modifying graphs. In addition, in order to simplify the presentation, we denote with v a vertex position, with e an edge position, and with o an object (element) stored at a vertex or edge. Also, we do not discuss error conditions that may occur.

General Methods

We begin by describing the fundamental methods for a graph, which ignore the direction of the edges. Each of the following methods returns global information about a graph G:

numVertices(): Return the number of vertices in G.

numEdges(): Return the number of edges in G.

vertices(): Return an enumeration of the vertex positions in G.

edges(): Return an enumeration of the edge positions in G.

Additionally, we include methods that take vertex and edge positions as arguments:

degree(v): Return the degree of v.

adjacentVertices(v): Return an enumeration of the vertices adjacent to v.

incidentEdges(v): Return an enumeration of the edges incident upon v.

endVertices(e): Return an array of size 2 storing the end vertices of e.

opposite(v, e): Return the endpoint of edge e distinct from v.

areAdjacent(v, w): Return whether vertices v and w are adjacent.

Methods Dealing with Directed Edges

When we allow for some or all the edges in a graph to be directed, then there are several additional methods we should include in the graph ADT:

directedEdges(): Return an enumeration of all directed edges (positions).

undirectedEdges(): Return an enumeration of all undirected edges.

inDegree(v): Return the in-degree of v.

outDegree(v): Return the out-degree of v.

inIncidentEdges(v): Return an enumeration of all the incoming edges to v.

outIncidentEdges(v): Return an enumeration of all the outgoing edges from v.

inAdjacentVertices(v): Return an enumeration of all the vertices adjacent to v along incoming edges to v.

outAdjacentVertices(v): Return an enumeration of all the vertices adjacent to v along outgoing edges from v.

destination(e): Return the destination of the directed edge e.

origin(e): Return the origin of the directed edge e.

isDirected(e): Return true if an only if the edge e is directed.

Methods for Updating Graphs

We can also allow for update methods that add or delete edges and vertices:

insertEdge(v, w, o): Insert and return an undirected edge between vertices v and w, storing the object o at this position.

insertDirectedEdge(v, w, o): Insert and return a directed edge from vertex v to vertex w, storing the object o at this position.

insertVertex(o): Insert and return a new (isolated) vertex storing the object o at this position.

removeVertex(v): Remove vertex v and all its incident edges.

removeEdge(e): Remove edge e.

makeUndirected(e): Make edge e undirected.

reverseDirection(e): Reverse the direction of directed edge e.

setDirectionFrom(e, v): Make edge e directed away from vertex v.

setDirectionTo(e, v): Make edge e directed into vertex v.

There are admittedly a lot of methods in the graph ADT. The number of methods is to a certain extent unavoidable, however, since graphs are such rich structures. Graphs support two kinds of positions—vertices and edges—and even then allow for edges to be either directed or undirected. We need to have different methods for accessing and updating all these different positions, as well as dealing with the relationships that can exist between these different positions.

9.2 Data Structures for Graphs

There are several ways to realize the graph ADT with a concrete data structure. In this section, we discuss three popular approaches, usually referred to as the *edge list* structure, the *adjacency list* structure, and the *adjacency matrix*. In all the three representations, we use a container (a sequence, for example) to store the vertices of the graph. Regarding the edges, there is a fundamental difference between the first two structures and the latter. The edge list structure and the adjacency list structure only store the edges actually present in the graph, while the adjacency matrix stores a placeholder for every pair of vertices (whether there is an edge between them or not). As we will explain in this section, this difference implies that, for a graph G with n vertices and m edges, an edge list or adjacency list representation uses $O(n+m)$ space, whereas an adjacency matrix representation uses $O(n^2)$ space.

9.2.1 The Edge List Structure

The edge list structure is possibly the simplest, though not the most efficient, representation of a graph G. In this representation, a vertex v of G storing an element o is explicitly represented by a vertex object that implements the Position interface. All such vertex objects are stored in a container V, which would typically be a sequence or dictionary. If we represent V as a ranked sequence, for example, then we would naturally think of the vertices as being numbered. If we represent V as a dictionary, on the other hand, then we would naturally think of each vertex as being identified by a key that we associate with it. Note that the elements of container V are the vertex positions of graph G.

The vertex object for a vertex v storing element o has instance variables that hold the following:

- A reference to o
- Counters for the number incident undirected edges, incoming directed edges, and outgoing directed edges
- A reference to the position (or locator) of the vertex-object in container V.

The distinguishing feature of the edge list structure is not how it represents vertices, however, but the way in which it represents edges. In this structure, an edge e of G storing an element o is explicitly represented by an edge object that implements the Position interface. The edge objects are stored in a container E, which would typically be a sequence or dictionary.

The edge object for an edge e storing element o has instance variables for:

- A reference to o
- A boolean indicator of whether e is directed or undirected
- References to the vertex objects in V associated with the endpoint vertices of e (if the edge e is undirected) or to the origin and destination vertices of e (if the e is directed)
- A reference to the position (or locator) of the edge-object in container E.

A schematic illustration of the edge list structure for a directed graph G is shown in Figure 9.3.

The reason this structure is called the ***edge list*** structure is that the simplest and most common implementation of the container E is with a sequence. Even so, in order to be able to conveniently search for specific objects associated with edges, we may wish to implement E with a dictionary, in spite of our calling this the "edge list." We may also wish to implement the container V as a dictionary for the same reason. Still, in keeping with tradition, we call this structure the edge list structure.

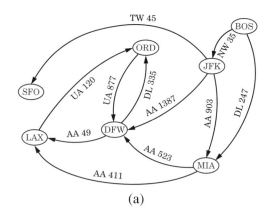

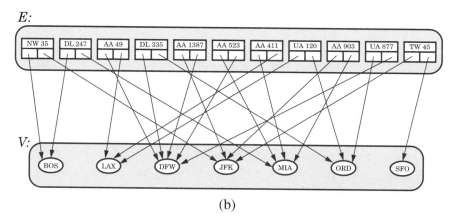

(b)

Figure 9.3: (a) A directed graph G: (b) schematic representation of the edge list structure for G. To avoid the clutter that would arise by showing with arrows the references to elements stored in the vertex and edge objects, we visualize such references with the objects' names.

The main feature of the edge list structure is that it provides direct access from edges to the vertices they are incident upon. This allows us to define very simple algorithms for implementing the different edge-based methods of the graph ADT (e.g., methods endVertices, origin, and destination). Nevertheless, the "inverse" operation—that of accessing the edges that are incident upon a vertex—requires an exhaustive inspection of all the edge objects in container E. Thus, for example, method incidentEdges(v) runs in time proportional to the number of edges in the graph, not in time proportional to the degree of vertex v.

Table 9.1 summarizes the performance of the edge structure implementation of a graph under the assumption that containers V and E are realized with sequences, which are, in turn, implemented with doubly linked lists (Section 4.1.4).

Operation	Time
size, isEmpty, replaceElement, swap	$O(1)$
numVertices, numEdges	$O(1)$
vertices	$O(n)$
edges, directedEdges, undirectedEdges	$O(m)$
elements, positions	$O(n+m)$
endVertices, opposite, origin, destination, isDirected, degree, inDegree, outDegree	$O(1)$
incidentEdges, inIncidentEdges, outIncidentEdges, adjacentVertices, inAdjacentVertices, outAdjacentVertices, areAdjacent	$O(m)$
insertVertex, insertEdge, insertDirectedEdge, removeEdge, makeUndirected, reverseDirection, setDirectionFrom, setDirectionTo	$O(1)$
removeVertex	$O(m)$

Table 9.1: Running times of methods of a graph implemented with an edge list structure, where V and E are realized with linked-list-based sequences. The space used is $O(n+m)$, where n is the number of vertices and m is the number edges.

Details of the implementations of selected methods are as follows:

- Methods numVertices(), numEdges(), and size() are implemented by returning V.size(), E.size(), and V.size() $+ E$.size(), respectively.
- The counters stored with the each vertex object allow us to perform, in constant time, methods degree, inDegree, and outDegree.
- Methods vertices() and edges() are implemented by calling V.elements() and E.elements(), respectively.
- We implement enumerations directedEdges() and undirectedEdges() by calling E.elements() and only returning those edges that are of the correct type.
- Since the containers V and E are sequences implemented with a doubly linked list, we can insert vertices, and insert and remove edges, in $O(1)$ time.
- Implementing enumeration methods for a vertex v is simple, but not very efficient, for to determine which edges are incident upon v, we must inspect all edges. Thus, methods incidentEdges, inIncidentEdges, outIncidentEdges, adjacentVertices, inAdjacentVertices, outAdjacentVertices, and areAdjacent all take $O(m)$ time.
- The update method removeVertex(v) takes $O(m)$ time, since it requires that we inspect all the edges to find and remove those incident upon v.

Thus, the edge list representation is simple but has its limitations.

9.2.2 The Adjacency List Structure

The adjacency list structure for a graph G extends the edge list structure, adding extra information that supports direct access to the incident edges (and thus to the adjacent vertices) of each vertex. While the edge list structure views the edge-vertex incidence relation only from the point of view of the edges, the adjacency list structure considers it from both viewpoints. This symmetric approach allows us to use the adjacency list structure to implement a number of vertex methods of the graph ADT much faster than what is possible with the edge list structure, even though these two representations both use an amount of space proportional to the number of vertices and edges in the graph.

The adjacency list structure includes all the structural components of the edge list structure and adds the follows additional elements:

- The vertex object for a vertex v holds a reference to a container $I(v)$, called the ***incidence container***, that stores the edge objects associated with the edges incident on v.
- The edge object for an edge (u,v) holds references to the positions of the edge in the incidence containers $I(u)$ and $I(v)$.

Traditionally, the incidence container $I(v)$ for a vertex v is realized by means of a sequence, which is why we call this way of representing a graph the "adjacency list" structure. Still, there may be some contexts where we wish to represent an incidence container $I(v)$ as, say, a dictionary or a priority queue, so let us stick with thinking of $I(v)$ as a generic container of edge objects.

Actually, we want to support a graph representation that can represent a graph G potentially containing both directed and undirected edges. So let us make a small modification to the adjacency list representation described above. Let us have, for each vertex, three incidence containers, $I_{in}(v)$, $I_{out}(v)$, and $I_{un}(v)$, that store references to the edge objects associated with the directed incoming, directed outgoing, and undirected edges incident on v, respectively.

A schematic illustration of the edge list structure for a directed graph G is shown in Figure 9.4. This figure provides a drawing of a flight network, together with an illustration of its edge list, vertex list, and the adjacency structures for each of the vertices in this graph.

The adjacency list structure provides direct access both from the edges to the vertices and from the vertices to their incident edges. Being able to provide access between vertices and edges in both directions allows us to speed up the performance of a number of the graph methods by using an adjacency list structure instead of an edge list structure.

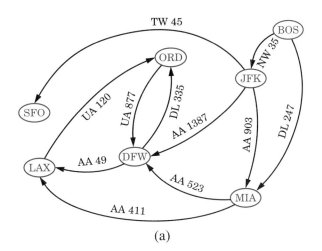

(a)

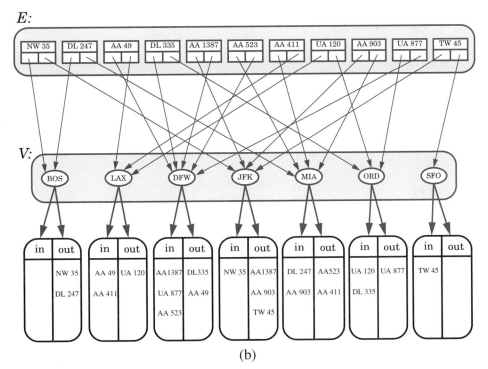

(b)

Figure 9.4: (a) A directed graph *G*: (b) schematic representation of the adjacency list structure of *G*. To avoid the confusion of showing extra references to edge objects in incidence containers, we show references to objects using their names. Also, we only show the incidence containers for directed edges, since there are no undirected edges in this graph.

Operation	Time
size, isEmpty, replaceElement, swap	$O(1)$
numVertices, numEdges	$O(1)$
vertices	$O(n)$
edges, directedEdges, undirectedEdges	$O(m)$
elements, positions	$O(n+m)$
endVertices, opposite, origin, destination, isDirected, degree, inDegree, outDegree	$O(1)$
incidentEdges(v), inIncidentEdges(v), outIncidentEdges(v), adjacentVertices(v), inAdjacentVertices(v), outAdjacentVertices(v)	$O(\deg(v))$
areAdjacent(u,v)	$O(\min(\deg(u),\deg(v)))$
insertVertex, insertEdge, insertDirectedEdge, removeEdge, makeUndirected, reverseDirection, setDirectionFrom	$O(1)$
removeVertex(v)	$O(\deg(v))$

Table 9.2: Running times for the methods of a graph implemented with an adjacency list structure such that containers V and E and the incidence containers are realized with sequences, which are in turn implemented with doubly linked lists. We denote with n and m the number of vertices and edges of the graph, respectively. The space used is $O(n+m)$.

Table 9.2 summarizes the performance of the adjacency structure implementation of a graph. Note that all of the methods that can be implemented with the edge list structure in $O(1)$ time can also be implemented in $O(1)$ time for the adjacency list structure using essentially the same algorithms. In addition, the adjacency list structure provides improved running time for the following methods:

- The methods that return enumerations of incident edges or adjacent vertices for a vertex v can be constructed in time proportional to their size, that is, in $O(\deg(v))$ time.
- Method areAdjacent(u,v) can be performed by inspecting either the incidence container of u or that of v. By choosing the smaller of the two, we get $O(\min(\deg(u),\deg(v)))$ running time.
- Method removeVertex(v) requires the inspection of the incidence container of v, and thus takes $O(\deg(v))$ time.

As we shall see in the future sections, the improvement achieved by using an adjacency list structure over an edge list structure is crucial. For the adjacency list structure allows us to perform several fundamental enumeration methods for a vertex v in $O(\deg(v))$ time, as opposed to the $O(m)$ time performance achievable using the edge list structure. Note that we can further improve the running time of the areAdjacent(u,v) method if we implement the container E with a fast dictionary whose keys are pairs of vertices (we explore this approach in further detail in an exercise).

9.2.3 The Adjacency Matrix Structure

Like the adjacency list structure, the adjacency matrix representation of a graph also extends the edge-structure with an additional component. In this case, we augment the edge list with a matrix A that allows us to determine adjacencies between pairs of vertices in constant time. As we shall see, achieving this speedup comes at a price in the space usage of the data structure.

In the adjacency matrix representation, we think of the vertices as being the integers in the set $\{0, 1, \ldots, n-1\}$ and the edges as being pairs of such integers. This allows us to store references to edges in the cells of a two dimensional $n \times n$ array A. Specifically, the adjacency matrix representation extends the edge list structure as follows (see Figure 9.5):

- A vertex object v also stores a distinct integer key in the range $0, 1, \ldots, n-1$, called the *index* of v. To simplify the discussion, we may refer to the vertex with index i simply as "vertex i."

- We keep a two dimensional $n \times n$ array A such that the cell $A[i,j]$ holds a reference to the edge object e that goes from the vertex with index i to the vertex with index j, if such an edge exists. If the edge e, connecting vertices i and j, is undirected, then we store references to e in both $A[i,j]$ and $A[j,i]$. If there is no edge from vertex i to vertex j, then $A[i,j]$ references the null object (or some other indicator that this cell is associated with no edge).

The adjacency matrix A allows us to perform the method areAdjacent(v,w) in $O(1)$ time. We achieve this performance by accessing the vertices v and w to determine their respective indices i and j, and then testing whether the cell $A[i,j]$ references the null object or not. This performance achievement is counteracted by an increase in the space usage, however, which is now $O(n^2)$, and in the running time of other methods. For example, the vertex methods, such as incidentEdges, adjacentVertices, inAdjacentVertices, and outAdjacentVertices, now require that we examine an entire row or column of array A, which takes $O(n)$ time. Moreover, any vertex insertions or deletions now require creating a whole new array A, of larger or smaller size, respectively, which takes time $O(n^2)$.

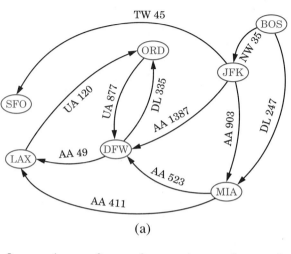

TW 45

UA 120

UA 877

DL 335

AA 1387

AA 903

DL 247

NW 35

AA 49

AA 523

AA 411

(a)

0	1	2	3	4	5	6
BOS	DFW	JFK	LAX	MIA	ORD	SFO

(b)

	0	1	2	3	4	5	6
0	Ø	Ø	NW 35	Ø	DL 247	Ø	Ø
1	Ø	Ø	Ø	AA 49	Ø	DL 335	Ø
2	Ø	AA 1387	Ø	Ø	AA 903	Ø	TW 45
3	Ø	Ø	Ø	Ø	Ø	UA 120	Ø
4	Ø	AA 523	Ø	AA 411	Ø	Ø	Ø
5	Ø	UA 877	Ø	Ø	Ø	Ø	Ø
6	Ø	Ø	Ø	Ø	Ø	Ø	Ø

(c)

Figure 9.5: Schematic of the adjacency matrix representation: (a) a directed graph G; (b) a numbering of the vertices in G; (c) the adjacency matrix A for G.

Operation	Time
size, isEmpty, replaceElement, swap	$O(1)$
numVertices, numEdges	$O(1)$
vertices	$O(n)$
edges, directedEdges, undirectedEdges	$O(m)$
elements, positions	$O(n+m)$
endVertices, opposite, origin, destination, isDirected, degree, inDegree, outDegree	$O(1)$
incidentEdges, inIncidentEdges, outIncidentEdges, adjacentVertices, inAdjacentVertices, outAdjacentVertices	$O(n)$
areAdjacent	$O(1)$
insertEdge, insertDirectedEdge, removeEdge, makeUndirected, reverseDirection, setDirectionFrom, setDirectionTo	$O(1)$
insertVertex, removeVertex	$O(n^2)$

Table 9.3: Running times of the methods of a graph implemented with an adjacency matrix. We denote with n and m the number of vertices and edges of the graph, respectively. The space used is $O(n^2)$.

Table 9.3 summarizes the performance of the adjacency matrix implementation of a graph. From this table we observe that the adjacency list structure is superior to the adjacency matrix in space, and is superior in time for all methods except for the areAdjacent method.

Historically, the adjacency matrix was the first representation used for graphs. We should not find this fact surprizing, however, for the adjacency matrix has a natural appeal as a mathematical structure (for example, an undirected graph has a symmetric adjacency matrix). The adjacency list structure came later, with its natural appeal to computer science due to its faster methods for most algorithms (many algorithms do not use method areAdjacent) and its space efficiency.

Most of the graph algorithms we examine in this book will run efficiently when acting upon a graph stored using the adjacency list representation. In some cases, however, a trade-off occurs, where graphs with few edges are most efficiently processed with an adjacency list structure and graphs with many edges are most efficiently processed with an adjacency matrix structure.

Next, we explore one of the most fundamental kinds of algorithmic operations we might wish to perform on a graph, which is to traverse the edges and the vertices of that graph.

9.3   Graph Traversal

A ***traversal*** is a systematic procedure for exploring a graph by examining all of its vertices and edges. A traversal is efficient if it visits all the vertices and edges in time proportional to their number, that is, in linear time. In this section and the next, we consider two efficient traversals of undirected graphs, called depth-first search and breadth-first search, respectively. In Section 9.4.2, we extend these techniques to traversals of directed graphs.

9.3.1   Depth-First Search

The first traversal algorithm we consider is ***depth-first search*** (DFS) in an undirected graph. Depth-first search is useful for performing a number of computations on graphs, including finding a path from one vertex to another, determining whether a graph is connected or not, and computing a spanning tree of a connected graph. In this section, we explain how DFS works and how it can be used to solve such problems as these.

Depth-first search in an undirected graph G is analogous to wandering in a labyrinth with a string and a can of paint, without getting lost. (See Figure 9.6.) We begin at a specific starting vertex s in G, which we initialize by fixing one end of our string to s and painting s as "visited." The vertex s is now our "current" vertex—call our current vertex u. We then traverse G by considering an (arbitrary) edge (u, v) incident to the current vertex u. If the edge (u, v) leads us to an already visited (that is, painted) vertex v, we immediately return to vertex u. If, on the other hand, (u, v) leads to an unvisited vertex v, then we unroll our string, and go to v. We then paint v as "visited," and make it the current vertex, repeating the above computation. Eventually, we will get to a "dead-end," that is a current vertex u such that all the edges incident on u lead to vertices already visited. Thus, taking any edge incident on u will cause us to return to u. To get out of this impasse, we roll our string back up, backtracking along the edge that lead us to u, to a previously visited vertex v. We then make v our current vertex, and repeat the above computation for any edges incident upon v that we hadn't looked at before. If all of v's incident edges lead to visited vertices, then we again roll up our string and backtrack to the vertex we came from to get to v, and repeat the procedure at that vertex. Thus, we continue to backtrack along the path that we have traced so far until we find a vertex that has yet unexplored edges, take one such edge, and continue the traversal. The process terminates when our backtracking leads us back to the start vertex s, and there are no more unexplored edges incident on s. This simple process traverses the edges of G in an elegant, systematic way.

We can visualize a DFS traversal by orienting the edges along the direction in which they are explored during the traversal, distinguishing the edges used to discover new vertices, called ***discovery edges***, or ***tree edges***, from those that lead to already visited vertices, called ***back edges***. (See Figure 9.6f.) In the analogy above, discovery edges are the edges where we unroll our string when we traverse them, and back edges are the edges where we immediately return without unrolling any string. As we will see, the discovery edges form a spanning tree of the connected component of the starting vertex s. We call the edges not in this tree "back edges," because each one leads back from a vertex in this tree to one of its ancestors in the tree.

The pseudo-code for a DFS traversal starting at a vertex v follows our analogy with string and paint. We use recursion to implement the string analogy, and we assume that we have a mechanism (the paint analogy) to determine if a vertex or edge has been explored or not, and to label the edges as discovery edges or back edges. This mechanism will require additional space and may affect the running time of the algorithm. A pseudo-code description of the recursive DFS algorithm is given in Code Fragment 9.1.

Algorithm DFS(v):

    Input: A vertex v in a graph

    Output: A labeling of the edges as "discovery" edges and "back edges"

  for each edge e incident on v **do**

    if edge e is unexplored **then**

      let w be the other endpoint of e

      if vertex w is unexplored **then**

        label e as a discovery edge

        recursively call DFS(w)

      else

        label e as a back edge

Code Fragment 9.1: The DFS algorithm.

There are a number of observations that we can make about the depth-first search algorithm, many of which derive from the way the DFS algorithm partitions the edges of the undirected graph G into two groups, the discovery edges and the back edges. For example, since back edges always connect a vertex v to a previously-visited vertex u, each back edge implies a cycle in G, consisting of the discovery edges from u to v plus the back edge (u, v).

Proposition '9.12, which follows, identifies some other important properties of the depth-first search traversal method.

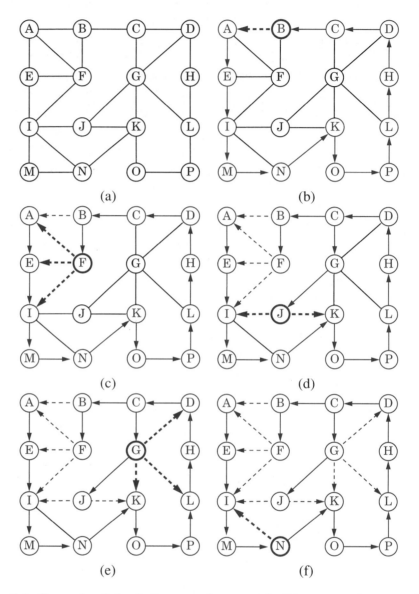

Figure 9.6: Example of depth-first search traversal. Discovery edges are shown with solid lines and back edges are shown with dashed lines: (a) input graph; (b) path of discovery edges traced from A until back edge (B,A) is hit; (c) reaching F, which is a dead end; (d) after backtracking to C, resuming with edge (C,G), and hitting another dead end, J; (e) after backtracking to G; (f) after backtracking to N.

Proposition 9.12: *Let G be an undirected graph on which a DFS traversal starting at a vertex s has been performed. Then:*

- *The traversal visits all vertices in the connected component of s*
- *The discovery edges form a spanning tree of the connected component of s.*

Justification: The justification for why we visit all the vertices in the connected component of s is based upon a simple contradiction argument. Suppose there is at least one vertex v in s's connected component not visited, and let w be the first unvisited vertex on some path from s to v (of course, we may have $v = w$). Since w is the first unvisited vertex on this path, it has a neighbor u that was visited. But when we visited u, we must have considered the edge (u, w); hence, it cannot be correct that w is unvisited. Therefore, there are no unvisited vertices in s's connected component.

Since we only mark edges when we go to unvisited vertices, we will never form a cycle with discovery edges, that is, discovery edges form a tree. Moreover, this is a spanning tree because, as we have just seen, the depth-first search visits each vertex in the connected component of s. ∎

In terms of its running time, depth-first search is an efficient method for traversing a graph. Note that DFS is called exactly once on each vertex, and that every edge is examined exactly twice, once from each of its end vertices. Thus, if n_s vertices and m_s edges are in the connected component of vertex s, a DFS starting at s runs in time $O(n_s + m_s)$, provided the following conditions are satisfied:

- The graph is represented by a data structure such that the vertex and edge methods each take $O(1)$ time. The adjacency list structure satisfies this condition, but the adjacency matrix structure does not.
- We have a way to "mark" a vertex as explored, and to test if a vertex has been explored in $O(1)$ time. One way to do such marking is extend vertex positions to store a variable used for marking. Another way, which we explore in a Java implementation, is to use a hash table mechanism, which satisfies this condition in the probabilistic sense, because it supports the mark and test operations in $O(1)$ *expected* time.
- We have a way of systematically considering the edges incident on the current vertex, so that we do not repeatedly examine the same edge. We can satisfy this condition by using the adjacency list structure to represent the graph and by implementing the DFS as a recursive method.

By Proposition 9.12 and the above discussion, we can solve a number of interesting problems for an undirected graph, as summarized in Proposition 9.13, which follows.

Proposition 9.13: *Let G be a graph with n vertices and m edges. A DFS traversal of G can be performed in time $O(n+m)$. Also, there exist $O(n+m)$ time algorithms based on DFS for the following problems:*

- *Testing whether G is connected*

- *Computing a spanning tree of G, if G is connected*

- *Computing the connected components of G*

- *Computing a path between two given vertices of G, or reporting that no such path exists*

- *Computing a cycle in G, or reporting that G has no cycles.*

The justification of Proposition 9.13 is based on algorithms that use the depth-first search algorithm or a slightly-modified versions of the DFS algorithm as subroutines. We explore the details in some interesting, but not too difficult, exercises.

In Code Fragments 9.2 and 9.3, we show a Java implementation of a generic depth-first search traversal by means of a class DFS whose behavior can be specialized for a particular application by redefining method execute, which activates the computation, and the following methods, which are called at various times by the recursive visit method dfsVisit.

- initResult(): called at the beginning of the execution of dfsVisit;

- startVisit(Vertex v): also called at the beginning of the execution of dfsVisit;

- traverseDiscovery(Edge e, Vertex v): called when a discovery edge e out of v is traversed;

- traverseBack(Edge e, Vertex v): called when a back edge e out of v is traversed;

- isDone(): called to determine whether to end the traversal early;

- finishVisit(Vertex v) called when all the incident edges of v have been traversed;

- result() called to return the output of dfsVisit.

The mechanism used to identify the explored vertices and edges is to insert them into a java.util.Hashtable. To use a different mechanism, we can redefine methods mark and isMarked. Our generic depth-first search traversal is based on the the template method pattern (see Section 5.3.4), which describes a generic computation mechanism that can be specialized by redefining certain steps.

```
public abstract class DFS {
  protected InspectableGraph graph;
  protected Object visitResult;
  protected Hashtable markedVerts = new Hashtable();
  protected Hashtable markedEdges = new Hashtable();
  public Object execute(InspectableGraph g, Vertex start, Object info) {
    graph = g;
    return null;
  }
  // recursive depth-first search starting at vertex v
  protected Object dfsVisit(Vertex v) {
    initResult();
    startVisit(v);
    mark(v);
    // check all incident edges
    for (Enumeration inEdges = graph.incidentEdges(v);
        inEdges.hasMoreElements(); ) {
      Edge nextEdge = (Edge)inEdges.nextElement();
      if (!isMarked(nextEdge)) {
        // found an unexplored edge, explore it
        mark(nextEdge);
        Vertex w = graph.opposite(v, nextEdge);
        if (!isMarked(w)) {
          // w is unexplored, this is a discovery edge
          mark(nextEdge);
          traverseDiscovery(nextEdge, v);
          if (!isDone()) {
            visitResult = dfsVisit(w);
          }
        } else {
          // w is explored, this is a back edge
          traverseBack(nextEdge, v);
        }
      }
    }
    finishVisit(v);
    return result();
  }
  // additional methods shown in Code Fragment 9.3
  ...
}
```

Code Fragment 9.2: Class DFS and method dfsVisit that performs a generic DFS traversal of a graph.

```
protected void mark(Vertex v) {
  markedVerts.put(v, v); // use the vertex as both key and value
}
protected void mark(Edge e) {
  markedEdges.put(e, e);
}
protected boolean isMarked(Vertex v) {
  return markedVerts.contains(v);
}
protected boolean isMarked(Edge e) {
  return markedEdges.contains(e);
}
// These methods will be defined in the subclasses of this class
protected void initResult() {}
protected void startVisit(Vertex v) {}
protected void traverseDiscovery(Edge e, Vertex from) {}
protected void traverseBack(Edge e, Vertex from) {}
protected boolean isDone() { return false; }
protected void finishVisit(Vertex v) {}
protected Object result() { return new Object(); }
```

Code Fragment 9.3: Auxiliary methods to mark vertices and edges, and methods that specialize the computation performed by the generic depth-first search traversal method dfsVisit of class DFS (Code Fragment 9.2).

Please note the following about Code Fragment 9.3:

- We mark a vertex by putting it into a hash table markedVerts.
- We mark an edge by putting it into a hash table markedEdges.
- We test if a vertex is marked by checking if the hash table contains that vertex, and perform a similar check for edges in markedEdges.

For us to do anything interesting with the dfsVisit we must extend the DFS class and redefine some of the trivial methods of Code Fragment 9.3 to do something nontrivial. This approach is in keeping with the template method pattern, for these methods are the modifiable functions of this template.

The code fragments that follow illustrate some interesting uses of the dfsVisit method in classes that extend DFS. In Code Fragment 9.4, we show a specialization of the generic depth-first search traversal that computes the vertices in the connected component of a given vertex. In Code Fragment 9.5, we show how to test whether a graph is connected as a simple application of the previous algorithm. In Code Fragments 9.6 and 9.7, we show specializations of the generic depth-first search traversal that find a path between two given vertices and a cycle, respectively.

```
// This class specializes DFS to return an enumeration of the vertices in
// the connected component of the start vertex.
public class FindAllVerticesDFS extends DFS {
  protected Sequence vertices;
  public Object execute(InspectableGraph g, Vertex start, Object info) {
    super.execute(g, start, info);
    vertices = new NodeSequence();
    dfsVisit(start);
    return vertices.elements();
  }
  // This will add vertices in DFS order
  public void startVisit(Vertex v) {
    vertices.insertLast(v);
  }
}
```

Code Fragment 9.4: Specialization of the generic depth-first search traversal to compute the vertices in the connected component of vertex start. An enumeration of such vertices is returned as output. Note the redefined startVisit method, which inserts into a sequence all the vertices encountered in the depth-first search traversal beginning at vertex start.

```
// This class uses a specialized DFS to test if a graph is connected.  It
// runs FindAllVerticesDFS and then checks if the number of vertices
// visited is equal to the total number of vertices in the graph.
public class ConnectivityTest {
  protected static DFS tester = new FindAllVerticesDFS();
  public static boolean isConnected(InspectableGraph g) {
    if (g.numVertices() == 0) return true; // an empty graph is connected
    Vertex start = (Vertex)g.vertices().nextElement();
    Enumeration compVerts = (Enumeration)tester.execute(g, start, null);
    // count now many elements are in the enumeration
    int count = 0;
    while (compVerts.hasMoreElements()) {
      compVerts.nextElement();
      count++;
    }
    if (count == g.numVertices())
      return true;
    return false;
  }
}
```

Code Fragment 9.5: An algorithm that uses the FindAllVerticesDFS specialization of the generic depth-first search traversal to test whether the graph is connected.

```
// This class specializes DFS to determine if there is a path from a
// start vertex to a target vertex. It returns an enumeration of
// vertices in the path, or an empty enumeration if such a path does
// not exist.  The algorithm performs a DFS beginning at the start vertex.
public class FindPathDFS extends DFS {
  protected Sequence path;
  protected boolean done;
  protected Vertex targetVert;
  public Object execute(InspectableGraph g, Vertex start, Object info) {
    super.execute(g, start, info);
    path = new NodeSequence();
    done = false;
    targetVert = (Vertex)info; // target vertex is stored in info parameter
    dfsVisit(start);
    return path.elements();
  }
  protected void startVisit(Vertex v) {
    path.insertFirst(v);
    if (v == targetVert) { done = true; }
  }
  protected void finishVisit(Vertex v) {
    if (!done) { path.remove(path.first()); }
  }
  protected boolean isDone() { return done; }
}
```

Code Fragment 9.6: Specialization of the generic depth-first search traversal to find a path between vertex start and another target vertex. A depth-first search traversal beginning at vertex start is performed. When we encounter an unexplored vertex, we add it to the beginning of the path, and when we finish processing a vertex, we remove it from the path. The traversal is terminated when the target vertex is encountered, and the path is returned as an enumeration of vertices. Note that the path found by this algorithm consists of discovery edges.

```
// This class specializes DFS to determine if the connected component of
// the start vertex contains a cycle and if so return it. The algorithm
// returns an enumeration of vertices in the cycle or an empty enumeration
// if there is no such cycle.
public class FindCycleDFS extends DFS {
  protected Sequence path;
  protected boolean done;
  protected Vertex cycleStart;
  public Object execute(InspectableGraph g, Vertex start, Object info) {
    super.execute(g, start, info);
    path = new NodeSequence();
    done = false;
    dfsVisit(start);
    // copy the vertices up to cycleStart from the path to the cycle sequence
    Sequence theCycle = new NodeSequence();
    Enumeration pathVerts = path.elements();
    while (pathVerts.hasMoreElements()) {
      Vertex v = (Vertex)pathVerts.nextElement();
      theCycle.insertFirst(v);
      if (v == cycleStart) {
        break;
      }
    }
    return theCycle.elements();
  }
  protected void startVisit(Vertex v) { path.insertFirst(v); }
  protected void finishVisit(Vertex v) {
    if (!done) { path.remove(path.first()); }
  }
  // When a back edge has been encountered, the graph has a cycle
  protected void traverseBack(Edge e, Vertex from) {
    Enumeration pathVerts = path.elements();
    cycleStart = graph.opposite(from, e);
    done = true;
  }
  protected boolean isDone() { return done; }
}
```

Code Fragment 9.7: Specialization of the generic depth-first search traversal to find a cycle in the connected component of the start vertex. A depth-first search traversal beginning at vertex start is performed, and is terminated when a back edge is encountered. When we encounter an unexplored vertex, we add it to the beginning of an initially empty path, and when we finish processing a vertex, we remove it from the path. The cycle reported consists of the vertices of the path up to the destination of the back edge.

9.3.2 Breadth-First Search

In this section, we consider the ***breadth-first search*** (BFS) traversal algorithm. Like DFS, BFS traverses a connected component of graph, and in so doing defines a spanning tree with useful properties. The BFS algorithm is less "adventurous" than DFS, however. Instead of wandering around the graph, BFS proceeds incrementally in rounds and subdivides the vertices into ***levels***. (See Figure 9.7.)

BFS can also be thought of as a traversal using a string and paint. The main difference is that BFS unrolls the string in a more conservative manner. The starting vertex s has level 0, and, as in DFS, s defines that "anchor" for our string. In the first round, we let out the string the length of one edge and we visit all the vertices we can reach without unrolling the string any farther. In this case, we visit, and paint as "visited," the vertices adjacent to the start vertex s—these vertices are placed into level 1. In the second round, we unroll the string the length of two edges and we visit all the new vertices we can reach without unrolling our string any farther. These new vertices, which are adjacent to level 1 vertices and were not previously assigned to a level, are placed into level 2. In a generic round i, we unroll our string the length of one more edge, and the vertices that are adjacent to level $(i-1)$ vertices and were not previously assigned to a level are placed into level i. The BFS traversal terminates when every vertex has been assigned to a level.

One of the nice properties of the BFS approach is that, in performing the BFS traversal, we can label each vertex by the length of a shortest path (in terms of the number of edges) from the start vertex s. In particular, if vertex v is placed into level i by a BFS starting at vertex s, then the length of a shortest path from s to v is i.

As with DFS, we can visualize the BFS traversal by orienting the edges along the direction in which they are explored during the traversal, and by distinguishing the edges used to discover new vertices, called ***discovery edges***, from those that lead to already visited vertices, called ***cross edges***. (See Figure 9.7f.) As with the DFS, the discovery edges form a spanning tree, which in this case we call the BFS tree. We do not call the nontree edges "back edges" in this case, however, for none of them connects a vertex to one of its ancestors. Every nontree edge connects a vertex v to another vertex that is neither v's ancestor nor its descendent.

The pseudo-code for a BFS traversal starting at a vertex s is shown in Code Fragment 9.8. Note that auxiliary space is used to label the edges, mark the visited vertices, and store the containers associated with the levels. Also note that the BFS algorithm is not recursive.

The BFS traversal algorithm has a number of interesting properties, some of which we explore in the proposition that follows.

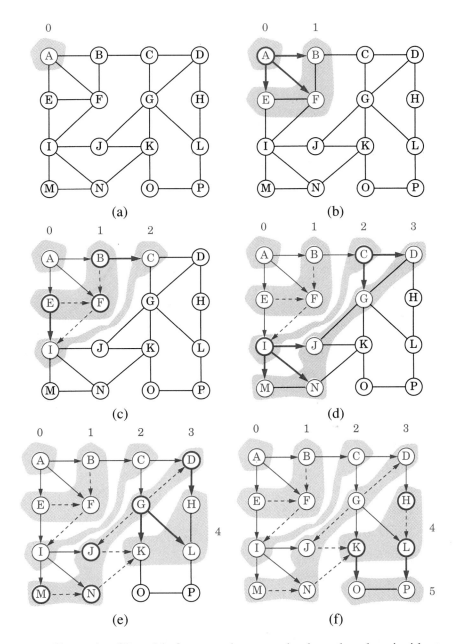

Figure 9.7: Example of breadth-first search traversal, where the edges incident on a vertex are explored by the alphabetical order of the adjacent vertices. The discovery edges are shown with solid lines and the cross edges are shown with dashed lines. (a) graph before the traversal; (b) discovery of level 1; (c) discovery of level 2; (d) discovery of level 3; (e) discovery of level 4; (f) discovery of level 5.

Algorithm BFS(s):

    initialize container L_0 to contain vertex s

    $i \leftarrow 0$

    while L_i is not empty **do**

      create container L_{i+1} to initially be empty

      for each vertex v in L_i **do**

        for each edge e incident on v **do**

          if edge e is unexplored **then**

            let w be the other endpoint of e

            if vertex w is unexplored **then**

              label e as a discovery edge

              insert w into L_{i+1}

            else

              label e as a cross edge

    $i \leftarrow i + 1$

Code Fragment 9.8: The BFS algorithm.

Proposition 9.14: *Let G be an undirected graph on which a BFS traversal starting at vertex s has been performed. Then*

- *The traversal visits all vertices in the connected component of s.*
- *The discovery-edges form a spanning tree T, which we call the BFS tree, of the connected component of s.*
- *For each vertex v at level i, the path of the BFS tree T between s and v has i edges, and any other path of G between s and v has at least i edges.*
- *If (u,v) is an edge that is not in the BFS tree, then the level numbers of u and v differ by at most 1.*

We leave the justification of this proposition as an exercise.

The analysis of the running time of BFS is similar to the one of DFS, which implies the following.

Proposition 9.15: *Let G be a graph with n vertices and m edges. A BFS traversal of G takes time $O(n+m)$. Also, there exist $O(n+m)$ time algorithms based on BFS for the following problems:*

- *Testing whether G is connected*
- *Computing a spanning tree of G*
- *Computing the connected components of G*
- *Computing, for every vertex v of G, the minimum number of edges of any path between s and v.*

By Proposition 9.15, the BFS traversal can do everything we claimed for the DFS traversal. There are a number of interesting differences between these two methods, however, and there are, in fact, a number of tasks that each can do better than the other. BFS traversals are better at finding shortest paths in a graph (where distance is measured by the number of edges), and the BFS traversal produces a spanning tree such that all the nontree edges are cross edges. DFS is better for answering complex connectivity questions, such as determining if every pair of vertices in a graph can be connected by two disjoint paths, and the DFS traversal produces a spanning tree such that all the nontree edges are back edges. These properties only hold for undirected graphs, however. Nevertheless, as we explore in the next section, there are a number of interesting properties for the directed analogues of DFS and BFS.

9.4 Directed Graphs

In this section, we consider issues that are specific to directed graphs. Recall that a directed graph, which is also known as a *digraph*, is a graph whose edges are all directed.

9.4.1 Reachability

One of the most fundamental issues with directed graphs is the notion of *reachability*, which deals with determining where we can get to in a directed graph. A traversal in a directed graph always goes along directed paths, that is, paths where all the edges are traversed according to their respective directions. Given vertices u and v of a digraph $\vec{G}$, we say that u *reaches* v (and v is *reachable* from u) if $\vec{G}$ has a directed path from u to v. We also say that a vertex v reaches an edge (w, z) if v reaches the origin vertex w of the edge.

A digraph $\vec{G}$ is *strongly connected* if for any two vertices u and v of $\vec{G}$, u reaches v and v reaches u. A *directed cycle* of $\vec{G}$ is a cycle where all the edges are traversed according to their respective directions. (Note that $\vec{G}$ may have a cycle consisting of two edges with opposite direction between the same pair of vertices.) A digraph $\vec{G}$ is *acyclic* if it has no directed cycles. (See Figure 9.8 for some examples.)

The *transitive closure* of a digraph $\vec{G}$ is the digraph $\vec{G}^*$ such that the vertices of $\vec{G}^*$ are the same as the vertices of $\vec{G}$, and $\vec{G}^*$ has an edge (u, v), whenever $\vec{G}$ has a directed path from u to v. That is, we define $\vec{G}^*$ by starting with the digraph $\vec{G}$ and adding in an extra edge (u, v) for each u and v such that v is reachable from u (and there isn't already an edge (u, v) in $\vec{G}$).

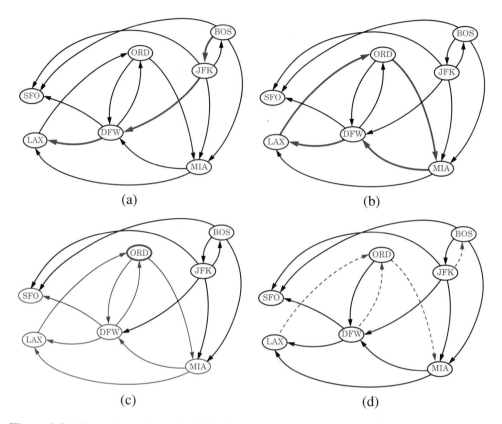

Figure 9.8: Examples of reachability in a digraph: (a) a directed path from BOS to LAX is drawn in blue; (b) a directed cycle (ORD, MIA, DFW, LAX, ORD) is shown in blue; its vertices induce a strongly connected subgraph; (c) the subgraph of the vertices and edges reachable from ORD is shown in blue; (d) removing the dashed blue edges gives an acyclic digraph.

Interesting questions that deal with reachability in a digraph $\vec{G}$ include the following:

- Given vertices u and v, determine whether u reaches v.
- Find all the vertices of $\vec{G}$ that are reachable from a given vertex s.
- Determine whether $\vec{G}$ is strongly connected.
- Determine whether $\vec{G}$ is acyclic.
- Compute the transitive closure $\vec{G}^*$ of $\vec{G}$.

In the remainder of this chapter, we explore some efficient algorithms for answering these questions.

9.4.2 Traversing a Digraph

As with undirected graphs, we can explore a digraph in a systematic way with methods akin to the depth-first search (DFS) and breadth-first search (BFS) algorithms defined previously for undirected graphs (Sections 9.3.1 and 9.3.2). Such explorations can be used, for example, to answer reachability questions. The directed depth-first search and breadth-first search methods we develop in this section for performing such explorations are very similar to their undirected counterparts. In fact, the only real difference is that the directed depth-first search and breadth-first search methods only traverse edges according to their respective directions.

The directed version of DFS starting at a vertex v can be described by the recursive algorithm in Code Fragment 9.9. (See Figure 9.9.)

Algorithm DirectedDFS(v):

Mark vertex v as visited.

for each outgoing edge (v, w) of v **do**

    if vertex w has not been visited **then**

        Recursively call DirectedDFS(w).

Code Fragment 9.9: The DirectedDFS algorithm.

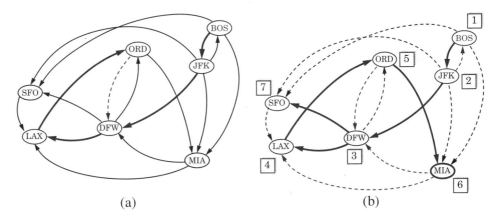

(a)   (b)

Figure 9.9: An example of a DFS in a digraph: (a) intermediate step, where, for the first time, an already visited vertex (DFW) is reached; (b) the completed DFS. The tree edges are shown with solid blue lines, the back edges are shown with dashed blue lines, and the forward and cross edges are shown with dashed black lines. The order in which the vertices are visited is indicated by a label next to each vertex. The edge (ORD,DFW) is a back edge, but (DFW,ORD) is a forward edge. Edge (BOS,SFO) is a forward edge, and (SFO,LAX) is a cross edge.

A DFS on a digraph $\vec{G}$ partitions the edges of $\vec{G}$ reachable from the starting vertex into *tree edges* or *discovery edges*, which lead us to discover a new vertex, and *nontree edges*, which take us to a previously visited vertex. The tree edges form a tree rooted at the starting vertex, called the *depth-first search* tree, and there are three kinds of nontree edges:

- **back edges**, which connect a vertex to an ancestor in the DFS tree
- **forward edges**, which connect a vertex to a descendent in the DFS tree
- **cross edges**, which connect a vertex to a vertex that is neither its ancestor nor its descendent.

Refer back to Figure 9.9b to see an example of each type of nontree edge.

Proposition 9.16: *Let $\vec{G}$ be a digraph. Depth-first search on $\vec{G}$ starting at a vertex s visits all the vertices of $\vec{G}$ that are reachable from s. Also, the DFS tree contains directed paths from v to every vertex reachable from s.*

Justification: Let V_s be the subset of vertices of $\vec{G}$ visited by DFS starting at vertex s. We want to show that V_s contains s and every vertex of V_s is reachable from s. Suppose now, for the sake of a contradiction, that there is a vertex w reachable from s that is not in V_s. Consider a directed path from s to w, and let (u, v) be the first edge on such a path taking us out of V_s, that is, u is in V_s but v is not in V_s. When DFS reaches u, it explores all the outgoing edges of u, and thus must reach also vertex v via edge (u, v). Hence, v should be in V_s, and we have obtained a contradiction. Therefore, V_s must contain every vertex reachable from s. ∎

Analyzing the running time of the directed DFS method is analogous to that for its undirected counterpart. In particular, a recursive call is made for each vertex exactly once, and each edge is traversed exactly once (from its origin). Hence, if n_s vertices and m_s edges are reachable from vertex s, a DFS starting at s runs in time $O(n_s + m_s)$, provided the digraph is represented with a data structure that supports constant-time vertex and edge methods. The adjacency list structure satifies this requirement, for example.

By Proposition 9.16, we can use DFS to find all the vertices reachable from a given vertex, and hence to find the transitive closure of $\vec{G}$. Also, by repeatedly traversing digraph $\vec{G}$ with a DFS, starting in turn at each vertex, we can easily test whether $\vec{G}$ is strongly connected. Namely, $\vec{G}$ is strongly connected if each DFS visits all the vertices of $\vec{G}$.

Thus, we may immediately derive the proposition that follows.

> **Proposition 9.17:** *Let $\vec{G}$ be a digraph with n vertices and m edges. The following problems can be solved by an algorithm that traverses $\vec{G}$ n times using DFS, runs in $O(n(n+m))$ time, and uses $O(n)$ auxiliary space:*
>
> - *Computing, for each vertex v of $\vec{G}$, the subgraph reachable from v*
> - *Testing whether $\vec{G}$ is strongly connected*
> - *Computing the transitive closure $\vec{G}^*$ of $\vec{G}$.*

Actually, we can determine if a directed graph $\vec{G}$ is strongly connected much faster than this, just using two depth-first searches. We begin by performing a DFS of our directed graph $\vec{G}$ starting at an arbitrary vertex s. If there is any vertex of $\vec{G}$ that is not visited by this DFS, and is not reachable from s, then the graph is not strongly connected. So, if this first DFS visits each vertex of $\vec{G}$, then we reverse all the edges of $\vec{G}$ (using the reverseDirection method) and perform another DFS starting at s in this "reverse" graph. If every vertex of $\vec{G}$ is visited by this second DFS, then the graph is strongly connected, for each of the vertices visited in this DFS can reach s. Since this algorithm makes just two DFS traversals of $\vec{G}$, it runs in $O(n+m)$ time.

As with DFS, we can easily extend the breadth-first search (BFS) method to work for directed graphs. The algorithm still visits vertices level by level and partitions the set of edges into **tree edges** (or **discovery edges**), which together form a directed **breadth-first search** tree rooted at the start vertex, and **nontree edges**. Unlike the directed DFS method, however, the directed BFS method only leaves two kinds of nontree edges: **back edges**, which connect a vertex to one of its ancestors in the BFS tree, and **cross edges**, which connect a vertex to another vertex that is neither its ancestor nor its descendent. There are no forward edges, which is a fact we explore in an exercise.

9.4.3 Transitive Closure

In this section, we explore an alternative technique for computing the transitive closure of a digraph, which can be efficiently implemented if the digraph is represented by a data structure that supports $O(1)$-time lookup and update of adjacency information (for example, by using the adjacency-matrix structure).

Let $\vec{G}$ be a digraph with n vertices and m edges. We compute the transitive closure of $\vec{G}$ in a series of rounds. We initialize $\vec{G}_0 = \vec{G}$. We also arbitrarily number the vertices of $\vec{G}$ as $v_1, v_2, \ldots, v_n$. We then begin the computation of the rounds, beginning with round 1. In a generic round k, we construct digraph $\vec{G}_k$ starting with $\vec{G}_k = \vec{G}_{k-1}$ and adding to $\vec{G}_k$ the directed edge (v_i, v_j) if digraph $\vec{G}_{k-1}$ contains both the edges (v_i, v_k) and (v_k, v_j). (See Figure 9.10.) In this way, we will enforce a simple rule embodied in the proposition that follows.

Proposition 9.18: *For* $i = 1, \ldots, n$, *digraph* $\vec{G}_k$ *has an edge* (v_i, v_j) *if and only if digraph* $\vec{G}$ *has a directed path from* v_i *to* v_j, *whose intermediate vertices (if any) are in the set* $\{v_1, \ldots, v_k\}$. *In particular,* $\vec{G}_n$ *is equal to* $\vec{G}^*$, *the transitive closure of* $\vec{G}$.

Proposition 9.18 suggests a simple algorithm for computing the transitive closure of $\vec{G}$ that is based on the series of rounds we described above. This algorithm is known as the ***Floyd-Warshall algorithm***, and its pseudo-code is given in Code Fragment 9.10. From this pseudo-code, we can easily analyze the running time of the Floyd-Warshall algorithm assuming that the data structure representing G supports methods areAdjacent and insertDirectedEdge in $O(1)$ time. The main loop is executed n times and the inner loop considers each of $O(n^2)$ pairs of vertices, performing a constant-time computation for each one. Thus, the total running time of the Floyd-Warshall algorithm is $O(n^3)$.

Algorithm FloydWarshall($\vec{G}$):
    Input: A digraph $\vec{G}$ with n vertices
    Output: The transitive closure $\vec{G}^*$ of $\vec{G}$

    let $v_1, v_2, \ldots, v_n$ be an arbitrary ordering of the vertices of $\vec{G}$
    $\vec{G}_0 \leftarrow \vec{G}$
    for $k \leftarrow 1$ to n **do**
        $\vec{G}_k \leftarrow \vec{G}_{k-1}$
        for each i, j in $\{1, \ldots, n\}$ with $i \neq j$ and $i, j \neq k$ **do**
            if both edges (v_i, v_k) and (v_k, v_j) are in $\vec{G}_{k-1}$ **then**
                add edge (v_i, v_j) to $\vec{G}_k$ (if it is not already present)
    return $\vec{G}_n$

Code Fragment 9.10: Pseudo-code for the Floyd-Warshall algorithm. This algorithm computes the transitive closure $\vec{G}^*$ of G by incrementally computing a series of digraphs $\vec{G}_0, \vec{G}_1, \ldots, \vec{G}_n$, where for $k = 1, \ldots, n$.

From this description and analysis we may immediately derive the following proposition.

Proposition 9.19: *Let* $\vec{G}$ *be a digraph with* n *vertices, and let* $\vec{G}$ *be represented by a data structure that supports lookup and update of adjacency information in* $O(1)$ *time. Then the Floyd-Warshall algorithm computes the transitive closure* $\vec{G}^*$ *of* $\vec{G}$ *in* $O(n^3)$ *time.*

The running time of the Floyd-Warshall algorithm might appear to be slower than performing a DFS of a directed graph from each of its vertices, but this depends upon the representation of the graph.

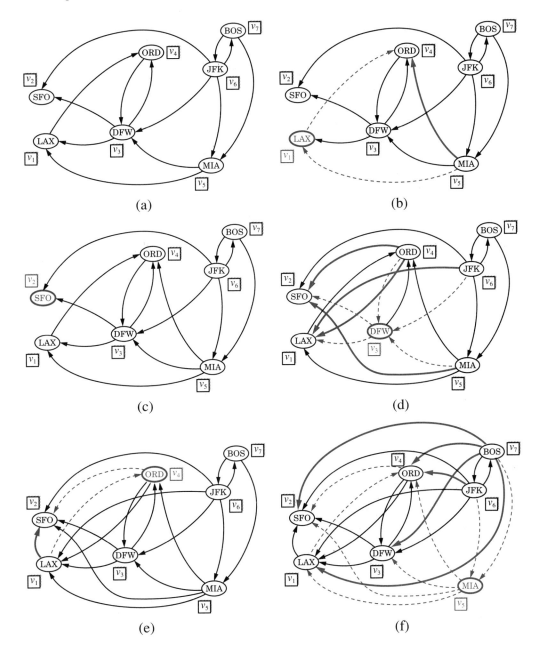

Figure 9.10: Sequence of digraphs computed by the Floyd-Warshall algorithm: (a) initial digraph $\vec{G} = \vec{G}_0$ and ordering of the vertices; (b) digraph $\vec{G}_1$; (c) $\vec{G}_2$; (d) $\vec{G}_3$; (e) $\vec{G}_4$; (f) $\vec{G}_5$, Note that $\vec{G}_5 = \vec{G}_6 = \vec{G}_7$. If digraph $\vec{G}_{k-1}$ has the edges (v_i, v_k) and (v_k, v_j), but not the edge (v_i, v_j), in the drawing of digraph $\vec{G}_k$, we show edges (v_i, v_k) and (v_k, v_j) with dashed blue lines, and edge (v_i, v_j) with a thick blue line.

If a graph is represented using an adjacency matrix, then running the DFS method once on a directed graph $\vec{G}$ takes $O(n^2)$ time (we explore the reason for this in an exercise). Thus, running DFS n times takes $O(n^3)$ time, which is no better than a single execution of the Floyd-Warshall algorithm, but the Floyd-Warshall algorithm would be much simpler to implement. Nevertheless, if the graph is represented using an adjacency list structure, then running the DFS algorithm n times would take $O(n(n+m))$ time to compute the transitive closure. Even so, if the graph is **dense**, that is, if it has $\Theta(n^2)$ edges, then this approach still runs in $O(n^3)$ time, and is more complicated than a single instance of the Floyd-Warshall algorithm. The only case where repeatedly calling the DFS method is better is when the graph is not dense and is represented using an adjacency list structure.

9.4.4 Directed Acyclic Graphs

Directed graphs without cycles are encountered in many applications. Such a digraph is often referred to as a **directed acyclic graph**, or **DAG**, for short. Applications of such graphs include the following:

- Inheritance between classes of a Java program
- Prerequisites between courses of a degree program
- Scheduling constraints between the tasks of a project.

Example 9.20: *In order to manage a large project, it is convenient for us to break it up into a collection of smaller tasks. The tasks, however, are rarely independent, because scheduling constraints exist between them. (For example, in a house building project, the task of ordering nails obviously precedes the task of nailing shingles to the roof deck.) Clearly, scheduling constraints cannot have circularities because this would make the project impossible. (For example, in order to get a job you need to have work experience, but in order to get work experience you need to have a job.) The scheduling constraints impose restrictions on the order in which the tasks can be executed. Namely, if a constraint says that task a must be completed before task b is started, then a must precede b in the order of execution of the tasks. Thus, if we model a feasible set of tasks as vertices of a directed graph, and we place a directed edge from v to w if the task for v must come before the task for w, then we define a directed acyclic graph.*

The above example motivates the following definition. Let $\vec{G}$ be a digraph with n vertices. A **topological ordering** of $\vec{G}$ is an ordering $v_1, \ldots, v_n$ of the vertices of $\vec{G}$ such that for every edge (v_i, v_j) of $\vec{G}$, $i < j$. That is, a topological ordering is an ordering such that any directed path in $\vec{G}$ traverses vertices in increasing order. (See Figure 9.11.) Note that a digraph may have more than one topological ordering.

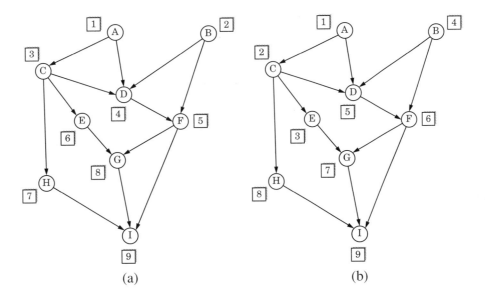

Figure 9.11: Two topological orderings of the same acyclic digraph.

Proposition 9.21: *Digraph $\vec{G}$ has a topological ordering if and only if it is acyclic.*

Justification: The necessity (the "only if" part of the statement) is easy to demonstrate. Suppose $\vec{G}$ is topologically ordered. Assume, for the sake of a contradiction, that $\vec{G}$ has a cycle consisting of edges $(v_{i_0}, v_{i_1}), (v_{i_1}, v_{i_2}), \ldots, (v_{i_{k-1}}, v_{i_0})$. Because of the topological ordering, we must have

$$i_0 < i_1 < \cdots < i_{k-1} < i_0,$$

which is clearly impossible. Thus, $\vec{G}$ must be acyclic.

We now argue the sufficiency of the condition (the "if" part of the statement). Suppose $\vec{G}$ is acyclic. We will give an algorithmic description of how to build a topological ordering for $\vec{G}$. Since $\vec{G}$ is acyclic, $\vec{G}$ must have a vertex with no incoming edges (that is, with in-degree 0). Let v_1 be this vertex. Indeed, if v_1 did not exist, then tracing a directed path from an arbitrary start vertex, we would eventually encounter a previously visited vertex, thus contradicting the acyclicity of $\vec{G}$. If we remove v_1 from $\vec{G}$, together with its outgoing edges, the resulting digraph is still acyclic. Hence, the resulting digraph also has a vertex with no incoming edges, and we let v_2 be this vertex. By repeating this process until the digraph becomes empty, we obtain an ordering $v_1, \ldots, v_n$ of the vertices of $\vec{G}$. Because of the above construction, if (v_i, v_j) is an edge of $\vec{G}$, then v_i must be deleted before v_j can be deleted, and thus $i < j$. This implies that $v_1, \ldots, v_n$ is a topological ordering. ∎

Proposition 9.21's justification suggests an algorithm (Code Fragment 9.11), called **topological sorting**, for computing a topological ordering of a digraph.

Algorithm TopologicalSort($\vec{G}$):

    Input: A digraph $\vec{G}$ with n vertices.

    Output: A topological ordering $v_1, \ldots, v_n$ of $\vec{G}$.

    Let Q be an initially empty queue.

    for each vertex u of $\vec{G}$ **do**

        Let incounter(u) be the in-degree of u.

        if incounter(u) $= 0$ **then**

            Q.enqueue(u)

    $i \leftarrow 1$

    while Q is not empty **do**

        $u \leftarrow Q$.dequeue()

        Let u be vertex number i in the topological ordering.

        $i \leftarrow i + 1$

        for each outgoing edge (u, w) of u **do**

            incounter(w) $\leftarrow$ incounter(w) $- 1$

            if incounter(w) $= 0$ **then**

                Q.enqueue(w)

Code Fragment 9.11: Pseudo-code for the topological sorting algorithm. (We show an example application of this algorithm in Figure 9.12.)

Proposition 9.22: *Let $\vec{G}$ be a digraph with n vertices and m edges. The topological sorting algorithm runs in $O(n+m)$ time using $O(n)$ auxiliary space, and either computes a topological ordering of $\vec{G}$ or fails to number some vertices, which indicates that $\vec{G}$ has a directed cycle.*

Justification: The initial computation of in-degrees and setup of the incounter variables can be done with a simple traversal of the graph, which takes $O(n + m)$ time. Say that a vertex u is **visited** by the topological sorting algorithm when u is dequeued from Q. A vertex u can be visited only when incounter(u) $= 0$, which implies that all its predecessors (vertices with outgoing edges into u) were previously visited. As a consequence, any vertex that is on a directed cycle will never be visited, and any other vertex will be visited exactly once. The algorithm traverses all the outgoing edges of each visited vertex once, so its running time is proportional to the number of outgoing edges of the visited vertices. Therefore, the algorithm runs in $O(n + m)$ time. Regarding the space usage, observe that the queue Q and the incounter variables attached to the vertices use $O(n)$ space. ∎

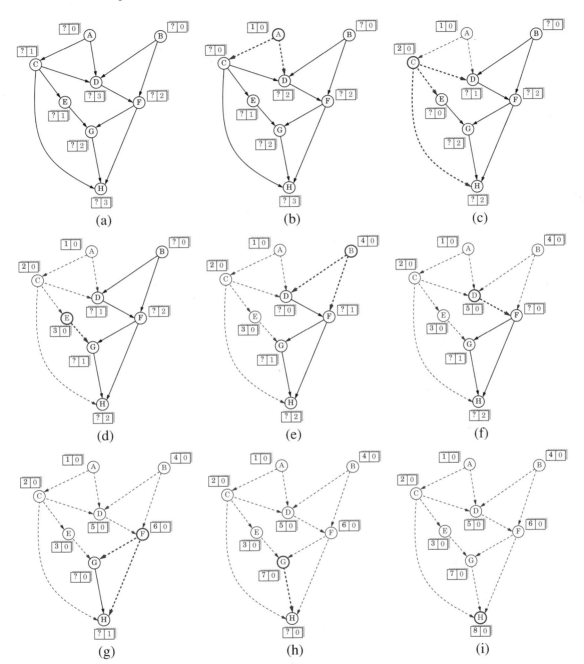

Figure 9.12: Example of a run of algorithm TopologicalSort (Code Fragment 9.11): (a) initial configuration, (b–i) after each while-loop iteration. The vertex labels show the vertex number and the current incounter value. The edges traversed are shown with dashed blue arrows. Thick lines denote the vertex and edges examined in the current iteration.

As a side effect, the topological sorting algorithm of Code Fragment 9.11 also tests whether the input digraph $\vec{G}$ is acyclic. Indeed, if the algorithm terminates without ordering all the vertices, then the subgraph of the vertices that have not been ordered must contain a directed cycle. (See Figure 9.13.)

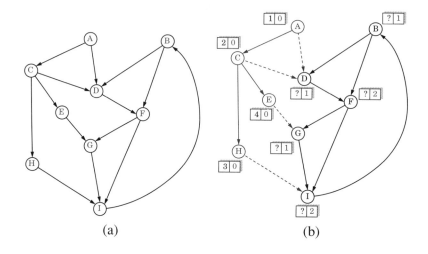

(a)   (b)

Figure 9.13: Detecting a directed cycle: (a) input digraph; (b) after algorithm TopologicalSort (Code Fragment 9.11) terminates, the subgraph of the vertices with undefined number contains a directed cycle.

We conclude this chapter with an application of directed graph traversal in Java.

9.4.5   Application: Garbage Collection in Java ★

In some languages, like C and C++, the memory space for objects must be explicitly allocated and deallocated by the programmer. This memory-allocation duty is often overlooked by beginning programmers, and, when done incorrectly, it can even be the source of frustrating programming errors for experienced programmers. Thus, the designers of other languages, like Java, place the burden of memory management on the run-time environment. A Java programmer does not have to explicitly deallocate the memory for some object when its life is over. Instead, the ***garbage collector*** mechanism deallocates the memory for such objects.

Recall that in Java the memory for most objects is allocated from the memory heap. In addition, the running threads in a Java program store the current space for their instance variables on their respective Java stacks. Since the instance variables in the Java stacks can refer to objects in the memory heap, all the variables and objects in the Java stack of running threads are called ***root objects***. All those objects that can be reached by following object references that start from a root object are called *live objects*. The live objects are the active objects currently being used by the running program; these objects should ***not*** be deallocated. For example, a running Java program may store in a variable a reference to a sequence S that is implemented using a doubly linked list. The reference variable to S is a root object, while the object for S is a live object, as are all the vertex objects that are referenced from this object and all the elements that are referenced from these vertex objects.

From time to time, a Java virtual machine (JVM) implementation may notice that available free space in the memory heap is becoming scarce. At such times, the JVM will probably elect to reclaim the space that is being used for objects that are no longer live. This reclamation process is known as *garbage collection*. There are several different algorithms for garbage collection, but one of the most-used is the *mark-sweep algorithm*. Therefore, let us consider the steps that we would need to implement to design a Java virtual machine that uses mark-sweep garbage collection.

In the mark-sweep garbage collection algorithm, we associate with each object a "mark" bit that identifies if that object is live or not. When we determine at some point that garbage collection is needed, we suspend all other running threads and clear all of the mark bits of objects currently allocated in the memory heap. We then trace through the Java stacks of the currently running threads and we mark as "live" all of the (root) objects in these stacks. We must then determine all of the other live objects—the ones that are reachable from the root objects. To do this efficiently, we should use the directed-graph version of the depth-first search traversal. In this case, each object in the memory heap is viewed as a vertex in a directed graph, and the reference from one object to another is viewed as an edge. By performing a directed DFS from each root object, we can correctly identify and mark each live object. This process is known as the "mark" phase. Once this process has completed, we then scan through the memory heap and reclaim any space that is being used for an object that has not been marked. This scanning process is known as the "sweep" phase, and when it completes, we resume running the suspended threads. Thus, this mark-sweep garbage collection algorithm will reclaim unused space in time proportional to the number of live objects and their references plus the size of the memory heap.

Performing DFS In-place

The mark-sweep algorithm is an effective way of reclaiming unused space in the memory heap, but there is an important issue we must face during the mark phase. Since we are probably reclaiming memory space at a time when free memory is scarce, we must take special care not to use much extra space during the garbage collection itself. The trouble is that the DFS algorithm, as we have described it, can use as much extra space as there are vertices in the graph. In the case of garbage collection, the vertices in our graph are the objects in the memory heap. We probably don't have this much memory to use, so our only alternative is to find a way to perform DFS in-place rather than recursively, that is, we must perform DFS using only a constant amount of additional storage. Fortunately, it is possible to perform DFS in-place.

The main idea for performing DFS in-place is to simulate the recursion stack using the edges of the graph (which in the case of garbage collection correspond to object references). Whenever we traverse an edge from a visited vertex v to a new vertex w, we change the edge (v, w) stored in v's adjacency list to point back to v's parent in the DFS tree. When we return back to v (simulating the return from the "recursive" call at w), we can now switch the edge we modified to point back to w as it did before. Of course, we need to have some way of identifying which edge we need to change back. One possibility is to number the references going out of v as 1, 2, and so on, and store, in addition to the mark bit (which we are using for the "visited" tag in our DFS), a count identifier that tells us which edges we have modified.

Using a count identifier of course requires an extra word of storage per object. This extra word can be avoided in some implementations, however. For example, many implementations of the Java Virtual Machine represent an object as a composition of a reference with a type identifier (which indicates if this object is an Integer or Vector or some other type) and as a reference to the other objects or data fields for this object. Since the type reference is always supposed to be the first element of the composition in such implementations, we can use this reference to "mark" the edge we changed when leaving an object v and going to some object w, in our DFS. We simply swap the reference at v that refers to the type of v with the reference at v that refers to w. When we return to v, we can quickly identify the edge (v, w) we changed, because it will be the first reference in the composition for v, and the position of the reference to v's type will tell us the place were this edge belongs in v's adjacency list. Thus, whether we use this edge-swapping trick or a count identifier, we can implement DFS in-place without affecting its asymptotic running time.

9.5   Exercises

Reinforcement

R-9.1   Draw an undirected graph G that has 12 vertices, 18 edges, and 3 connected components (with no two edges having the same end vertices and no edges that "loop" around to have both ends at the same vertex). Why would it be impossible draw G with 3 connected components if G had 66 edges?

R-9.2   Let G be a connected graph with n vertices and m edges such that no two edges have the same endpoints. Explain why $O(\log m)$ is $O(\log n)$.

R-9.3   Draw a directed graph with 8 vertices and 16 edges such that the in-degree and out-degree of each vertex is 2 (with no two edges having the same end vertices, and no edges that "loop" around to have both ends at the same vertex). Show that there is a single (nonsimple) cycle that includes all the edges of your graph, that is, you can trace all the edges in their respective directions without ever lifting your pencil. (Such a cycle is called an *Euler tour*.)

R-9.4   Repeat the previous problem and then remove one edge from the graph. Show that now there is a single (nonsimple) path that includes all the edges of your graph. (Such a path is called an *Euler path*.)

R-9.5   Bob loves foreign languages and wants to plan his course schedule for the following years. He is interested in the following nine language courses: LA15, LA16, LA22, LA31, LA32, LA126, LA127, LA141, and LA169. The course prerequisites are:

- LA15: (none)
- LA16: LA15
- LA22: (none)
- LA31: LA15
- LA32: LA16, LA31
- LA126: LA22, LA32
- LA127: LA16
- LA141: LA22, LA16
- LA169: LA32.

Find the sequence of courses that allows Bob to satisfy all the prerequisites.

R-9.6 Suppose we represent a graph G having n vertices and m edges with the edge list structure. Why, in this case, does the insertVertex method run in $O(1)$ time while the removeVertex method runs in $O(n)$ time?

R-9.7 Let G be a graph whose vertices are the integers 1 through 8, and let the adjacent vertices of each vertex be given by the table below:

vertex	adjacent vertices
1	(2, 3, 4)
2	(1, 3, 4)
3	(1, 2, 4)
4	(1, 2, 3, 6)
5	(6, 7, 8)
6	(4, 5, 7)
7	(5, 6, 8)
8	(5, 7)

Assume that, in a traversal of G, the adjacent vertices of a given vertex are returned in the same order as they are listed in the above table.

1. Draw G.
2. Give the sequence of vertices of G visited using a DFS traversal starting at vertex 1.
3. Give the sequence of vertices visited using a BFS traversal starting at vertex 1.

R-9.8 Would you use the adjacency structure or the adjacency matrix representation in each of the following cases? Justify your choice.

1. The graph has 10,000 vertices and 20,000 edges, and it is important to use as little space as possible.
2. The graph has 10,000 vertices and 20,000,000 edges, and it is important to use as little space as possible.
3. You need to answer as fast as possible query areAdjacent, no matter how much space you use.

R-9.9 Explain why the DFS method runs in $O(n^2)$ if the graph is represented with an adjacency matrix.

R-9.10 Draw the transitive closure of the directed graph shown in Figure 9.2.

R-9.11 Compute a topological ordering for the directed graph drawn with solid edges in Figure 9.8d.

Creativity

C-9.1 Describe the details of an $O(n+m)$ time algorithm for computing **all** the connected components of an undirected graph G with n vertices and m edges.

C-9.2 Let T be a spanning tree produced by the depth-first search of a connected undirected graph G. Argue why every edge of G, not in T, goes from a vertex v in T to one of its ancestors, that is, it is a **back edge**. (Hint: suppose that such a nontree edge is a cross edge, and argue based upon the order the DFS visits the end vertices of this edge.)

C-9.3 Suppose we wish to represent an n-vertex graph G using the edge list structure, assuming that we number the vertices with the integers in the set $\{0, 1, \ldots, n-1\}$. Describe how to implement the container E to support $O(\log n)$ time performance for the areAdjacent method. How are you implementing this method in this case?

C-9.4 Tamarindo University and many other schools worldwide are doing a joint project on multimedia. A computer network is built to connect these schools using communication links that form a tree. The schools decide to install a file server at one of the schools to share data among all the schools. Since the transmission time on a link is dominated by the link setup and synchronization, the cost of a data transfer is proportional to the number of links used. Hence, it is desirable to choose a "central" location for the file server.

Given a tree T and a node v of T, the *eccentricity* of v is the length of a longest path from v to any other node of T. A node of T with minimum eccentricity is called a *center* of T.

1. Design an efficient algorithm that, given an n-node tree T, computes a center of T.
2. Is the center unique? If not, how many distinct centers can a tree have?

C-9.5 Show that, if T is a BFS tree produced for a connected graph G, then, for each vertex v at level i, the path of T between s and v has i edges, and any other path of G between s and v has at least i edges. (Hint: justify this by induction on the length of a shortest path from the start vertex.)

C-9.6 The time delay of a long-distance call can be determined by multiplying a small fixed constant by the number of communication links on the telephone network between the caller and callee. Suppose the telephone network of a company named RT&T is a free tree. The engineers of RT&T want to compute the maximum possible time delay that may be experienced in a long-distance call. Given a tree T with N nodes, the *diameter* of T is the length of a longest path between two nodes of T. Give an efficient algorithm for computing the diameter of T.

C-9.7 A company named RT&T has a network of n switching stations connected by m high-speed communication links. Each customer's phone is directly connected to one station in his or her area. The engineers of RT&T have developed a prototype video-phone system that allows two customers to see each other during a phone call. In order to have acceptable image quality, however, the number of links used to transmit video signals between the two parties cannot exceed 4. Suppose that RT&T's network is represented by a graph. Design an efficient algorithm that computes, for each station, the set of stations it can reach using no more than 4 links.

C-9.8 An independent set of an undirected graph $G = (V, E)$ is a subset I of V such that no two vertices in I are adjacent. That is, if $u, v \in I$, then $(u, v) \notin E$. A *maximal independent set M* is an independent set such that, if we were to add any additional vertex to M, then it would not be independent any more. Every graph has a maximal independent set. (Can you see this? This question is not part of the exercise, but it is worth thinking about.) Give an efficient algorithm that computes a maximal independent set for a graph G.

C-9.9 Explain why there are no forward nontree edges with respect to a BFS tree constructed for a directed graph. (Hint: suppose there is such an edge and show why it would not be a nontree edge.)

C-9.10 An **Euler tour** of a directed graph G with n vertices and m edges is a cycle that traverses each edge of G exactly once according to its direction. Such a tour always exists if the in-degree equals the out-degree of each vertex in G. Describe an $O(n+m)$ time algorithm for finding a Euler tour of such a graph G.

C-9.11 Let G be an undirected graph G with n vertices and m edges. Describe an $O(n+m)$ time algorithm for traversing each edge of G exactly once in each direction.

C-9.12 Justify Proposition 9.14.

Projects

P-9.1 Write an implementation of an undirected graph ADT, not including the graph update methods, using an adjacency matrix representation. Your Graph class should include a constructor method that takes two containers (for example, sets or sequences)—a container V of vertex objects and a container E of pairs of vertex objects—and produces the graph G that these two containers represent. (Extra: design an applet that draws G by placing the vertices at points along a circle and draws the edges of G as straight lines joining pairs of such points.)

P-9.2 Implement an undirected graph ADT as described in the previous project, but use the adjacency list structure to represent the graph G.

P-9.3 Implement an undirected graph ADT using the adjacency list structure as described in the previous problem, but also include the graph update methods. (Extra: design an applet that draws the graph G being represented by placing the vertices of G along a circle and draws the edges of G as straight lines joining pairs of such points. Make our applet interactive, allowing a user to select graph update operations, and animate the insertion and removal of vertices and edges.)

P-9.4 Implement the mixed graph ADT using the adjacency list structure.

P-9.5 Implement the mixed graph ADT using the adjacency matrix structure.

P-9.6 Design an experimental comparison of repeated DFS versus the Floyd-Warshall algorithm for computing the transitive closure of a digraph.

Chapter Notes

The depth-first search method is a part of the "folklore" of computer science, but Hopcroft and Tarjan [73, 136] are the ones who showed how useful this algorithm is for solving several different graph problems. Knuth [89] discusses the topological sorting problem. The simple algorithm that we describe for determining if a directed graph is strongly connected in linear time is due to Kosaraju. The Floyd-Warshall algorithm appears in a paper by Floyd [50] and is based upon a theorem of Warshall [146]. The mark-sweep garbage collection we describe is one of many different algorithms for performing garbage collection. We encourage the reader interested in further study of garbage collection to examine the book by Jones [83]. The reader interested in further study of graph algorithms is referred to the books by Even [48], Gibbons [56], Mehlhorn [108], and Tarjan [138]. To learn about different algorithms for drawing graphs, please see the book chapter by Tamassia [135], the annotated bibliography of Di Battista *et al.* [40], or the book by Di Battista *et al.* [41].

Chapter

10

Weighted Graphs

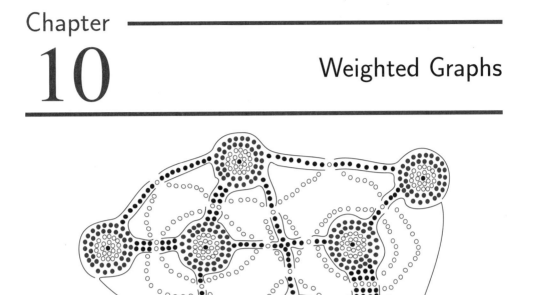

Contents

As we saw in the previous chapter, the breadth-first search strategy can be used to find the shortest path from some starting vertex to every other vertex in a connected graph. This approach makes sense in cases where each edge is as good as any other, but there are many situations where this approach is not appropriate. For example, we might be using a graph to represent the computers and connections in a computer network (such as the Internet), and we might then be interested in finding the fastest way to route a packet of information. In this case, it is probably not appropriate for all the edges to be equal to each other, for some connections in a computer network are typically much faster than others (for example, some edges might represent slow phone-line connections while others might represent high-speed, fiber-optic connections). Likewise, we might want to use a graph to represent the roads between cities, and we might be interested in finding the fastest way to travel cross-country. In this case, it is again probably not appropriate for all the edges to be equal to each other, for some inter-city distances will likely be much larger than others. Thus, it is natural to consider graphs whose edges are not weighted equally.

What is a Weighted Graph?

Let G be a graph, with a set V representing a collection of objects and a set E representing connections between these objects. Suppose further that there is a numeric (for example, integer) label $w(e)$ associated with each edge $e = (v,u)$. Then this graph is a ***weighted graph***. We illustrate an example undirected weighted graph in Figure 10.1.

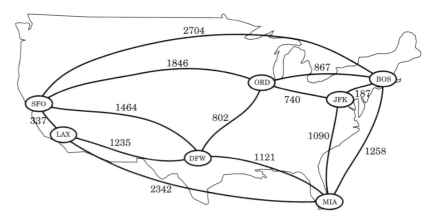

Figure 10.1: An example of a weighted graph. Vertices in this graph represent major U.S. airports and edge weights represent distances in miles. There is, for example, a path in this graph from JFK to LAX of 2,777 miles in length (and this is the shortest path from JFK to LAX in this graph).

In this chapter, we study weighted graphs. In the next section, we study the problem of finding a shortest path in a weighted graph, where weights correspond to distances between vertices. In Section 10.2, we study the classic problem of finding a minimum-weight spanning tree of a weighted graph, where the weights correspond to the costs of including edges in such a tree. Finally, in Section 10.3, we discuss maximum flows in a weighted graph, where weights correspond to the capacities of edges, which are viewed as "pipes" for shipping some commodity.

10.1 Shortest Paths

Let $G = (V, E)$ be a weighted graph. We define the *length* (or weight) of a path $P = ((v_1, v_2), (v_2, v_3), (v_3, v_4), \ldots, (v_{k-1}, v_k))$ in G as the sum of the weights of the edges on this path. That is,

$$w(P) = \sum_{i=1}^{k-1} w((v_i, v_{i+1})).$$

We define the *distance* from a vertex v to a vertex u in G, denoted $d(v, u)$, as the length of a shortest path from v to u, if such a path exists.

People often use the convention that $d(v, u) = +\infty$ if there is no path at all from v to u in G. Even if there is a path from v to u in G, the distance from v to u may not be defined, however, if there is a cycle in G whose total weight is negative. For example, suppose vertices in G represent cities, and the weights of edges in G represent how much money it costs to go from one city to another. If someone was willing to actually pay us to go from say JFK to ORD, then the "cost" of the edge (JFK,ORD) would be negative. If someone else was willing to pay us to go from ORD to JFK, then there would be a negative-weight cycle in G and distances would no longer be defined. That is, anyone can now build a path (with cycles) in G from any city A to another city B that first goes to JFK and then cycles as many times as he or she likes from JFK to ORD and back, before going on to B. The existence of such paths allows us to build arbitrarily low negative cost paths (and in this case make a fortune in the process). But distances cannot be arbitrarily low negative numbers. Thus, any time we use edge weights to represent distances, we must be careful not to introduce any negative-weight cycles.

Suppose we are given a weighted graph G, and we are asked to find a shortest path from some vertex v to each other vertex in G, viewing the weights on the edges as distances. In this section, we explore efficient ways of finding all such shortest paths, if they exist. The first algorithm we discuss is for the simple, yet common, case when all the edge weights in G are nonnegative (that is, $w(e) \geq 0$ for each edge $e \in G$); hence, we know in advance that there are no negative-weight cycles in G (the special case when all weights are 1 was considered in Section 9.3.2).

10.1.1   The Greedy Method

There is an interesting "greedy" approach for solving the ***single-source shortest-path*** problem, which consists of finding the shortest path in graph G from a vertex v, to every other vertex in G, for the case where the edges in G have nonnegative weights. The main idea in this approach is to perform what is essentially a "weighted" breadth-first search starting at v. In particular, we can use the greedy method to develop an algorithm that iteratively grows a "cloud" of vertices out of v, with the vertices of G entering the cloud in order of their distances from v. Thus, in each iteration, the next vertex chosen is the vertex outside the cloud that is closest to v. The algorithm is finished when there are no more vertices of G outside the cloud, at which point we will have found the shortest path from v to every vertex in G.

This approach might seem like a simple idea, but it is actually based on a powerful algorithmic paradigm—the ***greedy method***. Generically, this paradigm can be used in any situation where we are trying to optimize some function over a whole collection of objects (in this case, the function is the shortest path distance from the starting vertex v). The idea, as illustrated in the approach described above, is to add objects to a collection, one at a time, always picking the next object to be the one that optimizes the function from among those yet to be chosen.

In the case of the single-source, shortest-path problem, applying the greedy method results in a fully correct and complete algorithm, which is known as ***Dijkstra's algorithm***. When applied to other problems, however, the greedy method may not necessarily find the best solution (such as in the so-called ***traveling salesman problem***, in which we wish to find the shortest path that visits all the vertices in a graph exactly once). Nevertheless, there are a number of situations in which the greedy method allows one to come very close to the best solution. In this chapter, we discuss three such situations: computing shortest paths, constructing a minimum-spanning tree, and finding a maximum flow. We discuss other applications of the greedy method in Chapter 12, but here we concentrate on computing shortest paths.

10.1.2   Implementing Dijkstra's Algorithm

In Dijkstra's algorithm for finding shortest paths, the function we are trying to optimize in our application of the greedy method is also the function that we are trying to compute—shortest path distance. This may at first seem like circular reasoning until we realize that we can actually implement this approach by using a "bootstrapping" trick, consisting of using an approximation to the distance function we are trying to compute, which in the end will be equal to the true distance.

Specifically, let us define a label $D[u]$ for each vertex u in V, which we use to approximate the distance in G from v to u. The meaning of these labels is that $D[u]$ will always store the length of the best path we have found **so far** from v to u. Initially, $D[v] = 0$ and $D[u] = +\infty$ for each $u \neq v$, and we define the set C, which is our "**cloud**" of vertices, to initially be the empty set $\emptyset$. At each iteration in the algorithm, we select the vertex u not in C with smallest $D[u]$ label, and we pull u into C. In the very first iteration we will, of course, pull v into C. Once a new vertex u is pulled into C, we then update the label $D[z]$ of each vertex z that is adjacent to u and is outside of C, to reflect the fact that there may be a new and better way to get to z via u. This update operation is known as a **relaxation** procedure, for it takes an old estimate and checks if it can be improved to get closer to its true value. (A metaphor for why we call this a relaxation comes from a spring that is stretched out and then "relaxed" back to its true resting shape.) In the case of Dijkstra's algorithm, the relaxation is performed for an edge (u, z) such that we have computed a new value of $D[u]$ and wish to see if there is a better value for $D[z]$ using the edge (u, z). The specific edge relaxation operation is as follows:

Edge Relaxation: **if** $D[u] + w((u, z)) < D[z]$ **then**
$$D[z] \leftarrow D[u] + w((u, z))$$

We give the pseudo-code for Dijkstra's algorithm in Code Fragment 10.1, and we illustrate several iterations of Dijkstra's algorithm in Figures 10.2 and 10.3.

Algorithm ShortestPath(G, v):

    Input: A weighted graph G and a distinguished vertex v of G
    Output: A label $D[u]$, for each vertex u of G, such that $D[u]$ is the length of a
        shortest path from v to u in G

    initialize $D[v] \leftarrow 0$ and $D[u] \leftarrow +\infty$ for each vertex $u \neq v$
    let a priority queue Q contain all the vertices of G using the D labels as keys
    while $Q \neq \emptyset$ **do**
        {pull u into the cloud C}
        $u \leftarrow Q$.removeMinElement()
        for each vertex z adjacent to u such that z is in Q **do**
            {perform the **relaxation** operation on edge (u, z)}
            if $D[u] + w((u, z)) < D[z]$ **then**
                $D[z] \leftarrow D[u] + w((u, z))$
                change to $D[z]$ the key value of z in Q
    return the label $D[u]$ of each vertex u

Code Fragment 10.1: Pseudo-code for Dijkstra's algorithm. The priority queue Q stores the vertices of the graph that are not in the cloud C.

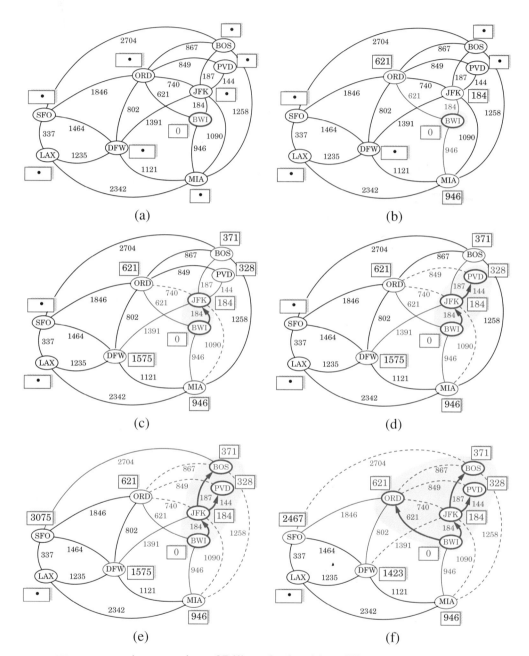

Figure 10.2: An execution of Dijkstra's algorithm. We use a box next to each vertex *v* to represent *D*[*v*]. The edges of the shortest-path tree are drawn with thick blue lines, and for each vertex *u* outside the "cloud" we show with a solid blue line the current best edge for pulling *u* in.

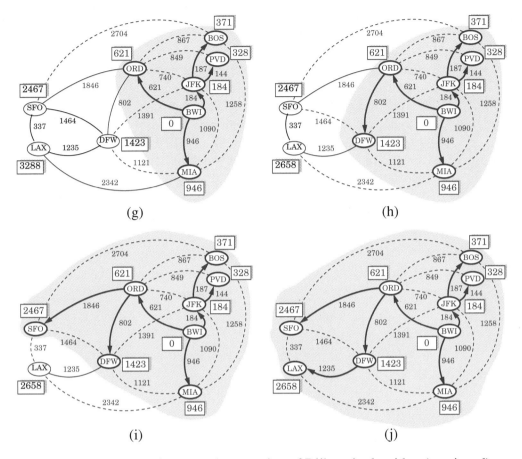

Figure 10.3: An example execution of Dijkstra's algorithm (continued).

The interesting, and possibly even a little surprising, aspect of the Dijkstra algorithm is that, at the moment a vertex u is pulled into C, its label $D[u]$ stores the correct length of a shortest path from v to u. Thus, when the algorithm terminates, it will have computed the shortest-path distance from v to every vertex of G. That is, it will have solved the single-source shortest path problem.

Why it Works

It is probably not immediately clear why Dijkstra's algorithm works. The key to its correctness is based upon an important fact about the value of label $D[u]$ at the time vertex u is pulled into the cloud C, that is, at the time u is removed from the priority queue Q.

Proposition 10.1: *For each vertex u of G, at the moment u is pulled into the cloud C, the label $D[u]$ is equal to $d(v,u)$, the length of a shortest path from v to u.*

Justification: Suppose, for the sake of a contradiction, that $D[u] > d(u,v)$ for some u in V. Indeed, let u be the **first** vertex pulled into the cloud C (that is, removed from the priority queue Q) by the algorithm such that $D[u] > d(v,u)$. There is a shortest path P from v to u (for otherwise $d(v,u) = +\infty = D[u]$). Let us therefore consider the specific moment when u is pulled into C, and let z be the first vertex of P (when going from v to u) that is not in C at this moment in time. Let y be the predecessor of z (note that we could have $y = v$). (See Figure 10.4.) We know, by our choice of z, that y is already in C at this point. Moreover, $D[y] = d(v,y)$, since u is the **first** incorrect vertex. When y was pulled into C, we tested (and possibly updated) $D[z]$ so that we had at that point:

$$D[z] = D[y] + w((y,z)) = d(v,y) + w((y,z)).$$

But since z is the next vertex on the shortest path from v to u, this implies that

$$D[z] = d(v,z).$$

But we are now at the moment when we are picking u, not z, to join C; hence,

$$D[u] \leq D[z].$$

It should be clear that a subpath of a shortest path is itself a shortest path. Hence, since z is on the shortest path from v to u,

$$d(v,z) + d(z,u) = d(v,u).$$

Moreover, $d(z,u) \geq 0$ because there are no negative-weight edges. Putting this all together,

$$D[u] \leq D[z] = d(v,z) \leq d(v,z) + d(z,u) = d(v,u).$$

But this contradicts the definition of u; hence, there can be no such vertex u.   ∎

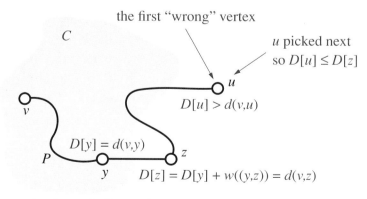

Figure 10.4: A schematic illustration for the justification of Proposition 10.1.

10.1.3   The Running Time of Dijkstra's Algorithm

Because of the high level of the description we gave for Dijkstra's algorithm, analyzing its running time requires that we give some more details about how some of the steps are implemented. Specifically, it requires that we think more about the data structures that are used and how they are implemented.

Let us first assume that we are representing the graph G using an adjacency list structure. This data structure allows us to step through the vertices adjacent to u during the relaxation step in time proportional to their number. It still does not settle all the details for the algorithm, however, for we must say more about how to implement the other principle data structure in the algorithm—the priority queue Q.

As we have observed in the chapter on priority queues, one possible implementation for the priority queue Q is a heap. This would allow us to extract the vertex u with smallest D label (call to the removeMinElement method) in $O(\log n)$ time. As noted in the pseudo-code, each time we update a $D[z]$ label we, of course, need to update the key of z in the priority queue. If Q is implemented as a heap, then this key update can, for example, be done by first removing and then inserting z with its new key. If our priority queue Q supports the locator pattern, then we can easily implement such key updates in $O(\log n)$ time, since a locator for z would allow Q to have immediate access to the item storing z in the heap (see Section 6.4). Thus, assuming this implementation of Q, we can implement Dijkstra's algorithm in $O((n+m)\log n)$ time, where n is the number of vertices in the graph G and m is the number of edges. If we express this running time as a function of only n, then it is $O(n^2 \log n)$ in the worst case.

There is nevertheless another efficient implementation for Q. We can implement Q using an unsorted sequence. This, of course, requires that we spend $\Theta(n)$ time when we wish to extract the minimum element, but it allows for very fast key updates, provided Q supports the locator pattern. Specifically, we can implement each key update done in a relaxation step in $O(1)$ time. This speed is due to the fact that key updates in a priority queue, such as Q, when realized with an unsorted sequence, can be performed by simply updating the key value once we locate the item in Q whose key must change. Since there are $n-1$ extractions of the minimum element and at most m relaxations done in Dijkstra's algorithm, this implementation results in a running time that is $O(n^2 + m)$, which can be simplified to $O(n^2)$.

Thus, we have two reasonable choices for implementing the priority queue in Dijkstra's algorithm: a locator-based heap implementation, which results in an $O((n+m)\log n)$ time algorithm, and a locator-based unsorted sequence implementation, which results in an $O(n^2)$ time algorithm. Since both of these implementations would be fairly simple to code up, they are about equal in terms of the programming sophistication needed. These two implementations are also about equal in terms of the constant factors in their worst-case running times. Looking only at these worst-case times, we prefer the heap implementation when the number of edges in the graph is small (that is, when $m < n^2/\log n$) and we prefer the sequence implementation when the number of edges is large (that is, when $m > n^2/\log n$).

In terms of average-case running time, the choice is not as clear. Even in the best case, the unsorted sequence implementation runs in $\Theta(n^2)$ time, for the bottleneck step with this implementation is extracting the minimum element, which must be performed $n-1$ times (but we leave the exact analysis of this as an exercise). For the heap implementation, however, the bottleneck step is updating the key of a vertex in Q after a successful relaxation step. From a worst-case point of view, we may need to perform as many updates as there are edges in the graph. This is a slight over-estimate, however, if, for each vertex in v, the neighbors of v are pulled into the cloud in what can be viewed as a random order.[1] In this case, we would expect only $O(\log n)$ updates to the key of a vertex (we leave the justification of this as an exercise for the more mathematically inclined). Thus, under this assumption, which we call the ***random neighbor-order*** assumption, the expected running time of the standard heap implementation of Dijkstra's algorithm is $O(n\log n + m)$, which is always $O(n^2)$. This would suggest, then, that the heap implementation should be preferred for all but the most degenerate graphs (which give rise to the higher worst-case running time). We summarize in Table 10.1 and Proposition 10.2.

Assumptions	Running Time
Q is a sequence	$O(n^2)$
Q is a heap	$O((n+m)\log n)$
Q is a heap and G satisfies the random neighbor-order property	expected $O(n\log n + m)$

Table 10.1: Time complexity of Dijkstra's algorithm under various implementation and distribution assumptions. We denote with n and m the number of vertices and edges of the graph G, respectively, and with Q the priority queue used.

Proposition 10.2: *Given a weighted graph G with n vertices and m edges, and such that that the weight of each edge is nonnegative, Dijkstra's algorithm computes the shortest path distance from any fixed vertex v in G to all other vertices in G in $O((n+m)\log n)$ worst-case time, or, alternately, in $O(n^2)$ worst-case time. Also, if the priority queue used by the algorithm is implemented with a heap, the running time is $O(n\log n + m)$ on average under the random neighbor-order assumption.*

---

[1]That is, G comes from a collection of graphs such that, for each vertex in G, the ordering of the neighbors pulled into the cloud before v is uniformly distributed.

We can easily modify Dijkstra's algorithm not only to output the distance from v to each vertex in G, but to also output a tree T rooted at v such that the path in T from v to a vertex u is actually a shortest path in G from v to u.

10.1.4 A Java Implementation of Dijkstra's Algorithm

In this section, we present in Code Fragments 10.2–10.4 a Java implementation of Dijkstra's algorithm that works for a generic undirected graph with positive integer weights. This implementation of Dijkstra's algorithm is generic in the sense that it does not make any explicit assumptions about the way the priority queue is implemented. Moreover, it is reusable in that it can be applied to any weighted graph G that is given together with a distinguished vertex and a priority queue object.

```java
public abstract class Dijkstra {
    private static final int INFINITE = Integer.MAX_VALUE;
    protected InspectableGraph graph;
    protected PriorityQueue Q; // priority queue used by the algorithm
    public Object execute(InspectableGraph g, Vertex start) {
        graph = g;
        dijkstraVisit(start);
        return distances();
    }
    // initialization
    abstract void init();
    // create an empty priority queue
    abstract PriorityQueue initPQ(Comparator comp);
    // return the weight of edge e
    abstract int weight(Edge e);
    // attach to u its locator loc in Q
    abstract void setLocator(Vertex u, Locator loc);
    // return the locator attached to u
    abstract Locator getLocator(Vertex u);
    // attach to u its distance dist
    abstract void setDistance(Vertex u, int dist);
    // return the vertex distances in a data structure
    abstract Object distances();
    // return as an int the key of a vertex in Q
    private int value(Locator u_loc) {
        return ((Integer) u_loc.key()).intValue();
    }
}
```

Code Fragment 10.2: A Java implementation of Dijkstra's algorithm: instance variables and auxiliary methods of class Dijkstra.

```
protected void dijkstraVisit (Vertex v) {
  // initialize the priority queue Q and store all the vertices in it
  init();
  Q = initPQ(new IntegerComparator());
  for (Enumeration vertices = graph.vertices();
       vertices.hasMoreElements(); ) {
    Vertex u = (Vertex) vertices.nextElement();
    int u_dist;
    if (u==v)
      u_dist = 0;
    else
      u_dist = INFINITE;
    Locator u_loc = Q.insert(new Integer(u_dist), u);
    setLocator(u, u_loc);
  }
  // grow the cloud, one vertex at a time
  while (! Q.isEmpty()) {
    // remove from Q and insert into cloud a vertex with minimum distance
    Locator u_loc = Q.min();
    Vertex u = (Vertex) u_loc.element();
    int u_dist = value(u_loc);
    Q.remove(u_loc);
    setDistance(u, u_dist); // the distance of u is final
    // examine all the neighbors of u and update their distances
    for (Enumeration u_edges = graph.incidentEdges(u);
         u_edges.hasMoreElements(); ) {
      Edge e = (Edge) u_edges.nextElement();
      Vertex z = graph.opposite(u,e);
      Locator z_loc = getLocator(z);
      // check if z is not in the cloud, i.e., z is in Q
      if (z_loc.isContained()) {
        // relaxation of edge e = (u,z)
        int e_weight = weight(e);
        int z_dist = value(z_loc);
        if ( u_dist + e_weight < z_dist )
          Q.replaceKey(z_loc, new Integer(u_dist + e_weight));
      }
    }
  }
}
```

Code Fragment 10.3: Method dijkstraVisit of class Dijkstra.

```
public class MyDijkstra extends Dijkstra {
  protected Hashtable locators = new Hashtable();
  protected Hashtable distances = new Hashtable();
  protected Hashtable weights = new Hashtable();
  public void init() { }
  public PriorityQueue initPQ(Comparator comp) {
    return (PriorityQueue) new SequenceLocPriorityQueue(comp);
  }
  public int weight(Edge e) {
    return ((Integer) weights.get(e)).intValue();
  }
  public void setWeight(Edge e, int w) {
    weights.put(e, new Integer(w));
  }
  public void setLocator(Vertex u, Locator loc) {
    locators.put(u, loc);
  }
  public Locator getLocator(Vertex u) {
    return (Locator) locators.get(u);
  }
  public void setDistance(Vertex u, int dist) {
    distances.put(u, new Integer(dist));
  }
  public int distance(Vertex u) {
    return ((Integer) distances.get(u)).intValue();
  }
  public  Object distances() {
    return distances;
  }
}
```

Code Fragment 10.4: Class MyDijkstra, extending Dijkstra, that provides concrete implementations of the auxiliary methods.

Following the template method pattern (Section 5.3.4), our implementation consists of a Java class Dijkstra that can be specialized with respect to the mechanisms used for:

- Storing and retrieving the edge weights
- Associating priority queue locators with the vertices
- Returning the vertex distances.

Indeed, these mechanisms are encapsulated in calls to several auxiliary methods that are declared abstract (see Code Fragment 10.2). An example of a concrete implementation of the auxiliary methods is shown in Code Fragment 10.4.

The main computation of Dijkstra's algorithm is performed by method dijkstraVisit (Code Fragment 10.3). Instead of using an explicit data structure for the labels $D(u)$, we exploit the fact that $D(u)$ is the key of vertex u in the priority queue Q, and thus $D(u)$ can be retrieved given the locator of u in Q. Thus, the algorithm "attaches" to each vertex its locator in Q by means of method setLocator, and retrieves the locator given the vertex by means of method getLocator.

10.1.5   The Bellman-Ford Algorithm ⋆

There is another algorithm, which is due to Bellman and Ford, that can find shortest paths in graphs that have negative-weight edges. We must, in this case, insist that the graph be directed, for otherwise any negative-weight undirected edge would immediately imply a negative-weight cycle, where we traverse this edge back and forth in each direction. We cannot allow such edges, since a negative cycle invalidates the notion of distance based on edge weights.

Let G be a weighted directed graph, possibly with some negative-weight edges. The Bellman-Ford algorithm for computing the shortest-path distance from some vertex v in G to every other vertex in G is very simple. It shares the notion of edge relaxation from Dijkstra's algorithm, but does not use it in conjunction with the greedy method (which would not work in this context; see Exercise C-10.3). That is, as in Dijkstra's algorithm, the Bellman-Ford algorithm uses a label $D[u]$ that is always an upper bound on the distance $d(v, u)$ from v to u, and which is iteratively "relaxed" until it exactly equals this distance.

The Bellman-Ford algorithm starts out the same way as Dijkstra's algorithm, with the label $D[v] = 0$ and the label $D[u] = +\infty$ for each other vertex u in the graph G. It then performs the computation shown in Code Fragment 10.5 on G. We illustrate an execution of the Bellman-Ford algorithm in Figure 10.5.

The following proposition shows that this algorithm is correct and even gives us a way of telling if G contains a negative-weight cycle.

```
for i ← 1 to n − 1 do
    for each (directed) edge (u, z) of G do
        {Perform the relaxation operation on (u, z)}
        if D[u] + w((u, z)) < D[z] then
            D[z] ← D[u] + w((u, z))
```

Code Fragment 10.5: The Bellman-Ford shortest-path algorithm.

Proposition 10.3: *If after performing the above computation there is an edge (u, z) that can be relaxed (that is, $D[u] + w((u, z)) < D[z]$), then the graph G contains a negative-weight cycle. Otherwise, $D[u] = d(v, u)$ for each vertex u in G.*

Justification: For the sake of this justification, let us introduce a new notion of distance in a graph. Specifically, let $d_i(v, u)$ denote the length of a path from v to u that is shortest among all paths from v to u that contain at most i edges. We call $d_i(v, u)$ the *i-edge distance* from v to u. We claim that after iteration i of the main for-loop in the Bellman-Ford algorithm $D[u] = d_i(v, u)$ for each vertex in G. This is certainly true before we even begin the first iteration, for $D[v] = 0 = d_0(v, v)$ and, for $u \neq v$, $D[u] = +\infty = d_0(v, u)$. Suppose this claim is true before iteration i (we will now show that if this is the case, then this claim will be true after iteration i as well). In iteration i, we perform a relaxation step for every edge in the graph. The i-edge distance $d_i(v, u)$, from v to a vertex u, is determined in one of two ways. Either $d_i(v, u) = d_{i-1}(v, u)$ or $d_i(v, u) = d_{i-1}(v, z) + w((z, u))$ for some vertex z in G. Because we do a relaxation for *every* edge of G in iteration i, if it is the former case, then after iteration i we have $D[u] = d_{i-1}(v, u) = d_i(v, u)$, and if it is the latter case, then after iteration i we have $D[u] = D[z] + w((z, u)) = d_{i-1}(v, z) + w((z, u)) = d_i(v, u)$. Thus, if $D[u] = d_{i-1}(v, u)$ for each vertex u before iteration i, then $D[u] = d_i(v, u)$ for each vertex u after iteration i.

Therefore, after $n - 1$ iterations, $D[u] = d_{n-1}(v, u)$ for each vertex u in G. Now observe that if there is still an edge in G that can be relaxed, then there is some vertex u in G such that the n-edge distance from v to u is less than the $(n - 1)$-edge distance from v to u, that is, $d_n(v, u) < d_{n-1}(v, u)$. But there are only n vertices in G; hence, if there is a shortest n-edge path from v to u, it must repeat some vertex z in G twice. That is, it must contain a cycle. Moreover, since the distance from a vertex to itself using zero edges is 0 (that is, $d_0(z, z) = 0$), this cycle must be a negative-weight cycle. Thus, if there is an edge in G that can still be relaxed after running the Bellman-Ford algorithm, then G contains a negative-weight cycle. If, on the other hand, there is no edge in G that can still be relaxed after running the Bellman-Ford algorithm, then G does not contain a negative-weight cycle. Moreover, in this case, every shortest path between two vertices will have at most $n - 1$ edges; hence, for each vertex u in G, $D[u] = d_{n-1}(v, u) = d(v, u)$. ∎

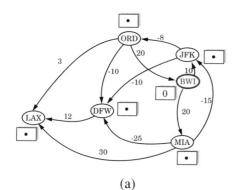

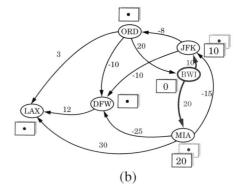

(a)

(b)

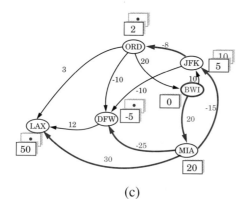

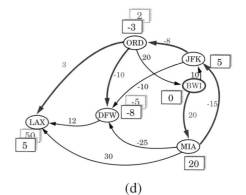

(c)

(d)

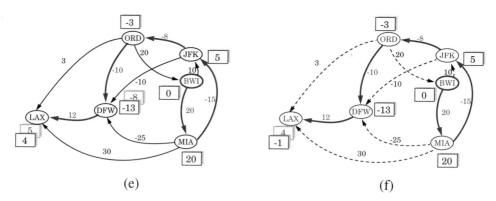

(e)

(f)

Figure 10.5: An illustration of an application of the Bellman-Ford algorithm. We show $D[u]$ values in boxes, with "shadows" showing values revised during relations; the thick edges are causing such relaxations. Blue edges are on true shortest paths.

Thus, the Bellman-Ford algorithm is correct and even gives us a way of telling when a graph contains a negative-weight cycle. The running time of the Bellman-Ford algorithm is easy to analyze. We perform the main for-loop $n-1$ times, and each such loop involves spending $O(1)$ time for each edge in G. Therefore, the running time for this algorithm is $O(nm)$. We summarize as follows:

Proposition 10.4: *Suppose we are given a weighted directed graph G. We can determine in $O(nm)$ time whether G contains a negative-weight cycle, and if G does not contain a negative-weight cycle, then we can determine the shortest-path distance from some distinguished vertex v to every other vertex in G.*

10.2 Minimum-Spanning Trees

Suppose we wish to connect all the computers in a new office building using the least amount of cable. We can model this as a weighted graph problem by creating a graph G such that each vertex in G is associated with a computer in the building, and we can assign a weight $w((v,u))$ for each edge (v,u) that is equal to the amount of cable needed to connect the computer for vertex v to the computer for vertex u. Rather than computing a shortest path tree from some particular vertex v, we are interested instead in finding a (free) tree T that contains all the vertices of G and has the least total weight over all such trees. That is, we want to find a tree T that contains all the vertices in G and minimizes the sum

$$w(T) = \sum_{(v,u) \in T} w((v,u)).$$

A tree, such as this, that contains every vertex of a connected graph G is said to be a *spanning tree*, and the problem of computing a spanning tree T with smallest total weight is known as the *minimum-spanning tree* (or *MST*) problem.

The development of efficient algorithms for the minimum-spanning tree problem is classic, predating the modern notion of computer science itself. In this section, we discuss three methods for solving the MST problem. These methods are all classic applications of the greedy method, which, as was discussed briefly in the previous section, is based on choosing objects to join a growing collection by iteratively picking an object that minimizes some function. The first method we discuss is Kruskal's algorithm, which "grows" the MST in clusters by considering edges in order of their weights. The second method we discuss is the Prim-Jarník algorithm, which grows the MST from a single root vertex, much in the same way as Dijkstra's shortest-path algorithm. Finally, we discuss Barůvka's algorithm, which grows the MST in clusters, by joining connected components that eventually merge to form the minimum-spanning tree.

The Crucial Fact about Minimum-Spanning Trees

Before we discuss the details of these methods, however, let us give the crucial fact about minimum-spanning trees that forms the basis for all three of these algorithms. (See Figure 10.6.)

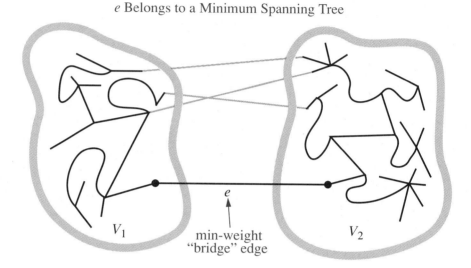

Figure 10.6: An illustration of the crucial fact about minimum-spanning trees.

Proposition 10.5: *Let $G = (V,E)$ be a weighted connected graph, and let V_1 and V_2 be two disjoint nonempty sets such that $V = V_1 \cup V_2$. Furthermore, let e be an edge in G with minimum weight from among those with one vertex in V_1 and the other in V_2. There is a minimum-spanning tree T that has e as one of its edges.*

Justification: Suppose, for the sake of a contradiction, that the proposition is false. That is, let us assume there is no minimum-spanning tree that has e as one of its edges. Let T be a minimum-spanning tree, and consider the addition of e to the edges of T. Since T is a spanning tree of G not containing e, the addition of e must create a cycle (that is, a path that starts and ends at the same vertex). Therefore, there is some edge f that is on this cycle and has one endpoint in V_1 and the other in V_2. Moreover, by the choice of e, $w(e) \le w(f)$. If we remove f from $T \cup \{e\}$, we will define a spanning tree whose total weight is no more than before. Since T was a minimum-spanning tree, this new tree must also be a minimum-spanning tree. But this contradicts our assumption that no minimum-spanning tree contains e. Thus, our assumption is false—there is an MST containing e after all. ■

In fact, if the weights in G are distinct, then the minimum-spanning tree is unique (we leave the justification of this less-crucial fact as an exercise). In addition, note that Proposition 10.5 remains valid even if the graph G contains negative-weight edges or negative-weight cycles, unlike the algorithms we presented for shortest paths.

10.2.1 Kruskal's Algorithm

The reason Proposition 10.5 is so important is that it can be used as the basis for building a minimum-spanning tree. In Kruskal's algorithm, it is used to build the minimum-spanning tree in clusters. Initially, each vertex is in its own cluster all by itself. The algorithm then considers each edge in turn, ordered by increasing weights. If an edge e connects two different clusters, then e is added to the set of edges identified as being in the minimum-spanning tree and the two clusters connected by e are merged into a single cluster. If, on the other hand, e connects two vertices that are already in the same cluster, then e is discarded. Once the algorithm has added enough edges to form a spanning tree, it terminates and outputs this tree as the minimum-spanning tree.

We give the pseudo-code for Kruskal's minimum-spanning tree algorithm in Code Fragment 10.6 and we illustrate the working of this algorithm in Figures 10.7, 10.8, and 10.9.

Algorithm Kruskal(G):

    Input: A connected weighted graph G with n vertices and m edges
    Output: A minimum-spanning tree T for G

  for each vertex v in G **do**
    Define a cluster $C(v) \leftarrow \{v\}$.
  Initialize a priority queue Q to contain all edges in G, using weights as keys.
  $T \leftarrow \emptyset$ $\{T$ will ultimately contain the edges of the MST$\}$
  while $Q \neq \emptyset$ **do**
    Extract (and remove) from Q an edge (v, u) with smallest weight.
    Let $C(v)$ be the cluster containing v, and let $C(u)$ be the cluster containing u.
    if $C(v) \neq C(u)$ **then**
      Add edge (v, u) to T.
      Merge $C(v)$ and $C(u)$ into one cluster, that is, union $C(v)$ and $C(u)$.
  return tree T

Code Fragment 10.6: Pseudo-code for Kruskal's algorithm.

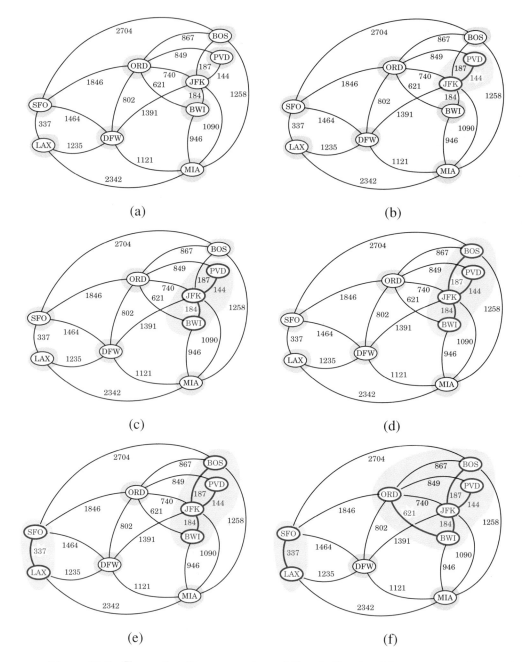

(a) (b)

(c) (d)

(e) (f)

Figure 10.7: Example of an execution of Kruskal's algorithm on a graph with integer weights. We show the clusters as shaded regions and we highlight the edge being considered in each iterstion. (Continued in Figure 10.8.)

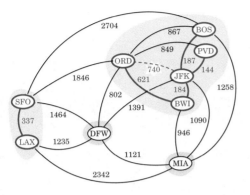

(g)

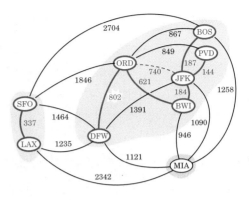

(h)

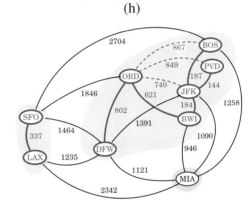

(i)

(j)

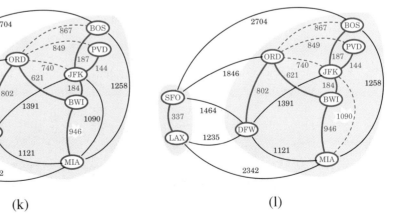

(k)

(l)

Figure 10.8: A continued example of an execution of Kruskal's algorithm. Rejected edges are shown dashed. (Continued in Figure 10.9.)

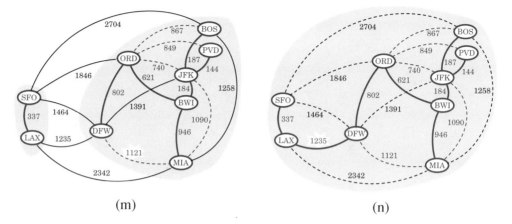

(m)   (n)

Figure 10.9: Example of an execution of Kruskal's algorithm (conclusion).

As mentioned before, the correctness of Kruskal's algorithm follows from the crucial fact about minimum-spanning trees, Proposition 10.5. Each time Kruskal's algorithm adds an edge (v, u) to the minimum spanning tree T, we can define a partitioning of the set of vertices V (as in the proposition) by letting V_1 be the cluster containing v and letting V_2 contain the rest of the vertices in V. This clearly defines a disjoint partitioning of the vertices of V and, more importantly, since we are extracting edges from Q in order by their weights, e must be a minimum-weight edge with one vertex in V_1 and the other in V_2. Thus, Kruskal's algorithm always adds a valid minimum-spanning tree edge.

Let us analyze the running time of Kruskal's algorithm. If we implement the priority queue Q using a heap, we can initialize Q in $O(m)$ time, as described in Section 6.3. In addition, this implies that we can perform the edge extract operation in each iteration of Kruskal's algorithm in $O(\log m)$ time, which actually is $O(\log n)$. We can think of each cluster $C(v)$ as a set, and the request for testing whether a cluster $C(v)$ is different than a cluster $C(u)$ as asking that we find the sets containing v and u, respectively, and test them for equality. In Section 12.1.4, we describe a simple scheme for supporting such a collection of sets, subject to union and find operations as found in Kruskal's algorithm, so that all the $O(n)$ unions and finds performed in Kruskal's algorithm would run in $O(n \log n)$ time. There are at most m iterations in the algorithm, since G is connected. Therefore, the total running time of Kruskal's algorithm is $O(n \log n + m \log n)$, which can be simplified as $O(m \log n)$. We summarize as follows:

Proposition 10.6: *Given a connected weighted graph G with n vertices and m edges, Kruskal's algorithm finds a minimum-spanning tree for G in $O(m \log n)$ time.*

10.2.2 The Prim-Jarník Algorithm

In the Prim-Jarník algorithm, we grow a minimum-spanning tree from a single cluster starting from some "root" vertex v. The main idea is similar to that of Dijkstra's algorithm. We begin with some vertex v, defining the initial "cloud" of vertices C. Then, in each iteration, we choose the smallest-weight edge $e = (v, u)$, connecting a vertex v in the cloud C to a vertex u outside of C. The vertex u is then brought into the cloud C and the process is repeated until a spanning tree is formed. Again, the crucial fact about minimum-spanning trees comes to play, for by always choosing the smallest-weight edge joining a vertex inside C to one outside C, we are assured of always adding a valid edge to the MST.

To efficiently implement this approach, we can take another cue from Dijkstra's algorithm. We can maintain a label $D[u]$ for each vertex u outside the cloud C, so that $D[u]$ stores the weight of the best current edge for joining u to the cloud C. This allows us to reduce the number of edges that we must consider in deciding which vertex is next to join the cloud. We give the pseudo-code in Code Fragment 10.7.

Algorithm PrimJarnik(G):

    Input: A weighted connected graph G with n vertices and m edges

    Output: A minimum-spanning tree T for G

  Pick any vertex v of G

  $D[v] \leftarrow 0$

  for each vertex $u \neq v$ **do**

    $D[u] \leftarrow +\infty$

  Initialize $T \leftarrow \emptyset$

  Initialize a priority queue Q whose keys are D labels and whose elements are vertex-edge pairs

  Insert the pair $(v, \cdot)$ into Q with priority $D(v)$

  while $Q \neq \emptyset$ **do**

    $(u, e) \leftarrow Q.\text{removeMinElement}()$

    add vertex u and edge e to T

    for each vertex z adjacent to u such that z is in Q **do**

      {Perform the relaxation operation on (u, z)}

      if $w((u, z)) < D[z]$ **then**

        $D[z] \leftarrow w((u, z))$

        change to $D[z]$ the key value of z in Q

        change to (u, z) the edge stored with z in Q

  return the tree T

    Code Fragment 10.7: Pseudo code for the Prim-Jarník algorithm.

We illustrate the Prim-Jarník algorithm in Figures 10.10 and 10.11.

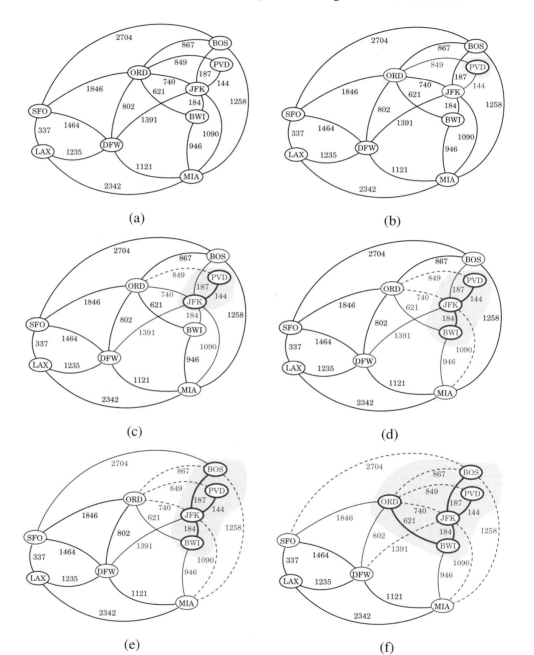

Figure 10.10: An illustration of the Prim-Jarník algorithm. (Continued in Figure 10.11.)

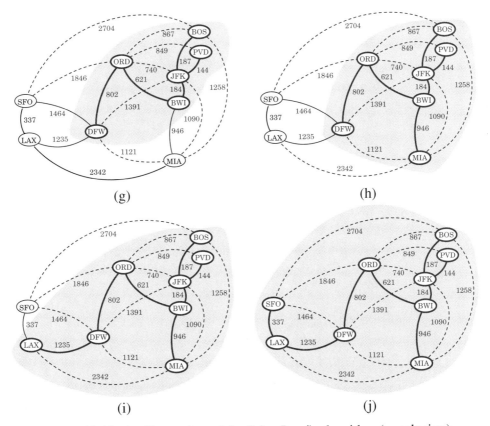

Figure 10.11: An illustration of the Prim-Jarník algorithm (conclusion).

The implementation issues for the Prim-Jarník algorithm are similar to those for Dijkstra's algorithm. If we implement the queue Q as a heap, we can extract the vertex u in each iteration in $O(\log n)$ time. In addition, we can update each $D[z]$ value in $O(\log n)$ time, as well, which is a computation considered at most twice for each edge (u,z): once for u and once for z. The other steps in each iteration can be implemented in constant time. Thus, the total running time is $O(n\log n + m\log n)$, which is $O(m\log n)$; hence, we can summarize as follows:

Proposition 10.7: *Suppose we are given a connected weighted graph G with n vertices and m edges. The Prim-Jarník algorithm finds a minimum-spanning tree for G in $O(m\log n)$ time.*

Incidentally, the running time for the Prim-Jarník algorithm, and also that of Dijkstra's algorithm, can actually be improved to be $O(n\log n + m)$ by implementing the priority queue Q with either of two more sophisticated data structures that we discuss in the chapter notes.

10.2.3   Barůvka's Algorithm

Each of the two minimum-spanning tree algorithms we have described previously has achieved its efficient running time by utilizing a priority queue Q, which could be implemented using a heap (or even a more-sophisticated data structure). This usage should seem natural, for minimum-spanning tree algorithms involve applications of the greedy method—and, in this case, the greedy method must explicitly be optimizing certain priorities among the vertices of the graph in question. It may be a bit surprising, but as we show in this section, we can actually design an efficient minimum-spanning tree algorithm without using a priority queue. Moreover, what may be even more surprising is that the insight behind this simplification comes from the oldest known minimum-spanning tree algorithm, the algorithm of Barůvka.

We present a pseudo-code description of Barůvka's minimum-spanning tree algorithm in Code Fragment 10.8, and we illustrate an execution of this algorithm in Figure 10.12.

Algorithm Barůvka(G):

  Input: A weighted connected graph $G = (V,E)$ with n vertices and m edges
  Output: A minimum-spanning tree T for G.

  Let T be a subgraph of G initally containing just the vertices in V.
  while T has fewer than $n-1$ edges $\{T$ is not yet an MST$\}$ **do**
    for each connected component C_i of T **do**
      $\{$Perform the MST edge addition procedure for cluster $C_i\}$
      Find the smallest-weight edge $e = (v,u)$, in E with $v \in C_i$ and $u \notin C_i$.
      Add e to T (unless e is already in T).
  return T

Code Fragment 10.8: Pseudo-code for Barůvka's algorithm.

Implementing Barůvka's algorithm is quite simple, requiring only that we be able to do the following:

- Maintain the forest T subject to edge insertion, which we can easily support in $O(1)$ time each using an adjacency list for T
- Traverse the forest T to identify connected components (clusters), which we can easily do in $O(n)$ time using a depth-first search of T
- Mark vertices with the name of the cluster they belong to, which we can do with an extra instance variable for each vertex
- Identify a smallest-weight edge in E incident upon a cluster C_i, which we can do by scanning the adjacency lists in G for the vertices in C_i.

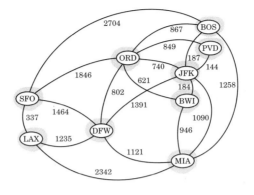

(a)

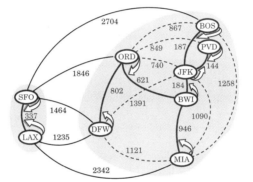

(b)

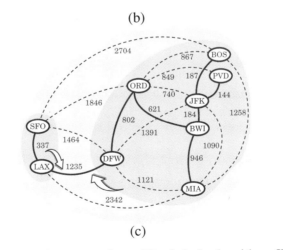

(c)

Figure 10.12: Example of an execution of Barůvka's algorithm. We show clusters as shaded regions. We highlight with an arrow the edge chosen by each cluster and we draw each such MST edge as a solid blue line. Edges determined not to be in the MST are shown dashed.

Like Kruskal's algorithm, Barůvka's algorithm builds the minimum-spanning tree by growing a number of clusters of vertices in a series of rounds, not just one cluster, as was done by the Prim-Jarník algorithm. But in Barůvka's algorithm, the clusters are grown by applying the crucial fact about minimum-spanning trees to each cluster simultaneously. This approach allows many more edges to be added in each round.

Why Is This Algorithm Correct?

In each iteration of Barůvka's algorithm, we choose the smallest-weight edge coming out of each connected component C_i of the current set T of minimum-spanning tree edges. In each case, this edge is a valid choice, for if we consider a partitioning of V into the vertices in C_i and those outside of C_i, then the chosen edge e for C_i satisfies the condition of the crucial fact about minimum-spanning trees (Proposition 10.5) for guaranteeing that e belongs to a minimum-spanning tree.

Let us analyze the running time of Barůvka's algorithm (Code Fragment 10.8). We can implement each round performing the searches to find the minimum-weight edge going out of each cluster by an exhaustive search through the adjacency lists of each vertex in each cluster. Thus, the total running time spent in searching for minimum-weight edges can be made to be $O(m)$, for it involves examining each edge (v, u) in G twice: once for v and once for u (since vertices are labeled with the number of the cluster they are in). The remaining computations in the main while-loop involve relabeling all the vertices, which takes $O(n)$ time, and traversing all the edges in T, which takes $O(n)$ time. Thus, each round in Barůvka's algorithm takes $O(m)$ time (since $n \leq m$). In each round of the algorithm, we choose one edge coming out of each cluster, and we then merge each new connected component of T into a new cluster. Thus, each old cluster of T must merge with at least one other old cluster of T. That is, in each round of Barůvka's algorithm, the total number of clusters is reduced by half. Therefore, the total number of rounds is $O(\log n)$; hence, the total running time of Barůvka's algorithm is $O(m \log n)$. We summarize:

Proposition 10.8: *Barůvka's algorithm computes a minimum-spanning tree for a connected weighted graph G with n vertices and m edges in $O(m \log n)$ time.*

10.2.4 Comparisons

Although each of the above algorithms for computing minimum-spanning trees has the same worst-case running time, each one achieves this running time using different data structures and different approaches to building the minimum-spanning tree.

Kruskal's algorithm uses both a priority queue Q (to store edges) and data structures to support disjoint sets under union and find operations. The Prim-Jarník algorithm requires the same data structure as used in Dijkstra's algorithm—a priority queue to store the values of vertex labels. Barůvka's algorithm requires a way of representing connected components. Thus, from an ease of programming viewpoint, the Prim-Jarník and Barůvka algorithms seem to be the best. Indeed, the Prim-Jarník algorithm is so similar to Dijkstra's algorithm that an implementation of Dijkstra's algorithm could be converted into an implementation for the Prim-Jarník algorithm without much effort.

In terms of the constant factors, the three algorithms are fairly similar in that they all have relatively small constant factors in their asymptotic running times. The asymptotic running time for Kruskal's algorithm can be improved if the edges are given in sorted order by their weights (which is something we explore in Section 12.1.4). Also, the running time of Barůvka's algorithm can be changed to be $O(n^2)$ in the worst case with a slight modification to the algorithm (which we explore in Exercise C-10.12). Thus, there is no clear winner among these three algorithms, although Barůvka's algorithm is the easiest of the three to implement from "scratch."

10.3 Maximum Flow ⋆

Another important problem involving weighted graphs, and one that can also be solved using the greedy method, is the **maximum flow** problem. In this problem, we are given a weighted directed graph G, with each edge being viewed as a "pipe" that can push some commodity from one end to the other, and each edge weight representing the maximum amount of that commodity that an edge can push. The maximum-flow problem is to find a way of legally pushing the maximum amount of the given commodity from some vertex s, called the **source**, to some vertex t, called the **sink**.

Example 10.9: *Let G be a computer communication graph in which each vertex in G represents a computer in some local area network, each edge (u, v) in G represents a communication channel from computer u to computer v, and the weight of each edge (u, v) in G represents the the maximum number of information packets of a certain size that can be sent from u to v in one second. If we have a huge file that we have to send from some computer s in G to some computer t in G, the fastest way to send this file is to divide it into packets and route these packets through G in a way specified by a solution to the maximum flow problem. (See Figure 10.13.)*

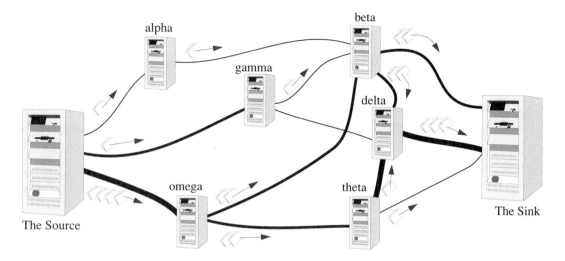

Figure 10.13: An example flow in a graph representing a computer network, with the capacity of thick edges being 4 packets/sec., the capacity of medium shaded edges being 2 packets/sec., and the capacity of thin solid edges being 1 packet/sec. The flow illustrated is not maximum, as there is one more packet-per-second that can be pushed from the source to gamma, from gamma to delta, and from delta to the sink. After this extra flow is added, the total flow will be maximum.

This example illustrates the rules that a legal flow must obey. In order to precisely say what these rules are, let us carefully define what we mean by a **flow**. So, let $G = (V, E)$ be a weighted directed graph where, for each edge e in E, there is a weight $c(e) \geq 0$ defined for e, which we call the **capacity** of e. We use the common convention of viewing the capacity of any edge not explicitly given in E as being 0. A flow for G is an assignment of a number $f(u, v)$ to each pair of vertices u and v in V. A flow is **valid** (or legal) if it satisfies the following intuitive rules:

1. **The Capacity Rule:**
$$f(u, v) \leq c((u, v)),$$
for each edge (u, v), where $c((u, v)) = 0$ if $(u, v) \notin E$.

2. **The Consistency Rule:**
$$f(u, v) = -f(v, u),$$
for each pair of vertices u and v in V. That is, the flow going from u to v is equal to the inverse of the amount going from v to u.

3. **The Conservation Rule.** For each vertex v in G, other than the source s and the sink t,
$$\sum_{u \in V} f(v, u) = 0.$$

In other words, a flow must satisfy the edge capacity constraints, must be consistent with itself, and must, for every vertex v other than s and t, have total amount of flow going out of v equal to the total amount of flow coming into v. Each of the above rules is satisfied, for example, by the flow illustrated in Figure 10.13. The value of a (valid) flow f, which we denote by $val(f)$, is equal to the total amount of flow coming out from the source s. That is,

$$val(f) = \sum_{u \in V} f(s,u).$$

The **maximum flow** problem is to find a valid flow, for a given weighted directed graph G, that has maximum value over all valid flows.

10.3.1 The Ford-Fulkerson Algorithm

Let $G = (V,E)$ be a weighted directed graph with positive edge weights that represent capacities. To make the algorithm description simple, let us assume that if (v,u) is an edge in E, then (u,v) is also an edge in E. This assumption is made without any loss of generality, for we can always add extra edges to E to make this so, giving each such added edge a capacity of 0. Ford and Fulkerson showed that the greedy method can be applied to solve the maximum flow problem for such a graph G. The main idea of their approach is to begin with the valid flow f for G with value $val(f) = 0$. That is, initially $f(u,v) = 0$ for every pair u and v in V. Then their method is to iteratively improve the value of f, always keeping f as a valid flow. Such an improvement can be made by finding a path from s to t, called an **augmenting path**, such that more flow can validly be pushed from s to t along this path (for example, the path source-gamma-delta-sink in Figure 10.13 is an augmenting path). Their algorithm continues to find augmenting paths in G and add the flow for these paths to f until there are no augmenting paths left. At this point, the flow is maximum (although formally proving this intuitive fact is equivalent to a proof of the important max-flow min-cut theorem, which is beyond the scope of this book). We illustrate an execution of this high-level description of the Ford-Fulkerson algorithm in Figures 10.14 and 10.15.

Implementation Details for the Ford-Fulkerson Algorithm

There are a number of important implementation details for the Ford-Fulkerson algorithm that impact how we represent a flow and how we compute augmenting paths. Representing a flow f is actually quite easy, for $f(v,u)$ will only be nonzero if (v,u) and (u,v) are edges in E (recall that we assume that every edge and edge inverse are in E). Thus, we can represent f by placing a flow label on every edge in E. Initially, every flow label in G is 0.

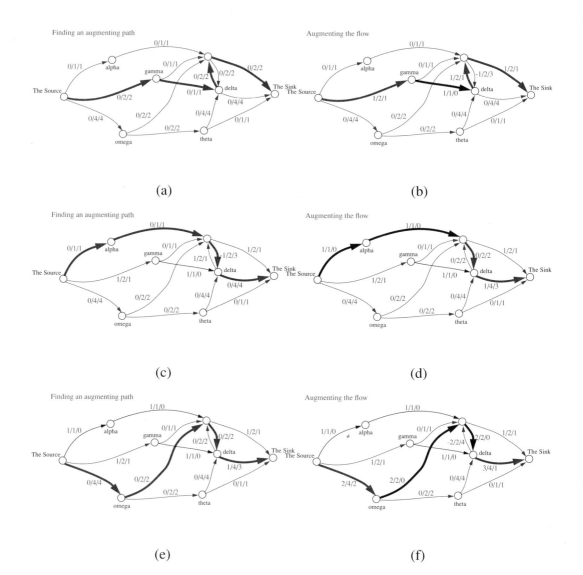

Figure 10.14: Example execution of the Ford-Fulkerson algorithm. We show each iteration as two phases: 1) finding an augmenting path and 2) augmenting the flow. Each edge e has three labels, the flow on e, the capacity of e, and the residual capacity on e. Augmenting path edges are shown with thick lines. Edges with some residual capacity are drawn in blue, and those without any residual capacity are drawn in black. (Note then that augmenting paths must be all blue.)

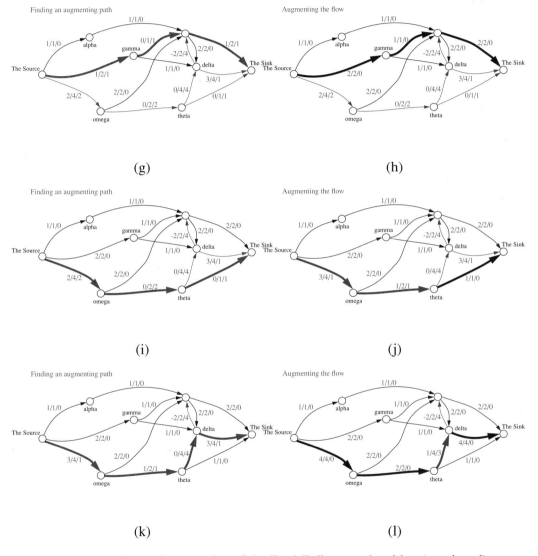

Figure 10.15: Example execution of the Ford-Fulkerson algorithm (continued).

The computation of an augmenting path can be reduced to a searching problem. Let $R = (V, F)$ be a weighted directed graph with the same set of vertices as G, but possibly different edges. An edge (u, v) is in the graph R if $c((u, v)) - f(u, v) > 0$. The value $c((u, v)) - f(u, v)$, which is called the ***residual capacity*** from u to v, is the amount of extra flow that can be pushed from u to v without violating the capacity rule. (Recall Figures 10.14–10.15.) The graph R is called the ***residual graph*** and the weight of each edge (u, v) in R is equal to the residual capacity from u to v. An ***augmenting path*** is a path from s to t in R. Thus, to find an augmenting path in G, we first construct the residual graph R from G and the current flow f, and then see if there is a path from s to t (for example, using our favorite graph-traversal method from Chapter 9). If we find such a path P in R, then we scan P to find an edge in P with the smallest amount of residual capacity, and we add this amount of flow to $f(u, v)$ for each edge (u, v) in P. If we cannot find a path P in R from s to t, then we are done—the current flow f is a maximum flow.

Analyzing the Ford-Fulkerson Algorithm

The analysis of the running time of the Ford-Fulkerson algorithm is a little tricky. This is because the algorithm never specifies the exact way to find augmenting paths, and the choice of augmenting path has a major impact on the algorithm's running time. Let $val(f^*)$ denote the value of a maximum flow, f^*. If the edge capacities are all integers, then each time we find an augmenting path we know we will increase the value of the flow by at least 1. Thus, $val(f^*)$ is an integer in this case. In addition, since we can find an augmenting path in a graph G by a simple graph traversal, such as a depth-first search, the total running time of the Ford-Fulkerson algorithm is $O((n+m)val(f^*))$ for a graph with integer capacities, where n is the number of vertices and m is the number of edges. Unfortunately, as illustrated in in Figure 10.16, this can be a very slow algorithm if the value of a maximum flow is very large and we choose augmenting paths poorly. In addition, if the edge capacities arbitrary real numbers, then the worst-case running time of the Ford-Fulkerson method can be made to be arbitrarily large.

Some Heuristics for Finding Augmenting Paths

Edmonds and Karp propose two heuristics, or "rules of thumb," for finding good augmenting paths that result in faster running times for the Ford-Fulkerson algorithm. Both of these heuristics are based on the notion of being a bit more "greedy" in our application of the greedy method to the maximum-flow problem. The first heuristic is to select an augmenting path that provides the maximum additional flow. Finding such a path can be done in $O((n+m)\log n)$ time (the details of which we leave as an exercise), which can be simplified to $O(m\log n)$ if we assume that

Finding an augmenting path   Augmenting the flow

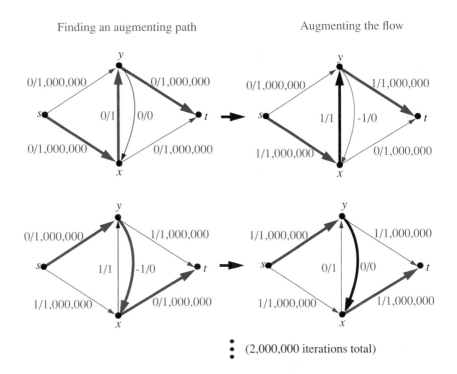

(2,000,000 iterations total)

Figure 10.16: An example of a network for which the standard Ford-Fulkerson algorithm runs slowly. If the augmenting path chosen in each iteration includes the edge (x,y) or the edge (y,x), then the algorithm will make a total of $2,000,000$ iterations, even though two iterations would have sufficed.

the graph is connected. We can show that, using this heuristic, the number of flow augmentations needed is $O(m \log val(f^*))$; hence, the total running time using this heuristic is $O(m^2 \log n \log val(f^*))$. The second heuristic proposed by Edmonds and Karp is to always use an augmenting path with the fewest number of edges. This heuristic can be implemented in $O(m)$ time by using a simple breadth-first search in the residual graph R to find augmenting paths. We can show that in this case, the number of augmentations needed is at most $O(nm)$; hence, the total running time needed to apply this heuristic is $O(nm^2)$. Thus, we can improve the running time of the Ford-Fulkerson algorithm for certain graphs.

There are a number of other algorithms and heuristics for computing maximum flows. The fastest of these methods have worst-case running times that are $O(n^3)$ or better. Rather than go into the details of these other maximum flow algorithms, let us instead examine an important application of the maximum flow problem—the maximum bipartite matching problem.

10.3.2   Maximum Bipartite Matching

A problem that arises in a number of important applications is the ***maximum bipartite matching*** problem. In this problem, we are given an undirected graph $G = (V, E)$ such that the vertices of V are divided into two sets, X and Y, with $V = X \cup Y$ and every edge in E joining a vertex in X to a vertex in Y. Such a graph is called a ***bipartite graph***. A ***matching*** in G is a set of edges from E that have no endpoints in common—such a set "pairs" up vertices in X with vertices in Y so that each vertex has at most one "partner" in the other set. The ***maximum bipartite matching*** problem is to find a matching that has the greatest number of edges (over all legal matchings).

Example 10.10: *Let $G = (V, E)$ be a bipartite graph with $V = X \cup Y$, where the set X represents a group of young men and the set Y represents a group of young women, who are all together at a community dance. Let there be an edge joining x in X and y in Y if x and y are willing to dance with one another. A maximum matching in G corresponds to a largest set of compatible pairs of men and women who can all be happily dancing at the same time.*

Example 10.11: *Let $G = (V, E)$ be a bipartite graph with $V = X \cup Y$, where the set X represents a group of college courses and the set Y represents a group of classrooms. Let there be an edge joining x in X and y in Y if, based on its enrollment and audio-visual needs, the course x can be taught in classroom y. A maximum matching in G corresponds to a largest set of college courses that can be taught simultaneously without conflicting.*

These two examples provide a small sample of the kinds of applications that the maximum bipartite matching problem can be used to solve. Fortunately, there is a very simple way of solving the maximum bipartite matching problem using a solution to the maximum flow problem.

Let $G = (V, E)$ be a bipartite graph with $V = X \cup Y$. We will create a new graph H such that a maximum flow in H can be immediately converted into a maximum matching in G. Let us begin our construction of H by including all the vertices in V plus a new "source" vertex s and a new "sink" vertex t. Add every edge in E to H, but direct each such edge (x, y) so that it is oriented from its vertex in X to its vertex in Y. In addition, create a directed edge from s to each vertex in X and a directed edge from each vertex in Y to t. Finally, assign to each of these edges in the new graph H a capacity of 1. If f^* is a maximum flow for H, then we use f^* to define a matching M in G using the rule that an edge e in E is in M if there is a flow of 1 on the edge corresponding to e in H.

We now show that the set M is a maximum matching. We have already observed in the previous section that if all the edge capacities in an instance of the maximum flow problem are integers, then a maximum flow will have all integer values. Again, this is because each time we augment, we are adding an integer value to the current flow along the edges of an augmenting path. Since the capacities in H are all 1, this means that a maximum flow in H will have flow values that are either 0 or 1 on each edge. Moreover, since there is only one edge coming into any vertex from X and only one edge coming out of any vertex in Y, the conservation rule implies that the flow going through any vertex of X or Y is either 0 or 1. Thus, each vertex in x will be paired with at most one vertex in Y. Finally, the fact that f^* is a maximum flow implies that the greatest possible number of edges in G are paired up.

Thus, any maximum flow algorithm can easily be used to solve the maximum bipartite matching problem. If we use, for example, the standard Ford-Fulkerson method, then the running time of this algorithm is $O(m|M|)$, where $|M|$ is the number of edges of the computed matching. Since $|M| \leq n/2$, we have that the bipartite matching problem can be solved in $O(nm)$ time.

We illustrate how maximum flow can be used to solve the maximum matching problem in Figure 10.17.

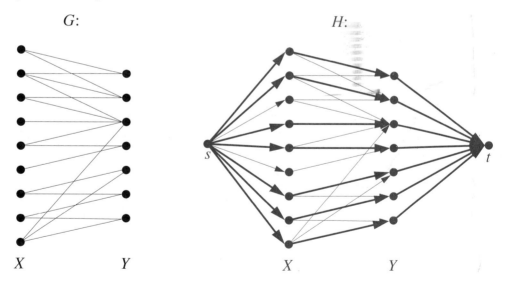

Figure 10.17: An example use of maximum flow to solve the bipartite maximum matching problem. The thick edges in the network on the right have unit flow, and the other edges have zero flow.

10.3.3   Minimum-Cost Flow

There is another variant of the maximum flow problem that applies in situations where there is a cost associated with moving a certain amount of flow across an edge. In this case, we are given a weighted directed graph G, with each weight $c((u,v)) \geq 0$ corresponding to a capacity, just as in the standard maximum flow problem, but we are also given another weight function $w((u,v)) \geq 0$ defined for each pair of vertices u and v in V, which corresponds to the *cost* of pushing a unit of flow along the edge (u,v). If (u,v) is an edge in E, then

$$w((u,v)) = w((v,u)) \geq 0,$$

and if neither (u,v) nor (v,u) is an edge in E, then $w((u,v)) = w((v,u)) = 0$. As was illustrated in the application of maximum flow to the bipartite matching problem (see Figure 10.17), for any given graph G, there may be a number of different ways to achieve a maximum flow in G. In the *minimum-cost flow* problem, we are interested in finding a maximum flow in G whose cost is lowest from among all possible maximum flows, where the *cost* of a flow f is defined as

$$w(f) = \sum_{(u,v) \ s.t. \ f(u,v)>0} w((u,v))f(u,v).$$

That is, the cost of a flow is the sum of the costs of all the positive flows along the edges of G.

Let G be a graph as described above. Computing a minimum-cost flow for G is surprisingly simple. We first find a maximum flow f^* using the Ford-Fulkerson algorithm. Let R be the residual graph defined for G and this maximum flow. We know that there is no path in R from the source s to t, but there are, nevertheless, still several edges in R. Recall that each edge e in R corresponds to some residual capacity for a corresponding edge in G. In this context of having a cost associated with each edge in G, there is also a cost associated with each edge in R. In particular, for each edge (u,v) in R, let $w((u,v))$ be the *cost* of the edge (u,v) in R, even if this cost is negative. If there is now a negative-cost cycle in R, then this corresponds to an *augmenting cycle*, which we can push flow across, just as we did with augmenting paths in the Ford-Fulkerson algorithm. Moreover, since its cost is negative, pushing additional flow around this cycle will reduce the cost of the current flow, and since it is a cycle, this will not reduce the total flow from s to t. Thus, by finding an augmenting cycle in R and adding the minimum residual capacity found on the edges of this cycle to each edge in this cycle, we can reduce the cost of the flow and still keep it being a maximum flow. After we do this, of course, we will *saturate* at least one edge on this cycle, which means we will increase its flow to match its capacity. Each saturated edge drops out of the residual graph. Thus, we can repeat this process of building the residual graph and finding a negative-cost augmenting cycle without fear of getting into an infinite loop. When we can find no more negative-cost augmenting cycles, the flow will be a minimum-cost maximum flow.

The running time of this algorithm can be analyzed using observations we have made in previous sections. First, we note that the Bellman-Ford algorithm can be used to find a negative cycle that contains some distinguished vertex v. Therefore, running the Bellman-Ford algorithm separately for every vertex v in G will determine whether there is some negative-weight cycle in G. Since one call to the Bellman-Ford algorithm takes $O(nm)$ time, calling it in this way takes (n^2m) time. After we find an augmenting cycle, we increment the flow in the edges of this cycle. If the flow capacities are integers, we will be adding at least an additional flow of 1 to each of these edges. If the edge costs are also integers, we are guaranteed to reduce the total cost by at least 1 with this augmentation. Thus, the total number of augmenting cycles that we would need to find is at most C, where

$$C = \sum_{e \in E} w(e)c(e),$$

which is called the **total weighted capacity** of G. Thus, if we have integer costs and capacities, the total time needed to solve the minimum-cost maximum-flow problem is $O(n^2mC)$. We can actually solve this problem faster using more complicated methods, but they are beyond the scope of this book.

10.4   Exercises

Reinforcement

R-10.1 Draw a (simple) connected weighted graph with 8 vertices and 16 edges, each with unique edge weights. Identify one vertex as a "start" vertex and illustrate a running of Dijkstra's algorithm on this graph.

R-10.2 Show how to modify the pseudo-code for Dijkstra's algorithm to not only output the distance from v to each vertex in G, but also to output a tree T rooted at v such that the path in T from v to a vertex u is actually a shortest path in G from v to u.

R-10.3 Draw a (simple) directed weighted graph G with 10 vertices and 18 edges such that G contains a minimum-weight cycle with at least 4 edges. Show that the Bellman-Ford algorithm will find this cycle.

R-10.4 There are eight small islands in a lake, and the state wants to build seven bridges to connect them so that each island can be reached from any other one via one or more bridges. The cost of constructing a bridge is proportional to its length. The distances between pairs of islands are given in the following table.

	1	2	3	4	5	6	7	8
1	–	240	210	340	280	200	345	120
2	–	–	265	175	215	180	185	155
3	–	–	–	260	115	350	435	195
4	–	–	–	–	160	330	295	230
5	–	–	–	–	–	360	400	170
6	–	–	–	–	–	–	175	205
7	–	–	–	–	–	–	–	305
8	–	–	–	–	–	–	–	–

Find which bridges to build so that the total construction cost is minimum.

R-10.5 Draw a (simple) connected undirected weighted graph with 8 vertices and 16 edges, each with unique edge weights. Illustrate the execution of Kruskal's algorithm on this graph. (Note that there is only one minimum-spanning tree for this graph.)

R-10.6 Repeat the previous problem for the Prim-Jarník algorithm.

R-10.7 Repeat the previous problem for Barůvka's algorithm.

R-10.8 Consider the unsorted sequence implementation of the priority queue Q used in Dijkstra's algorithm. Why is the best-case running time of Dijkstra's algorithm $\Omega(n^2)$ in this case? (Hint: consider the size of Q each time the minimum element is extracted.)

R-10.9 Draw a connected directed graph G with 9 vertices and 12 edges such that each edge in G has an integer capacity. Illustrate an execution of the Ford-Fulkerson algorithm on G.

Creativity

C-10.1 Give an example of an n-vertex graph G that causes Dijkstra's algorithm to run in $\Omega(n^2 \log n)$ time.

C-10.2 Show that the expected running time of Dijkstra's algorithm under the random neighbor-order assumption is $O(n \log n + m)$ if the priority queue Q is implemented with a heap. (Hint: observe that, for any vertex v, the probability that the ith neighbor of v pulled into the cloud causes a key change for v is $1/i$, and then refer to Appendix B to help determine the sum of all of these probabilities.)

C-10.3 Give an example of a weighted directed graph G with negative-weight edges, but no negative-weight cycle, such that Dijkstra's algorithm incorrectly computes the shortest-path distances from some vertex v.

C-10.4 Consider the following greedy strategy for finding a shortest path from vertex *start* to vertex *goal* in a given connected graph.

　　1: Initialize *path* to *start*.
　　2: Initialize *VisitedVertices* to $\{start\}$.
　　3: If *start=goal*, return *path* and exit. Otherwise, continue.
　　4: Find the edge *(start,v)* of minimum weight such that v is adjacent to *start* and v is not in *VisitedVertices*.
　　5: Add v to *path*.
　　6: Add v to *VisitedVertices*.
　　7: Set *start* equal to v and go to step 3.

Does this greedy strategy always find a shortest path from *start* to *goal*? Either explain intuitively why it works, or give a counter-example.

C-10.5 Show that if all the weights in a connected weighted graph G are distinct, then there is exactly one minimum spanning tree for G.

C-10.6 Suppose you are given a *timetable*, which consists of:

- A set $\mathcal{A}$ of N airports, and for each airport $a \in \mathcal{A}$, a minimum connecting time $c(a)$
- A set $\mathcal{F}$ of M flights, and the following information, for each flight $f \in \mathcal{A}$:
  - Origin airport $a_1(f) \in \mathcal{A}$
  - Destination airport $a_2(f) \in \mathcal{A}$
  - Departure time $t_1(f)$
  - Arrival time $t_2(f)$.

Give an efficient algorithm for the following problem:

Given airports a and b, and a time t, find a sequence of flights that allows one to arrive at the earliest possible time in b when departing from a at or after time t. Minimum connecting times at intermediate airports should be observed.

Also, give the running time of your algorithm as a function of N and M.

C-10.7 Let $\vec{G}$ be a weighted digraph with n vertices. Design a variation of Floyd-Warshall's algorithm for computing the lengths of the shortest paths from every vertex to every other vertex. Your algorithm should run in $O(n^3)$ time.

C-10.8 As your reward for saving the Kingdom of Bigfunnia from the evil monster, "Exponential Asymptotic," the king has given you the opportunity to earn a big reward. Behind the castle there is a maze, and along each corridor of the maze there is a bag of gold coins. The amount of gold in each bag varies. You will be given the opportunity to walk through the maze, picking up bags of gold. You may enter only through the door marked "ENTER" and exit through the door marked "EXIT." (These are distinct doors.) While in the maze you may not retrace your steps. Each corridor of the maze has an arrow painted on the wall. You may only go down the corridor in the direction of the arrow. There is no way to traverse a "loop" in the maze. You will receive a map of the maze, including the amount of gold in and the direction of each corridor. Describe an algorithm to help you pick up the most gold.

C-10.9 Design an efficient algorithm for finding a longest directed path from a vertex s to a vertex t of an acyclic weighted digraph $\vec{G}$. Specify the graph representation used and any auxiliary data structures used. Also, analyze the time complexity of your algorithm.

C-10.10 Suppose we are given a directed graph $\vec{G}$ with n vertices, and let M be the $n \times n$ adjacency matrix corresponding to G.

1. Let the product of M with itself (M^2) be defined, for $1 \le i, j \le n$, as follows:
$$M^2(i,j) = M(i,1) \odot M(1,j) \oplus \cdots \oplus M(i,n) \odot M(n,j),$$
where "$\oplus$" is the boolean **or** operator and "$\odot$" is boolean **and**. Given this definition, what does $M^2(i,j) = 1$ imply about the vertices i and j? What if $M^2(i,j) = 0$?

2. Suppose M^4 is the product of M^2 with itself. What do the entries of M^4 signify? How about the entries of $M^5 = (M^4)(M)$? In general, what information is contained in the matrix M^p?

3. Now suppose that $\vec{G}$ is weighted and assume the following:
   1: for $1 \le i \le n$, $M(i,i) = 0$.
   2: for $1 \le i, j \le n$, $M(i,j) = weight(i,j)$ if $(i,j) \in E$.
   3: for $1 \le i, j \le n$, $M(i,j) = \infty$ if $(i,j) \notin E$.
   Also, let M^2 be defined, for $1 \le i, j \le n$, as follows:
   $$M^2(i,j) = \min\{M(i,1) + M(1,j), \ldots, M(i,n) + M(n,j)\}.$$
   If $M^2(i,j) = k$, what may we conclude about the relationship between vertices i and j?

C-10.11 Suppose you are given a diagram of a telephone network, which is a graph G whose vertices represent switching centers, and whose edges represent communication lines between two centers. The edges are marked by their bandwidth. The bandwidth of a path is the bandwidth of its lowest bandwidth edge. Give an algorithm that, given a diagram and two switching centers a and b, will output the maximum bandwidth of a path between a and b.

C-10.12 NASA wants to link N stations spread over the country using communication channels. Each pair of stations has a different bandwidth available, which is known a priori. NASA wants to select $N-1$ channels (the minimum possible) in such a way that all the stations are linked by the channels and the total bandwidth (defined as the sum of the individual bandwidths of the channels) is maximum. Give an efficient algorithm for this problem and determine its worst-case time complexity.

C-10.13★ Show how to modify Barůvka's algorithm so that it runs in worst-case $O(n^2)$ time. (Hint: consider contracting the representation of the graph so that each connected component "cluster" is reduced to a single "super" vertex, with self-loops and parallel edges removed.)

Projects

P-10.1 Design and implement an applet that animates Dijkstra's algorithm.

P-10.2 Perform an experimental comparison of two of the minimum-spanning tree algorithms discussed in this chapter. Develop an extensive set of experiments to test the running times of these algorithms using both random graphs and graphs that you can find on the Internet.

P-10.3 Design and implement an applet that animates the Ford-Fulkerson flow algorithm. Try to be creative about how you illustrate flow augmentation, residual capacity, and the actual flow itself.

P-10.4 Implement the Ford-Fulkerson flow algorithm using three different heuristics for finding augmenting paths. Perform a careful experimental comparison of these heuristics.

P-10.5 Implement the Ford-Fulkerson flow algorithm and then show how to reuse this code to implement an algorithm for solving the maximum bipartite matching problem.

P-10.6 Implement the Ford-Fulkerson flow algorithm and the Bellman-Ford algorithm for finding negative-weight cycles. Show how the code for these two algorithms can be reused to develop a program for solving the minimum-cost flow problem.

Chapter Notes

The first known minimum-spanning tree algorithm is due to Barůvka [14], and was published in 1926. The Prim-Jarník algorithm was first published in Czech by Jarník [82] in 1930 and in English in 1957 by Prim [124]. Kruskal published his minimum-spanning tree algorithm in 1956 [94]. The reader interested in further study of the history of the minimum-spanning tree problem is referred to the paper by Graham and Hell [65]. The current asymptotically fastest minimum spanning tree algorithm is a randomized method of Karger, Klein, and Tarjan [85] that runs in $O(m)$ expected time. Dijkstra [42] published his single-source, shortest path algorithm in 1959. The average-case analysis of Dijkstra's algorithm, based on the random neighbor-order property, is due to Noshita [117].

The Bellman-Ford algorithm is derived from separate publications of Bellman [18] and Ford [52]. Ford and Fulkerson's network flow algorithm is described in their book [52], and Edmonds and Karp [47] describe heuristics that cause the Ford-Fulkerson algorithm to run in polynomial time. The reader interested in further study of graph algorithms is referred to the books by Ahuja, Magnanti, and Orlin [8], Cormen, Leiserson, and Rivest [36], Even [48], Gibbons [56], Mehlhorn [108], and Tarjan [138], and the book chapter by van Leeuwen [142].

Incidentally, the running time for the Prim-Jarník algorithm, and also that of Dijkstra's algorithm, can actually be improved to be $O(n \log n + m)$ by implementing the queue Q with either of two more-sophisticated data structures, the "Fibonacci Heap" [53] or the "Relaxed Heap" [43]. The reader interested in these implementations is referred to the papers that describe the implementation of these structures and how they can be applied to the shortest-path and minimum-spanning tree problems.

Chapter

11

Strings

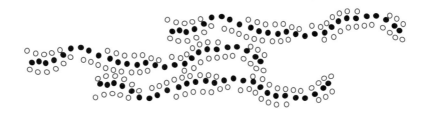

Contents

Document processing is rapidly becoming one of the dominant functions of computers. Computers are used to edit documents, to search documents, to transport documents over the Internet, and to display documents on printers and computer screens. Web "surfing" and Web searching are becoming significant and important computer applications, and many of the key computations in all of this document processing involve character strings and string pattern matching.

In this chapter, we explore the representations and methods that define the string abstract data type, and we study several of the fundamental algorithms for quickly performing important string operations. We pay particular attention to algorithms for string searching and pattern matching, since these can often be computational bottlenecks in many document-processing applications.

11.1 The String Abstract Data Type

Viewed abstractly, a string is just a sequence of characters that come from some *alphabet*, which is a set Σ of *characters*. Strings are almost always implemented as arrays of characters, so an individual character in a string can be accessed in constant time given its index in the string. Moreover, every modern computer language has a built-in primitive character data type, which defines an alphabet Σ that is typically based one the well-known character encoding schemes, such as the ASCII or Unicode character encodings. In addition, strings are also typically one of the built-in data types of modern computer languages, with the underlying characters for such strings being of the same primitive type as the built-in character type. In some applications, however, we may wish to restrict ourselves to a particular subset of characters, or we may wish to consider strings of characters that come from an unbounded alphabet. Thus, for full generality, we use the symbol Σ to refer to the specific alphabet that characters in any particular string we are considering can come from.

Let $P = P[0]P[1]P[2]\ldots P[m-1]$ be a string of m characters. For example, P could be the string `"hogs and dogs"`, which has length 13 and could have come from someone's Web page. In this case, $P[2] = $ 'g' and $P[5] = $ 'a', and the alphabet Σ could be the Unicode character set. Alternately, P could be the string `"CGTAATAGTTAATCCG"`, which has length 16 and could have come from a scientific application for DNA sequencing. In this case, the alphabet Σ is simply the set $\{A,C,G,T\}$.

Several of the typical string processing operations involve breaking large strings into smaller strings. In order to be able to speak about the pieces that result from such operations, we use the term *substring* of P to refer to a string of the form $P[i]P[i+1]P[i+2]\ldots P[j]$, for some $0 \le i \le j \le m-1$, that is, the string formed by the characters in P from index i to index j, inclusive. Technically, this means that a string is actually a substring of itself (taking $i = 0$ and $j = m - 1$), so if we want to rule this out as a possibility, we must restrict the definition to **proper** substrings, which require that either $i > 0$ or $j < m - 1$. To simplify the notation for referring to substrings, let us use $P[i..j]$ to denote the substring of P from index i to index j, inclusive. That is,

$$P[i..j] = P[i]P[i+1]\ldots P[j].$$

We use the convention that if $i > j$, then $P[i..j]$ is equal to the **null string** ε, which has length 0. In addition, in order to distinguish some special kinds of substrings, let us refer to any substring of the form $P[0..i]$, for $0 \le i \le m - 1$, as a **prefix** of P, and any substring of the form form $P[i..m - 1]$, for $0 \le i \le m - 1$, as a **suffix** of P. For example, if we again take P to be the string of DNA given above, then `"CGTAA"` is a prefix of P, `"CCG"` is a suffix of P, and `"TTAATC"` is a (proper) substring of P. Note that the null string is a prefix and a suffix of any other string.

String processing involves more than just dividing large strings into smaller ones. It also requires combining smaller strings into larger ones. The primary operation for combining strings is called **concatenation**, which takes a string

$$P = P[0]P[1]\ldots p[m - 1]$$

and a string

$$Q = Q[0]Q[1]\ldots Q[n - 1]$$

and combines them into a new string, denoted $P + Q$, with the following sequence of characters:

$$P[0]P[1]\ldots P[m - 1]Q[0]Q[1]\ldots Q[n - 1].$$

In Java, the "+" operation works exactly like this when acting on two strings. Thus, it is legal (and even useful) in Java to write the statement s = `"kilo"` + `"meters"`. Also, every object in Java is assumed to have a built-in method toString that returns a string associated with the object. Since strings are usually implemented as arrays, the concatenation of a length-n string with a length-m string typically takes time that is $O(n + m)$.

11.1.1 Immutable String Operations

String operations come in two flavors: those that modify the string they act upon and those that simply return information about the string they act upon without actually modifying the string itself. Therefore, let us distinguish two kinds of strings: the **immutable** strings, which cannot be modified, and the **mutable** strings, which can be modified. Java, for example, makes this distinction precise by defining the String class to represent immutable strings and the StringBuffer class to represent mutable strings.

The fundamental operations defined for an immutable string S of length n are as follows:

length(): Return the length, n, of S.
Input: None; **Output:** Integer.

charAt(i): Return the character at index i in S.
Input: Integer; **Output:** Character.

concat(Q): Return the concatenation of S and Q without modifying the string S.
Input: String; **Output:** String.

endsWith(Q): Determine if Q is a suffix of S.
Input: String; **Output:** Boolean.

equals(Q): Determine if Q is equal to S.
Input: String; **Output:** Boolean.

indexOf(Q): If Q is a substring of S, return the index of the beginning of the first occurrence of Q in S, else return -1.
Input: String; **Output:** Integer.

startsWith(Q): Determine if Q is a prefix of S.
Input: A string Q of length m; **Output:** true if Q is a prefix of S, false otherwise.

substring(i, j): Return the substring of S starting at index i and ending at index j.
Input: Two integers; **Output:** String.

We have chosen names for the above operations that are in keeping with the names used in the Java String class.

In terms of running times, if we assume that strings are implemented as arrays, then operation length() and charAt(i) can easily be implemented in $O(1)$ time. Likewise, it is straightforward to implement substring(i, j) in $O(i - j + 1)$ time, startsWith(Q) and endsWith(Q) in $O(m)$ time, and equals(Q) and concat(Q) in $O(n+m)$ time, where n is the length of S and m is the length of Q. Providing an efficient implementation of the indexOf(Q) operation is an interesting and important problem, for it has a number of applications in document retrieval and text editing programs. We discuss later in this chapter several possible implementations for this operation, some of which are more efficient than others.

11.1.2   Mutable String Operations

In addition to the operations for immutable strings given above, the fundamental operations for a mutable string S of length n are as follows:

> append(Q): Return $S + Q$, updating $S \leftarrow S + Q$.
> *Input:* String; *Output:* String.

> insert(i, Q): Return and update S to be the string obtained by inserting Q inside S starting at index i, that is, $S \leftarrow S[0..i-1] + Q + S[i..n-1]$.
> *Input:* String; *Output:* String.

> reverse(): Reverse the string S.
> *Input:* None; *Output:* None.

> setCharAt(i, ch): Set the ith character in S to be ch.
> *Input:* An integer i and a character ch; *Output:* Sets the ith character in S to be ch.

We have essentially kept the same names and meanings for these operations as for the Java StringBuffer class. Technically speaking, Java methods of the String class are not immediately available to a StringBuffer object S, but the Java String-Buffer class does provide a toString() method that returns a String version of S, which can then be used to access any of the standard String methods.

Recall that we are assuming that strings are implemented as arrays of characters. Thus, it is trivial to implement setCharAt(i, ch) to run in $O(1)$ time, and it is straightforward to design an implementation of append(Q) that runs in $O(m)$ time, and an implementation of insert(i, Q) that runs in $O(n+m)$ time. Also, with a little bit of care, one can design an implementation of the reverse() method that runs in $O(n)$ time (and is in-place). Thus, the standard operations for immutable and mutable strings all have simple and efficient implementations, with the exception of one operation—indexOf.

11.2   Pattern Matching Algorithms

In the classic *pattern matching* problem on strings, we are given a text string T of length n and a *pattern* string P of length m, and want to find whether P is a substring of T. The notion of a "match" is that there is a substring of T starting at some index i that matches P, character by character, so that $T[i] = P[0]$, $T[i+1] = P[1]$, ..., $T[i+m-1] = P[m-1]$. That is, $P = T[i..i+m-1]$. Thus, the output from a pattern matching algorithm could either be some indication that the pattern P does not exist in T or an integer indicating the starting index in T of a substring matching P. This is exactly the computation performed by the indexOf method. Alternatively, one may want to find all the indices where a substring of T matching P begins.

To allow for fairly general notions of a character string, we typically do not restrict the characters in T and P to explicitly come from a well-known character set, like the ASCII or Unicode character sets. Instead, we typically use the general symbol Σ to denote the character set, or alphabet, from which characters in T and P can come. This alphabet Σ can, of course, be a subset of the ASCII or Unicode character sets, but it could also be something more general and is even allowed to be infinite, like positive integers. Nevertheless, since most document processing algorithms are used in applications where the underlying character set is finite, we usually assume that the size of the alphabet Σ, denoted with $|\Sigma|$, is a fixed finite constant.

In this section, we present three pattern matching algorithms (with increasing levels of difficulty).

11.2.1 Brute-Force Pattern Matching

The ***brute-force pattern matching*** algorithm is probably the first algorithm that we might think of for solving the pattern matching problem—we simply test all the possible placements of P relative to T. This algorithm, shown in Code Fragment 11.1, is very simple and works even if the alphabet is unbounded.

Algorithm BruteForceMatch(T, P):

> *Input:* Strings T (text) with n characters and P (pattern) with m characters
> *Output:* Starting index of the first substring of T matching P, or an indication that P is not a substring of T

> **for** $i \leftarrow 0$ **to** $n - m$ {for each candidate index in T} **do**
>> **for** $j \leftarrow 0$ **to** $m - 1$ {for each candidate index in P} **do**
>>> **if** $T[i + j] = P[j]$ **then**
>>>> **if** $j \leftarrow m - 1$ **then**
>>>>> **return** i
>>> **else**
>>>> **break** out of the inner loop
> **return** "There is no substring of T matching P."

Code Fragment 11.1: Brute-force pattern matching.

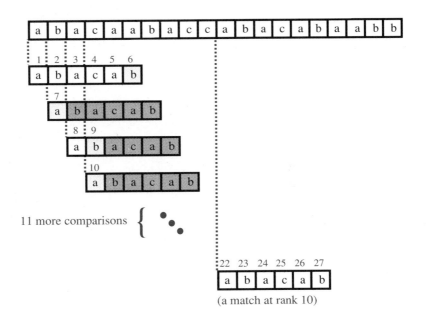

Figure 11.1: Example of a run of the brute-force pattern matching algorithm. The algorithm performs 27 character comparisons, which are indicated with numerical labels.

Example 11.1: *Suppose we are given the text string*

$$T = \text{"abacaabaccabacabaabb"}$$

and the pattern string

$$P = \text{"abacab"}.$$

In Figure 11.1 we illustrate the execution of the brute-force pattern matching algorithm on T and P.

The brute force algorithm could not be simpler. It consists of two nested for-loops, with the outer loop indexing through all possible starting indices of the pattern in the text, and the inner loop indexing through each character of the pattern, comparing it to its potentially corresponding character in the text. Thus, the correctness of the brute-force pattern matching algorithm follows immediately from this exhaustive search approach. The running time in the worst case is not good, however, because, for each candidate index in T, we can perform up to m character comparisons to discover that P does not match T at the current index. Referring to Code Fragment 11.1, we see that the outer for-loop is executed at most $n - m + 1$ times, and the inner loop is executed at most m times. Thus, the running time of the brute-force method is $O((n - m + 1)m)$, which is simplified as $O(nm)$. In the next section, we discuss a faster method for string pattern matching.

11.2.2   The Knuth-Morris-Pratt Algorithm

In studying the performance of the brute-force pattern matching algorithm on a specific instance of the problem, such as that given in Example 11.1, we should notice a major inefficiency. Specifically, we may perform many comparisons while testing a potential placement of the pattern against the text, yet if we discover a pattern character that does not match in the text, then we throw away all the information gained by these comparisons and start over again from scratch with the next incremental placement of the pattern. The Knuth-Morris-Pratt (or "KMP") algorithm, discussed in this section, avoids this waste of information and, in so doing, it achieves a running time of $O(n+m)$, which is optimal in the worst case.

The main idea of the KMP algorithm is to preprocess the pattern string P so as to compute a *failure function* f that indicates the proper shift of P so that, to the largest extent possible, we can reuse previously performed comparisons. Specifically, the failure function f is defined as the length of the longest prefix of P that is a suffix of $P[1..j]$ (note that we did *not* put $P[0..j]$ here). Later, we will discuss how to compute the failure function efficiently. The importance of this failure function is that it "encodes" repeated substrings inside the pattern itself, which is knowledge we can use to avoid unnecessary character comparisons.

Example 11.2: *Consider the pattern string $P =$ "abacab" from Example 11.1. The KMP failure function $f(j)$ for P is as follows:*

j	0	1	2	3	4	5
$P[j]$	a	b	a	c	a	b
$f(j)$	0	0	1	0	1	2

The KMP pattern matching algorithm, shown in Code Fragment 11.2, incrementally processes the text string T comparing it to the pattern string P. Each time there is a match, we increment the current indices. On the other hand, if there is a mismatch and we have previously made progress in P, then we consult the failure function to determine the new index in P where we need to continue checking P against T. Otherwise (there was a mismatch and we are at the beginning of P), we simply increment the index for T (and keep the index variable for P at its beginning). We repeat this process until we find a match of P in T or the index for T reaches n, the length of T (indicating that we did not find the pattern P in T).

In Figure 11.2, we illustrate the execution of the KMP pattern matching algorithm on the same input strings as in Example 11.1. Note the use of the failure function to avoid redoing one of the comparisons between a character of the pattern and a character of the text. Also note that the algorithm performs fewer overall comparisons than the brute-force algorithm run on the same strings (Figure 11.1).

Algorithm KMPMatch(T,P):

   Input: Strings T (text) with n characters and P (pattern) with m characters

   Output: Starting index of the first substring of T matching P, or an indication that P is not a substring of T

     $f \leftarrow$ KMPFailureFunction(P)   {construct the failure function f for P}

     $i \leftarrow 0$

     $j \leftarrow 0$

     while $i < n$ **do**

       if $P[j] = T[i]$ **then**

         if $j = m-1$ **then**

           return $i-m+1$ {a match!}

         $i \leftarrow i+1$

         $j \leftarrow j+1$

       else if $j > 0$ {no match, but we have advanced in P} **then**

         $j \leftarrow f(j-1)$ {j indexes just after prefix of P that must match}

       else

         $i \leftarrow i+1$

     return "There is no substring of T matching P."

Code Fragment 11.2: The KMP pattern matching algorithm.

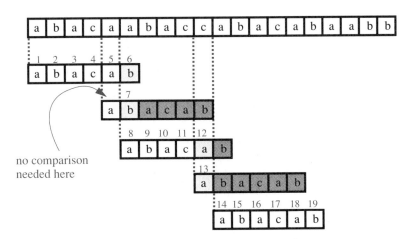

Figure 11.2: An illustration of the KMP pattern matching algorithm. The failure function f for this pattern is given in Example 11.2. The algorithm performs 19 character comparisons, which are indicated with numerical labels.

The main part of the KMP algorithm is the while-loop, which performs a comparison between a character in T and a character in P each iteration. Depending upon the outcome of this comparison, the algorithm either moves on to the next characters in T and P, consults the failure function for a new candidate character in P, or starts over with the next index in T. The correctness of this algorithm follows from the definition of the failure function. Any comparisons that are skipped are actually unnecessary, for the failure function guarantees that all the ignored comparisons are redundant—they would involve comparing the same matching characters over again.

Excluding the computation of the failure function, the running time of the KMP algorithm is clearly proportional to the number of iterations of the while-loop. For the sake of the analysis, let us define $k = i - j$. Intuitively, k is the total amount by which the pattern P has been shifted with respect to the text T. Note that throughout the execution of the algorithm, we have $k \leq n - 1$. One of the following three cases occurs at each iteration of the loop.

- If $T[i] = P[j]$, then i increases by 1, and k does not change, since j also increases by 1.
- If $T[i] \neq P[j]$ and $j > 0$, then i does not change and k increases by at least 1, since in this case k changes from $i - j$ to $i - f(j-1)$, which is an addition of $j - f(j-1)$, which is positive because $f(j-1) < j$.
- If $T[i] \neq P[j]$ and $j = 0$, then i increases by 1 and k increases by 1, since j does not change.

Thus, at each iteration of the loop, either i or k increases by at least 1 (possibly both); hence, total the number of iterations of the while-loop in the KMP pattern matching algorithm is at most $2n$. Achieving this bound, of course, assumes that we have already computed the failure function for P.

Constructing the KMP Failure Function

To construct the failure function, we use the method shown in Code Fragment 11.3, which is a "boot-strapping" process quite similar to the KMPMatch algorithm itself. We compare the pattern to itself as in the KMP algorithm. Each time we have two characters that match, we set $f(i) = j + 1$. Note that since we have $i > j$ throughout the execution of the algorithm, $f(j-1)$ is always defined when we need to use it.

Algorithm KMPFailureFunction runs in $O(m)$ time. Its analysis is analogous to that of algorithm KMPMatch. Thus, we have:

Proposition 11.3: *The Knuth-Morris-Pratt algorithm performs pattern matching on a text string of length n and a pattern string of length m in $O(n+m)$ time.*

Algorithm KMPFailureFunction(P):

  Input: String P (pattern) with m characters

  Output: The failure function f for P, which maps j to the length of the longest prefix of P that is a suffix of $P[1..j]$

  $i \leftarrow 1$

  $j \leftarrow 0$

  while $i \leq m - 1$ **do**

    if $P[j] = T[i]$ **then**

      {we have matched $j + 1$ characters}

      $f(i) \leftarrow j + 1$

      $i \leftarrow i + 1$

      $j \leftarrow j + 1$

    else if $j > 0$ **then**

      {j indexes just after a prefix of P that must match}

      $j \leftarrow f(j - 1)$

    else

      {we have no match here}

      $f(i) \leftarrow 0$

      $i \leftarrow i + 1$

Code Fragment 11.3: Computation of the failure function used in the KMP pattern matching algorithm. Note how the algorithm uses the previous values of the failure function to efficiently compute new values.

Portions of a Java implementation of the KMP pattern matching algorithm are shown in Code Fragment 11.4. This program assumes that the text and the pattern are stored in variables string and pattern, respectively. The failure function, constructed by method computeFailure, is represented by an array, failure[]. If a substring of the text matches the pattern, method match returns true and sets variable matchPoint equal to the index of the first substring of the text matching the pattern. Otherwise, method match returns false. (Please see Code Fragment 11.4 for details.)

The running time analysis of the Knuth-Morris-Pratt pattern matching algorithm may at first seem a little surprising, for it states that in time proportional to that needed just to read the strings T and P separately we can find the first occurrence of P in T. The intuition behind its efficiency comes from our being able to get the most out of each comparison that we do, and by our not performing comparisons we know to be redundant. Even so, there is an algorithm that can sometimes run even faster than this (at least when we consider constant factors), for it can skip over whole groups of comparisons at once. We discuss this algorithm next.

```java
public boolean match() {
  // Tries to find an occurrence of the pattern in the string
  int j = 0;
  if (string.length() == 0)
    return false;
  for (int i = 0; i < string.length(); i++) {
    while (j > 0 && pattern.charAt(j) != string.charAt(i))
      j = failure[j − 1];
    if (pattern.charAt(j) == string.charAt(i))
      j++;
    if (j == pattern.length()) {
      matchPoint = i − pattern.length() + 1;
      return true;
    }
  }
  return false;
}

private void computeFailure() {
  // Compute the failure function using a boot-strapping process,
  // where the pattern is matched against itself

  int j = 0;
  failure[0] = 0;
  for (int i = 1; i < pattern.length(); i++) {
    while (j > 0 && pattern.charAt(j) != pattern.charAt(i))
      j = failure[j − 1];
    if (pattern.charAt(j) == pattern.charAt(i))
      j++;
    failure[i] = j;
  }
}
```

Code Fragment 11.4: Portions of a Java implementation of the KMP pattern matching algorithm.

11.2.3 The Boyer-Moore Algorithm

At first, we might feel that it is always necessary to examine every character in T in order to locate a pattern P as a substring. But this is not always the case, for the Boyer-Moore pattern matching algorithm, which we study in this section, can sometimes avoid comparisons between P and a sizable fraction of the characters in T. The only caveat is that, whereas the KMP and brute-force algorithms can work even with a potentially unbounded alphabet, the Boyer-Moore algorithm assumes the alphabet is of fixed, finite size. It works the fastest when the alphabet is moderately sized and the pattern is relatively long.

The main idea of the Boyer-Moore algorithm is to return to the approach of the brute-force pattern matching algorithm, which involves testing the pattern P for each possible starting location i in T, but improve its running time by adding several potentially time-saving heuristics. Roughly stated, these heuristics are as follows:

Looking-Glass Heuristic: When testing a possible placement of P against T, begin the comparisons from the end of P and move backward to the front of P.

Character-Jump Heuristic: If, during the testing of a possible placement of P against T, we encounter a character in T that is not contained anywhere in P, then shift P completely past this character (for it cannot match any character in P). Otherwise, shift P to line up a matching character in P with this mismatched character.

Partial-Match Heuristic: If, during the testing of a possible placement of P against T, we encounter a mismatch at a location in P that allows us to shift P and automatically match a large group of characters in T and also possibly the mismatched character as well, then perform this shift.

We will formalize these heuristics shortly, but at an intuitive level they work as an integrated team. The looking-glass heuristic sets up the other two heuristics to allow the algorithm to avoid comparisons between P and whole groups of characters in T. In this case at least, we can get to the destination faster by going backwards. For if we encounter a mismatch during the consideration of P at a certain location in T, then we are likely to avoid lots of needless comparisons by significantly shifting P relative to T using one of the other two heuristics. These other two heuristics are in some ways complementary, for the character-jump heuristic pays off big if it can be applied early in the testing of a potential placement of P against T, and the partial-match heuristic can take advantage of situations where one encounters a mismatch after correctly matching a large number of characters in T. In fact, when the Boyer-Moore algorithm encounters a mismatch, it actually considers the shifts we get by applying either of these two heuristics, and it takes the shift that is larger.

Let us put this intuition aside, however, and get down to the business of saying precisely how these heuristics can be integrated into a string pattern matching algorithm. We begin with the character-jump heuristic. To implement this heuristic, we define a function $\text{last}(ch)$ that takes a character ch from the alphabet and indicates how far we may shift the pattern P if a character equal to ch is found in the text. In particular, we define $\text{last}(ch)$ as follows:

- $\text{last}(ch)$ is the index of the last occurrence of ch in P, if ch is in P, and otherwise, $\text{last}(ch) = -1$.

If characters can be used as indices in arrays, then the last function can be easily implemented as a lookup table. We leave, as a simple exercise, how to compute this table in $O(m + |\Sigma|)$ time, given P. This last function will give us all the information we need to perform the character-jump heuristic.

At the point the Boyer-Moore algorithm discovers a mismatch, it has matched the suffix $P[j+1..m-1]$ to the text (recall that the algorithm checks P against P backwards) and has mismatched the text at $P[j]$. To implement the partial-match heuristic, we need another function, $\text{match}(j)$, that maps indices in P to shifts. Specifically we define $\text{match}(j)$ as follows:

- $\text{match}(j)$ is the smallest $s \geq 1$ such that one of the following is satisfied:
  - $P[j+1-s..m-s-1]$ is a suffix of $P[j+1..m-1]$ (or $j = m-1$) and $P[j] \neq P[j-s]$, with $s \leq j$ (so all previously matched text characters will match the shifted pattern and there is a chance that $P[j-s]$ may match in the text the character that mismatched with $P[j]$).
  - $P[0..m-s-1]$ is a suffix of $P[j+1..m-1]$, with $j < s < m$ (so as many of the previously matched text characters will match a prefix of P as possible, because we are shifting P past the character that mismatched with $P[j]$).
  - $s = m$ (in which case we would shift the pattern completely past all the characters of the text that were previously compared with $P[j..m-1]$).

Intuitively, the match function indicates the best shift we can achieve so as to redo any comparisons that are "behind" the current position in the pattern (since we are comparing the pattern backwards). We will show how to compute a table representing the $\text{match}(j)$ function shortly. But before we give this method, we show in Code Fragment 11.5 how the last and match functions work together in the Boyer-Moore pattern matching algorithm.

In Figure 11.3, we illustrate the execution of the Boyer-Moore pattern matching algorithm on the same input strings as in Example 11.1.

Algorithm BMMatch(T, P):

 Input: Strings T (text) with n characters and P (pattern) with m characters

 Output: Starting index of the first substring of T matching P, or an indication that P is not a substring of T

 $i \leftarrow m - 1$

 $j \leftarrow m - 1$

 repeat

   if $P[j] = T[i]$ **then**

     if $j = 0$ **then**

       return i {a match!}

     else

       $i \leftarrow i - 1$

       $j \leftarrow j - 1$

   else

     $i \leftarrow i + m - j - 1$ {reset i to where it began in most-recent test}

     $i \leftarrow i + \max\{j - \mathsf{last}(T[i]), \mathsf{match}(j)\}$ {shift P relative to T }

     {Note that even if $j - \mathsf{last}(T[i])$ is negative, we will still perform a positive shift, because $\mathsf{match}(j)$ is always at least 1.}

     $j \leftarrow m - 1$

 until $i > n - 1$

 return "There is no substring of T matching P."

Code Fragment 11.5: The Boyer-Moore string pattern matching algorithm.

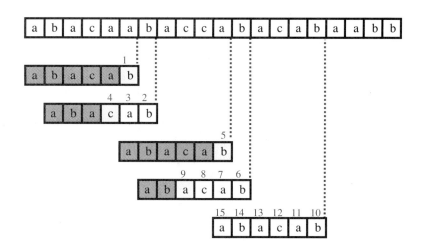

The last(ch) function:

ch	a	b	c	d
last(ch)	4	5	3	-1

The match(j) function:

j	0	1	2	3	4	5
$P[j]$	a	b	a	c	a	b
match(j)	4	4	4	4	6	1

Figure 11.3: An illustration of the Boyer-Moore pattern matching algorithm. The algorithm performs 15 character comparisons, which are indicated with numerical labels. Note that after comparison number 1, last(a) and match(6) indicated a shift of 1; after comparison number 4, last(a) indicated a shift of -1 and match(4) indicated a shift of 4; after comparison number 5, both last(a) and match(6) indicated a shift of 1, and after comparison number 9, last(c) indicated a shift of -1 and match(3) indicated a shift of 4.

The match function can be computed with a three-phase algorithm described informally below. (We leave the details of this algorithm to a (fairly intricate) exercise.) This algorithm is similar to the method for computing the KMP failure function, except that it proceeds in three phases, each of which corresponds to a part of the definition of match:

- In Phase 1, we initialize each entry in the match to be m, the maximum shift.
- In Phase 2, we compute each shift s such that $P[j+1-s..m-s-1]$ is a suffix of $P[j+1..m-1]$ (or $j = m-1$) and $P[j] \neq P[j-s]$, with $s < j$, and we store this shift value in match$[j]$. To facilitate the efficient computation of this phase, it is useful to utilize an auxiliary array, suffix, which is essentially a backwards version of the KMP failure function, for suffix$[i]$ will store the smallest $j > i$ such that the suffix $P[j..m-1]$ of P is a prefix of $P[i..m-1]$ (if there is no such suffix, then suffix$[i] = m$).
- Finally, in Phase 3, we again use the suffix array to compute each shift s such that $P[0..m-s-1]$ is a suffix of $P[j+1..m-1]$, with $j < s < m$, and we store the minimum of this shift and the previously computed shift for j in match$[j]$.

The correctness of the Boyer-Moore pattern matching algorithm follows from the fact that each time the method makes a shift, it is guaranteed to not "skip" over any possible matches. This is because last(ch) is the location of the *last* instance of ch in P, and match is the *smallest* shift that one can perform so as to achieve a partial match with the characters already successfully compared against P (and possibly also match the character that just mismatched against P).

Let us briefly discuss the running time of the Boyer-Moore algorithm. By a argument similar to that used to analyze the method for computing the KMP failure function, we can justify that the running time for computing a representation of the match function is $O(m)$. Likewise, we have already argued that computing a representation of the last function takes $O(m + |\Sigma|)$ time. What is perhaps a bit surprising is that the running time of the pattern-text comparison phase of the Boyer-Moore algorithm is $O(n)$ in the worst case. The justification of this fact is a bit involved, however, as it must carefully deal with various ways that small substrings may be repeated over and over inside P—a concept known as *periodicity*.

An interesting property of the Boyer-Moore algorithm is its ability to skip over large portions of the text. For example, there is experimental evidence that on English text, the average number of comparisons done per text character is approximately 0.24 for a five-character pattern string. The payoff is not as great for binary strings or for very short patterns, however, in which case the KMP algorithm (or, for very short patterns, the brute-force algorithm) may be better.

11.3 Regular Expression Pattern Matching

The brute-force, KMP, and Boyer-Moore pattern matching algorithms are all directed at solving the string pattern matching problem for the case when we are searching for a specific substring in a text. But there are instances when we are more interested in finding a substring that conforms to a general kind of pattern, not just a specific substring. Typically, as in the classic UNIX command "grep" for searching files, this general pattern is described as a ***regular expression***.

11.3.1 Regular Expressions

Regular expressions are a simple, yet powerful, notation for describing possibly infinite sets of strings, which are sometimes called "languages," over a given alphabet Σ. There are two rules for defining basic regular expressions:

1. ε is a regular expression that denotes the set $\{\varepsilon\}$, which contains only the null (or empty) string ε (that is, the zero-length string).
2. For each a in Σ, a is a regular expression that denotes the set $\{a\}$.

These basic regular expressions would be pretty boring were it not for the next three rules, which show how regular expressions can be combined to form new regular expressions:

1. If α and β are regular expressions describing sets A and B, respectively, then $(\alpha + \beta)$ is a regular expression describing the set $A \cup B$.
2. If α and β are regular expressions describing sets A and B, respectively, then $(\alpha\beta)$ is a regular expression describing the set of all strings formed by taking a string from A and concatenating a string from B to it.
3. If α is a regular expression describing the set A, then (α^*) is a regular expression that describes the set of all strings formed by concatenating i strings from A, allowing for repeats, for some $i \geq 0$ (we consider the case $i = 0$ to define the null string ε). This operation is called the ***Kleene closure*** of A. Sometimes this notation is given alternately as (α^+) to distinguish the case when $i \geq 1$.

Just as in arithmetic expressions, we can define a precedence for these expressions so that the parentheses can be removed if they conform to this precedence. Specifically, we let the Kleene closure operation have highest precedence, followed by concatenation, and we give + the lowest precedence. Thus, the expression $((ab) + (b^*))$ is the same as $ab + b^*$, and the expression $(((ab) + b)^*)$ is the same as $(ab + b)^*$.

Example 11.4: *Regular expressions can concisely express a number of interesting sets of strings, as the following examples illustrate, for the alphabet* $\Sigma = \{a,b\}$:

1. $ab+b$ is a regular expression denoting the set $\{ab,b\}$.
2. $(ab+ba)ba$ is a regular expression denoting the set $\{abba,baba\}$.
3. a^* is a regular expression denoting the set $\{\varepsilon,a,aa,aaa,aaaa,\dots\}$.
4. $(a+b)^*$ is a regular expression denoting the set of all strings formed from the alphabet $\Sigma = \{a,b\}$.
5. a^+b^+ is a regular expression denoting the set of all strings formed by the concatenation of a string of a's by a string of b's.
6. $b^*(ab^*a)^*b^*$ is a regular expression denoting the set of all strings with an even number of a's.

11.3.2 Regular Expressions and Finite State Automata

Given the simplicity and power of regular expressions, we would ideally like to have an algorithm that can take any regular expression α and any string x, and be able to quickly tell if x is in the set of strings described by α. Unfortunately, regular expressions are not in a form that is easily processed by computers. In order to use regular expressions in an efficient manner, we must first have a method for "compiling" any regular expression into a "machine" format that is easier for the computer to use in order to answer the regular-expression matching question.

A machine format that is most able to fill this role naturally is the **finite state automaton** (or "FSA"). In spite of its impressive-sounding name, an FSA is just a simple computer model for matching strings from regular languages. An FSA has five parts:

1. A finite set S of **states** (which usually are just numbered 1 to k, for some k).
2. An alphabet Σ that defines the characters the strings are defined over.
3. An initial, or **starting**, state $q_1 \in S$, which defines the initial configuration of the FSA.
4. A **final** state q_f, which is the accepting configuration when a string is recognized as fitting the pattern defined by the FSA.
5. A transition function δ, which defines the states in the FSA we can move into, given a current state and either ε or the next character in the string. Formally, δ maps a pair (q,a), where $q \in S$ is a state and $a \in \Sigma \cup \{\varepsilon\}$, to a subset of S, which contains the other candidate states we can move into if we are in state q and we read an a as the next character in the string (if $a = \varepsilon$, then we can move into one of the candidate states without reading the next character).

An FSA can be viewed as a directed graph whose vertices are states and whose edges, labeled with a character of Σ or with ε, are transitions. That is, if $\delta(q,a)=T$, then the graph associated with the FSA has a directed edge from state q to state r, labeled a, for every state $q \in T$. Given a string x to be processed, an FSA **accepts** x if there is a way for the FSA to start out in the initial state q_1 and processes x, left-to-right, character-by-character (allowing for ε-transitions), according to the rules specified by the transition function δ and end up in the final state after reading the last character in x. That is, an FSA accepts string x if the associated graph has a directed (possibly non-simple) path from the starting state to the final state, such that x is the string obtained by concatenating the labels of the edges of this path.

This way for an FSA to accept a string is said to be **nondeterministic**, because there are many potential legal paths that an FSA can take given a string x, and we say that the FSA accepts x so long as at least one leads to a final state. In addition, since we can only follow defined transitions, the nondeterministic acceptance rule also means that if a path leads to a state q has no defined transitions for the next character in x, then this path is terminated—it cannot lead to a final state. A string x is **not** accepted, therefore, if there are no legal paths through the FSA, starting from q_1, that lead to a final state on x. We show examples of FSA's in Figure 11.4.

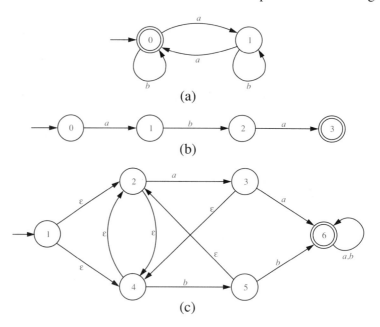

Figure 11.4: Examples of FSA's: (a) accepts any string containing an even number of a's; (b) accepts the string aba; (c) accepts any string containing aa or bb. The starting state has an arrow pointing to it; the final state is drawn as a double circle.

The Compilation Algorithm

Regular expressions are richly expressive, yet difficult to compute with, while FSAs are simple computational devices that are hard to design. An interesting relationship exists between these two concepts, however, in that any regular expression can be converted into an FSA that accepts the same strings as are expressed by the regular expression. In fact, although we will not describe it here, there is also a method for converting any FSA into an equivalent regular expression. Indeed, computer scientists have given a special name to the class of all sets of strings that can be denoted as regular expressions or accepted by FSAs, calling them the ***regular languages***. In the remainder of this section, we describe how to convert any regular expression to an equivalent FSA, and how to then simulate the processing of that FSA on a conventional computer.

Given the definition of FSA's and the way that they accept strings, it is actually a simple matter to compile any regular expression α into an FSA that only accepts the strings from the set that α denotes. The compilation process is defined in a recursive manner that mirrors that of the regular expressions themselves. FSA's for the basic regular expressions ε and a, for $a \in \Sigma$, are quite simple and are shown in Figure 11.5, parts a and b.

We construct FSA's for non-basic regular expressions recursively. If we are given the regular expression $(\alpha + \beta)$, then we recursively construct FSA's for α and β, and we compose these two FSA's into one accepting $(\alpha + \beta)$ as shown in Figure 11.5c. Likewise, if we are given the regular expression $(\alpha\beta)$, then we recursively construct FSA's for α and β, and we compose these two FSA's into one accepting $(\alpha\beta)$, as shown in Figure 11.5d. Finally, if we are given the regular expression (α^*), then we recursively construct an FSA for α, and we augment this FSA to create one accepting (α^*) as shown in Figure 11.5d (an FSA for (α^+) would not have the direct ε transition from q_1 to q_f). Since these are the three non-basic types of regular expressions, this completes the method for defining an FSA accepting the same set of strings as those described by a given regular expression.

There are a number of important observations that we can make about this construction. First, for any given symbol (be it part of a basic expression or non-basic one), we define at most two new states of the FSA. Thus, if a regular expression α is of length m, then there will be at most $2m$ states in the FSA we define for α. In addition, there is ultimately only one final state q_f, and there are no legal transitions out of this state. Finally, we define at most two legal transitions out of any state; the total number of transitions defined by our FSA is $4m$. Therefore, if we represent our FSA as a graph using a labeled adjacency list representation, then the entire description can be built in $O(m)$ time and space.

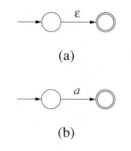

(a)

(b)

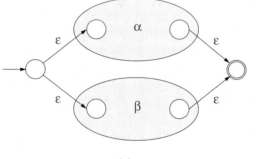

(c)

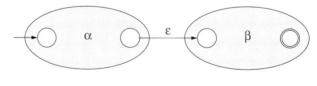

(d)

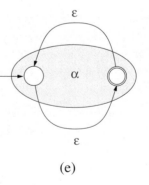

(e)

Figure 11.5: Composition of FSA's: (a) basic FSA for ε; (b) basic FSA for a; (c) FSA for $(\alpha + \beta)$, obtained from the ones for α and β; (d) FSA for $(\alpha\beta)$, obtained from the ones for α and β; (e) FSA for (α^*), obtained from the one for α.

11.3.3 Simulating a Finite State Automaton

We have shown how to efficiently take any regular expression α and "compile" α into a concise FSA F that only accepts strings in the language denoted by α. Viewing this FSA F as a compiled version of α, we can define an algorithm for determining whether a given string x is in the language denoted by α by simulating how F would process x.

The idea behind this simulation is pretty simple. A nondeterministic FSA will accept a string x if there is a sequence of transitions for a left-to-right processing of the characters of x that leads to a final state. This is simplified by the algorithm given above for converting a regular expression into a nondeterministic FSA, because there is only one final state to consider. The simulation is complicated somewhat, however, by the nondeterminism, since we have allowed the FSA to have ε transitions and even multiple transitions for the same character (or ε). Still, we can perform the simulation of such an FSA in a straightforward manner, simply by processing the characters of x in a left-to-right order, while maintaining at each stage, the set of **all** states that the FSA is allowed to be at that point in the processing.

We begin the simulation of an FSA F on a string x by initializing a set C of current states to contain q_1 (the start state for F) plus all those states reachable from q_1 by ε transitions. To process then next character a in x, we start from C, and we compute the set D of all the states reachable from states in C by a-transitions. We then define a new version of C to contain all the states in D plus those reachable from states in D by ε-transitions. We repeat this computation in order for each character in x. After processing the last character in x, we decide if we should accept x by determining whether the final state for F is in the final version of the set C.

The running time of each iteration of the FSA-simulation algorithm is $O(m)$, where m is the total size of the FSA (including all its five parts). Thus, the total time to simulate the processing of an n-length string x is $O(nm)$. Therefore, we have the following:

Proposition 11.5: *Given a regular expression α of length m and a string x of length n, we can determine if x is in the language denoted by α in $O(nm)$ time.*

Justification: The justification follows from the fact that the FSA compilation of a regular expression of size m produces an FSA of size $O(m)$, and the simulation of an $O(m)$ sized FSA on a string x of length n takes $O(nm)$ time. ∎

11.3.4 Finding a Substring Matching a Regular Expression

We have succeeded in showing how to test if a string x matches a regular expression, but we have not shown how to determine whether x contains a **substring** matching a given regular expression. Fortunately, as we now show, modifying the FSA simulation algorithm so that it can identify a substring pattern in a text is not very difficult.

Suppose we are given a text x and a regular expression α and wish to find a substring y of x such that y is in the language denoted by α. We can determine whether such a y exists by creating a new regular expression $\beta = (a_1 + a_2 + \cdots + a_d)^*\alpha$, which can be simplified to just $\Sigma^*\alpha$, where $\Sigma = \{a_1, a_2, \ldots, a_d\}$. If β matches a prefix of x, then α matches a substring y of x. We can modify the simulation algorithm to stop as soon as it completes any iteration, with one of the states in C being the final state, for this would identify the end of a prefix of x that matches β.

This approach doesn't give us the substring y; it gives us the index k where y ends. To determine where y begins we change the FSA simulation algorithm so that, in the processing the string x to match $\Sigma^*\alpha$, we identify when the FSA F makes the transition from the matching of Σ^* to the matching of α. Fortunately, this moment corresponds to a specific transition: the ε transition going from the recursively constructed FSA F_1 for Σ^* to the recursively constructed FSA F_2 for α. Moreover, once we enter F_2, we never leave F_2. Thus, in simulating F, we can associate with each state q_i of F_2 an index e_i that identifies the index in x where we made the transition from F_1 to F_2 that has ultimately led to this state, q_i. Let us call this the **cross-over** index associated with q_i. We initialize a new cross-over index each time we take a transition from the final state of F_1 to the start state of F_2.

During the simulation of F, if we make a transition from a state q_i in F_2 to a new state q_j in F_2, then the cross-over index e_i should travel to the new state q_j. Of course, in any given iteration of the FSA simulation algorithm, there may be multiple transitions to such a state q_j, each of which potentially brings along a different cross-over index. So, to break these potential conflicts, we need some kind of "tie breaking" rule. For example, if there are several different transitions into a state q_j of F_2, then one possible tie-breaking rule would be to associate with q_j the smallest cross-over index from a state we are coming from. This rule would have the effect of making y correspond to the longest substring matching α and ending at the index k. Even with this modification, the FSA simulation algorithm would still run in $O(nm)$ time. We may summarize, then, as follows:

Proposition 11.6: *Given a text string T of length n and a regular expression α of length m, we can find a substring of T in the language denoted by α or determine that no such substring exists, in $O(nm)$ time.*

11.4 Exercises

Reinforcement

R-11.1 How many prefixes of the string $P =$ "aaabbaaa" are also suffixes of P (not counting the empty string ε)?

R-11.2 Write a one-line Java Boolean expression that is true if and only if a string str is a *palindrome*, that is, the sequence of characters in str is the same whether it is listed forwards or backwards.

R-11.3 Write a Java program for reversing a string without using the built-in reverse() method of the String class.

R-11.4 Modify the method parentheticRepresentation given back in Section 5.2.2 to output a single string rather than print to standard output.

R-11.5 Draw a figure illustrating the comparisons done by the brute-force pattern matching algorithm for the case when the text is $T =$ "aaabaadaabaaa" and the pattern is $P =$ "aabaaa".

R-11.6 Repeat the previous problem for the KMP pattern matching algorithm, not counting the comparisons made to compute the failure function.

R-11.7 Compute a table representing the failure function for the following string:

"CGTACGTTCGTAC"

R-11.8 Assuming that the characters in Σ can be enumerated and can index arrays, give an $O(m + |\Sigma|)$ time method for constructing the last(ch) function from an m-length pattern string P.

R-11.9 Compute a table representing the last(ch) function used in the Boyer-Moore pattern matching algorithm for the following pattern string:

"the quick brown fox jumped over a lazy cat"

assuming the alphabet
$$\Sigma = \{'\,', a,b,c,d,e,f,g,h,i,j,k,l,m,n,o,p,q,r,s,t,u,v,w,x,y,z\}.$$

R-11.10 Compute a table representing the match(i) function used in the Boyer-Moore pattern matching algorithm for the following pattern string:

"hownowcow"

R-11.11 Construct a nondeterministic FSA for the regular expression $b^*(a+b)a^*$, as described in Section 11.3.2.

Creativity

C-11.1 Give an example of a text T of length n and a pattern P of length m that force the brute-force pattern matching algorithm to have a running time that is $\Omega(nm)$.

C-11.2 Give a justification of why the KMPFailureFunction method (Code Fragment 11.3) runs in $O(m)$ time.

C-11.3 Show how to modify the KMP string pattern matching algorithm so as to find *every* occurrence of a pattern string P that appears as a substring in T, while still running in $O(n+m)$ time. (Be sure to catch even those matches that overlap.)

C-11.4 Let T be a text of length n, and let P be a pattern of length m. Describe an $O(n+m)$ time method for finding the longest prefix of P that is a substring of T.

C-11.5 Say that a pattern P of length m is a *circular* substring of a text T of length n if P is a (normal) substring of T or if there is an index $0 \le i < m$, such that $P = T[n-m+i..n-1]+T[0..i-1]$, that is, P is equal to the concatenation of a suffix of T and a prefix of T. Give an $O(n+m)$ time algorithm for determining whether P is a circular substring of T.

C-11.6 The KMP pattern matching algorithm can be modified to run faster on binary strings by redefining the failure function as

$$f(j) = \text{the largest } k < j \text{ such that } P[0..k-2]\bar{p}_k \text{ is a suffix of } P[1..j],$$

where $\bar{p}_k$ denotes the complement of the kth bit of P. Describe how to modify the KMP algorithm to be able to take advantage of this new failure function and also give a method for computing this failure function. Show that this method makes at most n comparisons between the text and the pattern (as opposed to the $2n$ needed by the standard KMP algorithm given in Section 11.2.2).

C-11.7 Show how to modify the Boyer-Moore pattern matching algorithm, so that it only uses the looking-glass and character-shift heuristics, not the partial-match heuristic. (Hint: be careful; the obvious modification is wrong.)

C-11.8 Describe in detail the algorithm for computing the functions last and match used the Boyer-Moore pattern matching algorithm.

C-11.9 Describe nondeterministic FSA's for the following families of strings for $\Sigma = \{a, b\}$:

1. All strings with an odd number of a's.
2. All strings starting with an a.
3. All strings with three consecutive b's.
4. All strings without three consecutive b's.

C-11.10 Design regular expressions to denote each of the families of strings given in the previous problem.

Projects

P-11.1 Implement the brute-force and KMP pattern matching algorithms. Perform an experimental analysis, using documents found on the Internet, on the relative speed of these algorithms for varying-length patterns.

P-11.2 Implement the Boyer-Moore pattern matching algorithm. Perform an experimental analysis, using documents found on the Internet, on the average number of comparisons done for each passed character using varying-length patterns.

P-11.3 Perform an experimental comparison, possibly as a project utilizing groups of two or three programmers, of the relative speeds of the brute-force, KMP, and Boyer-Moore pattern matching algorithms. Document the time taken for coding up each of these algorithms as well as their relative running times on documents found on the Internet that are then searched using varying length patterns.

Chapter Notes

The KMP algorithm is described by Knuth, Morris, and Pratt in their journal article [92], and Boyer and Moore describe their algorithm in a journal article published the same year [27]. In their article, however, Knuth *et al.* [92] also prove that the Boyer-Moore algorithm runs in linear time. More recently, Cole [34] shows that the Boyer-Moore algorithm makes at most $3n$ character comparisons in the worst case, and this bound is tight. All of the algorithms discussed above are also discussed in the book chapter by Aho [5], albeit in a more theoretical framework, including the methods for regular-expression pattern matching. The reader interested in further study of string pattern matching algorithms is referred to the book by Stephen [134] and the book chapters by Aho [5] and Crochemore and Lecroq [38].

Chapter

12

Fundamental Techniques

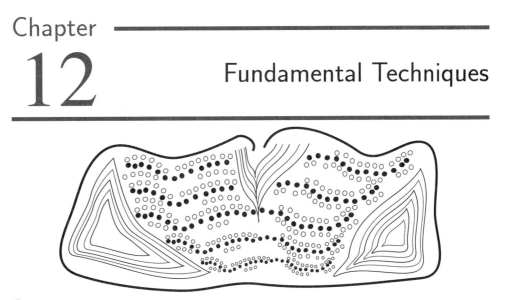

Contents

Television shows about carpentry are becoming common, yet the approaches they take to the subject can be quite divergent. In one show, the host builds furniture using very specialized power tools, and in another the host builds furniture using only general-purpose hand tools. The specialized tools, used in the first show, are all very good at the jobs they are intended for, but none of them is very versatile. The tools in the second show are fundamental, however, because they can be effectively used for a number of different tasks. In short, the first show demonstrates the power of specialization, whereas the second demonstrates the power of craftsmanship using fundamental tools and techniques.

These two television shows provide an interesting metaphor for data structure and algorithm design. There are some algorithmic tools, such as those used in the string pattern matching algorithms discussed in Chapter 11, that are very specialized. These specialized methods are very good for the problems they are intended to solve, but they are not very versatile. There are other algorithmic tools, however, that are *fundamental* in that they can be applied to a wide variety of different data structure and algorithm design problems. Learning to use these fundamental techniques is a craft, and this chapter is dedicated to developing the knowledge for using these techniques effectively.

The fundamental techniques covered in this chapter are amortization, divide-and-conquer, dynamic programming, and the greedy method. These techniques are rather versatile, and examples of them have already been presented in earlier chapters of this book.

Amortization was used on a number of different occasions, including in the analysis of the graph traversal algorithms in Chapter 9. In this chapter, we describe the amortization technique in a general way and give an application to the analysis of Java vectors and of a simple union-find partition data structure (which arises in Kruskal's minimum-spanning tree algorithm).

Divide-and-conquer was used in the merge-sort, quick-sort, and quick-select algorithms of Chapter 8. In this chapter, we show how to design and analyze general kinds of divide-and-conquer algorithms and we give an additional application of this technique to the problem of multiplying big integers.

The dynamic programming technique underlies the Floyd-Warshall transitive closure algorithm of Chapter 9. In this chapter, we describe the general framework of dynamic programming and give several applications, including the longest common subsequence problem.

The greedy method was used in several of the algorithms for weighted graphs discussed in Chapter 10. In this chapter, we give the general structure for the greedy method and show how it can be applied to a data compression problem.

12.1   Amortization

The first technique we discuss is an interesting method for data structure analysis known as **amortization**. It is technically not a methodology for designing efficient data structures; it is just an analysis tool. Even so, it influences many data structure designs. The term "amortization" itself comes from the field of accounting, which provides an intuitive monetary metaphor for analysis, as we shall see in this section.

12.1.1   Amortized Running Time

The typical data structure usually supports a wide variety of different methods for accessing and updating the elements it stores. Throughout this book, we have studied a variety of data structures, and we have analyzed their performance on the basis of the worst-case running time of each individual operation. Amortization takes a different viewpoint. Rather than focusing on each operation separately, it considers the interactions between operations by studying the running time of a series of operations.

As an example, we introduce a new ADT, the **clearable stack**, which supports the usual stack operations, push, pop, top, size, and isEmpty (Section 3.1), plus the following operation:

> clearStack(): Empty the stack by removing all its elements.
> **Input:** None; **Output:** None.

Let S be a clearable stack with n elements implemented by means of an array. Operation clearStack takes $\Theta(n)$ time, since we should dereference all the elements in the stack (see, for example, operation pop in Code Fragment 3.3).

Now consider a series of n operations on an initially empty clearable stack S. If we take a worst-case viewpoint, we may say that the running time of this series of operations is $O(n^2)$, since the worst case of a single clearStack operation in the series is $O(n)$, and there may be as many as $O(n)$ clearStack operations in this series. While this analysis is correct, it is also an overstatement, since an analysis that takes into account the interactions between the operations shows that the running time of the entire series is actually $O(n)$.

Proposition 12.1: *A series of n operations on an initially empty clearable stack implemented with an array takes $O(n)$ time.*

Justification: Let $M_0, \ldots, M_{n-1}$ be the series of operations performed on S, and let $M_{i_0}, \ldots, M_{i_{k-1}}$ be the k clearStack operations within the series. We have

$$0 \le i_0 < \ldots < i_{k-1} \le n-1.$$

Let us also define $i_{-1} = -1$. The running time of operation M_{i_j} (a clearStack operation) is $O(i_j - i_{j-1})$, because at most $i_j - i_{j-1} - 1$ elements could have been pushed into the stack since the previous clearStack operation $M_{i_{j-1}}$ or since the beginning of the series. Thus, the running time of all the clearStack operations is

$$O\left(\sum_{j=0}^{k-1}(i_j - i_{j-1})\right).$$

A summation such as this is known as a ***telescoping sum***, for all terms other than the first and last cancel each other out. That is, this summation is $O(i_{k-1} - i_{-1})$, which is $O(n)$. All the remaining operations of the series take $O(1)$ time each. Thus, we conclude that a series of n operations performed on an initially empty clearable stack takes $O(n)$ time.   ∎

Proposition 12.1 indicates that the average running time of any operation on a clearable stack is $O(1)$, where the average is taken over an arbitrary series of operations, starting with an initially empty clearable stack.

This example provides a motivation for the amortization technique, which gives us a worst-case way of performing an average-case analysis. Formally, we define the ***amortized running time*** of an operation within a series of operations as the worst-case running time of the series of operations divided by the number of operations. When the series of operations is not specified, it is usually assumed to be a series of operations from the repertory of a certain data structure, starting from an empty structure. Thus, by Proposition 12.1, we can say that the amortized running time of each operation in the clearable stack ADT is $O(1)$ when we implement that stack with an array. Note that the actual running time of an operation may be much higher than its amortized running time (for example, a particular clearStack operation may take $O(n)$ time).

The advantage of using amortization is that it gives us a way to do a robust average-case analysis without using any probability. It simply requires that we have some way of characterizing the worst-case running time for performing a series of operations. We can even extend the notion of amortized running time so as to assign each individual operation in a series of operations its own amortized running time, provided the total actual time taken to process the entire series of operations is no more than the sum of amortized bounds given to the individual operations.

There are several ways of doing an amortized analysis. The most obvious way is to use a direct argument to derive bounds on the total time needed to perform a series of operations, which is what we did in the justification of Proposition 12.1. While direct arguments can often be found for a simple series of operations, performing an amortized analysis of a nontrivial series of operations is often easier using another method of amortized analysis—the ***accounting method***.

12.1.2   The Accounting Method

The ***accounting method*** for performing an amortized analysis is to use a scheme of credits and debits for keeping track of the running time of the different operations in the series. The basis of the accounting method is simple. We view the computer as a coin-operated appliance that requires the payment of one ***cyber-dollar*** for a constant amount of computing time. We also view an operation as a sequence of constant time ***primitive operations***, which each cost one ***cyber-dollar*** to be executed. When an operation is executed, we should have enough cyber-dollars available to pay for its running time. Of course, the most obvious approach is to charge an operation a number of cyber-dollars equal to the number of primitive operations performed. However, the interesting aspect of using the accounting method is that we do not have to be fair in the way we charge the operations. Namely, we can overcharge some operations that execute few primitive operations and use the profit made on them to help out other operations that execute many primitive operations. This mechanism may allow us to charge the same amount a of cyber-dollars to each operation in the series, without ever running out of cyber-dollars to pay for the computer time. Hence, if we can set up such a scheme, called an ***amortization scheme***, we can say that each operation in the series has an amortized running time that is $O(a)$. When designing an amortization scheme, it is often convenient to think of the unspent cyber-dollars as being "stored" in certain places of the data structure, for example, at the elements of a stack or the nodes of a tree.

An alternative amortization scheme charges different amounts to the various operations. In this case, the amortized running time of an operation is proportional to the total charges made divided by the number of operations.

We now go back to the clearable stack example and present an amortization scheme for it that yields an alternative justification of Proposition 12.1. Let us assume that one cyber-dollar is enough to pay for the execution of operation push, pop, top, size, or isEmpty, and for the time spent by operation clearStack to dereference one element. We shall charge each operation two cyber-dollars. This means undercharging operation clearStack and overcharging all the other operations by one cyber-dollar. The cyber-dollar profited in a push operation will be stored at the element inserted by the operation. (See Figure 12.1.) When a clearStack operation is executed, the cyber-dollar stored at each element in the stack is used to pay for the time spent dereferencing it. Hence, we have a valid amortization scheme, where each operation is charged two cyber-dollars, and all the computing time is paid for. This simple amortization scheme implies the result of Proposition 12.1.

Notice that the worst case for the running time occurs for a series of push operations followed by a single clearStack operation. In other cases, at the end of the series of operations, we may end up with some unspent cyber-dollars, which

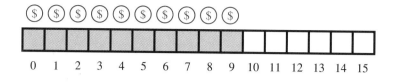

Figure 12.1: Cyber-dollars stored at the elements of a clearable stack S in the amortized analysis of a series of operations on S.

are those profited from operations top, size, or isEmpty, and those stored at the elements still in the sequence. Indeed, the computing time for executing a series of n operations can be paid for with the amount of cyber-dollars between n and $2n$. Our amortization scheme accounts for the worst case by always charging two cyber-dollars per operation.

We should stress at this point that the accounting method is simply an analysis tool. It does not require that we modify the data structure or the execution of the operations in any way. In particular, it does not require that we add objects for keeping track of the cyber-dollars spent or accumulated to the data structure. Even so, performing an amortized analysis on a data structure using the accounting method can have an impact on design decisions we make for that data structure. In order to drive this point home, we next perform an amortized analysis of a familiar data structure that is standard in Java.

12.1.3 An Amortized Analysis of Java Vectors

As we observed in Section 4.1.3, the java.util.Vector class provides a convenient expandable array type in Java. The Vector class supports the insertion of new elements at specified ranks (with automatic shifting up of elements at higher ranks). It is expandable in the sense that the size of a Java vector can grow as the number of elements being stored in the vector grows. When an insertion causes an *overflow*, that is, makes the number of elements exceed the capacity n of the current array, the Java run-time environment allocates a new array of larger capacity and copies all the elements from the current array into the new array. Thus, growing a Java vector takes $O(n)$ time.

When a Java Vector object is created, an array of size capacity is created. Also, a parameter capacityIncrement is provided, which determines how the size of this array will increase in the event of an overflow. If capacityIncrement is positive, then the array capacity is increased by this amount. If capacityIncrement is zero, however, the size of the array is doubled when an overflow occurs. The Vector class provides three methods for constructing a new vector, one with no parameters, one with just a capacity parameter, and one with both capacity and capacity increment parameters. In the case of the first two constructor methods, the default capacity increment is 0. In addition, the Vector allows the capacityIncrement variable to be changed over time. Of course, when we use a Java Vector object, we have full freedom in how it is created, and we have full freedom in how to use this object over time. This choice should not be made lightly, however, for it has significant implications, as we will see.

Consider now a Java implementation of the stack ADT based on a Java Vector (this is, in fact, the way Java implements the java.util.Stack class). In Chapter 3, we observed that a good stack implementation should support the push and pop methods in $O(1)$ time, and we also observed that a reasonable way to achieve this is to use an array. Recall that the problem with an array implementation is that it imposes an artificial cap on the total number of elements that can be stored in a stack. This objection is overcome, however, when we implement a stack using a Java Vector, for it grows as needed. Unfortunately, growing a Java vector of current size n takes $O(n)$ time, since a new array is created and all the elements have to be copied from the old to the new array. As a consequence, the worst-case running time of a push operation, when a stack is implemented with a Java Vector, now becomes $O(n)$, not $O(1)$. But this is a situation where an amortized analysis can help greatly, as the following proposition shows.

Proposition 12.2: *Let S be a stack implemented by means of a Java Vector initialized with capacity = 1 and capacityIncrement = 0. In a series of operations on S, starting with S being empty, the amortized running time of each operation is $O(1)$.*

Justification: Let us assume that one cyber-dollar is enough to pay for the execution of each operation, excluding the time spent for growing the array. Also, let us assume that growing the array from size k to size $2k$ requires k cyber-dollars for the time spent copying the elements. We shall charge each operation executed three cyber-dollars. Thus, we overcharge by two cyber-dollars each operation that does not cause an overflow. The two cyber-dollars profited in a push operation will be stored at the element inserted by the operation. An overflow occurs when stack S has 2^i elements, for some integer $i \geq 0$, and the size of the array used by the Vector representing S is 2^i. Thus, doubling the size of the array will require 2^i cyber-dollars. Such cyber-dollars will be found at the elements stored in cells 2^{i-1} through $2^i - 1$. (See Figure 12.2.) Note that the previous overflow occurred when the number of elements became larger than 2^{i-1} for the first time, and thus the cyber-dollars stored in cells 2^{i-1} through $2^i - 1$ were not previously spent. Therefore, we have a valid amortization scheme in which each operation is charged three cyber-dollars and all the computing time is paid for. ∎

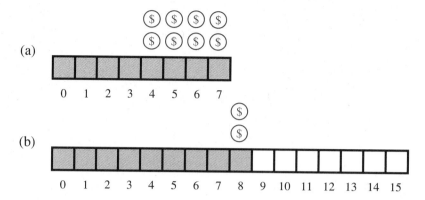

Figure 12.2: Illustration of the amortized analysis of a series of operations on a stack implemented with a Java vector: (a) the 8-cell array is full and there are two cyber-dollars stored at the cells 4 through 7; (b) a push operation causes an overflow and a doubling of the array capacity. The time spent for copying the eight old elements to the new array is paid for by the cyber-dollars already stored in the stack; the time spent for inserting the new element is paid for by one of the cyber-dollars charged to the push operation; and the two cyber-dollars profited are stored at cell 8.

The requirement that the capacityIncrement parameter be set to 0 might at first seem like a technicality, but it is not, as the following proposition shows.

Proposition 12.3: *If we implement a stack using a Java Vector with any fixed positive* capacityIncrement *value, then performing a series of n push operations on an initially empty stack takes $\Omega(n^2)$ time, that is, each operation has amortized running time $\Omega(n)$.*

Justification: Let $c > 0$ be the capacityIncrement value, and $c_0 > 0$ denote the initial size of the array. An overflow will be caused by a push operation when the current number of elements in the stack is $c_0 + ic$, for $i = 0, \ldots, m-1$, where

$$m = \lfloor (n - c_0)/c \rfloor .$$

Hence, the total time for handling the overflows is proportional to

$$\sum_{i=0}^{m-1} (c_0 + ci) \;=\; c_0 m + c \sum_{i=0}^{m-1} i$$

$$=\; c_0 m + c \frac{m(m-1)}{2} \quad \text{(by Proposition 2.4)},$$

which is $\Omega(n^2)$. Thus, performing the n push operations takes $\Omega(n^2)$ time.   ∎

Figure 12.3 compares the running times of a series of push operations on an initially empty stack implemented with a Vector, for two cases; in the first case, we have capacityIncrement $= 0$, and in the second, capacityIncrement $= 3$.

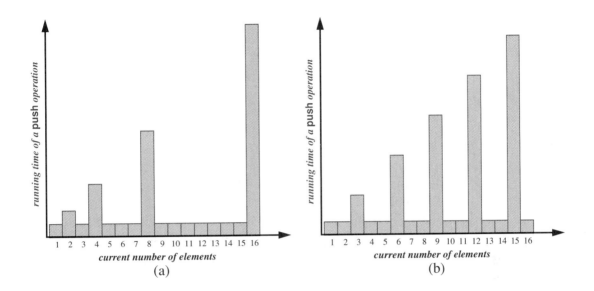

Figure 12.3: Running times of a series of push operations on an initially empty stack, implemented with a Java Vector: (a) capacityIncrement $= 0$; (b) capacityIncrement $= 3$.

A lesson to be learned from Propositions 12.2 and 12.3 is that a careful amortized analysis provides important insights into how a data structure ought to be used. This lesson is reinforced even further in the following subsection, which contains an interesting usage of the accounting method.

12.1.4   Partitions with Union-Find Operations

A **partition** is a collection of disjoint sets. As an abstract data type, a partition P supports the following three operations:

makeSet(e): Create a singleton set containing the element e and return a locator ℓ for e.
    Input: Object; *Output:* Locator (see Section 6.4).

union(A, B): Either assign $A \leftarrow A \cup B$, destroy B, and return A, or assign $B \leftarrow A \cup B$, destroy A, and return B .
    Input: Two sets; *Output:* Set.

find(ℓ): Return the set containing the element with locator ℓ.
    Input: Locator; *Output:* Set.

We examine a simple implementation of this ADT next.

Sequence Implementation

A simple implementation of a partition with a total of n elements is with a collection of sequences, one for each set, where the sequence for a set A stores **node** objects as its elements. We define each such node so that it implements the locator interface (needed in the find operation), and so that each node holds an element of a set A and a reference to to that set A. (See Figure 12.4.) Thus, the nodes serve as locators for the partition, and we can perform a find operation for a locator (node) ℓ in $O(1)$ time simply by returning $\ell.A$. Likewise, makeSet also takes $O(1)$ time. Operation union(A,B) requires that we join the two sequences into one and update the set references in the locators (that is, nodes) of one of the two. We choose to implement this operation by removing all the locators from the sequence with smaller size, and inserting them in the sequence with larger size. Hence, the operation union(A,B) takes time $O(\min(|A|,|B|))$, which is $O(n)$. Nevertheless, as shown below, an amortized analysis shows this implementation to be much better than appears from this worst-case analysis.

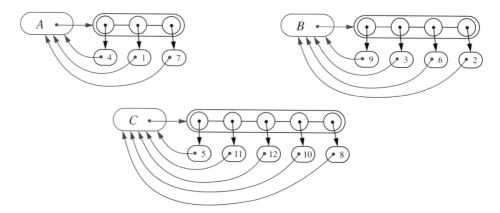

Figure 12.4: Sequence-based implementation of a partition consisting of three sets: $A = \{1,4,7\}, B = \{2,3,6,9\}$, and $C = \{5,8,10,11,12\}$.

Proposition 12.4: *Performing a series of n* makeSet, union, *and* find *operations, using the above implementation, starting from an initially-empty partition P takes $O(n \log n)$ time.*

Justification: We use the accounting method and assume that one cyber-dollar can pay for the time to perform a find operation, a makeSet operation, or the movement of a locator (node) from one sequence to another in a union operation. In the case of a find or makeSet operation, we charge the operation itself 1 cyber-dollar.

In the case of a union operation, however, we charge 1 cyber-dollar to each locator that we move from one set to another. Note that we charge nothing to the union operations themselves. Clearly, the total charges to find and makeSet operations is $O(n)$. Consider, then, the number of charges made to locators on behalf of union operations. The important observation is that each time we move a locator from one set to another the size of the new set at least doubles. Thus, each locator ℓ is moved from one set to another at most $\lceil \log n \rceil$ times; hence, each such ℓ can be charged at most $O(\log n)$ times. Since we assume that the partition is initially empty, there are $O(n)$ different elements referenced in the given series of operations, which implies that the total time to perform this series is $O(n \log n)$. ■

We can conclude from the above proposition that the amortized running time of an operation in a series of n makeSet, union, and find operations on a partition P implemented using sequences is proportional to the total time taken for the series divided by the number of operations:

$$\frac{O(n \log n)}{n},$$

which is $O(\log n)$.

We show in Code Fragments 12.1, 12.2, and 12.3 a complete Java implementation of a partition by means of a sequence.

```java
public interface Partition extends Container {
    public Locator makeSet(Object element);
    public PartitionSet union(PartitionSet A, PartitionSet B)
                    throws InvalidArgumentException;
    public PartitionSet find(Locator l) throws InvalidLocatorException;
}
public interface PartitionSet {
    // empty interface
}
class SeqPartitionSet extends VectorSequence implements PartitionSet {
    private SeqPartition container;
    public SeqPartition container() {
        return container;
    }
    public void setContainer(SeqPartition p) {
        container = p;
    }
}
```

Code Fragment 12.1: Interfaces Partition and PartitionSet and class SeqPartitionSet in the Java implementation of a partition by means of a sequence.

```java
public class SeqPartition implements Partition {
  int numSets; // number of sets in the partition
  public SeqPartition() { numSets = 0; }
  public int size() { return numSets; }
  public boolean isEmpty() { return numSets == 0; }
  public Locator makeSet(Object element) {
    SeqPartitionSet set = new SeqPartitionSet();
    set.setContainer(self);
    numSets++;
    SeqPartitionLocator loc = new SeqPartitionLocator(element, set);
    set.insertLast(loc);
    return loc;
  }
  public PartitionSet union(PartitionSet A, PartitionSet B)
                            throws InvalidArgumentException {
    try {
      if (((SeqPartitionSet)A).container() != self ||
          ((SeqPartitionSet)B).container() != self)
        throw new InvalidArgumentException();
    } catch (ClassCastException e) {
      throw new InvalidArgumentException();
    }
    if (A.size() < B.size()) {
      Set temp = A;
      A = B;
      B = temp;
    }
    Enumeration enumB = B.positions();
    while (enumB.hasMoreElements()) {
      SeqPartitionLocator elem = (SeqPartitionLocator)
                         ((Position)enumB.nextElement()).element();
      elem.newOwnerSet(A);
      A.insertLast(elem);
    }
    numSets--;
    return A;
  }
  ...
```

Code Fragment 12.2: Class SeqPartition in the Java implementation of a partition by means of a sequence (continues in Code Fragment 12.3).

. . .

```java
    public PartitionSet find(Locator l) throws InvalidLocatorException {
      try {
        if (((SeqPartitionLocator) l).container() != self)
          throw new InvalidLocatorException();
        return ((SeqPartitionLocator) l).getOwnerSet();
      } catch (ClassCastException e) {
        throw new InvalidLocatorException();
      }
    }
  }


class SeqPartitionLocator implements Locator {
  private Object data;
  private SeqPartitionSet ownerSet;
  public SeqPartitionLocator(Object d, SeqPartitionSet s) {
    data = d;
    ownerSet = s;
  }
  public Object element() throws InvalidLocatorException {
    return data;
  }
  public Object key() throws InvalidLocatorException {
    return null; // not used
  }
  public SeqPartition container() throws InvalidLocatorException {
    return ownerSet.container();
  }
  public SeqPartitionSet getOwnerSet() {
    return ownerSet;
  }
  public void newOwnerSet(SeqPartitionSet c) {
    ownerSet = c;
  }
}
```

Code Fragment 12.3: Method find of class SeqPartition and class SeqPartitionLocator in the Java implementation of a partition by means of a sequence.

In the sequence-based implementation of a partition, each find operation takes worst-case $O(1)$ time. In the next section, we show a tree-based implementation of a partition that does not guarantee constant-time find operations, but has amortized time better than $O(\log n)$ per operation.

12.1.5 A Tree-Based Partition Implementation ★

An alternative data structure for a partition with n elements uses a collection of trees to store the elements in sets, where each tree is associated with a different set. (See Figure 12.5.) In particular, we implement a tree T with a linked data structure, where each node u of T is represented by an object holding two references:

- A reference element to an element of the set associated with T
- A reference parent pointing to the object associated with the parent node of u, if node u is not the root, and to the object itself, if u is the root.

As with our sequence-based implementation, the objects associated with nodes serve as the locators for the elements in the partition. In this case, however, we identify the "name" of a set to be the root of its associated tree.

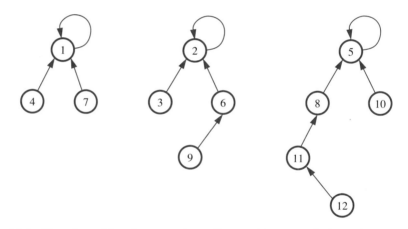

Figure 12.5: Tree-based implementation of a partition consisting of three disjoint sets: $A = \{1,4,7\}$, $B = \{2,3,6,9\}$, and $C = \{5,8,10,11,12\}$.

Note that this representation of a tree is a specialized data structure used to implement a partition, and is not meant to be a realization of the tree abstract data type (Section 5.1). Indeed, the representation has only "upward" links, and does not provide a way to access the children of a given node.

With this tree-based partition data structure, operation find for a locator (node) ℓ is performed by walking up to the root of the tree containing the locator ℓ (Figure 12.6b), which takes $O(n)$ time in the worst case. Operation union is performed by making one of the two trees a subtree of the other (Figure 12.6a), which can be done in $O(1)$ time by setting the parent reference of the root of one tree to point to the root of the other tree.

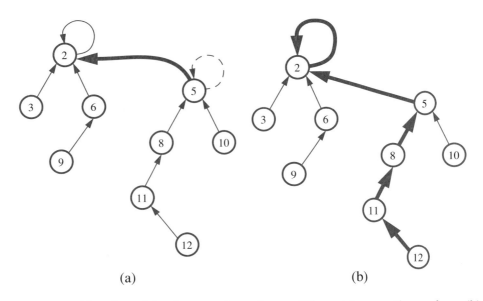

Figure 12.6: Tree-based implementation of a partition: (a) operation union; (b) operation find(ℓ), where ℓ denotes the locator for 12.

At first, this may seem to be no better than the sequence-based data structure, but we add the following simple heuristics to make it run faster.

Union-by-Size: Add a size field to each node v, which stores the size of the subtree rooted at v. In a union operation, make the tree of the smaller set a subtree of the other tree, and update the size field of the root of the resulting tree.

Path Compression: In a find operation, for each node v that the find visits, reset the parent pointer from v to point to the root. (See Figure 12.7.)

These heuristics increase the actual running time of an operation by a constant factor, but as we show below, they significantly improve the amortized running time.

Defining a Rank Function

Let us analyze the running time of a series of n union and find operations on an partition that initially consists of n single-element sets.

For each node v that is a root, we recall that we have defined v.size to be the size of the subtree rooted at v (including v), and that we identified a set with the root of its associated tree.

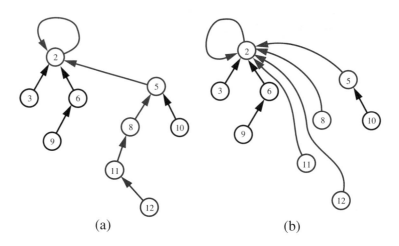

(a)   (b)

Figure 12.7: Path-compression heuristic: (a) path traversed by operation find on element 12; (b) restructured tree.

We update this size field each time a set is unioned into v. Thus, if v is not a root, then v.size is the largest the subtree rooted at v can be, which occurs just before we union v into some other node whose size is at least as large as v's. For any set-object node v, then, define the **rank** of v, which we denote as $rank(v)$, as

$$rank(v) = \lfloor \log(v.\text{size}) \rfloor.$$

Thus, we immediately get that $v.\text{size} \geq 2^{rank(v)}$. Also, since there are at most n nodes in the tree of v, $rank(v) \leq \lfloor \log n \rfloor$, for each node v.

Proposition 12.5: *If node w is the parent of node v, then*

$$rank(v) < rank(w).$$

Justification: We make v point to w only if the size of w before the union is at least as large as the size of v. Let w.size denote the size of w before the union and let $w.\text{size}'$ denote the size of w after the union. Thus, after the union we get

$$
\begin{aligned}
rank(v) &= \lfloor \log(v.\text{size}) \rfloor \\
&< \lfloor \log(v.\text{size}) + 1 \rfloor \\
&= \lfloor \log 2(v.\text{size}) \rfloor \\
&\leq \lfloor \log(v.\text{size} + w.\text{size}) \rfloor \\
&= \lfloor \log(w.\text{size}') \rfloor \\
&\leq rank(w).
\end{aligned}
$$

■

Put another way, this proposition states that ranks are ***monotonically*** increasing as we follow parent pointers up a tree. It also implies the following:

Proposition 12.6: *There are at most $n/2^s$ nodes of rank s, for $0 \leq s \leq \lfloor \log n \rfloor$.*

Justification: By the previous proposition, $rank(v) < rank(w)$, for any node v with parent w, and ranks are monotonically increasing as we follow parent pointers up any tree. Thus, if $rank(v) = rank(w)$ for two nodes v and w, then the nodes counted in v.size must be separate and distinct from the nodes counted in w.size. By the definition of rank, if a node v is of rank s, then v.size $\geq 2^s$. Therefore, since there are at most n nodes total, there can be at most $n/2^s$ that are of rank s. ■

Amortized Analysis

A surprising property of the tree-based partition data structure, when implemented using the union-by-size and path-compression heuristics, is that performing a series of n union and find operations takes $O(n \log^* n)$ time, where $\log^* n$ is the "iterated logarithm" function, which is the inverse of the ***tower-of-twos*** function $t(i)$:

$$t(i) = \begin{cases} 1 & \text{if } i = 0 \\ 2^{t(i-1)} & \text{if } i \geq 1. \end{cases}$$

That is,

$$\log^* n = \min\{i: t(i) \geq n\}.$$

Intuitively, $\log^* n$ is the number of times that one can iteratively take the logarithm (base 2) of a number before getting a number smaller than 2. Table 12.1 shows a few sample values of this function.

minimum n	$\log^* n$
1	0
2	1
$2^2 = 4$	2
$2^{2^2} = 16$	3
$2^{2^{2^2}} = 65,536$	4
$2^{2^{2^{2^2}}} = 2^{65,536}$	5

Table 12.1: Some sample values of $\log^* n$ and the minimum value of n needed to obtain this value.

As is demonstrated in Table 12.1, for all practical purposes, $\log^* n \leq 4$. It is an amazingly slow-growing function (but one that is growing nonetheless).

In order to justify our surprising claim that the time needed to perform n union and find operations is $O(n \log^* n)$, we divide the nodes into **rank groups**. Nodes v and u are in the same rank group g if

$$g = \log^*(rank(v)) = \log^*(rank(u)).$$

Since the largest rank is $\lfloor \log n \rfloor$, the largest rank group is $\log^*(\log n) = \log^* n - 1$. We use rank groups to derive rules for an amortized analysis via the accounting method. We have already observed that performing a union takes $O(1)$ time. We charge each union operation 1 cyber-dollar to pay for this. Thus, we can concentrate on the find operations to justify our claim that performing all n operations takes $O(n \log^* n)$ time.

The main computational task in performing a find operation is following parent pointers up from a node u to the root of the tree containing u. We can account for all of this work by paying one cyber-dollar for each parent reference we examine. Let v be some node along this path, and let w be v's parent (that is, $w = v.\mathsf{parent}$). We use two rules for paying for the examination of this parent reference:

- If w is the root or if w is in a different rank group than v, then charge the find operation one cyber-dollar.
- Otherwise (w is not a root and v and w are in the same rank group), charge the node v one cyber-dollar.

Since there are most $\log^* n - 1$ rank groups, this rule guarantees that any find operation is charged at most $\log^* n$ cyber-dollars. This accounts for the find operation, but we must still account for all the cyber-dollars we charged to nodes.

Observe that after we charge a node v then v will get a new parent, which is a node higher up in v's tree. Moreover, since ranks are monotonically increasing up a tree, the rank of v's new parent will be greater than the rank of v's old parent (w). Thus, any node v can be charged at most the number of different ranks that are in v's rank group. Also, since any node in rank group 0 has a parent in a higher rank group, we can restrict our attention to nodes in rank groups higher than 0 (for we will always charge the find operation for examining a node in rank group 0). If v is in rank group $g > 0$, then v can be charged at most $t(g) - t(g-1)$ times before v has a parent in a higher rank group (and from that point on, v will never be charged again). In other words, the total number, C, of cyber-dollars that can ever be charged to nodes can be bound as

$$C \leq \sum_{g=1}^{\log^* n - 1} n(g) \cdot (t(g) - t(g-1)),$$

where $n(g)$ denotes the number of nodes in rank group g.

Therefore, if we can derive an upper bound for $n(g)$, we can then plug that into the above equation to derive an upper bound for C. To derive a bound on $n(g)$, the number of nodes in rank group g, recall that the total number of nodes of any given rank s is at most $n/2^s$ (by Proposition 12.6). Thus, for $g > 0$,

$$
\begin{aligned}
n(g) \;\le\;& \sum_{s=t(g-1)+1}^{t(g)} \frac{n}{2^s} \\
=\;& \frac{n}{2^{t(g-1)+1}} \sum_{s=0}^{t(g)-t(g-1)-1} \frac{1}{2^s} \\
<\;& \frac{n}{2^{t(g-1)+1}} \cdot 2 \\
=\;& \frac{n}{2^{t(g-1)}} \\
=\;& \frac{n}{t(g)}.
\end{aligned}
$$

Plugging this bound into the bound given above for the total number of node charges C, we get

$$
\begin{aligned}
C \;<\;& \sum_{g=1}^{\log^* n-1} \frac{n}{t(g)} \cdot (t(g)-t(g-1)) \\
\le\;& \sum_{g=1}^{\log^* n-1} \frac{n}{t(g)} \cdot t(g) \\
=\;& \sum_{g=1}^{\log^* n-1} n \\
\le\;& n\log^* n.
\end{aligned}
$$

Therefore, we have shown that the total cyber-dollars charged to nodes is at most $n\log^* n$. This implies the following:

Proposition 12.7: *Let P be a partition with n elements implemented by means of a collection of trees and using the union-by-size and path-compression heuristics. In a series of* union *and* find *operations on P, starting with a collection of single-element sets, the amortized running time of each operation is $O(\log^* n)$.*

We can actually prove that the amortized running time of an operation in a series of n partition operations is $O(\alpha(n))$, where $\alpha(n)$ is a function, called the inverse of the **Ackerman function**, that asymptotically grows even slower than $\log^* n$, but proving this is beyond the scope of this book.

12.2   Divide-and-Conquer

The next technique we discuss is the divide-and-conquer technique, which is a general methodology for using recursion to design efficient algorithms. The divide-and-conquer technique involves solving a particular computational problem by dividing it into one or more subproblems of smaller size, recursively solving each subproblem, and then "merging" the solutions to the subproblem(s) to produce a solution to the original problem. We can model this approach by using a parameter n to denote the size of the original problem, and let $S(n)$ denote this problem. We solve the problem $S(n)$ by solving subproblems $S(n_1)$, $S(n_2)$, ..., $S(n_a)$, where each $n_i < n$, and then merging the solutions to these problems. In the classic merge-sort algorithm, $S(n)$ denotes the problem of sorting n numbers. Recall that in the merge-sort algorithm, we solve $S(n)$ by dividing it into two subproblems $S(\lfloor n/2 \rfloor)$ and $S(\lceil n/2 \rceil)$, recursively solving these two sorting problems, and then merging the two sorted lists produced to build a solution to $S(n)$. This merging step takes $O(n)$ time, and results in a total running time of $O(n \log n)$ for the merge-sort algorithm. As with the merge-sort algorithm, the general divide-and-conquer technique can be used to build algorithms that have fast running times.

12.2.1   Divide-and-Conquer Recurrence Relations

To analyze the running time of a divide-and-conquer algorithm we can use a ***recurrence relation***. That is, we can let a function $T(n)$ denote the running time of the algorithm, and we then characterize $T(n)$ using an equation that relates $T(n)$ to values of the function T for problem sizes smaller than n. In the case of the merge-sort procedure, we get the recurrence relation

$$T(n) = \begin{cases} b & \text{if } n < 2 \\ 2T(n/2) + bn & \text{if } n \geq 2, \end{cases}$$

for some constant $b \geq 1$, taking the simplifying assumption that n is a power of 2. In fact, throughout this section, we take the simplifying assumption that n is an appropriate power, so that we can avoid using floor and ceiling functions. Every asymptotic thing we say about recurrence relations will still be true, even if we relax this assumption, but justifying this formally involves long and boring proofs. As we observed above, one can show that $T(n)$ is $O(n \log n)$ in this case. In general, however, one will possibly get a recurrence equation that is more challenging to solve than this one. Thus, it is useful to develop some general ways of solving the kinds of recurrence equations that arise in the analysis of divide-and-conquer algorithms.

The Iterative Substitution Method

One way to solve a divide-and-conquer recurrence relation is to use the ***iterative substitution*** method, which is more colloquially known as the "plug-and-chug" method. In using this method, we assume that n is fairly large and we then substitute the general form of the recurrence for each occurrence of the function T on the right-hand side. For example, performing such a substitution with the merge-sort recurrence relation yields the equation

$$T(n) = 2(2T(n/2^2) + b(n/2)) + bn$$
$$= 2^2 T(n/2^2) + 2bn.$$

Plugging the general equation for T in again yields the equation

$$T(n) = 2^2(2T(n/2^3) + b(n/2^2)) + 2bn$$
$$= 2^3 T(n/2^3) + 3bn.$$

The hope in applying the iterative substitution method is that, at some point, we will see a pattern that can be converted into a general closed-form equation (with T only appearing on the left-hand side). In the case of the merge-sort recurrence equation, the general form is

$$T(n) = 2^i T(n/2^i) + ibn.$$

Note that the general form of this equation shifts to the base case, $T(n) = b$, when $n = 2^i$, that is, when $i = \log n$, which implies

$$T(n) = bn + bn\log n.$$

In other words, $T(n)$ is $O(n\log n)$. In a general application of the iterative substitution technique, we hope we can easily determine a general pattern for $T(n)$ and that we can also easily determine the point in which the general form of $T(n)$ shifts to the base case.

From a mathematical point-of-view, there is one point in the use of the iterative substitution technique that involves a bit of a logical "jump." This jump occurs at the point where we try to characterize the general pattern emerging from a sequence of substitutions. Often, as was the case with the merge-sort recurrence equation, this jump is quite reasonable. Other times, however, it may not be so obvious what a general form for the equation should look like. In these cases, the jump may be more dangerous. To be completely safe in making such a jump, we must fully justify the general form of the equation, possibly using induction. Combined with such a justification, use of the iterative substitution method is completely correct and an often useful way of characterizing recurrence equations. By the way, the colloquialism "plug-and-chug," used to describe the iterative substitution method, comes from the way this method involves "plugging" in the recursive part of an equation for $T(n)$ and then often "chugging" though a considerable amount of algebra in order to get this equation into a form where we can infer a general pattern.

Caution

The Recursion Tree

Another way of characterizing recurrence equations is to use the ***recursion tree*** method. Like the iterative substitution method, this technique uses repeated substitution to solve a recurrence equation, but it differs from the iterative substitution method in that, rather than being an algebraic approach, it is a visual approach. In using the recursion tree method, we draw a recursion tree R in which each node in the tree R represents a different substitution of the recurrence equation. Thus, each node in R has a value of n associated with it. In addition, we associate with each node v in R the value of the nonrecursive part of the recurrence equation for v, which in the case of divide-and-conquer recurrences corresponds to the running time needed to merge the subproblem solutions coming from the children of v. The recurrence equation is then solved by summing the values associated with each node in R. This is commonly done by first summing values across the levels of R and then summing up these partial sums for all the levels of R. This final sum is the value of the recurrence equation.

Example 12.8: *Consider the following recurrence equation:*

$$T(n) = \begin{cases} b & \text{if } n < 3 \\ 3T(n/3) + bn & \text{if } n \geq 3. \end{cases}$$

This is the recurrence equation that we get, for example, by modifying the merge-sort algorithm so that we divide a given unsorted sequence into three equal-sized sequences, recursively sort each one, and then do a three-way merge of three sorted sequences to produce a sorted version of the original sequence. Let us analyze this recurrence equation using the recursion tree method. We define a tree R such that each node in R corresponds to an application of the equation (that is, a recursive call in our algorithm). Thus, each internal node v in R has three children and has associated with it a size value n and a work bound of bn, which corresponds to the time needed to merge the subproblem solutions produced by v's children. We illustrate the resulting recursion tree R in Figure 12.8. Note the extra work performed by each recursive call sums to at most bn for each level of R. Thus, observing that the depth of R is $\log_3 n$, we have that $T(n)$ is $O(n \log n)$.

As with the iterative substitution method, there is a logical jump needed to generalize the equation bounding the work performed by each level in the recursion tree. If this value is obvious, as it was in Example 12.8, this is a reasonable jump to make, but it should always be a well-justified jump that is made. The advantage of the recursion tree method is that it provides a nice visual way of analyzing a recurrence equation and this can often make the analysis (and the sophistication of the logical jump needed) much simpler.

Overhead

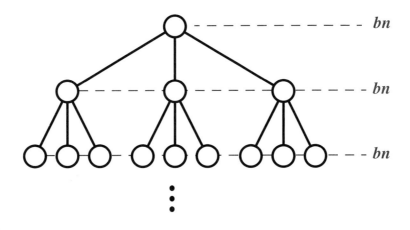

Figure 12.8: The recursion tree R used to characterize the recurrence equation $T(n)$ of Example 12.8.

The Guess-and-Test Method

Another method for solving recurrence relations is the ***guess-and-test*** technique. This technique involves first making an educated guess as to what a closed-form solution of the recurrence equation might look like and then justifying that guess, usually by induction. The educated guess itself could come from intuition gained by using either the iterative substitution method of the recursion tree method, or it could come simply because the recurrence equation looks very similar to an equation that one has seen before.

Let us say that we wish to bound a recurrence equation using the big-Oh notation; that is, we are looking for an upper bound. Then we can use the guess-and-test method as a kind of "binary search" for good upper bounds on a given recurrence relation. If the justification of our current guess fails, then it is possible that we need to use a faster-growing function, and if our current guess is justified "too easily," then it is possible that we need to use a slower-growing function. Using this technique requires our being careful in each mathematical step we take in trying to justify that a certain hypothesis holds with respect to our current "guess." Fortunately, the mathematics needed in each step is typically no more sophisticated than high school algebra.

We explore an application of the guess-and-test method in the example that follows.

Example 12.9: *Consider the following recurrence relation (assuming the base case $T(n) = b$ for $n < 2$):*

$$T(n) = 2T(n/2) + bn\log n.$$

This looks very similar to the recurrence relation for the merge-sort routine, so we might make as our first guess the following:

First guess: $T(n) \le cn\log n,$

for some constant $c \ge 1$. We can choose c large enough to make this true for the base case, certainly, so consider the case when $n \ge 2$. If we assume our first guess as an inductive hypothesis that is true for input sizes smaller than n, then we have

$$
\begin{aligned}
T(n) &= 2T(n/2) + bn\log n \\
&\le 2(c(n/2)\log(n/2)) + bn\log n \\
&= cn(\log n - \log 2) + bn\log n \\
&= cn\log n - cn + bn\log n.
\end{aligned}
$$

But there is no way that we can make this last line less than or equal to $cn\log n$ for $n \ge 2$. Thus, this first guess was not sufficient. Let us therefore try

Better guess: $T(n) \le cn\log^2 n,$

for some constant $c \ge 1$. We can again choose c large enough to make this true for the base case, so consider the case when $n \ge 2$. If we assume this guess as an inductive hypothesis that is true for input sizes smaller then n, then we have

$$
\begin{aligned}
T(n) &= 2T(n/2) + bn\log n \\
&\le 2(c(n/2)\log^2(n/2)) + bn\log n \\
&= cn(\log^2 n - 2\log n + 1) + bn\log n \\
&= cn\log^2 n - 2cn\log n + cn + bn\log n \\
&\le cn\log^2 n,
\end{aligned}
$$

provided $c \ge b$. Thus, we have shown that $T(n)$ is indeed $O(n\log^2 n)$ in this case.

The guess-and-test method has the advantage of not having any logical jumps needed in order to characterize a recurrence equation. Thus, it is one of the more mathematically sound methods for solving recurrence equations. We must take care, however, in using this method. Just because one inductive hypothesis for $T(n)$ does not work, that does not necessarily imply that another one proportional to this one will not work.

Caution

Example 12.10: *Consider the following recurrence relation (assuming the base case $T(n) = b$ for $n < 2$):*

$$T(n) = 2T(n/2) + \log n.$$

This recurrence is the running time for the bottom-up heap construction discussed in Section 6.3.4, which we have shown is $O(n)$. Nevertheless, if we try to prove this fact with the most straightforward inductive hypothesis, we will run into some difficulties. In particular, consider the following:

First guess: $T(n) \leq cn$,

for some constant $c \geq 1$. We can choose c large enough to make this true for the base case, certainly, so consider the case when $n \geq 2$. If we assume this guess as an inductive hypothesis that is true for input sizes smaller than n, then we have

$$
\begin{aligned}
T(n) &= 2T(n/2) + \log n \\
&\leq 2(c(n/2)) + \log n \\
&= cn + \log n.
\end{aligned}
$$

But there is no way that we can make this last line less than or equal to cn for $n \geq 2$. Thus, this first guess was not sufficient, even though $T(n)$ is indeed $O(n)$. Still, we can show this fact is true by using

Better guess: $T(n) \leq c(n - \log n)$,

for some constant $c \geq 1$. We can again choose c large enough to make this true for the base case; in fact, we can show that it is true any time $n < 8$. So consider the case when $n \geq 8$. If we assume this guess as an inductive hypothesis that is true for input sizes smaller than n, then we have

$$
\begin{aligned}
T(n) &= 2T(n/2) + \log n \\
&\leq 2c((n/2) - \log(n/2)) + \log n \\
&= cn - 2c \log n + 2c + \log n \\
&= c(n - \log n) - c \log n + 2c + \log n \\
&\leq c(n - \log n),
\end{aligned}
$$

provided $c \geq 3$ and $n \geq 8$. Thus, we have shown that $T(n)$ is indeed $O(n)$ in this case.

The guess-and-test method can be used to establish either an upper or lower bound for the asymptotic complexity of a recurrence equation. Even so, as the above example demonstrates, it requires that we have developed some skill with induction. It also requires that we have gained experience and intuition about recurrence equations in general, which requires some usage of other methods for solving recurrence equations.

The Master Method

Each of the methods we have described so far for solving recurrence relations is ad hoc, and each requires a certain amount of mathematical sophistication in order to be used effectively. There is, nevertheless, one method for solving divide-and-conquer recurrence relations that is quite general. It is the **master method**. The master method is a "cook-book" method for determining the asymptotic character-ization of a wide variety of recurrence relations. Namely, it is used for recurrence relations of the form

$$T(n) = \begin{cases} c & \text{if } n < d \\ aT(n/b) + f(n) & \text{if } n \geq d, \end{cases}$$

where $c \geq 1$ and $d \geq 1$ are integer constants, $a \geq 1$ and $b > 1$ are real constants, and $f(n)$ is a real function that is positive for $n \geq d$. Such a recurrence equation would arise in the analysis of a divide-and-conquer algorithm that divides a given problem into a subproblems of size at most n/b each, solves each subproblem recursively, and then "merges" the subproblem solutions into a solution to the entire problem. The function $f(n)$, in this equation, denotes the total additional time needed to divide the problem into subproblems and merge the subproblem solutions into a solution to the entire problem. Each of the recurrence equations given above uses this form, as do each of the recurrence equations used to analyze divide-and-conquer algorithms given earlier in this book. Thus, it is indeed a general form for divide-and-conquer recurrence relations.

The master method for solving such recurrence equations involves simply writing down the answer based on whether one of the three cases applies. Each case is distinguished by comparing $f(n)$ to the special function $n^{\log_b a}$ (we will show later why this special function is so important).

1. If there is a small constant $\varepsilon > 0$ such that $f(n)$ is $O(n^{\log_b a - \varepsilon})$, then $T(n)$ is $\Theta(n^{\log_b a})$.

2. If there is a constant $k \geq 0$ such that $f(n)$ is $\Theta(n^{\log_b a} \log^k n)$, then $T(n)$ is $\Theta(n^{\log_b a} \log^{k+1} n)$.

3. If there are small constants $\varepsilon > 0$ and $\delta < 1$ such that $f(n)$ is $\Omega(n^{\log_b a + \varepsilon})$ and $af(n/b) \leq \delta f(n)$, for $n \geq d$, then $T(n)$ is $\Theta(f(n))$.

Case 1 characterizes the situation where $f(n)$ is polynomially smaller than the special function, $n^{\log_b a}$. Case 2 characterizes the situation when $f(n)$ is asymp-totically close to the special function, and Case 3 characterizes the situation when $f(n)$ is polynomially larger than the special function. We illustrate the usage of the master method with a few examples (with each taking the assumption that $T(n) = c$ for $n < d$, for constants $c \geq 1$ and $d \geq 1$).

Example 12.11: *Consider the recurrence*
$$T(n) = 4T(n/2) + n.$$
In this case, $n^{\log_b a} = n^{\log_2 4} = n^2$. Thus, we are in Case 1, for $f(n)$ is $O(n^{2-\varepsilon})$ for $\varepsilon = 1$. This means that $T(n)$ is $\Theta(n^2)$ by the master method.

Example 12.12: *Consider the recurrence*
$$T(n) = T(n/2) + 1,$$
which is the running time of a recursive version of the binary search algorithm. In this case, $n^{\log_b a} = n^{\log_2 1} = n^0 = 1$. Thus, we are in Case 2, with $k = 0$, for $f(n)$ is $\Theta(1)$. This means that $T(n)$ is $\Theta(\log n)$ by the master method.

Example 12.13: *Consider the recurrence*
$$T(n) = 2T(n/2) + n \log n,$$
which is one of the recurrences given above. In this case, $n^{\log_b a} = n^{\log_2 2} = n$. Thus, we are in Case 2, with $k = 1$, for $f(n)$ is $\Theta(n \log n)$. This means that $T(n)$ is $\Theta(n \log^2 n)$ by the master method.

Example 12.14: *Consider the recurrence*
$$T(n) = T(n/3) + n,$$
which is the recurrence for a geometrically decreasing summation that starts with n. In this case, $n^{\log_b a} = n^{\log_3 1} = n^0 = 1$. Thus, we are in Case 3, for $f(n)$ is $\Omega(n^{0+\varepsilon})$, for $\varepsilon = 1$, and $af(n/b) = n/3 = (1/3)f(n)$. This means that $T(n)$ is $\Theta(n)$ by the master method.

Example 12.15: *Consider the recurrence*
$$T(n) = 9T(n/3) + n^{2.5}.$$
In this case, $n^{\log_b a} = n^{\log_3 9} = n^2$. Thus, we are in Case 3, for $f(n)$ is $\Omega(n^{2+\varepsilon})$, for $\varepsilon = 1/2$, and $af(n/b) = 9(n/3)^{2.5} = (1/3)^{1/2} f(n)$. This means that $T(n)$ is $\Theta(n^{2.5})$ by the master method.

Example 12.16: *Finally, consider the recurrence*
$$T(n) = 2T(n^{1/2}) + \log n.$$
This equation is unfortunately not in a form that allows us to use the master method. We can put it into such a form, however, by introducing the variable $k = \log n$, which lets us write
$$T(n) = T(2^k) = 2T(2^{k/2}) + k.$$
Substituting into this the equation $S(k) = T(2^k)$, we get that
$$S(k) = 2S(k/2) + k.$$
Now, this recurrence equation allows us to use master method, which specifies that $S(k)$ is $O(k \log k)$. Substituting back for $T(n)$ implies $T(n)$ is $O(\log n \log \log n)$.

Rather than rigorously justify a proposition encapsulating the master method, we instead discuss the justification behind the master method at a high level. If we apply the iterative substitution method to the general divide-and-conquer recurrence relation, we get

$$
\begin{aligned}
T(n) &= aT(n/b) + f(n) \\
&= a(aT(n/b^2) + f(n/b)) + f(n) = a^2 T(n/b^2) + af(n/b) + f(n) \\
&= a^3 T(n/b^3) + a^2 f(n/b^2) + af(n/b) + f(n) \\
&\;\;\vdots \\
&= a^{\log_b n} T(1) + \sum_{i=1}^{\log_b n - 1} a^i f(n/b^i) \\
&= n^{\log_b a} T(1) + \sum_{i=1}^{\log_b n - 1} a^i f(n/b^i),
\end{aligned}
$$

where the last substitution is based on the identity $a^{\log_b n} = n^{\log_b a}$. Indeed, this equation is where the special function comes from. Given this closed-form characterization of $T(n)$, we can intuitively see how each of the three cases is derived. Case 1 comes from the situation when $f(n)$ is small and the first term above dominates. Case 2 denotes the situation when each of the terms in the summation above are proportional to one another, so the characterization of $T(n)$ is $f(n)$ times a logarithmic factor. Finally, Case 3 denotes the situation when the first term is smaller than the second and the summation above is a sum of geometrically decreasing terms that start with $f(n)$; hence, $T(n)$ is itself proportional to $f(n)$.

Rather than formally justifying this intuition, however, we instead give another algorithmic application of the master method.

12.2.2 Integer Multiplication

So as to demonstrate one more application of the divide-and-conquer technique and the way we characterize divide-and-conquer algorithms using recurrence relations, let us consider, in this subsection, the problem of multiplying big integers. There are a number of applications for an integer type that does not have an upper bound on the maximum number of bits used to represent integers. These applications include data security, where big integers are used to encrypt and decrypt secret messages, and geometric computing, where big integers are used in pairs to support a rational number type that does not produce any round-off errors in arithmetic operations. Indeed, in recognition of such applications, the Java package java.math includes a BigInteger class. Therefore, let us consider the situation where we represent big integers using a variable number of bits.

Given two big integers I and J that use at most n bits each, it is a straightforward exercise to derive algorithms for computing $I + J$ and $I - J$ in $O(n)$ time. In fact, binary versions of the arithmetic algorithms taught in grade school will work. Efficiently computing the product $I \cdot J$ is not so straightforward, however. A binary version of the common grade-school multiplication algorithm requires $O(n^2)$ time in the worst case (do you see why?). In this section, we show how to use the divide-and-conquer technique to derive an algorithm that is asymptotically faster than this.

Suppose we are given two n-bit big integers I and J. Let us assume that n is a power of two (and if this is not the case, assume that we pad I and J with 0's until their number of bits n, is a power of two). We can therefore divide the bit representations of I and J in half, with one half representing the ***higher-order*** bits and the other representing the ***lower-order*** bits. In particular, if we split I into I_h and I_l and J into J_h and J_l, then

$$I = I_h 2^{n/2} + I_l,$$
$$J = J_h 2^{n/2} + J_l.$$

Also, observe that multiplying a binary number I by a power of two, 2^k, is trivial—it simply involves shifting the number I in the higher-order direction by k bit positions. Thus, multiplying an integer by a power of two, 2^k, for any k that is $O(n)$, can also be performed in $O(n)$ time.

Therefore, let us focus on the problem of computing the product $I \cdot J$. Given the expansion of I and J above, we can rewrite $I \cdot J$ as

$$I \cdot J = (I_h 2^{n/2} + I_l) \cdot (J_h 2^{n/2} + J_l)$$
$$= I_h J_h 2^n + I_l J_h 2^{n/2} + I_h J_l 2^{n/2} + I_l J_l.$$

Thus, we can compute $I \cdot J$ by applying a divide-and-conquer algorithm that divides the bit representations of I and J in half, partitions the product $I \cdot J$ into four products of $n/2$ bits each (as above), recursively produces each subproduct, and then merges the solutions to these subproducts in $O(n)$ time using addition and multiplication by powers of two. We can terminate the recursion when we get down to the multiplication of two 1-bit numbers, which is trivial. Thus, this divide-and-conquer algorithm has a running time that can be characterized by the following recurrence:

$$T(n) = \begin{cases} c & \text{if } n < 2 \\ 4T(n/2) + cn & \text{if } n \geq 2, \end{cases}$$

for some constant $c \geq 1$. We can then apply the master theorem to note that the special function $n^{\log_b a} = n^{\log_2 4} = n^2$ in this case; hence, we are in Case 3 and $T(n)$ is $\Theta(n^2)$. Unfortunately, this is no better than applying the simple algorithm taught in grade school to compute $I \cdot J$.

Still, the master method gives us some insight into how we might improve this algorithm. If we can reduce the number of recursive calls, then we will reduce the complexity of the special function used in the master theorem, which is currently the dominating factor in the running time of our divide-and-conquer algorithm. Fortunately, if we are a little more clever in how we define subproblems to solve recursively, we can in fact reduce the number of recursive calls by one. In particular, consider the product

$$(I_h - I_l) \cdot (J_l - J_h) = I_h J_l - I_l J_l - I_h J_h + I_l J_h.$$

This is admittedly a strange product to consider, but it has an interesting property. When expanded out, it contains two of the products we want to compute (namely, $I_h J_l$ and $I_l J_h$) and two products that can be computed recursively (namely, $I_h J_h$ and $I_l J_l$). Thus, we can compute $I \cdot J$ as the following:

$$I \cdot J = I_h J_h 2^n + [(I_h - I_l) \cdot (J_l - J_h) - I_h J_h - I_l J_l] 2^{n/2} + I_l J_l.$$

This computation requires the recursive computation of three products of $n/2$ bits each, plus $O(n)$ additional work. Thus, it results in a divide-and-conquer algorithm with a running time characterized by the following recurrence relation:

$$T(n) = \begin{cases} c & \text{if } n < 2 \\ 3T(n/2) + cn & \text{if } n \geq 2, \end{cases}$$

for some constant $c \geq 1$. We can then again apply the master theorem to note that the special function is now $n^{\log_b a} = n^{\log_2 3}$ in this case; hence, we are in Case 3 and $T(n)$ is $\Theta(n^{\log_2 3})$, which is itself $O(n^{1.585})$. Therefore, we have designed a divide-and-conquer algorithm that is asymptotically faster than the straightforward quadratic-time method.

We can actually do even better than this so as to achieve a running time that is "almost" $O(n \log n)$, by using a divide-and-conquer algorithm called the *fast Fourier transform*, but a discussion of this method is beyond the scope of this book.

12.3   Dynamic Programming

In this section, we discuss the *dynamic programming* technique for building data structures and algorithms. This technique is similar to the divide-and-conquer technique, in that it can be applied to a wide variety of different problems. Conceptually, the dynamic programming technique is different from divide-and-conquer, however, because the divide-and-conquer technique can be easily explained in a sentence or two, and can be well illustrated with a single example. Dynamic programming takes a bit more explaining and multiple examples before it can be fully appreciated.

The extra effort needed to fully appreciate dynamic programming is well worth it, though. There are few algorithmic techniques that can take problems that seem to require exponential time and produce polynomial-time algorithms to solve them. Dynamic programming is one such technique. In addition, the algorithms that result from applications of the dynamic programming technique are usually quite simple—often needing little more than a few lines of code to describe some nested loops for filling in a table.

12.3.1 Matrix Chain-Product

Rather than starting out with an explanation of the general components of the dynamic programming technique, we start out instead by giving a classic, concrete example. Suppose we are given a collection of n two-dimensional matrices for which we wish to compute the product

$$A = A_0 \cdot A_1 \cdot A_2 \cdots A_{n-1},$$

where matrix A_i is a $d_i \times d_{i+1}$ matrix, for $i = 0, 1, 2, \ldots, n-1$. In the standard matrix multiplication algorithm (which is the one we will use), to multiply a $d \times e$-matrix A times an $e \times f$-matrix B, we compute the (i, j)th entry of the product as

$$\sum_{k=0}^{e-1} A[i,k] \cdot A[k,j].$$

This definition implies that matrix multiplication is associative, that is, it implies that $B \cdot (C \cdot D) = (B \cdot C) \cdot D$. Thus, we can parenthesize the expression for A any way we wish and we will end up with the same answer. We will not necessarily perform the same number of primitive (that is, scalar) multiplications in each parenthesization, however, as is illustrated in the following example.

Example 12.17: *Let B be a 2×10-matrix, let C be a 10×50-matrix, and let D be a 50×20-matrix. Computing $B \cdot (C \cdot D)$ requires $2 \cdot 10 \cdot 20 + 10 \cdot 50 \cdot 20 = 10,400$ multiplications, whereas computing $(B \cdot C) \cdot D$ requires $2 \cdot 10 \cdot 50 + 2 \cdot 50 \cdot 20 = 3,000$ multiplications.*

The *matrix chain-product* problem is to determine the parenthesization of the expression defining A that minimizes the total number of scalar multiplications performed. Of course, one way to solve this problem is to simply enumerate all the possible ways of parenthesizing the expression for A, determine the number of multiplications performed by each one, and then keep the parenthesization that produces the smallest number of multiplications. Unfortunately, the set of all different parenthesizations of the expression for A is equal in number to the set of all different binary trees that have n external nodes. This number is exponential in n. Thus, this straightforward ("brute force") algorithm runs in exponential time.

We can improve this performance significantly, however, by making a few observations about the nature of the matrix chain-product problem. The first observation is that the problem can be split into *subproblems*. In this case, we can define a number of different subproblems, each of which is to compute the best parenthesization for some subexpression $A_i \cdot A_{i+1} \cdots A_j$. As a concise notation, we use $N_{i,j}$ to denote the minimum number of multiplications needed to compute this subexpression. Thus, the original matrix chain-product problem can be characterized as that of computing the value of $N_{0,n-1}$. This observation is important, but we need one more in order to apply the dynamic programming technique.

The other important observation we can make about the matrix chain product problem is that it is possible to characterize an optimal solution to a particular subproblem in terms of optimal solutions to its subproblems. We call this property the *subproblem optimality* condition. In the case of the matrix chain product, we observe that, no matter how we parenthesize a subexpression, there has to be some final matrix multiplication that we perform. That is, a full parenthesization of a subexpression $A_i \cdot A_{i+1} \cdots A_j$ has to be of the form $(A_i \cdots A_k) \cdot (A_{k+1} \cdots A_j)$, for some $k \in \{i, i+1, \ldots, j-1\}$. Moreover, for whichever k is the right one, the products $(A_i \cdots A_k)$ and $(A_{k+1} \cdots A_j)$ must also be solved optimally. If this were not so, then there would be a global optimal that had one of these subproblems solved suboptimally. But this is impossible, since we could then reduce the total number of multiplications by replacing the current subproblem solution by an optimal solution for the subproblem. This observation implies a way of explicitly defining the optimization problem for $N_{i,j}$ in terms of other optimal subproblem solutions. Namely, we can compute $N_{i,j}$ by considering each place k where we could put the final multiplication and taking the minimum over all such choices. This approach results in the following equation:

$$N_{i,j} = \min_{i \le k < j} \{N_{i,k} + N_{k+1,j} + d_i d_{k+1} d_{j+1}\},$$

where we note that

$$N_{i,i} = 0,$$

since no multiplication is needed to compute a subexpression containing a single matrix. That is, $N_{i,j}$ is the minimum, taken over all possible places to perform the final multiply, of the number of multiplications needed to compute each subexpression plus the number of multiplications needed to perform the final matrix multiply.

The equation for $N_{i,j}$ looks similar to the recurrence equations we derive for divide-and-conquer algorithms, but this is only a superficial resemblance, for there is an aspect of the equation $N_{i,j}$ that makes it difficult to use divide-and-conquer to compute $N_{i,j}$. In particular, there is a *sharing of subproblems* going on that prevents us from dividing the problem into completely independent subproblems (as we would need to do to apply the divide-and-conquer technique). We can, nevertheless, use the equation for $N_{i,j}$ to derive an efficient algorithm by computing $N_{i,j}$ values in a bottom-up fashion, and storing intermediate solutions in a table of $N_{i,j}$ values. We can begin simply enough by assigning $N_{i,i} = 0$ for $i = 0, 1, \ldots, n-1$. We can then apply the general equation for $N_{i,j}$ to compute $N_{i,i+1}$ values, since they depend only on $N_{i,i}$ and $N_{i+1,i+1}$ values, which are available. Given the $N_{i,i+1}$ values, we can then compute the $N_{i,i+2}$ values, and so on. Therefore, we can build $N_{i,j}$ values up from previously computed values until we can finally compute the value of $N_{0,n-1}$, which is the number that we are searching for. The details of this *dynamic programming* algorithm are given in Code Fragment 12.4.

Algorithm MatrixChain($d_0, \ldots, d_n$):

    Input: Sequence $d_0, \ldots, d_n$ of integers

    Output: For $i, j = 0, \ldots, n-1$, the minimum number of multiplications $N_{i,j}$
        needed to compute the product $A_i \cdot A_{i+1} \cdots A_j$, where A_k is a $d_k \times d_{k+1}$ matrix

    for $i \leftarrow 0$ **to** $n-1$ **do**

        $N_{i,i} \leftarrow 0$

    for $b \leftarrow 1$ **to** $n-1$ **do**

        for $i \leftarrow 0$ **to** $n-b-1$ **do**

            $j \leftarrow i + b$

            $N_{i,j} \leftarrow +\infty$

            for $k \leftarrow i$ **to** $j-1$ **do**

                $N_{i,j} \leftarrow \min\{N_{i,j}, N_{i,k} \mid N_{k+1,j} + d_i d_{k+1} d_{j+1}\}.$

Code Fragment 12.4: Dynamic programming algorithm for the matrix chain-product problem.

Thus, we can compute $N_{0,n-1}$ with an algorithm that consists primarily of three nested for-loops. The outside loop is executed n times. The loop inside is executed at most n times. And the inner-most loop is also executed at most n times. Therefore, the total running time of this algorithm is $O(n^3)$.

Proposition 12.18: *Given a chain-product of n two-dimensional matrices, we can compute a parenthesization of this chain that achieves the minimum number of scalar multiplications in $O(n^3)$ time.*

Justification: We have shown above how we can compute the optimal *number* of scalar multiplications. But how do we recover the actual parenthesization? The method is actually quite simple. We modify the algorithm for computing $N_{i,j}$ values so that any time we find a new minimum value for $N_{i,j}$, we store, with $N_{i,j}$, the index k that allowed us to achieve this minimum. ∎

We illustrate in Figure 12.9 the way the dynamic programming solution to the matrix chain-product problem fills in the array N.

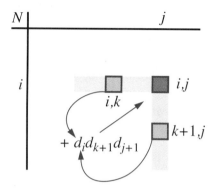

Figure 12.9: Illustration of the way the matrix chain-product dynamic-programming algorithm fills in the array N.

Now that we have worked through one complete example use of the dynamic programming method, while highlighting the important features of the problem that allowed us to derive an efficient algorithm, let us discuss the general aspects of the dynamic programming technique as it can be applied to other problems.

12.3.2   The General Technique

The dynamic programming technique is used primarily for *optimization* problems, where we wish to find the "best" way of doing something. Often the number of different ways of doing that "something" is exponential, so a brute-force search for the best is computationally infeasible for all but the smallest problem sizes. We can apply the dynamic programming technique in such situations, however, if the problem has a certain amount of structure that we can exploit. This structure involves the following three components:

Simple Subproblems: There has to be some way of breaking the global optimization problem into subproblems. Moreover, there should be a simple way of defining subproblems with just a few indices, like i, j, k, and so on.

Subproblem Optimization: An optimal solution to the global problem must be a composition of optimal subproblem solutions. We should not be able to find a globally optimal solution that contains suboptimal subproblems.

Subproblem Overlap: Optimal solutions to unrelated subproblems can contain subproblems in common.

The transitive closure reachability algorithm of Floyd and Warshall, which we discuss in Chapter 9, has all of these components. Recall that in this problem we are given a directed graph G and asked to determine, for each pair of nodes v and w, whether w is reachable from v. The Floyd-Warshall approach to this problem is first to define simple subproblems. Such subproblems are defined by assigning number labels $1, 2, \ldots, n$ to the vertices and then using an index k to define each subproblem, which is the problem of determining whether w is reachable from v using only intermediate vertices whose number labels are less than or equal to k. Second, the Floyd-Warshall algorithm is based on the concept of subproblem optimization, for we can define the reachability problem for index k as solving the subproblem for index $k - 1$ optimally and then possibly adding one more vertex. Finally, there is subproblem overlap, for the subproblem of determining the reachability of the vertex labeled k from vertex v will be reused in several different reachability problems (one for each vertex not equal to v or k). Thus, Warshall's algorithm can be thought of as a classic application of the dynamic programming technique.

Now that we have given the general components of a dynamic programming algorithm, we next give another example of its use.

12.3.3 The Longest Common Subsequence Problem

A common problem in computational genetics is to test the similarity between two strands of DNA. There are many different ways we can define the similarity between two such strands, but we can abstract a simple, yet common, version of this problem using character strings and their subsequences. Given a character string $X = x_0 x_1 x_2 \ldots x_{n-1}$, a **subsequence** of X is any string that is of the form $x_{i_1} x_{i_2} \ldots x_{i_k}$, where $i_j < i_{j+1}$, that is, it is a sequence of characters that are not necessarily contiguous but are nevertheless taken in order from X. For example, the string $AAAA$ is a subsequence of the string $CGATAATTGAGA$. The specific problem we address in this section is the **longest common subsequence** problem. In this problem, we are given two character strings, $X = x_0 x_1 x_2 \ldots x_{n-1}$ and $Y = y_0 y_1 y_2 \ldots y_{m-1}$, over some alphabet (such as the alphabet $\{A, C, G, T\}$ common in computational genetics) and are asked to find a longest string S that is a subsequence of both X and Y. The motivation from computational genetics is that two individuals are genetically related if they have a long subsequence common to their respective DNA sequences.

One way to solve the longest common subsequence problem is to enumerate all subsequences of x, and take the largest one that is also a subsequence of Y. Since each character of X is either in or not in a subsequence, there are potentially 2^n different subsequences of X, each of which requires $O(m)$ time to determine whether it is a subsequence of Y. Thus, this brute-force approach yields an exponential algorithm that runs in $O(2^n m)$ time, which is very inefficient.

We can solve the longest common subsequence problem much faster than exponential time using the dynamic programming technique. As we saw in the previous section, one of the key components of the dynamic programming technique is the definition of simple subproblems that satisfy the subproblem optimization and subproblem overlap properties. Since X and Y are character strings, we have a natural set of indices with which to define subproblems—indices into the strings X and Y. Let us define a subproblem as that of computing the value $L[i,j]$, the length of a longest string that is a subsequence of both $X[0..i] = x_0x_1x_2\ldots x_i$ and $Y[0..j] = y_0y_1y_2\ldots y_j$. This allows us to define $L[i,j]$ in terms of optimal subproblem solutions. This definition depends on which of two cases we are in. (See Figure 12.10.)

- $x_i = y_j$. In this case, we have a match between the last character of $X[0..i]$ and $Y[0..j]$. We claim that this character belongs to a longest common subsequence of $X[0..i]$ and $Y[0..j]$. To justify this claim, let us suppose it is not true. There has to be some longest common subsequence $x_{i_1}x_{i_2}\ldots x_{i_k} = y_{j_1}y_{j_2}\ldots y_{j_k}$. If $x_{i_k} = x_i$ or $y_{j_k} = y_j$, then we get the same sequence by setting $i_k = i$ and $j_k = j$. Alternately, if $x_{j_k} \neq x_i$, then we can get an even longer common subsequence by adding x_i to the end. Thus, a longest common subsequence of $X[0..i]$ and $Y[0..j]$ ends with x_i. Therefore, we can set

$$L[i,j] = L[i-1, j-1] + 1 \quad \text{if } x_i = y_j.$$

- $x_i \neq y_j$. In this case, we cannot have a common subsequence that includes both x_i and y_j. That is, we can have a common subsequence end with x_i or one that ends with y_j (or possibly neither), but certainly not both. Therefore, we can set

$$L[i,j] = \max\{L[i-1, j], L[i, j-1]\} \quad \text{if } x_i \neq y_j.$$

In order to make both of these equations make sense in the boundary cases when $i = 0$ or $j = 0$, we assign $L[i, -1] = 0$ for $i = -1, 0, 1, \ldots, n-1$ and $L[-1, j] = 0$ for $j = -1, 0, 1, \ldots, m-1$.

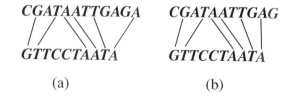

(a)   (b)

Figure 12.10: The two cases in the longest-common-subsequence algorithm: (a) $x_i = y_j$; (b) $x_i \neq y_j$.

The above definition of $L[i, j]$ satisfies subproblem optimization, for we cannot have a longest common subsequence without also having longest common subsequences for the subproblems. Also, it uses subproblem overlap, because a subproblem solution $L[i, j]$ can be used in several other problems (namely, the problems $L[i+1, j], L[i, j+1]$ and $L[i+1, j+1]$).

Turning this definition of $L[i, j]$ into an algorithm is straightforward. We start by defining the boundary cases and then iteratively build up values until we have $L[n, m]$, the length of a longest common subsequence of X and Y.

We give a pseudo-code description of how this approach results in a dynamic programming solution to the longest common subsequence (LCS) problem in Code Fragment 12.5.

Algorithm LCS(X, Y):

    Input: Strings X and Y with n and m elements, respectively

    Output: For $i = 0, \ldots, n-1$, $j = 0, \ldots, m-1$, the length $L[i, j]$ of a longest string that is a subsequence of both the string $X[0..i] = x_0 x_1 x_2 \ldots x_i$ and the string $Y[0..j] = y_0 y_1 y_2 \ldots y_j$

    for $i \leftarrow -1$ **to** $n-1$ **do**

        $L[i, -1] \leftarrow 0$

    for $j \leftarrow 0$ **to** $n-1$ **do**

        $L[-1, j] \leftarrow 0$

    for $i \leftarrow 0$ **to** $n-1$ **do**

        for $j \leftarrow 0$ **to** $m-1$ **do**

            if $x_i = y_j$ **then**

                $L[i, j] \leftarrow L[i-1, j-1] + 1$

            else

                $L[i, j] \leftarrow \max\{L[i-1, j], L[i, j-1]\}$

    return a matrix representing L

Code Fragment 12.5: Dynamic programming algorithm for the longest common subsequence (LCS) problem.

The running time of the algorithm of Code Fragment 12.5 is easy to analyze, for it is dominated by two nested for-loops, with the outer one iterating n times and the inner one iterating m times. Since the if-statement and assignment inside the loop each requires $O(1)$ primitive operations, this algorithm runs in $O(nm)$ time. Thus, the dynamic programming technique can be applied to the longest common subsequence problem to improve significantly over the exponential-time brute-force solution to the LCS problem.

Proposition 12.19: *Suppose we are given a string X of n characters and a string Y of m characters. Then we can find the longest common subsequence of X and Y in $O(nm)$ time.*

Justification: We have already explained how to compute $L[n,m]$, the ***length*** of a longest common subsequence, in $O(nm)$ time. Given the table of $L[i,j]$ values, constructing a longest common subsequence is actually quite simple. The method is to start from $L[n,m]$ and work back through the table, reconstructing a longest common subsequence from back to front. At any position $L[i,j]$, we can determine whether $x_i = y_j$. If this is true, then we take x_i as the next character of the subsequence (noting that x_i is ***before*** the previous character we found, if any), and we move next to $L[i-1,j-1]$. If $x_i \neq y_j$, then we move to the larger of $L[i,j-1]$ and $L[i-1,j]$. (See Figure 12.11.) We stop when we reach a boundary cell (with $i=-1$ or $j=-1$). This method constructs a longest common subsequence in $O(n+m)$ additional time. ∎

L	-1	0	1	2	3	4	5	6	7	8	9	10	11
-1	0	0	0	0	0	0	0	0	0	0	0	0	0
0	0	0	1	1	1	1	1	1	1	1	1	1	1
1	0	0	1	1	2	2	2	2	2	2	2	2	2
2	0	0	1	1	2	2	2	3	3	3	3	3	3
3	0	1	1	1	2	2	2	3	3	3	3	3	3
4	0	1	1	1	2	2	2	3	3	3	3	3	3
5	0	1	1	1	2	2	2	3	4	4	4	4	4
6	0	1	1	2	2	3	3	3	4	4	5	5	5
7	0	1	1	2	2	3	4	4	4	4	5	5	6
8	0	1	1	2	3	3	4	5	5	5	5	5	6
9	0	1	1	2	3	4	4	5	5	5	6	6	6

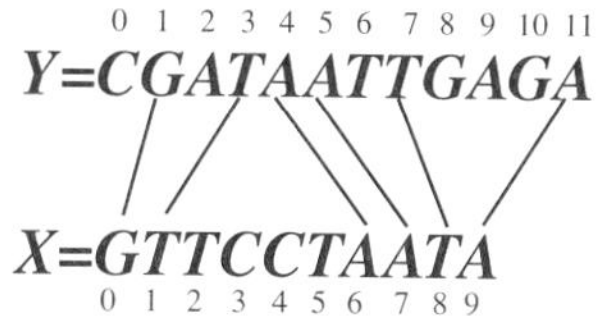

0 1 2 3 4 5 6 7 8 9 10 11
$Y = CGATAATTGAGA$

$X = GTTCCTAATA$
0 1 2 3 4 5 6 7 8 9

Figure 12.11: Illustration of the algorithm for constructing a longest common subsequence from the array L.

The dynamic programming technique is also used in the next problem we study, the 0-1 knapsack problem. As with its use in the longest common subsequence problem, its use to solve the 0-1 knapsack problem can provide significant speedups over a brute-force approach in many cases.

12.3.4   The 0-1 Knapsack Problem

Suppose an experienced hiker is about to go on a long hike through a rain forest, but she can only carry a single knapsack. Suppose further that, because of her experience, she knows the maximum total weight W that she can carry, and she knows of n different useful items that she can potentially take with her, such as a sleeping bag, a box of matches, a propane stove, and a copy of this book. Let us assume that each item i has an integer weight w_i and a benefit value b_i, which is the utility value that our hiker assigns to item i based on her experience (say as a real number scaled between 0 and 10). Her problem, of course, is to optimize the total value of the set of items that she takes with her, without going over the weight limit W. More generally speaking, her problem is an instance of the **0-1 knapsack problem**, where we are given a set S of n items, such that each item i in S has a benefit b_i and a weight w_i, and we wish to find the subset of items whose total benefit is the maximum from among all subsets of S whose total weight does not exceed some value W. This problem is called a "0-1" problem, because each item must be entirely accepted or rejected (we consider a fractional version of this problem in the next section).

We can easily solve the 0-1 knapsack problem in $\Theta(2^n)$ time, of course, by enumerating all subsets of S and keeping the one that has highest total benefit from among all those with total weight not exceeding W. This would be an inefficient algorithm, however. Fortunately, we can derive a dynamic programming algorithm for the 0-1 knapsack problem that runs much faster than this in most cases.

As with many dynamic programming problems, one of the hardest parts of designing such an algorithm for the 0-1 knapsack problem is to find a nice characterization for subproblems (so that we satisfy the three properties of a dynamic programming algorithm). To simply the discussion, number the items in S as $1, 2, \ldots, n$ and define, for each $k \in \{1, 2, \ldots, n\}$, the subset

$$S_k = \{\text{items in } S \text{ labeled } 1, 2, \ldots, k\}.$$

One possibility is for us to use this definition to define subproblems in a way reminiscent of the Floyd-Warshall algorithm by using a parameter k so that subproblem k is the best way to fill the hiker's knapsack using only items from the set S_k. This

| Caution |

would certainly be a valid subproblem definition, but it is not at all clear how to define an optimal solution for index k in terms of optimal subproblem solutions. Our hope would be that we would be able to derive an equation that takes the best solution using items from S_{k-1} and considers how to add the item k to that. Unfortunately, if we stick with this definition for subproblems, then this approach is fatally flawed. For, as we show in Figure 12.12, if we use this characterization for subproblems, then an optimal solution to the global problem may actually contain a suboptimal subproblem.

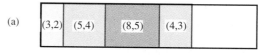

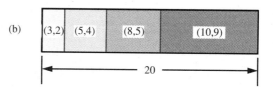

Figure 12.12: An example showing that our first approach to defining a knapsack subproblem does not work: (a) best solution with the first four items; (b) best solution with the first five items. We label each item with a benefit-weight pair, and shade each item in proportion to its benefit.

One of the reasons that defining subproblems in terms of only an index k is fatally flawed is that there is not enough information represented in a subproblem to provide much help for solving the global optimization problem. We can correct this difficulty, however, by adding a second parameter w. Let us therefore now define each subproblem as that of computing $B[k,w]$, which we define as the maximum total value of a subset of S_k from among all those subsets having total weight *exactly* w. Now we can define $B[0,w] = 0$ for each $w \leq W$ and derive the following relationship for the general case

$$B[k,w] = \begin{cases} B[k-1,w] & \text{if } w_k > w \\ \max\{B[k-1,w], B[k-1,w-w_k]+b_k\} & \text{else.} \end{cases}$$

That is, the best subset of S_k that has total weight w is either the best subset of S_{k-1} that has total weight w or the best subset of S_{k-1} that has total weight $w - w_k$ plus the item k. Since the best subset of S_k that has total weight w must either contain item k or not, one of these two choices must be the right choice. Thus, we have a subproblem definition that is simple (it involves just two parameters, k and w) and satisfies the subproblem optimization condition. Moreover, it has subproblem overlap, for the optimal way of summing exactly w to weight may be used by many future subproblems.

In deriving an algorithm from this definition, we can make one additional observation, namely, that the definition of $B[k,w]$ is built from $B[k-1,w]$ and possibly $B[k-1,w-w_k]$. Thus, we can implement this algorithm using only a single array B, which we update in each of a series of iterations indexed by a parameter k so that at the end of each iteration $B[w] = B[n,w]$. This gives us the algorithm shown in Code Fragment 12.6.

Algorithm 01Knapsack($W, w_1, \ldots, w_n, b_1, \ldots, b_n$):

> *Input:* Set of n items, such that item i has integer weight w_i, and real-number benefit b_i, and an integer W
>
> *Output:* For $w = 0, \ldots, W$, maximum benefit $B[w]$ of a subset of S with total weight w

> **for** $w \leftarrow 0$ to W **do**
> > $B[w] \leftarrow 0$
> **for** $k \leftarrow 1$ to n **do**
> > **for** $w \leftarrow w_k$ to W **do**
> > > **if** $B[w - w_k] + b_k > B[w]$ **then**
> > > > $B[w] \leftarrow B[w - w_k] + b_k$

Code Fragment 12.6: Dynamic programming algorithm for the 0-1 knapsack problem.

The running time of this algorithm is dominated by the two nested for-loops, where the outer one iterates n times and the inner one iterates at most W times. After it completes we can find the optimal value by locating the value $B[w]$ that is greatest among all $w \leq W$. Thus, we have the following:

Proposition 12.20: *Given an integer W and a set S of n items, each of which having an integer weight and a real-number benefit, we can find the highest benefit subset of S with total weight at most W in $O(nW)$ time.*

Justification: We have given an algorithm above for constructing the *value* of the maximum-benefit subset of S that has total weight at most W using an array B of benefit values. We can easily convert our algorithm into one that outputs the items in a best subset, however. We leave the details of this conversion as an exercise. ∎

In addition to being another useful application of the dynamic programming technique, this proposition states something very interesting. In particular, it states that the running time of our algorithm depends on a parameter W that, strictly speaking, is not proportional to the size of the input (the n items, together with their weights and benefits, plus the *number* W). Assuming that W is encoded in some standard way (such as a binary number), then it takes only $O(\log W)$ bits to encode W. Moreover, if W is very large (say $W = 2^n$), then this dynamic programming algorithm would actually be asymptotically slower than the brute force method. Thus, technically speaking, this algorithm is not a polynomial-time algorithm, for its running time is not actually a function of the *size* of the input.

It is common to refer to an algorithm such as our knapsack dynamic programming algorithm as being a *pseudo-polynomial time* algorithm, for its running time depends on the magnitude of a number given in the input, not its encoding size. In practice, such algorithms should run much faster than any brute-force algorithm, but it is not correct to say they are true polynomial-time algorithms. In fact, there is a theory known as **NP-completeness**, which is beyond the scope of this book, that states that it is very unlikely that anyone will ever find a true polynomial-time algorithm for the 0-1 knapsack problem.

12.4   The Greedy Method

The final algorithmic technique we consider in this chapter is the **greedy method**. This technique is used throughout the weighted graphs chapter (Chapter 10) to derive efficient algorithms for a number of optimization problems for weighted graphs. In this chapter we characterize the greedy method in terms of a general **greedy-choice** property, and we give two additional applications of its use.

12.4.1   The Greedy-Choice Property

Like the dynamic programming technique, the greedy method is applied to optimization problems. The general formula of the greedy method could not be simpler. In order to solve a given optimization problem, we proceed by a sequence of choices. The sequence starts from some well-understood starting condition, and then iteratively makes the decision that seems best from all of those that are currently possible. As we saw in Figure 12.12, this approach does not always lead to an optimal solution. But there are several problems that it does work for, and such problems are said to possess the **greedy-choice** property, which is the property that a global optimal condition can be reached by a series of locally optimal choices (that is, choices that are each the current best from among the possibilities available at the time), starting from a well-defined starting condition.

12.4.2   The Fractional Knapsack Problem

Consider again the knapsack problem, where we are given a set S of n items, such that each item i has a benefit b_i and an integer weight w_i, and we wish to find the maximum-benefit subset that does not exceed a given weight W. If we are restricted to entirely accepting or rejecting each item, then we would have the 0-1 version of this problem (for which we give a dynamic programming solution in the previous section). Let us now allow ourselves to take arbitrary fractions of some elements.

The motivation for this **fractional knapsack problem** is that we now have a knapsack that can can carry items that together have weight at most W, but we can break items into fractions arbitrarily. Consider, for example, a student that is going to an outdoor sporting event and must fill a knapsack full of foodstuffs to take along, where each candidate foodstuff is something that can be easily divided into fractions, such as soda pop, potato chips, popcorn, and pizza.

This is one place where greed is good, for we can can solve the fractional knapsack problem using the greedy algorithm shown in Code Fragment 12.7.

Algorithm FractionalKnapsack(S):

    Input: A number W and set S, with item i in S having benefit b_i and weight w_i

    Output: A subset of (possibly fractional) items from S having maximum benefit while not exceeding weight W

  for $i \leftarrow 1$ to n **do**

    Compute a ***value index*** $v_i \leftarrow b_i/w_i$ for item i.

  $K \leftarrow \emptyset$ {K is the set of the items chosen so far}

  $w \leftarrow 0$ {w is the current weight of K}

  while $w < W$ **do**

    Let i be the item remaining in S with highest value index.

    Remove an amount of item i with weight $w' \leftarrow \min\{w_i, W - w\}$ from S and add it to K. That is, either take all of item i or an amount with weight $W - w$ if adding all of i would produce a weight overflow.

    Update $w \leftarrow w + w'$.

Code Fragment 12.7: A pseudo-code description of a greedy algorithm for the fractional knapsack problem.

This algorithm can be implemented in $O(n \log n)$ time, where n is the number of items in S, if we use a heap-based priority queue (Section 6.3) to store the items in S prioritized by their value indices. To see that the fractional knapsack problem satisfies the greedy-choice property, consider an optimal set K. If there is any amount of some item i left in S (that is, in $S - K$) with value index strictly greater than some item j in K, then we could remove as much of j as is in K, and substitute an equal weight amount of i, which would increase the total value of K. Since this is not possible, there can be no item i left in S with value index greater than items in K. Therefore, have the following:

Proposition 12.21: *Given a collection S of n items, such that each item i has a benefit b_i and weight w_i, we can construct a maximum-benefit subset of S, allowing for fractional amounts, that has a total weight W in $O(n \log n)$ time.*

12.4.3   Huffman Coding

Let us consider another application of the greedy method, this time to a string compression problem (we give another string compression algorithm in Section 14.1.6). In this problem, we are given a string $X = x_1x_2 \ldots x_n$ defined over some alphabet, such as the ASCII or Unicode character sets, and we want to efficiently encode X into a small binary string Y (using only the characters 0 and 1). The method we explore in this section is to use a **Huffman code**. Standard encoding schemes, such as the ASCII and Unicode systems, use fixed-length binary strings to encode characters (with 7 bits in the ASCII system and 16 in the Unicode system). A Huffman code, on the other hand, uses a variable-length encoding optimized for the string X. The optimization is based on the use of character **frequencies**, where we have, for each character c, a count $f(c)$ of the number of times c appears in the string X. The Huffman code saves space over a fixed-length encoding by using short code-word strings to encode high-frequency characters and long code-word strings to encode low-frequency characters.

To encode the string X, we convert each character in X from its fixed-length code word to its variable-length code word using a Huffman code optimized for X, and we concatenate all these characters in order to produce the encoding Y for X. In order to avoid ambiguities when using such a variable-length code, we insist that no code word in our encoding is a prefix of another code word in our encoding. Such a code is called a **prefix code**, and it simplifies the decoding of Y so as to get back X. (See Figure 12.13.) Even with this restriction, the savings produced by using Huffman's method to define a variable-length prefix code to encode X into Y can be significant, particularly if there is a wide variance in character frequencies (as is the case for natural language text in almost every spoken language).

Huffman's algorithm for producing an optimal variable-length prefix code for X is based on the construction of a binary tree T that represents the code. Each edge in T represents a bit in a code word, with each left child edge representing a "0" and each right child edge representing a "1." Each external node v is associated with a specific character, and the string for that character is defined by the listing of edges in the path from the root of T to v. (See Figure 12.13.) Each external node v has a **frequency** $f(v)$, which is simply the frequency in X of the character associated with v. In addition, we give each internal node v in T a frequency, $f(v)$, that is the sum of the frequencies of all the external nodes in the subtree rooted at v.

Huffman's algorithm for building the tree T is based on the greedy method. It begins with each of the n given characters being the root node of a single-node tree, and proceeds in a series of rounds. In each round, the algorithm takes the two root nodes with smallest frequencies and merges them into a single tree. It repeats this process until only one node is left. (See Code Fragment 12.8.)

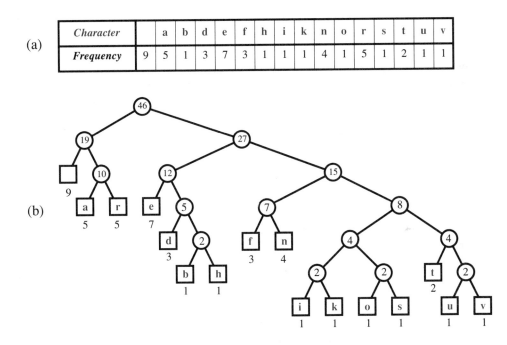

Figure 12.13: An illustration of an example Huffman code for the input string $X = $ "a fast runner need never be afraid of the dark": (a) frequency of each character of X; (b) Huffman tree T for string X. The code for a character c is obtained by tracing the path from the root of T to the external node where c is stored, and associating a left child with 0 and a right child with 1. For example, the code for "a" is 010, and the code for "f" is 1100.

Algorithm Huffman(X):

   Input: String X of length n

   Output: Coding tree for X

   Compute the frequency $f(c)$ of each character c of X.

   Initialize a priority queue Q.

   for each character c in X **do**

      Create a single-node tree T storing c.

      Insert T into Q with key $f(c)$.

   while Q.size() > 1 **do**

      $f_1 \leftarrow Q$.minKey()

      $T_1 \leftarrow Q$.removeMinElement()

      $f_2 \leftarrow Q$.minKey()

      $T_2 \leftarrow Q$.removeMinElement()

      Create a new tree T with left subtree T_1 and right subtree T_2.

      Insert T into Q with key $f_1 + f_2$.

   return tree Q.removeMinElement()

Code Fragment 12.8: Huffman coding algorithm.

Each iteration of the while loop in the Huffman coding algorithm can be implemented in $O(\log n)$ time using a heap. In addition, each iteration takes two nodes out of Q and adds one in, a process that will be repeated $n - 1$ times before there is exactly one node left in Q. Thus, this algorithm runs in $O(n \log n)$ time. A formal justification of the correctness of this algorithm is beyond the scope of this book, however. The main idea in this justification is to show that any optimal code can be converted into an optimal code in which the code words for the two lowest-frequency characters, a and b, differ only in their last bit. Given this fact, one then repeats the argument for a string X, replacing each a and b by a new character c. This gives us the following:

Proposition 12.22: *Huffman's algorithm constructs an optimal prefix code for a string of length n in $O(n \log n)$ time.*

12.5 Exercises

Reinforcement

R-12.1 What is the amortized running time of an operation in a series of n push and pop operations on an initially empty stack implemented with a Java Vector such that the capacityIncrement parameter is always maintained to be $\lceil \log(m+1) \rceil$, where m is the number of elements of the stack?

R-12.2 Characterize each of the following recurrence relations using the master method (assuming that $T(n) = c$ for $n < d$, for constants $c, d \geq 1$).

1. $T(n) = 2T(n/2) + \log n$
2. $T(n) = 8T(n/2) + n^2$
3. $T(n) = 16T(n/2) + (n \log n)^4$
4. $T(n) = 7T(n/3) + n$
5. $T(n) = 9T(n/3) + n^3 \log n$

R-12.3 Suppose we implement the tree-based partition (union-find) data structure using only the union-by-size heuristic. What is the amortized running time of a sequence of n union and find operations in this case?

R-12.4 Use the divide-and-conquer algorithm, from Section 12.2.2, to compute $10110011 \cdot 10111010$ in binary. Please show your work.

R-12.5 What is the best way to multiply a chain of matrices with dimensions that are respectively 10×5, 5×2, 2×20, 20×12, 12×4, and 4×60? Please show your work.

R-12.6 Show how to use dynamic programming to compute the longest common subsequence between the two strings "*babbabab*" and "*bbabbaaab*."

R-12.7 Let $S = \{a, b, c, d, e, f, g\}$ be a collection of objects with the following benefit-weight values:

$a{:}(12,4)$, $b{:}(10,6)$, $c{:}(8,5)$, $d{:}(11,7)$, $e{:}(14,3)$, $f{:}(7,1)$, $g{:}(9,6)$.

What is the best solution to the 0-1 knapsack problem for a sack that can hold objects with total weight 18? Please show your work.

R-12.8 Repeat the previous exercise for the fractional knapsack problem.

R-12.9 Draw a Huffman tree for the following string (remember to include the space character ' '):

```
the file is only found when it is on fire
```

Creativity

C-12.1 What is the amortized running time of the operations in a sequence of n operations $P = p_1 p_2 \ldots p_n$ if the running time of p_i is $\Theta(i)$ if i is a multiple of 3, and is constant otherwise?

C-12.2 Let $P = p_1 p_2 \ldots p_n$ be a sequence of n operations, each either a red or blue operation, with p_1 being a red operation and p_2 being a blue operation. The running time of the blue operations is always constant. The running time of the first red operation is constant, but each red operation p_i after that runs in time that is twice as long as the previous red operation, p_j (with $j < i$). What is the amortized time of the red and blue operations under the following conditions?

1. There are always $\Theta(1)$ blue operations between consecutive red operations.
2. There are always $\Theta(\sqrt{n})$ blue operations between consecutive red operations.
3. The number of blue operations between a red operation p_i and the previous red operation p_j is always twice the number between p_j and its previous red operation.

C-12.3 What is the total running time of counting from 1 to n in binary if the time needed to add 1 to the current number i is proportional to the number of bits in the binary expansion of i that must change in going from i to $i+1$?

C-12.4 Suppose we wish to implement a partial Dictionary ADT that supports the operations insertItem and findElement, using $O(\log n)$ sorted arrays $A_0, A_1, \ldots, A_{\lceil \log n \rceil}$ where the size of A_i is 2^i. Array A_i is full of elements if the ith bit of the binary expansion of n is 1, and A_i is empty otherwise.

1. Describe how to support a fast findElement(k) dictionary lookup method. What is the worst-case running time for this method?
2. Describe how to support an efficient insertItem(k, x) dictionary insertion method. What is the amortized running time for this method?

C-12.5 Suppose we implement the tree-based partition (union-find) data structure using the union-by-size heuristic and a *partial* path-compression heuristic. The partial path compression in this case means that after performing a sequence of pointer hops for a find operation, we update the parent pointer for each node u along this path to point to its grandparent. Show that the total running time of performing n union and find operations is still $O(n \log^* n)$.

C-12.6 Recalling a similar problem from Chapter 3, describe a method for implementing the Queue ADT using two stacks so that the amortized running time for dequeue and enqueue is $O(1)$, assuming that the stacks support constant time push, pop, and size methods.

C-12.7 Suppose we implement the tree-based partition (union-find) data structure using the union-by-size and path-compression heuristics. Show that the total running time of performing n union and find operations is $O(n)$ if all the unions come before all the finds.

C-12.8 Suppose we are given a weighted graph G with n vertices and m edges such that the weight on each edge is an integer between 0 and n. Show that we can find a minimum spanning tree for G in $O(n\log^* n)$ time.

C-12.9 Suppose we are given a series $P = p_1 p_2 \ldots p_n$ of operations on a priority queue whose keys are integers between 0 and n. Show that we can output the answers to all the removeMinElement operations in $O(n\log^* n)$ time. (Hint: break the series of operations up into chains of insertions separated by removeMinElement operations.)

C-12.10 Suppose we are given a collection S of n intervals of the form $[a_i, b_i]$. Design an efficient algorithm for computing the union of all the intervals in S. What is the running time of your method?

C-12.11 How can we modify the dynamic programming algorithm from simply computing the best benefit value for the 0-1 knapsack problem to computing the assignment that gives this benefit?

C-12.12 Suppose we are given a collection $A = \{a_1, a_2, \ldots, a_n\}$ of n positive integers that add up to N. Design an $O(nN)$ time algorithm for determining whether there is a subset $B \subset A$ such that

$$\sum_{a_i \in B} a_i = \sum_{a_i \in A-B} a_i.$$

C-12.13 Let P be a convex polygon (Section 15.1). A *triangulation* of P is an addition of diagonals connecting the vertices of P so that each interior face is a triangle. The *weight* of a triangulation is the sum of the lengths of the diagonals. Assuming that we can compute lengths and add and compare them in constant time, give an efficient algorithm for computing a minimum-weight triangulation of P. (Hint: there is a surprising similarity between this problem and the matrix chain-product problem.)

C-12.14 Suppose we are given a sequence $A = (a_1, a_2, \ldots, a_n)$ of numbers. Describe an $O(n^2)$ time algorithm to find the longest subsequence of A such that the numbers in this subsequence are monotonically increasing. (Hint: think about computing for each a_i the length of a longest increasing subsequence that ends with a_i.)

C-12.15 Describe an $O(n \log n)$ time algorithm for the previous problem.

C-12.16 A native Australian named Anatjari wishes to cross a desert carrying only a single water bottle. He has a map that marks all the watering holes along the way. Assuming he can walk k miles on one bottle of water, design an efficient algorithm for determining where Anatjari should refill his bottle in order to make as few stops as possible. Argue why your algorithm is correct.

C-12.17 Describe an efficient greedy algorithm for making change for a specified value using a minimum number of coins, assuming there are four denominations of coins (called quarters, dimes, nickels, and pennies), with values 25, 10, 5, and 1, respectively. Argue why your algorithm is correct.

Projects

P-12.1 Implement the partition (union-find) ADT using the tree-based approach with the union-by-size and path-compression heuristics.

P-12.2 Design and implement a big integer package supporting the four basic arithmetic operations.

P-12.3 Design and implement dynamic programming and greedy methods for solving the longest common subsequence (LCS) problem. Run experiments comparing the running times of these two methods to the quality of the solutions they produce.

P-12.4 Implement an algorithm that can take any string of text and produce a Huffman code for it.

Chapter Notes

The topics discussed in this chapter come from diverse sources. Amortization has been used to analyze a number of different data structures and algorithms, but it was not a topic of study in its own right until the mid 1980's. For more information about amortization, please see the paper by Tarjan [139] or the book by Tarjan [138]. The analysis we give for the partition data structure comes from Hopcroft and Ullman [74] (see also [6]). Tarjan [137] shows that a sequence of n union and find operations, implemented as described in this chapter, can be performed in $O(n\alpha(n))$ time, where $\alpha(n)$ is the very slow growing inverse of the Ackermann function, and this bound is tight in the worst case (see also [138]). Gabow and Tarjan [54] show that one can in some cases achieve a running time of $O(n)$, however.

The divide-and-conquer technique is a part of the folklore of data structure and algorithm design. The master method for solving divide-and-conquer recurrences traces it origins to a paper by Bentley, Haken, and Saxe [23]. The divide-and-conquer algorithm for multiplying two large integers in $O(n^{1.585})$ time is generally attributed to the Russians Karatsuba and Ofman [84]. The asymptotically fastest known algorithm for multiplying two n-digit numbers is an algorithm by Schönhage and Strassen [129] that runs in $O(n\log n\log\log n)$ time.

Dynamic programming was developed in the operations research community and formalized by Bellman [19]. The matrix chain-product solution we described is due to Godbole [57]. The asymptotically fastest method is due to Hu and Shing [77, 78]. The dynamic programming algorithm for the knapsack problem is found in the book by Hu [76]. Hirchsberg [71] shows how to solve the longest common substring problem in the same time given above, but with linear space (see also [38]).

The term "greedy algorithm" was coined by Edmonds [46] in 1971, although the concept existed before then. For more information about the greedy method and the theory that supports it, which is known as matroid theory, please see the book by Papadimitriou and Steiglitz [121]. The application we gave to the coding problem comes from Huffman [80].

Chapter

13

Balanced Search Trees

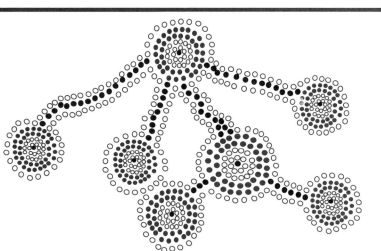

Contents

People like choices. We like to have a number of different ways of solving the same problem, so that we can explore different trade-offs and efficiencies. This chapter is devoted to the exploration of different ways of solving a problem we discussed in an earlier chapter—the implementation of an ordered dictionary (Chapter 7). Namely, we study several alternative data structures based on trees for realizing ordered dictionaries.

In Section 13.1, we introduce the concept of a multi-way search tree, which is an ordered tree where each internal node can store several items and have several children. A multi-way search tree is a generalization of the binary search tree studied in Section 7.3, and like the binary search tree, it can be specialized into an efficient data structure for dictionaries by imposing additional constraints. One of the advantages of using these multi-way trees is that they often require fewer internal nodes than binary search trees to store the items.

Section 13.2 is devoted to the discussion of $(2,4)$ trees, which are also known as 2-4 trees or 2–3–4 trees. These are multi-way search trees, such that all the external nodes have the same depth and each node stores 1, 2, or 3 keys and has 2, 3, or 4 children, respectively. The advantage of these trees is that they have algorithms for inserting and deleting keys that are simple and intuitive. Update operations rearrange a $(2,4)$ tree by means of natural operations that split and merge "nearby" nodes or transfer keys between them. A $(2,4)$ tree storing n items uses $O(n)$ space and supports searches, insertions, and deletions in $O(\log n)$ worst-case time, matching the asymptotic performance of an AVL tree (see Section 7.4).

We present red-black trees in Section 13.3. These are binary search trees whose nodes are colored "red" and "black" in such a way that the coloring scheme guarantees logarithmic height. There is a simple, yet illuminating, correspondence between red-black and $(2,4)$ trees. Using this correspondence, we motivate and provide intuition for the somewhat more complex algorithms for insertion and removal in red-black trees, which are based on rotations and recolorings. Like an AVL tree, a red-black tree storing n items uses $O(n)$ space and supports searches, insertions, and deletions in $O(\log n)$ time. The advantage that a red-black tree achieves over an AVL tree is that it can be restructured after an insertion or deletion with only $O(1)$ rotations (albeit at the expense of more complex operations).

We conclude the chapter by presenting, in Section 13.4, splay trees, which are attractive due to the simplicity of their search and update methods. Splay trees are binary search trees that after each search, insertion, or deletion, move the node accessed up to the root by means of a carefully choreographed sequence of rotations. This simple "move-to-the-top" heuristic helps this data structure to *adapt* itself to the kinds of operations being performed. One of the results of this heuristic is that splay trees guarantee that the amortized running time of each dictionary operation is logarithmic (the concept of amortized analysis is introduced in Section 12.1).

13.1   Multi-Way Search Trees

All of the data structures we discuss in this chapter are multi-way trees, that is, trees with nodes that have two or more children. In this section, we describe how multi-way trees can be used as search trees, including how multi-way trees store items and how we can perform search operations in multi-way search trees. Recall that the **items** that we store in a search tree are pairs of the form (k, x), where k is the **key** and x is the element associated with the key.

13.1.1   Definition

Let v be a node of an ordered tree. We say that v is a d-**node** if v has d children. A **multi-way search tree** is an ordered tree T that has the following properties (which are illustrated in Figure 13.1a):

- Each internal node of T has at least two children.
- Each internal node of T stores a collection of items of the form (k, x), where k is a key and x is an element.
- Each d-node v of T, with children $v_1, \ldots, v_d$, stores $d - 1$ items $(k_1, x_1), \ldots, (k_{d-1}, x_{d-1})$, where $k_1 \leq \cdots \leq k_{d-1}$.
- Let us conventionally define $k_0 = -\infty$ and $k_d = +\infty$. For each item (k, x) stored at a node in the subtree of v rooted at v_i, $i = 1, \cdots, k$, we have $k_{i-1} \leq k \leq k_i$.

That is, if we think of the set of keys stored at v as including the special fictitious keys $k_0 = -\infty$ and $k_d = +\infty$, then a key k stored in the subtree of T rooted at a child node v_i must be "in between" two keys stored at v. This simple viewpoint gives rise to the rule that a node with d children stores $d - 1$ regular keys, and it also forms the basis of the algorithm for searching in a multi-way search tree.

We use the additional convention that in a multi-way search tree, the external nodes do not store any items and serve only as "placeholders." This convention allows us to view a binary search tree (Section 7.3) as a special case of a multi-way search tree, where each internal node stores one item and has two children. At the other extreme, this convention allows a multi-way search tree to have only a single internal node storing many items. Whether internal nodes of a multi-way tree have two children or many, however, we still have the following relationship between the number of items and the number of external nodes.

Proposition 13.1: *A multi-way search tree storing n items has $n + 1$ external nodes.*

We leave the justification of this proposition as an exercise.

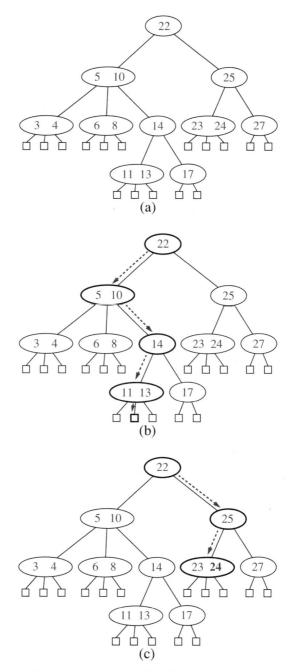

Figure 13.1: (a) A multi-way search tree T; (b) search path in T for key 12 (unsuccessful search); (c) search path in T for key 24 (successful search).

13.1.2 Searching in a Multi-way Tree

Given a multi-way search tree T, searching for an element with key k is quite simple. We perform such a search by tracing a path in T starting at the root. (See Figure 13.1(b–c).) When we are at a d-node v during this search, we compare the key k with the keys $k_1, \ldots, k_{d-1}$ stored at v. If $k = k_i$ for some i, the search is successfully completed. Otherwise, we continue the search in the child v_i of v such that $k_{i-1} < k < k_i$. (Recall that we consider $k_0 = -\infty$ and $k_d = +\infty$.) If we reach an external node, then we know that there is no item with key k in T, and the search terminates unsuccessfully.

13.1.3 Data Structures for Multi-way Search Trees

In Chapter 5, we discuss different ways of representing general trees. Each of these representations can also be used for multi-way search trees. In fact, in using a general multi-way tree to implement a multi-way search tree, the only additional information that we need to store at each node is the set of items (or keys) associated with that node.

When we use a binary tree to represent an ordered dictionary D, we simply store a reference to a single item at each internal node. In using a multi-way search tree T to represent D, we must store at each internal node v of T a reference to the ordered set of items associated with v, which may at first seem like a circular argument, since we need a representation of an ordered dictionary to represent an ordered dictionary. We can avoid any circular arguments, however, by using the *bootstrapping* technique, where we use a previous (less advanced) solution to a problem to create a new (more advanced) solution. In this case, bootstrapping consists of representing the ordered set associated with each internal node by means of a dictionary data structure that we have previously constructed (for example, a dictionary based on ordered sequence, as shown in Section 7.2.1). In particular, assuming we already have a way of implementing ordered dictionaries, we can realize a multi-way search tree by taking a tree T and storing such a dictionary at each d-node v of T. The dictionary we store at each node v is known as a *secondary* data structure, for we are using it to support the bigger, *primary* data structure.

We denote the dictionary stored at a node v of T with $D(v)$. The items we store in $D(v)$ will allow us to find which child node to move to next during a search operation. Specifically, for each node v of T, with children $v_1, \ldots, v_d$ and items $(k_1, x_1), \ldots, (k_{d-1}, x_{d-1})$, we store in the dictionary $D(v)$ the items (k_1, x_1, v_1), $(k_2, x_2, v_2), \ldots, (k_{d-1}, x_{d-1}, v_{d-1})$, $(+\infty, null, v_d)$. That is, an item (k_i, x_i, v_i) of dictionary $D(v)$ has key k_i and element (x_i, v_i). Note that the last item stores the special key $+\infty$.

With the above realization of a multi-way search tree T, processing a d-node v while searching for an element of T with key k can be done by performing a search operation to find the item (k_i, x_i, v_i) in $D(v)$ with smallest key greater than or equal to k, such as in the closestElemAfter(k) operation (see Section 7.1.2). We distinguish two cases.

- If $k < k_i$, then we continue the search by processing child v_i. (Note that if the special key $k_d = +\infty$ is returned, then k is greater than all the keys stored at node v, and we continue the search processing child v_d).
- Otherwise ($k = k_i$), then the search terminates successfully.

Consider the space requirement for the above realization of a multi-way search tree T storing n items. By Proposition 13.1, using any of the common realizations of dictionaries (Chapter 7) for the secondary structures of the nodes of T, the overall space requirement for T is $O(n)$.

Consider next the time spent answering a search in T. The time spent at a d-node v of T during a search depends on how we realize the secondary data structure $D(v)$. If $D(v)$ is realized with an array-based sorted sequence or with an AVL tree, then we can process v in $O(\log d)$ time. If instead $D(v)$ is realized by means of an unsorted sequence or a list-based sorted sequence, then processing v takes $O(d)$ time. Let $d_{\max}$ denote the maximum number of children of any node of T, and let h denote the height of T. The search time in a multi-way search tree is either $O(h d_{\max})$ or $O(h \log d_{\max})$, depending on the specific implementation of the secondary structures at the nodes of T (the dictionaries $D(v)$). If $d_{\max}$ is a constant, the running time for performing a search is $O(h)$, irrespective of the implementation of the secondary structures. Thus, the prime efficiency goal for a multi-way search tree is to keep the height as small as possible, that is, we want h to be a logarithmic function of n, the number of total items stored in the dictionary. A search tree with logarithmic height, such as this, is called a ***balanced search tree***. We discuss next in this chapter a balanced search tree that caps $d_{\max}$ at 4.

13.2   (2,4) Trees

A multi-way search tree that keeps the secondary data structures stored at each node small and also keeps the primary multi-way tree balanced is the $(2,4)$ tree, which is sometimes called 2-4 tree or 2-3-4 tree. This data structure achieves these goals by maintaining two simple properties (see Figure 13.2):

Size Property: Every node has at most four children.

Depth Property: All the external nodes have the same depth.

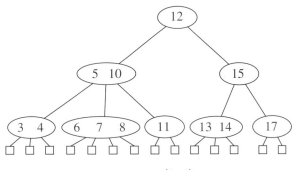

Figure 13.2: A $(2,4)$ tree.

Enforcing the size property keeps the nodes in the multi-way search tree simple. It also gives rise to the alternative name "2-3-4 tree," since it implies that each node in the tree has 2, 3, or 4 children. Another implication of this rule is that we can represent the dictionary $D(v)$ stored at each internal node v using a sequence, and still achieve $O(1)$ time performance for all operations (since $d_{\max} = 4$). The depth property, on the other hand, enforces the following bound on the height of a $(2,4)$ tree:

Proposition 13.2: *The height of a $(2,4)$ tree storing n items is $\Theta(\log n)$.*

Justification: Let h be the height of a $(2,4)$ tree T storing n items. We justify the proposition by establishing the following relationships:

$$\frac{1}{2}\log(n+1) \leq h \leq \log(n+1). \tag{13.1}$$

By the size and depth properties, the number of external nodes in T is at least 2^h and at most 4^h. In addition, by Proposition 13.1, the number of external nodes in T is $n+1$. Thus, we obtain

$$2^h \leq n+1 \leq 4^h.$$

Taking the logarithm in base 2 of each term, we get

$$h \leq \log(n+1) \leq 2h,$$

which justifies our claim (13.1). ∎

Proposition 13.2 states that the size and depth properties are sufficient for keeping a multi-way tree balanced (Section 13.1.3). Moreover, this proposition implies that performing a search in a $(2,4)$ tree takes $O(\log n)$ time, and that the specific realization of the secondary structures at the nodes is not a crucial design choice, since the maximum number of children $d_{\max}$ is a constant (4). We can, for example, use the simplest previous dictionary implementation for each secondary structure—an array-based or list-based sequence.

Maintaining the size and depth properties requires some effort after performing insertions and deletions in a $(2,4)$ tree, however. We discuss these operations next.

13.2.1 Insertion

To insert a new item (k,x), with key k, into a $(2,4)$ tree T, we first perform a search for k. Assuming that T has no element with key k, this search terminates unsuccessfully at an external node z. Let v be the parent of z. We insert the new item into node v, and add a new child w (an external node) to v on the left of z. That is, we add item (k,x,w) to the dictionary $D(v)$. We show a sequence of insertions in a $(2,4)$ tree in Figures 13.3 and 13.5. In particular, we highlight the insertion of an item with key 5 into the tree of Figure 13.3g, resulting in the tree of Figure 13.3i.

Our insertion method preserves the depth property, since we add a new external node at the same level as existing external nodes. Nevertheless, it may violate the size property. Indeed, if a node v was previously a 4-node, then it may become a 5-node after the insertion, which causes the tree T to no longer be a $(2,4)$ tree. This type of violation of the size property is called an *overflow* at node v, and it must be resolved in order to restore the properties of a $(2,4)$ tree.

Let $v_1,\ldots,v_5$ be the children of v, and let $k_1,\ldots,k_4$ be the keys stored at v. To remedy the overflow at node v, we perform a *split* operation on v, which is currently a 5-node, as follows (Figure 13.4):

- We replace v with two nodes v' and v'', where
    - v' is a 3-node with children v_1,v_2,v_3 storing keys k_1 and k_2
    - v'' is a 2-node with children v_4,v_5 storing key k_4.
- If v was the root of T, we create a new root node u. Otherwise, we let u be the parent of v.
- We insert key k_3 into u and make v' and v'' children of u, such that if v was the ith child of u, then v' and v'' become the ith and $(i+1)$st children of u, respectively.

A split operation affects a constant number of nodes of the tree and $O(1)$ items stored at such nodes. Thus, it can be implemented to run in $O(1)$ time.

As a consequence of a split operation on node v, a new overflow may occur at the parent u of v. If such an overflow occurs, it triggers in turn a split at node u. (See Figure 13.5.) A split operation either eliminates the overflow or propagates it into the parent of the current node. Hence, the number of split operations is bounded by the height of the tree, which is $O(\log n)$ by Proposition 13.2. Therefore, the total time to perform an insertion in a $(2,4)$ tree is $O(\log n)$.

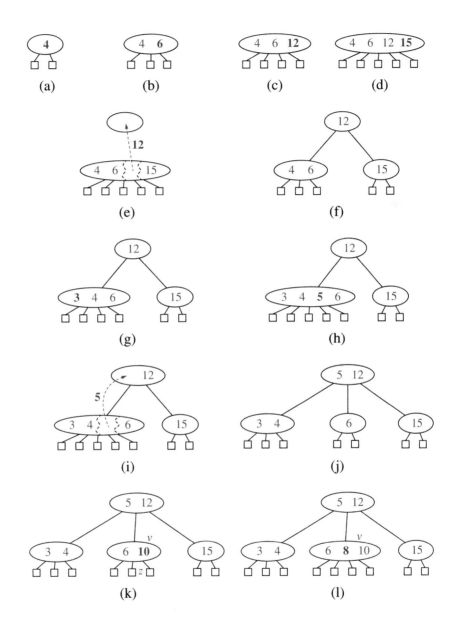

Figure 13.3: A sequence of insertions into a (2,4) tree: (a) initial tree with one item; (b) insertion of 6; (c) insertion of 12; (d) insertion of 15, which causes an overflow; (e) split, which causes the creation of a new root node; (f) after the split; (g) insertion of 3; (h) insertion of 5, which causes an overflow; (i) split; (j) after the split; (k) insertion of 10; (l) insertion of 8.

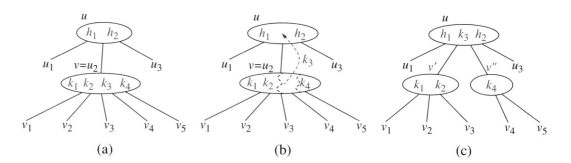

Figure 13.4: Split operation at a node of a $(2,4)$ tree: (a) overflow at a 5-node v; (b) the third key of v is inserted into the parent u of v; (c) node v is replaced with a 3-node v' and a 2-node v''.

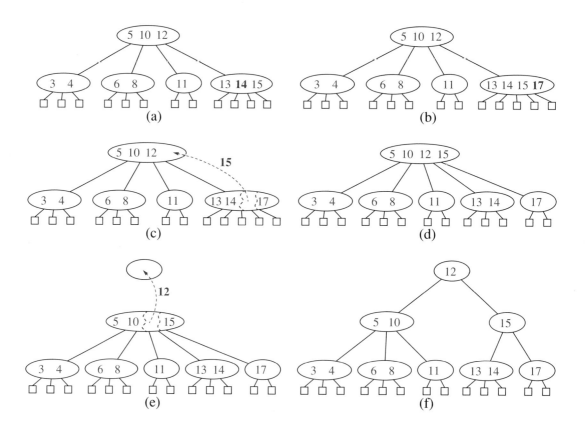

Figure 13.5: An insertion in a $(2,4)$ tree that causes a cascading split: (a) before the insertion; (b) insertion of 17, causing an overflow; (c) a split; (d) after the split a new overflow occurs; (e) another split, creating a new root node; (f) final tree.

13.2.2 Deletion

Let us now consider the deletion of an item with key k from a $(2,4)$ tree T. We begin such an operation by performing a search in T for an item with key k. Deleting such an item from a $(2,4)$ tree can always be reduced to the case where the item to be deleted is stored at a node v whose children are external nodes. Suppose, for instance, that the item with key k that we wish to delete is stored in the ith item (k_i, x_i) at a node z that has only internal-node children. In this case, we swap the item (k_i, x_i) with an appropriate item that is stored at a node v with external-node children as follows (Figure 13.6d):

1. We find the right-most internal node v in the subtree rooted at the ith child of z, noting that the children of node v are all external nodes.

2. We swap the item (k_i, x_i) at z with the last item of v.

Once we ensure that the item to remove is stored at a node v with only external-node children (because either it was already at v or we swapped it into v), we simply remove the item from v (that is, from the dictionary $D(v)$) and delete the ith external node of v.

Deleting an item (and a child) from a node v as described above preserves the depth property, for we always remove an external node child from a node v with only external-node children. However, in removing such an external node we may violate the size property at v. Indeed, if v was previously a 2-node, then it becomes a 1-node with no items after the deletion (Figure 13.6(d–e)), which is not allowed in a $(2,4)$ tree. This type of violation of the size property is called an ***underflow*** at node v.

To remedy an underflow, we check whether a sibling of v is a 3-node or a 4-node. If we find such a sibling w, then we perform a ***transfer*** operation, in which we move a child of w to v, a key of w to the parent u of v and w, and a key of u to v. (See Figure 13.6(b–c).) If v has only one sibling, or if both siblings of v are 2-nodes, then we perform a ***fusion*** operation, in which we merge v with a sibling, creating a new node v', and move a key from the parent u of v to v'. (See Figure 13.7(e–f).)

A fusion operation at node v may cause a new underflow to occur at the parent u of v, which in turn triggers a transfer or fusion at u. (See Figure 13.7.) Hence, the number of fusion operations is bounded by the height of the tree, which is $O(\log n)$ by Proposition 13.2. If an underflow propagates all the way up to the root, then the root is simply deleted. (See Figure 13.7(c–d).) We show a sequence of deletions from a $(2,4)$ tree in Figures 13.6 and 13.7.

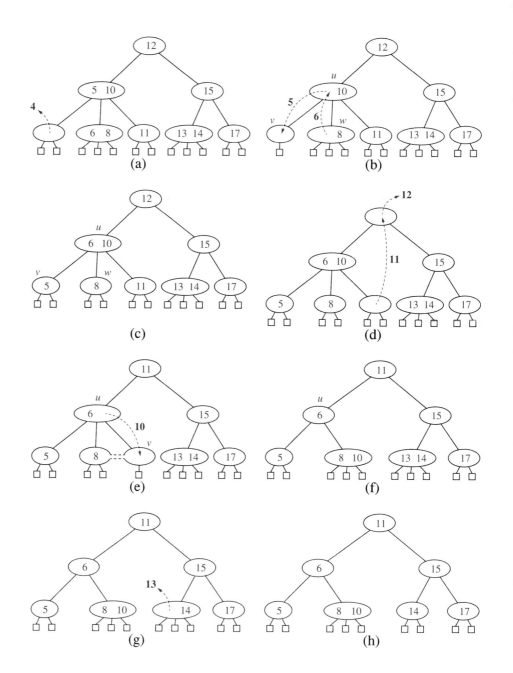

Figure 13.6: A sequence of deletions from a $(2,4)$ tree: (a) deletion of 4, causing an underflow; (b) a transfer operation; (c) after the transfer operation; (d) deletion of 12, causing an underflow; (e) a fusion operation; (f) after the fusion operation; (g) deletion of 13; (h) after deleting 13.

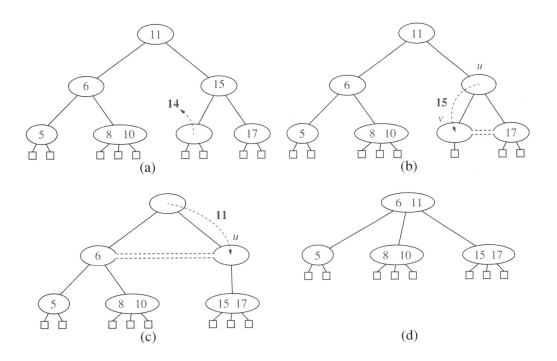

Figure 13.7: A propagating sequence of fusions in a $(2,4)$ tree: (a) deletion of 14, which causes an underflow; (b) fusion, which causes another underflow; (c) second fusion operation, which causes the root to be removed; (d) final tree.

13.2.3 Analysis

Table 13.1 shows the running times of the main operations of a dictionary realized with a $(2,4)$ tree. The time bounds in Table 13.1 are based on the following facts:

- The height of a $(2,4)$ tree storing n items is $O(\log n)$, by Proposition 13.1.
- A split, transfer, or fusion operation takes $O(1)$ time.
- A search, insertion, or deletion of an item visits $O(\log n)$ nodes.

Method	Time
findElement	$O(\log n)$
insertItem	$O(\log n)$
remove	$O(\log n)$

Table 13.1: Running times of methods of a dictionary realized by a $(2,4)$ tree.

Thus, (2,4) trees provide logarithmic-time performance for dictionary search and update operations. In addition, (2,4) trees have an interesting correspondence to the dictionary data structure we discuss next.

13.3 Red-Black Trees

A *red-black tree* is a binary search tree (see Section 7.3) with nodes colored red and black in a way that satisfies the following properties:

Root Property: The root is black.

External Property: Every external node is black.

Internal Property: The children of a red node are black.

Depth Property: All the external nodes have the same *black depth*, which is defined as the number of black ancestors minus one.

An example of a red-black tree is shown in Figure 13.8.

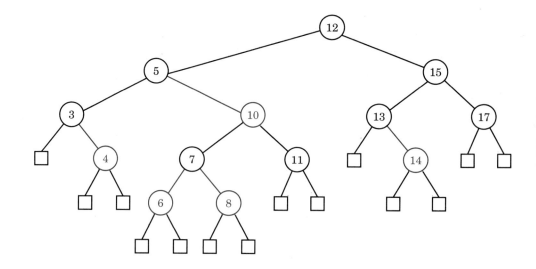

Figure 13.8: Red-black tree associated with the (2,4) tree of Figure 13.2. The external nodes of this red-black have black depth 3. We use the color blue instead of red. Also, we use the convention of giving an edge of the tree the same color as the child node.

We can make the red-black tree definition more intuitive by noting an interesting correspondence between red-black and $(2,4)$ trees, as illustrated in Figure 13.9. Namely, given a red-black tree, we can construct a corresponding $(2,4)$ tree by merging every red node v into its parent and storing the item from v at its parent. Conversely, we can transform any $(2,4)$ tree into a corresponding red-black tree by coloring each node black and performing the following transformation for each internal node v:

- If v is a 2-node, then keep the (black) children of v as is.

- If v is a 3-node, then create a new red node w, give v's first two (black) children to w, and make w and v's third child be the two children of v.

- If v is a 4-node, then create two new red nodes w and z, give v's first two (black) children to w, give v's last two (black) children to z, and make w and z be the two children of v.

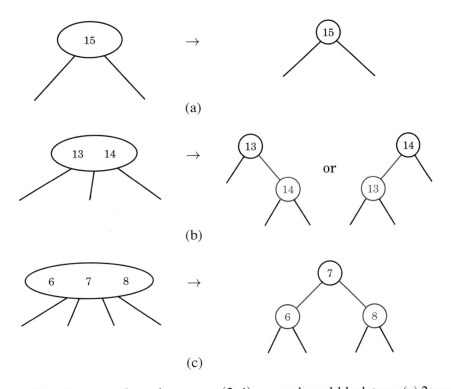

Figure 13.9: Correspondence between a $(2,4)$ tree and a red-black tree: (a) 2-node; (b) 3-node; (c) 4-node.

The correspondence between $(2,4)$ trees and red-black trees provides important intuition that we will use throughout our discussion of how to perform updates in red-black trees. In fact, the update algorithms for red-black trees are mysteriously complex without this intuition. The correspondence between $(2,4)$ trees and red-black trees also gives us the following property for red-black trees:

Proposition 13.3: *The height of a red-black tree storing n items is $\Theta(\log n)$.*

Justification: Let T be a red-black tree storing n items, and let h be the height of T. We justify this proposition by establishing the following fact

$$\log(n+1) \leq h \leq 2\log(n+1).$$

Let d be the common black depth of all the external nodes of T. Let T' be the $(2,4)$ tree associated with T, and let h' be the height of T'. We know that $h' = d$. Hence, by Proposition 13.2, $d = h' \leq \log(n+1)$. By the internal node property, $h \leq 2d$. Thus, we obtain $h \leq 2\log(n+1)$. The other inequality, $\log(n+1) \leq h$, follows from Proposition 5.10 and the fact that T has n internal nodes. ∎

We assume that a red-black tree is realized by means of a linked structure for binary trees (Section 5.4.2), in which we store a dictionary item and a color bit at each node. Thus the space requirement for a red-black tree storing n keys is $O(n)$. The algorithm for searching in a red-black tree T is the same as that for a standard binary search tree (Section 7.3). Thus, the running time for searching in a red-black tree is $O(\log n)$.

13.3.1 Insertion

Consider now the insertion of an element x with key k into a red-black tree T, keeping in mind the correspondence between T and its associated $(2,4)$ tree T' and the insertion algorithm for T'. The insertion algorithm initially proceeds as in a binary search tree (Section 7.3.2). Namely, we search for k in T until we reach an external node of T, and we replace this node with an internal node z, storing (k,x) and having two external-node children. We color z red and its children black. This action corresponds to inserting (k,x) into a node of the $(2,4)$ tree T' with external children. In addition, this action preserves the root, external and depth properties of T, but it may violate the internal property. Indeed, if the parent v of z is red, then we have a parent and a child (namely, v and z) that are both red. Note that by the root property, v cannot be the root of T, and by the internal property (which was previously satisfied), the parent u of v must be black. Since z and its parent are red, but z's grandparent u is black, we call this violation of the internal property a *double red* at node z.

To remedy a double red, we consider two cases.

Case 1: *The Sibling w of v is Black.* (See Figure 13.10.) In this case, the double red denotes the fact that we have created in our red-black tree T a malformed replacement for a corresponding 4-node of the $(2,4)$ tree T', which has as its children the four black children of u, v, and z. Our malformed replacement has one red node (v) that is the parent of another red node (z), while we want it to have the two red nodes as siblings instead. To fix this problem, we perform a *restructuring* of T. The restructuring begins by performing operation Rotate(z), which consists of the following steps (see again Figure 13.10; this operation is also discussed in Section 7.4):

- Take node z, its parent v, and grandparent u, and temporarily relabel them as a, b, and c, in left-to-right order, so that a, b, and c will be visited in this order by an inorder tree traversal.

- Replace the grandparent u with the node labeled b, and make nodes a and c the children of b, keeping inorder relationships unchanged.

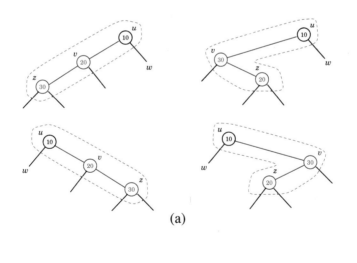

(a)

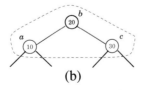

(b)

Figure 13.10: Restructuring a red-black tree to remedy a double red: (a) the four configurations for u, v, and z before restructuring; (b) after restructuring.

After performing the Rotate(z) operation, we color b black and we color a and c red. Thus, the restructuring eliminates the double red problem. Examples of restructurings are shown in Figures 13.12 and 13.13.

Case 2: ***The Sibling w of v is Red.*** (See Figure 13.11.) In this case, the double red denotes an overflow in the corresponding $(2,4)$ tree T. To fix the problem, we perform the equivalent of a split operation. Namely, we do a ***recoloring***: we color v and w black and their parent u red (unless u is the root, in which case, it is colored black). It is possible that, after such a recoloring, the double red problem reappears, albeit higher up in the tree T, since u may have a red parent. If the double red problem reappears at u, then we repeat the consideration of the two cases at u. Thus, a recoloring either eliminates the double red problem at node z, or propagates it to the grandparent u of z. We continue going up T performing recolorings until we finally resolve the double red problem (with either a final recoloring or a restructuring). Thus, the number of recolorings caused by an insertion is no more than half the height of tree T, that is, no more than $\log(n+1)$ by Proposition 13.3.

Figures 13.12 and 13.13 show a sequence of insertion operations.

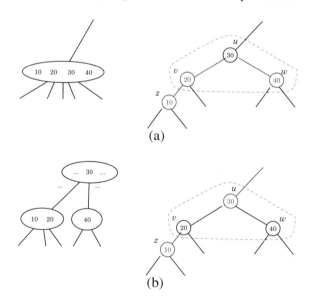

Figure 13.11: Recoloring a red-black tree to remedy the double red problem: (a) configuration before recoloring and corresponding 5-node in the associated $(2,4)$ tree before the split; (b) after the recoloring (and corresponding nodes in the associated $(2,4)$ tree after the split).

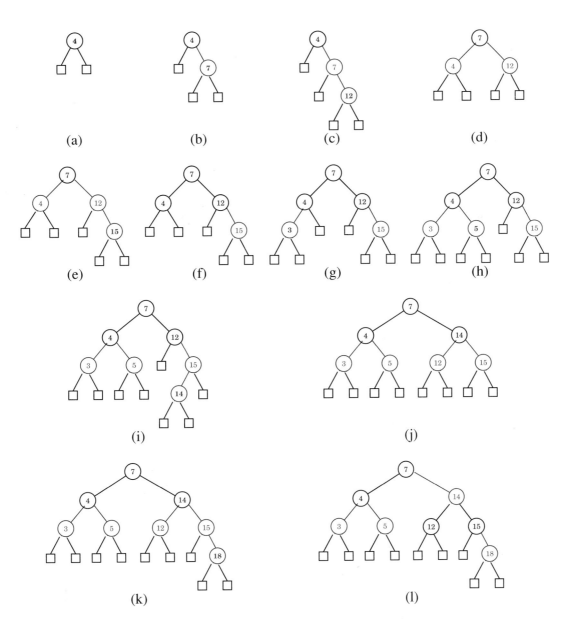

Figure 13.12: A sequence of insertions in a red-black tree: (a) initial tree; (b) insertion of 7; (c) insertion of 12, which causes a double-red; (d) after restructuring; (e) insertion of 15, which causes a double-red; (f) after recoloring (the root remains black); (g) insertion of 3; (h) insertion of 5; (i) insertion of 14, which causes a double-red; (j) after restructuring; (k) insertion of 18, which causes a double-red; (l) after recoloring. Continued in Figure 13.13.

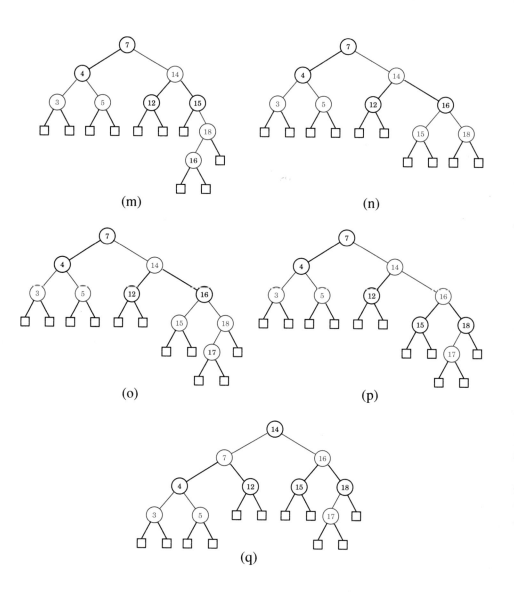

Figure 13.13: A sequence of insertions in a red-black tree (continued from Figure 13.12): (m) insertion of 16, which causes a double-red; (n) after restructuring; (o) insertion of 17, which causes a double-red; (p) after recoloring there is again a double-red, to be handled by a restructuring; (r) after restructuring.

Code Fragment 13.1 shows a Java implementation of the insertion algorithm for a red-black tree. It reuses the code for a binary search tree, and accesses the structure of that tree using the position pattern.

```java
public void insertItem(Object key, Object element)
  throws InvalidKeyException  {
  super.insertItem(key, element); // may throw an InvalidKeyException
  Position posZ = actionPos; // start at the insertion position
  T.replace(posZ, new RBTItem(key, element, Red));
  if(T.isRoot(posZ))
    setBlack(posZ);
  else
    remedyDoubleRed(posZ);
}
protected void remedyDoubleRed(Position posZ)  {
  Position posV = T.parent(posZ);
  if(T.isRoot(posV))
    return;
  if(!isPosRed(posV))
    return;
  // we have a double red: posZ and posV
  if(!isPosRed(T.sibling(posV)))  { // Case 1: restructuring
    posV = ((RestructurableNodeBinaryTree) T).restructure(posZ);
    setBlack(posV);
    setRed(T.leftChild(posV));
    setRed(T.rightChild(posV));
  }
  else  { // Case 2: recoloring
    setBlack(posV);
    setBlack(T.sibling(posV));
    Position posU = T.parent(posV);
    if(T.isRoot(posU))
      return;
    setRed(posU);
    remedyDoubleRed(posU);
  }
}
```

Code Fragment 13.1: A Java implementation of the insertItem method of the dictionary ADT in the Java implementation of a red-black tree. Note how it performs the two cases in red-black tree insertion algorithm.

The two cases for red-black tree insertion provide an additional interesting property of red-black trees. Namely, since the Case 1 action eliminates the double-red problem with a single restructuring of the binary search tree and the Case 2 action performs no restructuring operations, at most one restructuring is needed for a red-black tree in an insertion operation. By the above analysis and the fact that a restructuring or recoloring takes $O(1)$ time, we have the following:

Proposition 13.4: *The insertion of an item in a red-black tree storing n items can be done in $O(\log n)$ time, and requires at most $O(\log n)$ recolorings and one restructuring (a* Rotate *operation).*

13.3.2   Deletion

Suppose now that we are given a key k and are asked to remove an item with key k from a red-black tree T. Removing such an item initially proceeds as for a binary search tree (Section 7.3.2). First, we search for a node u storing such an item. If node u does not have an external child, we find the internal node v following u in the inorder traversal of T, move the item at v to u, and then perform the deletion at v. Thus, we may consider only the deletion of an item with key k stored at a node v with an external child w. Also, as we did for insertions, we keep in mind the correspondence between red-black tree T and its associated $(2,4)$ tree T' (and the deletion algorithm for T').

To delete the item with key k from a node v of T with an external child w we proceed as follows. Let r be the sibling of w and x be the parent of v. We remove nodes v and w, and make r a child of x. If r is red, we color it black and we are done. If r is instead black, then, to preserve the depth property, we give r a fictitious **double black** color. We now have a violation of the coloring scheme of T, which we call the double black problem. A double black in T denotes an underflow in the corresponding $(2,4)$ tree T'. Recall that x is the parent of the double black node r. To remedy the double-black problem at r, we consider three cases.

Case 1: *The Sibling y of r Is Black and Has a Red Child z.* (See Figure 13.14.)
   Resolving this case corresponds to a transfer operation in the $(2,4)$ tree T'. We perform a **restructuring** by means of an operation Rotate(z). Recall that the operation Rotate(z) takes the node z, its parent y, and grandparent x, labels them temporarily left-to-right as a, b, and c, and replaces x with the node labeled b, making it the parent of the other two. (See also the description of Rotate in Section 7.4.) We color a and c black, give b the former color of x, and color r black. This restructuring eliminates the double black problem. Hence, at most one restructuring is performed in a deletion operation in this case.

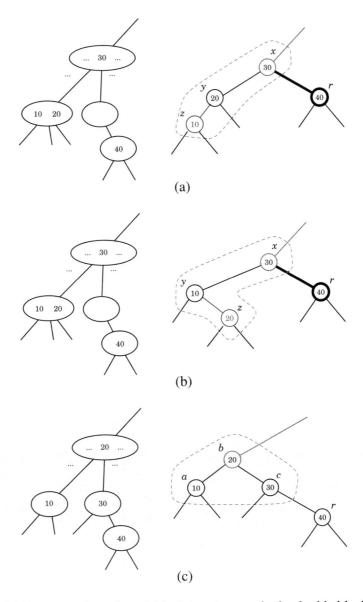

Figure 13.14: Restructuring of a red-black tree to remedy the double black problem: (a) and (b) configurations before the restructuring, where r is a right child and the associated nodes in the corresponding $(2, 4)$ tree before the transfer (two other symmetric configurations where r is a left child are possible); (c) configuration after the restructuring and the associated nodes in the corresponding $(2, 4)$ tree after the transfer. The grey color for node x in parts (a) and (b) and for node b in part (c) denotes the fact that this node may be colored either red or black.

Case 2: *The Sibling y of r Is Black and Both Children of y are Black.* (See Figures 13.15 and 13.16.) Resolving this case corresponds to a fusion operation in the corresponding $(2,4)$ tree T'. We do a ***recoloring***; we color r black, we color y red, and, if x is red, we color it black (Figure 13.15), else, we color x ***double black*** (Figure 13.16). Hence, after this recoloring, the double black problem may reappear at the parent x of r. (See Figure 13.16.) That is, this recoloring either eliminates the double black problem or propagates it into the parent of the current node. We then repeat a consideration of these three cases at the parent. Thus, since Case 1 performs a restructuring operation and stops (and, as we will soon see, Case 3 does so as well), the number of recolorings caused by a deletion is no more than $\log(n+1)$.

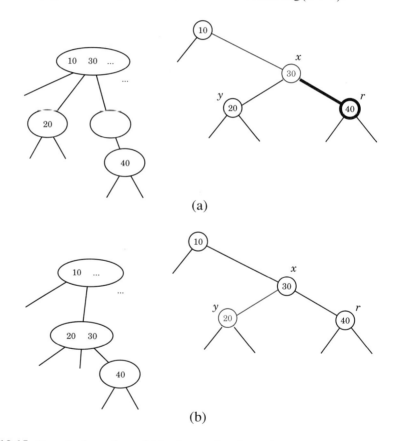

Figure 13.15: Recoloring of a red-black tree that fixes the double black problem: (a) before the recoloring and corresponding nodes in the associated $(2,4)$ tree before the fusion (other similar configurations are possible); (b) after the recoloring and corresponding nodes in the associated $(2,4)$ tree after the fusion.

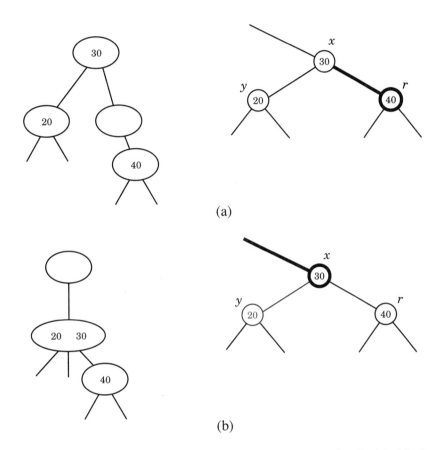

(a)

(b)

Figure 13.16: Recoloring of a red-black tree that propagates the double black problem: (a) configuration before the recoloring and corresponding nodes in the associated (2,4) tree before the fusion (other similar configurations are possible); (b) configuration after the recoloring and corresponding nodes in the associated (2,4) tree after the fusion.

Case 3: ***The Sibling y of r Is Red.*** (See Figure 13.17.) In this case, we perform an ***adjustment*** operation, as follows. If y is the right child of x, let z be the right child of y, else, let z be the left child of y. Execute operation Rotate(z), which makes y the parent of x. Color y black and x red. An adjustment corresponds to choosing a different representation of a 3-node in the $(2,4)$ tree T'. After the adjustment operation, the sibling of r is black, and either Case 1 or Case 2 applies, with a different meaning of x and y. Note that if Case 2 applies, the double-black problem cannot reappear. Thus, to complete Case 3 we make one more application of either Case 1 or Case 2 above and we are done. Therefore, at most one adjustment is performed in a deletion operation.

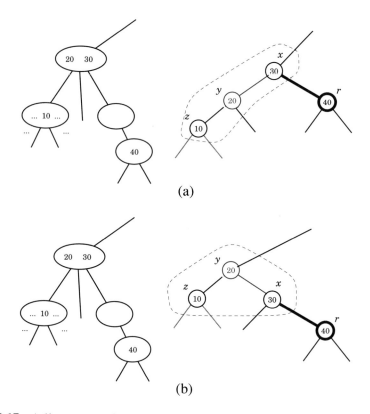

Figure 13.17: Adjustment of a red-black tree in the presence of a double black problem: (a) configuration before the adjustment and corresponding nodes in the associated $(2,4)$ tree (a symmetric configuration is possible); (b) configuration after the adjustment with the same corresponding nodes in the associated $(2,4)$ tree.

From the above algorithm description, we see that the tree updating needed after a deletion involves an upward march in the tree T, while performing at most a constant amount of work (in a restructuring, recoloring, or adjustment) per node. Thus, since any changes we make at a node in T during this upward march takes $O(1)$ time (because it affects a constant number of nodes), we have the following:

Proposition 13.5: *The algorithm for deleting an item from a red-black tree with n items takes $O(\log n)$ time and performs $O(\log n)$ recolorings and at most one adjustment and one restructuring. Thus, it performs at most three* Rotate *operations.*

We show in Figures 13.18 and 13.19 a sequence of deletion operations on a red-black tree. We illustrate Case 1 restructurings in Figure 13.18(c–d). We illustrate Case 2 recolorings at several places in Figures 13.18 and 13.19. Finally, in Figure 13.19(i–j) we show an example of a Case 3 adjustment.

13.3.3 Analysis

Table 13.2 summarizes the running times of the main operations of a dictionary realized by means of a red-black tree. The running times for the fundamental dictionary operations are all logarithmic in the number of elements being stored in the dictionary.

Method	Time
findElement	$O(\log n)$
insertItem	$O(\log n)$
remove	$O(\log n)$

Table 13.2: Running times of the main methods of a dictionary realized by a red-black tree. We denote the number of items in the dictionary at the time the method is executed with n. The space used is $O(n)$.

Thus, a red-black tree achieves logarithmic worst-case running times for both searching and updating in a dictionary. The red-black tree data structure is slightly more complicated than an AVL tree or even its corresponding $(2,4)$ tree. Even so, a red-black tree has the conceptual advantage that only a constant number of restructuring operations are ever needed to restore the balance in a red-black tree after an update.

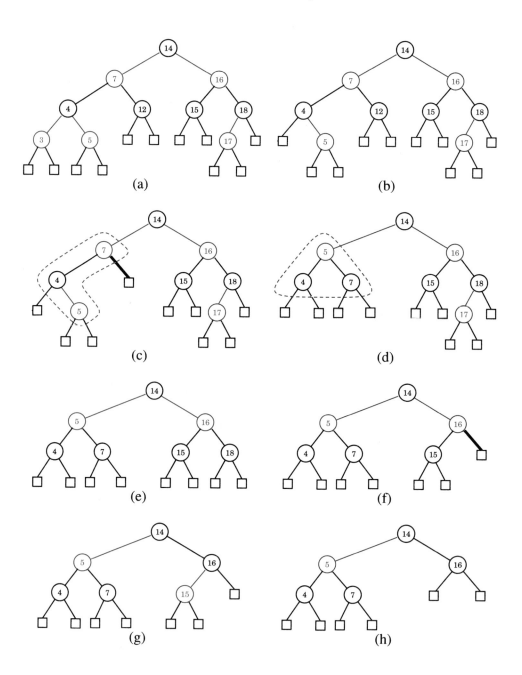

Figure 13.18: Sequence of removals from a red-black tree: (a) initial tree; (b) deletion of 3; (c) deletion of 12, causing a double black (handled by restructuring); (d) after restructuring; (e) deletion of 17; (f) deletion of 18, causing a double black (handled by recoloring); (g) after recoloring; (h) deletion of 15.

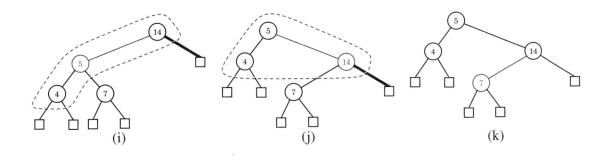

Figure 13.19: Sequence of deletions in a red-black tree (continued): (i) deletion of 16, causing a double black (handled by an adjustment); (j) after the adjustment the double black needs to be handled by a recoloring; (k) after the recoloring.

13.4   Splay Trees

The final balanced search tree data structure we discuss in this chapter is the *splay tree*. This structure is conceptually quite different from the previously discussed balanced search trees (AVL, red-black, and $(2,4)$ trees), for a splay tree does not use any explicit rules to enforce its balance. Instead, it applies a certain move-to-root operation, called *splaying* after every access, in order to keep the search tree balanced in an amortized sense. The splaying operation is performed at the bottom-most node x reached during an insertion, deletion, or even a search. The surprising thing about splaying is that it allows us to guarantee an amortized running time for insertions, deletions, and searches that is logarithmic.

The structure of a *splay tree* is simply a binary search tree T. In fact, there are no additional height, balance, or color labels that we associate with the nodes of this tree. The only tool used to maintain balance in T is the splaying step done after every search, insertion, and deletion in T.

13.4.1   Splaying

Given an internal node x of a binary search tree T, we *splay* x by moving x to the root of T through a sequence of restructurings. The particular restructurings we perform are important, for it is not sufficient to move x to the root of T by just any sequence of restructurings. The specific operation we perform to move x up depends upon the relative positions of x, its parent y, and (if it exists) x's grandparent z. There are three cases that we consider.

zig-zig: The node x and its parent y are both left children or both right children. (See Figure 13.20.) We replace z by x, making y a child of x and z a child of y, while maintaining the inorder relationships of the nodes in T. This restructuring is equivalent to performing Rotate(x) followed by Rotate(w), where w is the right child of x if x is a right child, and is the left child of x if x is a left child.

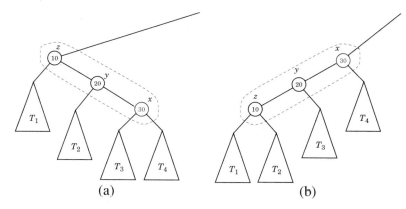

Figure 13.20: Zig-zig: (a) before; (b) after. There is another symmetric configuration where x and y are left children.

zig-zag: One of x and y is a left child and the other is a right child. (See Figure 13.21.) In this case, we replace z by x and make x have as its children the nodes y and z, while maintaining the inorder relationships of the nodes in T. This restructuring operation is equivalent to performing Rotate(x).

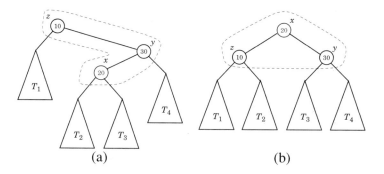

Figure 13.21: Zig-zag: (a) before; (b) after. There is another symmetric configuration where x is a right child and y is a left child.

zig: x does not have a grandparent (or we are not considering x's grandparent for some reason). (See Figure 13.22.) In this case, we rotate x over y, making x's children be the node y and one of x's former children w, so as to maintain the relative inorder relationships of the nodes in T. Note that this restructuring operation is equivalent to performing Rotate(w), where w is the right child of x if x is a right child, and is the left child of x if x is a left child.

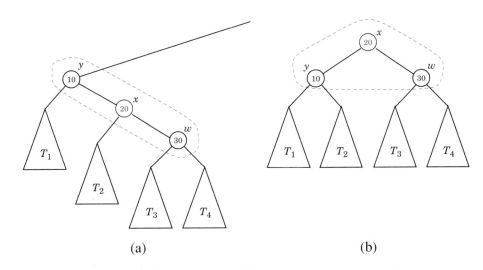

(a)   (b)

Figure 13.22: Zig: (a) before; (b) after. There is another symmetric configuration where x and w are left children.

We perform a zig-zig or a zig-zag when x has a grandparent, and we perform a zig when x has a parent but not a grandparent. A ***splaying*** step consists of repeating these restructurings at x until x becomes the root of T. Note that this is not the same as a sequence of simple rotations that brings x to the root. An example of the splaying of a node is shown in Figures 13.23 and 13.24.

After a zig-zig or zig-zag, the depth of x decreases by two, and after a zig the depth of x decreases by one. Thus, if x has depth d, splaying x consists of a sequence of $\lfloor d/2 \rfloor$ zig-zigs and/or zig-zags, plus one final zig if d is odd. Since a single zig-zig, zig-zag, or zig affects a constant number of nodes, it can be done in $O(1)$ time. Thus, splaying a node x in a binary search tree T takes time $O(d)$, where d is the depth of x in T. In other words, the time for performing a splaying step for a node x is asymptotically the same as the time needed just to reach that node in a top-down search from the root of T.

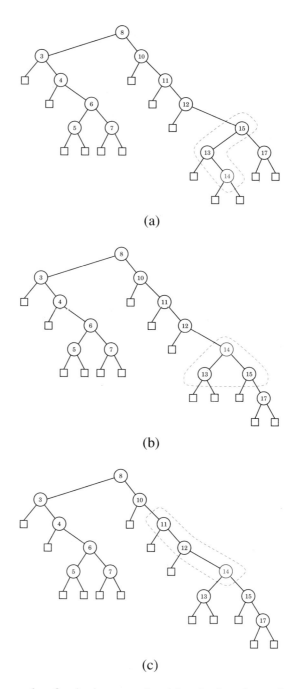

(a)

(b)

(c)

Figure 13.23: Example of splaying a node: (a) splaying the node storing 14 starts with a zig-zag; (b) after the zig-zag; (c) the next step is a zig-zig.

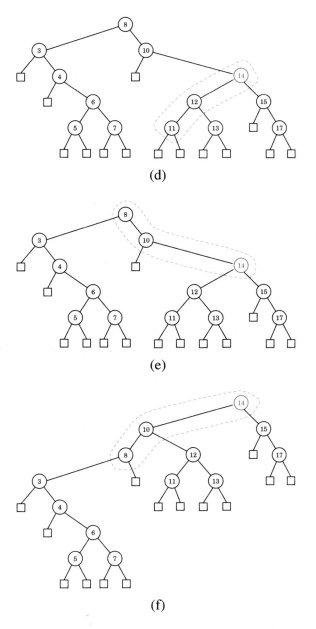

Figure 13.24: Example of splaying a node (continued from Figure 13.23):(d) after the zig-zig; (e) the next step is again a zig-zig; (f) after the zig-zig.

13.4.2 When to Splay

The rules that dictate when splaying is performed are as follows:

- When searching for key k, if k is found at a node x, we splay x, else we splay the parent of the external node at which the search terminates unsuccessfully. For example, the splaying in Figures 13.23 and 13.24 would be performed after searching successfully for key 14 or unsuccessfully for key 14.5.
- When inserting key k, we splay the newly created internal node where k gets inserted. For example, the splaying in Figures 13.23 and 13.24 would be performed if 14 were the newly inserted key. We show a sequence of insertions in a splay tree in Figure 13.25.

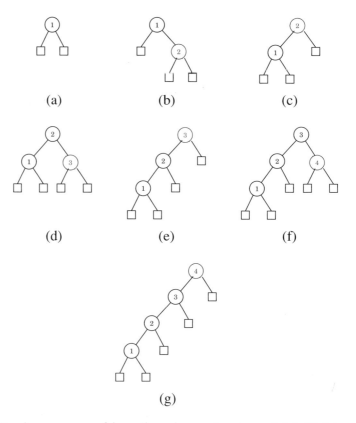

Figure 13.25: A sequence of insertions in a splay tree: (a) initial tree; (b) after inserting 2; (c) after splaying; (d) after inserting 3; (e) after splaying; (f) after inserting 4; (g) after splaying.

- When deleting a key k, we splay the parent of the node w that gets removed, that is, w is either the node storing k or one of its descendents. (Recall the deletion algorithm for binary search trees given in Section 7.3). An example of splaying following a deletion is shown in Figure 13.26.

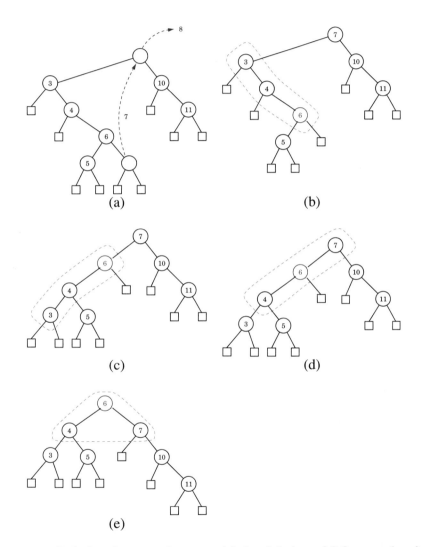

Figure 13.26: Deletion from a splay tree: (a) the deletion of 8 from node r is performed by moving to r the key of the right-most internal node v, in the left subtree of r, deleting v, and splaying the parent u of v; (b) splaying u starts with a zig-zig; (c) after the zig-zig; (d) the next step is a zig; (e) after the zig.

In the worst case, the overall running time of a search, insertion, or deletion in a splay tree of height h is $O(h)$, since the node we splay might be the deepest node in the tree. Moreover, it is possible for h to be $\Omega(n)$, as shown in Figure 13.25. Thus, from a worst-case point of view, a splay tree is not an attractive data structure.

13.4.3 Amortized Analysis of Splaying

In spite of its poor worst-case performance, a splay tree performs well in an amortized sense. That is, in a sequence of intermixed searches, insertions, and deletions, each operation takes on average logarithmic time. We perform the amortized analysis of splay trees using the accounting method introduced in Section 12.1. Before we begin our analysis, we recall the simple observation that the time for performing a search, insertion, or deletion is proportional to the time for the associated splaying. Hence, in our analysis, we consider only the splaying time.

Let T be a splay tree with n keys, and let v be a node of T. We define the **size** $n(v)$ of v as the number of nodes in the subtree rooted at v. Note that this definition implies that the size of an internal node is one more than the sum of the sizes of its two children. We define the **rank** $r(v)$ of a node v as the logarithm in base 2 of the size of v, that is, $r(v) = \log(n(v))$. Clearly, the root of T has the maximum size $(2n+1)$ and the maximum rank, $\log(2n+1)$, while each external node has size 1 and rank 0.

We use cyber-dollars to pay for the work we perform in splaying a node x in T, and we assume that one cyber-dollar pays for a zig, while two cyber-dollars pay for a zig-zig or a zig-zag. Hence, the cost of splaying a node at depth d is d cyber-dollars. We keep at each internal node of T a virtual account storing cyber-dollars. Note that this account exists only for the purpose of our amortized analysis, and does not need to be included in a data structure implementing the splay tree T.

When we perform a splaying, we pay a certain number of cyber-dollars (the exact value of the payment will be determined at the end of our analysis). We distinguish three cases:

- If the payment is equal to the splaying work, then we use it all to pay for the splaying.
- If the payment is greater than the splaying work, we deposit the excess in the accounts of several nodes.
- If the payment is less than the splaying work, we make withdrawals from the accounts of several nodes to cover the deficiency.

We will show, in the rest of this section, that a payment of $O(\log n)$ cyber-dollars per operation is sufficient to keep the system working, that is, to ensure that each node keeps a nonnegative account balance.

We use a scheme in which transfers are made between the accounts of the nodes to ensure that there will always be enough cyber-dollars to withdraw for paying for splaying work when needed. We also maintain the following invariant:

> **Before and after a splaying, each node v of T has $r(v)$ cyber-dollars in its account.**

Note that the invariant is "financially sound," since it does not require us to make a preliminary deposit to endow a tree with zero keys.

Let $r(T)$ be the sum of the ranks of all the nodes of T. To preserve the invariant after a splaying, we must make a payment equal to the splaying work plus the total change in $r(T)$. We refer to a single zig, zig-zig, or zig-zag operation in a splaying as a splaying **substep**. Also, we denote the rank of a node v of T before and after a splaying substep with $r(v)$ and $r'(v)$, respectively. The following proposition gives an upper bound on the change of $r(T)$ caused by a single splaying substep.

Proposition 13.6: *Let δ be the variation of $r(T)$ caused by a single splaying substep (a zig, zig-zig, or zig-zag) for a node x in T. We have the following:*

- *$\delta \le 3(r'(x) - r(x)) - 2$ if the substep is a zig-zig or zig-zag.*
- *$\delta \le 3(r'(x) - r(x))$ if the substep is a zig.*

Justification: We shall make use of the following mathematical fact (see Appendix B): If $a > 0$, $b > 0$ and $c > a + b$, then

$$\log a + \log b \le 2\log c - 2. \tag{13.2}$$

Let us consider the change in $r(T)$ caused by each type of splaying substep.

zig-zig: (Recall Figure 13.20.) Since the size of each node is one more than the size of its two children, note that only the ranks of x, y, and z change in a zig-zig operation, where y is the parent of x and z is the parent of y. Also, $r'(x) = r(z)$, $r'(y) \le r'(x)$, and $r(y) \ge r(x)$. Thus

$$
\begin{aligned}
\delta &= r'(x) + r'(y) + r'(z) - r(x) - r(y) - r(z) \\
&\le r'(y) + r'(z) - r(x) - r(y) \\
&\le r'(x) + r'(z) - 2r(x). \tag{13.3}
\end{aligned}
$$

Observe now that $n(x) + n'(z) \le n'(x)$. Thus, by 13.2,

$$r(x) + r'(z) \le 2r'(x) - 2,$$

that is,

$$r'(z) \le 2r'(x) - r(x) - 2.$$

This inequality and 13.3 imply

$$
\begin{aligned}
\delta &\le r'(x) + (2r'(x) - r(x) - 2) - 2r(x) \\
&\le 3(r'(x) - r(x)) - 2.
\end{aligned}
$$

zig-zag: (Recall Figure 13.21.) Again, by the definition of size and rank, only the ranks of x, y, and z change, where y denotes the parent of x and z denotes the parent of y. Also, $r'(x) = r(z)$ and $r(x) \le r(y)$. Thus

$$
\begin{aligned}
\delta &= r'(x) + r'(y) + r'(z) - r(x) - r(y) - r(z) \\
&\le r'(y) + r'(z) - r(x) - r(y) \\
&\le r'(y) + r'(z) - 2r(x).
\end{aligned}
\tag{13.4}
$$

Observe now that $n'(y) + n'(z) \le n'(x)$. Thus, by 13.2,

$$
r'(y) + r'(z) \le 2r'(x) - 2,
$$

This inequality and 13.4 imply

$$
\begin{aligned}
\delta &\le 2r'(x) - 2 - 2r(x) \\
&\le 3(r'(x) - r(x)) - 2.
\end{aligned}
$$

zig: (Recall Figure 13.22.) In this case, only the ranks of x and y change, where y denotes the parent of x. Also, $r'(y) \le r(y)$ and $r'(x) \ge r(x)$. Thus

$$
\begin{aligned}
\delta &= r'(y) + r'(x) - r(y) - r(x) \\
&\le r'(x) - r(x) \\
&\le 3(r'(x) - r(x)).
\end{aligned}
$$

■

We can now bound the total variation of $r(T)$ caused by splaying a node x.

Proposition 13.7: *Let T be a splay tree with root t, and let Δ be the total variation of $r(T)$ caused by splaying a node x at depth d. We have*

$$
\Delta \le 3(r(t) - r(x)) - d + 2.
$$

Justification: Splaying node x consists of $p = \lceil d/2 \rceil$ splaying substeps, each of which is a zig-zig or a zig-zag, except possibly the last one, which is a zig if d is odd. Let $r_0(x) = r(x)$ be the initial rank of x, and for $i = 1, \ldots, p$, let $r_i(x)$ be the rank of x after the ith substep and δ_i be the variation of $r(T)$ caused by the ith substep. By Proposition 13.6, the total variation Δ of $r(T)$ caused by splaying node x is given by

$$
\begin{aligned}
\Delta &= \sum_{i=1}^{p} \delta_i \\
&\le \sum_{i=1}^{p} (3(r_i(x) - r_{i-1}(x)) - 2) + 2 \\
&= 3(r_p(x) - r_0(x)) - 2p + 2 \\
&\le 3(r(t) - r(x)) - d + 2.
\end{aligned}
$$

■

By Proposition 13.7, if we make a payment of $3(r(t) - r(x)) + 2$ cyber-dollars towards the splaying of node x, we have enough cyber-dollars to maintain the invariant, keeping $r(v)$ cyber-dollars in the account of each node v in T, and pay for the entire splaying work, which costs d dollars. Since the size of the root t is $2n + 1$, its rank $r(t) = \log(2n + 1)$. In addition, we have $r(x) < r(t)$. Thus, the payment to be made for splaying is $O(\log n)$ cyber-dollars. To complete our amortized analysis, we have to compute the cost associated with maintaining the invariant when a node is inserted or deleted.

When inserting a new node v into a splay tree with n keys, the ranks of all the ancestors of v are increased. Namely, let $v_0, v_i, \ldots, v_d$ be the ancestors of v, where $v_0 = v$, v_i is the parent of v_{i-1}, and v_d is the root. For $i = 1, \ldots, d$, let $n'(v_i)$ and $n(v_i)$ be the size of v_i before and after the insertion, respectively, and let $r'(v_i)$ and $r(v_i)$ be the rank of v_i before and after the insertion, respectively. We have

$$n'(v_i) = n(v_i) + 1.$$

Also, since $n(v_i) + 1 \le n(v_{i+1})$, for $i = 0, 1, \ldots, d - 1$, we have the following for each i in this range:

$$r'(v_i) = \log(n'(v_i)) = \log(n(v_i) + 1) \le \log(n(v_{i+1})) = r(v_{i+1}).$$

Thus, the total variation of $r(T)$ caused by the insertion is

$$
\begin{aligned}
\sum_{i=1}^{d} \left(r'(v_i) - r(v_i) \right) &\le r'(v_d) + \sum_{i=1}^{d-1} \left(r(v_{i+1}) - r(v_i) \right) \\
&= r'(v_d) - r(v_0) \\
&\le \log(2n + 1).
\end{aligned}
$$

Thus, a payment of $O(\log n)$ cyber-dollars is sufficient to maintain the invariant when a new node is inserted.

When deleting a node v from a splay tree with n keys, the ranks of all the ancestors of v are decreased. Thus, the total variation of $r(T)$ caused by the deletion is negative, and we do not need to make any payment to maintain the invariant when a node is deleted. Therefore, we may summarize our amortized analysis in the following proposition (which is sometimes called the "Balance" proposition for splay trees):

Proposition 13.8: *Consider a sequence of m operations on a splay tree, each a search, insertion, or deletion, starting from a splay tree with zero keys. Also, let n_i be the number of keys in the tree after operation i, and n be the total number of insertions. The total running time for performing the sequence of operations is*

$$O\left(m + \sum_{i=1}^{m} \log n_i \right),$$

which is $O(m \log n)$.

In other words, the amortized running time of performing a search, insertion, or deletion in a splay tree is $O(\log n)$, where n is the size of the splay tree at the time. Thus, a splay tree can achieve logarithmic time amortized performance for implementing an ordered dictionary ADT. This amortized performance matches the worst-case performance of AVL trees, $(2,4)$ trees, and red-black trees, but it does so using a simple binary tree that does not need any extra balance information stored at each of its nodes. In addition, splay trees have a number of other interesting properties that are not shared by these other balanced search trees. We explore one such additional property in the following proposition (which is sometimes called the "Static Optimality" proposition for splay trees):

Proposition 13.9: *Consider a sequence of m operations on a splay tree, each a search, insertion, or deletion, starting from a splay tree T with zero keys. Also, let $f(i)$ denote the number of times the item i is accessed in the splay tree, that is, its* **frequency,** *and let n denote the total number of items. Assuming that each item is accessed at least once, then the total running time for performing the sequence of operations is*

$$O\left(m + \sum_{i=1}^{n} f(i)\log(m/f(i)) \right).$$

We leave the proof of this proposition as an exercise, for it is not as hard to justify as one might imagine.

The remarkable thing about this proposition is that it states that the amortized running time of accessing an item i is $O(\log(m/f(i)))$. For example, if a sequence of operations accesses some item i as many as $m/4$ times, then the amortized running time of each of these accesses is $O(1)$ when the dictionary is implemented with a splay tree. Contrast this to the $\Omega(\log n)$ time needed to access this item if the dictionary is implemented with an AVL tree, $(2,4)$ tree, or red-black tree. Thus, an additional nice property of splay trees is that they can "adapt" to the ways in which items are being accessed in a dictionary, so as to achieve faster running times for the frequently accessed items.

13.5 Exercises

Reinforcement

R-13.1 Is the multi-way search tree of Figure 13.1a a $(2,4)$ tree? Justify your answer.

R-13.2 An alternative way of performing a split at a node v in a $(2,4)$ tree is to partition v into v' and v'', with v' being a 2-node and v'' being a 3-node. Which of the keys k_1, k_2, k_3, or k_4 do we store at v's parent in this case? Why?

R-13.3 Consider the following sequence of keys:
$$(5, 16, 22, 45, 2, 10, 18, 30, 50, 12, 1).$$
Consider the inserton of items with this set of keys in the order given into:

1. An initially-empty $(2,4)$ tree T'
2. An initially-empty red-black tree T''.

Draw T' and T'' after each insertion.

R-13.4 Professor Amongus claims that a $(2,4)$ tree storing a set of items will always have the same structure, regardless of the order in which the items are inserted. Show that Professor Amongus is wrong.

R-13.5 Draw four different red-black trees that correspond to the same $(2,4)$ tree, using the correspondence rules described in the chapter.

R-13.6 For each of the following statements about red-black trees, determine whether it is true or false. If you think it is true, provide a justification. If you think it is false, give a counterexample.

1. A subtree of a red-black tree is itself a red-black tree.
2. The sibling of an external node is either external or it is red.
3. Given a red-black tree T, there is an unique $(2,4)$-tree T' associated with T.
4. Given a $(2,4)$ tree T, there is a unique red-black tree T' associated with T.

R-13.7 Draw an example red-black tree that is not an AVL tree. Your tree should have at least 6 nodes, but no more than 16.

R-13.8   Consider a tree T storing 100,000 items. What is the worst-case height of T in the following cases?

1. T is an AVL tree.
2. T is a $(2,4)$-tree.
3. T is a red-black tree.
4. T is a splay tree.
5. T is a binary search tree.

R-13.9   Perform the following sequence of operations in an initially empty splay tree and draw the tree after each operation.

1. Insert keys 0, 2, 4, 6, 8, 10, 12, 14, 16, 18, in this order.
2. Search for keys 1, 3, 5, 7, 9, 11, 13, 15, 17, 19, in this order.
3. Delete keys 0, 2, 4, 6, 8, 10, 12, 14, 16, 18, in this order.

R-13.10   What does a splay tree look like if its items are accessed in increasing order by their keys?

Creativity

C-13.1   Let T and U be $(2,4)$ trees storing n and m items, respectively, such that all the items in T have keys less than the keys of all the items in U. Describe an $O(\log n + \log m)$ time method for **joining** T and U into a single tree that stores all the items in T and U (destroying the old versions of T and U).

C-13.2   Repeat the previous problem for red-black trees T and U.

C-13.3   Justify Proposition 13.1.

C-13.4   The extra bit used to mark nodes in a red-black tree as being "red" or "black" is not strictly needed. Describe a scheme for implementing a red-black tree without adding any extra space to standard binary search tree nodes. How does your scheme affect the running times for searching and updating a red-black tree?

C-13.5   Let T be a red-black tree storing n items, and let k be the key of an item in T. Show how to construct from T in $O(\log n)$ time two red-black trees T' and T'' such that T' contains all the keys of T less than k, and T'' contains all the keys of T greater than k. This operation destroys T.

C-13.6 Consider a variation of splay trees, called ***half-splay trees***, where splaying a node at depth d stops as soon as the node reaches depth $\lfloor d/2 \rfloor$. Perform an amortized analysis of half-splay trees.

C-13.7 Show that the nodes of any AVL tree T can be colored "red" and "black" so that T becomes a red-black tree.

C-13.8 The ***mergeable heap*** ADT consists of operations insert(k,x), remove(k), unionWith(h), and minElement$()$, where the unionWith(h) operation performs a union of the mergeable heap h with the present one, destroying the old versions of both. Describe a concrete implementation of the mergeable heap ADT that achieves $O(\log n)$ performance for all its operations. For simplicity, you may assume that all keys in existing mergeable heaps are distinct, although this is not strictly necessary.

C-13.9 The standard splaying step requires two passes, one downward pass to find the node x to splay, followed by an upward pass to splay the node x. Describe a method for splaying and searching for x in one downward pass. Each substep now requires that you consider the next two nodes in the path down to x, with a possible zig substep performed at the end. Describe the details for performing each of the zig-zig, zig-zag, and zig substeps. (Hint: since you know the node x will eventually become the root, maintain a tree of nodes to the left of x and a tree of nodes to the right of x, which will eventually become the two children of x.)

C-13.10 Describe a sequence of accesses to an n-node splay tree T, where n is odd, that results in T consisting of a single chain of internal nodes with external node children, such that the internal-node path down T alternates between left children and right children. (Hint: if you are having trouble with this problem, you may wish to gain some intuition about splay trees by "playing" with an interactive splay tree program.)

C-13.11 Justify Proposition 13.9. A way to establish this justification is to note that we can redefine the "size" of a node as the sum of the access frequencies of its children and show that the entire justification of Proposition 13.7 still goes through.

Projects

P-13.1 Write a Java class that implements all the methods of an ordered dictionary given in Chapter 7 by means of a $(2,4)$ tree.

P-13.2 Write a Java class that can take any red-black tree and convert it into its corresponding $(2,4)$ tree and can take any $(2,4)$ tree and convert it into its corresponding red-black tree.

P-13.3 Write a Java class that implements all the methods of a dictionary given in Chapter 7 by means of a red-black tree.

P-13.4 Write a Java class that implements all the methods of a dictionary given in Chapter 7 by means of a splay tree.

P-13.5 Form a three-programmer team and have each member implement a different one of the previous three projects. Perform extensive experimental studies to compare the speed of these three implementations. Try to design three sets of experiments such that each favors a different implementation.

P-13.6 Prepare an implementation of splay trees that uses bottom-up splaying as described in this chapter and another that uses top-down splaying as described in Exercise C-13.9. Perform extensive experimental studies to see which implementation is better in practice, if any.

Chapter Notes

Aho, Hopcroft, and Ullman [6] discuss $(2,3)$ trees, which are similar to $(2,4)$ trees. Red-black trees were defined by Bayer [15]. Variations and interesting properties of red-black trees are presented in a paper by Guibas and Sedgewick [67]. Splay trees were invented by Sleator and Tarjan [133] (see also [138]). The reader interested in learning more about different balanced tree data structures is referred to the books by Mehlhorn [109] and Tarjan [138], and the book chapter by Mehlhorn and Tsakalidis [112]. Knuth [90] is an excellent additional reading that includes early approaches to balancing trees.

Chapter

14

Multi-Dimensional Search Trees

Contents

We live in a multi-dimensional world. Physical space itself is three-dimensional, for we can use three coordinates, x, y, and z, to describe points in space. Completely describing the orientation of the tip of a robot arm actually requires six dimensions, for we use three dimensions to describe the position of the tip in space, plus three more dimensions to describe the angles the tip is in (which are typically called pitch, roll, and yaw). Describing the state of an airplane in flight takes at least nine dimensions, for we need six to describe its orientation in the same manner as for the tip of a robot arm, and we need three more to describe the plane's velocity. In fact, these physical representations are considered "low-dimensional," particularly in applications in machine learning or computational biology, where 100- and 1,000-dimensional spaces are not unusual. This chapter is directed at data structures for storing **multi-dimensional** data, where keys are vectors of the form $(x_0, x_1, \ldots, x_{d-1})$, for $d \geq 2$.

There are actually a great number of different data structures for storing and querying multi-dimensional data, and it is beyond the scope of this chapter to discuss all of them. Rather than discuss all such structures, we provide a small sampling of some of the more interesting ones in this chapter. We begin with a discussion of **tries**, which are useful for storing and searching sets of strings. We then present **range trees**, which can store multi-dimensional data so as to support a special kind of query called a **range-searching query**, and we also include an interesting variant of the range tree called the **priority search tree**. Finally, we discuss a class of data structures, called **partition trees**, which partition space into cells, and focus on variants known as **k-d trees**, **quadtrees**, and **octrees**.

14.1   Tries

A **trie** (pronounced "try") is a tree-based data structure for storing strings in order to support fast pattern matching. Since strings can be viewed as variable-length vectors, the trie is properly viewed as a multi-dimensional data structure. In fact, it is related to the quadtree data structure we discuss in Section 14.3. We describe the trie here as a string-based structure, however, for that is its primary use.

The main application for tries is in information retrieval. Indeed, the name "trie" comes from the word "re*trie*val." In an information retrieval application, such as a search for a certain DNA sequence in a genomic database, we are given a collection S of strings, all defined using the same alphabet. The primary query operation that tries support is a **prefix query**. Such an operation involves being given a string X, and looking for the longest prefix of X that matches a prefix of some string in the collection. Another important application of tries and prefix queries is data compression, as we will see in Section 14.1.6.

We consider the following operations on a set S of strings:

insert(X): Insert the string X into S.
Input: String; *Output:* None.

remove(X): Remove string X from S.
Input: String; *Output:* None.

prefixes(X): Return all the strings in S that have a longest prefix of X as a common prefix.
Input: String; *Output:* Enumeration of strings.

Note that the prefixes operation does not return the prefix of X that was matched, but we can easily determine this. For example, we can take any string Y in the enumeration returned, and compare X and Y's prefixes until we find a mismatch or reach the end of X or Y.

Example 14.1: *We show below a series of* insert, remove, *and* prefixes *operations on an initially empty set S of sequences.*

Operation	*Output*	S
insert("abaab")	–	{abaab}
insert("aabab")	–	{abaab, aabab}
insert("babbb")	–	{abaab, aabab, babbb}
insert("bbaaa")	–	{abaab, aabab, babbb, bbaaa}
insert("bbbab")	–	{abaab, aabab, babbb, bbaaa, bbbab}
prefixes("bbbb")	bbbab	{abaab, aabab, babbb, bbaaa, bbbab}
remove("babbb")	–	{abaab, aabab, bbaaa, bbbab}
prefixes("bbabab")	bbaaa	{abaab, aabab, bbaaa, bbbab}
prefixes("bb")	bbaaa, bbbab	{abaab, aabab, bbaaa, bbbab}

14.1.1 Standard Tries

Let S be a set of strings from alphabet Σ such that no string in S is a prefix of another string. A **standard trie** for S is an ordered tree T with the following properties (see Figure 14.1):

- Each edge of T is labeled with a character from Σ.
- The ordering of the edges going to the children of an internal node in T is determined by a canonical ordering of the alphabet Σ.
- The path from the root of T to any node in T represents a prefix of a string in S that is equal to the concatenation of the characters encountered while traversing this path.

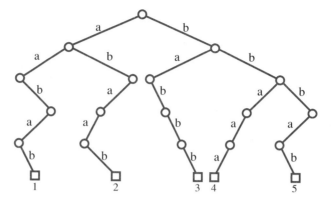

Figure 14.1: The standard trie over the alphabet $\Sigma = \{a, b\}$ for the set of strings $\{aabab, abaab, babbb, bbaaa, bbbab\}$.

Thus, a trie T represents the set S by associating strings of S with paths from the root to nodes of T. A node v that is reached after traversing the edges corresponding to the characters in a string X in S is **labeled** by X. If no string in S is a prefix of another, then the nodes in T labeled by strings will all be external nodes, as shown in Figure 14.1. We can always impose the restriction that strings only label external nodes, however, by adding a special symbol "$" at the end of each string we store in T, where $\$ \notin \Sigma$. With this restriction, there will always be a one-to-one correspondence between the external nodes of T and the strings of S.

An internal node in a standard trie T can have anywhere between 1 and d children, where d is the size of the alphabet. There is an edge going from the root r to one of its children for each character that is first in some string in the collection S. In addition, a path from the root of T to an internal node v at depth i corresponds to an i-character prefix $X[0..i-1]$ of a string of S. In fact, for each character x that can follow the prefix $X[0..i-1]$ in a string of the set S, there is an edge labeled with x that goes from v to one of v's children. In this way, a trie concisely represents all the common prefixes that exist among a set of strings.

If there are only two characters in the alphabet, as in Example 14.1 and Figure 14.1, then the trie is essentially a binary tree, although some internal nodes may have only one child. In general, if there are d characters in the alphabet, then the trie will be a multi-way tree where each internal node has between 1 and d children. In addition, there are likely to be several internal nodes in a standard trie that have fewer than d children. For example, the trie shown in Figure 14.1 has several internal nodes with only one child. Indeed, the only way an internal node v can have d children is if there are d different strings in the collection that have, as a common prefix, the prefix represented by the path from the root r to node v followed by a different character from the alphabet.

Since an ordered tree stores elements at its nodes (Section 5.1), we can implement a trie with a data structure that realizes the ordered tree interface by storing the character associated with an edge at the child node below the edge. This implementation allows us to refer to the character associated with an edge without explicitly storing characters at edge objects.

Example 14.2: *A trie T can be used to implement a dictionary whose keys are strings. Consider the trie illustrated in Figure 14.1. We perform a search in T for a string X by tracing down the path from the root that is indicated by the characters in X. If we reach a node labeled with X at then end of this search, then we know X is in the dictionary (for example, tracing the path for* babbb *in the trie of Figure 14.1 ends up at an external node labeled by string number 3). If such a search stops at an internal node v because there is no outgoing edge from v with the correct label, then the string is not in the set. For example, a search for the string* babba *terminates at the parent of external node number 3.*

From a worst-case point of view, the standard trie definition does not provide any asymptotic space improvement over simply storing all the strings of a set S in a sequence or dictionary. In the worst case, a standard trie must use a constant amount of space for each character in each string in S; hence, the worst-case space usage of a trie is $O(m)$, where m is the sum of the lengths of all the strings in S. A standard trie is still a better data structure than a sequence or dictionary, however, for performing prefix queries on the strings in S. Still, this potential space inefficiency has prompted the development of a more space-efficient version of the trie data structure, known as the ***compressed trie*** or (for historical reasons) the ***Patricia trie*** structure.

14.1.2 Compressed Tries

A ***compressed trie*** is similar to a standard trie but it ensures that each internal node in the trie has degree at least 2. It enforces this rule by compressing chains of single-child nodes into individual edges. (See Figure 14.2.) Call a node v in a standard trie ***critical*** if v is labeled with a string in S, if v has at least two children, or if v is the root. We convert a standard trie into a compressed by try by replacing with an edge (v_0, v_k) each chain of nodes $(v_0, v_1, v_2, \ldots, v_k)$, for $k \geq 2$, such that

- The nodes v_0 and v_k are critical, but no v_i is critical for $0 < i < k$.
- Each node v_i, for $0 < i < k$, has only one child, the node v_{i+1}.

Thus, edges in a compressed trie are associated with strings, which are substrings of strings in the collection S, rather than individual characters.

We do not need to explicitly store the strings associated with each edge. Instead, we can use three variables for each edge e in a compressed trie that together represent the substring associated with e:

- A reference to a string X in the set associated with an external descendant node further down the trie from edge e
- The index of the beginning of the substring of X associated with e
- The index of the end of the substring of X associated with e.

Thus, we store a compound object containing three instance variables with each edge in a compressed trie. Since each internal node in a compressed trie has at least two children, and each external node is associated with a different string in S, this compression scheme allows us to reduce the total space for the trie itself from $O(m)$ for the standard trie to $O(n)$ for the compressed trie, where n is the number of strings in S and m is the sum of the lengths of the strings in S. We must still have some way of representing the diffcrent strings in S, of course, but we nevertheless reduce the space for the tree T using this compression scheme.

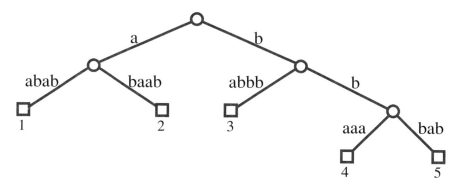

Figure 14.2: The compressed trie over the alphabet $\Sigma = \{a,b\}$ for the set of strings $\{aabab, abaab, babbb, bbaaa, bbbab\}$. Compare this with the standard trie for the same set of strings shown in Figure 14.1.

This reduction in space may seem to be insignificant, and indeed it is insignificant if we explicitly store all the strings in S, for this in itself requires $\Theta(m)$ space. There are many applications where the strings in S need not be stored explicitly, however, and in these applications the reduction in space from $O(m)$ to $O(n)$ can be important.

Suffix Tries

One of the primary applications for tries is for the case when the strings in S are the suffixes of a string X, each followed by a special character $ that is not in Σ. That is, if X has length n, S contains the n strings $X[i..n-1]$$, for $i = 0, \ldots, n-1$. The special character $ is used to ensure that no string of S is a prefix of another string.

A suffix trie can be used for pattern matching. Namely, we can determine whether a string Y is a substring of X by performing operation prefixes(Y) on the suffix trie of X. Indeed, Y is a substring of X if and only if Y is a prefix of a suffix of X. Thus, we can immediately test if Y is a substring of X by checking if Y is a prefix of one of the strings of the enumeration returned by prefixes(X).

The compressed trie we derive in this case is the *suffix trie* (also known as a *suffix tree* or *position tree*). A standard trie representing all of the suffixes of X requires $O(n^2)$ space in the worst case, and this is also the space needed to explicitly store all the suffixes of X. But if we use a compressed trie, then we only need $O(n)$ space.

14.1.3 Searching

Let S be a collection of n strings defined over the same alphabet Σ and stored in a (standard or compressed) trie T. To be consistent in how we deal with T if it is a standard trie, let us refer to the single character associated with each edge e in a standard trie as a (one-character) string associated with e.

Suppose we are now given a string X, and asked to perform a prefix query prefixes(X). That is, we want to return the strings in S that have a longest prefix of X in common. We perform this query using the prefixQuery algorithm described in Code Fragment 14.1. Let us denote by prefix(v) the concatenation of characters that label the edges on the path from the root of T to a node v in T. The prefixQuery algorithm will terminate in one of two ways, returning a node v in either case: it will either stop at the node v itself, indicating that a prefix of the query string X matches prefix(v), or it will stop at an edge e with parent u and child v, indicating that a prefix of X matches prefix(u) and a portion of the string associated with e. In either case, the strings of S with a longest prefix in common with X are stored at the labeled nodes of the subtree of T rooted at node v.

The correctness of algorithm prefixQuery follows from the fact that we search down the trie T, matching characters of X until we come to the first mismatch. This mismatch either occurs in the middle of some edge (which is caught as a match to a proper prefix of an edge string Y) or at a node (which is caught by our terminating the for-loop without a break out). Note that if T is a standard trie, then we will never terminate a search in the middle of an edge. In any case, this top-down greedy search strategy guarantees that the strings returned in the enumeration will all have the same longest prefix in common with X. Also, if the outgoing edges of each node are ordered alphabetically, then an inorder traversal of the labeled nodes in the subtree rooted at that node will enumerate the strings in lexicographic order.

The running time algorithm prefixQuery is $O(dn)$, where d is the size of the alphabet and n denotes the length of X. This time bound derives from the following observations:

- We spend $O(1)$ time for each character comparison we do for an edge e.
- There are at most d edges out of any node v that we visit.
- There are at most n internal nodes that we visit.

We usually assume that the alphabet size d is a constant, so that the running time for answering a prefix query can be simplified to $O(n)$, and, in most cases, we will not have to perform character comparisons for all of X, just the prefix that matches.

Algorithm prefixQuery(T, X):

    Input: Trie T for a set S of strings and a query string X

    Output: The node v of T such that the labeled nodes of the subtree of T rooted at v store the strings of S with a longest prefix in common with X

    $v \leftarrow T.\text{root}()$

    $i \leftarrow 0$ $\{i$ is an index into the string $X\}$

    repeat

        for each child w of v **do**

            let e be the edge (v, w)

            $Y \leftarrow \text{string}(e)$ $\{Y$ is the substring associated with $e\}$

            $l \leftarrow Y.\text{length}()$ $\{l = 1$ if T is a standard trie$\}$

            $Z \leftarrow X.\text{substring}(i, i + l - 1)$ $\{Z$ holds the next l characters of $X\}$

            if $Z = Y$ **then**

                $v \leftarrow w$

                $i \leftarrow i + l$ $\{$move to w, incrementing i past $Z\}$

                break out of the **for** loop

            else if a proper prefix of Z matches a proper prefix of Y **then**

                $v \leftarrow w$ $\{$we stop "inside" $e\}$

                break out of the **repeat** loop

    until v is external **or** $v \neq w$

    $\{$we have gone as far down T as we can$\}$

    return v

Code Fragment 14.1: Prefix query on a trie. We assume that the string associated with an edge e is returned by method string(e).

Let v be the node returned by prefixQuery(T,X). To complete the prefix query prefixes(X), we output the k strings stored at the labeled nodes of the subtree of trie T rooted at v by performing a traversal of this subtree (for example, an inorder traversal). Assuming we use an efficient tree traversal algorithm, this enumeration will run in $O(k)$ time.

14.1.4   Insertion

The first update operation we consider for a (standard or compressed) trie T is the insertion of a new string X into the set S of strings represented by T. As with the prefix query algorithm, we describe the insertion algorithm assuming that T is a compressed trie, since a standard trie can be viewed as a special case of a compressed trie.

The insertion algorithm is fairly simple. We first perform a prefix query for string X using the prefixQuery algorithm of Code Fragment 14.1. Recall that there are two possible ways this algorithm terminates. It either terminates at an edge in the trie, returning the longest prefix for X ends in the middle of a string Y associated with some edge e, or it terminates at a vertex v, returning that there is no edge out of v that begins with the next character of X. Also recall that we denote by prefix(v) the concatenation of characters that label edges on the path from the root of T to a node v in T. Let us consider each case in turn. (See Figure 14.3.)

1. The search terminates at a node v. (This will be the only case for the standard trie.) Let X_1 be the prefix of X that matched in the trie up to the node v, and let X_2 denote the rest of X. Then $X = X_1 + X_2 = \text{prefix}(v) + X_2$. If X_2 is the empty string (that is, $X = \text{prefix}(v)$), then we label v with X, and we are done. Otherwise, we create a new external node w and label it with the string X. If this trie is a standard trie, then we create a path of edges corresponding to the characters in the string X_2 and we attach this path to go from the node v to the node w. If this trie is a compressed trie, however, we simply create a single new edge (v, w) and we associate it with the string X_2. (See Figure 14.3a.)

2. The search terminates at an edge $e = (v, w)$, for a prefix of X matches prefix(v) and a proper prefix of the string Y associated with e. (This case can only occur if we are working with a compressed trie.) Let Y_1 be the part of Y that X matched to, and let Y_2 be the rest of Y (so Y is a concatenation of Y_1 and Y_2). Likewise, let X_1 be the prefix of X that matched in the trie up to and including the string Y_1, and let X_2 denote the rest of X. Then $X = X_1 + X_2 = \text{prefix}(v) + Y_1 + X_2$. We create a new node u and split the edge e into the edges (v, u) and (u, w), where w was previously a child of v (now u is a child of v). We associate the string Y_1 with (v, u) and we asso-

ciate the string Y_2 with (u,w). If X_2 is empty, then we label u with X, since $X = \mathsf{prefix}(u)$. Otherwise, we create another new node z, which is an external node we label with X, and we associate the string X_2 with the new edge (u,z). (See Figure 14.3b.)

The running time for inserting a new string X is $O(dn)$, where d is the size of the alphabet and n is the length of X, that is, it is proportional to the size of X, if the alphabet has constant size.

An interesting property about tries, which follows immediately from the string insertion algorithm given above, is that we will always get the same trie for a collection of strings S, regardless of the order they are inserted. This property would not hold, for example, if we were to store the strings of S in a binary search tree or even a balanced binary search tree, for, in these cases, the order of insertion matters.

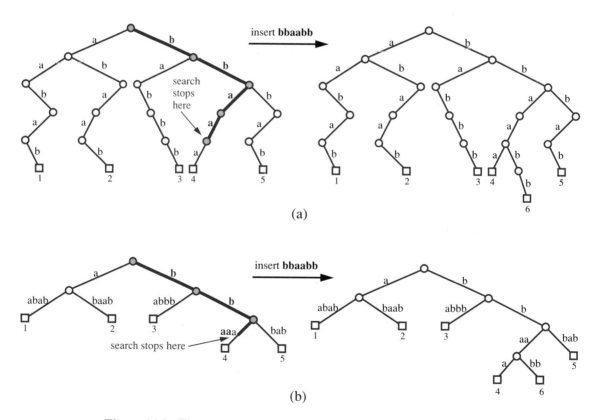

Figure 14.3: The two cases for insertion into a trie: (a) an insertion that stops at a vertex (in a standard trie); (b) an insertion that stops in the middle of an edge (in a compressed trie).

14.1.5 Deletion

The algorithm for deletion in a trie is more-or-less insertion in reverse. Suppose we are given a string X and asked to remove X from a trie T. We first perform a search from the root in T to locate the labeled node z associated with X. We begin by removing the label for X from z. If z is an external node, then we traverse up the trie T starting at z to locate the lowest ancestor v of z that is either labeled itself or has at least two children (let v be the root if there is no such last ancestor of z, for X is the only string in T in this case). During this traversal, we remove from T every node and edge we encounter (except for the node v). Of course, if T is a compressed trie, then v is z's parent. Otherwise, we remove a chain of edges and nodes from z up to v in T. If T is a standard trie, then we are done. If T is a compressed trie, on the other hand, then we need to check if v is no longer critical (for example, v may now have only one child). If so, then we also remove v and replace the edges (x, v) and (v, u) by a single edge (x, u), where x is the parent of v, and we associate with this edge the concatenation of the strings previously associated with the edges (x, v) and (v, u). (See Figure 14.4.)

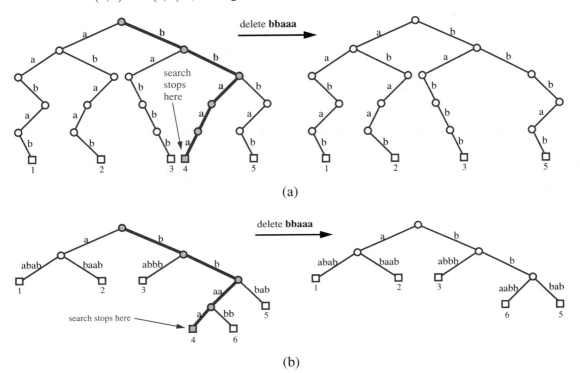

Figure 14.4: Deletion of a string from a trie: (a) deletion of bbaaa in a standard trie; (b) deletion of bbaaa in a compressed trie.

The string deletion algorithm takes time $O(dn)$ in the worst case, where d is the size of the alphabet and n is the length of string X. This bound is dominated by $O(dn)$ time to search for the string X, because the time needed to update the trie T is $O(n)$. Since the update time is dominated by the searching step, we can actually improve this time to $O(n)$ if the trie T supports the locator pattern, and the deletion method is given a locator for string X that accesses the labeled node associated with X (instead of the string X itself). In either case, the trie data structure provides an efficient way of storing a collection of strings, as we summarize:

Proposition 14.3: *A trie T for a collection S of strings defined over an alphabet of size d supports a prefix query, an insertion, or a deletion of a string X of length n in $O(dn)$ time. If T is a standard trie, then it uses $O(m)$ space, where m is the total length of the strings in S. If T is a compressed trie, then it uses $O(s)$ space, in addition to the space used for the strings themselves, where s is the number of strings in S.*

As we mentioned in Section 14.1.2, one of the primary applications of tries is for storing a collection of all suffixes of a single string X, in which case the trie is called a **suffix** trie. Constructing such a trie using a series of insertions into an empty trie would take $O(n^2)$ time in the worst case, but we can actually construct a suffix trie for a string X in $O(n)$ time. The method for achieving this is not too difficult, but it is rather involved, so we do not include it here. Instead, let us assume that such a trie can be constructed in linear time and give an example application.

Example 14.4: *Let X and Y be two strings of length n and m, defined over the same d-character alphabet. Suppose we wish to find the longest prefix of Y that is a substring of X. We can do this efficiently by first constructing a suffix trie for X and then performing a prefix query for Y. The running time is $O(d(n+m))$.*

We explore another application of tries in the next subsection.

14.1.6 Application: Data Compression

One of the chief modern uses of computers is to transmit and process documents, often over networks of limited bandwidth (such as slow modem lines) or in memory-limited situations (such as hand-held computers). In contexts where memory or bandwidth is limited, there are great advantages to be gained by compressing text files, and then either transmitting or storing their compressed versions. In order for a file to be effectively compressed, it must contain repeated patterns, but this is often the case in compiled programs that contain repeated sequences of instructions, and in natural language text that contains repeated words and phrases.

A well-known method for performing such compression is an algorithm that is historically known as "adaptive Lempel-Ziv" encoding or the **LZ78 algorithm**. The standard Unix compression command "compress" uses a variant of the LZ78 algorithm, for example.

Suppose we are given a string X defined over some alphabet. The LZ78 method for compressing X is defined in a somewhat greedy fashion. The string X is scanned from left to right in a series of "rounds," and parsed into a collection of numbered substrings called **phrases**. Each phrase is defined to have a prefix that is equal to a previously encoded phrase plus one additional character in the alphabet. We begin the compression by defining phrase 0 to be the null string. At the beginning of a round i, the text to the left of the current position k is already encoded using the phrases $0, 1, 2, \ldots, i-1$, and the text starting at k and continuing to the right is yet to be processed. The round i computation involves finding the index j of the longest phrase in the current set that is a prefix of the text yet to be encoded starting at position k. Given this phrase index j, the algorithm defines phrase i to be phrase j concatenated with the next character c in the text X. This substring in the text can then be replaced by the the pair (j, c). Round i completes by resetting the current position k to be the index of the character of X following this character c. The string X is therefore encoded as a sequence of number-character pairs. (See Figure 14.5.)

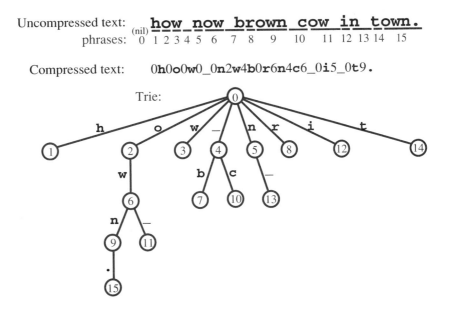

Figure 14.5: An example text compression using the LZ78 algorithm. An underscore in the compressed text and in the trie denotes a blank space.

One of the attractions of the LZ78 algorithm is that it is fairly simple to implement using a standard trie data structure, where we allow for a string to be a prefix of another string. Namely, we use a trie to store each of the phrases used during compression. Since every phrase is defined in terms of a previous phrase plus an additional character, each node in the trie is labeled with a different phrase. Thus, we can store at each node in the trie the index number of the phrase that node represents.

This indexing mechanism makes processing of the next phrase in the text string quite simple. We simply traverse down the trie, matching text characters to edges until we come to a node j that has no out-going edge defined for the next character c. (See Figure 14.5.) Our stopping at this point implies that the phrase j matches the longest prefix in the remaining text to be encoded, and we can then define the next phrase i as the phrase j plus the character c. Moreover, we can insert phrase i into the trie in $O(1)$ additional time, for the node i should be a child of node j and the edge from j to i should be labeled with the character c. Thus, a text string of length n defined over an alphabet of size d (which is usually taken to be a fixed constant), can be encoded using the LZ78 algorithm in $O(dn)$ time. Such a string can be decoded in $O(n)$ time, independent of d, but we leave the details of this algorithm as an exercise.

The compression achieved by the LZ78 algorithm in practice can be as high as 50% or better, especially when it is combined with various heuristics for describing each pair (j, c) with as few bits as possible. For example, we can remove each reference to phrase 0, since we can detect a missing phrase number and take that to mean that the next character defines a new (one-character) phrase. In fact, variants of the LZ78 algorithm are claimed to be able to achieve better compression performance in practice than the Huffman encoding method, which is described in Section 12.4.3.

We have shown how to use the trie data structure to solve an interesting problem for strings. There is actually nothing "magical" about our use of strings with tries, however. We also could have used vectors of numbers or even bit sequences just as easily. In fact, our description using strings is general enough to include these other kinds of data types, since we allow for arbitrary kinds of "alphabets." The main purpose of tries is to support prefix queries, however, which have more applications among collections of strings, such as data compression and searching for strings in the World Wide Web or in DNA sequences. Thus, it is probably most natural to use tries for strings.

Another popular kind of query to perform on multidimensional data is range searching, which we discuss next.

14.2 Range Trees

Multi-dimensional data arise in a number of different applications, and in many cases the different dimensions are most naturally represented by numbers, not characters from some alphabet. In such applications a key is actually a d-dimensional *vector* $(x_0, x_1, \ldots, x_{d-1})$, where each coordinate x_i is referred to as an *attribute*. Such data can come from business applications, where each vector represents various attributes of products or personnel. For example, televisions in an electronics catalog would probably have different attribute values for price, screen-size, weight, height, width, and depth. Multi-dimensional data can also come from scientific applications, where each vector represents attributes of individual experiments or observations. For example, heavenly objects in an astronomy sky survey would probably have different attribute values for brightness (or apparent magnitude), diameter, distance, and position in the sky (which is itself two-dimensional). In applications such as these, where the attributes are numbers, a natural query to perform is a *range search* query.

A range-search query is a request to retrieve all items in a multi-dimensional collection whose keys have attribute values that fall within a given set of ranges. For example, a consumer wishing to buy a new television may request, from an electronic store's catalog, all units that have a screen-size between 24 and 27 inches, and have a price between \$400 and \$800. Alternately, an astronomer interested in studying asteroids may request all heavenly objects that are at a distance between 1.5 and 10 astronomical units, have an apparent magnitude between +1 and +15, and have a diameter between 0.5 and 1,000 kilometers. The range tree data structure, which we discuss in this section, can be used to answer such queries.

To keep the discussion simple, we focus on two-dimensional range-searching queries. Later, we will sketch how the corresponding two-dimensional range tree data structure can be extended to higher dimensions. A *two-dimensional dictionary* D is an ADT for storing key-element items each of which have a key that is a pair (x, y) of numbers, called the *coordinates* of the element. A two-dimensional dictionary supports the following operations:

findAllInRange(a, b, c, d): Return all the elements of D with coordinates (x, y) such that $a \leq x \leq b$ and $c \leq y \leq d$.
Input: Four numbers; *Output:* Enumeration.

insert(x, y, o): Insert into D an element o with coordinates (x, y).
Input: Two numbers and an object; *Output:* None.

remove(x, y): Remove from D an element with coordinates (x, y).
Input: Two numbers; *Output:* Object.

Operation findAllInRange is the ***reporting*** version of the range-searching query, because it asks for an enumeration of all the objects satisfying the range constraints. There is also a functional version of the range query:

applyToRange(a, b, c, d, f): Return the value of the associative function f applied to all the elements of D with coordinates (x, y) such that $a \leq x \leq b$ and $c \leq y \leq d$.
Input: Four numbers and a function; *Output:* The object returned from f.

Examples of popular choices for function f include the *count* function, which simply counts the number of elements in the range, the *sum* function, which adds up the elements in the range (assuming they have a numeric value), and the *max* function, which returns the maximum of all the elements in the range (assuming an order relation is defined over them). Since any implementation of the standard findAllInRange method can immediately be converted into an implementation for the applyToRange method, we will concentrate on the findAllInRange method.

We present data structures for realizing a two-dimensional dictionary in the remainder of this section. We discuss, only briefly, the methods for the insert and remove operations, since their analysis is beyond the scope of this book.

14.2.1   One-Dimensional Range Searching

Before we proceed, we make a slight digression into the problem of finding and reporting the elements of an ordered dictionary whose keys are in a given one-dimensional range. This problem is called ***one-dimensional range searching***. Namely, given an ordered dictionary D, we want to perform the following operation:

findAllInRange(k_1, k_2): Return an enumeration of all the elements in D with key k, such that $k_1 \leq k \leq k_2$.
Input: Two objects (keys); *Output:* Enumeration.

This operation is useful for database and statistical applications. For example, for marketing purposes, we may want to screen prospective buyers of a product by selecting from a large database only those people whose age falls in a certain range. In addition to database applications such as this, we explore applications of the findAllInRange operation to geometric algorithms in the next chapter.

Let us discuss how we can use a binary search tree T (Section 7.3) representing D to perform operation findAllInRange(k_1, k_2). The algorithm is fairly straightforward. We use a recursive method treeRangeSearch that takes as arguments the range parameters k_1 and k_2 and a node v in T. If the node v is external, we are done.

If the node v is internal, but key(v), the key at v, is outside the range $[k_1, k_2]$, then we recurse on the child of v whose key might be in this range. On the other hand, if the node v is internal and key(v) is inside the range $[k_1, k_2]$, then we recurse on both of v's children. We give the pseudo-code for this algorithm in Code Fragment 14.2 and illustrate it in Figure 14.6. We execute findAllInRange(k_1, k_2) by calling treeRange-Search$(k_1, k_2, T.\text{root}())$. Intuitively, the treeRangeSearch method can be thought of as a modification of the standard searching algorithm for binary search trees (Code Fragment 7.2) so as to search for "both" of the keys k_1 and k_2.

Algorithm treeRangeSearch(k_1, k_2, v):

  Input: Search keys k_1 and k_2, and a node v of a binary search tree T

  Output: The elements stored in the subtree of T rooted at v, whose keys are greater than or equal to k_1 and less then or equal to k_2

  if v is an external node **then**
    return the empty set
  if $k_1 \leq$ key$(v) \leq k_2$ **then**
    $E_L \leftarrow$ treeRangeSearch$(k_1, k_2, T.\text{leftChild}(v))$
    $E_R \leftarrow$ treeRangeSearch$(k_1, k_2, T.\text{rightChild}(v))$
    return $E_L \cup \{\text{element}(v)\} \cup E_R$
  else if key$(v) < k_1$ **then**
    return treeRangeSearch$(k_1, k_2, T.\text{rightChild}(v))$
  else if $k_2 <$ key(v) **then**
    return treeRangeSearch$(k_1, k_2, T.\text{leftChild}(v))$

Code Fragment 14.2: Range search in a binary search tree.

A Java implementation of the range-searching algorithm is shown in Code Fragment 14.3.

The running time of the algorithm treeRangeSearch is proportional to the number of nodes visited. We will show that treeRangeSearch visits at most $2h + 2s + 1$ nodes, where h is the height of T and s is the number of elements reported. This bound will establish that the running time of treeRangeSearch is $O(h + s)$. To establish this bound, we identify each node v of T as belonging to one of three groups with respect to the range $[k_1, k_2]$:

- We say v is an ***outside node*** if the subtree rooted at v can contain only items with keys outside the range $[k_1, k_2]$.
- We say v is an ***inside node*** if the subtree rooted at v can contain only items with keys inside the range $[k_1, k_2]$.
- We say v is a ***boundary node*** if the subtree rooted at v can contain some items with keys inside the range $[k_1, k_2]$ and some with keys outside this range.

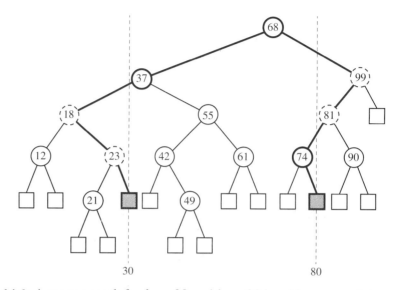

Figure 14.6: A range search for $k_1 = 30$ and $k_2 = 80$ in a binary search tree. Visited nodes are drawn in blue and outside nodes are drawn in black. The boundary nodes are on the paths (drawn with thick lines) from the root to the nodes reached when searching for keys k_1 and k_2 (boundary nodes not storing answers are drawn with dashes). The inside nodes are the 10 blue nodes that are not on these two paths.

```
public Enumeration findAllInRange(Object k1, Object k2) {
    return TreeRangeSearch(k1, k2, T.root()).elements();
}

protected Set TreeRangeSearch(Object k1, Object k2, Position v) {
    Object key = keyAtPos(v);
    if (T.isExternal(v))
        return new SequenceSet();
    if (C.isLessThan(k1, key) && C.isLessThan(key, k2)) {
        Set elemL = TreeRangeSearch(k1, k2, C, T.leftChild(v));
        elemL.insert(elementAtPos(v));
        Set elemR = TreeRangeSearch(k1, k2, C, T.rightChild(v));
        return elemL.unionWith(elemR);
    } else if (C.isLessThan(key, k1))
        return TreeRangeSearch(k1, k2, C, T.rightChild(v));
    else if (C.isLessThan(k2, key))
        return TreeRangeSearch(k1, k2, C, T.leftChild(v));
}
```

Code Fragment 14.3: Java implementation of the range-searching algorithm, which uses an auxiliary data structure for sets.

Note that we identify nodes based on the potential of their descendants to contain items in the range, and not on their actual descendants, since we visit nodes in a top-down fashion. When we come to a node, we do not yet know what its descendants store. The potential of a node v's descendents to store certain keys is of course determined by the keys stored at v's ancestors.

Consider the execution of a particular call to the treeRangeSearch method. Starting at the root r of T, we traverse a path of boundary nodes until we come to the first boundary node w (which may be the root) with key in the range $[k_1, k_2]$. In this case, we recursively search at both of w's children. This is the only boundary node in T that has both of its children searched. In fact, node w is the bottommost common node of the two paths that would respectively be traced by findElement(k_1) and findElement(k_2) in T. For each boundary node v visited from this point on, we will either make a single call at a child of v, which is also a boundary node, or we will make a call at one child of v that is a boundary node and the other child that is an inside node. Once we visit an inside node, we will visit all of its (inside node) descendents. We will never visit an outside node. Thus, since we spend a constant amount of work per node in T, we can account for all the time we spend by counting the number of nodes we visit.

Consider next the number of nodes we visit in T. We visit 0 outside nodes and at most $2h$ boundary nodes, where h is the height of T, since boundary nodes are on the search paths to k_1 and k_2 in T. Some of these boundary nodes may store items in the range $[k_1, k_2]$, but let us ignore this possibility (since we are considering a worst-case scenario). Each time we visit an inside node v, we visit the entire subtree $T(v)$ of T rooted at v. Since v is an inside node, however, the traversal of $T(v)$ will result in our adding to the enumeration all the items stored at internal nodes of $T(v)$, for these items are all in the range $[k_1, k_2]$. Thus, if $T(v)$ holds s_v items, then we visit $2s_v + 1$ nodes of $T(v)$. (To see this, note that an inorder traversal of $T(v)$ alternates between internal nodes and external nodes.) Adding up the costs for all the internal nodes we visit, we see that the total number of nodes we visit is at most $2h + 2s + 1$. Therefore, operation findAllInRange runs in $O(h + s)$ time.

For the sake of efficiency, we choose an AVL tree (Section 7.4), or some other balanced binary search tree, instead of a generic binary search tree, to implement T. So, if we store n items in T, then T has height $O(\log n)$. Therefore, one-dimensional range searching in a dictionary with n items can be implemented in $O(\log n + s)$ time, where s is the number of elements in the range that are reported.

In the next section, we show how to use the one-dimensional range tree structure for two-dimensional range searching.

14.2.2   Two-Dimensional Range Trees

The two-dimensional range tree (Figure 14.7) is a data structure that realizes the two-dimensional dictionary ADT. It consists of a ***primary*** structure, which is a binary search tree T (Section 7.3), together with a number of smaller ***auxiliary*** structures. Specifically, as we describe below, each internal node in the primary structure T stores a reference to a related auxiliary structure.

The primary structure T is a binary search tree built assuming the x-coordinates of the items are their only keys. For a node v of T, we denote with $\text{key}(v)$ the x-coordinate of the item stored at v. In addition, each node v of T stores an interval $[\min_x(v), \max_x(v)]$, where $\min_x(v)$ is the smallest x-coordinate for any item stored in the subtree rooted at v (including v itself), and $\max_x(v)$ is the largest x-coordinate for any item stored in the subtree rooted at v.

This additional information that we store at the nodes of T does not pose much of an additional computational burden. For, given a standard binary search tree T built on the x-coordinates of our set of elements, we can compute all the $\min_x$ and $\max_x$ values in linear time. We leave the details of this computation to an exercise, however.

In order to guarantee an efficient running time for insertions and deletions, the primary structure T must be a so called "$BB[\alpha]$-tree," which is an advanced type of balanced search tree whose description is beyond the scope of this book. Instead, we describe the running times of range tree methods in terms of the height of the primary tree T, which we denote as $h(T)$. There are many cases in the context of range-searching queries, however, where $h(T)$ will be $O(\log n)$. For example, if all the x-coordinates of the points are known in advance, then the tree T can be statically built to have logarithmic height. Alternately, if the insertion and removal of points can be viewed as a random process, then the expected height of T is $O(\log n)$, where n is the number of points in the two-dimensional dictionary. So the term $h(T)$ can in many cases be thought of simply as being $O(\log n)$.

To also support searching in terms of the y-coordinates, we use a collection of auxiliary data structures, which are themselves one-dimensional range trees that use y-coordinates as their keys. Specifically, each internal node v of T holds a one-dimensional range tree $T(v)$ that stores the same set of items as the subtree rooted at v in T (including v itself), but using the y-coordinates as keys. Each one-dimensional range tree $T(v)$ is implemented exactly as described in the previous subsection. That is, it is a balanced binary search tree, such as an AVL tree or a red-black-tree. The total space used by the primary structure T and all its auxiliary structures is more than linear, but not by a large factor, as the following proposition shows.

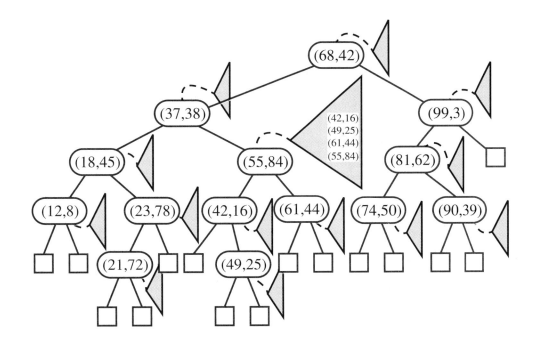

Figure 14.7: An example of a two-dimensional range tree. We draw the nodes of the primary structure in blue, and we schematically indicate the auxiliary structures as black triangles. We illustrate the contents of one of the auxiliary structures as well.

Proposition 14.5: *A range tree T storing n items uses $O(nh(T))$ space, where $h(T)$ is the height of T.*

Justification: The justification is based upon a simple counting argument. Let o be some item stored in the range tree. Item o is first stored in the primary tree T at some node v, which requires $O(1)$ space. In addition, o is stored in $T(v)$ and each auxiliary tree $T(u)$ such that u is an ancestor of v. In the worst case, v has h ancestors (including itself); hence, in the worst case there are $h(T)$ copies of o stored in the range tree. Thus, the total space required by the range tree is $O(nh(T))$. ∎

Thus, if the primary structure T is balanced, then the total space used by the range tree with T as its primary structure is $O(n \log n)$.

We next discuss how we can use a two-dimensional range tree to answer 2-D range-searching queries.

14.2.3 Two-Dimensional Range Searching

Suppose we are now given four parameters, a, b, c, and d, and asked to return the elements with coordinates (x, y) such that $a \leq x \leq b$ and $c \leq y \leq d$. That is, we are asked to return all points with x-coordinates in the range $[a, b]$ and y-coordinates in the range $[c, d]$, which can be viewed geometrically as the problem of determining all points in the rectangle with vertices (a, c), (a, d), (b, c), and (b, d).

The algorithm for answering a two-dimensional range-searching query begins by performing what is essentially a one-dimensional range searching query on the primary structure T, using a and b to specify a one-dimensional range of x-coordinates. Recall that performing a one-dimensional range query such as this involves performing a search along the boundary nodes and visiting the inside nodes with respect to the range $[a, b]$. In adapting this algorithm for two-dimensional range searching, we still traverse down T in search of inside nodes. We make one important modification, however. As soon as we realize we are at a node v in T, such that the subtree rooted at v only contains elements with x-coordinates in the range $[a, b]$, then, rather than returning all these elements, we perform instead a one-dimensional range-searching query in $T(v)$, the auxiliary structure for v. We give in Code Fragment 14.4 the pseudo-code for algorithm 2DTreeRange-Search (a, b, c, d, v), which performs this search, when invoked as 2DTreeRange-Search$(a, b, c, d, T.\text{root}())$. (See Figure 14.8.)

Algorithm 2DTreeRangeSearch(a, b, c, d, v):
    Input: Search keys a, b, c, and d, and node v in a range tree T
    Output: The elements stored in the subtree of T rooted at v whose keys are in
        the x-range $[a, b]$ and the y-range $[c, d]$

    if v is an external node **then**
        return the empty set
    if $[\min_x(v), \max_x(v)] \subseteq [a, b]$ **then**
        return $T(v).\text{findAllInRange}(c, d)$
    else if $a \leq \text{key}(v) \leq b$ **then**
        $E_L \leftarrow$ 2DTreeRangeSearch$(a, b, c, d, T.\text{leftChild}(v))$
        $E_R \leftarrow$ 2DTreeRangeSearch$(a, b, c, d, T.\text{rightChild}(v))$
        return $E_L \cup \{\text{element}(v)\} \cup E_R$
    else if $\text{key}(v) < a$ **then**
        return 2DTreeRangeSearch$(a, b, c, d, T.\text{rightChild}(v))$
    else if $b < \text{key}(v)$ **then**
        return TreeRangeSearch$(a, b, c, d, T.\text{leftChild}(v))$

Code Fragment 14.4: Two-dimensional range searching in a 2-D range tree.

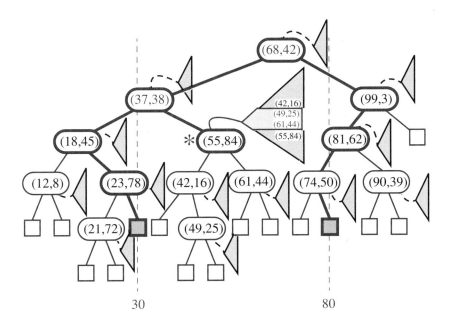

Figure 14.8: An example two-dimensional range search, for the range $[30, 80] \times [20, 50]$. We show the edges traversed in bold, and we mark with an asterix (*) the one node, in this case, for which we perform a range search in its auxiliary structure. We also highlight, in blue, two elements in boundary nodes that are also included in the range.

We summarize the performance of the two-dimensional range-searching algorithm in the following proposition.

Proposition 14.6: *A two-dimensional range tree T storing n items performs a two-dimensional range searching query in time $O(h(T)\log n + k)$, where k is the number of elements returned and $h(T)$ is the height of the primary tree T.*

Justification: We have already mentioned that one-dimensional range queries can be solved in $O(\log n + k)$ time using a one-dimensional range tree implemented with a balanced binary search tree, such as an AVL tree or a red-black tree, which is what we are assuming for each auxiliary tree. The claimed bounds follow, then, from the observation that there are $O(h(T))$ inside nodes in the primary structure T that we will visit with respect to any two-dimensional range-searching query, and each item in the range is output exactly once. ■

Thus, assuming that the height of primary structure is $O(\log n)$, then we can answer two-dimensional range-searching queries in $O(\log^2 n + k)$ time.

There are a number of interesting schemes that can improve the running time for performing two-dimensional range queries to be $O(\log n + k)$. We explore one such scheme in Section 14.2.5. Before we do this, however, let us discuss how we can perform insertions and deletions in a two-dimensional range tree.

14.2.4   Insertion and Deletion

Suppose now that we are given an object o with key pair (x, y), which we would like to insert into a range tree. The method for doing this insertion follows naturally from the definition of the two-dimensional range tree.

We begin by first performing an insertion of x into the primary structure, the binary search tree T. For example, if we are assuming T is a standard (unbalanced) binary search tree, we can do this using the insertion method described in Section 7.3.2. Recall that this method places the new item o in an external node v, and then adds external-node children to make v internal. Independent of the details of how we insert the new item in the primary structure T, if we were simply performing a binary search tree insertion, then we would be done at this point. But in our case this insertion simply sets up the structure of the primary structure T. We must still update the auxiliary structures. Specifically, in order to maintain the property that, for each node u in T, the auxiliary tree $T(u)$ holds all the objects in the subtree of T rooted at u, then we have to insert the new object o into each auxiliary tree $T(u)$ such that u is an ancestor of v. We can do this by traversing up the tree T from the node v and using the appropriate balanced binary search tree insertion method at each node u we encounter. Recall that we are maintaining each auxiliary tree as a balanced binary search tree, such as an AVL tree, red-black tree, or splay tree. (See Figure 14.9.) Since insertion in a balanced search tree can be done in $O(\log n)$ time, this entire insertion algorithm runs in $O(h(T) \log n)$ time in the worst case, where $h(T)$ denotes the height of T (which will typically be $O(\log n)$).

Now suppose that we wish to delete some object o, with key pair (x, y), that is already in the range tree. As with object insertion, we begin by changing the primary structure T, and, as we did with insertion, we use the standard binary search tree method for object removal. We first locate the vertex v in T that is holding the object o (either by an explicit search or by using a locator). There are two cases.

1. The node v has an external-node child u. In this case, we simply replace v with u's sibling w. This has the effect of removing the vertex v (and, hence the object o) from the tree T. It does not, however, change any of the ancestor-descendent relationships for pairs of nodes not including v. Thus, the only auxiliary trees that we need to change are those on the path from the old node

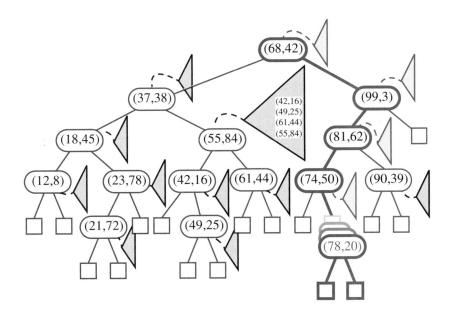

Figure 14.9: An example insertion in a two-dimensional range tree. We show the key, $(78, 20)$ of the new element in blue, and we highlight, in blue, each auxiliary structure into which the new element must be inserted.

v (which is now w, the former sibling of u) to the root, and the only change required for them is that we remove from them the object o. We therefore traverse the path up T from w to the root, removing o from the auxiliary structure $T(z)$ for each node z along this path. (See Figure 14.10.) Since each such removal can be implemented to run in $O(\log n)$ time, the worst-case running time to remove o from the range tree in this case is $O(h(T)\log n)$.

2. The node v has no external-node children. In this case, we find the parent w of the external node u that is the immediate successor of v in an inorder listing. We then move the object p stored at w to be at v, and we replace w by u's sibling. This effectively updates the primary structure T. To update all the auxiliary structures that need to change, we traverse up T from the old node w (which is now the former sibling of u). Since we moved p up to the vertex v, as we now move up T, we delete p from the auxiliary tree of each node we visit until we reach the node v. Once we reach v and for the remainder of the traversal up T, we delete from each auxiliary tree the object o. Since each such removal can be implemented to run in $O(\log n)$ time, the worst-case running time to remove o from the range tree in this case is also $O(h(T)\log n)$.

Thus, we may summarize as in the proposition that follows.

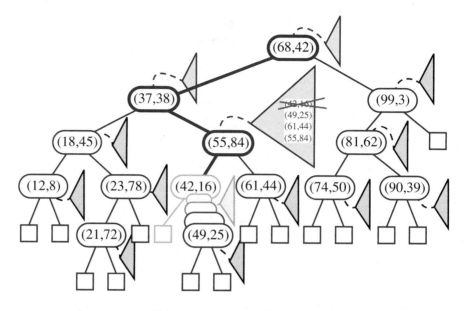

Figure 14.10: An example object removal from a two-dimensional range tree. We illustrate the removal of the element with key $(42, 16)$, and we highlight, in blue, each auxiliary structure from which we need to remove this element.

Proposition 14.7: *We can perform object insertion and removal from a two-dimensional range tree that has as its primary structure a binary search tree T, that holds n objects in $O(h(T)\log n)$ time, where $h(T)$ denotes the height of T.*

As we have observed before, if we have additional knowledge about the application domain, for our range tree that keeps $h(T)$ being $O(\log n)$, then this implies that we can perform object insertion and removal in $(\log^2 n)$ time. This running time might at first seem to be the best we can do for any of the two-dimensional range tree operations, but we can actually do better in some cases. We discuss one such case in the following subsection.

14.2.5 Priority Search Trees

In this subsection, we discuss the ***priority search tree*** data structure, which is also known as a ***Cartesian tree*** or ***treap***, and we give an application of priority search trees to the problem of performing range-searching queries. Throughout this subsection, we will be making the simplifying assumption that the x-coordinates of objects are known in advance. This will allow us to achieve a running time of $O(\log n + k)$ for answering range queries.

The priority search tree data structure is not actually designed to answer general kinds of two-dimensional range-searching queries—it is designed to answer what are often called ***three-sided*** or ***semi-infinite*** range searching:

threeSidedRange(a, b, c):   Return an enumeration of all the objects in the current set that have key-value coordinates (x, y) such that $a \leq x \leq b$ and $c \leq y$.
Input: Three numbers; ***Output:*** An enumeration.

Geometrically, this range query asks us to return all points between two vertical lines ($x = a$ and $x = b$) and above a horizontal line ($y = c$). We could also consider other variants, of course, where we use the numbers a, b, and c to define a different set of three out of the usual four boundaries in a range query. For concreteness, we stick with the above definition for three-sided range queries, remembering that any data structure we devise for this kind of three-sided range query can be easily converted into a data structure for any other kind of three-sided range query. (Intuitively, each other choice simply amounts to a "turning of the head" to change the names we give to coordinates.)

An elegant data structure for answering three-sided range queries is the ***priority search tree***. This data structure is similar to the range tree, in that it uses as its primary structure a binary search tree T that is built using x-coordinates as key values. As we have observed already, such a tree can be used to easily answer one-dimensional range queries involving x-coordinates. The auxiliary information we add to T to handle three-sided range queries is much simpler than that added for the range tree, however. Specifically, for each internal node v in T, we add a reference, high_y, that points to the object stored in the subtree rooted at v (including v itself) that has the highest y-coordinate and has not already been referenced by an ancestor of v. If there is no such object (because all the objects in v's subtree have already been referenced by ancestors of v), then let high_y point to the null object. It might not be immediately obvious, but these simple rules imply that the high_y values satisfy the heap-order property in the nodes of T (Section 6.3). That is, the high_y value stored at any node with a parent will never be more than the high_y value stored at the parent. In fact, this simple property motivates the term "priority search tree." This simple property also implies that the total space needed for a priority search tree holding n objects is $O(n)$. (See Figure 14.11.)

Constructing a Priority Search Tree

It is fairly easy to convert any binary search tree T into a priority search tree. To do so, we take a binary search tree T and examine its root r. If r holds no object, then we set high_y to point to the null object, and we are done. In addition, if r itself

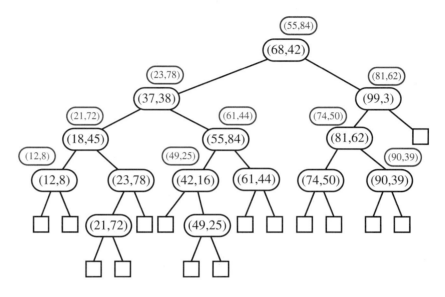

Figure 14.11: An example priority search tree. If a node has a nonnull high_y reference, then we show the (x, y) key of that reference next to the node in blue.

holds an object, but has no descendants holding objects, then we simply define high_y $= r$, and we are done. Otherwise, we recursively form a priority search tree for each child u and v of r. After the recursive calls return for r's children, we must set the high_y reference for r. To do this, we compare r.element, u.high_y, and v.high_y, and we set r.high_y to the one that has largest y-coordinate. If we set r.high_y $= r$.element in this case, then we are done. But if we set r.high_y to the high_y reference of one of r's children, then we have just violated the priority search property at that child. Without loss of generality, let us assume that it is the node v from which r got its high_y reference, so we are now violating the priority search tree rule at v that requires that no ancestor of v has the same high_y reference as v. To repair this situation, we perform a kind of down-heap bubbling action to restore the property that each node's high_y value is correct. Unlike the down-heap bubbling action in the heap construction algorithm, in this case we are bubbling down an "empty" slot in the structure. We give the details of this modified down-heap bubbling method, which we call FixHighY, in Code Fragment 14.5, calling it with the node v that just lost its high_y value to r.

The FixHighY fix-up method is initially called at r's child v, and continues recursively down the tree T until we reach an external node or run out of available objects. Thus, this update operation runs in $O(\log n)$ time (remember that we are assuming that we know all the x-coordinates of the pairs in our set in advance, which implies that we can build T as a balanced tree from the start without using

Algorithm FixHighY(v):

    Let u and w denote v's children.

    if $y(v.\text{high\_y}) > y(v.\text{element})$ **then**

        $C \leftarrow \{v.\text{element}, u.\text{high\_y}, w.\text{high\_y}\}$

        $\{C$ is a set of candidate replacements for $v.\text{high\_y}\}$

    else

        $C \leftarrow \{u.\text{high\_y}, w.\text{high\_y}\}$

    Set $v.\text{high\_y}$ to point to the element in C with largest y-coordinate.

    if $v.\text{high\_y} = w.\text{high\_y} \neq$ **null** **then**

        Call FixHighY(w).

    else if $v.\text{high\_y} = u.\text{high\_y} \neq$ **null** **then**

        Call FixHighY(u).

    else

        return $\{$for we are done fixing high_y references$\}$

Code Fragment 14.5: The method for restoring the heap-order property to the high_y values in a priority search tree. We use $y(p)$ to denote p's y-coordinate.

rotations). This completes the algorithm for converting a balanced binary search tree T into a priority search tree. Using an amortized argument like the one used in Section 6.3.4, for bottom-up heap construction, we can show that the running time for converting an n-node balanced search tree into a priority search tree is $O(n)$.

Searching in a Priority Search Tree

Let us now discuss how we can use a priority search tree to answer a three-sided range query. Therefore, let a, b, and c be three parameters for which we wish to determine all objects in our current collection that have (x, y) key pairs that satisfy the inequalities $a \leq x \leq b$ and $c \leq y$. To answer this query, we traverse down the primary structure T, in a fashion similar to that for performing a one-dimensional range-searching query on x-coordinates for the parameters a and b. One important difference, however, is that we only continue searching in a subtree if the high_y reference for the current node has a y-coordinate at least as big as c. We also check to see if this reference satisfies the range-searching query, and if so, we add it to the output. In addition, if the element at the current node satisfies the query and it has not been output previously (because it was a high_y for some other node), then we output this element as well. We then recurse as necessary. We give the pseudo-code for this method in Code Fragment 14.6, describing a method 3SideTreeRangeSearch(a, b, c, v), which we call by passing it the three parameters a, b, and c, and the root of the priority search tree T. (See Figure 14.12.)

Algorithm 3SideTreeRangeSearch(a,b,c,v):

> *Input:* Search range $[a,b]$ of x-coordinates, lower bound c on y-coordinates, and a node v of a priority search tree T
>
> *Output:* The elements stored in the subtree of T rooted at v with x-coordinates in $[a,b]$ and y-coordinates at least c
>
> **if** v.high_y = **null or** $y(v.\text{high\_y}) < c$ **then**
> > **return** the empty set
>
> **if** $x(v.\text{high\_y}) \in [a,b]$ **then**
> > $C \leftarrow \{v.\text{high\_y}\}$ {we should output v.high_y}
>
> **else**
> > $C \leftarrow \emptyset$
>
> **if** $a \le \text{key}(v) \le b$ **then**
> > $E_L \leftarrow$ 3SideTreeRangeSearch($a,b,c,T.\text{leftChild}(v)$)
> > $E_R \leftarrow$ 3SideTreeRangeSearch($a,b,c,T.\text{rightChild}(v)$)
> > **if** $y(v.\text{high\_y}) > y(v.\text{element})$ **then**
> > > **return** $C \cup E_L \cup \{v.\text{element}\} \cup E_R$
> >
> > **else**
> > > **return** $C \cup E_L \cup E_R$ {v.element has already been output}
>
> **else if** $\text{key}(v) < a$ **then**
> > **return** 3SideTreeRangeSearch($a,b,c,T.\text{rightChild}(v)$)
>
> **else if** $b < \text{key}(v)$ **then**
> > **return** 3SideTreeRangeSearch($a,b,c,T.\text{leftChild}(v)$)

Code Fragment 14.6: Three-sided range searching in a priority search tree.

Let us analyze the running time of using a priority search tree to answer three-sided range-searching queries. We will use an amortized argument based on the accounting method. Let us pay one cyber-dollar for each time we visit a node in a priority search tree. Since we spend $O(1)$ time for each node we visit, this charging scheme is sufficient to pay for all the computations needed to answer a three-sided range query. If we visit a node that is a boundary node with respect to the x-range $[a,b]$, then we charge the cyber-dollar for this visit to the node. Suppose, on the other hand, that we visit a node that is an inside node with respect to the x-range $[a,b]$. If this node holds an element that we need to output, then we charge one cyber-dollar to this element. Otherwise, if this node produces no output, then we charge one cyber-dollar to the same thing we charged the parent of this node. Since we do not recurse beyond this later case, we know that each output element will be charged at most three times (once by the node and at most once from each of its children) and each boundary node will be charged at most twice (once from itself and at most once from an inside child).

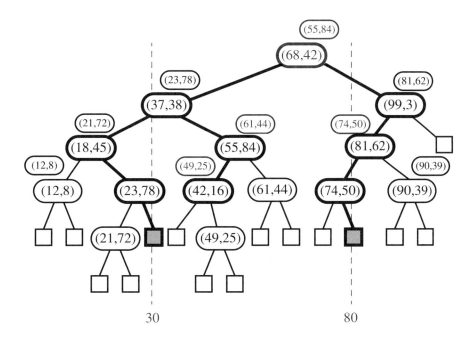

Figure 14.12: An example implementation of three-sided range-searching query in a priority search tree. We highlight in blue each element that is output, and we draw in bold each edge and node that is visited. Note that $(74, 50)$ and $(55, 84)$ are both output as high_y values before their nodes are visited.

Therefore, the total time spent answering a three-sided range query with a priority search tree holding n objects is $O(\log n + k)$, where k is the number of elements in the enumeration (assuming, of course, that the tree T is balanced). To sum up, we have the following:

Proposition 14.8: *A priority search tree holding n objects can be constructed in $O(n)$ time and $O(n)$ space, from a balanced binary search tree, to answer three-sided range queries in $O(\log n + k)$ time, where k is the number of elements returned.*

14.2.6 Priority Range Trees

Priority search trees can be used to speed up the running time of answering standard four-sided, two-dimensional range queries. The resulting data structure, which is known as the ***priority range tree***, is quite ingenious actually, as it uses priority search trees as auxiliary structures in a way that achieves the same space bound as traditional range trees.

Let T be a given balanced binary search tree built for the x-coordinates of a set of n objects with (x, y) pairs as keys. To convert T into a priority range tree, we simply visit each internal node v other than the root in T and construct as an auxiliary structure a priority search tree $T(v)$ for v. If v is a left child, then we construct $T(v)$ to answer three-sided range queries of the form $a \leq x$, $c \leq y \leq d$, for three parameters a, c, and d. If v is a right child, then we construct $T(v)$ to answer three-sided range queries of the form $x \leq b$, $c \leq y \leq d$, for three parameters b, c, and d. Thus, for any internal node u in T, u's left child can quickly answer three-sided range queries that are open on the right, and u's right child can quickly answer three-sided range queries that are open on the left. This preprocessing step requires $O(n \log n)$ time and space to accomplish.

Suppose we are now given four parameters a, b, c, and d, and asked to construct an enumeration of all objects in our collection that have (x, y) key pairs such that $a \leq x \leq b$ and $c \leq y \leq d$. To answer this query, we search down the search tree T, until we come to the first vertex v such that the element o stored at v has x-coordinate in the interval $[a, b]$. We then ask v's left child to solve a three-sided range query to return all objects with (x, y) keys such that $a \leq x$ and $c \leq y \leq d$ (assuming v's left child is internal, of course). Next, we ask v's right child to solve a three-sided range query to return all objects with (x, y) keys such that $x \leq b$ and $c \leq y \leq d$ (assuming v's right child is internal, of course). That completes the algorithm.

The reason that this algorithm works is that, in searching down T, each node we bypass is guaranteed to hold objects that fall strictly outside the specified x-range until we get to the node v. This node may have descendant objects within the range. Rather than continue to traverse down T, however, we perform two three-sided range queries at v's children. These queries return objects within the specified four-sided range, because the objects in the subtree, rooted at v's left child, must have x-coordinates less than or equal to o's, which in turn is less than or equal to b. Likewise, the objects in the subtree, rooted at v's right child, must have x-coordinates greater than or equal to o's, which in turn is greater than or equal to a. The total running time for performing this search is $O(\log n + k)$. Therefore, we may summarize as follows:

Proposition 14.9: *A priority range tree can be constructed from a balanced binary search tree holding n elements in $O(n \log n)$ time and space. It can be used to answer (four-sided) two-dimensional range queries in $O(\log n + k)$ time, where k is the number of answers.*

Higher-Dimensional Range Searching

We have been restricting our attention to two-dimensional range queries, but the approach of using auxiliary structures extends naturally to higher dimensions. For example, to construct a three-dimensional range tree, we can take a binary search tree T, and attach at each node in T an auxiliary tree that is a two-dimensional range tree. This will result in an $O(n \log^2 n)$ space data structure that can answer three-dimensional range-searching queries in $O(\log^2 n + k)$ time. Extending this further to $d \geq 1$ dimensions, for some fixed constant d, results in a data structure that uses $O(n \log^{d-1} n)$ space and answers d-dimensional range queries in $O(\log^d n + k)$ time. The running time can be improved slightly to $O(\log^{d-1} n + k)$, if we utilize priority range trees at the level that calls for a data structure for answering two-dimensional range queries. These results are quite impressive, but they come at a price. For one thing, they require that we know the set of coordinates in advance, for otherwise we cannot easily achieve the polylogarithmic query times. More importantly, however, these results require that we allow for a super-linear amount of space to be used. In fact, the space usage increases significantly for higher-dimensional spaces, thus it is natural to consider what kinds of results can be achieved when we are limited to a linear amount of space. We explore this topic in the next section.

14.3 Partition Trees

Multi-dimensional data sets often come from large applications; hence, memory space is often a scarce commodity when it comes to data structures for storing and querying multi-dimensional data. The multi-dimensional objects in such collections are viewed as points in some d-dimensional space. In order to save memory, a large number of different tree-based data structures have been invented and reinvented for storing d-dimensional points using a linear amount of memory space, where the dimensionality d is assumed to be a fixed constant. There a number of linear-space multi-dimensional search trees, including quadtrees, octrees, k-d trees, balanced box decompositions, fair-split trees, linear decision trees, binary space partition (BSP) trees, and hierarchical cutting trees, to name just a few. These structures have important differences between them, some of which we will explore in this section, but they all nevertheless fall into the same general framework. They are ***partition trees***.

A partition tree is a rooted tree T that has n external nodes, where n is the number of d-dimensional points in our given set S. Each external node of a partition tree T stores a different point from S. Internal nodes in a partition tree do not store points. Instead, each internal node v in a partition tree T corresponds to a region of d-dimensional space, which is then divided into some number c of different cells or regions associated with v's children. For each region R associated with a child u of v, we require that all the points in u's subtree fall inside the region R. Ideally, the c different cells for v's children are easily distinguished using a constant number of comparisons and arithmetic calculations, so that if we are searching down T for a specific point, we can go from one level to the next in constant time.

Partition trees are used to quickly answer a number of different queries for a collection S of points, including the following:

- **Range Searching Queries**: Return all the points in S that are inside a given axis-aligned rectangle (or hyper-rectangle in higher-dimensions).
- **Fixed-Radius Searching**: Return all the points in S that are within a given distance l from a given query point p.
- **Nearest-Neighbor Searching**: Return the point in S that is closest to a given query point p.
- **Generalized Range Searching**: return all the points in S that fall inside a given region R, which may be a half-space, a tetrahedron, or some other easily described shape in d-dimensional space.

Also, partition trees can often be updated to insert and remove points in the collection S. Modifying partition trees in such "dynamic" environments is often rather complicated, however, so we will restrict our attention in this section to the *static* case, in which the collection S of n points in d-dimensional space is given in advance. The motivation for this is that S may be a stable database of information that needs to have a large number of different queries performed on it. For example, S may be a collection of heavenly bodies taken from a sky survey that will then be searched repeatedly by astronomers to make new and interesting discoveries about the observable universe.

In this section, we discuss some of the important variants of partition tree data structures and illustrate their usefulness by describing how they can be used to answer some of the queries listed above.

14.3.1 Quadtrees and Octrees

The first partition tree data structures we discuss are *quadtrees* and *octrees*, which are different dimensional versions of essentially the same data structure. Quadtrees are designed for two-dimensional data and octrees are designed for 3-dimensional data. In order to keep our discussion (and our figures) simple, let us concentrate on the quadtree data structure, and later outline how it can be extended to three dimensions to give rise to the octree structure. The main application for quadtrees is for sets of points that come from images, where x- and y-coordinates are integers, because the data points come from image pixels. In addition, they exhibit their best properties if the distributions of points is fairly nonuniform, with some areas being mostly empty and others being dense.

Suppose we are given a set S of n points in the plane. In addition, let R denote a square region that contains all the points of S (for example, R could be a bounding box of a 2048×2048 image that produced the set S). The quadtree data structure is a partition tree T such that the root r of T is associated with the region R. To get to the next level in T, we subdivide R into four equal-sized squares R_1, R_2, R_3, and R_4, and we associate each square R_i with a potential child of the root r. Specifically, we create a child v_i of r, if the square R_i contains a point in S. If a square R_i contains no points of S, then we create no child of r for it. This process of refining R into the squares R_1, R_2, R_3, and R_4 is called a *split*.

The *quadtree* T is defined by recursively performing a split at each child v of r if necessary. That is, each child v of r has a square region R_i associated with it, and if the region R_i for v contains more than one point of S, then we perform a split at v, subdividing R_i into four equal-sized squares and repeating the above subdivision process at v. We continue in this manner, splitting squares that contain more than one point into four subsquares, and recursing on the nonempty subsquares, until we have separated all the points of S into individual squares. We then store each point p in S at the external node of T that corresponds to the smallest square in the subdivision process that contains p. We store at each internal node v a concise representation of the split that we performed for v. We illustrate an example point set and an associated quadtree in Figure 14.13.

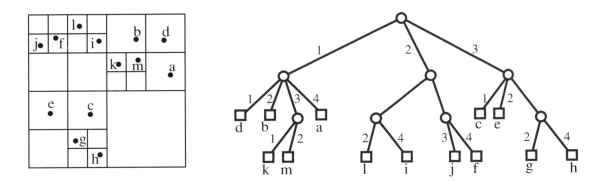

Figure 14.13: A quadtree. We illustrate an example point set and its corresponding quadtree data structure. We number the edges by quadrants in a counterclockwise fashion.

As we have just defined it, there is potentially no upper bound on the depth of the quadtree T defined on a set S of n points. For example, S could contain two points that happen to be very close to one another, and it may take a long sequence of splits before we separate these two points. Thus, it is customary for quadtree designers to specify some upper bound D on the depth of T. In this case, we stop performing splits any time we reach a node of T at depth D. Given a set S of n points in the plane, we can construct a quadtree T for S so as to spend $O(n)$ time building each level of T. Thus, in the worst case, constructing such a depth-bounded quadtree takes $O(Dn)$ time.

Range Searching in a Quadtree

One of the queries that quadtrees are often used to answer is range searching. Suppose then that we are given a rectangle A aligned with the coordinate axes, and are asked to use a quadtree T to return all the points in S that are contained in A. The method for answering this query is quite simple. We start with the root r of T, and we compare the region R for r to A. If A and R do not intersect at all, then we are done—there are no points in the subtree rooted at r that fall inside A. Alternatively, if A completely contains R, then we simply enumerate all the external node descendants of r. These are two simple cases. If instead R and A intersect, but A does not completely contain R, then we recursively perform this search on each child v of r.

In performing such a range-searching query, we can in the worst case traverse the entire tree T and not produce any output. Thus, the worst-case running time for performing a range query in a depth D quadtree, with n external nodes is $O(Dn)$. From a worst-case point of view, answering a range-searching query with a quadtree is actually worse than a brute-force search through the set S, which would take $O(n)$ time to answer a two-dimensional range query. In practice, however, the quadtree typically allows for range-searching queries to be processed faster than this. In fact, under some uniformity assumptions about the distribution of points in S, we can show that the expected time to perform a range query in a quadtree is $O(\sqrt{n}+k)$, where k is the number of answers.

Octrees

The quadtree and the related range query method can be extended into three dimensions, as well. In this case, we let the bounding region R be a cube, and if R needs to be split, then we subdivide R into eight equal-sized cubes in the natural way. Thus, each node in the partition tree T that results can have as many as eight children, which is why this structure is called an *octree*. The methods for constructing such a tree and for performing three-dimensional range queries with it are natural extensions of the two-dimensional methods we have outlined above.

The quadtree and octree data structures are effective ways of storing two- and three-dimensional point data, but they have some drawbacks. One drawback, of course, is that there is no implicit bound on the depth of a quadtree or octree. The size and depth of such a tree T may have no relationship at all to the number, n, of points in the collection S. In practice, however, this is not a big concern, because the depth of a quadtree rarely goes over $O(\log n)$, if one stops splitting when cells contain at most some small constant number of points. Still, even in practice, it is common to have nodes in a quadtree or octree with only one child, which can be a source of inefficiency. Even then, the depth of a quadtree (or octree) is not a very big drawback.

There is another drawback to quadtrees and octrees, which is that they do not generalize well to higher dimensions. In particular, each node in a four-dimensional analogue of an octree (typically called a four-dimensional "octree") can have as many as 16 children. Each internal node in a d-dimensional octree can have has many as 2^d children. Thus, as we go to higher-dimensional domains, the time to process each node in an octree (for both construction and search) goes up exponentially in the dimension. This is probably the reason that the quadtree/octree approach is used almost exclusively in two- and three-dimensions, where the out-degree of nodes is not a serious drawback. To overcome the out-degree drawback for storing data from dimensions higher than three data, structure designers often consider alternative partition tree structures that are binary.

14.3.2 k-d Trees

Another kind of partition data structure is the k-d tree, which has a number of similarities and differences with the quadtree structure. The k-d tree data structure is actually a family of partition tree data structures, all of which are binary partition trees for storing k-dimensional data (which motivates the name "k-d tree"). Like the quadtree data structure, each node v in a k-d tree is associated with a rectangular region R, although in the case of k-d trees this region is not necessarily square. The difference is that, when it comes time to perform a split operation for a node v in a k-d tree, it is done with a single line that is perpendicular to one of the coordinate axes. For three- or higher-dimensional data sets, this "line" is an axis-aligned hyperplane. Thus, no matter the dimensionality, a k-d tree is a binary tree, for we resolve a split by associating the part of v's region R to the "left" of the splitting line with v's left child, and associating the part of v's region R to the "right" of the splitting line with v's right child. As with the quadtree structure, we do not perform splits at nodes whose region R contains only one point, or, alternately, we may stop performing splits if the number of points in a region falls below some fixed constant threshold. (See Figure 14.14.)

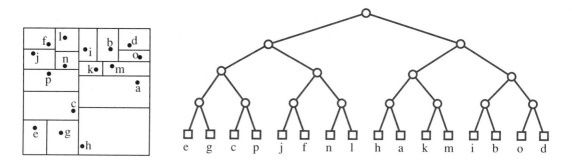

Figure 14.14: An example *k*-d tree. This figure illustrates a point-based *k*-d tree in two-dimensions.

There are fundamentally two different kinds of *k*-d trees, ***region-based*** *k*-d trees and ***point-based*** *k*-d trees. Region-based *k*-d trees are essentially binary versions of quadtrees and octrees. Each time a rectangular region *R* needs to be split in a region-based *k*-d tree, the region *R* is divided exactly in half by a line perpendicular to the longest side of *R*. If there is more than one longest side of *R*, then they are split in a "round robin" fashion. On the other hand, point-based *k*-d trees, which are also known as ***optimized*** *k*-d trees or ***adaptive*** *k*-d trees, perform splits based on the distribution of points inside a rectangular region.

The method for splitting a rectangular region *R* containing a subset $S' \subseteq S$ in a point-based *k*-d tree involves two steps. In the first step, we determine the dimension *i* that has the largest variation in dimension *i* from among those points in S'. This can be done, for example, by finding for each dimension *j* the points in S' with minimum and maximum dimension *j* value, and taking *i* to be the dimension with the largest gap between these two values. In the second step we determine the median dimension *i* value from among all those points in S', and we split *R* with a line going through this median perpendicular to the dimension *i* axis. Thus, the split for *R* divides the set of points in S' in half, but may not divide the region *R* itself very evenly. Using a linear-time median-finding method (Section 8.6), this splitting step can be performed in $O(k|S'|)$ time. Therefore, the running time for building a *k*-d tree for a set of *n* points can be characterized by the following recurrence relation

$$T(n) = 2T(n/2) + kn,$$

which is $O(kn\log n)$. Moreover, since we divide in two the size of the set of points associated with a node with each split, the height of *T* is $\lceil \log n \rceil$. Figure 14.14 illustrates a point-based *k*-d tree that could be built using this algorithm.

The advantage of point-based *k*-d trees is that they are guaranteed to have nice depth and construction times. The drawback of point-based schemes is that they may give rise to "long-and-skinny" rectangular regions, which are usually considered bad for most k-d tree query methods. In practice, however, such long-and-skinny regions are quite rare, and most of the rectangular regions associated with the nodes of a k-d tree are "boxy."

Nearest Neighbor Searching with k-D Trees

Let us discuss how k-d trees can be used to answer queries. They can, for example, be used to answer range-searching queries using an algorithm similar to that used for quadtrees and octrees, but without the exponential overhead in the dimension. Since the method is similar to that given for quadtrees and octrees, let us consider here a different kind of query that can be answered efficiently by a k-d tree: nearest-neighbor searching.

Recall that in nearest-neighbor searching we are given a query point p and asked to find the point in S that is closest to p. The standard way to use a k-d tree T to answer such a query is as follows. We first search down the tree T to locate the external node v with smallest rectangular region R that contains p. Any points of S that fall in R or in the region associated with v's sibling are then compared to find a current closest neighbor q. We can then define a sphere centered at p and containing q as a current nearest-neighbor sphere s. Given this sphere, we then perform a traversal of T (with a bottom-up traversal being preferred) to find any regions associated with external nodes of T that intersect s. If, during this traversal, we find a point closer than q, then we update the reference q to refer to this new point and we update the sphere s to contain this new point. We do not visit any nodes that have regions not intersecting s. When we have exhausted all possible alternatives, we output the current point q as the nearest-neighbor of p. In the worst case, this method may take $O(n)$ time, but there are many different analytic and experimental analyses that suggest that the average running time is more like $O(\log n)$, using some reasonable assumptions about the distribution of points in S. In addition, there are a number of useful heuristics for speeding up this search in practice, with one of the best being the *priority* searching strategy, which says that we should explore subtrees of T in order of the distance of their associated regions to p.

14.3.3 Other Partitioning Schemes

Although quadtrees, octrees, and k-d trees are some of the most well-known partition tree data structures, there are many others that also have a number of interesting properties. We briefly highlight three such structures in this subsection.

Balanced Box Decomposition Trees

The **balanced box decomposition** tree, or BBD tree, combines the best aspects of quadtree/octree data structures and k-d trees. It is a tree that is guaranteed to have $O(\log n)$ depth and to also have "boxy" rectangular regions (that is, regions with aspect ratios that are bounded by a constant). This combined property allows BBD trees to be used to achieve worst-case logarithmic query times for **approximate** nearest-neighbor searching and range querying, where we are interested in answers that may not be optimal, but are, nevertheless, within a factor of $(1+\varepsilon)$ from being optimal for a small fixed constant $\varepsilon > 0$.

Binary Space Partition Trees

Another variant of k-d trees are **binary space partition** trees, or BSP trees, which are used in computer graphics applications. These data structures are like k-d trees in that, each time a region associated with a node of a BSP tree is split, it is partitioned using a single line. The difference is that BSP trees do not restrict the splitting line to be perpendicular to a coordinate axis. Such planes are certainly allowed, however, so any k-d tree is automatically also a BSP tree, but such axis-aligned planes are not required. The typical domain, where BSP trees are employed is partitioning a collection of polygons that make up some geometric object in three-dimensional space. Experimental evidence suggests that, in such domains, it is more useful, for performing rendering and other computer graphics tasks, to use splitting planes that contain polygons from the input collection.

Hierarchical-Cutting Trees

The last variants of partition trees we would highlight are the **hierarchical-cutting** trees which were invented by Matoušek. These partition trees are more complicated than those considered above, but can be used to efficiently answer a very general kind of range query, **simplicial range queries**. In this query, we are given a d-dimensional "triangle" t (which is more properly called a **simplex**), and asked to return all the points in a set S of d-dimensional points that are contained in t. The hierarchical-cutting trees can answer such queries in $O(n^{1-1/d})$ time. The main idea behind these trees is still the partition tree approach, but taken to a higher level of sophistication. Each node v in a hierarchical-cutting tree is still associated with a region R and a subset S' of S, but to subdivide R, we now compute a collection of d-dimensional "triangles" that divide up R, and associate with each child of v a more-or-less equal sized subset of S' that falls into each such triangle. However, the details of this construction are beyond the scope of this book.

14.4 Exercises

Reinforcement

R-14.1 Draw a standard trie for the following set of strings:
$$\{abab, baba, ccccc, bbaaaa, caa, bbaacc, cbcc, cbca\}.$$

R-14.2 Draw a compressed trie for the set of strings given in the previous exercise.

R-14.3 Show the phrases, trie, and compressed string resulting from applying the LZ78 compression algorithm to the following string:

```
right sight fights might's fright
```

R-14.4 What would be the worst-case space usage of a range tree, if the primary structure were not required to have $O(\log n)$ height?

R-14.5 Given a binary search tree T built on the x-coordinates of a set of n objects, describe an $O(n)$ time method for computing $\min_x(v)$ and $\max_x(v)$ for each node v in T.

R-14.6 Show that the high_y values in a priority search tree satisfy the heap-order property.

R-14.7 Argue that the algorithm for answering three-sided range-searching queries with a priority search tree is correct.

R-14.8 What is the worst-case depth of a k-d tree defined on n points in the plane? What about in higher dimensions?

R-14.9 Suppose a set S contains n two-dimensional points whose coordinates are all integers in the range $[0, N]$. What is the worst-case depth of a quadtree defined on S?

R-14.10 Draw a quadtree for the following set of points, assuming a 16×16 bounding box:
$$\{(1,2), (4,10), (14,3), (6,6), (3,15), (2,2), (3,12), (9,4), (12,14)\}.$$

R-14.11 Construct a k-d tree for the point set of Exercise R-14.10.

R-14.12 Construct a priority search tree for the point set of Exercise R-14.10.

Creativity

C-14.1 Show that we can perform all the trie query and update operations in a compressed trie, even if we simply store with each edge in the compressed trie the first character of the string associated with it, and store with each vertex v in the compressed trie the depth v would have in the standard trie.

C-14.2 The $\min_x(v)$ and $\max_x(v)$ labels used in the two-dimensional range tree are not strictly needed. Describe an algorithm for performing a two-dimensional range-searching query in a 2-D range tree, where each internal node of the primary structure only stores a $key(v)$ label (which is the x-coordinate of its element). What is the running time of your method?

C-14.3 Give a pseudo-code description of an algorithm for constructing a range tree from a set of n points in the plane. What is the running time of your method?

C-14.4 Describe an efficient data structure for storing a set S of n items with ordered keys so as to support a rankRange(a,b) method, which enumerates all the items with keys whose **rank** in S is in the range $[a,b]$, where a and b are integers in the interval $[0,n-1]$. Describe methods for object insertions and deletion, and characterize the running times for these and the rankRange method.

C-14.5 Design a static data structure (which does not support insertions and deletions) that stores a two-dimensional set S of n points and can answer in $O(\log^2 n)$ time queries of the form countAllInRange(a,b,c,d), which return the number of points in S with x-coordinates in the range $[a,b]$ and y-coordinates in the range $[c,d]$. What is the space used by this structure?

C-14.6 Suppose we are given a range-searching data structure D that can answer range-searching queries for a set of n points in d-dimensional space for any fixed dimension d (like 8, 10, or 20) in time that is $O(\log^d n + k)$, where k is the number of answers. Show how to use D to answer the following queries for a set S of n rectangles in the plane:

- findAllContaining(x,y): Return an enumeration of all rectangles in S that contain the point (x,y).
- findAllIntersecting(a,b,c,d): Return an enumeration of all rectangles that intersect the rectangle with x-range $[a,b]$ and y-range $[c,d]$.

What is the running time needed to answer each of these queries?

C-14.7 Let S be a set of n intervals of the form $[a,b]$, where $a < b$. Design an efficient data structure that can answer, in $O(\log n + k)$ time, queries of the form contains(x), which asks for an enumeration of all intervals in S that contain x, where k is the number of such intervals. What is the space usage of your data structure? (Hint: think about a one-dimensional version of the priority range tree.)

C-14.8 Describe an efficient method for inserting an object into a (balanced) priority search tree. What is the running time of this method?

C-14.9 Design a data structure for answering countAllInRange queries (as defined in the previous exercise) in $O(\log n)$ time. (Hint: think of storing auxiliary structures at each node that are "linked" to the structures at neighboring nodes.)

Projects

P-14.1 Implement the trie data structure and use it to develop a system for data compression based on the LZ78 algorithm. Download documents from the World Wide Web and perform an experimental study on the compression that your method can achieve on these files.

P-14.2 Implement a class supporting range-searching queries with a range tree data structure.

P-14.3 Implement a class supporting range-searching queries with a priority range tree data structure.

P-14.4 Pair up with another programmer and each provide a solution to one of the previous two problems. Design an extensive experimental study to see which implementation is preferred for answering range searching queries.

P-14.5 Implement the quadtree and k-d tree data structures and perform an experimental study comparing the performance of these two data structures for answering range-searching queries.

P-14.6 Perform the previous project for answering nearest-neighbor queries.

P-14.7 Suppose we are only interested in approximate solutions to the range searching and nearest neighbor problems. Implement a way of answering such queries that guarantees that the answers are correct to within a factor of $1 + \varepsilon$, where ε is a small error factor.

Chapter Notes

Multi-dimensional search trees are discussed in books by Mehlhorn [107], Samet [126, 127], and Wood [149]. Please see these books for an extensive discussion of the history of multi-dimensional search trees, including various data structures for solving range queries.

The trie was invented by Morrison [114] and is discussed extensively in the classic *Sorting and Searching* book by Knuth [90]. The name "Patricia" is short for "Practical Algorithm to Retrieve Information Coded in Alphanumeric" [114]. McCreight [104] shows how to construct suffix tries in linear time. The LZ78 text compression algorithm we discuss is due to Ziv and Lempel [152], and they also have another well-known text compression method known as LZ77 [151]. For more information about text compression, please see the book chapter by Crochemore and Lecroq [38] or the book by Bell, Cleary, and Witten [17].

Priority search trees are due to McCreight [105], although Vuillemin [145] introduced this structure earlier under the name "Cartesian trees." The term "treap" comes from McCreight [105], but is used more extensively by Aragon and Seidel [9]. Edelsbrunner [44] shows how priority search trees can be used to answer two-dimensional range queries. Arya and Mount [11] present the balanced box decomposition tree, and they show how it can be used to solve approximate range searching [12]. Matoušek [101, 102] discovered the data structure we call hierarchical-cutting trees, although he simply calls his structure the "partition tree."

The reader interested in recent developments for range-searching data structures is referred to the book chapters by Agarwal [2, 3] or the survey paper by Matoušek [103].

Chapter
15
Computational Geometry

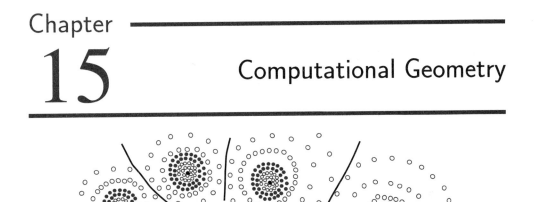

Contents

Computer graphics, mechanical engineering, geographic information systems, robotics, and computer vision are among the many applications of *computational geometry*, the discipline that investigates algorithms for geometric problems. In this chapter, we present some basic algorithmic techniques for solving geometric problems that deal with points and segments in the plane.

15.1   Points, Lines, Segments, and Polygons

Geometric algorithms take geometric objects of various types as their inputs. The basic geometric objects in the plane are points, lines, segments, and polygons.

15.1.1   Representations of Geometric Objects

There are many ways of representing planar geometric objects. Rather than give separate ADT's for points, lines, segments, and polygons, which would be appropriate for a book on geometric algorithms, we assume instead we have intuitive representations for these objects. Even so, we briefly mention some of the choices that we can make regarding geometric representations.

We can represent a point in the plane by a pair (x, y) that stores the x and y Cartesian coordinates for that point. While this representation is quite versatile, it is not the only one. There may be some applications where a different representation may be better (such as representing a point as the intersection between two nonparallel lines).

We can represent a line l as a triple (a, b, c) such that these values are the coefficients a, b, and c of the linear equation

$$ax + by + c = 0$$

associated with l. Alternatively, we may specify instead two different points, q_1 and q_2, and associate them with the line that goes through both. Given the Cartesian coordinates (x_1, y_1) of q_1 and (x_2, y_2) of q_2, the equation of the line l through q_1 and q_2 is given by

$$\frac{x - x_1}{x_2 - x_1} = \frac{y - y_1}{y_2 - y_1},$$

from which we derive

$$a = (y_2 - y_1); \quad b = -(x_2 - x_1); \quad c = y_1(x_2 - x_1) - x_1(y_2 - y_1).$$

A line segment s is typically represented by the pair (p, q) of points in the plane that form s's endpoints. We may also represent s by giving the line through it, together with a range of x- and y-coordinates, that restrict this line to the segment s. (Why is it insufficient to include just a range of x- or y-coordinates?)

We can represent a polygon P by a circular sequence of points, called the *vertices* of P. (See Figure 15.1.) The segments between consecutive vertices of P are called the *edges* of P. Polygon P is said to be *nonintersecting*, or *simple*, if intersections between pairs of edges of P happen only at a common endpoint vertex. A polygon is *convex* if it is simple and all its internal angles are less than π.

Our discussion of different ways of representing points, lines, segments, and polygons is not meant to be exhaustive. It is meant simply to indicate the different ways we can implement these geometric objects. In the remainder of this section, we explore some of the fundamental operations that are required of the objects in typical geometric algorithms.

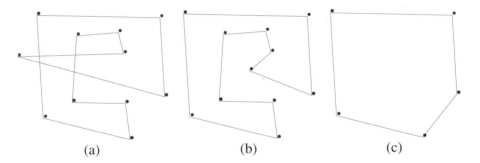

(a)   (b)   (c)

Figure 15.1: Examples of polygons: (a) intersecting, (b) simple, (c) convex.

15.1.2 Intersection of Two Segments

One of the most important operations that geometric objects should support is the *intersection* operation. For example, given two lines l_1 and l_2, we may want to know whether they *intersect*, that is, if they have one or more points in common. If l_1 and l_2 are represented by their equations

$$a_1 x + b_1 y + c_1 = 0 \quad \text{and} \quad a_2 x + b_2 y + c_2 = 0,$$

then l_1 and l_2 intersect if and only if one of the following two conditions is satisfied.

- The determinant

$$\begin{vmatrix} a_1 & b_1 \\ a_2 & b_2 \end{vmatrix} = a_1 b_2 - a_2 b_1$$

  is nonzero, which implies that the two lines intersect in exactly one point.
- There exists a positive constant k such that: $a_2 = k a_1$, $b_2 = k b_1$, and $c_2 = k c_1$, which implies that the two lines are coincident.

These tests are easily carried out in $O(1)$ time.

Testing whether two segments s_1 and s_2 intersect, that is, if they have one or more points in common, is disappointingly more complicated, however. The reader is encouraged to think about this problem before reading on.

The first approach that might come to mind is to test whether the lines l_1 and l_2 through s_1 and s_2, respectively, intersect. We distinguish three cases:

- If l_1 and l_2 do not intersect, then we know that s_1 and s_2 also do not intersect and we return a negative answer.
- If l_1 and l_2 intersect and are coincident, we test whether the ranges of x-coordinates of s_1 and s_2 overlap, and similarly for the y-coordinates.
- Otherwise, we compute the intersection point q of l_1 and l_2. The coordinates of q are given by the solution of the system of two equations in two unknowns that are derived from the equations of lines l_1 and l_2 (which can be specified as formulas, with a little extra work). Given the intersection point q, we can then test whether point q is included both in s_1 and s_2. This can be done by checking that the x-coordinate of q lies in the range of the x-coordinates of both s_1 and s_2, and similarly for the y-coordinate of q.

This testing method is admittedly somewhat complicated. An alternative approach is based on the concept of **orientation**, which we discuss next.

15.1.3   Orientation of Three Points

Another important geometric relationship, which arises in many geometric algorithms, is **orientation**. Given an ordered triplet (p, q, r) of points, we say that (p, q, r) makes a **left turn** and is oriented **counterclockwise** if the angle that stays on the left-hand side when going from p to q and then to r is less than π. (See Figure 15.2a.) If the angle on the right-hand side is less than π instead, then we say that (p, q, r) makes a **right turn** and is oriented **clockwise**. (See Figure 15.2b.) It is possible that the angles of the left- and right-hand sides are both equal to π, in which case the three points do not actually make any turn, and we say that their orientation is **collinear**.

Given a triplet (p_1, p_2, p_3) of three points $p_1 = (x_1, y_1)$, $p_2 = (x_2, y_2)$, and $p_3 = (x_3, y_3)$, in the plane, let $\Delta(p_1, p_2, p_3)$ be the determinant defined by

$$\Delta(p_1, p_2, p_3) = \begin{vmatrix} x_1 & y_1 & 1 \\ x_2 & y_2 & 1 \\ x_3 & y_3 & 1 \end{vmatrix} = x_1 y_2 - x_2 y_1 + x_3 y_1 - x_1 y_3 + x_2 y_3 - x_3 y_2. \quad (15.1)$$

The function $\Delta(p_1, p_2, p_3)$ is often called the "signed area" function, because its absolute value is twice the area of the (possibly degenerate) triangle formed by the points p_1, p_2, and p_3. In addition, we have the following important fact relating this function to orientation testing.

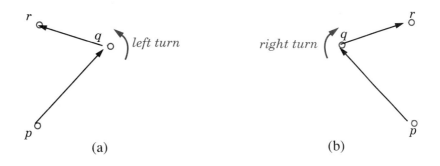

(a)   (b)

Figure 15.2: Orientation of a triplet (p,q,r) of points in the plane: (a) left turn and counterclockwise orientation; (b) right turn and clockwise orientation.

Proposition 15.1: *The orientation of a triplet (p_1, p_2, p_3) of points in the plane is counterclockwise, clockwise, or collinear, depending on whether $\Delta(p_1, p_2, p_3)$ is positive, negative, or zero, respectively.*

We provide a sketch of the justification of Proposition 15.1. The details are left as an exercise. We show in Figure 15.3 a triplet (p_1, p_2, p_3) of points such that $x_1 < x_2 < x_3$. Clearly, this triplet makes a left turn if the slope of segment $p_2 p_3$ is greater than the slope of segment $p_1 p_2$. This is expressed by the question

$$\text{Is } \quad \frac{y_3 - y_2}{x_3 - x_2} > \frac{y_2 - y_1}{x_2 - x_1} \quad ? \tag{15.2}$$

By the expansion of $\Delta(p_1, p_2, p_3)$ shown in 15.1, we can verify that inequality 15.2 is equivalent to $\Delta(p_1, p_2, p_3) > 0$.

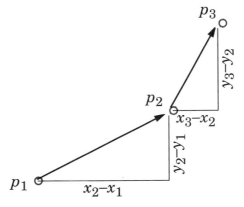

Figure 15.3: Schematic justification for Proposition 15.1.

Intersection of Two Segments Revisited

Using the notion of orientation, let us revisit the problem of testing whether two segments s_1 and s_2 intersect.

Proposition 15.2: *Let* $s_1 = \overline{p_1q_1}$ *and* $s_2 = \overline{p_2q_2}$ *be two segments in the plane.* s_1 *and* s_2 *intersect if and only if* **one of** *the following two conditions is verified:*

1. (a) (p_1, q_1, p_2) *and* (p_1, q_1, q_2) *have different orientations,* **and**
    (b) (p_2, q_2, p_1) *and* (p_2, q_2, q_1) *have different orientations.*
2. (a) (p_1, q_1, p_2), (p_1, q_1, q_2), (p_2, q_2, p_1) *and* (p_2, q_2, q_1) *are all collinear,* **and**
    (b) *the x-projections of* s_1 *and* s_2 *intersect,* **and**
    (c) *the y-projections of* s_1 *and* s_2 *intersect.*

Condition 1 of Proposition 15.2 is illustrated in Figure 15.4. Table 15.1 gives the orientation of the triplets (p_1, q_1, p_2), (p_1, q_1, q_2), (p_2, q_2, p_1) and (p_2, q_2, q_1) in each of the four cases for Condition 1. A complete justification is left as an exercise. Note that Proposition 15.2 holds also if s_1 and/or s_2 is a degenerate segment with coincident endpoints.

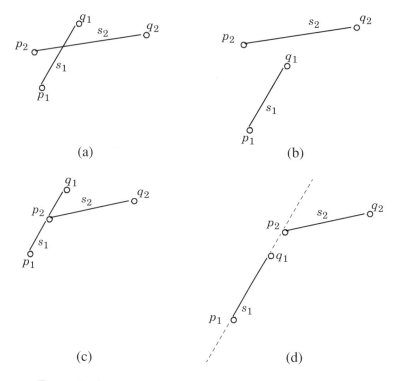

Figure 15.4: Examples illustrating four cases of Condition 1 of Proposition 15.2.

case	(p_1, q_1, p_2)	(p_1, q_1, q_2)	(p_2, q_2, p_1)	(p_2, q_2, q_1)	intersection?
(a)	CCW	CW	CW	CCW	yes
(b)	CCW	CW	CW	CW	no
(c)	COLL	CW	CW	CCW	yes
(d)	COLL	CW	CW	CW	no

Table 15.1: The four cases shown in Figure 15.4 for the orientations specified by Condition 1 of Proposition 15.2, where CCW stands for counterclockwise, CW stands for clockwise, and COLL stands for collinear.

15.1.4   Inclusion of a Point in a Polygon

The final geometric relation we consider in this section is the ***inclusion*** of one geometric object in another. In particular, we address the problem of testing whether a point q is inside or outside a nonintersecting polygon P. This test is called a ***point inclusion*** test.

We present, in Code Fragment 15.1, a simple algorithm for the point inclusion test that works for the special case where the y-coordinate of point q is different from the y-coordinate of any vertex of P. We leave the extension to the general case as an exercise. The algorithm is based on the following idea. (See Figure 15.5.) Consider a horizontal ray emanating leftward towards the point q, and imagine traversing the ray starting somewhere outside P and going towards q. After the first time we intersect an edge of P, we go inside P, after the second time, we go outside P, after the third time, we again go inside P, and so on. If the number of intersections is odd, this means that q is inside P; otherwise, q is outside P.

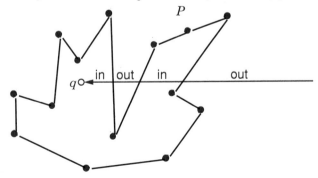

Figure 15.5: Point inclusion test for a polygon. Point q is inside polygon P if and only if a ray emanating rightward from point q intersects P an odd number of times.

Algorithm PointInPolygon(q,P):

> *Input:*   A point q and a nonintersecting polygon P whose vertices have y-coordinate distinct from $y(q)$
>
> *Output:*   An indication of whether q is inside or outside P

> Compute the maximum x-coordinate x_M of the vertices of P.
> Let s be the segment with endpoints q and $(x_M, y(q))$.
> $i \leftarrow 0$
> **for** each edge e of P **do**
>> **if** segments s and e intersect **then**
>>> $i \leftarrow i + 1$
>
> **if** i is odd **then**
>> **return** "inside"
>
> **else**
>> **return** "outside"

Code Fragment 15.1: An algorithm for testing the inclusion of a point in a simple polygon. Note the restriction on the y-coodinates of q and the vertices of P.

15.2   Convex Hulls

One of the most studied geometric problems is that of computing the convex hull of a set of points. Informally speaking, the ***convex hull*** of a set of points in the plane is the shape taken by a rubber band that is placed "around the points" and allowed to shrink to a state of equilibrium. (See Figure 15.6.)

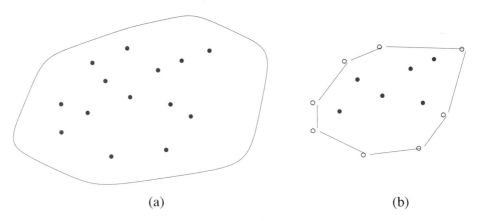

(a)   (b)

Figure 15.6: The convex hull of a set of points in the plane: (a) an example "rubber band" placed around the points; (b) the convex hull of the points.

The convex hull corresponds to the intuitive notion of a "boundary" of a set of points and can be used to approximate the shape of a complex object. Indeed, computing the convex hull of a set of points is a fundamental operation in computational geometry. We say that a region R is **convex** if any time two points p and q are in R, the entire line segment $\overline{pq}$ is also in R. The **convex hull** of a set of points S is the boundary of the smallest convex region that contains all the points of S inside it or on its boundary. The notion of "smallest" refers to either the perimeter or area of the region, both definitions being equivalent. The convex hull of a set of points S in the plane defines a convex polygon, and the points of S on the boundary of the convex hull define the vertices of this polygon. The following example describes an application of the convex hull problem in a robot motion planning problem.

Example 15.3: *A common problem in robotics is to identify a trajectory from a start point s to a target point t that avoids a certain obstacle. Among the many possible trajectories, we would like to find one that is as short as possible. Let us assume that the obstacle is a polygon P. We can compute a shortest trajectory from s to t that avoids P with the following strategy (see Figure 15.7):*

- *We determine if the line segment $\ell = \overline{st}$ intersects P. If it does not intersect, then ℓ is the shortest trajectory avoiding P.*
- *Otherwise, if $\overline{st}$ intersects P, then we compute the convex hull H of the vertices of polygon P plus points s and t. Note that s and t subdivide the convex hull H into two polygonal chains, one going clockwise from s to t and one going counterclockwise from s to t.*
- *We select and return the shortest of the two polygonal chains with endpoints s and t on H.*

This shortest chain is the shortest path in the plane that avoids the obstacle P.

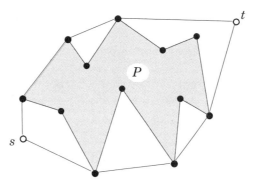

Figure 15.7: An example shortest trajectory from a point s to a point t that avoids a polygonal obstacle P; in this case the trajectory is the clockwise chain from s to t.

There are a number of other applications of the convex hull problem, including partitioning problems, shape testing problems, and separation problems. For example, if we wish to determine whether there is a half-plane (that is, a region of the plane on one side of a line) that completely contains a set of points A but completely avoids a set of points B, it is enough to compute the convex hulls of A and B and determine whether they intersect each other. We study a number of other interesting properties of convex hulls in the next subsection.

15.2.1   Basic Properties of Convex Hulls

There are many interesting geometric properties associated with convex hulls. The following proposition provides an alternate characterization of the points that are on the convex hull and of those that are not.

Proposition 15.4: *Let P be a set of points in the plane, and let H be the convex hull of P. We have:*

- *A pair of points a and b of P form an edge of H if and only if all the other points of P are contained in the same half-plane delimited by the line through a and b.*
- *A point p of P is a vertex of H if and only if there exists a line l through p such that all the other points of P are contained in the same half-plane delimited by l (that is, they are all on the same side of l).*
- *A point p of P is not a vertex of H if and only if p is contained in the interior of a triangle formed by three other points of P or in the interior of a segment formed by two other points of P.*

The properties expressed by Proposition 15.4 are illustrated in Figure 15.8. A complete justification of them is left as an exercise. As a consequence of Proposition 15.4, we can immediately verify that in any set S of points in the plane the following ***critical*** points are always on the convex hull of S:

- The point with minimum x-coordinate (and minimum y-coordinate if there are ties)
- The point with maximum x-coordinate (and maximum y-coordinate if there are ties)
- The point with minimum y-coordinate (and minimum x-coordinate if there are ties)
- The point with maximum y-coordinate (and maximum x-coordinate if there are ties).

The four critical points may not be unique or distinct, of course, but if there are at least two distinct points in the set S, there will be at least two distinct critical points identified by the above tests to be on the convex hull of S. Thus, any such point, say the one with minimum y-coordinate, provides an initial starting configuration for an algorithm that computes the convex hull.

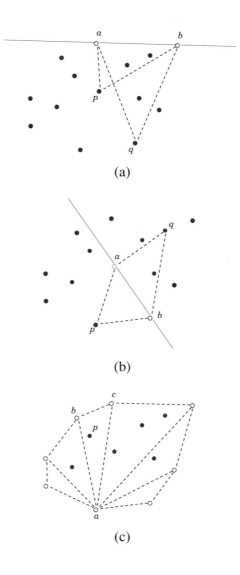

Figure 15.8: Illustration of the properties of the convex hull given in Proposition 15.4: (a) points a and b form an edge of the convex hull; (b) points a and b do not form an edge of the convex hull; (c) point p is not on the convex hull.

15.2.2   The Gift Wrapping Algorithm

The *gift wrapping* algorithm for computing the convex hull of a set of points in the plane can be intuitively described as follows (see Figure 15.9):

1. View the points as pegs implanted in a level field, and imagine that we tie a rope to the peg corresponding to the point *a* with minimum *y*-coordinate (and minimum *x*-coordinate if there are ties). Call *a* the **anchor point**, and note that *a* is a vertex of the convex hull.

2. Pull the rope to the right of the anchor point and rotate it counterclockwise until it touches another peg, which corresponds to the next vertex of the convex hull.

3. Continue rotating the rope counterclockwise, identifying at each step a new vertex of the convex hull, until the rope gets back to the anchor point.

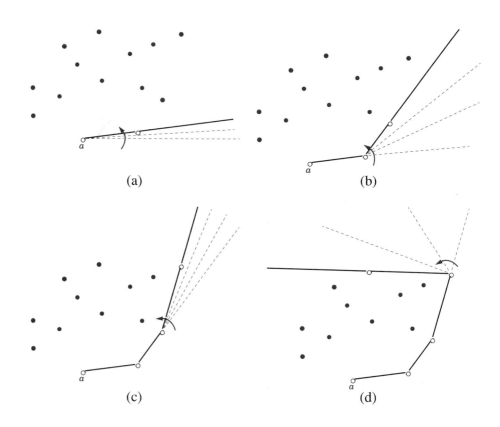

Figure 15.9: Initial four wrapping steps of the gift wrapping algorithm.

Each time we rotate our "rope" around the current peg until it hits another point, we perform an operation called a ***wrapping*** step. Geometrically, a wrapping step involves starting from a given line L known to be tangent to the convex hull at the current anchor point a, and determining the line through a and another point in the set making the smallest angle with L. Implementing this wrapping step does not require trigonometric functions and angle calculations, however. Instead, we can perform a wrapping step by means of the following proposition, which follows from Proposition 15.4.

Proposition 15.5: *Let P be a set of points in the plane, and let a be a point of P that is a vertex of the convex hull H of P. The next vertex of H, going counterclockwise from p, is the point p such that triplet (a, p, q) makes a left turn with every other point q of P.*

Recalling the discussion from Section 6.1.4, let us define a comparator $C(a)$ that uses the orientation of (a, p, q) to compare two points p and q of P. That is, $C(a).\text{isLess}(p, q)$ returns true if triplet (a, p, q) makes a left turn. We call the comparator $C(a)$ the ***radial*** comparator, as it compares points in terms of their radial relationships around the anchor point a. By Proposition 15.5, the vertex following a counterclockwise on the hull is simply the minimum point with respect to the radial comparator $C(a)$.

We can now analyze the running time of the gift wrapping algorithm. Let n be the number of points of P, and let $h \le n$ be the number of vertices of the convex hull H of P. Let $p_0, \ldots, p_{h-1}$ be the vertices of H. Finding the anchor point $a = p_0$ takes $O(n)$ time. Since with each wrapping step of the algorithm we discover a new vertex of the convex hull, the number of wrapping steps is equal to h. Step i is a minimum-finding computation based on radial comparator $C(p_{i-1})$, which runs in $O(n)$ time, since determining the orientation of a triplet takes $O(1)$ time and we must examine all the points of P to find the smallest with respect to $C(p_{i-1})$. We conclude that the gift wrapping algorithm runs in time $O(hn)$, which is $O(n^2)$ in the worst-case. Indeed, the worst-case for the gift wrapping algorithm occurs when $h = n$, that is, when all the points are on the convex hull.

The worst-case running time of the gift wrapping algorithm in terms of n is therefore not very efficient. This algorithm is nevertheless reasonably-efficient in practice, however, for it can take advantage of the (common) situation when h, the number of hull points is small relative to the number of input points, n. That is, this algorithm is an ***output sensitive*** algorithm—an algorithm whose running time depends on the size of the output. Gift wrapping has a running time that varies between linear and quadratic, and is efficient if the convex hull has few vertices. We will see in the next section an algorithm that is efficient for all hull sizes, although it is slightly more complicated.

15.2.3   The Graham Scan Algorithm

A convex hull algorithm that has an efficient running time no matter how many points are on the boundary of the convex is the ***Graham scan*** algorithm. The Graham scan algorithm for computing the convex hull H of a set P of n points in the plane consists of the following three phases:

1. We find a point a of P that is a vertex of H and call it the ***anchor point***. We can, for example, pick as our anchor point a the point in P with minimum y-coordinate (and minimum x-coordinate if there are ties).

2. We sort the remaining points of P (that is, $P - \{a\}$) using the radial comparator $C(a)$, and let S be the resulting sorted sequence of points. (See Figure 15.10.) In the sequence S, the points of P appear sorted counterclockwise "by angle" with respect to the anchor point a, although no explicit computation of angles is performed by the comparator.

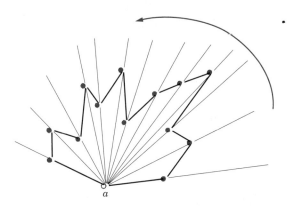

Figure 15.10: Sorting around the anchor point in the Graham scan algorithm.

3. After adding the anchor point a at the first and last position of S, we ***scan*** through the points in S in (radial) order, maintaining at each step a sequence H storing a convex chain "surrounding" the points scanned so far. Each time we consider new point p, we perform the following test:

   (a) If p forms a left turn with the last two points in H, or if H contains fewer than two points, then add p to the end of H.

   (b) Otherwise, remove the last point in H and repeat the test for p.

   We stop when we return to the anchor point a, at which point H stores the vertices of the convex hull of P in counterclockwise order.

The details of the scan phase (Phase 3) are spelled out in Algorithm Scan, described in Code Fragment 15.2. (See Figures 15.11–15.12.)

Algorithm Scan(*S,a*):

Input: A sequence *S* of points in the plane beginning with point *a* such that:

- *a* is a vertex of the convex hull of the points of *S*;
- the remaining points of *S* are sorted according to the radial comparator *C*(*a*), that is, counterclockwise around *a*

Output: Sequence *S* from which the points that are not vertices of the convex hull have been removed

S.insertLast(*a*) 　　{add a copy of *a* at the end of *S*}
prev ← *S*.first() 　　{so that *prev* = *a* initially}
curr ← *S*.after(*prev*) 　　{the next point is on the current convex chain}
repeat
  next ← *S*.after(*curr*) 　　{advance}
  if points point(*prev*), point(*curr*), point(*next*)) make a left turn **then**
    prev ← *curr*
  else
    S.remove(*curr*) 　　{ point *curr* is not in the convex hull}
    prev ← *S*.before(*prev*)
  curr ← *S*.after(*prev*)
until *curr* = *S*.last()
S.remove(last()) 　　{remove the duplicate copy of *a*}

Code Fragment 15.2: The scan phase of the Graham scan algorithm for computing the convex hull. (See Figures 15.11–15.12.) Variables *prev*, *curr*, and *next* are positions (Section 4.2.2) of sequence *S*. We assume that an accessor method point(*pos*) is defined that returns the point stored at position *pos*. We give a simplified description of the algorithm that works only if *S* has at least three points, and no three points of *S* are collinear.

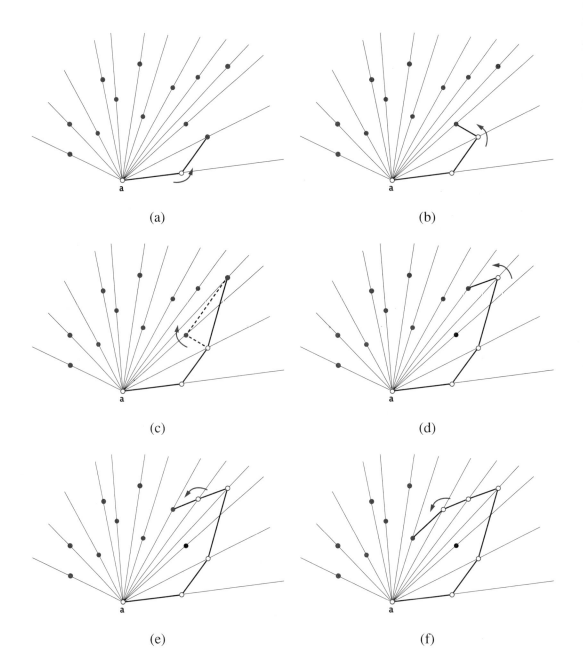

(a)   (b)

(c)   (d)

(e)   (f)

Figure 15.11: Third phase of the Graham scan algorithm (Code Fragment 15.2). (The illustration of this algorithm is continued in Figure 15.12.)

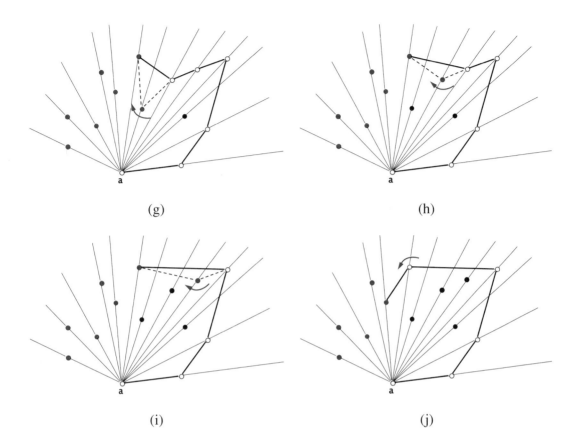

Figure 15.12: Third phase of the Graham scan algorithm (see Code Fragment 15.2). (Continued from Figure 15.11.)

Let us now analyze the running time of the Graham scan algorithm. We denote the number of points in P (and S) with n. The first phase (finding the anchor point) clearly takes $O(n)$ time. The second phase (sorting the points around the anchor point) takes $O(n \log n)$ time provided we use one of the asymptotically optimal sorting algorithms, such as heap-sort (Section 6.3.3) or merge-sort (Section 8.1). The analysis of the scan (third) phase is more subtle.

To analyze the scan phase of the Graham scan algorithm, let us look more closely at the **repeat** loop of Code Fragment 15.2. At each iteration of the loop, either variable *next* advances forward by one position in the sequence S (successful **if** test), or variable *next* stays at the same position but a point is removed from S (unsuccessful **if** test). Hence, the number of iterations of the **repeat** loop is at most $2n$. Therefore, each statement of algorithm Scan is executed at most $2n$ times. Since each statement requires in turn the execution of $O(1)$ elementary operations, algorithm Scan takes $O(n)$ time. In conclusion, the running time of the Graham scan algorithm is dominated by the second phase, where sorting is performed. Thus, the Graham scan algorithm runs in $O(n \log n)$ time.

15.2.4   Implementing the Graham Scan Algorithm

We described the Graham scan algorithm (Code Fragment 15.2) assuming it avoided any *degeneracies*, that is, input configurations that involve annoying special cases (such as coincident or collinear points). When implementing the Graham scan algorithm, however, it is important to handle all possible input configurations.

We show in Code Fragments 15.3–15.5 a Java implementation of the Graham scan algorithm. The main method is grahamScan (Code Fragment 15.3), which uses several auxiliary methods. Because of the degenerate point configurations that may occur, several special situations are handled by method grahamScan.

- The input sequence is first copied into sequence hull, which will be returned at the end of the execution (method copyInputPoints of Code Fragment 15.4).

- If the input has zero or one point (the output is the same as the input) return.

- If there are two input points, then if the two points are coincident, remove one of them and return.

- The anchor point is computed and removed, together with all the points coincident with it (method anchorPointSearchAndRemove of Code Fragment 15.4). If zero or one point is left, reinsert the anchor point and return.

- If none of the above special cases arises, that is, at least two points are left, sort the points counterclockwise around the anchor point with method sortPoints (Code Fragment 15.4), which passes a ConvexHullComparator (corresponding to to the radial comparator $C(a)$ of Code Fragment 15.2) to the generic sorting algorithm ListMergeSort (Code Fragment 8.3).

- In preparation for the scan, we remove any initial collinear points in the sorted sequence, except the farthest one from the anchor point (method removeInitialIntermediatePoints of Code Fragment 15.5).

- The scan phase of the algorithm is performed calling method scan of Code Fragment 15.5.

```
public class ConvexHull {
  private static Sequence hull;
  private static Point2D anchorPoint;
  private static GeomTester2D geomTester = new GeomTester2DImpl();
  // public class method
  public static Sequence grahamScan (Sequence points) {
    Point2D p1, p2;
    copyInputPoints(points); // copy into hull the sequence of input points
    switch (hull.size()) {
    case 0: case 1:
      return hull;
    case 2:
      p1 = (Point2D)hull.first().element();
      p2 = (Point2D)hull.last().element();
      if (geomTester.areEqual(p1,p2))
        hull.remove(hull.last());
      return hull;
    default: // at least 3 input points
      // compute anchor point and remove it together with coincident points
      anchorPointSearchAndRemove();
      switch (hull.size()) {
      case 0: case 1:
        hull.insertFirst(anchorPoint);
        return hull;
      default:   // at least 2 input points left besides the anchor point
        sortPoints();// sort the points in hull around the anchor point
        // remove the (possible) initial collinear points in hull except the
        // farthest one from the anchor point
        removeInitialIntermediatePoints();
        if (hull.size() == 1)
          hull.insertFirst(anchorPoint);
        else { // insert the anchor point as first and last element in hull
          hull.insertFirst(anchorPoint);
          hull.insertLast(anchorPoint);
          scan(); // Graham's scan
          // remove one of the two copies of the anchor point from hull
          hull.remove(hull.last());
        }
        return hull;
      }
    }
  }
}
```

Code Fragment 15.3: Method grahamScan in the Java implementation of the Graham scan algorithm.

```
private static void copyInputPoints (Sequence points) {
  // copy into hull the sequence of input points
  hull = new NodeSequence();
  Enumeration pe = points.elements();
  while (pe.hasMoreElements()) {
    Point2D p = (Point2D)pe.nextElement();
    hull.insertLast(p);
  }
}
private static void anchorPointSearchAndRemove () {
  // compute the anchor point and remove it from hull together with
  // all the coincident points
  Enumeration pe = hull.positions();
  Position anchor = (Position)pe.nextElement();
  anchorPoint = (Point2D)anchor.element();
  // hull contains at least three elements
  while (pe.hasMoreElements()) {
    Position pos = (Position)pe.nextElement();
    Point2D p = (Point2D)pos.element();
    int aboveBelow = geomTester.aboveBelow(anchorPoint,p);
    int leftRight = geomTester.leftRight(anchorPoint,p);
    if (aboveBelow == GeomTester2D.BELOW ||
        aboveBelow == GeomTester2D.ON &&
        leftRight == GeomTester2D.LEFT) {
      anchor = pos;
      anchorPoint = p;
    }
    else
      if (aboveBelow == GeomTester2D.ON &&
          leftRight == GeomTester2D.ON)
        hull.remove(pos);
  }
  hull.remove(anchor);
}
private static void sortPoints() {
  // sort the points in hull around the anchor point
  SortObject sorter = new ListMergeSort();
  ConvexHullComparator comp = new ConvexHullComparator(anchorPoint,
                                                       geomTester);
  sorter.sort(hull,comp);
}
```

Code Fragment 15.4: Auxiliary methods copyInputPoints, anchorPointSearchAndRemove, and sortPoints called by method grahamScan of Code Fragment 15.3.

```
private static void removeInitialIntermediatePoints() {
  // remove the (possible) initial collinear points in hull except the
  // farthest one from the anchor point
  boolean collinear = true;
  while (hull.size() > 1 && collinear) {
    Position pos1 = hull.first();
    Position pos2 = hull.after(pos1);
    Point2D p1 = (Point2D)pos1.element();
    Point2D p2 = (Point2D)pos2.element();
    if (geomTester.leftRightTurn(anchorPoint,p1,p2) ==
        GeomTester2D.COLLINEAR)
      if (geomTester.closest(anchorPoint,p1,p2) == p1)
        hull.remove(pos1);
      else
        hull.remove(pos2);
    else
      collinear = false;
  }
}
private static void scan() {
  // Graham's scan
  Position first = hull.first();
  Position last = hull.last();
  Position prev = hull.first();
  Position curr = hull.after(prev);
  do {
    Position next = hull.after(curr);
    Point2D prevPoint = (Point2D)prev.element();
    Point2D currPoint = (Point2D)curr.element();
    Point2D nextPoint = (Point2D)next.element();
    if (geomTester.leftRightTurn(prevPoint,currPoint,nextPoint) ==
        GeomTester2D.LEFT_TURN)
      prev = curr;
    else {
      hull.remove(curr);
      prev = hull.before(prev);
    }
    curr = hull.after(prev);
  }
  while (curr != last);
}
```

Code Fragment 15.5: Auxiliary methods removeInitialIntermediatePoints and scan called by method grahamScan of Code Fragment 15.3.

15.3 Orthogonal Segment Intersection

In this section, we study the problem of finding all the intersecting pairs among a set of n segments. As we have seen in Section 15.1.2, testing whether two segments intersect can be performed in constant time. Suppose we are now given a set of n line segments in the plane and are asked to find each pair of intersecting segments in this set. A straightforward approach to this problem is to check every pair of segments to see whether they intersect. Since the number of pairs is $n(n-1)/2$, this "brute-force" algorithm takes $O(n^2)$ time. Of course, if indeed all the pairs intersect, this algorithm is optimal, for just reporting the intersecting pairs would take this much time. Still, we would like to have a faster method for the case where the number of intersecting pairs is small, or there are no intersections at all. Specifically, if s is the number of intersecting pairs, we would like to have an output sensitive algorithm whose running time depends on both n and s. (Recall the concept of an output sensitive algorithm that was introduced in Section 15.2.2.)

We shall present an algorithm that runs in $O(n \log n + s)$ time for the case when the input set of segments consists of n **orthogonal segments**, meaning that each segment in the set is either horizontal or vertical.

One-Dimensional Range Searching Revisited

Before we proceed with our algorithm, we make a slight digression to review a problem discussed in the previous chapter. This problem is the one-dimensional range searching problem, in which we wish to dynamically maintain a dictionary of numbers (that is, points on a number line), subject to insertions and deletions and queries of the following form:

findAllInRange(k_1, k_2): Return an enumeration of all the elements in D with key k such that $k_1 \leq k \leq k_2$.
Input: Two objects (keys); *Output:* Enumeration.

We show in Section 14.2.1 how we can use any balanced binary search tree, such as an AVL tree or a red-black tree, to maintain such a dictionary in order to achieve $O(\log n)$ time for point insertion and removal, and $O(\log n + s)$ time for answering findAllInRange queries, where n is the number of points in the dictionary at the time, and s is the number of returned points in the range. We will not make use of the details of this algorithm, only its existence, so a reader who skipped Section 14.2.1 can safely take this result on faith and not have to worry about how it is achieved.

15.3.1 A Collection of Range Searching Problems

Let us return to the problem at hand, which is to compute all intersecting pairs of segments from a collection of n horizontal and vertical segments. The main idea of the algorithm for solving this problem is to reduce this two-dimensional problem to a collection of one-dimensional range-searching problems. Namely, for each vertical segment v, we consider the vertical line $l(v)$ through v, and plunge into the "one-dimensional world" of line $l(v)$. (See Figure 15.13(a–b).) Only the vertical segment v and the intersections of horizontal segments with $l(v)$ exist in this world. In particular, segment v corresponds to an interval of $l(v)$, a horizontal segment h intersecting $l(v)$ corresponds to a point on $l(v)$, and the horizontal segments crossing v correspond to the points on $l(v)$ contained in the interval.

Thus, if we are given the set $S(v)$ of horizontal segments intersecting line $l(v)$, then determining those that intersect segment v is equivalent to performing a range search in $S(v)$ using the y coordinates of the segments as keys and the interval given by the y-coordinates of the endpoints of segment v as the selection range.

As we have reviewed above (and seen in Section 14.2.1), range searching in an n-element ordered dictionary can be performed in $O(\log n + s)$ time, using $O(n)$ space, where s is the number of items reported. Let $n(v)$ be the size of set $S(v)$, and let $s(v)$ be the number of horizontal segments in $S(v)$ that intersect v. Range searching in $S(v)$ can be done in time $O(\log n(v) + s(v))$. Thus, we have only to show how to compute a dictionary representation of the set $S(v)$ for each vertical segment v (so that we can query this dictionary to determine which horizontal segments intersect v).

15.3.2 The Plane Sweep Technique

Suppose we are given a set of n horizontal and vertical segments in the plane. We will determine all pairs of intersecting segments in this set by using a powerful technique known as the ***plane sweep*** technique. This technique involves simulating the sweeping of a vertical line l, over the segments, moving from left to right, starting at a location to the left of all the input segments. During the sweep, the set of horizontal segments currently intersected by the sweep line is maintained by means of insertions into and removals from a dictionary ordered by y-coordinate. When the sweep encounters a vertical segment v, a range query on the dictionary is performed to find the horizontal segments intersecting v.

Specifically, during the sweep, we maintain an ordered dictionary S storing horizontal segments with key given by the y-coordinate. The sweep pauses at certain ***events*** that trigger the ***actions*** shown in Table 15.2 and are illustrated in Figure 15.13c–f and Figure 15.14).

Event	Action
left endpoint of a horizontal segment h	insert h into dictionary S
right endpoint of a horizontal segment h	remove h from dictionary S
vertical segment v	perform a range search on S with selection range given by the y-coordinates of the endpoints of v

Table 15.2: Events triggering actions in the plane sweep algorithm for orthogonal segment intersection.

In order to perform the sweep, we need to identify all the events and sort them by x-coordinate. An event is either an endpoint of a horizontal segment or a vertical segment. Hence, the number of events is at most $2n$. When sorting the events, we compare them by x-coordinate, which takes $O(1)$ time.

Let us now analyze the running time of this plane sweep algorithm. Using one of the asymptotically optimal sorting algorithms, such as heap-sort (Section 6.3.3) or merge-sort (Section 8.1), we can order the events in $O(n\log n)$ time. The operations performed on dictionary S are insertions, removals, and range searches. Each time an operation is executed, the size of S is at most $2n$. We implement S as an AVL tree (Section 7.4), or as a red-black tree (Section 13.3), so that insertions and deletions each take $O(\log n)$ time, and a range search triggered by a vertical segment v takes time $O(\log n + s(v))$, where $s(v)$ is the number of horizontal segments currently in dictionary S that intersect v. Thus, indicating with V the set of vertical segments, we have that the running time of the sweep is

$$O\left(2n\log n + \sum_{v \in V}(\log n + s(v))\right).$$

Since the sweep goes through all the segments, the sum of $s(v)$ over all the vertical segments encountered is equal to the total number s of intersecting pairs of segments. Hence, we conclude that the sweep takes time $O(n\log n + s)$.

In summary, the complete segment intersection algorithm, outlined above, consists of the event sorting step followed by the sweep step. Sorting the events takes $O(n\log n)$ time, while sweeping takes $O(n\log n + s)$ time. Thus, the running time of the algorithm is $O(n\log n + s)$.

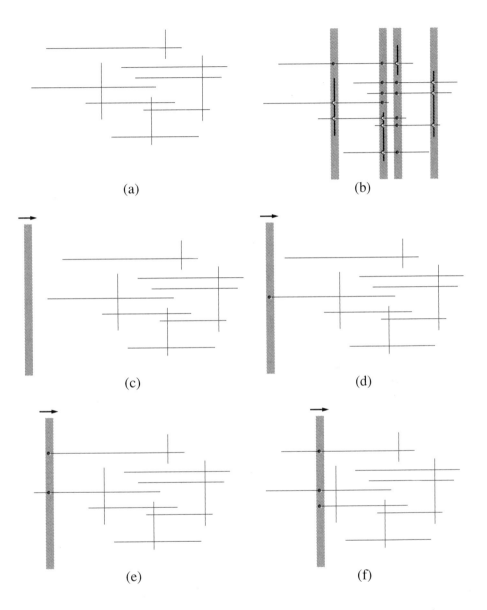

Figure 15.13: Plane sweep for orthogonal segment intersection: (a) a set of horizontal and vertical segments; (b) the collection of one-dimensional range search problems; (c) beginning of the plane sweep (the ordered dictionary S of horizontal segments is empty); (d) the first (left-endpoint) event, causing an insertion into S; (e) the second (left-endpoint) event, causing another insertion into S; (f) the third (left-endpoint) event, causing yet another insertion into S. (The plane-sweep is continued in Figure 15.14.)

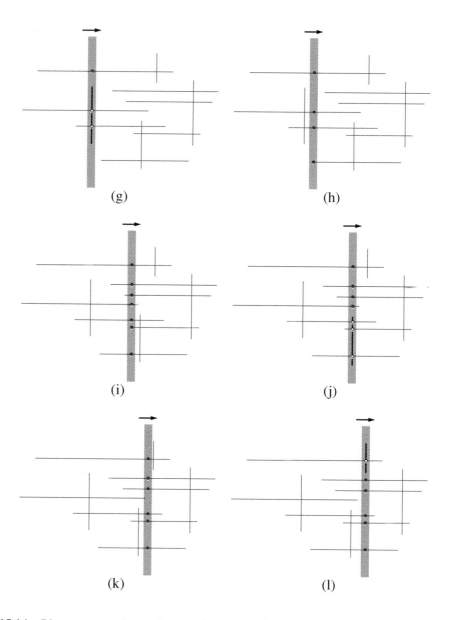

Figure 15.14: Plane sweep for orthogonal segment intersection (continued): (g) the first vertical-segment event, causing a range search in S (two intersections reported); (h) the next (left-endpoint) event, causing an insertion into S; (i) a left-endpoint event three events later, causing an insertion into S; (j) the next (vertical-segment) event, causing a range search in S; (k) a right-endpoint event, causing a removal from S; (l) a vertical-segment event, causing a range search in S. We skip the remaining events.

15.4   Closest Pairs and Proximity

The final geometric concept we discuss in this chapter is **proximity**, which is the relationship of **distance** that exists between geometric objects. We begin this discussion by studying the **closest pair** problem, which consists of finding in a set of n points a pair of points p and q that are at a minimum distance from each other. (See Figure 15.15.) This pair is said to be a closest pair. Recall that the distance between two points a and b in the plane is given by

$$\sqrt{(x(a) - x(b))^2 + (y(a) - y(b))^2},$$

which we denote by $\text{dist}(a, b)$. Applications of the closest pair problem include the verification of mechanical parts and integrated circuits, where it is important that certain separation rules between components be respected.

Figure 15.15: Closest pair in a set of points.

A straightforward "brute-force" solution to the closest pair problem is to compute the distance between every pair of points and select a pair with minimum distance. Since the number of pairs is $n(n-1)/2$, this algorithm takes $O(n^2)$ time. We can apply a more clever strategy, however, which avoids checking all the pairs of points.

15.4.1   A Plane-Sweep Algorithm

It turns out that we can effectively apply the plane-sweep technique, which was introduced in Section 15.3.2, to the closest pair problem. We solve the closest pair problem by imagining that we sweep the plane by a vertical line from left to right, starting at a position to the left of all n of the input points. In this case, as we sweep the line across the plane, we keep track of the closest pair seen so far, and of all those points that are "near" the sweep line. We also keep track of the distance, d, between the closest pair seen so far. In particular, as we illustrate in Figures 15.16 and 15.17, while sweeping through the points from left to right, we maintain the following data:

- A closest pair (a,b) among the points encountered, and the distance $d = \text{dist}(a,b)$
- An ordered dictionary S that stores the points lying in a strip of width d to the left of the sweep line and uses the y-coordinates of points as keys.

Each input point p corresponds to an event in this plane sweep. When the sweep line encounters a point p, we perform the following actions:

1. We update dictionary S by removing the points at horizontal distance greater than d from p, that is, each point r such that $x(p) - x(r) > d$.
2. We find the closest point q to the left of p by searching in dictionary S (we will say in a moment how this is done). If $\text{dist}(p,q) < d$, then we update the current closest pair and distance by setting $a \leftarrow p$, $b \leftarrow q$, and $d \leftarrow \text{dist}(p,q)$.
3. We insert p into S.

Clearly, we can restrict our search of the closest point q to the left of p to the points in dictionary S, since all other points will have distance greater than d. What we want are those points in S that lie within the half-circle $C(p,d)$ of radius d centered at and to the left of point p. (See Figure 15.18.) As a first approximation, we can get the points in the enclosing $d \times 2d$ rectangular box $B(p,d)$ of $C(p,d)$ (Figure 15.18) by performing a range search (Section 14.2.1) on S for the points in S with y-coordinates in the interval of keys $[y(p) - d, y(p) + d]$. We examine such points, one by one, and find the closest to p, denoted q. Since the operations performed on dictionary S are range searches, insertions, and removals of points, we implement S by means of an AVL tree or red-black tree.

The following intuitive property, whose proof is left as an exercise, is crucial to the analysis of the running time of the algorithm.

Proposition 15.6: *A rectangle of width d and height $2d$ can contain at most six points such that any two points are at distance at least d.*

By Proposition 15.6, the number of points of S that lie in the box $B(p,d)$ is at most six. Thus, the range search operation on S, to find the points in $B(p,d)$, takes time $O(\log n + 6)$, which is $O(\log n)$. Also, we can find the point in $B(p,d)$ closest to p in $O(1)$ time.

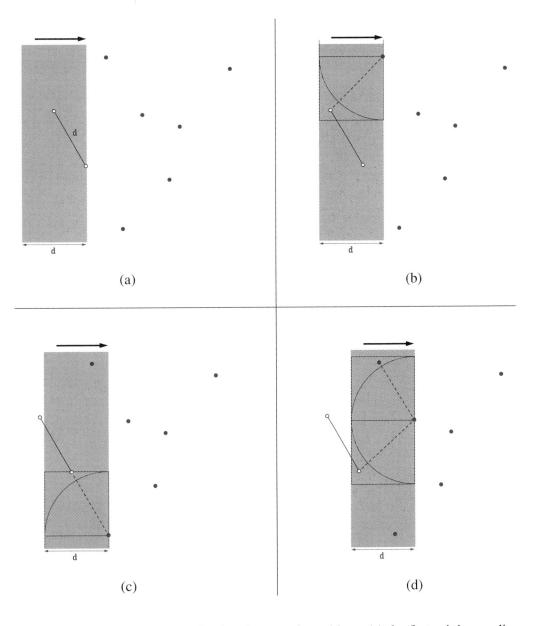

Figure 15.16: Plane sweep for the closest pair problem: (a) the first minimum distance d and closest pair (highlighted); (b) the next event (box $B(p,d)$ contains a point, but the half-circle $C(p,d)$ is empty); (c) next event ($C(p,d)$ again is empty, but a point is removed from S); (d) next event (with $C(p,d)$ again empty). The dictionary S contains the points in the grey strip of width d. (The plane sweep continues in Figure 15.17.)

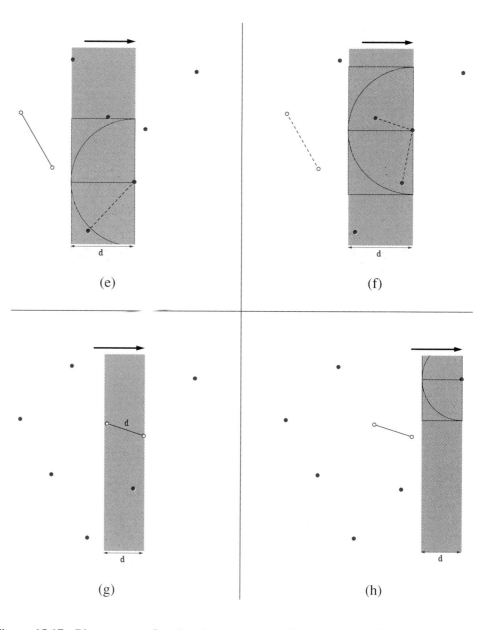

Figure 15.17: Plane sweep for the closest pair problem (continued): (e) a point p is encountered (and a point removed from S), with $B(p,d)$ containing 1 point, but $C(p,d)$ containing none; (f) a point p encountered with $C(p,d)$ containing 2 points (and a point is removed from S); (g) minimum distance d and closest pair (a,b) are updated by setting $a \leftarrow p$, $b \leftarrow q$, and $d \leftarrow \text{dist}(p,q)$, where q is the point in $C(p,d)$ closest to p; (h) the end of the sweep.

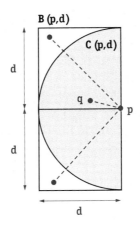

Figure 15.18: Box $B(p,d)$ and half-circle $C(p,d)$.

Before we begin the sweep, we sort the points by x-coordinate, and store them in an ordered sequence X. The sequence X is used for two purposes:

- To get the next point to be processed
- To identify the points to be removed from dictionary S.

We keep references to two positions in sequence X, which we denote as firstInStrip and lastInStrip. Position lastInStrip keeps track of the new point to be inserted into S, while position firstInStrip keeps track of the left-most point in S. By advancing lastInStrip one step at a time, we find the new point to be processed. By using firstInStrip, we identify the points to be removed from S. Namely, while we have

$$x(\text{point}(\text{firstInStrip})) < x(\text{point}(\text{lastInStrip}) - d,$$

we perform operation remove(y(point(firstInStrip))) on dictionary S and advance firstInStrip.

Let n be the number of input points. The analysis of the running time of the plane-sweep algorithm for the closest pair problem is based on the following observations:

- The preliminary sorting by x-coordinate takes time $O(n \log n)$.
- Each point is inserted once and removed once from dictionary S, which has size at most n; hence, the total time for inserting and removing elements in S is $O(n \log n)$.
- By Proposition 15.6, each range query in S takes $O(\log n)$ time. We execute such a range query each time we process a new point. Thus, the total time spent for performing range queries is $O(n \log n)$.

We conclude that we can compute a closest pair in a set of n points in time $O(n \log n)$.

15.4.2   Voronoi Diagrams

There are a number of other interesting problems that deal with proximity. For example, we may be interested in determining the closest point to p in S, for each point p in a set S of n points in the plane. This problem is known as the all-nearest neighbors problem. Alternately, we may be interested in building a data structure for a set S of n points in the plane that can determine, for any query point q, which point in S is closest to q. Many such problems can be solved by using a geometric structure known as the ***Voronoi diagram***.

The Voronoi diagram V of a set S of points in the plane is a subdivision of the plane into ***cells***. Each cell $C(p)$ of V is associated with a point p of S and is defined to be the region of the plane containing all the points that have p as a their closest point in S. (See Figure 15.19.)

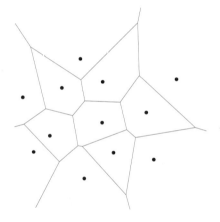

Figure 15.19: An example Voronoi diagram.

There are a number of interesting properties of Voronoi diagrams. For example, each cell of a Voronoi diagram is convex, and if the point p is inside the convex hull of S, then $C(p)$ is a convex polygon. In fact, a point p in S is on the convex hull of S if and only if $C(p)$ is unbounded. Also, for any point p in S, if q is the nearest neighbor of p in S, then the Voronoi cells $C(p)$ and $C(q)$ touch (that is, they share an edge). In addition, note that if no four points in S are all on the same circle, then the Voronoi diagram defines a graph whose vertices have degree three. A vertex of the Voronoi diagram is the center of an empty circle defined by three of the input points. It is beyond the scope of this book to go into the justification of all these facts (though we explore some of them in exercises). We remark without justification that the number of vertices and edges in a Voronoi diagram of n points in the plane is $O(n)$, and that such a Voronoi diagram can be constructed in $O(n \log n)$ time.

15.5 Exercises

Reinforcement

R-15.1 Verify that the absolute value of the function $\Delta(p_1, p_2, p_3)$ is twice the area of the triangle formed by the points p_1, p_2, and p_3 in the plane.

R-15.2 Provide a complete justification of Proposition 15.1.

R-15.3 Provide a complete justification of Proposition 15.2.

R-15.4 Provide a complete justification of Proposition 15.4.

R-15.5 Provide a complete justification of Proposition 15.5.

Creativity

C-15.1 Give an $O(n)$ time algorithm for testing whether a point q is inside, outside, or on the boundary of a nonintersecting polygon P with n vertices. Unlike the algorithm given in Code Fragment 15.1, your algorithm should also work correctly for the case when the y-coordinate of q is equal to the y-coordinate of one or more vertices of P.

C-15.2 Design an $O(n)$ time algorithm to test whether a given n-vertex polygon is convex. You should not assume that P is nonintersecting.

C-15.3 Let S be a collection of segments. Give an algorithm for determining whether the segments of S form a polygon. Allow the polygon to be intersecting, but do not allow two vertices of the polygon to be coincident.

C-15.4 Show how to perform the point inclusion test for a triangle with a method that is simpler than the one for general polygons given in Section 15.1.4.

C-15.5 Design a data structure for convex polygons that uses linear space and supports the point inclusion test in logarithmic time.

C-15.6 Given a set P of n points, design an efficient algorithm for constructing a nonintersecting polygon whose vertices are the points of P.

C-15.7 Design an $O(n^2)$ time algorithm for testing whether a polygon with n vertices is nonintersecting. Assume that the polygon is given by the sequence of its vertices.

C-15.8 Suppose we are given an array-based sequence S of n non-intersecting segments $s_0, \ldots, s_{n-1}$ with endpoints on the lines $y = 0$ and $y = 1$, and ordered from left to right. Given a point q with $0 < y(q) < 1$, design an algorithm that in $O(\log n)$ time computes the segment s_i of S immediately to right of q, or reports that q is to the right of all the segments.

C-15.9 Give examples of configurations of input points for which the simplified Graham scan algorithm, given in Code Fragment 15.2, does not work correctly.

C-15.10 Let P be a set of n points in the plane. Modify the Graham scan algorithm to compute, for every point p of P that is not a vertex of the convex hull, either a triangle with vertices in P, or a segment with endpoints in P that contains p in its interior.

C-15.11 Show that each cell in a Voronoi diagram is convex.

C-15.12 Show that if p and q are a closest pair of points in a set S of n points in the plane, then the Voronoi cells $C(p)$ and $C(q)$ touch.

C-15.13 Show that a point p is on the boundary of the convex hull of a set S of points in the plane if and only if the Voronoi cell for p is unbounded.

C-15.14 Show that for any point p in a set S of points in the plane, if q is the nearest neighbor of p in S, then the Voronoi cells $C(p)$ and $C(q)$ touch.

Projects

P-15.1 Implement the gift wrapping algorithm for computing the convex hull of a set of points.

P-15.2 Produce an animation of the gift wrapping and Graham scan algorithms for computing the convex hull of a set of points.

P-15.3 Implement the plane-sweep algorithm for computing the intersecting pairs of a set of horizontal and vertical segments.

P-15.4 Implement the plane-sweep algorithm for computing the closest pair of a set of points.

Chapter Notes

The convex hull algorithm we present in this chapter is a variant of an algorithm given by Graham [64]. The plane sweep algorithm we present for intersecting orthogonal line segments is due to Bentley and Ottmann [24]. The closest point algorithm we present combines ideas of Bentley [20] and Hinrichs *et al.* [70].

There are several excellent books for computational geometry, including books by Edelsbrunner [45], Mehlhorn [107], O'Rourke [118], Preparata and Shamos [123], and handbooks edited by Goodman and O'Rourke [61], and Pach [119]. Other sources for further reading include survey papers by Aurenhammer [13], Lee and Preparata [96], and book chapters by Goodrich [62], Lee [95], and Yao [150]. Also, the books by Sedgewick [130, 131] contain several chapters on computational geometry, which have some very nice figures. Indeed, the figures in Sedgewick's books have inspired many of the figures we present in this book.

Chapter

16

Caches and Disks

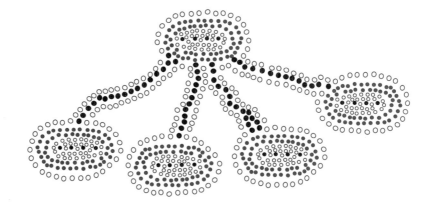

Contents

There are several computer applications that must deal with a large amount of data. Examples include the analysis of scientific data sets, the processing of financial transactions, and the organization and maintenance of databases (such as telephone directories). In fact, the amount of this data that must be dealt with is typically too large to fit entirely in the internal memory of a computer.

In order to accommodate large data sets, computers have a *hierarchy* of different kinds of memories, which vary in terms of their size and distance from the CPU. Closest to the CPU are the internal registers that the CPU itself uses. Access to such locations is very fast, but there are relatively few such locations. At the second level in the hierarchy is the *cache* memory. This memory is considerably larger than the register set of a CPU, but accessing it takes longer (and there may even be multiple caches with progressively slower access times). At the third level in the hierarchy is the *internal memory*, which is also known as *main memory*, *core memory*, or random-access memory (RAM). The internal memory is considerably larger than the cache memory, but also requires more time to access. Finally, at the highest level in the hierarchy is the *external memory*, which usually consists of disks, CDs, or tapes. This memory is very large, but it is also very slow. Thus, the memory hierarchy for computers can be viewed as consisting of four levels, each of which is larger and slower than the previous level. (See Figure 16.1.) In most applications, however, only two levels really matter.

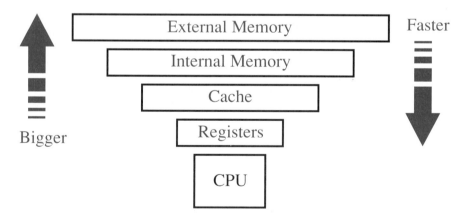

Figure 16.1: The memory hierarchy.

The specific two levels that matter most depend on the size of the problem we are trying to solve. For a problem that can fit entirely in main memory, the important two levels are the cache memory and the internal memory. Access times for internal memory can be as much as ten to 100 times longer than those for cache memory. It is desirable, therefore, to be able to perform most memory accesses in cache memory. For a problem that does not fit entirely in main memory, on the other hand, the important two levels are the internal memory and the external memory. Here the differences are even more dramatic, for access times for disks, the typical general-purpose external-memory device, are typically as much as $100,000$ to $1,000,000$ times longer than those for internal memory.

To put this latter figure into perspective, imagine there is a student in Baltimore who wants to send a request-for-money message to his parents in Chicago. If the student sends his parents an e-mail message, it can arrive at their home computer in about five seconds. Think of this mode of communication as corresponding to an internal-memory access by a CPU. A mode of communication, corresponding to an external-memory access that is $500,000$ times slower, would be for the student to walk to Chicago and deliver his message in person, which would take about a month if he can average twenty miles per day. Thus, one should make as few accesses to external memory as possible.

In this chapter, we discuss general strategies for hierarchical memory management and present methods for performing searching and sorting in two-level memory hierarchies that minimize second-level memory accesses. Since these discussions all involve a certain degree of device dependence, we do not provide any Java examples in this chapter.

16.1 Hierarchical Memory Management

Most algorithms are not designed with memory hierarchy in mind, in spite of the great variance between access times for different levels. Indeed, all of the algorithm analyses described so far in this book have assumed that all memory accesses are equal. This assumption might seem, at first, to be a great oversight (and one we are only addressing now in the final chapter), but there are two fundamental justifications for why it is actually a reasonable assumption to make.

The first justification is that it is often necessary to the assumption that all memory accesses take the same amount of time. since specific device-dependent information about memory sizes is often hard to come by. In fact, information about memory size may be impossible to get. Indeed, a Java program that is designed to run on many different computer platforms cannot be defined in terms of a specific computer architecture configuration. We can certainly use architecture-specific information, if we have it (and we will show how to exploit such information later in this chapter). But once we have optimized our software for a certain architecture configuration, our software will no longer be device-independent. Fortunately, such optimizations are not always necessary, primarily because of the second justification for the equal-time memory-access assumption.

The second justification for the memory-access equality assumption is that operating system designers have developed general mechanisms that allow for most memory accesses to be fast. These mechanisms are based on two important *locality-of-reference* properties that most software possesses:

- **Temporal Locality**: If a program accesses a certain memory location, then it is likely to access this location again in the near future. For example, it is quite common to use the value of a counter variable in several different expressions, including one to increment the counter's value. In fact, a common adage among computer architects is that "a program spends ninety percent of its time in ten percent of its code."
- **Spatial Locality**: If a program accesses a certain memory location, then it is likely to access other locations that are near this one. For example, a program using an array is likely to access the locations of this array in a sequential or near-sequential manner.

Computer scientists have performed extensive software profiling experiments to justify the claim that most software possesses both of these kinds of locality-of-reference.

16.1.1 Caching and Blocking

Temporal and spatial localities have, in turn, given rise to two fundamental design choices for two-level computer memory systems (which are present in the interface between cache memory and internal memory, and also in the interface between internal memory and external memory).

The first design choice is called *virtual memory*, and consists of providing an address space as large as the capacity of the secondary-level memory, and of transferring into the primary-level memory data located in the secondary level, when they are addressed. Virtual memory does not limit the programmer to the constraint of the internal memory size. The concept of bringing data into primary memory is called *caching*, and it is motivated by temporal locality, for, by bringing data into primary memory, we are hoping that it will be accessed again soon, and we will be able to quickly respond to all the requests for this data that come in the near future.

The second design choice is motivated by spatial locality. Specifically, if data stored at a secondary-level memory location *l* is accessed, then we bring into primary-level memory a large block of contiguous locations that include the location *l*. (See Figure 16.2.) This concept is known as *blocking*, and it is motivated by the expectation that other secondary-level memory locations close to *l* will soon be accessed. In the interface between cache memory and internal memory such blocks are often called *cache lines*, and in the interface between internal memory

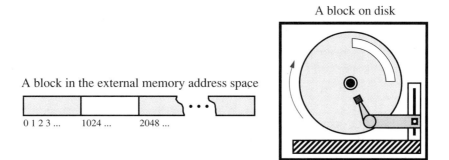

Figure 16.2: Blocks in external memory.

and external memory such blocks are often called **pages**. Incidentally, blocking for disk and CD-ROM drives is also motivated by the properties of these hardware technologies, for a reading arm on a disk or CD-ROM takes a relatively long time to position itself for reading a certain location, but, once the arm is positioned, it can quickly read many contiguous locations, because the medium it is reading is spinning very fast. (See Figure 16.2.) Even without this motivation, however, blocking is fully justified by the spatial locality property that most programs have.

Thus, when implemented with caching and blocking, virtual memory often allows us to perceive secondary-level memory as being faster than it really is. There is still a problem, however. Primary-level memory is much smaller than secondary-level memory. Moreover, because memory systems use blocking, any program of substance will likely reach a point where it requests data from secondary-level memory that is not in primary memory, but the primary memory is already full of blocks. In order to fulfill the request and maintain our use of caching and blocking, we must remove some block from primary memory to make room for a new block from secondary memory. Deciding how to do this brings up a number of data structure and algorithm design issues that we discuss in the remainder of this section.

16.1.2 Block Replacement Policies

Suppose we have a primary-level memory that has m "slots" that can contain blocks from secondary-level memory. Adopting standard terminology, we call the primary-level memory the **cache**, and we call the secondary-level memory **external memory**. We assume that a block from external memory can be placed in any slot of the cache. This is known as a **fully associative** cache. Caches with other more limited kinds of associativity can also use the methods we discuss in this section, but only for groups of slots that are fully associative.

As a program executes, it requests access to different locations in external memory. Each time a program accesses such a location l, the CPU determines (at the hardware level) if l is currently contained in the cache, and if so, where. If l is contained in the cache, then the CPU performs the access for this location (either a read or write) and moves on to the next instruction. If l is not in the cache, however, the block in external memory containing l must be transferred into the cache. Let b denote this block. If one of the m slots in the cache is available, then the computer brings in the block b, and performs the access for l in it. But if all of the m cells of the cache are occupied, then the computer must determine which block to move back to external memory before bringing in b to take its place. There are, of course, many different policies that can be used to determine the block to evict. Some of the better-known block replacement policies include the following (see Figure 16.3):

- **Random**: Choose a block at random to evict from the cache.
- **First-In, First-out (FIFO)**: Evict from the cache the block that has been in the cache the longest, that is, the block that was transferred to the cache furthest in the past.
- **Least Frequently Used (LFU)**: Evict from the cache the block that has been accessed the least often.
- **Least Recently Used (LRU)**: Evict from the cache the block whose last access occurred furthest in the past.

Among these policies, the easiest to implement is the Random policy, for it only requires a pseudo-random number generator. The overhead involved in implementing this policy is an $O(1)$ additional amount of work per block replacement. Moreover, there is no additional overhead for each memory access, other than the hardware check to determine whether a memory request is in internal memory or not. Still, this policy makes no attempt to take advantage of any temporal or spatial localities that a program exhibits.

The FIFO strategy is also quite simple to implement, as it only requires a queue Q to store references to the blocks in the cache. Block references are enqueued in Q when blocks are brought into the cache. When a block needs to be evicted, the computer simply performs a dequeue operation on Q to determine which block to evict. Thus, assuming the queue Q is implemented efficiently (Section 3.2), this policy also requires $O(1)$ additional work per block replacement. Also, like the Random policy, the FIFO policy incurs no additional overhead for memory accesses. Therefore, the FIFO strategy has the same asymptotic overhead as the Random policy, but it tries to take some advantage of temporal locality. In particular, the FIFO policy assumes that the block inserted first among all those present is the least likely to be accessed in the near future.

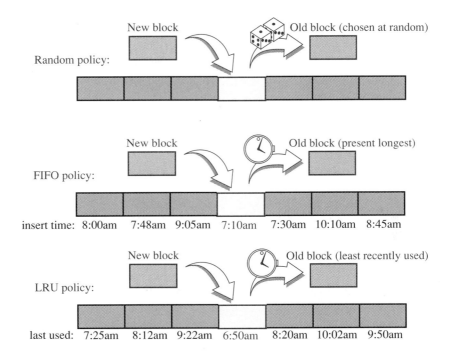

Figure 16.3: Illustrating the Random, FIFO, and LRU block replacement policies.

The LFU strategy, on the other hand, requires more overhead, for both memory access and block replacement. In particular, this strategy requires that we store block references in a priority queue, where the key of a block is the number of times (a location in) the block has been accessed. With a bit of creativity (which we explore in Exercise C-16.1), one can implement this strategy to have only a constant time additional overhead per memory access. Nevertheless, although the LFU policy tries to take advantage of temporal and spatial locality, it can penalize recently added blocks that haven't been accessed often enough to be "mature."

The LRU strategy overcomes the drawbacks in the FIFO and LFU strategies by explicitly taking advantage of temporal locality as much as possible. From a policy point of view, this is an excellent approach, but it is costly from an implementation point of view. That is, its way of optimizing temporal and spatial locality is fairly costly. Implementing the LRU strategy requires the use of a priority queue Q that supports locators (Section 6.4.1). Namely, each time we access a block b in the cache, we use the locator ℓ for b in Q as the argument of a replaceKey(ℓ, k) operation, which assigns to b a key k equal to the current time. If Q is implemented with a sorted sequence based on a linked list, then the overhead for each memory access and block replacement is $O(1)$. Whenever we insert a block in Q or update its key, the block is assigned the highest key in Q and is placed at the end of the list.

Even though the LRU strategy has $O(1)$ overhead, the constant factors involved, in terms of the additional time overhead and the extra space for the priority queue Q, make this policy less attractive from a practical point of view.

Since these different block replacement policies have different trade-offs between implementation difficulty and the degree in which they seem to take advantage of localities, it is natural for us to ask for some kind of comparative analysis of these methods to see which one, if any, is the best.

16.1.3 Competitive Analysis ★

We have already examined how much computational overhead each of these block replacement policies impose on memory accesses and block replacements. We have observed that each requires only $O(1)$ overhead for both of these activities. Nevertheless, since memory access is the single most common thing that a CPU does, the constant factors in these running times are very important. In terms of constant factors, and inherent degree of implementation difficulty, the ordering of these policies from best to worst is as follows: (1) Random, (2) FIFO, (3) LFU, and (4) LRU.

Degree of implementation difficulty is not necessarily the most important factor, however, given the great benefits that can come from avoiding unnecessary accesses to external memory. Perhaps even more important is the number of block transfers that each policy requires. We can try to measure this using the worst-case approach we have advocated for most of the analysis done in this book, but this type of analysis is not as useful here. For example, suppose we have a cache containing m blocks, and consider the FIFO and LRU methods performing block replacement for a program that has a loop that repeatedly accesses $m+1$ blocks in a cyclic order. Both the FIFO and LRU policies perform very badly on such a sequence of memory accesses because they perform a block replacement on every access. Thus, from a worst-case point of view, these policies are the worst we can imagine—they require a block replacement on every memory access!

This worst-case analysis is a little too pessimistic, however, for it focuses on each protocol's behavior for one bad sequence of accesses. An ideal analysis would be to compare these methods over all possible memory access sequences. Of course, this is impossible to do exhaustively, but there have been a great number of experimental simulations done on memory access sequences derived from real programs. The experiments have focused primarily on the Random, FIFO, and LRU policies (since LFU has such a large overhead and does not take full advantage of temporal locality). Based on these experimental comparisons, the ordering of policies, from best to worst, is as follows: (1) LRU, (2) FIFO, and (3) Random. In fact, LRU is significantly better than the others on typical access sequences.

Thus, from a strategic viewpoint, LRU is the best policy in the group, but, from an implementation-difficulty viewpoint, it is the worst. In fact, this benefit-cost trade-off for the LRU strategy has motivated computer scientists to consider other block-replacement policies that are easier to implement, but nevertheless try to emulate the LRU policy. One such policy is the Marker strategy:

- **Marker**: Associate, with each block in the cache, a Boolean variable marked, which is initially set to "false" for every block in the cache. If a program accesses a block that is already in the cache, that block's marked variable is set to "true." Otherwise, if a program accesses a block that is not in the cache, a random block whose marked variable is "false" is evicted and replaced with the new block, whose marked variable is immediately set to "true." If all the blocks in the cache have marked variables set to "true," then all of them are reset to "false." (See Figure 16.4.)

Experimental studies that compare the Marker policy to the LRU, FIFO, and Random policies show that it consistently beats the FIFO and Random policies and comes very close to the performance of the LRU policy.

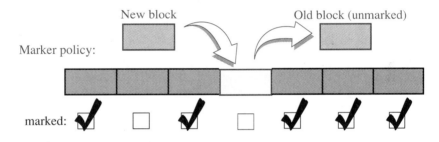

Figure 16.4: Illustrating the Marker block-replacement policy.

There is another kind of analysis that we can perform on policies such as these block-replacement policies, however, that avoids experimentation yet still yields interesting insights into performance. It is called the ***competitive*** analysis, and it is useful for analyzing all kinds of ***on-line*** algorithms, including the block-replacement policies described above.

An on-line algorithm is an algorithm that responds to a sequence of ***service requests*** which have different ***costs*** associated with them. For example, a block-replacement policy maintains blocks in cache and external memory, subject to a sequence of access requests, with the cost of a block access being zero if the block is in the cache and one if the block is outside the cache. In an "on-line" setting, the algorithm must completely finish responding to a service request before it can receive the next request in the sequence.

If an algorithm is given the entire sequence of service requests in advance, it is said to be an **off-line** algorithm. In the competitive analysis, we compare a particular on-line algorithm A to an optimal off-line algorithm, OPT. Given a sequence $P = (p_1, p_2, \ldots, p_n)$ of service requests, let $cost(A, P)$ denote the cost of A on P and let $cost(OPT, P)$ denote the cost of the optimal algorithm on P. The algorithm A is said to be c-**competitive** for a sequence P if

$$cost(A, P) \le c \cdot cost(OPT, P) + b,$$

for some constant $b \ge 0$. If A is c-competitive for every sequence P, then we simply say that A is c-competitive, and we call c the **competitive ratio** of A.

Proposition 16.1: *The FIFO and LRU block replacement policies for a cache with m blocks have competitive ratio m.*

Justification: We observed above that there is a sequence $P = (p_1, p_2, \ldots, p_n)$ of memory-access requests causing FIFO and LRU to perform a block replacement with each request (the loop of $m + 1$ accesses). We compare this performance with that of the optimal off-line algorithm, OPT, which, in the case of the block replacement problem, is to evict the block that is referenced the furthest into the future. This strategy can only be implemented, of course, in the off-line case, when we are given the entire sequence P in advance, unless the algorithm is "prophetic." When applied to the loop sequence, the OPT policy will perform a block replacement once every m requests (for it evicts the most recently referenced block each time, as this one is referenced furthest in the future). Thus, both FIFO and LRU are c-competitive on this sequence P, where

$$c = \frac{n}{n/m} = m.$$

Observe that if any portion $P' = (p_i, p_{i+1} \ldots, p_j)$ of a sequence P of requests makes requests to m different blocks (with p_{i-1} and/or p_{j+1} not being one of them), then even the optimal algorithm must evict one block. In addition, the most number of blocks the FIFO and LRU policies evict for such a portion P' is m, each time evicting a block that was referenced prior to p_i. Therefore, FIFO and LRU have a competitive ratio of m, and this is the best possible competitive ratio for these strategies in the worst case.   ∎

Even though FIFO and LRU can have poor worst-case competitive ratios compared to the "prophetic" optimal algorithm, several computer science researchers have shown that LRU actually has a much better competitive ratio when the analysis is performed in a more realistic model. This analysis is beyond the scope of this book, however. Still, we can show that the Marker policy, which simulates LRU (and is very close to LRU's performance in practice), has a good competitive ratio.

Before we can examine the Marker policy's competitive ratio, however, we must first define what we mean by the competitive ratio of a randomized on-line algorithm. Since a randomized algorithm A, like the Marker policy, can have many different possible runs, depending upon the random choices it makes, we define such an algorithm to be c-***competitive*** for a sequence of requests P if

$$E(cost(A,P)) \leq c \cdot cost(OPT,P) + b,$$

for some constant $b \geq 0$, where $E(cost(A,P))$ denotes the expected cost of algorithm A on the sequence P (with this expectation taken over all possible random choices for the algorithm A). If A is c-competitive for every sequence P, then we simply say that A is c-competitive, and we call c the ***competitive ratio*** for A.

Proposition 16.2: *The Marker block policy for a cache with m blocks has competitive ratio $O(\log m)$.*

Justification: Let $P = (p_1, p_2, \ldots, p_n)$ be a sufficiently long sequence of access requests to memory. The Marker policy implicitly partitions the requests in P into ***rounds***. Each round begins with all the blocks in the cache having "false" marked labels, and a round ends when all the blocks in the cache have "true" marked labels (with the next request beginning the next round, since the policy then resets each such label to "false"). Consider the ith round in P, and call a block accessed in round i as being ***fresh*** if it is not in the Marker policy's cache at the beginning of round i. Also, we refer to a block in the Marker's cache that has a false marked label as being ***stale***. Thus, at the beginning of a round i, all the blocks in the Marker policy's cache are stale. Let m_i denote the number of fresh blocks referenced in the ith round, and let b_i denote the number of blocks that are in the cache for the OPT algorithm at the beginning of round i and are not in the cache for the Marker policy at this time. Since the Marker policy has to perform a block replacement for each of the m_i requests, algorithm OPT must perform at least $m_i - b_i$ block replacements in round i. (See Figure 16.5.) In addition, since each of the blocks in the Marker policy's cache at the end of round i are requested in round i, algorithm OPT must perform at least b_{i+1} block replacements in round i. Thus, the algorithm OPT must perform at least

$$\max\{m_i - b_i, b_{i+1}\} \geq \frac{m_i - b_i + b_{i+1}}{2}$$

block replacements in round i. Summing over all k rounds in P then, we see that algorithm OPT must perform at least the following number of block replacements:

$$L = \sum_{i=1}^{k} \frac{m_i - b_i + b_{i+1}}{2} = (b_{k+1} - b_1)/2 + \frac{1}{2}\sum_{i=1}^{k} m_i.$$

Let us next consider the expected number of block replacements performed by the Marker policy.

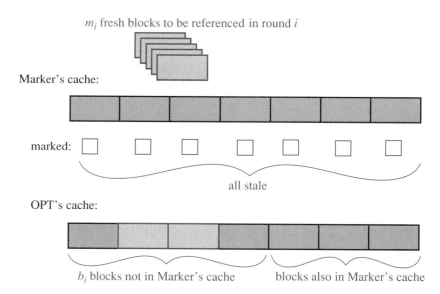

Marker's cache:

marked:

all stale

OPT's cache:

b_i blocks not in Marker's cache   blocks also in Marker's cache

Figure 16.5: Illustrating the state of Marker's cache and OPT's cache at the beginning of round i.

We have already observed that the Marker policy has to perform at least m_i block replacements in round i. It may actually perform more than this, however, if it evicts stale blocks that are then requested later in the round. Thus, the expected number of block replacements performed by the Marker policy is $m_i + n_i$, where n_i is the expected number of stale blocks that are referenced in round i after having been evicted from the cache. The value n_i is equal to the sum, over all stale blocks referenced in round i, of the probability that these blocks are outside of the cache when referenced. At the point in round i when a stale block v is referenced, the probability that v is out of the cache is at most f/g, where f is the number of fresh blocks referenced before block v and g is the number of stale blocks that have not yet been referenced. This is because each reference to a fresh block evicts some unmarked stale block at random. The cost to the Marker policy will be highest then, if all m_i requests to fresh blocks are made before any requests to stale blocks. So, assuming this worst-case viewpoint, the expected number of evicted stale blocks referenced in round i can be bounded as

$$n_i \;\leq\; \frac{m_i}{m} + \frac{m_i}{m-1} + \frac{m_i}{m-2} + \cdots + \frac{m_i}{m_i+1}$$

$$\leq\; m_i \sum_{j=0}^{m} \frac{1}{j},$$

since there are $m - m_i$ references to stale blocks in round i. Noting that this summation is known as the *m*th harmonic number, which is denoted H_m, we have

$$n_i \leq m_i H_m.$$

Thus, the expected number of block replacements performed by the Marker policy is at most

$$U = \sum_{i=1}^{k} m_i (H_m + 1) = (H_m + 1) \sum_{i=1}^{k} m_i.$$

Therefore, the competitive ratio for the Marker policy is at most

$$\frac{U}{L} = \frac{(H_m + 1) \sum_{i=1}^{k} m_i}{(1/2) \sum_{i=1}^{k} m_i}$$

$$= 2(H_m + 1).$$

Using an approximation for H_m, the *m*th harmonic number (see Appendix B), we have that the competitive ratio for the Marker policy is $O(\log m)$. ∎

Thus, the competitive analysis shows that the Marker policy is fairly efficient.

16.1.4 Living with Caches and Disks

In general, block replacement policies provide an abstraction to programmers that allows them to not be overly concerned with the memory hierarchy. Nevertheless, there are some lessons that a good programmer should take to heart, even if he or she is relying on the operating system to handle block replacement:

- **Use Temporal Locality.** If an algorithm calls for several accesses to the same variable, try to group all these accesses as close together as possible in time.
- **Use Spatial Locality.** If an algorithm calls for accessing a certain location in an array or a certain field in an object, try to group other spatially nearby accesses as close in time to this one as possible.

These may seem like obvious bits of advice coming at the end of this section, but they actually have some surprising implications. One such implication, which is explored further in the next example, is that one may prefer an asymptotically slower algorithm to a faster one if it can make better use of temporal and spatial locality.

Example 16.3: *Suppose we want to sort a sequence S of n items with integer keys in the range $[1, n]$. Consider the radix-sort and merge-sort methods discussed in Chapter 8 for sorting S. Based on an asymptotic operation count, radix-sort runs in $\Theta(n)$ time and merge-sort runs in $\Theta(n \log n)$ time. Moreover, since the constant factors for both of these algorithms are relatively small, it would appear that radix-sort should be the preferred algorithm for sorting S. This is not necessarily so.*

Suppose n is so large that S and the working storage for the two sorting algorithms must be stored in external memory. The radix-sort algorithm does not exhibit any locality in terms of its working storage, temporally or spatially. It "bounces" all around the bucket array it uses. Thus, since each access to the bucket array can cause a new block replacement, radix sort requires $O(n)$ block replacements in the worst case. The merge-sort algorithm, on the other hand, exhibits a great deal of spatial locality if the sequences it uses are implemented as arrays. This is because the merging process scans sequentially through the arrays (including both input arrays and the output array). Thus, if the size of a block is B, then the merge-sort algorithm performs only $O((n/B)\log n)$ block replacements in the worst case. Therefore, if $B > \log n$ (which will often be the case), then merge-sort should be preferred over radix-sort for large-scale sorting applications.

This example shows the benefits of programming with caches and disks in mind, while still relying on the operating system to handle block replacement. In the next two sections, we study situations in which the algorithm designer can take control of block replacement and improve what can be achieved by the operating system alone.

16.2   External Searching

In this section, we study the problem of implementing a dictionary for a large collection of items that do not fit in primary memory. Since one of the main applications of large dictionaries is in database systems, we refer to the secondary-memory blocks as **disk blocks**. Likewise, we refer to the transfer of a block between secondary memory and primary memory as a **disk transfer**. Even though we use this terminology, the search techniques we discuss in this section apply also when the primary memory is the CPU cache and the secondary memory is the main (RAM) memory. We use the disk-based viewpoint because it is concrete and also because it is more prevalent.

Recalling the great time difference that exists between main memory accesses and disk accesses, the main goal of maintaining a dictionary in external memory is to minimize the number of disk transfers needed to perform a query or update. In fact, the difference in speed between disk and internal memory is so great that we should be willing to perform a considerable number of internal-memory accesses if they allow us to avoid a few disk transfers. Let us, therefore, analyze the performance of dictionary implementations by counting the number of disk transfers each would require to perform the standard dictionary search and update operations.

Let us consider first the simple dictionary realizations that use a sequence to store the items. If the sequence is implemented as an unsorted doubly linked list, then insert and delete can be performed with $O(1)$ transfers each, but searching requires $\Theta(n)$ transfers in the worst case, since each link hop we perform could access a different block. This search time can be improved to $O(n/B)$ transfers (using a method we explore in Exercise C-16.3), where B denotes the number of nodes of the list that can fit into a block, but this is still poor performance. We could alternately implement the sequence using a sorted array. In this case, a search performs $O(\log_2 n)$ transfers, which is a nice improvement. But this solution requires $\Theta(n/B)$ transfers to implement an insert or remove operation in the worst case, for we may have to access all the blocks holding the array to move elements up or down. Thus, sequence implementations of a dictionary are not efficient from an external memory standpoint.

If sequence implementations are inefficient, then perhaps we should consider the logarithmic-time, internal-memory strategies that use balanced binary trees (for example, AVL trees or red-black trees) or other search structures with logarithmic average-case query and update times (for example, skip lists or splay trees). These methods store the dictionary items at the nodes of a binary tree or of a graph (for skip lists). In the worst case (and also the average case), each node accessed for a query or update in one of these structures will be in a different block. Thus, these methods all require $O(\log_2 n)$ transfers in the worst case to perform a query or update operation. This is pretty good, but we can do much better. In particular, we describe in the remainder of this section how to perform dictionary query and update operations using only $O(\log_B n) = O(\log n / \log B)$ transfers.

16.2.1 (a,b) Trees and B-Trees

The main idea behind improving the external-memory performance of the dictionary implementations discussed above is that we should be willing to perform up to $O(B)$ internal-memory accesses to avoid a single disk transfer, where B denotes the size of a disk block. The hardware and software that drives the disk performs this many internal-memory accesses just to bring a block into internal memory, and, even then, this is only a small part of the cost of a disk transfer. Thus, $O(B)$ high-speed, internal-memory accesses are a small price to pay to avoid a time-consuming disk transfer.

(a,b) Trees

To reduce the importance of the performance difference between internal-memory accesses and external-memory accesses for searching, we can represent our dictionary using a multi-way search tree (Chapter 13). This approach gives rise to a generalization of the $(2,4)$ tree data structure to a structure known as the (a,b) tree.

An (a, b) tree is a multi-way search tree such that each node has between a and b children and stores between $a - 1$ and $b - 1$ items. The algorithms for searching, inserting, and deleting elements in an (a, b) tree are straightforward generalizations of the corresponding ones for $(2, 4)$ trees. The advantage of generalizing $(2, 4)$ trees to (a, b) trees is that a generalized class of trees provides a flexible search structure, where the size of the nodes and the running time of the various dictionary operations depends on the parameters a and b. By setting the parameters a and b appropriately with respect to the size of disk blocks, can derive a data structure that achieves good external-memory performance.

An (a, b) *tree*, where a and b are integers, such that $2 \le a \le (b + 1)/2$, is a multi-way search tree T with the following additional restrictions:

Size Property: Each internal node has at least a children, unless it is the root, and has most b children.

Depth Property: All the external nodes have the same depth.

Proposition 16.4: *The height of an (a, b) tree storing n items is $\Omega(\log n / \log b)$ and $O(\log n / \log a)$.*

Justification: Let T be an (a, b) tree storing n elements, and let h be the height of T. We justify the proposition by establishing the following bounds on h:

$$\frac{1}{\log b} \log(n + 1) \le h \le \frac{1}{\log a} \log \frac{n + 1}{2} + 1.$$

By the size and depth properties, the number n'' of external nodes of T is at least $2a^{h-1}$ and at most b^h. By Proposition 13.1, $n'' = n + 1$. Thus

$$2a^{h-1} \le n + 1 \le b^h.$$

Taking the logarithm in base 2 of each term, we get

$$(h - 1) \log a + 1 \le \log(n + 1) \le h \log b.$$

∎

We recall that in a multi-way search tree T, each node v of T holds a secondary structure $D(v)$, which is itself a dictionary (Section 13.1.3). If T is an (a, b) tree, then $D(v)$ stores at most b items. Let $f(b)$ denote the time for performing a search in a $D(v)$ dictionary. The search algorithm in an (a, b) tree is exactly like the one for multi-way search trees given in Section 13.1.3. Hence, searching in an (a, b) tree T with n items takes $O(\frac{f(b)}{\log a} \log n)$. Note that if b is a constant (and thus a is also), then the search time is $O(\log n)$, independent of the specific implementation of the secondary structures.

The main application of (a,b) trees is for dictionaries stored in external memory (for example, on a disk or CD-ROM). Namely, to minimize disk accesses, we select the parameters a and b that each tree node occupies a single disk block (so that $f(b) = 1$ if we wish to simply count block transfers). Providing the right a and b values in this context gives rise to a data structure known as the B-tree, which we will describe shortly. Before we describe this structure, however, let us discuss how insertions and deletions are handled in (a,b) trees.

Insertion and Deletion in an (a,b) Tree

The insertion algorithm for an (a,b) tree is similar to that for a $(2,4)$ tree. An overflow occurs when an item is inserted into a b-node v, which becomes an illegal $(b+1)$-node. (Recall that a node in a multi-way tree is a d-node if it has d children.) To remedy an overflow, we split node v by moving the median item of v into the parent of v and replacing v with a $\lceil (b+1)/2 \rceil$-node v' and a $\lfloor (b+1)/2 \rfloor$-node v''. We can now see the reason for requiring $a \le (b+1)/2$ in the definition of an (a,b) tree. Note that as a consequence of the split, we need to build the secondary structures $D(v')$ and $D(v'')$.

Deleting an element from an (a,b) tree is also similar to what was done for $(2,4)$ trees. An underflow occurs when a key is removed from an a-node v, distinct from the root, which causes v to become an illegal $(a-1)$-node. To remedy an underflow, we either perform a transfer with a sibling of v that is not an a-node or we perform a fusion of v with a sibling that is an a-node. The new node w resulting from the fusion is a $(2a-1)$-node. Here, we see another reason for requiring $a \le (b+1)/2$. Note that as a consequence of the fusion, we need to build the secondary structure $D(w)$.

Table 16.1 shows the running time of the main operations of a dictionary realized by means of an (a,b) tree T.

Method	Time
findElement	$O\left(\dfrac{f(b)}{\log a} \log n \right)$
insertItem	$O\left(\dfrac{g(b)}{\log a} \log n \right)$
remove	$O\left(\dfrac{g(b)}{\log a} \log n \right)$

Table 16.1: Time complexity of the main methods of a dictionary realized by an (a,b) tree. Only the main dictionary methods are shown. We denote the number of elements in the dictionary at the time the method is executed with n. The space complexity is $O(n)$.

The time bounds in Table 16.1 are based on the following assumptions and facts:

- The (a,b) tree T is realized by means of the data structure described in Section 13.1.3, and the secondary structure of the nodes of T support search in $f(b)$ time, and split and fusion operations in $g(b)$ time, for some functions $f(b)$ and $g(b)$, which can be made to be $O(1)$ in the context where we are only counting disk transfers.

- The height of an (a,b) tree storing n elements is $O((\log n)/(\log a))$ (Proposition 16.4).

- A search visits $O((\log n)/(\log a))$ nodes on a path between the root and an external node, and spends $f(b)$ time per node.

- A transfer operation takes $f(b)$ time.

- A split or fusion operation takes $g(b)$ time and builds a secondary structure of size $O(b)$ for the new node(s) created.

- An insertion or deletion of an element visits $O((\log n)/(\log a))$ nodes on a path between the root and an external node, and spends $f(b)$ time per node.

B-Trees

A specialized version of the (a,b) tree data structure, which is the best known method for maintaining a dictionary in external memory, is the data structure known as the "B-tree." (See Figure 16.6.) A *B-tree of order* d is simply an (a,b) tree with $a = \lceil d/2 \rceil$ and $b = d$. Since we discussed the standard dictionary query and update methods for (a,b) trees above, we restrict our discussion here to the analysis of the external-memory performance of B-trees.

The most important observation about B-trees is that we can choose d so that the d children references and the $d-1$ keys stored at a node can all fit into a single disk block, which implies that d is $\Theta(B)$. This choice also implies that we may assume that a and b are $\Theta(B)$ in the analysis of the search and update operations on (a,b) trees. This choice also implies that $f(b)$ and $g(b)$ are both $O(1)$, for each time we access a node to perform a search or an update operation, we need only perform a single disk transfer. As we have already observed above, each search or update requires that we examine at most $O(1)$ nodes for each level of the tree. Therefore, any dictionary search or update operation on a B-tree requires only

$$O(\log_{\lceil d/2 \rceil} n) = O(\log n / \log B)$$

disk transfers. For example, an insert operation proceeds down the B-tree to locate the node in which to insert the new item. If the node would *overflow* (to have $d+1$

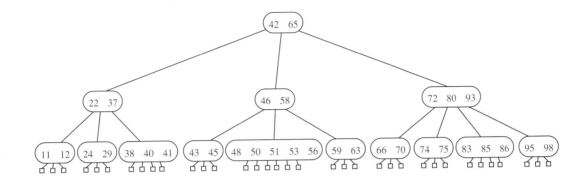

Figure 16.6: A B-tree of order 6.

children) because of this addition, then this node is *split* into two nodes that have $\lfloor (d+1)/2 \rfloor$ and $\lceil (d+1)/2 \rceil$ children, respectively. This process is then repeated at the next level up, and will continue for at most $O(\log_B n)$ levels. Likewise, in a delete operation, we remove an item from a node, and, if this results in a a node *underflow* (to have $\lceil d/2 \rceil - 1$ children), then we either move references from a sibling node with at least $\lceil d/2 \rceil + 1$ children or we need to perform a *fusion* operation of this node with its sibling (and repeat this computation at the parent). As with the insert operation, this will continue up the B-tree for at most $O(\log_B n)$ levels. Thus, we have the following:

Proposition 16.5: *A B-tree with n items executes $O(\log_B n)$ disk transfers in a search or update operation, where B is the number of items that can fit in one block.*

The requirement that each internal node have at least $\lceil d/2 \rceil$ children implies that each disk block used to support a B-tree is at least half full. Analytical and experimental study of the average block usage in a B-tree is that it is closer to 67%, which is quite good.

16.2.2 Achieving "Near" Machine Independence

Using B-trees can produce significant reductions in the number of block transfers. The most important piece of information that made such reductions possible was knowing the value of B, the size of a disk block (or cache line). This information is, of course, machine-dependent, but it is one of the few truly machine-dependent pieces of information that are needed, with one of the others being the ability to store keys continuously in arrays.

From our description of B-trees, one may think that we also require low-level access to the external-memory device driver, but this is not strictly needed in order to achieve the claimed results to within a constant factor. In particular, in addition to knowing the block size, the only other thing we need to know is that large arrays of keys are partitioned into blocks of continuous cells. This allows us to implement the "blocks" in B-trees as separate size B arrays, which we call ***pseudo-blocks***. If arrays are allocated to blocks in the natural way, any such pseudo-block will be allocated to at most two real blocks. Thus, even if we are relying on the operating system to perform block replacement (for example, using FIFO, LRU, or the Marker policy), we can be sure that accessing any pseudo-block takes at most two, that is, $O(1)$, real block transfers. By using pseudo-blocks then, instead of real blocks, we can implement the dictionary ADT to achieve search and update operations that use only $O(\log_B n)$ block transfers. We can, therefore, design external-memory data structures without taking control of the memory hierarchy from the operating system. In fact, this same technique also works for external-memory algorithms, such as the external-memory sorting algorithm we discuss next.

16.3 External Sorting

In addition to data structures, such as dictionaries, that need to be implemented in external memory, there are many algorithms that must also operate on input sets that are too large to fit entirely into internal memory. In this case, the objective is to solve the algorithmic problem using as few block transfers as possible. The most classic domain for such external-memory algorithms is the sorting problem.

16.3.1 A Lower Bound for External-Memory Sorting

As we discussed in Example 16.3, there can be a big difference between an algorithm's performance in internal memory and its performance in external memory. For example, the performance of the radix-sorting algorithm is bad in external memory, yet good in internal memory. Other algorithms, such as the merge-sort algorithm, are reasonably good in both internal memory and external memory, however. The number of block transfers performed by the traditional merge-sorting algorithm is $O((n/B) \log_2 n)$, where B is the size of disk blocks. While this is much better than the $O(n)$ block transfers performed by an external version of radix sort, it is, nevertheless, not the best that is achievable for the sorting problem. In fact, we can show the following lower bound, whose justification is beyond the scope of this book.

Proposition 16.6: *Sorting n elements stored in external memory requires*

$$\Omega\left(\frac{n}{B}\cdot\frac{\log(n/B)}{\log(M/B)}\right)$$

block transfers, where M is the size of the internal memory.

The ratio M/B is the number of external memory blocks that can fit into internal memory. Thus, this proposition is saying that the best performance we can achieve for the sorting problem is equivalent to the work of scanning through the input set (which takes $\Theta(n/B)$ transfers) at least a logarithmic number of times, where the base of this logarithm is the number of blocks that fit into internal memory. We will not formally justify this proposition, but we will show how to design an external-memory sorting algorithm whose running time comes within a constant factor of this lower bound.

16.3.2 Multi-way Merge-Sort

An efficient way to sort a set S of n objects in external memory amounts to a simple external-memory variation on the familiar merge-sort algorithm. The main idea behind this variation is to merge many recursively sorted lists at a time, thereby reducing the number of levels of recursion. Specifically, a high-level description of this ***multi-way merge-sort*** method is to divide S into d subsets $S_1, S_2, \ldots, S_d$ of roughly equal size, recursively sort each subset S_i, and then simultaneously merge all d sorted lists into a sorted representation of S. If we can perform the merge process using only $O(n/B)$ disk transfers, then, for large enough values of n, the total number of transfers performed by this algorithm satisfies the following recurrence:

$$t(n) = d\cdot t(n/d) + cn/B,$$

for some constant $c \geq 1$. We can stop the recursion when $n \leq B$, since we can perform a single block transfer at this point, getting all of the objects into internal memory, and then sort the set with an efficient internal-memory algorithm. Thus, the stopping criterion for $t(n)$ is

$$t(n) = 1 \quad \text{if } n/B \leq 1.$$

This implies a closed-form solution that $t(n)$ is $O((n/B)\log_d(n/B))$, which is

$$O((n/B)\log(n/B)/\log d).$$

Thus, if we can choose d to be $\Theta(M/B)$, then the worst-case number of block transfers performed by this multi-way merge-sort algorithm will be within a constant factor of the lower bound given in Proposition 16.6. We choose

$$d = (1/2)M/B.$$

The only aspect of this algorithm left to specify, then, is how to perform the d-way merge using only $O(n/B)$ block transfers.

We perform the d-way merge by running a "tournament." We let T be a complete binary tree with d external nodes, and we keep T entirely in internal memory. We associate each external node i of T with a different sorted list S_i. We initialize T by reading into each external node i, the first object in S_i. This has the effect of reading into internal memory the first block of each sorted list S_i. For each internal-node parent v of two external nodes, we then compare the objects stored at v's children and we associate with v the smaller of the two. We then repeat this comparison test at the next level up in T, and the next, and so on. When we reach the root r of T, we will associate with r the smallest object from among all the lists. This completes the initialization for the d-way merge. (See Figure 16.7.)

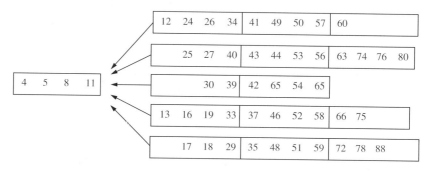

Figure 16.7: A d-way merge. We show a five-way merge with $B = 4$.

In a general step of the d-way merge, we move the object o associated with the root r of T into an array we are building for the merged list S'. We then trace down T, following the path to the external node i that o came from. We then read into i the next object in the list S_i. If o was not the last element in its block, then this next object is already in internal memory. Otherwise, we read in the next block of S_i to access this new object (if S_i is now empty, associate with the node i a pseudo-object with key $+\infty$). We then repeat the minimum computations for each of the internal nodes from i to the root of T. This again gives us the complete tree T. We then repeat this process of moving the object from the root of T to the merged list S', and rebuilding T until T is empty of objects. Each step in the merge takes $O(\log d)$ time; hence, the internal time for the d-way merge is $O(n \log d)$. The number of transfers performed in a merge is $O(n/B)$, since we scan each list S_i in order once and we write out the merged list S' once. Thus, we have:

Proposition 16.7: *Given an array-based sequence S of n elements stored in external memory, we can sort S using $O((n/B) \log(n/B) / \log(M/B))$ transfers and $O(n \log n)$ internal CPU time, where M is the size of the internal memory and B is the size of a block.*

16.4 Exercises

Reinforcement

R-16.1 What is the best running time overhead for implementing the LRU policy if we use a priority queue that does not support the locator pattern? Why is this worse than the locator-based implementation?

R-16.2 Describe, in detail, the insertion and deletion algorithms for an (a,b) tree.

R-16.3 Suppose T is a multi-way tree such that each internal node has at least five and at most eight children. For what values of a and b is T a valid (a,b) tree?

R-16.4 For what values of d is the tree T of the previous exercise an order-d B-tree?

R-16.5 Draw the order-7 B-tree resulting from inserting the following keys (in this order) into an initially empty tree T:
$$(4,40,23,50,11,34,62,78,66,22,90,59,25,72,64,77,39,12).$$

R-16.6 Show each level of recursion in performing a four-way merge-sort of the sequence given in the previous exercise.

Creativity

C-16.1 Show how to implement the LFU replacement policy to have only $O(1)$ time additional overhead per memory access. (Hint: choose a simple priority queue implementation that takes advantage of additional knowledge about block priorities as blocks are inserted and accessed.)

C-16.2 What is the expected number of block replacements performed by the Random policy on a cache of size m, for an access sequence of length n, that iteratively accesses $m+1$ blocks in a cyclic fashion (assuming n is much larger than m)?

C-16.3 Show how to implement a dictionary in external memory, using an unordered sequence so that updates require only $O(1)$ transfers and updates require $O(n/B)$ transfers in the worst case, where n is the number of elements and B is the number of list nodes that can fit into a disk block. (Hint: consider an alternate linked list implementation that uses "fat" nodes.)

C-16.4 Change the rules that define red-black trees so that each red-black tree T has a corresponding $(4,8)$ tree, and vice versa.

C-16.5 Describe a modified version of the B-tree insertion algorithm so that each time we create an overflow because of a split of a node v, we redistribute keys among all of v's siblings such that each sibling holds roughly the same number of keys (possibly cascading the split up to the parent of v). What is the minimum fraction of each block that will always be filled using this scheme?

C-16.6 Another possible external-memory dictionary implementation is to use a skip list, but to collect in individual blocks consecutive groups of $O(B)$ nodes on any level in the skip list. In particular, we define an *order-d B-skip list* to be such a representation of a skip list structure, where each block contains at least $\lceil d/2 \rceil$ list nodes and at most d list nodes. Let us also choose d in this case to be the maximum number of list nodes from a level of a skip list that can fit into one block. Describe how we should modify the skip-list insertion and deletion algorithms for a B-skip list so that the expected height of the structure is $O(\log n/\log B)$.

C-16.7 Suppose that instead of having the node-search function $f(d)=1$ in an order-d B-tree T, we instead have $f(d)=\log d$. What does the asymptotic running time of performing a search in T now become?

C-16.8 Describe how to use a B-tree to implement the queue ADT so that the total number of disk transfers needed to process a sequence of n enqueue and dequeue operations is $O(n/B)$.

C-16.9 Describe how to use a B-tree to implement the partition (union-find) ADT (from Section 12.1.4) so that the union and find operations each use at most $O(\log n/\log B)$ disk transfers.

C-16.10 Suppose we are given a sequence S of n elements with integer keys such that some items in S are colored "blue" and some elements in S are colored "red." In addition, say that a red element e *pairs* with a blue element f if they have the same key value. Describe an efficient external-memory algorithm for finding all the red-blue pairs in S. How many disk transfers does your algorithm perform?

C-16.11 Describe an external-memory algorithm for computing the convex hull of a set of n points in the plane. Your algorithm should not use more than $O((n/B)\log(n/b)/\log(M/B))$ disk transfers.

Projects

P-16.1 Write a Java class that implements all the methods of a dictionary given in Chapter 7 by means of an (a, b) tree, where a and b are integer constants.

P-16.2 Implement the B-tree data structure, assuming a block size of $1,000$ and that keys are integers. Test the number of "disk transfers" needed to process a sequence of dictionary operations.

P-16.3 Implement the multi-way merge-sort algorithm.

Chapter Notes

Knuth [90] has very nice discussions about external-memory sorting and searching, and Ullman [141] discusses external memory structures for database systems. The reader interested in the study of the architecture of hierarchical memory systems is referred to the book chapter by Burger *et al.* [30] or the book by Hennessy and Patterson [69]. The handbook by Gonnet and Baeza-Yates [59] compares the performance of a number of different sorting algorithms, many of which are external-memory algorithms.

Memory management is treated in elegant detail by Aho, Hopcroft, and Ullman [7]. The reader interested in further study of the competitive analysis of other on-line algorithms is referred to the paper by Koutsoupias and Papadimitriou [93].

B-trees were invented by Bayer and McCreight [16] and Comer [35] provides a very nice overview of this data structure. The books by Mehlhorn [109] and Samet [127] also have nice discussions about B-trees and their variants. Aggarwal and Vitter [4] study the I/O complexity of sorting and related problems, establishing upper and lower bounds, including the lower bound for sorting given in this chapter. Goodrich *et al.* [63] study the I/O complexity of several computational geometry problems. The reader interested in further study of I/O-efficient algorithms is encouraged to examine the survey paper of Vitter [143].

Appendix

A

A Java Primer

Contents

In this appendix, we give a brief overview of the Java programming language, assuming the reader is familiar with some existing high-level language, such as Pascal, C, or C++. Java possesses a number of features that make it an excellent pedagogical tool for exploring the implementation of data structures and algorithms. Java was designed to allow for secure platform-independent software execution, which is a big advantage in heterogeneous educational computing environments. Java is powerful enough to allow us to efficiently implement sophisticated linked structures, but it restricts dangerous programming styles, such as pointer arithmetic and arbitrary array indexing. It is strongly typed but is flexible enough to allow for safe type casting. In addition, it provides for several levels of data protection (such as public and private variables and methods), and it has an extensive collection of meaningfully named error conditions (together with an easy-to-use mechanism for exception handling). It has a simple built-in mechanism for memory management and garbage collection, which can be used transparently by the novice programmer, but which has several "behind-the-scenes" hooks for expert programmers. And, finally, it contains simple constructs for performing some fairly sophisticated kinds of computing, such as multiprocessing (through the use of Thread objects), network computing (including a built-in knowledge of the Internet), and graphical user interfaces (through windows and applets). The specific topics of the Java language we focus on in this primer are those that are directly related to the implementation of data structures and algorithms, including the following:

- Classes and objects (Section A.1)
- Methods (Section A.2)
- Variables and expressions (Section A.3)
- Control flow (Section A.4)
- Packages (Section A.5)
- Interfaces (Section A.6)
- Casting (Section A.7)
- Exceptions (Section A.8).

We discuss some other important aspects of the Java language elsewhere in this book, including:

- Object-oriented design (Sections 1.3 and 1.4)
- Applets (discussed briefly in Section 1.4.2)
- The method stack (Section 3.1.3)
- Dynamic memory allocation (Section 3.2.3)
- Garbage collection (Section 9.4.5)
- Strings (Section 11.1)
- Vectors (Sections 4.1.3 and 12.1.3).

This primer does not provide a complete description of the Java language, however. There are major aspects of the language that are not directly relevant to data structure and algorithm design. These language features are, therefore, not included here, but are, nevertheless, fundamental parts of the language. These include:

- The abstract windowing toolkit (AWT)
- Remove method invocation
- Threads
- Input and output
- JavaBeans
- Sockets.

For the reader interested in learning more about these topics, we refer some of the fine books about Java, including the books by Arnold and Gosling [10], Campione and Walrath [31], Cornell and Horstmann [37], Flanagan [49], and Horstmann [75], as well as the Javasoft web site (http://www.javasoft.com).

A.1   Classes and Objects

We begin our Java primer by discussing Java classes and objects, which are central to Java programming. The main "actors" in a Java program are objects. Objects store data and provide methods for accessing and modifying them. Every object is an instance of a *class*, which defines the kind of data that the object stores, as well as the operations that can act on that data. In particular:

- Data of Java objects are stored in *instance variables* (also called *fields*). Therefore, if an object from some class is to store data, then its class must specify the instance variables for such objects. Instance variables can either come from base types (such as integers, floating-point numbers, or Booleans) or they can refer to objects of other classes.
- The operations that can act upon data, and which express the "messages" that objects respond to, are called *methods*. The methods of a class consist of constructors, procedures, and functions. They define the behavior of objects from that class.

As in other object-oriented languages, a class in Java can *inherit* data and methods from another Java class (Chapter 1). In Java, we say that one class *extends* another class in this case. A class in Java can only directly extend one other class. Every class extends the superclass Object at the highest level of inheritance. In fact, if we omit the extends keyword in a class declaration, the Java compiler assumes the new class directly extends the Object class.

Java provides a limited form of multiple inheritance, however, by using a variant form of class called an ***interface***. An interface is like a class that has only methods with no instance variables. All the methods of an interface are abstract, which means that they are empty. The purpose of interfaces is to allow the programmer to write generic methods of other classes, which can accept objects that ***implement*** the functionality specified in an interface as arguments. A class in Java can extend only one other class, but it can implement any number of interfaces.

How Classes Are Declared

The syntax for a Java class definition is as follows:

[⟨class_modifiers⟩] **class** ⟨class_name⟩ [**extends** ⟨superclass_name⟩]
                 [**implements** ⟨interface_1⟩, ⟨interface_2⟩, . . .] {
        // class methods and instance variable definitions . . .
    }

where use a syntax shorthand where optional material is enclosed in square brackets ("[" and "]") and identifiers and keywords are indicated by words inside angle brackets ("⟨" and "⟩"). Below is an example of definition of a class:

```
class MythicalCreature extends Creature {
    protected int age;        // the creature's age
    protected String name;    // the creature's name
    boolean magical;          // an indicator of magical powers

    public MythicalCreature() {
        // default constructor's body . . .
    }
    public MythicalCreature(String name, int age, boolean magical) {
        // alternate constructor's body . . .
    }
    public void doMagic() {
        // procedure body . . .
    }
    public int getAge() {
        // function body . . .
    }
}
```

In this case, we do not use any class modifiers (which we discuss next), but we include definitions of three instance variables and three methods, one of which is the class constructor, one is a procedure (with no return type), and the other is a function. Notice that the class definition begins with a " { " and ends with a " }."

Class Modifiers

Class Modifiers are optional keywords that precede the **class** keyword. They modify a class' scope and status in a program in the following ways:

- The **abstract** class modifier describes a class that has abstract methods. Abstract methods are methods declared with the **abstract** keyword and are empty. A class that has nothing but abstract methods and no instance variables is more properly called an interface, so an **abstract** class usually has a mixture of abstract methods and actual methods. Abstract classes may not be instantiated, that is, no object can be created from an abstract class. Instead, we must define another class that is not abstract and extends (subclasses) an abstract superclass—and this new class must fill in code for all abstract methods.

- The **final** class modifier describes a class that can have no subclasses.

- The **public** class modifier describes a class that can be instantiated or extended by anything in the same package or by anything that *imports* the class. (This is explained in more detail in the packages section.) All public classes are declared in their own separate file called ⟨classname⟩.java. There can only be one public class per file.

- If the **public** class modifier is not used, the class is considered *friendly*. This means that it can be used and instantiated by all classes in the same *package*. This is the default class modifier.

Commenting

Java allows for two kinds of comments—block comments and inline comments—which define text ignored by the compiler. Java uses a /* to begin a block comment and a */ to close it. In addition, Java uses a // to begin inline comments and ignores everything else on the line.
For example:

```
/*
 * This is a block comment.
 */

// This is an inline comment.
```

A.1.1   Instance Variables

Java classes can define instance variables. Instance variables must have a *type*, which can either be a *base type* (such as **int, float, double**) or it can be a *reference* to another class. The syntax for declaring an instance variable is as follows:

[⟨variable_modifier⟩] ⟨variable_type⟩ ⟨variable_name⟩ [=⟨initial_value⟩];

We have already given the syntax for ⟨variable_name⟩ and ⟨variable_type⟩. The syntax of the optional ⟨initial_value⟩ is that it must match the variable's type. Here are some examples of instance variables for a class Gnome:

```
class Gnome extends MythicalCreature {
    protected String name;
    protected int age;
    protected Gnome gnome_buddy;
    public static final int MAX_HEIGHT = 3; // This is a constant.

    // Constructor for a Gnome:
    public Gnome (String n, int a, Gnome gb) {
        super ();                              // Calls MythicalCreature();
        name = n;
        age = a;
        gnome_buddy = gb;
    }

    // Other methods for Gnome objects . . .

}
```

Note the use of instance variables in this example. The variable age is a base type, the variable name is a reference to the built-in class String, and the variable gnome_buddy is a reference to an object of the class we are now defining. Our declaration of the instance variable MAX_HEIGHT is taking advantage of a number of variable modifiers to define a "variable" that has a fixed constant value.

Variable Modifiers

The scoping of instance variables can be controlled through the use of the following *variable modifiers*:

- **public**: Anyone can access public instance variables.
- **protected**: Only methods of the same class or of subclasses can access protected instance variables.
- **private**: Only methods of the same class (not methods of a subclass) can access private instance variables.

Base Types

Java has the following base types, which are also called *primitive types*:

boolean	Boolean value: true or false
char	16-bit Unicode character
byte	8-bit signed two's complement integer
short	16-bit signed two's complement integer
int	32-bit signed two's complement integer
long	64-bit signed two's complement integer
float	32-bit floating-point number (IEEE 754-1985)
double	64-bit floating-point number (IEEE 754-1985)

- If none of the above modifiers are used, the instance variable is considered friendly. Friendly instance variables can be accessed by any class in the same package. Packages are discussed in more detail in Section A.5.

In addition to scoping variable modifiers, there are also the following usage modifiers:

- **static**: A static instance variable is used to declare a variable that is associated with the class, not to individual instances of that class. Static variables are used to store "global" information about a class (for example, a static variable could be used to maintain the total number of Gnome objects created). Static variables exist even if no instance of their class is created.
- **final**: A final instance variable is one that *must* be assigned an initial value, and then can never be assigned a new value after that. If it is a base type, then it is a constant (like the MAX_HEIGHT constant in the Gnome class above). If an object variable is **final**, then it will always refer to the same object (even if that object changes its internal state).

Constant values associated with a class should be declared to be both **static** and **final**.

A.1.2 Object Creation

In Java, a new object is created from a defined class by using the new operator. The **new** operator creates a new object from a specified class and returns a *reference* to that object. Here is the syntax for using the **new** operator:

⟨variable_name⟩ = **new** ⟨class_type⟩([param, param, ...]);

We use ⟨variable_name⟩ to denote an identifier that is the name of an object variable. Identifiers in Java must begin with a letter and be a string of letters and numbers (where "letter" and "number" can be from any written language defined in the Unicode character set). The ⟨class_type⟩ is an identifier defining the name of the class, and the list of parameters is optional. C/alling the **new** operator on a class type causes three events to occur:

- A new object is dynamically allocated in memory, and all instance variables are initialized to standard default values. The default values are **null** for object variables and 0 for all base types except **boolean** variables (which are **false** by default).
- The constructor for the new object is called with the parameters specified.
- After the constructor is called, the **new** operator returns a reference (that is, a memory address) to the newly created instance.

Illegal Identifiers

Java restricts method and variable names. In particular, none of the following words can be used as a Java identifier:

abstract	else	interface	switch
boolean	extends	long	synchronized
break	false	native	this
byte	final	null	throw
case	finally	new	throws
catch	float	package	transient
char	for	private	true
class	goto	protected	try
const	if	public	void
continue	implements	return	volatile
default	import	short	while
do	instanceof	static	
double	int	super	

In general, the reference returned by **new** must be assigned to some variable. In the following statement, a new object of class Point is instantiated with a constructor that takes as arguments the coordinates of the point, and variable myPoint becomes a reference to the object:

```
myPoint = new Point (3,6);
```

Before we go into more detail about instance variables and their uses (which we do in Section A.3), let us discuss the methods that can act upon them.

A.2 Methods

Methods in Java are conceptually similar to functions and procedures in other high-level languages. In general, they are "chunks" of code that can be called on a particular object (from some class). Methods can accept parameters as arguments, and they modulate their behavior depending upon the object they belong to and the values of any parameters that are passed. Every method in Java is specified in the body of some class. A method definition has two parts: the *signature*, which defines the name and parameters for a method, and the *body*, which defines what the method actually does.

A.2.1 Declaring Methods

The syntax for defining a method is as follows:

```
[⟨method_modifiers⟩] ⟨return_type⟩ ⟨method_name⟩ ([⟨params⟩]) {
    // method body . . .
}
```

where ⟨params⟩ is an optional comma-separated list of parameter declarations that has the following syntax:

```
⟨param_type⟩ ⟨param_name⟩, [⟨param_type⟩ ⟨param_name⟩, . . .]
```

Methods in a class are associated with a specific instance of that class (unless they are **static**), and can be used to change the state of that object. Here is a simple example:

```
public void renameGnome (String s) {
    name = s;     // Reassign the name instance variable of this gnome.
}
```

The syntax rule for the name of a method is the same as for instance variables, and this rule also applies to parameter names. Parameters can be either base types or object references. We discuss each of the components of a method declaration in more detail below.

Method Modifiers

As with instance variables, method modifiers can restrict the scope of a method as follows:

- **public**: Anyone can call public methods.
- **protected**: Only methods of the same class or of subclasses can call a protected method.
- **private**: Only methods of the same class (not methods of a subclass) can call a private method.
- If none of the above modifiers are used, then the method is friendly. Friendly methods can only be called by objects of classes in the same package.

The above method modifiers may be preceded by the following additional modifiers, which further restrict a method:

- **abstract**: A method declared as **abstract** will have no code. The parameter list of an abstract method is followed by a semicolon with no method body. For example:

    public abstract int giveSize (**int** weight);

    Abstract methods may only appear within an abstract class. A subclass of an abstract class must provide an implementation for the abstract methods of its superclass, unless it is itself abstract.
- **final**: This is a method that cannot be overridden by a subclass.
- **static**: This is a method that is associated with the class, not any instance of the class. Examples of static methods include the mathematical functions in the java.lang.Math class. Static methods can also be used to change the state of static variables associated with a class (provided these variables are not declared to be **final**).

Return Types

A method definition must specify the type of value the method will return. If the method does not return a value, then the keyword **void** must be used. If the return type is **void**, the method is called a *procedure*; otherwise, it is called a *function*. To return a value in Java, a method must use the **return** keyword (and the type returned must match the return type of the method). Here is an example of a method (from inside the Gnome class) that is a function:

```
public boolean isAdult () {
    return (age > 17);
}
```

As soon as a **return** is performed in a Java function, the method invocation ends.

Java functions can return only one value. To return multiple values in Java, we should instead combine all the values we wish to return in a ***compound object*** and then return a reference to that object. In addition, we can change the internal state of an object that is passed to a method as another way of "returning" multiple results. We discuss parameter passing next.

A.2.2 Parameter Passing

A method's parameters are defined in a comma-separated list enclosed in parentheses after the name of the method. A parameter consists of two parts, the parameter type and the parameter name. If a method has no parameters, then only an empty pair of parentheses is used.

All parameters in Java are passed ***by value***. This means that any time we pass a parameter to a method, a copy of that parameter is made for use within the method body. So if we pass an **int** variable to a method, then that variable is copied. The method can change the copy but not the original. If we pass an object reference as a parameter to a method, then the reference is copied as well. Remember that we can have many different variables that all refer to the same object. Changing the internal reference inside a method will not change the reference that was passed in. For example, if we pass a Gnome reference g to a method that calls this parameter h, then this method can change the reference h to point to a different object, but g will still refer to the same object it did before. Of course, the method can use the reference h to change the internal state of the object, and this will change g's object as well (since g and h are currently referring to the same object). Consider the following (***incorrect***) example:

```
public static void makeKing (Gnome h) {
    // This is wrong:
    Gnome king = new Gnome ("King " + h.name, h.age, true);
    h = king;
}
```

If we call this as Gnome.makeKing(g), it will not change g at all. It will simply create a new "king gnome" object and then terminate with no variable outside the makeKing method referring to this object (at which point this object becomes a candidate for garbage collection). The correct way to do this is as follows:

```
public static void makeKing (Gnome h) {
    h.name = "King " + h.name;
    h.magical = true;
}
```

This method modifies what h refers to; hence, if we call it as Gnome.makeKing(g), it will change the state of g so that it now refers to a "king gnome."

Local Variables

Methods may also have local variables. These variables are declared in the body of the method. Usually this is done at the beginning of the main method body (between the { and }). Local variables are similar to instance variables, but only exist while the method is being invoked. A local variable can be either a **base type** (such as **int, float, double**) or a **reference** to an instance of some class.

Here is the syntax for declaring local variables:

⟨variable_type⟩ ⟨variable_name⟩ [= ⟨initial_value⟩];

where the rules for the type, name, and initial value are the same as for instance variables.

Here are some examples of local variable declarations:

```
double radius = computeRadius ();
Point p1 = new Point (3, 4);
Point p2 = new Point (8, 2);
int i = 512;
float p = 2.71818;
```

Notice that we can assign an initial value to a variable when we declare it.

A.2.3 Constructor Methods

A **constructor** is a special kind of method that is used to initialize newly created objects. Java has a special way to declare the constructor and a special way to invoke the constructor. First, let's look at the syntax for declaring a constructor:

```
[constructor_modifiers] ⟨constructor_name⟩ ([⟨params⟩]) {
    // Constructor body . . .
}
```

Thus, its syntax is essentially the same as that of any other method. The name of the constructor must be the same as the name of the class it constructs, however. So, if the class is called Fish, the constructor must be called Fish as well. In addition, a constructor has no return value. So its return type is implicitly void. The constructor modifier follows the same rules as for normal methods. An **abstract, static**, or **final** constructor is not allowed, however.

Here is an example:

```
public Fish (int weight, String n) {
    super(weight);
    name = n;
}
```

The body of a constructor begins with an inherited call to the class' superclass constructor. This call *must* be the first statement of the body of a constructor and can appear nowhere else. In Java, the **super** keyword is used instead of the superclass' constructor name. If the **super** call is not used, then the constructor body is implicitly assumed to begin with the statement:

super();

In other words, the default in Java is to make a call to the constructor of the superclass with no parameter list. The rest of a constructor's body is like a normal method's body.

The only other unique aspect of a construct method is the way it is invoked. A constructor method from some class *must* be invoked with the **new** operator. So, upon invocation, a new instance of this class is automatically created and its constructor is then called (to initialize its instance variables and perform other setup tasks). For example, consider the following constructor invocation (which is also a declaration for the myFish variable):

Fish myFish = **new** Fish ("Wally");

A class can have multiple constructor methods, but each must have a different *signature*, that is, each must be distinguished by the type and number of parameters it takes.

A.2.4   The main() Method

Some Java classes are meant to be utilized by other classes, others are meant to define stand-alone programs. Classes that define stand-alone programs must contain one other special kind of method for a class—the **main()** method. When we wish to execute a stand-alone Java program, we reference the name of class that defines this program, say by issuing the following command (in DOS or UNIX):

java Aquarium

The Java run-time system then looks for a compiled version of the Aquarium class, and then invokes the special **main()** method in that class. This method must be declared as follows:

```
public static void main(String[] args) {
    // main method body . . .
}
```

The arguments passed as a parameter to the main method are the command-line arguments given when the program is called. For example, we may have defined the Aquarium program to take an optional argument that specifies the number of fish in the aquarium.

We could then invoke the program by typing

    java Aquarium 4

to specify that we want an aquarium with four fish in it. In this case, args[0] refers to the string "4." One nice feature of the **main()** method is that it allows each class to define a stand-alone program, and one of the uses for this method is to test all the other methods in a class. Thus, thorough use of the **main()** method is an effective tool for debugging large collections of Java classes.

A.3   Expressions

Variables and constants are used in *expressions* to define new values and to modify variables. In this section, we discuss how expressions work in Java in more detail.

Expressions involve the use of *literals*, *variables*, and *operators*. We have already discussed variables, so let us now focus on literals and operators.

A.3.1   Literals

A Java *literal* or "constant" can be one of the following:

- The **null** object reference (this is the only object literal).
- Boolean: **true** and **false**.
- Integer: The default for an integer like 176 or -52 is that it is of type **int**. A long integer literal must end with an "L," for example, 176L or -52L.
- Floating Point: The default for floating point numbers, such as 3.1415 and 10035.23, is that they are **double**. To specify that a literal is a **float**, it must end with an "F." Floating-point literals, in exponential notation, are also allowed, such as 3.14E2 or .19E10; the base is assumed to be 10.
- Character: Java recognizes character constants enclosed in single quotes, for example, 'a' and '?', as well as the following special character constants:

'\n'	(newline)	'\t'	(tab)
'\b'	(backspace)	'\r'	(return)
'\f'	(form feed)	'\\'	(backslash)
'\''	(single quote)	'\"'	(double quote).

- Strings: A string is a sequence of characters enclosed in double quotes, for example, "dogs all around" or "jump".

A.3.2 Operators

The Dot Operator

As we have mentioned above, creating a new object in Java involves the use of the **new** operator to allocate space for the object, and then the use of a constructor of the object to initialize this space. The location (or ***address***) of this space is then assigned to a ***reference*** variable. Therefore, a reference variable can be viewed as a link or "pointer" to some object. There can be many references to the same object, and each reference to a specific object can be used to call methods on that object. All references either have to be "newed" or have to be assigned to refer to already existing objects.

One of the primary uses of reference variables is to access the methods and instance variables associated with an object. This is done with the dot ('.') operator. We call a method associated with an object by using the following syntax:

⟨object_reference⟩.⟨method_name⟩([⟨param⟩,⟨param⟩, ...]);

This calls the method with the specified name for the object referred to by this object reference. It can optionally be passed multiple parameters. If there are several methods with this same name defined for this object, then the Java run-time system uses the one that is lowest in the inheritance hierarchy that matches the number of parameters, and most closely matches their type (together with a method's name, the number and types of its parameters are called a method's ***signature***). Consider the following examples:

```
oven.cookDinner();
oven.cookDinner(food);
oven.cookDinner(food,seasoning);
```

Each of these method calls is actually referring to a different method with the same name defined in the class that oven belongs to.

We refer to the instance variables associated with an object by using the following syntax:

⟨object_reference⟩.⟨variable_name⟩

Assuming, of course, that the scoping rule defined for such a variable allows access, then this use can appear anywhere in an expression.

If an object reference is not **final**, then it can appear on the left-hand side of an assignment as well. Consider the following examples:

```
gnome.name = "Professor Smythe";
gnome.age = gnome.age + 1;
```

The ⟨object_reference⟩ can also be any expression that returns an object reference.

So something like the following is also syntactically correct:

```
System.out.println("The oldest is "+(Gnome.oldestGnome()).name);
```

Array Indexing

Arrays in Java are defined to be one-dimensional, but we can compose them to define multi-dimensional arrays. They are created with a declaration statement like the following:

```
int[] a = new int[10];
float[][] x = new float[8][10];
```

The first creates a new array "a" that is of type **int** and has ten cells, which are indexed using the set of integers $\{0,1,2,3,4,5,6,7,8,9\}$ (arrays in Java always start indexing at 0). The second creates a two-dimensional "array of arrays." The following are then valid uses of the above arrays:

```
i = 5;
a[i] = 138;
x[i][i+1] = 2.189 + x[i][i];
```

Array indices are checked in Java to see if they are ever out of bounds, and if so, the run-time environment throws an IndexOutOfBoundsException. The size of an array is stored in an instance variable length, and can be accessed as follows:

```
⟨array_name⟩.length
```

So the following are valid uses for the above arrays:

```
i = a.length;
j = x[4].length;
```

Arithmetic Operators

The following are the binary arithmetic operators in Java:

$+$	addition
$-$	subtraction
$*$	multiplication
$/$	division
$\%$	the modulo operator

Java also provides a unary minus $(-)$, which can be placed in front of an arithmetic expression to invert its sign. Parentheses can be used in any expression to define the order of evaluation. Java also uses a fairly intuitive operator precedence rule to determine the order of evaluation when parentheses are not used. Unlike C++, Java does not allow operator overloading.

Operator Precedence

Java performs operations assuming the following ordering (or ***precedence***) rules if parentheses are not used to determine the order of evaluation (operators on the same line are evaluated in left-to-right order subject to the conditional evaluation rule for && and ||). The operations are listed below from highest to lowest precedence (we use ⟨exp⟩ to denote an atomic or parenthesized expression):

postfix ops	[] . (⟨exp⟩) ⟨exp⟩ ++ ⟨exp⟩ −−
prefix ops	++⟨exp⟩ −−⟨exp⟩ −⟨exp⟩ ˜⟨exp⟩ !⟨exp⟩
creation/cast	**new** (⟨type⟩)⟨exp⟩
mult./div.	* / %
add./subt.	+ −
shift	<< >> >>>
comparison	< <= > >= **instanceof**
equality	== !=
bitwise-and	&
bitwise-xor	^
bitwise-or	|
and	&&
or	||
conditional	⟨bool_exp⟩? ⟨true_val⟩: ⟨false_val⟩
assignment	=
op assignment	+= −= *= /= %=
bitwise assign.	>>= <<= >>>=
boolean assign.	&= ^= |=

String Concatenation

Strings in Java can be composed using the ***concatenation*** operator (+), so that the following code

```
String rug = "carpet";
String dog = "spot";
String mess = rug + dog;
System.out.println(mess + " costs " + 50 + " dollars!");
```

would produce the output

```
carpetspot costs 50 dollars!
```

This example also shows how Java converts nonstring constants into strings, when they are involved in a string concatenation operation.

Increment and Decrement Operators

Like C and C++, Java provides increment and decrement operators. Specifically, it provides the plus-one increment (++) and decrement (−−) operators. If such an operator is used in front of a variable reference, then 1 is added to (or subtracted from) the variable and its value is read into the expression. If it is used after a variable reference, then the value is first read and then the variable is incremented or decremented by 1. So, for example, the code fragment

```
int i = 8;
System.out.println(i++ + "," + ++i + "," + i−−);
```

produces the output

8,10,10

after which i will have the value 9.

Logical Operators

Java allows for the standard comparison operators between numbers:

<	less than
<=	less than or equal to
==	equal to
!=	not equal to
>=	greater than or equal to
>	greater than

The operators == and != can also be used for object references. The type of the result of a comparison is a **boolean**.

Operators that operate on **boolean** values are the following:

!	not (prefix)
&&	conditional and
||	conditional or

The Boolean operators && and || will not evaluate the second operand in their expression if it is not needed to determine the value of the expression. Thus, a statement like the following will never generate an index out-of-bounds exception:

```
if (((i >= 0) && (i < a.length)) && (a[i] > 0.5) )
    System.out.println(a[i]);
```

for the comparison " a[i] > 0.5" will only be performed if the first two comparisons succeed.

Bitwise Operators

Java also provides the following bitwise operators for integers and Booleans:

~	bitwise complement (prefix unary operator)
&	bitwise and
|	bitwise or
^	bitwise exclusive-or
<<	shift bits left, filling in with zeros
>>	shift bits right, filling in with sign bit
>>>	shift bits right, filling in with zeros

Assignment Operators

Besides the standard assignment operator (=), Java also provides a number of other assignment operators that have operational side effects. These other kinds of operators are of the following form:

⟨variable⟩ ⟨op⟩= ⟨expression⟩;

This is equivalent to

⟨variable⟩ = ⟨variable⟩ ⟨op⟩ ⟨expression⟩;

except that if ⟨variable⟩ contains an expression (for example, an array index), the expression is evaluated only once. Thus, the code fragment

```
a[5] = 10;
i = 5;
a[i++] += 2;
```
leaves a[5] with value 12 and i with value 6.

A.4   Control Flow

Control flow in Java is similar to that of other high-level languages. We review the basic structure and syntax of control flow in Java in this section, including method returns, if statements, switch statements, loops, and restricted forms of "jumps" (the **break** and **continue** statements).

A.4.1   Returning from Methods

If a Java method is declared with return type of **void**, then flow of control returns
when it reaches the last line of code in the method or when it encounters a **return**
statement with no argument. If a method is declared with a return type, however,
the method must exit by returning the functions value as an argument to a **return**
statement. The method will exit when the **return** statement is reached, returning
the specified value if the method is a function. The following (correct) example
illustrates such a function:

```
public boolean checkBDay (int date) {
    if (date == BirthdayList.MIKES_BDAY)
        return true;
    }
    return false;
}
```

It follows that the **return** statement *must* be the last statement executed in a
function, as the rest of the code will never be reached.

Note that there is a significant difference between a statement being the last line
of code that is *executed* in a method and the last line of code in the method itself.
In the above example, the line **return true;** is clearly not the last line of code that
is written in the function, but it may be the last line that is executed (if the condition
involving date is **true**).

A.4.2   If Statements

In Java, conditionals work the same as in other languages. They provide a way of
making a decision and then executing one or more different statement blocks based
on the outcome of that decision. The syntax of an if statement is as follows:

```
if (⟨boolean_expr⟩)
    ⟨true_statement⟩
[else if (⟨boolean_expr⟩)
    ⟨else_if_statement⟩]
[else
    ⟨else_statement⟩]
```

where each statement can be a block of statements enclosed in braces ({ and }). In
addition, the "else if" and "else" parts are optional; either or both may be omitted
from a valid if statement.

Unlike in C and C++, the expression in an if statement in Java *must* be a
Boolean expression.

This rule helps us avoid a common programming error, for the following bug will be caught by the compiler:

```
i = 5;
// intermediate code ...
if (i = 5)                          // (THIS IS WRONG!)
    System.out.println("i is unchanged.");
```

The "condition" in this case is really an assignment, which is of type **int**. Thus, this is not a syntactically correct if statement. The following is correct, however:

```
if (snowLevel < 2) {
    goToClass();
    comeHome();
}
else if (snowLevel < 5) {
    goSledding();
    haveSnowballFight();
}
else
    stayAtHome();
```

A.4.3 Switch Statements

Java provides for multiple-value control flow using the **switch** statement. The following is an indicative example:

```
public Candy getCandy (int money) {
    Candy candy;
    int tax=1;
    switch (money+tax) {
      case 5:
          candy = new Gumball ();
          break;
      case 25:
          candy = new Peanuts ();
          break;
      case 50:
          candy = new Candybar ();
          break;
      default:
          candy = new EmptyWrapper();
          break;
    }
    return candy;
}
```

The **switch** statement evaluates an integer expression (such as " money+tax") and causes control flow to jump to the code location labeled with the value of this expression. If there is no such label, then control flow jumps to the location labeled "**default**." This is the only explicit jump performed by the **switch** statement, however, so flow of control "falls through" to other cases if the code for each case is not ended with a **break** statement (which causes control flow to jump to the next line after the **switch** statement).

A.4.4 Loops

Another important control flow mechanism in a programming language is looping. Java provides for three types of loops.

For Loops

In their simplest form, **for** loops provide for repeated code based on an integer index. In Java, we can do that and much more. The functionality of a **for** loop is significantly more flexible. In particular, the usage of a **for** loop is split into four sections; the initialization, the condition, the increment, and the body. Here is the syntax for a Java **for** loop:

```
for ([⟨initialization⟩];[⟨condition⟩];[⟨increment⟩])
    ⟨body_statement⟩
```

In the ⟨initialization⟩ section, we can declare an index variable that will only be in the scope of the **for** loop. For example, if we want a loop that indexes on a counter, and we have no need for the counter variable outside of the **for** loop, then declaring

```
for (int counter = 0; ⟨condition⟩; ⟨increment⟩)
```

will declare a variable counter whose scope is the loop body only.

In the ⟨condition⟩ section, we specify the repeat (while) condition of the loop. This must be a Boolean expression. The body of the **for** loop will be executed each time the ⟨condition⟩ is **true** when evaluated at the beginning of a potential iteration. As soon as ⟨condition⟩ evaluates to be **false**, then the loop body is not executed, and, instead, the program executes the next statement after the **for** loop.

In the ⟨increment⟩ section, we declare the incrementing statement for the loop. The incrementing statement can be any legal statement, allowing for significant flexibility in coding.

The following example shows a simple **for** loop in Java:

```java
public void eatApples (Apples apples) {
    numApples = apples.getNumApples ();
    for (int x = 0; x < numApples; x++) {
        eatApple (apples.getApple (x));
        spitOutCore ();
    }
}
```

In the above Java example, the loop variable x was declared as **int** x = 0. Before each iteration the loop tests the condition " x < numApples" and executes the loop body only if this is true. Finally, at the end of each iteration the loop uses the statement x++ to increment the loop variable x before again testing the condition.

Java has two other kinds of loops besides **for** loops, the standard **while** loop and the **do-while** loop. One loop tests a Boolean condition before performing an iteration of the loop body and the other tests a condition after.

While Loops

The syntax for testing a condition before a loop body is executed is as follows:

```
while (⟨boolean_expression⟩)
    ⟨loop_body_statement⟩
```

At the beginning of each iteration the loop tests the boolean expression and then executes the loop body only if this expression evaluates to true. As with the **for** loop, the loop body statement can also be a block of statements.

Consider, for example, a gnome that is trying to water all of the carrots in his carrot patch, which he does until his watering can is empty. Since his can might be empty to begin with, we would write the code to perform this task as follows:

```java
public void waterCarrots () {
    Carrot current = garden.findNextCarrot ();

    while (!waterCan.isEmpty ()) {
        water (current, waterCan);
        current = garden.findNextCarrot ();
    }
}
```

Recall that "!" in Java is the "not" operator.

Do-While Loops

The syntax for a **while** loop that tests a condition after the loop body is as follows:

> **do**
> 　　⟨loop_body_statement⟩
> **while** (⟨boolean_expression⟩)

Consider, for example, that we want to prompt the user for input and then do something useful with that input. The condition for exiting the loop is when the user enters an empty string. However, even in this case, we want to handle that input and inform the user that she has quit. The following example illustrates this:

```
public void getUserInput() {
    String input;
    do {
        input = getInputString();
        handleInput(input);
    } while (input.length()>0);
}
```

Notice the exit condition for the above example—in Java **do-while** loops exit when the condition is *not* true (unlike the repeat-until construct in other languages).

A.4.5 Explicit Control-Flow Statements

Java also provides statements that allow for explicit change in the flow of control of a program. In fact, we have already discussed one such statement, the **return** statement, which terminates the flow of control in a function and returns a specified value. There are two other such explicit control-flow statements.

The break Statement

The typical usage of a **break** statement has the following simple syntax:

> **break**;

It is used to "break" out of the innermost **switch**, **for**, **while**, or **do-while** statement body. It causes the flow of control to jump to the next line after the statement body containing the **break**. The **break** statement can also be used in a labeled form to jump out of an outer-nested loop or **switch** statement. In this case, it has the syntax

> **break** ⟨label⟩;

where ⟨label⟩ is a Java identifier that is used to label a loop or **switch** statement.

We illustrate the use of a label with a **break** statement in the following example:

```
public static boolean hasZeroEntry (int[][] a) {
    boolean foundFlag = false;

zeroSearch:
    for (int i=0; i<a.length; i++) {
        for (int j=0; j<a[i].length; j++) {
            if (a[i][j] == 0) {
                foundFlag = true;
                break zeroSearch;
            }
        }
    }
    return foundFlag;
}
```

The continue Statement

The other statement to explicitly change the flow of control in a Java program is the **continue** statement, which has the following syntax:

```
continue [⟨label⟩];
```

The **continue** can only be used inside loops (**for**, **while**, and **do-while**). It skips over remaining steps in a loop body and then repeats the condition for the loop.

A.5   Packages

The Java language takes a general and useful approach to the organization of classes into programs. Every public class defined in Java must be given in a separate file. The file name is the name of the class with a *.java* extension. So the class, **public class** SmartBoard, is defined in a file, *SmartBoard.java*. A set of related classes, all defined in a common subdirectory, can be a Java **package**. Every file in a package starts with the line:

```
package ⟨package_name⟩;
```

The subdirectory containing the package must be the same as the package name. We can also define a package in a single file that contains several class definitions, but when it is compiled, all the classes will be be compiled into separate files in the same subdirectory.

A.5.1   Using Other Packages

In Java, we can use classes that are defined in other packages by prefixing class names with dots (that is, using the '.' character) that correspond to the other packages' directory structure.

```
public boolean Temperature(TA.Measures.Thermometer thermometer,
                                    int temperature) {
    // . . .
}
```

Here, the function Temperature takes a class Thermometer as a parameter. Thermometer is defined in the TA package in a subpackage called Measures. The dots in TA.Measures.Thermometer correspond directly to the directory structure in the TA package.

A.5.2   The Import Command

All the extra typing needed to refer to a class outside of the current package can get tiring. In Java, we can use the **import** keyword to include external classes or entire packages in the current file. This is done as follows:

To Import Individual Classes

To import an individual class from a specific package, we type the following at the beginning of the file:

```
import ⟨packageName⟩.⟨classNames⟩;
```

For example we could type:

```
package Project;

import TA.Measures.Thermometer;
import TA.Measures.Scale;
```

at the beginning of a Project package to indicate that we are importing the classes named TA.Measures.Thermometer and TA.Measures.Scale. The Java run-time environment will now search these classes to match identifiers to classes, methods, and instance variables that we use in our program.

To Import a Whole Package

We can also import an entire package, by using the following syntax:

```
import ⟨packageName⟩.*;
```

For example:
```
package student;

import TA.Measures.*;

public boolean Temperature(Thermometer thermometer, int temperature) {

}
```

In the case where two packages have classes of the same name, we ***must*** specifically reference the package that contains a class. For example, suppose both the package Gnomes and package Cooking have a class named Mushroom.

If we provide an **import** statement for both packages, then we must specify which class we mean as follows:
```
Gnomes.Mushroom shroom = new Gnomes.Mushroom ("purple");
Cooking.Mushroom topping = new Cooking.Mushroom ();
```

If we do not specify the package (that is, in the previous example we just use a variable of type Mushroom), the compiler will give an "ambiguous class" error.

To sum up the structure of a Java program, we can have instance variables and methods inside a class, and classes inside a package.

A.6 Interfaces

Another kind of structural element that we can have in Java is an ***interface***. A Java interface is similar to an abstract superclass. Classes are collections of data and methods. An interface is a collection of methods with no data. The methods of an interface are always empty. When a class implements an interface, it must implement all of the methods declared in the interface.

Suppose we want to define a data structure like a hash table. We know that every element in the hash table must support some simple functions like HashValue or DisplayValue. So, we can define an interface that declares these functions:
```
public interface Hashable {
    public int hashValue ();
    public void displayValue ();
}
```

Notice that functions are declared, but no implementation is given.

Now we can define a hash table that holds Hashable things:

```
public class HashTable {
  public HashTable () {
    // . . .
  }
  public void insert (Hashable element) {
    // . . .
  }
  public Hashable remove (Hashable element) {
    // . . .
  }
}
```

Our hash table stores Hashable things as if Hashable were a class. Any class that implements the interface Hashable must be able to execute all of Hashable's functions. As long as we have a reference to a Hashable object, we can call Hashable's methods no matter what the class actually is. But, each class will execute the methods of Hashable in its own specific way.

We can then define an element to go into our hash table. Let us say we want to store point elements. Then we can do the following:

```
public class HashPoint extends MyPoint implements Hashable {

  public hashPoint (int x, int y) {
    super (x,y);
  }
  public int hashFunc () {
    return x_ / 10;
  }
  public void displayValue () {
    super.displayValue ();
  }
}
```

In the definition for HashPoint, the functions in Hashable are all implemented, and we can use them in our HashTable.

A.6.1   Implementing Multiple Interfaces

Another nice thing about interfaces is that, although a class can only extend one class, it can implement as many different interfaces as it wants. So, we could define the following:

```
public class Snake extends Reptile
                   implements Slitherer, Biter, Predator {

}
```

When we do this, the class Snake must define all the methods declared in the Slitherer, Biter, and Predator interfaces.

Interfaces are useful for making classes compatible with container data structures, such as priority queues and dictionaries. In some cases, however, *casting* might be necessary to implement certain interfaces. We say more about this in the next section.

A.7 Casting

Casting is an operation that allows us to change the type of a variable. In essence, we can take a variable of one type and *cast* it into an equivalent variable of another type. The ability to change the type of a variable extends from simple base types like **int** and **double** all the way to class types. Casting can be useful for doing certain numerical operations and for building and using abstract data types (ADT's).

The syntax for casting involves putting the cast type in parentheses before the variable to cast.

$$(\langle \text{desired\_type} \rangle)\langle \text{variable} \rangle;$$

So, if we wanted to cast the variable, papa_gnome of type MythicalCreature to type Gnome we would write :

(Gnome) papa_gnome

So, papa_gnome, a variable of type MythicalCreature, can now be used as if it were of type Gnome.

There are two fundamental types of casting that can be done in Java. We can either cast with respect to the base numerical types or we can cast with respect to objects.

A.7.1 Casting in Numerical Operations

It is often the case that we need to perform numerical operations on numbers of different base types. For instance, it might be helpful to cast an **int** to a **double** in order to perform operations like division.

Ordinary Casting

When casting from a **double** to an **int**, we may lose precision. This means that the resulting double value will be rounded down.

```
double d1 = 3.2;
double d2 = 3.9999;

int iresult;

iresult = (int)d1;          // iresult has value 3
iresult = (int)d2;          // iresult has value 3
```

We can also cast an **int** to a **double**.

```
int i = 3;

double dresult = (double)i;     // dresult has value 3.0
```

Casting with Operators

Certain binary operators, like division, will have different results depending on the variable types they are used with. We must take care to make sure operations perform their computations on values of the intended type. When used with integers, division does not keep track of the fractional part, for example. When used with doubles, division keeps this part, as is illustrated in the following example:

```
int i1 = 3;
int i2 = 6;

dresult = (double)i1 / (double)i2;     // dresult has value 0.5
dresult = i1 / i2;                     // dresult has value 0.0
```

Notice that when i1 and i2 were cast to doubles, regular division for real numbers was performed. When i1 and i2 were not cast, the " /" operator performed an integer division and the result of i1 / i2 was the **int** 0. Java then did an *implicit cast* to assign an **int** value to the **double** result. We discuss implicit casting next.

Implicit Casting

If an *explicit cast*, that is, a cast that is not syntactically included in the code, is not specified, then there are cases where Java will need to perform an *implicit cast*. This means that Java will go ahead and change the types of variables, even though the programmer did not explicitly include the cast. Java will perform a cast according to the type of the assignment variable, provided there is no loss of precision.

For example:
```
int iresult, i = 3;
double dresult, d = 3.2;

dresult = i / d;              // dresult has value 0.9375. i1 was
                              // cast to a double because dresult is a double.

iresult = i / d;              // this results in a compilation error;
                              // an explicit cast is needed where
                              // precision will be lost.
```

Java will not perform implicit casts where precision is lost. In the above example, the line
```
iresult = i / d;
```
needs an explicit cast to an **int**. In this case, casting the **double** d to an **int** would loose d's decimal precision.

The general rule with casting then is to ***play it safe***. If we are not sure whether the compiler will be implicitly casting our variables, it is better to spell it out. Explicitly casting variables guarantees the right results.

A.7.2   Casting with Interfaces and Generic Classes

In Java, we can define abstract data structures that organize elements of a common class or a common interface. We can use these data structures to hold any class of elements we like as long as the class extends the common class or implements the common interface. Suppose, for example, we want to declare a Person interface for all classes that are associated with persons. We could specify this as follows:
```
public interface Person {
    public boolean equalTo (Geometric other);
    public String getName ();
    public int getAge ();
}
```
Thus, the Person interface declares three functions. The first of these functions takes one parameter of type Person. So, any class implementing the Person comparison function is passed another object from a class implementing the Person interface to compare to. Now, suppose we want to build a dictionary data structure for storing ***students***, which we assume come as an implementation of the Person interface. But a Student object only knows how to compare itself to other Student objects. To resolve this difficulty, we cast a Person object into a Student. We can do this because we know that only Student objects are in our dictionary; hence, we know a reference to the Person object is also a reference to a Student. This knowledge assures us that the run-time environment will let us perform the cast.

Thus, the following is correct:

```
public class Student implements Person {
    String name;
    int age;
    public Student (String n, int a) {
        name = n;
        age = a;
    }
    // no. of hrs. spent studying weekly:
    protected int studyHours() {return age/3;}
    // The next three methods are for implementing the Person interface.
    public String getName() {return name;}
    public String getAge() {return age;}
    public boolean equalTo (Person other) {
        Student other_student = (Student)other;  // Cast Person to Student
        return (name.equals (other_student.getName()));
    }
}
```

In order to compare two student names, we did an explicit cast of the Person parameter other into a Student.

This type of generic casting also allows us to write general kinds of data structures, which only make minimal assumptions about the elements that they store. In the following example, we sketch how to build a person-pair directory data structure that stores pairs of objects that implement the Person interface.

```
public class PersonPairDirectory {
    // instance variables...

    public PersonPairDirectory() {
        // constructor code body...
    }
    public void insert (Person person, Person other) {
        // insertion code for a person pair...
    }
    public Person findOther (Person person) {
        // code for finding a pair containing person... (uses equalTo)
    }
    public void remove (Person person, Person other) {
        // code for removing a specified person pair...
    }
}
```

This directory contains pairs of elements that implement the interface Person. The remove performs a search on the directory contents and removes the specified person pair, if it exists, and like the findOther method it uses the equalTo method to do this.

Now, suppose we have filled a directory, myDirectory, full of pairs of Student objects that represent roommate pairs. In order to find the roommate of a given Student object, smart_one, we may try to do the following (which is wrong):

```
// THIS IS WRONG:
Student cute_one = myDirectory.findOther(smart_one);
```

Compiling this gives an explicit-cast-required compilation error. The problem here is that we are trying to assign something of type Person to something of type Student. To solve this problem, we write something like the following:

```
// THIS IS RIGHT:
Student cute_one = (Student) (myDirectory.findOther(smart_one));
```

We cast the Person return value of findOther to the Student type. This works fine as long as we are sure that myDirectory.findOther() is really giving us a Student object.

One way to make absolutely sure our generic class always gives us objects of the expected type is to define an *adapter class*, which implements the *adapter pattern*, to guarantee that only objects of the correct type go in and out of the dictionary. For our running example, we can guarantee that only Student pairs go into our directory as follows:

```
public class StudentPairDirectory {
    protected PersonPairDirectory directory;

    public StudentPairDirectory() {
        directory = new PersonPairDirectory ();
    }
    public void insert(Student s, Student t) {
        directory.insert(s,t);
    }
    public Student findOther(Student s) {
        return (Student)(directory.findOther(s));
    }
    public void remove(Student s, Student t) {
        directory.remove(Student s, Student t);
    }
}
```

Such an adapter class *specializes*, or "adapts," the generic directory data structure to only work for pairs of Student objects. It performs the casting for us inside its implementation of the findOther method.

Thus, interfaces can be a valuable tool for the design of general data structures, which can then be specialized by other programmers through the use of casting. If our data structure is to be used infrequently in another program, then it is probably reasonable to do the casting explicitly with each use, as needed. If our data structure is to be used extensively, however, it saves typing time and eases readability to design an adapter class that hides all the casting inside its internal methods.

A.8   Exceptions

Exceptions are surprising events that occur during the execution of a program.

A.8.1   Throwing and Catching Exceptions

In Java, exceptions are objects that are ***thrown*** by code that encounters some sort of unexpected condition. They can also be thrown by the Java runtime environment should it encounter an unexpected condition, like running out of object memory. An thrown exception is ***caught*** by other code that "handles" the exception somehow, or the program is terminated unexpectedly. Those terms aren't very precise, but please accept them as metaphors for now. The technical details are given in the remainder of this section.

Throwing Exceptions

Exceptions originate when a piece of Java code finds some sort of problem during execution and ***throws*** an exception, which is identified with a descriptive name. For instance, if we try to delete the tenth element from a sequence that has only five elements, the code may throw a BoundaryViolationException. This could be done, for example, using the following code fragment:

```
if (insertIndex > size()) {
    throw new BoundaryViolationException("Sequence overflow.");
}
```

The general syntax for the **throw** statement is as follows:

```
throw new ⟨exception_constructor⟩([⟨param⟩,⟨param⟩,...]);
```

Exceptions are also thrown by the Java run-time environment itself. For example, the counterpart to the example above is ArrayIndexOutOfBoundsException. If we have a six-element array and asks for element number 9, then the exception called ArrayIndexOutOfBoundsException will be thrown by the Java run-time system.

Catching Exceptions

When an exception is thrown, it must be *caught* or the program will terminate. When an exception is caught, it can be analyzed and dealt with. The general methodology for dealing with exceptions then is to *try* to execute some fragment of code that might throw an exception. If it does throw an exception, then that exception is *caught* by having the flow of control jump to a predefined **catch** statements. Within the catch block we can then deal with the exceptional circumstance.

The general syntax for a try-catch block in Java is as follows:

```
try
    ⟨block_of_statements_1⟩
catch (⟨exception_type⟩ ⟨identifier⟩)
    ⟨block_of_statements_2⟩
[catch (⟨exception_type⟩ ⟨identifier⟩)
    ⟨block_of_statements_3⟩]
        . . .
[finally
    ⟨block_of_statements_n⟩]
```

The Java environment begins by executing ⟨block_of_statements_1⟩. If this execution generates no exceptions, then the flow of control continues with the first statement after the last line of the **try** block.

Consider the following example code fragment:

```
int index = Integer.MAX_VALUE;    // 2.14 Billion
try                               // This code might have a problem...
{
    String toBuy = shoppingList[index];
}
catch (ArrayIndexOutOfBoundsException aioobx)
{
    System.out.println(``The index ``+index+'' is outside the array.'');
}
```

If this code does not catch the exception, the flow of control will immediately exit the method and return to the code which called our method. There the Java run-time environment will look again for a catch block. If there is no catch block in the code that called this method, the flow of control will jump to the code that called this, and so on. Eventually, if no code catches the exception, the Java run-time system (the origin of our program's flow of control) will catch the exception. At this point, an error message and a stack trace is printed to the screen.

The following is an actual (hopefully unfamiliar) run-time error message:

```
java.lang.NullPointerException: Returned a null locator
    at java.awt.Component.handleEvent(Component.java:900)
    at java.awt.Component.postEvent(Component.java:838)
    at java.awt.Component.postEvent(Component.java:845)
    at sun.awt.motif.MButtonPeer.action(MButtonPeer.java:39)
    at java.lang.Thread.run(Thread.java)
```

Once an exception is caught, there are several things a programmer might want to do. An unsophisticated, but sometimes useful, approach is to print out an error message. There are also some interesting cases in which the best way to handle an exception is to ignore it (this can be done by having an empty **catch** block). This approach is usually taken when the programmer doesn't care whether there was an exception or not. Another legitimate way of handling exceptions is to create and throw another exception, possibly one that specifies the exceptional condition more precisely.

The following is an example of this exception-handling approach:

```
catch (ArrayIndexOutOfBoundsException aioobx) {
    throw new ShoppingListTooSmallException(
            "Product index is not in the shopping list");
}
```

Perhaps the best way to handle an exception (although this is not always possible) is to find the problem, fix it, and continue execution.

A.8.2 The Throws Clause

When a method is declared, it must also declare the exceptions it might throw. This has both a functional and courteous purpose. For one, it lets users know what to expect. It also lets the Java compiler know which exceptions to prepare for. The following is an example of such a method definition:

```
public void goShopping() throws ShoppingListTooSmallException,
                            OutOfMoneyException {
    // method body . . .
}
```

By specifying all the exceptions that might be thrown by a method, we prepare others to be able to handle all of the exceptional cases that might arise from using this method. Another benefit of declaring exceptions is that we do not need to catch those exceptions in our method. Sometimes this is appropriate in the case where the other code is responsible for causing the circumstances leading up to the exception.

The following illustrates an exception that is "passed through:"

```
public void getReadyForClass() throws ShoppingListTooSmallException,
                                        OutOfMoneyException {
    goShopping();   // I don't have to try or catch the exceptions
                    // which goShopping() might throw because
                    // getReadyForClass() will just pass these along.

    makeCookiesForTAs();
}
```

A function can declare that it throws as many exceptions as it likes. This can be simplified somewhat if all exceptions that can be thrown are subclasses of the same exception. In this case, we only have to declare that a method throws the appropriate superclasses.

A.8.3   Kinds of Throwables

As illustrated in Figure A.1, the classes Exception and Error are subclasses of Throwable, which is a subclass of Object. A Throwable is anything that can be thrown or caught. Errors can be caught but probably should not be, because they usually deal with problems that cannot really be handled, like running out of memory. In these cases, an error message or a sudden program termination is about as much grace as we can expect.

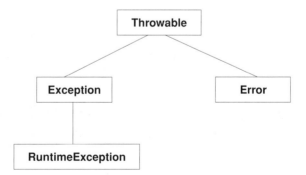

Figure A.1: The class hierarchy of throwable objects.

Run-time exceptions indicate errors that could come up just about anywhere and anytime. Run-time exceptions can be caught when catching them is useful, but need not be either caught or declared. The ability to catch exceptions by their superclasses leads to the possibility of intercepting more exceptions than we probably should, by catching too generic a superclass—in the worst case, catching everything of class Exception. We should not be overly general.

Appendix B

Useful Mathematical Facts

Contents

In this appendix we give several useful mathematical facts.

B.1   Combinatorial Facts

We begin with some combinatorial definitions and facts.

B.1.1   Logarithms and Exponents

The logarithm function is defined as

$$\log_b a = c \qquad \text{if} \qquad a = b^c.$$

The following identities hold for logarithms and exponents:

1. $\log_b ac = \log_b a + \log_b c$
2. $\log_b a/c = \log_b a - \log_b c$
3. $\log_b a^c = c \log_b a$
4. $\log_b a = (\log_c a)/\log_c b$
5. $b^{\log_c a} = a^{\log_c b}$
6. $(b^a)^c = b^{ac}$
7. $b^a b^c = b^{a+c}$
8. $b^a/b^c = b^{a-c}$

In addition, we have the following:

Proposition B.1: *If $a > 0$, $b > 0$, and $c > a + b$, then*

$$\log a + \log b \leq 2 \log c - 2.$$

The ***natural logarithm*** function $\ln x = \log_e x$, where $e = 2.71828\ldots$, is the value of the following progression

$$e = 1 + \frac{1}{1!} + \frac{1}{2!} + \frac{1}{3!} + \cdots.$$

In addition,

$$e^x = 1 + \frac{x}{1!} + \frac{x^2}{2!} + \frac{x^3}{3!} + \cdots$$

$$\ln(1+x) = x - \frac{x^2}{2!} + \frac{x^3}{3!} - \frac{x^4}{4!} + \cdots.$$

There are a number of useful inequalities relating to these functions (which derive from these definitions).

Proposition B.2:

$$\frac{x}{1+x} \leq \ln(1+x) \leq x.$$

Proposition B.3: *For* $0 \leq x \neq 1$

$$1 + x \leq e^x \leq \frac{1}{1-x}.$$

Proposition B.4: *For any real number* x *and positive integer* n

$$\left(1 + \frac{x}{n}\right)^n \leq e^x \leq \left(1 + \frac{x}{n}\right)^{n+x/2}.$$

B.1.2 Integer Functions and Relations

The "floor" and "ceiling" functions are defined respectively as follows:

1. $\lfloor x \rfloor$ = the largest integer less than or equal to x.
2. $\lceil x \rceil$ = the smallest integer greater than or equal to x.

The *modulus* function is defined for integers $a \geq 0$ and $b > 0$ as

$$a \bmod b = a - \left\lfloor \frac{a}{b} \right\rfloor b.$$

The *factorial* function is defined as

$$n! = 1 \cdot 2 \cdot 3 \cdot \cdots \cdot (n-1)n.$$

The binomial coefficient is

$$\binom{n}{k} = \frac{n!}{k!(n-k)!},$$

which is equal to the number of different *combinations* one can define by choosing k different items from a collection of n items (where the order does not matter). The name "binomial coefficient" derives from the *binomial expansion*:

$$(a+b)^n = \sum_{k=0}^{n} \binom{n}{k} a^k b^{n-k}.$$

We also have the following relationships:

Proposition B.5: *If* $0 \leq k \leq n$, *then*

$$\left(\frac{n}{k}\right)^k \leq \binom{n}{k} \leq \frac{n^k}{k!}.$$

Proposition B.6 (Stirling's Approximation):

$$n! = \sqrt{2\pi n} \left(\frac{n}{e}\right)^n \left(1 + \frac{1}{12n} + \varepsilon(n)\right),$$

where $\varepsilon(n)$ *is* $O(1/n^2)$.

The *Fibonacci progression* is a numeric progression such that $F_0 = F_1 = 1$ and $F_n = F_{n-1} + F_{n-2}$ for $n \geq 2$.

Proposition B.7: *If F_n is defined by the Fibonacci progression, then F_n is $\Theta(g^n)$, where $g = (1 + \sqrt{5})/2$ is the so-called* **golden ratio.**

B.1.3   Summations

There are a number of useful facts about summations.

Proposition B.8: *Factoring summations:*

$$\sum_{i=1}^{n} af(i) = a \sum_{i=1}^{n} f(i),$$

provided a does not depend upon i.

Proposition B.9: *Reversing the order:*

$$\sum_{i=1}^{n} \sum_{j=1}^{m} f(i, j) = \sum_{j=1}^{m} \sum_{i=1}^{n} f(i, j).$$

One special form of summation is a **telescoping sum**:

$$\sum_{i=1}^{n} (f(i) - f(i-1)) = f(n) - f(0),$$

which arises often in the amortized analysis of a data structure or algorithm.

The following are some other facts about summations that arise often in the analysis of data structures and algorithms.

Proposition B.10:

$$\sum_{i=1}^{n} i = \frac{n(n+1)}{2}.$$

Proposition B.11:

$$\sum_{i=1}^{n} i^2 = \frac{n(n+1)(2n+1)}{6}.$$

Proposition B.12: *If $k \geq 1$ is an integer constant, then*

$$\sum_{i=1}^{n} i^k \text{ is } \Theta(n^{k+1}).$$

Another common summation is the **geometric sum**

$$\sum_{i=0}^{n} a^i,$$

for any fixed real number $0 < a \neq 1$.

Proposition B.13:

$$\sum_{i=0}^{n} a^i = \frac{1 - a^{n+1}}{1 - a}$$

for any real number $0 < a \neq 1$.

Proposition B.14:

$$\sum_{i=0}^{\infty} a^i = \frac{1}{1 - a}$$

for any real number $0 < a < 1$.

There is also a combination of the two common forms, called the ***linear exponential*** summation, which has the following expansion:

Proposition B.15: *For* $0 < a \neq 1$, *and* $n \geq 2$,

$$\sum_{i=1}^{n} i a^i = \frac{(n-2)a^n - (n-1)a^{n-1} + a}{(1-a)^2}.$$

The *n*th ***harmonic number*** H_n is defined as

$$H_n = \sum_{i=1}^{n} \frac{1}{i}.$$

Proposition B.16: *If* H_n *is the nth harmonic number, then* H_n *is* $\ln n + \Theta(1)$.

B.2 Basic Probability

In this section, we review some basic facts from probability theory. The most basic such fact is that any statement about a probability is defined upon a ***sample space*** S, which is defined as the set of all possible outcomes from some experiment. We leave the terms "outcomes" and "experiment" undefined in any formal sense, but an intuitive understanding will suffice for the probabilistic arguments presented in this book.

Example B.17: *Consider an experiment that consists of the outcome from flipping a coin five times. This sample space has* 2^5 *different outcomes, one for each different ordering of possible flips that can occur.*

Sample spaces can also be infinite, as the following example illustrates.

Example B.18: *Consider an experiment that consists of flipping a coin until it comes up heads. This sample space is infinite, with each outcome being a sequence of i tails followed by a single flip that comes up heads, for* $i \in \{1, 2, 3, \ldots\}$.

A *probability space* is defined from a sample space S and a probability function Pr that maps subsets of S to real numbers in the interval $[0, 1]$. It captures mathematically the intuitive notion of the probability of certain "events" occurring. Formally, each subset A of S is called an *event*, and the probability function Pr is assumed to possess the following basic properties with respect to events defined from S:

1. $\Pr(\emptyset) = 0$.
2. $\Pr(S) = 1$.
3. $0 \leq \Pr(A) \leq 1$, for any $A \subseteq S$.
4. If $A, B \subseteq S$ and $A \cap B = \emptyset$, then $\Pr(A \cup B) = \Pr(A) + \Pr(B)$.

Two events A and B are *independent* if
$$\Pr(A \cap B) = \Pr(A) \cdot \Pr(B).$$
A collection of events $\{A_1, A_2, \ldots, A_n\}$ is *mutually independent* if
$$\Pr(A_{i_1} \cap A_{i_2} \cap \cdots \cap A_{i_k}) = \Pr(A_{i_1}) \Pr(A_{i_2}) \cdots \Pr(A_{i_k}).$$
for any subset $\{A_{i_1}, A_{i_2}, \ldots, A_{i_k}\}$.

The *conditional probability* that an event A occurs, given an event B, is denoted as $\Pr(A|B)$, and is defined as the ratio
$$\frac{\Pr(A \cap B)}{\Pr(B)},$$
assuming that $\Pr(B) > 0$.

An elegant way for dealing with events is in terms of *random variables*. Intuitively, random variables are variables whose values depend upon the outcome of some experiment. Formally, a *random variable* is a function X that maps outcomes from some sample space S to real numbers. An *indicator random variable* is a random variable that maps outcomes to the set $\{0, 1\}$. Often in data structure and algorithm analysis we use a random variable X to characterized the running time of a randomized algorithm. In this case, the sample space S is defined by all possible outcomes of the random sources used in the algorithm.

We are most interested in the typical, average, or "expected" value of such a random variable. The *expected value* of a random variable X is defined as
$$\mathbf{E}(X) = \sum_{x} x \Pr(X = x),$$
where the summation is defined over the range of X (which in this case is assumed to be discrete).

Proposition B.19 (The Linearity of Expectation): *Let X and Y be two arbitrary random variables. Then*
$$\mathbf{E}(X + Y) = \mathbf{E}(X) + \mathbf{E}(Y).$$

Example B.20: *Let X be a random variable that assigns the outcome of the roll of two fair dice to the sum of the number of dots showing. Then $E(X) = 7$.*

Justification: *To justify this claim, let X_1 and X_2 be random variables corresponding to the number of dots on each die. Thus, $X_1 = X_2$ (i.e., they are two instances of the same function) and $E(X) = E(X_1 + X_2) = E(X_1) + E(X_2)$. Each outcome of the roll of a fair die occurs with probability $1/6$. Thus*

$$E(X_i) = \frac{1}{6} + \frac{2}{6} + \frac{3}{6} + \frac{4}{6} + \frac{5}{6} + \frac{6}{6} = \frac{7}{2},$$

for $i = 1, 2$. Therefore, $E(X) = 7$. ∎

Two random variables X and Y are **independent** if
$$\Pr(X = x | Y = y) = \Pr(X = x),$$
for all real numbers x and y.

Proposition B.21: *If two random variables X and Y are independent, then*
$$E(XY) = E(X)E(Y).$$

Example B.22: *Let X be a random variable that assigns the outcome of a roll of two fair dice to the product of the number of dots showing. Then $E(X) = 49/4$.*

Justification: *Let X_1 and X_2 be random variables denoting the number of dots on each die. The variables X_1 and X_2 are clearly independent; hence*
$$E(X) = E(X_1 X_2) = E(X_1)E(X_2) = (7/2)^2 = 49/2.$$
∎

B.3 Useful Mathematical Techniques

To determine whether a function is little-oh or little-omega of another, it is sometimes helpful to apply the following rule.

Proposition B.23 (L'Hôpital's Rule): *If we have $\lim_{n\to\infty} f(n) = +\infty$ and we have $\lim_{n\to\infty} g(n) = +\infty$, then $\lim_{n\to\infty} f(n)/g(n) = \lim_{n\to\infty} f'(n)/g'(n)$, where $f'(n)$ and $g'(n)$ respectively denote the derivatives of $f(n)$ and $g(n)$.*

In deriving an upper or lower bound for a summation, it is often useful to **split a summation** as follows:

$$\sum_{i=1}^{n} f(i) = \sum_{i=1}^{j} f(i) + \sum_{i=j+1}^{n} f(i).$$

Another useful technique is to **bound a sum by an integral**. If f is a nondecreasing function, then

$$\int_{a-1}^{b} f(x)\,dx \le \sum_{i=a}^{b} f(i) \le \int_{a}^{b+1} f(x)\,dx,$$

provided these terms are defined.

There is a general form of recurrence relation that arises in the analysis of divide-and-conquer algorithms

$$T(n) = aT(n/b) + f(n).$$

for constants $a \ge 1$ and $b > 1$.

Proposition B.24: *Let $T(n)$ be defined as above. Then*

1. *If $f(n)$ is $O(n^{\log_b a - \varepsilon})$, for some constant $\varepsilon > 0$, then $T(n)$ is $\Theta(n^{\log_b a})$.*
2. *If $f(n)$ is $\Theta(n^{\log_b a} \log^k n)$, for a fixed non-negative integer $k \ge 0$, then $T(n)$ is $\Theta(n^{\log_b a} \log^{k+1} n)$.*
3. *If $f(n)$ is $\Omega(n^{\log_b a + \varepsilon})$, for some constant $\varepsilon > 0$, and if $af(n/b) \le cf(n)$, then $T(n)$ is $\Theta(f(n))$.*

This proposition is known as the **master method** for characterizing divide-and-conquer recurrence relations asymptotically.

Bibliography

[1] G. M. Adel'son-Vel'skii and Y. M. Landis, "An algorithm for the organization of information," *Doklady Akademii Nauk SSSR*, vol. 146, pp. 263–266, 1962. English translation in *Soviet Math. Dokl.*, **3**, 1259–1262.

[2] P. K. Agarwal, "Geometric partitioning and its applications," in *Computational Geometry: Papers from the DIMACS special year* (J. E. Goodman, R. Pollack, and W. Steiger, eds.), American Mathematical Society, 1991.

[3] P. K. Agarwal, "Range searching," in *Handbook of Discrete and Computational Geometry* (J. E. Goodman and J. O'Rourke, eds.), ch. 31, pp. 575–598, CRC Press LLC, 1997.

[4] A. Aggarwal and J. S. Vitter, "The input/output complexity of sorting and related problems," *Commun. ACM*, vol. 31, pp. 1116–1127, 1988.

[5] A. V. Aho, "Algorithms for finding patterns in strings," in *Handbook of Theoretical Computer Science* (J. van Leeuwen, ed.), vol. A. Algorithms and Complexity, pp. 255–300, Amsterdam: Elsevier, 1990.

[6] A. V. Aho, J. E. Hopcroft, and J. D. Ullman, *The Design and Analysis of Computer Algorithms*. Reading, MA: Addison-Wesley, 1974.

[7] A. V. Aho, J. E. Hopcroft, and J. D. Ullman, *Data Structures and Algorithms*. Reading, MA: Addison-Wesley, 1983.

[8] R. K. Ahuja, T. L. Magnanti, and J. B. Orlin, *Network Flows: Theory, Algorithms, and Applications*. Englewood Cliffs, NJ: Prentice Hall, 1993.

[9] C. Aragon and R. Seidel, "Randomized search trees," in *Proc. 30th Annu. IEEE Sympos. Found. Comput. Sci.*, pp. 540–545, 1989.

[10] K. Arnold and J. Gosling, *The Java Programming Language*. The Java Series, Reading, Mass.: Addison-Wesley, 1996.

[11] S. Arya and D. M. Mount, "Approximate nearest neighbor queries in fixed dimensions," in *Proc. 4th ACM-SIAM Sympos. Discrete Algorithms*, pp. 271–280, 1993.

[12] S. Arya and D. M. Mount, "Approximate range searching," in *Proc. 11th Annu. ACM Sympos. Comput. Geom.*, pp. 172–181, 1995.

[13] F. Aurenhammer, "Voronoi diagrams: A survey of a fundamental geometric data structure," *ACM Comput. Surv.*, vol. 23, pp. 345–405, 1991.

[14] O. Baruvka, "O jistem problemu minimalnim," *Praca Moravske Prirodovedecke Spolecnosti*, vol. 3, pp. 37–58, 1926. (in Czech).

[15] R. Bayer, "Symmetric binary B-trees: Data structure and maintenance," *Acta Informatica*, vol. 1, no. 4, pp. 290–306, 1972.

[16] R. Bayer and McCreight, "Organization of large ordered indexes," *Acta Inform.*, vol. 1, pp. 173–189, 1972.

[17] T. C. Bell, J. G. Cleary, and I. H. Witten, *Text Compression*. Prentice Hall, 1990.

[18] R. Bellman, "On a routing problem," *Quarterly of Applied Mathematics*, vol. 16, no. 1, pp. 87–90, 1958.

[19] R. E. Bellman, *Dynamic Programming*. Princeton, NJ: Princeton University Press, 1957.

[20] J. L. Bentley, "Multidimensional divide-and-conquer," *Commun. ACM*, vol. 23, no. 4, pp. 214–229, 1980.

[21] J. L. Bentley, "Programming pearls: Writing correct programs," *Communications of the ACM*, vol. 26, pp. 1040–1045, 1983.

[22] J. L. Bentley, "Programming pearls: Thanks, heaps," *Communications of the ACM*, vol. 28, pp. 245–250, 1985.

[23] J. L. Bentley, D. Haken, and J. B. Saxe, "A general method for solving divide-and-conquer recurrences," *SIGACT News*, vol. 12, no. 3, pp. 36–44, 1980.

[24] J. L. Bentley and T. A. Ottmann, "Algorithms for reporting and counting geometric intersections," *IEEE Trans. Comput.*, vol. C-28, pp. 643–647, 1979.

[25] G. Booch, *Object-Oriented Analysis and Design with Applications*. Redwood City, CA: Benjamin/Cummings, 1994.

[26] C. B. Boyer and U. C. Merzbach, *A History of Mathematics*. New York: John Wiley & Sons, Inc., 2nd ed., 1991.

[27] R. S. Boyer and J. S. Moore, "A fast string searching algorithm," *Communications of the ACM*, vol. 20, no. 10, pp. 762–772, 1977.

[28] G. Brassard, "Crusade for a better notation," *SIGACT News*, vol. 17, no. 1, pp. 60–64, 1985.

[29] T. Budd, *An Introduction to Object-Oriented Programming*. Reading, Mass.: Addison-Wesley, 1991.

[30] D. Burger, J. R. Goodman, and G. S. Sohi, "Memory systems," in *The Computer Science and Engineering Handbook* (A. B. Tucker, Jr., ed.), ch. 18, pp. 447–461, CRC Press, 1997.

[31] M. Campione and H. Walrath, *The Java Tutorial: Programming for the Internet*. Reading, Mass.: Addison Wesley, 1996.

[32] L. Cardelli and P. Wegner, "On understanding types, data abstraction and polymorphism," *ACM Computing Surveys*, vol. 17, no. 4, pp. 471–522, 1985.

[33] S. Carlsson, "Average case results on heapsort," *BIT*, vol. 27, pp. 2–17, 1987.

[34] R. Cole, "Tight bounds on the complexity of the Boyer-Moore pattern matching algorithm," *SIAM Journal on Computing*, vol. 23, no. 5, pp. 1075–1091, 1994.

[35] D. Comer, "The ubiquitous B-tree," *ACM Comput. Surv.*, vol. 11, pp. 121–137, 1979.

[36] T. H. Cormen, C. E. Leiserson, and R. L. Rivest, *Introduction to Algorithms*. Cambridge, MA: MIT Press, 1990.

[37] G. Cornell and C. S. Horstmann, *Core Java*. Mountain View, CA: SunSoft Press, 1996.

[38] M. Crochemore and T. Lecroq, "Pattern matching and text compression algorithms," in *The Computer Science and Engineering Handbook* (A. B. Tucker, Jr., ed.), ch. 8, pp. 162–202, CRC Press, 1997.

[39] S. A. Demurjian, Sr., "Software design," in *The Computer Science and Engineering Handbook* (A. B. Tucker, Jr., ed.), ch. 108, pp. 2323–2351, CRC Press, 1997.

[40] G. Di Battista, P. Eades, R. Tamassia, and I. G. Tollis, "Algorithms for drawing graphs: an annotated bibliography," *Comput. Geom. Theory Appl.*, vol. 4, pp. 235–282, 1994.

[41] G. Di Battista, P. Eades, R. Tamassia, and I. G. Tollis, *Graph Drawing: Algorithms for Geometric Representations of Graphs*. Englewood Cliffs, NJ: Prentice Hall, 1998.

[42] E. W. Dijkstra, "A note on two problems in connexion with graphs," *Numerische Mathematik*, vol. 1, pp. 269–271, 1959.

[43] J. R. Driscoll, H. N. Gabow, R. Shrairaman, and R. E. Tarjan, "Relaxed heaps: An alternative to Fibonacci heaps with applications to parallel computation.," *Commun. ACM*, vol. 31, pp. 1343–1354, 1988.

[44] H. Edelsbrunner, "A note on dynamic range searching," *Bull. EATCS*, vol. 15, pp. 34–40, 1981.

[45] H. Edelsbrunner, *Algorithms in Combinatorial Geometry*, vol. 10 of *EATCS Monographs on Theoretical Computer Science*. Heidelberg, West Germany: Springer-Verlag, 1987.

[46] J. Edmonds, "Matroids and the greedy algorithm," *Mathematical Programming*, vol. 1, pp. 126–136, 1971.

[47] J. Edmonds and R. M. Karp, "Theoretical improvements in the algorithmic efficiency for network flow problems," *Journal of the ACM*, vol. 19, pp. 248–264, 1972.

[48] S. Even, *Graph Algorithms*. Potomac, Maryland: Computer Science Press, 1979.

[49] D. Flanagan, *Java in Nutshell*. O'Reilly, 2nd ed., 1997.

[50] R. W. Floyd, "Algorithm 97: Shortest path," *Communications of the ACM*, vol. 5, no. 6, p. 345, 1962.

[51] R. W. Floyd, "Algorithm 245: Treesort 3," *Communications of the ACM*, vol. 7, no. 12, p. 701, 1964.

[52] L. R. Ford, Jr. and D. R. Fulkerson, *Flows in Networks*. Princeton, NJ: Princeton University Press, 1962.

[53] M. Fredman and R. E. Tarjan, "Fibonacci heaps and their uses in improved network optimization problems," *J. ACM*, vol. 34, pp. 596–615, 1987.

[54] H. N. Gabow and R. E. Tarjan, "A linear-time algorithm for a special case of disjoint set union," *SIAM Journal on Computing*, vol. 30, no. 2, pp. 209–221, 1985.

[55] E. Gamma, R. Helm, R. Johnson, and J. Vlissides, *Design Patterns: Elements of Reusable Object-Oriented Software*. Reading, Mass.: Addison-Wesley, 1995.

[56] A. M. Gibbons, *Algorithmic Graph Theory*. Cambridge, UK: Cambridge University Press, 1985.

[57] S. S. Godbole, "On efficient computation of matrix chain products," *IEEE Transactions on Computers*, vol. C-22, no. 9, pp. 864–866, 1973.

[58] A. Goldberg and D. Robson, *Smalltalk-80: The Language*. Reading, Mass.: Addison-Wesley, 1989.

[59] G. H. Gonnet and R. Baeza-Yates, *Handbook of Algorithms and Data Structures in Pascal and C*. Reading, Mass.: Addison-Wesley, 1991.

[60] G. H. Gonnet and J. I. Munro, "Heaps on heaps," *SIAM Journal on Computing*, vol. 15, no. 4, pp. 964–971, 1986.

[61] J. E. Goodman and J. O'Rourke, eds., *Handbook of Discrete and Computational Geometry*. CRC Press LLC, 1997.

[62] M. T. Goodrich, "Parallel algorithms in geometry," in *Handbook of Discrete and Computational Geometry* (J. E. Goodman and J. O'Rourke, eds.), ch. 36, pp. 669–682, CRC Press LLC, 1997.

[63] M. T. Goodrich, J.-J. Tsay, D. E. Vengroff, and J. S. Vitter, "External-memory computational geometry," in *Proc. 34th Annu. IEEE Sympos. Found. Comput. Sci.*, pp. 714–723, 1993.

[64] R. L. Graham, "An efficient algorithm for determining the convex hull of a finite planar set," *Inform. Process. Lett.*, vol. 1, pp. 132–133, 1972.

[65] R. L. Graham and P. Hell, "On the history of the minimum spanning tree problem," *Annals of the History of Computing*, vol. 7, no. 1, pp. 43–57, 1985.

[66] R. L. Graham, D. E. Knuth, and O. Patashnik, *Concrete Mathematics*. Reading, Mass.: Addison-Wesley, 1989.

[67] L. J. Guibas and R. Sedgewick, "A dichromatic framework for balanced trees," in *Proc. 19th Annu. IEEE Sympos. Found. Comput. Sci.*, Lecture Notes Comput. Sci., pp. 8–21, Springer-Verlag, 1978.

[68] Y. Gurevich, "What does $O(n)$ mean?," *SIGACT News*, vol. 17, no. 4, pp. 61–63, 1986.

[69] J. Hennessy and D. Patterson, *Computer Architecture: A Quantitative Approach*. San Francisco: Morgan Kaufmann, 2nd ed., 1996.

[70] K. Hinrichs, J. Nievergelt, and P. Schorn, "Plane-sweep solves the closest pair problem elegantly," *Inform. Process. Lett.*, vol. 26, pp. 255–261, 1988.

[71] D. S. Hirchsberg, "A linear space algorithm for computing maximal common subsequences," *Communications of the ACM*, vol. 18, no. 6, pp. 341–343, 1975.

[72] C. A. R. Hoare, "Quicksort," *The Computer Journal*, vol. 5, pp. 10–15, 1962.

[73] J. E. Hopcroft and R. E. Tarjan, "Efficient algorithms for graph manipulation," *Communications of the ACM*, vol. 16, no. 6, pp. 372–378, 1973.

[74] J. E. Hopcroft and J. D. Ullman, "Set merging algorithms," *SIAM Journal on Computing*, vol. 2, no. 4, pp. 294–303, 1979.

[75] C. S. Horstmann, *Computing Concepts in Java*. New York: John Wiley, and Sons, 1998.

[76] T. C. Hu, *Combinatorial Algorithms*. Reading, Mass.: Addison-Wesley, 1981.

[77] T. C. Hu and M. T. Shing, "Computations of matrix chain products, part i," *SIAM Journal on Computing*, vol. 11, no. 2, pp. 362–373, 1982.

[78] T. C. Hu and M. T. Shing, "Computations of matrix chain products, part ii," *SIAM Journal on Computing*, vol. 13, no. 2, pp. 228–251, 1984.

[79] B. Huang and M. Langston, "Practical in-place merging," *Communications of the ACM*, vol. 31, no. 3, pp. 348–352, 1988.

[80] D. A. Huffman, "A method for the construction of minimum-redundancy codes," *Proceedings of the IRE*, vol. 40, no. 9, pp. 1098–1101, 1952.

[81] J. JáJá, *An Introduction to Parallel Algorithms*. Reading, Mass.: Addison-Wesley, 1992.

[82] V. Jarnik, "O jistem problemù minimalnim," *Praca Moravske Prirodovedecke Spolecnosti*, vol. 6, pp. 57–63, 1930. (in Czech).

[83] R. E. Jones, *Garbage Collection: Algorithms for Automatic Dynamic Memory Management*. John Wiley and Sons, 1996.

[84] A. Karatsuba and Y. Ofman, "Multiplication of multidigit numbers on automata," *Doklady Akademii Nauk SSSR*, vol. 145, pp. 293–294, 1962. (In Russian).

[85] D. R. Karger, P. Klein, and R. E. Tarjan, "A randomized linear-time algorithm to find minimum spanning trees," *Journal of the ACM*, vol. 42, pp. 321–328, 1995.

[86] R. M. Karp and V. Ramachandran, "Parallel algorithms for shared memory machines," in *Handbook of Theoretical Computer Science* (J. van Leeuwen, ed.), pp. 869–941, Amsterdam: Elsevier/The MIT Press, 1990.

[87] P. Kirschenhofer and H. Prodinger, "The path length of random skip lists," *Acta Informatica*, vol. 31, pp. 775–792, 1994.

[88] D. E. Knuth, *Fundamental Algorithms*, vol. 1 of *The Art of Computer Programming*. Reading, MA: Addison-Wesley, 1968.

[89] D. E. Knuth, *Fundamental Algorithms*, vol. 1 of *The Art of Computer Programming*. Reading, MA: Addison-Wesley, 2nd ed., 1973.

[90] D. E. Knuth, *Sorting and Searching*, vol. 3 of *The Art of Computer Programming*. Reading, MA: Addison-Wesley, 1973.

[91] D. E. Knuth, "Big omicorn and big omega and big theta," in *SIGACT News*, vol. 8, pp. 18–24, 1976.

[92] D. E. Knuth, J. H. Morris, Jr., and V. R. Pratt, "Fast pattern matching in strings," *SIAM Journal on Computing*, vol. 6, no. 1, pp. 323–350, 1977.

[93] E. Koutsoupias and C. H. Papadimitriou, "On the k-server conjecture," *Journal of the ACM*, vol. 42, no. 5, pp. 971–983, 1995.

[94] J. B. Kruskal, Jr., "On the shortest spanning subtree of a graph and the traveling salesman problem," *Proc. Amer. Math. Soc.*, vol. 7, pp. 48–50, 1956.

[95] D. T. Lee, "Computational geometry," in *The Computer Science and Engineering Handbook* (A. B. Tucker, Jr., ed.), ch. 6, pp. 111–140, CRC Press, 1997.

[96] D. T. Lee and F. P. Preparata, "Computational geometry: a survey," *IEEE Trans. Comput.*, vol. C-33, pp. 1072–1101, 1984.

[97] N. G. Leveson and C. S. Turner, "An investigation of the Therac-25 accidents," *IEEE Computer*, vol. 26, no. 7, pp. 18–41, 1993.

[98] R. Levisse, "Some lessons drawn from the history of the binary search algorithm," *The Computer Journal*, vol. 26, pp. 154–163, 1983.

[99] T. Lindholm and F. Yellin, *The Java Virtual Machine Specification*. Reading, Mass.: Addison-Wesley, 1997.

[100] B. Liskov and J. Guttag, *Abstraction and Specification in Program Development*. Cambridge, Mass./New York: The MIT Press/McGraw-Hill, 1986.

[101] J. Matoušek, "Efficient partition trees," *Discrete Comput. Geom.*, vol. 8, pp. 315–334, 1992.

[102] J. Matoušek, "Range searching with efficient hierarchical cuttings," *Discrete Comput. Geom.*, vol. 10, no. 2, pp. 157–182, 1993.

[103] J. Matoušek, "Geometric range searching," *ACM Comput. Surv.*, vol. 26, pp. 421–461, 1994.

[104] E. M. McCreight, "A space-economical suffix tree construction algorithm," *Journal of Algorithms*, vol. 23, no. 2, pp. 262–272, 1976.

[105] E. M. McCreight, "Priority search trees," *SIAM J. Comput.*, vol. 14, pp. 257–276, 1985.

[106] C. J. H. McDiarmid and B. A. Reed, "Building heaps fast," *Journal of Algorithms*, vol. 10, no. 3, pp. 352–365, 1989.

[107] K. Mehlhorn, *Data Structures and Algorithms 3: Multi-dimensional Searching and Computational Geometry*, vol. 3 of *EATCS Monographs on Theoretical Computer Science*. Heidelberg, West Germany: Springer-Verlag, 1984.

[108] K. Mehlhorn, *Graph Algorithms and NP-Completeness*, vol. 2 of *Data Structures and Algorithms*. Heidelberg, West Germany: Springer-Verlag, 1984.

[109] K. Mehlhorn, *Sorting and Searching*, vol. 1 of *Data Structures and Algorithms*. Heidelberg, West Germany: Springer-Verlag, 1984.

[110] K. Mehlhorn and S. Näher, "LEDA: a platform for combinatorial and geometric computing," *Commun. ACM*, vol. 38, pp. 96–102, 1995.

[111] K. Mehlhorn and S. Näher, *The LEDA Platform for Combinatorial and Geometric Computing*. Cambridge, UK: Cambridge University Press, 1997.

[112] K. Mehlhorn and A. Tsakalidis, "Data structures," in *Handbook of Theoretical Computer Science* (J. van Leeuwen, ed.), vol. A. Algorithms and Complexity, pp. 301–341, Amsterdam: Elsevier, 1990.

[113] M. H. Morgan, *Vitruvius: The Ten Books on Architecture*. New York: Dover Publications, Inc., 1960.

[114] D. R. Morrison, "PATRICIA—practical algorithm to retrieve information coded in alphanumeric," *Journal of the ACM*, vol. 15, no. 4, pp. 514–534, 1968.

[115] R. Motwani and P. Raghavan, *Randomized Algorithms*. New York, NY: Cambridge University Press, 1995.

[116] D. R. Musser and A. Saini, *STL Tutorial and Reference Guide: C++ Programming with the Standard Template Library*. Reading, Mass.: Addison-Wesley, 1996.

[117] K. Noshita, "A theorem on the expected complexity of Dijkstra's shortest path algorithm," *Journal of Algorithms*, vol. 6, pp. 400–408, 1985.

[118] J. O'Rourke, *Computational Geometry in C*. Cambridge University Press, 1994.

[119] J. Pach, ed., *New Trends in Discrete and Computational Geometry*, vol. 10 of *Algorithms and Combinatorics*. Springer-Verlag, 1993.

[120] T. Papadakis, J. I. Munro, and P. V. Poblete, "Average search and update costs in skip lists," *BIT*, vol. 32, pp. 316–332, 1992.

[121] C. H. Papadimitriou and K. Steiglitz, "Some complexity results for the traveling salesman problem," in *Proc. 8th Annu. ACM Sympos. Theory Comput.*, pp. 1–9, 1976.

[122] P. V. Poblete, J. I. Munro, and T. Papadakis, "The binomial transform and its application to the analysis of skip lists," in *Proceedings of the European Symposium on Algorithms (ESA)*, pp. 554–569, 1995.

[123] F. P. Preparata and M. I. Shamos, *Computational Geometry: An Introduction*. New York, NY: Springer-Verlag, 1985.

[124] R. C. Prim, "Shortest connection networks and some generalizations," *Bell Syst. Tech. J.*, vol. 36, pp. 1389–1401, 1957.

[125] W. Pugh, "Skip lists: a probabilistic alternative to balanced trees," *Commun. ACM*, vol. 35, pp. 668–676, 1990.

[126] H. Samet, *Applications of Spatial Data Structures: Computer Graphics, Image Processing, and GIS*. Reading, MA: Addison-Wesley, 1990.

[127] H. Samet, *The Design and Analysis of Spatial Data Structures*. Reading, MA: Addison-Wesley, 1990.

[128] R. Schaffer and R. Sedgewick, "The analysis of heapsort," *Journal of Algorithms*, vol. 15, no. 1, pp. 76–100, 1993.

[129] A. Schönhage and V. Strassen, "Schnelle multiplikation grosser zahlen," *Computing*, vol. 7, no. 1, pp. 37–44, 1971.

[130] R. Sedgewick, *Algorithms*. Reading, MA: Addison-Wesley, 1983.

[131] R. Sedgewick, *Algorithms in C++*. Reading, MA: Addison-Wesley, 1992.

[132] R. Sedgewick and P. Flajolet, *An Introduction to the Analysis of Algorithms*. Reading, Mass.: Addison-Wesley, 1996.

[133] D. D. Sleator and R. E. Tarjan, "Self-adjusting binary search trees," *J. ACM*, vol. 32, no. 3, pp. 652–686, 1985.

[134] G. A. Stephen, *String Searching Algorithms*. World Scientific Press, 1994.

[135] R. Tamassia, "Graph drawing," in *Handbook of Discrete and Computational Geometry* (J. E. Goodman and J. O'Rourke, eds.), CRC Press LLC, 1997.

[136] R. E. Tarjan, "Depth first search and linear graph algorithms," *SIAM Journal on Computing*, vol. 1, no. 2, pp. 146–160, 1972.

[137] R. E. Tarjan, "A class of algorithms which require nonlinear time to maintain disjoint sets," *J. Comput. System Sci.*, vol. 18, pp. 110–127, 1979.

[138] R. E. Tarjan, *Data Structures and Network Algorithms*, vol. 44 of *CBMS-NSF Regional Conference Series in Applied Mathematics*. Society for Industrial Applied Mathematics, 1983.

[139] R. E. Tarjan, "Amortized computational complexity," *SIAM J. Algebraic Discrete Methods*, vol. 6, no. 2, pp. 306–318, 1985.

[140] A. B. Tucker, Jr., *The Computer Science and Engineering Handbook*. CRC Press, 1997.

[141] J. D. Ullman, *Principles of Database Systems*. Potomac, MD: Computer Science Press, 1983.

[142] J. van Leeuwen, "Graph algorithms," in *Handbook of Theoretical Computer Science* (J. van Leeuwen, ed.), vol. A. Algorithms and Complexity, pp. 525–632, Amsterdam: Elsevier, 1990.

[143] J. S. Vitter, "Efficient memory access in large-scale computation," in *Proc. 8th Sympos. Theoret. Aspects Comput. Sci.*, Lecture Notes Comput. Sci., Springer-Verlag, 1991.

[144] J. S. Vitter and P. Flajolet, "Average-case analysis of algorithms and data structures," in *Algorithms and Complexity* (J. van Leeuwen, ed.), vol. A of *Handbook of Theoretical Computer Science*, pp. 431–524, Amsterdam: Elsevier, 1990.

[145] J. Vuillemin, "A unifying look at data structures," *Commun. ACM*, vol. 23, pp. 229–239, 1980.

[146] S. Warshall, "A theorem on boolean matrices," *Journal of the ACM*, vol. 9, no. 1, pp. 11–12, 1962.

[147] J. W. J. Williams, "Algorithm 232: Heapsort," *Communications of the ACM*, vol. 7, no. 6, pp. 347–348, 1964.

[148] M. R. Williams, *A History of Computing Technology*. Prentice-Hall, Inc., 1985.

[149] D. Wood, *Data Structures, Algorithms, and Performance*. Reading, Mass.: Addison-Wesley, 1993.

[150] F. F. Yao, "Computational geometry," in *Algorithms in Complexity* (R. A. Earnshaw and B. Wyvill, eds.), pp. 345–490, Amsterdam: Elsevier, 1990.

[151] J. Ziv and A. Lempel, "A universal algorithm for sequential data compression," *IEEE Trans. Information Theory*, vol. 23, no. 3, pp. 337–343, 1977.

[152] J. Ziv and A. Lempel, "Compression of individual sequences via variable-rate coding," *IEEE Transactions on Information Theory*, vol. IT-24, pp. 530–536, 1978.